A HISTORY OF THE
CZECHOSLOVAK REPUBLIC
1918-1948

•

A HISTORY OF THE
CZECHOSLOVAK REPUBLIC

1918-1948

•

Edited by
Victor S. Mamatey and
Radomír Luža

PRINCETON UNIVERSITY PRESS

PRINCETON, NEW JERSEY

LC Card: 79-39791

ISBN: 0-691-05205-0

THIS BOOK HAS BEEN COMPOSED
IN LINOTYPE TIMES ROMAN

PRINTED IN THE UNITED STATES OF AMERICA
BY PRINCETON UNIVERSITY PRESS

The Publisher and Editors gratefully acknowledge permission from
New York University Press to reproduce Maps 2 and 5,
which were first published in Radomír Luža,
The Transfer of the Sudeten Germans, 1964.

To those Czech and Slovak historians,
past and present, who have had the courage
to tell their history as
it really happened

Czechoslovakia's shortlived "springtime" in 1968 revived Western interest in that country. The resolute rejection of Stalinism by the Czechs and Slovaks in that year, and their earnest search for a form of socialism "with a human face," revived memories of "Masaryk's democracy" in prewar Czechoslovakia. Soviet armed intervention in Czechoslovakia in August, 1968, which ruthlessly crushed the Czech and Slovak search for a freer, more humane way of life, revived poignant memories of Hitler's intervention against Czechoslovakia, which destroyed the first Czechoslovak democracy thirty years before.

The part played by France, Britain, and the United States in the establishment of Czechoslovakia in 1918 created a certain paternalistic feeling in those countries for her. The feeling was stimulated in the 1930's when Czechoslovakia remained the last outpost of Western democracy in East Central Europe. The assistance France and Britain unwittingly gave Hitler in destroying the first Czechoslovak democracy in 1938 provoked deep embarrassment among their peoples. The Allied powers, during World War II, tacitly recognized their obligation to make amends to the Czechs and Slovaks by including the restoration of a democratic Czechoslovakia among their war aims.

The destruction of the second Czechoslovak democracy by a communist coup in 1948 did not provoke the same sympathetic concern in the West. The fact that it had been destroyed by an internal coup rather than overt external intervention cast doubts on its genuine character. The fact also that the communist coup provoked no armed resistance on the part of the Czech and Slovak people raised the question of whether they really wanted democracy, since they appeared unwilling to fight for it. This impression was based on a gross oversimplification of the facts, but it was widely spread in the West. Whether in anger or dismay, Western opinion generally turned against Czechoslovakia, and for twenty years virtually ignored her.

In the 1950's Communist Czechoslovakia bore a harder Stalinian face, and bore it longer, than some of her neighbors, who had not a democratic tradition comparable to hers. In the 1960's, however, there were signs, at first faint but later unmistakable, that behind the hard Stalinian façade of Czechoslovakia the Czech and Slovak people still deeply longed for freedom. The events of 1968 left no doubt about it.

The explanation of the paradox—and the tragedy—of the repeated

vii

failures of the Czechs and Slovaks to establish a durable democracy, despite their manifest desire for it, is not simple. It may be found only in a careful study of their history. It is to this task that the authors of this symposium addressed themselves, by critically examining all aspects of Czechoslovak democracy, its strengths and shortcomings, and its triumphs and failures, from its inception in 1918 to its final collapse in 1948.

No comparable study exists in Western historiography on Czechoslovakia, which is not abundant. The outstanding English-language histories of Czechoslovakia—the symposium *Czechoslovakia* (Berkeley, 1940), edited by the late Prof. Robert J. Kerner; *A History of the Czechs and Slovaks* (London, 1943), by the late Prof. Robert W. Seton-Watson; and *Czechoslovakia in European History* (Princeton, 1944; rev. ed. 1953), by Prof. S. Harrison Thomson—give brilliant insights into the history of the First Czechoslovak Republic. However, they were written during World War II, a period too hectic and chronologically too close to the collapse of the first Czechoslovak democracy to allow the authors the necessary detachment and perspective to examine it critically. The authors of the present volume have had the benefit of a much longer perspective and of much new evidence, which has been published since Professors Kerner, Seton-Watson, and Thomson prepared and published their studies.

The editors of the present volume wish to emphasize that they have made no attempt to impose a uniform point of view on the individual contributions; each represents the views of its author alone. Conversely, each author bears responsibility for the content of his or her contribution alone. Finally, the editors wish to acknowledge that in preparing this volume they have greatly profited from the valuable help of the Council of Free Czechoslovakia in Washington, D. C. The editors wish to thank the advisory board, consisting of Dr. S. Harrison Thomson, professor emeritus of the University of Colorado, Dr. Edward Taborsky, professor at the University of Texas and former Czechoslovak diplomat, and Dr. Petr Zenkl, chairman of the Council of Free Czechoslovakia, former lord mayor of Prague and Czechoslovak deputy premier, for their advice and encouragement in organizing this study. The editors wish to give particular thanks to Dr. Zenkl and the late Dr. Matej Josko, likewise of the Council of Free Czechoslovakia, who generously provided assistance and facilities. The editors would also like to thank Prof. Herman Freudenberger of Tulane University for valuable assistance in reading the article of this symposium dealing with Czechoslovak economic development.

The Editors

· CONTENTS ·

CONTENTS

PART THREE

Czechoslovakia between East and West
1945 to 1948

· ILLUSTRATIONS ·

following page 210

· MAPS ·

· PART ONE ·

The Czechoslovak Republic
1918 to 1938

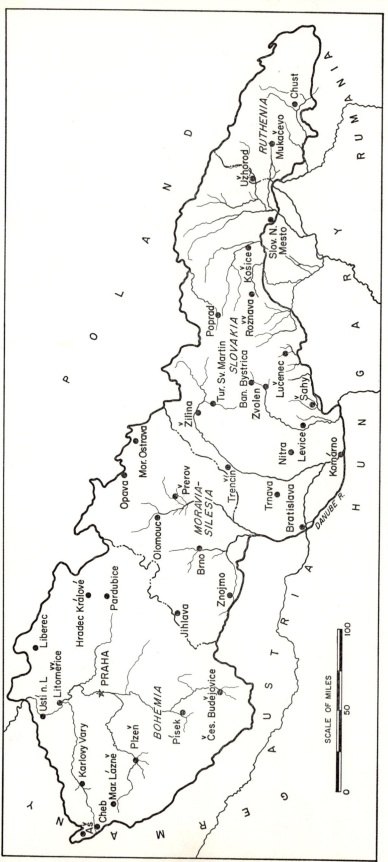

1. The Czechoslovak Republic, 1918-1938

· 1 ·

THE ESTABLISHMENT OF THE REPUBLIC

Victor S. Mamatey
University of Georgia

Popular historical studies tend to describe the creation of the Czechoslovak Republic and the other "successor states" of the Austro-Hungarian monarchy as an accidental product of Allied diplomacy in World War I and at the Paris Peace Conference. This is a simplification of history. Actually, the dissolution of the multinational Habsburg empire and the formation of the successor states was a product of complex historical forces that began long before the outbreak of World War I. The emergence of the Czechoslovak Republic in 1918 had its origins largely in the sentiments of the Czechs and Slovaks.[1]

CZECH REVIVAL

After the loss of their national independence at the outset of the Thirty Years' War (1618-48), the Czechs of Bohemia were reduced largely to a nation of peasants. In the nineteenth century, however, they effected a remarkable national revival. Owing partly to the general progress of the Austrian half of the Habsburg empire—especially its industrialization, of which Bohemia became the center[2]—but also to their own efforts, the Czechs achieved by 1914 a level of social, economic, and cultural development second only to that of the Germans in the empire. From a nation of peasants they had raised themselves to a nation consisting of a large, well-educated, and often wealthy bourgeoisie; a large, politically and nationally conscious working class; and a progressive, literate peasantry. However, they had failed to achieve their political

---

[1] The Czech and Slovak literature on their national revival and struggle for independence is very large. The following syntheses may be usefully consulted: Zdeněk Tobolka, *Politické dějiny československého národa od r. 1848 do dnešní doby* [*Political History of the Czechoslovak People from 1848 to the Present*] (4 vols. in 5; Prague, 1932-37); Československá akademie věd, *Přehled československých dějin* [*Survey of Czechoslovak History*] (3 vols. in 4; Prague, 1958-60), hereafter *Přehled*; Jozef Butvin and Jan Havránek, *Dějiny Československa* [*History of Czechoslovakia*] (Prague, 1968); and František Bokes, *Dejiny Slovenska a Slovákov od najstarších čias po oslobodenie* [*History of Slovakia and the Slovaks from the Oldest Times to their Liberation*] (Bratislava, 1946).

[2] Just before World War I between 70 and 80 percent of the industries of Austria-Hungary were concentrated in the provinces of the kingdom of Bohemia. See *Přehled*, III, 47.

ambition, which was to restore the historic "state rights" (*Staatsrecht*) of the kingdom of Bohemia and to secure for it a place in the empire analogous to that of the kingdom of Hungary after the Austro-Hungarian Compromise (*Ausgleich*) of 1867.

Emperor Francis Joseph I (1848-1916) might, perhaps, have conceded this demand to the Czechs. Three times he promised to have himself crowned with the crown of St. Venceslas and to confirm Bohemia's historic state rights. However, the Germans of Bohemia (called Sudeten Germans after 1918), who feared isolation in an autonomous Bohemian state with a Czech majority, were always able to frustrate an agreement between Vienna and the Czechs by mobilizing German opinion in other parts of the empire in support of their stand.

In 1906 universal male suffrage was adopted in the Austrian half of the Dual Monarchy, which assured the Czechs and other non-German nationalities fair representation in the Reichsrat (parliament) in Vienna. The Czech agrarian deputy and future Czechoslovak prime minister, František Udržal (1886-1938), bluntly stated the Czech aim in the Reichsrat: "We wish to save the Austrian parliament from utter ruin, but we wish to save it for the Slavs of Austria, who form two-thirds of the population. The empire is ours by right."[3] The Czechs sought to achieve their objective by forming an alliance with other Slavs. The Reichsrat became the scene of Homeric battles between the nationalities. In the end, however, the Czechs failed to gain their objective, because only the Yugoslavs (but not the Poles or the Ukrainians) would cooperate with them. Frustrated, the Czechs became increasingly alienated from the dynasty and the empire. Yet, with characteristic realism they did not consider withdrawal from the empire. They continued to agitate for its reform, not its destruction.

In 1909 Prof. Tomáš G. Masaryk (1850-1937), sole representative of the small but intellectually influential Czech Realist party in the Reichsrat, clearly stated the reasons for the Czech attitude: "We want a federal Austria. We cannot be independent outside of Austria, next to a powerful Germany, having Germans on our territory."[4] It was thus fear of the Germans, historical enemies of the Czechs, that stifled their desire for independence. The dissolution of the weak and inefficient Austrian empire might bring them under the rule of the powerful and efficient German empire. Masaryk was not singular in his views on the empire. For different reasons, Czech leaders of all political hues believed in the necessity of maintaining the Habsburg empire.

Bohumír Šmeral (1880-1941), leader of the Czech Social Democratic

[3] Arthur J. May, *The Hapsburg Monarchy, 1867-1914* (Cambridge, Mass., 1951), p. 427.

[4] Evžen Štern, *Názory T. G. Masaryka* [*Opinions of T. G. Masaryk*] (Prague, 1918), p. 60.

party, a left-wing, internationalist socialist and one of the founders of the future Czechoslovak Communist party, supported the maintenance of the Austrian empire for peculiarly Marxist reasons. In common with other Marxists, he believed that the triumph of socialism depended on industrialization, and industrialization on "large-area economy" (*Grossraumwirtschaft*). In its "Žofín program" of 1913, the Czech Social Democratic party, which had emerged from the last Austrian election in 1911 as the largest Czech party, proclaimed: "It is necessary, in the interest of the nations inhabiting Central Europe and their proletariat, not the least in the interest of the Czech nation and its proletariat, to strengthen everything that . . . contributes to the maintenance and development of a large state-organized economic area in Central Europe, the historical expression of which today is Austria-Hungary."[5]

On the opposite side of the Czech political spectrum, Karel Kramář (1860-1937), leader of the Young Czech party in the Reichsrat, a future Czechoslovak prime minister, and a conservative nationalist politician noted for his Russophile sentiments, accepted the empire *faute de mieux*. On July 4, 1914, under the impression of the assassination of Archduke Francis Ferdinand, Kramář declared in a speech in Prague—and no doubt sincerely meant at the moment: " . . . we protest most resolutely against anyone thinking that because of our sincere Slavism we are hostile to the empire. . . . We lean in no direction outside the empire."[6] On the eve of World War I the Czechs, though deeply frustrated in the Habsburg empire, could not conceive of living outside of it.

SLOVAK REVIVAL AND DECLINE

The Slovaks, *a fortiori*, dared not look outside the empire before 1914. Like the Czechs, the Slovaks who inhabited northern Hungary, of which they formed an integral part, experienced a national awakening at the beginning of the nineteenth century. However, they did not make progress commensurate with that of the Czechs. Unlike the earlier technical breakthrough in Austria, the Industrial Revolution in Hungary did not begin until the end of the nineteenth century. Through most of the century Hungary was largely an agrarian country. The socioeconomic structure of the Slovaks therefore differed markedly from that of the Czechs. They had no large urban industrial proletariat or bourgeoisie, but consisted largely of peasants and rural laborers. The modest commercial enterprise of Slovakia was owned almost exclusively by the Hungarian Jewish community, by Germans, or by other nonindigenous elements.

---

[5] Tobolka, *Politické dějiny*, IV, 52; *Přehled*, II-2, 1044.

[6] Jaroslav Werstadt, "Politické plány české Maffie v prvním roce války" ["The Political Plans of the Czech Mafia in the First Year of the War"], *Naše revoluce*, VII, 1, 385.

The Slovak middle class consisted of the "intelligentsia"—a ha village priests and ministers and a sprinkling of country docto smalltown lawyers.

Nevertheless, at the beginning of the nineteenth century Slovak c tural life was lively enough. Briefly, in the 1820's and 1830's, the Slovak Jan Kollár (1793-1852) and Pavel Jozef Šafárik (1795-1861) were not only the leading Slovak literary figures but also the intellectual mentors of the Czechs and other Austrian Slavs. Both were members of the Slovak Protestant (Lutheran) minority. Perhaps because they were a religious as well as an ethnic minority in the "Apostolic" kingdom of Hungary, the Slovak Protestants felt less at home in it than the Slovak Catholics and tended to look outside of it. Traditionally, their ministerial students went to Lutheran Germany to complete their theological training. There, at the beginning of the nineteenth century, they imbibed romantic nationalism at its very fountainhead—the German universities—while the Czechs and other Austrian Slavs received it second-hand, through Vienna.

Kollár and Šafárik had studied at the University of Jena in the immediate post-Napoleonic period when this university was a center of German nationalist fermentation. To the movement for German unification that they had observed in Germany, they offered a seeming analogy —a movement for Slavic unity. For the Slovaks, this meant first unity with the Czechs and then with other Slavs. Contrary to a common assumption, it was Slovak Protestant intellectuals rather than Czechs who first suggested the idea of Czechoslovak unity, and it was the same men rather than Russians who first began to propagate the idea of Panslavic solidarity. Both movements represented attempts by a beleaguered minority to find strength by leaning on stronger peoples. Typical of the influence of the Slovak Protestants on the Czechs was the famous historian and political leader František Palacký (1798-1876). A *rara avis*—a Czech Protestant, he was educated in Protestant schools at Trenčín and Bratislava in Slovakia before going to the University of Prague. He bore a heavy impress of the peculiarly romantic atmosphere of Slovak Protestantism.

Until the nineteenth century Latin was the official language as well as the language of intellectual intercourse in Hungary. One of the features of the national awakening of Hungary's nationalities was that they discarded Latin and elevated their vernaculars to the dignity of literary tongues. Among the Slovaks, a Catholic priest, Father Anton Bernolák (1762-1813), promoted a western Slovak dialect as the Slovak literary language. His linguistic reform failed to gain the support of the Slovak Protestants, however. They had used Czech as their liturgical language since the sixteenth century, when the Protestant Reformation was introduced in Slovakia partly by Protestant preachers from Bohemia. Now they proposed to use it also as the Slovak literary language. As a result, a linguistic schism developed between the Slovak Catholics and Protestants. However, in the 1840's, alarmed by legislation then passed by the Hungarian diet that replaced Latin with Magyar as the official language in all of Hungary, a younger Slovak Protestant intellectual, Ľudovít Štúr (1815-56), felt that the importance for the Slovaks of closing their ranks for a struggle for survival against the threat of Magyar assimilation outweighed the advantage of linguistic unity with the Czechs. Therefore, as a compromise with the Catholics, he promoted a central Slovak dialect as the Slovak literary language. Unlike Bernolák's reform, Štúr's gradually gained general acceptance among the Slovaks, despite the protests of Kollár, Šafárik, and the older generation of Slovak Protestant intellectuals. The reform healed the temporary linguistic schism between the Slovak Catholics and Protestants, but created a permanent one between the Slovaks as a whole and the Czechs.

In the second half of the nineteenth century Slovak cultural life was stifled, first by the reaction that followed the Revolution of 1848 and then by the aftermath of the Austro-Hungarian Compromise of 1867, under which Emperor Francis Joseph sacrificed the interests of the Hungarian minorities that had supported the dynasty during the Revolution of 1848 for the sake of coming to an agreement with the Hungarian ruling classes. In principle, the rights of the Hungarian minorities were to be regulated by the Law of the Equal Rights of the Nationalities of 1868, which postulated the existence of a unitary Hungarian political nation but provided for a fair amount of cultural autonomy for non-Magyar nationalities. Unfortunately, the law was never enforced. Instead, the Hungarian government adopted a policy that sought to "magyarize," i.e. culturally and linguistically assimilate, the non-Magyar minorities and to transform Hungary, in which the Magyars constituted less than half the population at the time, into an ethnically and culturally homogeneous Magyar state.

The harsh policy of magyarization, combined with the unenlightened social policy of the Hungarian government, which sought to keep the peasant masses—the Magyar peasants included—ignorant and obedient, seriously impeded Slovak cultural life. Instead of progressing like the Czechs, the Slovaks actually regressed. Their only escape from the oppressive Hungarian policies was emigration. In the first years of the present century, Slovak emigration, particularly to the United States, reached the proportions of a mass flight. This further weakened the Slovak people by depriving them of their most enterprising elements. On the eve of World War I Slovak cultural life had come to a virtual standstill.

Politically, the Slovaks were likewise in full retreat as the war ap-

7

proached. Unlike the enfranchisement prevailing in Austria, universal male suffrage was never adopted in Hungary. Franchise remained extraordinarily limited, and discriminated against the non-Magyar minorities and the working classes. In 1910 out of a population of about 20 million, only about 1.2 million, or 6 percent, had the right to vote. In the same year, according to Hungarian statistics, the Slovaks numbered about 1.95 million, or about 10 percent of the population. The lower house of the Hungarian parliament comprised 413 deputies. On a proportionate basis, the Slovaks should have been represented in it by about 40 deputies. Instead, in the elections of 1906 they succeeded in electing only seven, and in the elections of 1910, the last before the war, only three. One of them was soon forced to resign. The remaining two Slovak deputies made up less than 0.5 percent of the lower house's membership. Consequently, Slovak political activity took place largely outside the Hungarian parliament.

Unlike the Czechs who had a full range of well-organized political parties based on class and ideological divisions, before 1918 the Slovaks had, properly speaking, only one political party, the Slovak National party. It was a loose political organization of leaders without a mass following, and reflected several political trends, from liberal-democratic to conservative-clerical. As the Hungarian pressure on them increased, the older generation of Slovak political leaders, typified by Svetozár Hurban Vajanský (1847-1917), a poet and editor of the party's organ, *Národnie noviny* (*National News*), lapsed into complete political passivity. If they thought of the future at all, they dreamed of the day when the great "white tsar" of Russia would come to liberate them. Among the younger leaders who had not yet given up the fight, three trends were discernible.

One trend, a liberal-democratic one, was represented by the Hlasisti (so-called after their review, *Hlas* [*Voice*]) who comprised notably the physicians Vavro Šrobár and Pavel Blaho, the journalists Anton Štefánek and Igor Hrušovský, and the lawyer Ivan Dérer, all of whom were to play prominent roles in Czechoslovak politics after the war. Influenced by Professor Masaryk, the Hlasists professed to believe in reason, progress, and democracy and deplored the conservative-clerical influence in Slovak life. Looking to Prague for support, they believed firmly in "Czechoslovak unity" (*československá jednota*) or, more accurately, Czechoslovak identity, for they insisted that the Czech and Slovak peoples were completely identical, despite the patent social, economic, and cultural differences imposed on them by a thousand years of different history.

The Hlasist program elicited a more ready response from the Slovak Protestants than from the Catholics, but Hlasism was by no means a Protestant movement. As a matter of fact, the two original Hlasists,

Šrobár and Blaho, were both Catholics. Among the Czechs, the Hlasists were supported by a small but dedicated band of Slovakophiles, organized in the society "Czechoslav Unity" in Prague. With the exception of Masaryk, however, who took a very active interest in the Slovaks, the Czech politicians, though sympathetic toward them, were reluctant to interfere in their behalf in Hungary, for this would constitute a violation of Hungary's state rights and might jeopardize the Czech program that was based on Bohemia's historic state rights.

A second trend in the Slovak National party, Catholic populism, was best represented by Andrej Hlinka (1864-1938). A courageous Catholic priest and fiery popular orator, with a remarkable ability to hold a peasant audience enthralled, Father Hlinka did not hesitate to denounce publicly the harsh Hungarian policy toward the Slovaks or to defy the Church hierarchy that supported it. After the war he became critical of the Czechs and a vocal spokesman of Slovak "distinctness" (*samobytnost'*) and political autonomy. Before 1918, however, he endorsed the principle of Czechoslovak unity on several occasions, and his relations with the Czechs were cordial. In 1907, at the invitation of the "Czechoslav Unity," Hlinka toured Bohemia and Moravia to speak about the "massacre of Černová"—a brutal outrage perpetrated against the helpless Slovak villagers of Černová that caused a Europe-wide stir. He was warmly applauded by Czech audiences, and on his return to Slovakia promptly imprisoned by the Hungarian authorities.

While Hlinka had no quarrel with the principle of Czechoslovak unity, he was suspicious of Czech anticlericalism. The Czechs, it should be noted, identified their national disaster in the seventeenth century with the triumph of the Catholic Counter-Reformation, and tended to be increasingly secular in outlook and critical of the Catholic Church. On the other hand, they had no analogy to the Slovak Catholic-Protestant rivalry, the Counter-Reformation having whittled the Czech Protestant majority down to an insignificant minority as early as the eighteenth century. In 1912, alarmed by the growing influence of the "free-thinking" Hlasists on younger Slovak intellectuals and the appeal of socialism to the growing ranks of Slovak workers, Hlinka took the lead in founding the Slovak People's party on the model of the Hungarian Christian Social party. However, before the new party could properly organize and test itself in elections, the outbreak of the war suspended all Slovak political activity.

The third trend in the Slovak National party, agrarianism, was represented by Milan Hodža (1878-1943), a member of the Hungarian parliament and future Czechoslovak prime minister, who because of his energy and resourcefulness held a special place in Slovak politics. A realistic and pragmatic politician, Hodža believed that the Slovak National party should try to acquire a mass basis by appealing to the class interests of the peasants, who constituted the largest Slovak class. Although he contributed to the Hlas and subscribed to the ideal of Czechoslovak unity, he did not look to Prague alone for support, but explored every possible avenue of escape from the Hungarian pressure. In the Hungarian parliament, he promoted a Slovak-Rumanian-Serb coalition against the Magyars. Later he found his way into Archduke Francis Ferdinand's "political workshop," an informal group of advisers on whom the heir-presumptive occasionally called for advice.[7] What the archduke's plans with regard to the Slovaks were—if, indeed, he had any—is uncertain, because he never had an opportunity to carry out any plan. His assassination at Sarajevo, among other things, extinguished the last Slovak hope in the Habsburg dynasty.

In the early years of the present century when the Hungarian Industrial Revolution gained momentum, a Slovak socialist movement began. In 1905 Emanuel Lehocký (1876-1930), a tailor by training and editor of the first Slovak socialist newspaper, organized with the help of Czech Social Democrats in Vienna the Slovak Social Democratic party. Only a year later, however, the party was obliged to merge with the Hungarian Social Democratic party, whose internationalist, left-wing leaders frowned on any attempt to organize workers on an ethnic basis as being a manifestation of bourgeois nationalism and a threat to the unity of the proletarian movement in Hungary. Nevertheless, the Slovak Social Democratic leaders continued to maintain relations with, and to receive help from, their Czech comrades in Vienna and the Czech provinces.

Thus, while the Czechs and Slovaks had no plans to seek independence and unity before World War I, they had little reason to feel loyalty to the Habsburg dynasty or the empire.

Outbreak of World War I

When the Austro-Hungarian government declared war on Serbia on July 28, 1914, Czech and Slovak soldiers responded to the mobilization orders obediently, if indifferently or even sullenly. There were, however, no stirring scenes of enthusiasm for the war in Bohemia and Slovakia as in Vienna and Budapest. The spread of the Austro-Serb conflict into a great world conflagration raised the possibility of defeat of Austria-Hungary and its German ally, which caused a gradual shift in Czech and Slovak opinion. They watched to see what the Allies, especially Russia,

---

[7] Milan Hodža, *Federation in Central Europe* (London, 1942), pp. 41-43; "Listy Milana Hodžu šéfovi vojenskej kancelárie následníka tronu Františka Ferdinanda v rokoch 1907-1911" ["Milan Hodža's Letters to the chief of the Military Chancellery of the Heir-Presumptive Francis Ferdinand in 1907-1911"], *Historický časopis*, XVIII (1970), 427-47.

would do. Their particular interest in Russian action reflected not so much their traditional Russophile sentiment as the simple fact that at the beginning of the war Russia was the only major Allied power that fought Austria-Hungary directly. From the point of view of Prague, Vienna, and Budapest alike, Russia was the Allied power that counted. France was very secondary, and insular Britain hardly figured at all.

On August 20, 1914, Tsar Nicholas II received a Czechoslovak delegation in the Kremlin in Moscow. The group expressed the hope that the "free and independent crown of St. Venceslas shine in the rays of the crown of the Romanovs."[8] A month later, Tsar Nicholas received another Czechoslovak delegation in Petrograd. On the same day, September 15, the Russian government issued over the signature of Grand Duke Nicholas, the Russian commander-in-chief, a manifesto addressed to all "peoples of Austria-Hungary" but meant primarily for the Austrian Slavs. It expressed Russia's hope that they would "develop and prosper" and preserve the heritage of their ancestors, their "language and faith."[9] A few days later, after a ceremony in Kiev, a Czech volunteer unit, the Česká družina, departed for the front.

Czech and Slovak emigrants in Russia had been settled there for some time. They had for the most part become Russian subjects and, therefore, had hardly the right to dispose of the Bohemian crown. Nevertheless, when the news of their political activity filtered through to Bohemia, it was widely acclaimed. The grand duke's manifesto, which was widely circulated in Bohemia despite Austrian censorship, likewise produced great excitement. As the Russian "steamroller" rolled into Galicia and advanced toward Bohemia, liberation by the Russians was expected daily. The Russophile Kramář, who was generally looked upon as the future prime minister of a Russian-sponsored Bohemian kingdom, passed the word to Czech politicians to sit tight and wait, for the "Russians will do it for us alone."[10] So prompted, Czech politicians adopted a cautious wait-and-see attitude. Slovak leaders, under the harsh Hungarian rule, were even more cautious.[11]

---

[8] František Šteidler, Československé hnutí na Rusi [The Czechoslovak Movement in Russia] (Prague, 1922), p. 7. For a more recent, Marxist, view of the Czechoslovak movement in Russia, see Karel Pichlík, Zahraniční odboj 1914-1918 bez legend [The Resistance Movement abroad in 1914-1918 without Legends] (Prague, 1968), pp. 47-59.

[9] Edvard Beneš, Světová válka a naše revoluce [The World War and Our Revolution] (3 vols.; Prague, 1927-29), III Dokumenty, No. 236, 553-54. Hereafter this third volume of Beneš's World War I memoirs, which contains documents, will be cited as Beneš, Dokumenty.

[10] Tobolka, Politické dějiny, IV, 53.

[11] Czech political resistance to Austrian rule, though nonviolent, had the character of a mass movement. With remarkable national solidarity, all Czech classes joined in it. On the other hand, Slovak political resistance to Hungarian rule was limited to a handful of intellectuals. According to Hungarian police records cited

The Russophile sentiment of the Czech people put the Czech socialists in a difficult position. Since the days of Marx and Engels all socialists had regarded Imperial Russia as the most powerful bastion of reaction and a foe of socialism. Hostility to Russia was, therefore, the touchstone of revolutionary sincerity. Caught between the aspirations of Czech nationalism and socialist duty, the Czech Social Democrats remained aloof from the struggle for independence until the Russian Revolution. However, the Czech socialists never displayed the same ardor to fight Russia as their German-Austrian comrades, whose "social patriotism" at the beginning of the war scarcely exceeded by the patriotism of the German-Austrian "bourgeois-nationalist" parties. Many rank-and-file Czech socialists were unable to resist the call of Slav brotherhood. Among the Czech soldiers who deserted en masse to the Russians in 1914 were many Czech socialists.

MASARYK AND THE PARIS NATIONAL COUNCIL

Not all Czechs, however, were content to wait, hopefully or uneasily, for the Cossack liberators. A few—very few—looked also to the Western democracies for support. Among them was, notably, Professor Masaryk. A man of humble background, he had acquired a culture that was unusually broad not only for a Czech but also for a continental European intellectual at the time; he was equally at home in the Russian and Anglo-Saxon cultures. A Russophile like the rest of the Czechs, but also a democrat, he had convinced himself from his Russian studies[12] that liberation and consequent domination by autocratic Imperial Russia might not be quite the blessing that his sentimentally Russophile compatriots supposed. His was, in his own words, an "open-eyed love" of

---

by Vavro Šrobár, *Osvobodené Slovensko: Pamäti z rokov 1918-1920* [*Liberated Slovakia: Memories of the Years 1918-1920*] (Bratislava, 1928), pp. 163-83. Hungarian authorities kept only 526 Slovaks and their families under surveillance because they were known to be Slovak nationalists, and of these the authorities regarded only 101 persons as potentially subversive. On the other hand, Slovak social discontent was more intense than the Czech. It was vented only after the war when the Hungarian rule collapsed. Likewise, insubordination and mutinies of Slovak soldiers were more frequent and violent and desertion to the "green cadres" more common than among Czech soldiers. The weapon of the Czech soldier against Austrian oppression was either desertion to the enemy or evasion, the classical expression of which was the "Good Soldier Švejk"—the fictional but true-to-life character created by Czech communist writer Karel Hašek. A good study of Czech and Slovak soldiers in both the Austro-Hungarian army and the Czechoslovak legions with the Allied armies is Karel Pichlík *et al.*, *Červenobílá a rudá: Vojáci ve válce a revoluci, 1914-1918* [*Red-white and Red: Soldiers in War and Revolution, 1914-1918*] (Prague, 1967).

[12] In 1911 Masaryk published his well-known book *Russland und Europa*. Translated into English as *The Spirit of Russia* (3 vols.; New York, 1955-67), it remains to this day a standard study of pre-Marxist Russian thought.

Russia.[13] Above all, the course of the war convinced him that for tactical reasons it was not wise for the Czech and Slovaks to bet on the Russian card alone.

The battles of Tannenberg and the Marne shattered the general expectation that the conflict would be short, and opened the prospect of a long-drawn-out war of attrition, for which the Austrian and Russian empires, with their antiquated administrative, social, and economic structures, were ill-prepared. This prospect convinced Masaryk that the Central Powers might be defeated, which was the *sine qua non* of Czechoslovak liberation, and also that in the end Russia, more weakened by war than the Western powers, might have less, and the latter more, to say about the peace settlement in Central Europe than was generally supposed in 1914. Therefore, to Kramář's tactic of waiting for the Russians to do it for them, Masaryk opposed the tactic that the Czechs and Slovaks must do it alone; that is, that they must take the initiative toward their liberation, political and military, at home and abroad, and that they must seek to commit not only Russia but also the Western powers to support their cause. Events were to prove him a singularly accurate prophet.

In the fall of 1914, Masaryk made three trips to neutral countries to sound out, cautiously, Western opinion about support for the Czechoslovak cause. During his third trip, while in Switzerland, he was warned that he was under suspicion by the Austrian authorities and might be arrested upon his return home. He decided to stay abroad, therefore, and work openly for Czechoslovak independence. Before his departure from Prague he had made arrangements to stay in touch with Czech opinion and politicians through a small group of dedicated followers, who later became known as the "Czech Mafia." From Switzerland he traveled to neutral Rome and then to belligerent Paris and London. In Paris, in September, 1915, he was joined by Edvard Beneš (1884-1948), a young professor of sociology and one of his intellectual followers, who thereafter became his lifelong collaborator. In Paris Masaryk also encountered another of his disciples, the colorful Slovak Milan Rastislav Štefánik (1880-1918), a scientist, astronomer, meteorologist, traveler, and, since the war, an officer in the French air force. Together the three scholars formed an extraordinarily effective team.

Through his connections in Paris, Štefánik arranged an interview for Masaryk with French Premier Aristide Briand. In London, Masaryk was introduced to Prime Minister Herbert Asquith by Wickham Steed, the political editor of the *Times* and former correspondent in Vienna. The French and British premiers, though sympathetic, remained noncommittal. Being primarily concerned with defeating Germany, they did not

[13] Thomas G. Masaryk, *The Making of a State: Memories and Observations, 1914-1918* (London, 1927), p. 38.

13

wish to prejudice the possibility of detaching Austria-Hungary from the Central Alliance by committing themselves to the cause of her disaffected nationalities. In order to work on British opinion, Masaryk settled in London, where he lectured at King's College and carried on propaganda for the Czechoslovak cause.

In the meantime, Czech politicians at home, knowing that Masaryk was *persona non grata* in Russia because of his criticism of the Russian autocracy, decided to send abroad Josef Dürich, an Agrarian deputy in the Reichsrat, to represent the Czechoslovak cause in Russia. Before Dürich's departure from Prague in May, 1915, Kramář instructed him to work for a "great Slav empire"[14] in which Bohemia would be an autonomous kingdom. However, the Russian government refused to admit Dürich to Russia, despite his conservative and Russophile reputation, because Russian military reverses had altered the situation. In May, 1915, the German and Austrian armies broke through the Russian lines and proceeded to roll back the whole Russian front. By September, when their offensive ended, the Russians had been forced to evacuate not only Austrian Galicia but also Russian Poland and Lithuania, and had suffered irreparable losses. Early Russian optimism had given way to increasing defeatism. Doubtful of victory, the Russian government did not wish to add to its commitments another one to the Czechs and Slovaks, which might stand in the way of peace with the Central Powers. Instead of going to Russia, Dürich joined the exiles in Paris.

On November 14, 1915, the Paris exiles formally launched the Czechoslovak movement for independence with the issuance by the "Czech Foreign Committee" of a declaration demanding the establishment of an independent Czechoslovak state.[15] The declaration said nothing of the future form of the Czechoslovak state, but it was a foregone conclusion that it would be a monarchy under a Romanov prince. Even Masaryk took it for granted,[16] although he had misgivings about it. In 1916, the Czech Foreign Committee was transformed into the "National Council of the Czech Lands"[17] with headquarters in Paris. Masaryk became its chairman; Dürich and Štefánik, vice chairmen; and Beneš, secretary-general.

[14] Josef Dürich, *V českých službách* [*In Czech Service*] (Klášter nad Jizerou, 1921), p. 13.

[15] Beneš, *Dokumenty*, No. 80, pp. 264-68. See also Pichlík, *Zahraniční odboj*, pp. 144-58.

[16] See Masaryk's confidential memorandum "Independent Bohemia," given to the British government in 1915, in R. W. Seton-Watson, *Masaryk in England* (London, 1943), pp. 133-34.

[17] According to Beneš, *Světová válka*, I, 116-17n., it was on Štefánik's insistence that the council was called "Czech," rather than "Czechoslovak," in order not to confuse Allied opinion, which was very imperfectly informed about the Czechs and Slovaks of that time.

The diligent work of the exiles bore fruit on January 10, 1917, when, in response to President Woodrow Wilson's appeal to belligerent governments to state their war aims, the Allied governments issued a statement of their own war aims that included the "liberation of Italians, of Slavs, of Roumanians and of *Czechoslovaks* from foreign domination."[18]

This success, however, was presently threatened by Russian action. In 1916, as the Russian military situation temporarily improved, the Russian government, alarmed by the progress of the Czechoslovak movement in the Western countries, renewed its own interest. In May it admitted Dürich to Russia. He became the tool of the extremely conservative, Panslav, and antidemocratic elements among the exiles in Russia, which had the ear of the Russian Foreign Ministry. Dürich was persuaded to repudiate the Paris National Council and form a rival national council in Petrograd. On January 31, 1917, the Russian government approved the formation of the Petrograd council and undertook to finance it.[19] Fortunately for the unity of the Czechoslovak cause, this East-West schism proved shortlived. With the fall of the Russian monarchy March, 1917, the Petrograd council disappeared and Dürich passed into oblivion. More lasting were the repercussions of the Allied statement of war aims in Austria-Hungary.

The Allied statement of January 10, 1917, taken at face value, was a threat to dismember the Habsburg empire. The statesmen of Vienna and Budapest were greatly alarmed. To check the effect of the declaration, Count Ottokar Czernin, the foreign minister, exacted from the parliamentary representatives of the nationalities, including the Czechs, statements repudiating the Allied promise to liberate them.[20] The young Emperor Charles (1916-18), who had succeeded Francis Joseph the previous November, showed little liking for the war that he had not started. Alarmed by the Allied declaration, he began to put out peace-feelers to the Allies. These overtures convinced the Allied governments that Austria-Hungary was ready to conclude a separate peace if it was given a guarantee against dismemberment.

In March, 1917, secret peace negotiations began between Vienna on one hand and Paris, London, and Washington on the other, and went on intermittently until April, 1918. The French, British, and United States governments, in turn, tried to wean Austria from Germany by giving

[18] Sharp to Lansing, January 10, 1971, U. S. Department of State, *Papers Relating to the Foreign Relations of the United States: The World War, 1917*, Supplement 1 (Washington, 1931), p. 8. Hereafter this collection will be cited as *Foreign Relations*.

[19] Josef Kudela, *Profesor Masaryk a Čs. vojsko na Rusi [Professor Masaryk and the Czechoslovak Army in Russia]* (Prague, 1923), p. 31; Beneš, *Dokumenty*, No. 254, pp. 592-99.

[20] Beneš, *Dokumenty*, Nos. 89-90, pp. 264-87.

15

Vienna assurances against radical dismemberment and holding out hope of compensations for possible territorial losses to Allied nations. The negotiations ultimately failed because Austria would not, or could not, separate herself from Germany. However, while they lasted, the Allies were reluctant to commit themselves to support Czechoslovak independence.

THE RUSSIAN REVOLUTION

The outbreak of the Russian Revolution in March and the American entry into the war in April, 1917, gave the war an entirely new dimension. Both the Russian revolutionaries and the American crusaders for democracy put national self-determination on their banner, which caused the latent forces of social and nationalist discontent on both sides of the fighting lines to surface. Of the two events, the Russian Revolution had the more immediate effect on the Czechs and Slovaks; the American declaration of war was for the moment secondary, for it was limited to Germany.

The outbreak of the Russian Revolution brought about the second major shift in Czech and Slovak opinion since the beginning of the war. The fall of the Russian monarchy freed the Czech socialists from an old socialist bogey and made it possible for them to be good socialists and Czech patriots all at the same time. In the fall of 1917, after considerable behind-the-scenes struggle, the right-wing and nationalist Gustav Habrman replaced the left-wing internationalist Šmeral as leader of the Czech Social Democratic party. Under Habrman's guidance the party took an increasingly important part in the Czech struggle for national independence.

In London, Masaryk, who represented the Czech democratic center, was heartened by the fall of the Russian monarchy, which buried the prospect that Czechoslovakia would become a conservative monarchy under a Russian prince—a prospect which he had accepted but had never cherished. He also shared the view then widely held in the West that the Russian Revolution would rekindle Russia's dying fighting spirit. In a telegram to Prof. Paul N. Milyukov, the foreign minister and strong man in the Russian provisional government, he confidently affirmed: "The solution of Slav questions is now assured."[21] On the other hand, the conservative Czech nationalists were disheartened by the fall of the Russian monarchy, which buried their dream of a "Slav imperium" and a Romanov king in the Hradčany castle in Prague. When Alois Rašín, a Young Czech leader and future Czechoslovak finance minister, heard of the Russian Revolution, he told Kramář in jail, where they were both

21 Ibid., No. 257, pp. 615-16.

awaiting execution under sentences of death for alleged treason to Austria: "We are finished."[22]

Whether they were heartened or disheartened by the Russian Revolution, the Czech politicians were encouraged by the principle of national self-determination, which the Russian Revolution and the American declaration of war made the order of the day, to abandon their cautious wait-and-see policy and adopt a more active one. The convocation of the Reichsrat by Emperor Charles in May, 1917—for the first time since the beginning of the war—provided them with a tribune from which to voice their aspirations. Shaken by the fall of the Romanovs and fearful lest the Russian Revolution spread to the Habsburg empire, the young monarch had determined upon a policy of conciliation toward the nationalist and socialist opposition. Kramář, Rašín, and other political offenders were amnestied, and returned in triumph to Prague to lead the Czech people.

In the very first session of the Reichsrat on May 30, František Staněk, chairman of the Czech Club (the organization of the Czech deputies in the Reichsrat), read a statement in which the Czech deputies, basing themselves on the "natural rights of nations to self-determination" and the "inalienable rights" of the kingdom of Bohemia, announced that they would press for "union of all branches of the Czechoslovak nation into a democratic Bohemian state."[23] Although the declaration still professed Czech loyalty to the Habsburg dynasty, it was a far cry from the abject declaration in January by the same men, repudiating Allied liberation. Moreover, in a separate declaration, Antonín Kalina, spokesman of the small Czech Progressive State-Rights party, went farther than the Czech Club: he simply demanded the establishment of a Czechoslovak state, that is, *without* the Habsburgs.[24] It should also be noted that the Czech Social Democrats submitted a memorandum to the Socialist Conference in Stockholm in June-July, 1917, in which they likewise demanded the establishment of an independent Czechoslovak state within a Danubian confederation, without referring to the Habsburg dynasty.[25]

The new democratic spirit emanating from Russia and America affected also the Slovaks. While the conservative Slovak Russophiles were disheartened by the Tsar's downfall, the progressive Hlasists were encouraged by the promise of self-determination, and the socialists by the hope of social emancipation. Living under the harsh Hungarian regime,

---

[22] Tobolka, *Politické dějiny*, IV, 54.

[23] Ibid., pp. 245-46; František Soukup, *28. říjen 1918* [*October 28, 1918*] (2 vols.; Prague, 1928), I, 421-22; and Milada Paulová, *Tajný výbor Maffie a spolupráce s Jihoslovany v letech 1916-1918* [*The Mafia's Secret Committee and Cooperation with the Yugoslavs in 1916-1918*] (Prague, 1968), pp. 248-49. For the text of the declaration, see Beneš, *Dokumenty*, No. 93, pp. 291-92.

[24] Tobolka, *Politické dějiny*, IV, 246; Paulová, *Tajný výbor*, pp. 249-50.

[25] Paulová, *Tajný výbor*, pp. 270-74; and Soukup, *28. říjen 1918*, I, 538-39.

however, the Slovaks were unable to voice their feelings or formulate programs freely. In April, therefore, when the convocation of the Reichsrat was announced, Šrobár hastened to Prague to appeal to the Czech leaders to champion the Slovak cause.[26]

To include Slovak liberation in the Czech program would complicate it, because it was based on the historic state rights of Bohemia. Nevertheless, in the end, the Czech leaders decided to do it, partly because of sympathy for their Slovak kinsmen and partly because they realized that only by uniting with the Slovaks could the Czechs escape German encirclement and reach out across Slovakia to Russia for support. As noted, in the Reichsrat declaration of May 30, they not only reiterated the old demand for the restoration of Bohemia's historic state rights but included the new demand for "union of all branches of the *Czechoslovak* nation." Thereafter, the Czech and Slovak leaders remained in touch—in Vienna where Hodža, Dérer, and others had sought refuge from Hungarian harassment. The Czechs continued to speak up for their "gagged" Slovak brethren, despite the vehement protests of the Hungarian government, which denounced Czech championship of the Slovaks as crass interference in Hungary's internal affairs and a violation of the spirit of the *Ausgleich.*

The hopes placed in democratic Russia by the Czech and Slovak democrats were not borne out. Masaryk, to whom the Russian Revolution had opened the gates to Russia, arrived in Petrograd in the midst of the "May crisis" of the Provisional Government. The crisis resulted in the fall of Milyukov, who had been the staunchest supporter of Russia's continued participation in the war and of the aspirations of the Austrian Slavs. The new strong man in the Provisional Government, War Minister Alexander F. Kerensky, favored continuation of the war effort, but was not sympathetic to the cause of the Austrian Slavs. He believed that Russia could not encourage them without also encouraging Russia's own subject peoples and thus threatening the integrity of the Russian empire. If the Czechs and Slovaks wanted freedom, he felt that they should go home and overthrow the Habsburgs as the Russians had overthrown the Romanovs. However, Russia, in travail of revolution, was in no position to help the Austrian Slavs.[27]

When the Czechoslovak unit distinguished itself in the Russian July offensive (Battle of Zborov), Kerensky modified his attitude toward the Czechoslovaks to the extent that he authorized the Russian high command to conclude an agreement with Masaryk for the organization of an autonomous Czechoslovak army in Russia.[28] Masaryk considered this

[26] Vavro Šrobár, *Pamäti z vojny a väzenia, 1914-1918* [*Memories of War and Imprisonment, 1914-1918*] (2nd ed., Turčiansky Svätý Martin, 1946), pp. 54-55.
[27] Kudela, *Profesor Masaryk*, p. 69. [28] Ibid., p. 75.

an important achievement, for in harmony with his belief that the Czechs and Slovaks had to do it alone, he had stressed all along the importance of the Czechoslovak military effort, not only in Russia but also in France and later in Italy. Unfortunately, the Czechoslovak army could render little further service in fighting the Germans and Austrians, because after the failure of its July offensive the Russian army disintegrated, and fighting on the Eastern front came to a virtual standstill. In Lenin's memorable phrase, the Russian soldiers "voted for peace with their feet." The Bolsheviks, needless to say, were opposed to the aspirations of the Austrian Slavs, in which they saw manifestations of "bourgeois nationalism" and an obstacle to the conclusion of an immediate peace.

On November 8, the morrow of the Bolshevik coup d'état, Lenin issued the famous "Peace Decree," which unilaterally *decreed* Russia to be at peace and called on all belligerents to conclude an immediate peace on the basis of the Russian formula: no annexations, no indemnities, and self-determination of peoples. On December 5, the Central Powers granted Russia an armistice, and two weeks later the Brest-Litovsk peace conference opened. On Christmas Day Count Czernin, speaking for all members of the Central Alliance, accepted the Russian peace formula, with the reservation, however, that the question of national minorities was an internal one and should be solved by constitutional, rather than diplomatic, means by the states concerned.[29]

This casuistic interpretation of the Russian peace formula denied self-determination to the Austrian nationalities even while paying lip-service to it. On January 6 (Epiphany), 1918, the Czech parliamentary leaders protested, in the name of "the Czech people and the subjected and politically gagged Slovak branch," and demanded representation at the Brest-Litovsk conference.[30] Needless to say, the Central Powers ignored the Czech protest. The Czech "Epiphany Declaration" ("Tříkrálová deklarace"), however, which restated the demand for a Czechoslovak state without any reference to the Habsburg dynasty, was duly noted in Allied countries.

The Russian armistice (December 5, 1917) and the American declaration of war on Austria-Hungary (December 7, 1917) marked the third major shift in Czechoslovak opinion since the beginning of the war. After her withdrawal from the war, Russia could be of no further assistance to them. By declaring war on Austria-Hungary, the United States became their great hope. The American crusade for democracy also encouraged those Czechs and Slovaks who hoped to establish a democratic Czecho-

---

[29] James B. Scott (ed.), *Official Statements of War Aims and Peace Proposals, December 1916 to November 1918* (Washington, 1921), p. 221.

[30] Text of declaration in Beneš, *Dokumenty*, No. 107, pp. 318-21. See also Tobolka, *Politické dějiny*, IV, 314-16; Paulová, *Tajný výbor*, pp. 372-78; and Soukup, *28 říjen 1918*, I, 607-14.

slovak republic. In March, 1918, after making arrangements to transfer the Czechoslovak army from Russia to the Western front, Masaryk set out, via Siberia and Japan, for the United States to win President Wilson to the Czechoslovak cause.

PRESIDENT WILSON AND ALLIED RECOGNITION

After the war the Czechs and Slovaks hailed the American president as one of their liberators. The accolade was well warranted, even though Wilson's attitude toward them and other oppressed nationalities had not been constant but had undergone a gradual evolution.

As early as May 27, 1916, in an address to the League to Enforce Peace in Washington, Wilson stated as the foremost principle of an equitable peace that "every people has a right to choose the sovereignty under which they shall live."[31] The principle of government by the consent of the governed or national self-determination, that the founding fathers had invoked to justify the American Revolution, was for him a self-evident truth, a natural right, and an indispensable corollary of democracy, but not yet a principle of action. He appears to have been unaware at the time of its revolutionary implications if applied to multinational empires or reluctant to accept its logical conclusion, namely, their dismemberment. A year later, in August, 1917, in declining the peace proposal of Pope Benedict XV, he wrote that "dismemberment of empires . . . we deem inexpedient."[32]

In his memorable address to Congress on April 2, 1917, Wilson recommended a declaration of war on Germany, but counseled against a declaration of war on Germany's allies because he hoped to separate them from Germany. In his annual address to Congress on December 4, 1917, he recommended a declaration of war on Austria-Hungary, largely to bolster the shaken morale of Italy, which had recently suffered a grievous defeat at Caporetto. However, he hastened to give Vienna an assurance against dismemberment: "We owe it, however, to ourselves to say that we do not wish in any way to impair or to rearrange the Austro-Hungarian Empire. It is no affair of ours what they do with their own life, either industrially or politically."[33] Finally, in his celebrated Fourteen Points address on January 8, 1918, he called for "the freest opportunity of autonomous development" for "the peoples of Austria-Hungary" (Point Ten) but not for their independence.[34]

It was not until after the collapse of the secret negotiations with

[31] *The Messages and Papers of Woodrow Wilson* (2 vols.; New York, 1924), I, 274.

[32] Ibid., 424.   [33] Ibid., 447.   [34] Ibid., 469.

Vienna for a separate peace in April, 1918, that Wilson accepted—quite reluctantly at first, it appears—the alternate policy toward Austria-Hungary of encouraging its disaffected nationalities to revolt by holding out to them the prospect of freedom.[35] The new American policy was announced by Secretary of State Robert Lansing in a declaration on May 29, which stated that the "nationalistic aspirations of the Czecho-Slovaks and Jugo-Slavs for freedom" had the "earnest sympathy" of the United States government.[36] Five days later, on June 3, the French, British, and Italian prime ministers, who had gathered at Versailles for the meeting of the Allied Supreme War Council, noted the American declaration "with pleasure" and hastened to "associate themselves" with it.[37]

Masaryk has often been credited—approvingly by critics of the Habsburg empire and disapprovingly by its sympathizers—with converting Wilson to an anti-Austrian policy. This, indeed, had been Masaryk's intention when he first became aware of the president's intention to maintain Austria-Hungary intact on hearing Wilson's address of December 4, 1917.[38] However, by the time Masaryk arrived in the United States in May, 1918, Wilson's attitude toward Austria-Hungary had changed. Masaryk's task, therefore, was no longer to prejudice the president against the Dual Monarchy but to seek to commit him as firmly as possible to support the Czechoslovak aspirations.

In this task Masaryk was assisted by an unexpected circumstance: the outbreak of a conflict between the Czechoslovak army and the Soviet government in Siberia in May, 1918. The speed and ease with which the Czechoslovak army seized the Siberian railway in May and June convinced the Russian anti-Bolsheviks and the Allied governments that the Soviet government was weak and could easily be overthrown. The Soviet-Czechoslovak conflict precipitated the Russian Civil War and Allied intervention in Russia.

On June 30, preparing to intervene in Russia, the French government recognized the Czechoslovak National Council in Paris as an official agency authorized to represent the Czechoslovak cause. On August 9, the British government followed suit. On September 3, going much farther than the French and British governments, the United States government recognized the Czechoslovak National Council as "a *de facto*

---

[35] Victor S. Mamatey, *The United States and East Central Europe, 1914-1918: A Study in Wilsonian Diplomacy and Propaganda* (Princeton, 1957), pp. 252-61.

[36] Lansing to Page, May 29, 1918, *Foreign Relations: 1918, The World War, 1918*, Supplement 1 (2 vols.; Washington, 1933), I, 808-809.

[37] Frazier to Lansing, June 4, 1918, ibid., pp. 809-10.

[38] Kudela, *Profesor Masaryk*, pp. 142-45; Masaryk, *The Making of a State*, p. 273.

belligerent government, clothed with proper authority to direct the military and political affairs of the Czecho-Slovaks."[39] Unlike the Fourteen Points, which spoke only of "autonomous development" for the Austrian peoples, or the later expressions of "sympathy" for the Czechoslovak and Yugoslav movements, the American and Allied recognition of the Czechoslovak National Council committed them to support Czechoslovak independence.

RESISTANCE AT HOME

The Czech political leaders at home were encouraged by the gradual shift of Allied policy from a pro-Austrian to an anti-Austrian course, of which they were informed by Beneš through the secret channels of the Mafia and by Allied public statements, to intensify their anti-Austrian activity. On May 15-17, they invited representatives of all the disaffected Austrian nationalities to Prague, ostensibly to observe the fiftieth anniversary of the foundation of the Czech National Theater, actually to stage a demonstration of their solidarity and anti-Austrian feeling, in imitation of the well-publicized Congress of Oppressed Nationalities of Austria-Hungary held in Rome in April.[40]

Two months later, on July 13, the Czech political leaders formed under Kramář's chairmanship a thirty-member "Czechoslovak National Committee" in Prague. All Czech political parties were represented in it on the basis of the results of the last Austrian Reichsrat election in 1911.[41] Under the impression of war and revolution, Czech public opinion had shifted considerably to the left since 1911. The Czech Social Democratic and Socialist parties felt that they and the Czech working class, which they claimed to represent, were under-represented in the Prague National Committee. Therefore, on September 6, they formed a "Socialist Council," consisting of thirteen members, most of whom were also members of the National Committee.[42] In this way, without breaking Czech national solidarity, a special body to represent the interests of Czech workers was created. It cooperated closely with the National Committee. The National Committee styled itself "Czechoslovak," although—for obvious reasons—it included no Slovak. Nevertheless, despite protests from Budapest, it continued to speak out for the Slovaks.

Meanwhile, Slovak political activity had revived. The Slovak National

---

[39] *Foreign Relations, 1918*, Suppl. 1, I, 824-25.

[40] Soukup, *28. říjen 1918*, II, 690-704; Paulová, *Tajný výbor*, pp. 454-64; Tobolka, *Politické dějiny*, IV, 359-61.

[41] Tobolka, *Politické dějiny*, pp. 361-64; Soukup, *28. říjen 1918*, II, 825-28; Paulová, *Tajný výbor*, pp. 497-98.

[42] Paulová, *Tajný výbor*, p. 499; Soukup, *28. říjen 1918*, II, 903-904; Tobolka, *Politické dějiny*, IV, 370-71.

22

party had been forbidden all public activity since the beginning of the war. When the Hungarian authorities permitted a Social Democratic rally to be held at Liptovský Svätý Mikuláš on May 1 to observe International Labor Day, however, the Slovak politicians seized the opportunity to express—for the first time since the beginning of the war—Slovak national aspirations. At the meeting, Vavro Šrobár read a resolution that demanded, in addition to the usual workers' social goals, the "unconditional right of self-determination" for all Austro-Hungarian peoples, including "the Hungarian branch of the Czechoslovak family."[43] The Mikuláš Declaration constituted the first Slovak public endorsement of the principle of Czechoslovak unity.

Encouraged by the Prague manifestations in mid-May which many of them had attended, the leaders of the Slovak National party met secretly at Turčiansky Svätý Martin on May 24—for the first time since the beginning of the war—to consult on a course of action. During the debate the impetuous Hlinka urged: "Let us openly declare ourselves for the Czechoslovak orientation! Our thousand-year marriage with the Magyars has failed. We must part ways!"[44] Indeed, to part ways with the Hungarians proved to be the sense of the meeting. It was also decided to form a Slovak national council representing all Slovak political trends. However, the Mikuláš and Prague manifestations had aroused the vigilance of the Hungarian authorities. Šrobár was arrested and police surveillance of the Slovak politicians was tightened, which delayed the formation of the Slovak National Council until October.

DISSOLUTION OF THE HABSBURG EMPIRE

On August 9, the Allies launched a great offensive on the Western Front, which rolled on relentlessly until the Compiègne armistice. The Austrian leaders became alarmed even before the Germans, for it was obvious that if the Central Powers were defeated Germany would survive, though bleeding and humiliated, but Austria might not. In August, Vienna proposed to Berlin a joint peace overture to the Allies. However, the Germans were still hopeful of a reversal of fortunes on the Western Front and declined the suggestion. Vienna went ahead alone, therefore. On September 14, it proposed that all belligerents enter into secret nonbinding discussions of the "fundamental principles" of peace.[45] With victory

---

[43] Šrobár, *Pamäti z vojny a väzenia*, pp. 73-74; a partial English translation of the Mikuláš declaration may be found in Jozef Lettrich, *History of Modern Slovakia* (New York, 1955), Document 2, p. 287.

[44] Karol A. Medvecký, *Slovenský prevrat* [*Slovak Revolution*] (4 vols.; Trnava, 1930-31), III, 346; for the resolution of the meeting, see Lettrich, *History*, Doc. 3, p. 288.

[45] Scott, *Official Statements*, p. 389.

in sight, however, the Allies were not inclined to discuss peace principles. All of them rejected the Austrian proposal, the United States on the grounds that the president had "repeatedly and with entire candor" stated his peace terms and that, therefore, further discussions of peace principles would be superfluous.[46]

By the end of September, the German high command panicked over the continued Allied advance and advised the German government to seek peace. On October 4, Germany and Austria-Hungary addressed separate but similar notes to President Wilson, offering to discuss peace on the basis of the Fourteen Points. This put Wilson in a quandary as far as Austria-Hungary was concerned, because Point Ten of the Fourteen Points had been superseded and voided by the American expressions of sympathy for the Czechoslovaks and Yugoslavs and especially by the American recognition of the Czechoslovak National Council. He delayed a reply to Vienna for two weeks, therefore, even while replying to Berlin at once. The delay caused extreme uneasiness and wild speculation in Vienna. In an effort to show Austrian readiness to comply with the Fourteen Points, Emperor Charles issued on October 16 a manifesto on the federalization of the Austrian half of the empire (the Hungarians had refused to go along and federalize Hungary).[47] The manifesto authorized the nationalities to form national committees or sanctioned existing ones.

In Washington, Masaryk, fearing that the manifesto might lead to new negotiations between Washington and Vienna, hastily countered it by issuing a Czechoslovak declaration of independence (October 18).[48] His fear proved unwarranted, however. In his reply to Vienna on October 19, President Wilson stated that he could no longer negotiate with Austria-Hungary on the basis of the Fourteen Points, because since their issuance the United States had recognized the aspirations of the Czechoslovaks and the Yugoslavs to freedom, and therefore they, and not he, had to determine what action on the part of the Austro-Hungarian government would satisfy them.[49] Wilson's note caused panic in Vienna, for the Austrian statesmen knew that if the matter were left up to the Czechoslovaks and Yugoslavs they would demand nothing less than complete independence. It was not the Czechs or the Southern Slavs, however, but the German Austrians who took the initiative to dissolve the empire.

On October 21, basing themselves on the imperial manifesto, the German-Austrian deputies withdrew from the Reichsrat and constituted themselves a provisional national assembly of an independent German-

[46] Ibid., p. 396.

[47] Stovall to Lansing, October 18, 1918, *Foreign Relations, 1918*, Suppl. 1, I, 367-68.

[48] Masaryk to Lansing, October 18, 1918, ibid., pp. 847-49.

[49] Lansing to Ekengren, October 19, 1918, ibid., p. 368.

Austrian state.[50] For the moment, they left in abeyance the question of whether they would enter into a confederation with other independent national states of the former Habsburg empire, or join Germany.

While the emperor and his advisers desperately cast about for a way out, the Italians launched their last offensive against the Austrian army (October 24). Austrian resistance soon collapsed and the army disintegrated. Like the Russian soldiers in July, 1917, the Austrian soldiers voted for peace with their feet. On frantic appeals from the Austrian high command that feared a Bolshevik revolution, the Austro-Hungarian government unconditionally accepted Wilson's last note and asked him to arrange an immediate armistice (October 27).[51] Wilson's ponderous diplomacy, however, proved too slow for Austria. In the end, unable to wait for his mediation, the Austrian high command entered into direct negotiations with the Italian high command. On November 3, the Austro-Hungarian armistice was signed at Padua. In a sense, it was a hollow legal ceremony, for not only the Austro-Hungarian army but the Habsburg empire itself had already largely disintegrated.

Contrary to a common myth, the Habsburg empire was not *dismembered from without* by the Allies at the Paris Peace Conference, but *broke up from within* in the days immediately preceding and following the Padua armistice. The disappearance of the Habsburg empire left a legal vacuum in East Central Europe, which the Allied powers, too preoccupied with their own affairs, failed to fill. No Allied armies occupied Vienna and Budapest in 1918 to fill the vacuum left by the fall of the Habsburg government, as Allied armies were to occupy Berlin in 1945 to fill the vacuum left by the fall of Hitler's government. When the Allied Supreme War Council drafted the terms of the Padua armistice early in October, the Allied powers assumed that Austria-Hungary could remain whole, at least until the peace conference. The armistice provided for Italian occupation of the Austrian territories that Italy hoped to annex, but made no provision for the disposal of the rest of the empire. In this *vacuum juris*, which lasted until the opening of the Paris Peace Conference more than two months later, the successor states of the Habsburg empire were left to fend for themselves. Each sought to protect its interests by its own means.

ESTABLISHMENT OF THE CZECHOSLOVAK REPUBLIC

When the news of the Austrian note of October 27 to Wilson reached Prague on the morning of October 28, the Czechs took it to mean that

[50] Otto Bauer, *The Austrian Revolution* (London, 1925), p. 48.
[51] Ekengren to Lansing, October 29, 1918, *Foreign Relations, 1918*, Suppl. 1, I, 404-405.

Vienna recognized their right of independence. On the evening of October 28, after securing the acquiescence of the Austrian military authorities in Prague by professing to act in the limits of Emperor Charles' federalization manifesto, the Prague National Committee issued its first "law": "The independent Czechoslovak state has come into being."[52] It was not until October 30, however, that the National Committee was free from a threat of a coup by the Austrian command in Prague, thanks to the refusal of the Prague garrison, consisting largely of Rumanian and Hungarian troops, to engage in any action against the Czech population and their insistence on returning to their homes. On the same day, October 30, the Slovak leaders met at Turčiansky Svätý Martin and formed the Slovak National Council that had been planned since May. Unaware of the declaration of Czechoslovak independence in Prague, the Slovak National Council adopted a resolution that merely demanded the right of self-determination for the Slovaks and endorsed the principle of Czechoslovak unity ("The Slovak nation is a part of the Czechoslovak nation, united in language and in the history of its culture.").[53]

On October 31, Kramář, leading a delegation of the Prague National Committee, and Beneš, representing the Paris National Council, concluded a three-day conference in Geneva at which the practical aspects of setting the new Czechoslovak state afloat were agreed upon. It was definitely decided that Czechoslovakia would be a democratic parliamentary republic and that Masaryk would be its first president. More delicate were the negotiations concerning the composition of the first Czechoslovak cabinet under Kramář as premier and with Beneš as foreign minister and Štefánik as minister of war.[54] The delegation returned to Prague on November 5, amidst frenzied public acclaim. However, it was not until after Emperor Charles' abdication on November 11 and the proclamation of the German-Austrian Republic and its *Anschluss* to Germany on

[52] Alois Kocman et al. (eds.), *Boj o směr vývoje československého státu* [Struggle for the Direction of the Development of the Czechoslovak State] (2 vols.; Prague, 1965-69), I, No. 89, p. 113. On October 14 the Socialist Council issued a proclamation calling for a general strike and the establishment of a Czechoslovak republic. However, the National Committee regarded the move as premature and also as a threat to its leadership of the Czech people, and frustrated it. For descriptions of the crowded October events in Prague, see Soukup, *28. říjen 1918*, II, 954-56 and 983-1051; Tobolka, *Politické dějiny*, IV, 379-95; Jan Opočenský, *The Collapse of the Austro-Hungarian Monarchy and the Rise of the Czechoslovak State* (Prague, 1928), pp. 36-51 and 93-152; and Richard G. Plaschka, *Cattaro-Prag: Revolte und Revolution* (Graz, 1963), pp. 195-297.

[53] Martin Grečo, *Martinská deklárácia* [The Martin Declaration] (2nd ed., Turčiansky Svätý Martin, 1947), pp. 105-13; Medvecký, *Slovenský prevrat*, I, 342-46. An English translation of the Martin declaration may be found in Lettrich, *History*, Doc. No. 4, pp. 288-89.

[54] Tobolka, *Politické dějiny*, IV, 395-98; Opočenský, *The Collapse*, pp. 51-65; Pichlík, *Zahraniční odboj*, pp. 466-71; Beneš, *Světová válka*, II, 394. For the Geneva declaration, see Beneš, *Dokumenty*, No. 195, pp. 492-93.

November 12,[55] which definitely buried the possibility of a confederation of the successor states of the Habsburg empire, that the Prague National Committee proceeded to implement the Geneva agreement. On November 13, it adopted a provisional constitution providing for the creation of a provisional ("revolutionary") national assembly.[56] On the following day, the National Assembly formally elected Masaryk (then still in Washington) president and invested the cabinet under Kramář.

The first task of the new government was to establish its authority throughout the territory of Czechoslovakia. This was no simple task, because the government had neither legal title to the territory nor armed forces with which to secure it.

OCCUPATION OF THE SUDETEN GERMAN AREAS

In their wartime memoranda to the Allies, Masaryk, Beneš, and Štefánik had made it clear that they regarded the historic boundaries of Bohemia, Moravia, and Silesia as the natural boundaries of the future Czechoslovakia, but had been somewhat uncertain about the limits of Slovakia. The Czech leaders at home were likewise determined to preserve the historic boundaries of the Czech provinces. However, this aim encountered the opposition of the Sudeten Germans. On October 21, the Sudeten German deputies had joined other German deputies in the Reichsrat in forming the German-Austrian National Assembly and had declared the German parts of Bohemia, Moravia, and Silesia to be parts of German-Austria. The difficulty of this arrangement was that the Sudeten Germans did not inhabit one well-defined area adjoining Austria, but were spread in a band of varying width all along the Bohemian, Moravian, and Silesian boundary, facing both Germany and Austria. The largest concentration of them occurred in northern Bohemia, adjoining Germany, not Austria. For this reason, they were forced to create not one but four separate provinces: (1) Deutschböhmen (in northern Bohemia adjoining Germany); (2) Sudetenland (in Silesia and northern Moravia adjoining Germany); (3) Böhmerwaldgau (in southern Bohemia facing Bavaria); and (4) Deutschsüdmähren (in southern Moravia adjoining Austria).[57] The four provinces could not communicate with one another or the two

---

[55] David F. Strong, *Austria, October 1918—March 1919* (New York, 1939), pp. 115-18.

[56] For the text of the provisional constitution, see Kocman, *Boj o směr*, I, No. 118, pp. 133-35.

[57] Johann Wolfgang Brügel, *Tschechen und Deutsche, 1918-1938* (Munich, 1967), pp. 48-51; Ferdinand Peroutka, *Budování státu: Československá politika v letech popřevratových* [*The Building of the State: Czechoslovak Politics in the Postwar Years*] (2nd ed., 5 vols. in 6; Prague, 1936), I, 159-62.

northern ones with Austria, except across Czech territory. With the exception of Deutschsüdmähren, they were largely industrial areas in character, and depended for food on the Czech areas. Their supply of fuel and raw materials was likewise centrally controlled through Prague. Because of geography, Bohemia, Moravia, and Silesia constituted one of the most natural and best-integrated economic units in Europe. It was no accident that the boundaries of Bohemia and Moravia, if not of Silesia, had scarcely changed since Charlemagne.

On October 30, the Sudeten German nationalist Reichsrat deputy Rudolf Lodgman von Auen and on November 4 the Sudeten German Social Democratic Reichsrat deputy Josef Seliger arrived in Prague to seek food and supplies for the Sudeten German areas. The Czech leaders then suggested to them that they and the other representatives of Sudeten German parties join the Prague National Committee and share in the task of building the new Czechoslovak state. If the Sudeten Germans had accepted the Czech offer, Czech-German relations and the whole history of Czechoslovakia might have taken a different course. However, apart from being affected by the old German-Czech antagonism, they tended to regard Czechoslovakia at that time as an "artificial" and "ephemeral" state (*künstliche Staat, Saisonstaat*) and did not see any wisdom in boarding a sinking ship, as it were. They therefore declined the Czech offer and kept their Austrian connection.[58]

It would have made more sense for Deutschböhmen, Sudetenland, and Böhmerwaldgau to seek admission to Germany which they adjoined, rather than to Austria from which they were separated by Czech territory. However, Germany, in the throes of revolution, was not interested in the Sudeten Germans at that time. Nevertheless, they did not exclude the possibility of joining Germany. All along, their assumption was that if the plans for a confederation of the successor states of the Habsburg empire did not materialize, German-Austria would join Germany. Indeed, as already noted, the German-Austrian National Assembly voted for *Anschluss* to Germany on November 12. Therefore, by joining Austria, the Sudeten Germans would be joining Germany. Once this was accomplished, the absorption of the Czech parts of Bohemia, Moravia, and Silesia into Greater Germany would inevitably follow, for—as the events in 1938-39 were to prove—the Czech and German parts of the historic provinces could not live apart. Either the Sudeten German areas would belong to Czechoslovakia or the whole of Bohemia, Moravia, and Silesia to Greater Germany. *Tertium non datur*—there was no third possibility. Both the Czech and Sudeten German leaders were well aware of it, and acted accordingly.

[58] Ibid., pp. 185-88; Brügel, *Tschechen und Deutsche*, pp. 61-66.

Given equal resolve on both sides, the issue could be decided only by force. In theory, the Sudeten Germans, numbering about 3 million, stood a fair chance of standing off the Czechs, numbering about 6 million, especially if the former were aided by their kinsmen in Austria and Germany. Neither side possessed any organized armed forces at the time. The Czechoslovak legions were still abroad. Both sides, therefore, depended on volunteers, to be recruited among the Czech or Sudeten German soldiers of the disbanded Austro-Hungarian army then straggling home from the fronts. Both were warweary. Still, the Czechs were elated over their newly-acquired independence, while the Sudeten Germans were depressed by the defeat of Austria and Germany. In the end, this psychological difference decided the issue. While enough Czechs responded to the Czechoslovak government's call for volunteers, the Sudeten Germans failed completely to respond to the appeals of their leaders to resist the Czechs. Austria and Germany likewise declined their appeals to intervene in the situation. The Czechoslovak occupation of the Sudeten German areas, which began in the latter part of November and was over in about a month, proved therefore to be little more than a military parade. Except at Most (Brüx), where minor skirmishes occurred on November 27-29, the Sudeten German resistance was token or none.[59]

After the occupation, the Sudeten German leaders fled to Vienna, where they resumed their seats in the German-Austrian National Assembly until the signing of the St. Germain peace. On November 22, 1918, the Vienna National Assembly passed a law formally incorporating the Sudeten German areas in German-Austria.[60] In notes to the Allied governments on December 13 and 16, the German-Austrian government protested the Czechoslovak occupation of the Sudeten German areas and asked for Allied arbitration of the conflict. Beneš, who had returned to Paris after the Geneva conference with the Prague leaders, then took up the matter with the French government. The French leaders saw at once the danger to their own interests in allowing Austria, which had just declared for *Anschluss* to Germany, jurisdiction over the Sudeten German areas. They were determined that Germany must not come out of the war with one square foot of additional territory. Therefore, they not only approved but positively insisted on the Czechoslovak occupation of the Sudeten German areas. On December 19, without consulting Britain or the United States, Foreign Minister Stephen Pichon replied to Vienna that Czechoslovakia had been recognized as an Allied nation and that, "at least until the decision of the Peace Conference," she should have

---

[59] Brügel, *Tschechen und Deutsche*, pp. 59-60; Pichlík, *Červenobílá a rudá*, pp. 396-400.

[60] Strong, *Austria*, pp. 131-32.

the boundaries of the historic provinces of Bohemia, Moravia, and Austrian Silesia."[61] The British and United States governments, with whom Beneš next took up the matter,[62] acquiesced in the French decision, with the proviso that it should not prejudice the final decision of the peace conference.

OCCUPATION OF SLOVAKIA

The occupation of Slovakia proved more difficult and complicated than that of the Sudeten German areas. On November 1, Hungary withdrew from the Habsburg empire, but the new liberal-democratic Hungarian government of Count Michael Károlyi was as reluctant as the old royal government to allow the non-Magyars to withdraw from Hungary. At first, however, the Károlyi government was too preoccupied with internal as well as external difficulties to attend to the Slovaks.

As soldiers, often armed, straggled home from the fronts, Hungary was swept by a great wave of social turbulence. Peasants and workers revenged centuries of ruthless exploitation by looting and burning landowners' mansions in the countryside and merchants' shops in the towns.[63] In many parts of Slovakia Hungarian authority collapsed. The Slovak National Council at Turčiansky Svätý Martin made no attempt to fill the void. Completely inexperienced in the exercise of political power, the Slovak politicians tended to confuse it with abstract political rights, which should be granted them from above by some superior authority—presumably, President Wilson at the peace conference. They did not think it proper or necessary to try to seize power by their own efforts. While they sat back and awaited developments, however, the more experienced Czechs acted.

On November 4, the Prague National Committee appointed a four-member Slovak "government" under Vavro Šrobár, gave it some money and seventy Czech gendarmes, and sent it to Slovakia. On the following day the small band crossed the Moravian-Slovak boundary, proclaimed the Czechoslovak Republic in Slovakia, and set up headquarters in the small town of Uhorská Skalica. Šrobár was soon recalled to Prague and the "Skalica government" was abolished on November 14, when the Czechoslovak government was constituted. However, Šrobár's colleague Pavel Blaho remained at Skalica as Czechoslovak commissioner. With

[61] Beneš, *Světová válka*, II, 499-501; *Foreign Relations, 1919: The Paris Peace Conference* (13 vols.; Washington, 1942-47), II, 379-83. Hereafter *The Paris Peace Conference*.

[62] Ibid.

[63] Medvecký, *Slovenský prevrat*, III, 3 ff.

the aid of Czech and local Slovak volunteers, he managed to maintain and expand the small enclave in Slovakia under Prague's authority.[64]

The Padua armistice provided that the Allied armies could continue to advance into Austro-Hungarian territory until the surrender of Germany. Consequently, until the Compiègne armistice on November 11, the Allied armies of the southeastern command (Macedonian front) under Gen. Louis Franchet d'Espérey, which had freed Serbia by the end of October, continued to advance into Hungary. In order to halt their advance, Count Károlyi solicited from Gen. Franchet d'Espérey a separate armistice. It was concluded at Belgrade on November 13, and laid down a demarcation line between the Hungarian and Serbian armies in southern Hungary. However, it made no provision for the Czechoslovak occupation of Slovakia in the north or the Rumanian occupation of Transylvania in the east.[65] The Hungarians assumed that this assured them the control of these areas, at least until the peace conference. They were to be disappointed. The conclusion of the separate Belgrade armistice proved to be a tactical blunder on Károlyi's part.

The Padua armistice in no way affected Hungary. Its terms had been drafted to accommodate Italy, the only major Allied power that had fought Austria-Hungary directly. The Italians, who were responsible for its enforcement, had no quarrel with the Hungarians. On the contrary, they felt a certain sympathy for them, based on their common hostility to Yugoslavia. On the other hand, the Belgrade armistice, for the enforcement of which the French were responsible, put Hungary under direct Allied control. An Allied armistice commission was established at Budapest under a French officer, Lt. Col. Ferdinand Vyx (Vix).[66] The French sympathized with Hungary's hostile neighbors, especially with Serbia, which provided the bulk of the Allied troops in Hungary.

At first, the Hungarian government made no effort to resist Šrobár's effort to establish Czechoslovak authority in Slovakia. However, on November 13, the day of the Belgrade armistice, it sent troops into Slovakia to reassert its authority there. On November 15, they entered Turčiansky Svätý Martin, dispersed the Slovak National Council, and arrested its chairman. They forced the feeble Czechoslovak forces in western Slovakia to fall back toward the Moravian boundary, but did not succeed in driving them out altogether. The Czechoslovak government, lacking suf-

---

[64] Šrobár, *Osvobodené Slovensko*, pp. 194-203; Pichlík, *Červenobílá a rudá*, pp. 402-404.

[65] Francis Deak, *Hungary at the Peace Conference* (New York, 1942), pp. 359-61.

[66] Peter Pastor, "The Vix Mission in Hungary, 1918-1919: A Re-examination," *Slavic Review*, XXIX (September, 1970), 481-98.

ficient military strength to dispute Slovakia with the Hungarians, then turned to diplomacy for help.

In Paris, Beneš protested to Pichon and Marshal Foch against Gen. Franchet d'Espérey's failure to include any provision in the Belgrade armistice with regard to Slovakia, and asked that the Czechoslovak government, as a recognized Allied government, be permitted to occupy the area. Since no administrative boundary existed separating Slovakia from the rest of Hungary, he proposed a demarcation line between the Czechoslovak and Hungarian forces that was to run along the Danube and the Ipeľ' (Ipoly) rivers and would place the fertile, largely Magyar-inhabited, plain north of the Danube under Czechoslovak control. The French government agreed to his request readily enough. On November 27, it sent instructions to Colonel Vyx in Budapest to inform the Hungarian government to evacuate Slovakia. However, the instructions failed to include the demarcation line proposed by Beneš.[67] Apparently, the French whose knowledge of the political geography of East Central Europe was quite limited, assumed that *le pays slovaque* was as definite a term as, for instance, Bohemia or Alsace-Lorraine, and thought that inclusion of a demarcation line was superfluous.

The matter was further confused by unauthorized negotiations carried on with the Hungarian government by the Czechoslovak commissioner in Budapest, Milan Hodža. In an effort to induce the Hungarian government to evacuate Slovakia, Hodža had entered into negotiations with Oscar Jászi, the Hungarian Minister of Nationalities, for Slovak autonomy *within Hungary* until a decision of the peace conference. Moreover, when he was informed by Colonel Vyx of the French instruction to the Hungarian government to evacuate Slovakia which lacked a demarcation line, he proposed to negotiate one. On December 6, acting again without Prague's authorization, Hodža concluded an agreement with Béla Bártha, the Hungarian Minister of Defense, providing for a demarcation line that was much less advantageous to the Slovaks than the one that Beneš had proposed. It provided for Hungarian evacuation of only the poor, mountainous, purely Slovak districts of northern and central Slovakia.[68] It left the principal towns of Slovakia, Bratislava and Košice, under Hungarian control, as well as all of eastern Slovakia, where on the same day, December 6, a Slovak renegade, Victor Dvorčák, set up an "East Slovak Republic," claiming that the eastern Slovaks were a distinct nationality.

[67] Ibid., 486-87; Deak, *Hungary*, p. 13; Beneš, *Světová válka*, II, 489.
[68] Beneš, *Světová válka*, 488-95; Beneš, *Dokumenty*, Nos. 214, 215, 223, 224, and 226, pp. 526-35, 537-41; Václav Chaloupecký, *Zápas o Slovensko 1918* [*Struggle for Slovakia, 1918*] (Prague, 1930), pp. 104-95 *passim*; for Hodža's explanation, see his collection of articles *Slovenský rozchod s Maďarmi roku 1918* [*The Slovak Break with the Magyars in 1918*] (Bratislava, 1928).

When the news of Hodža's action reached Prague, it produced an uproar. The Czechoslovak government disavowed it. Beneš, who was much embarrassed by Hodža's inopportune initiative, undertook new negotiations with the French to undo it. The French were disgruntled by the discordant voices of the Czechoslovak representatives in Paris and Budapest which put them in an embarrassing position too, but agreed to correct their oversight in the instructions of November 27. On December 19, at the same time as he informed Vienna of Czechoslovakia's right to the historic boundaries of Bohemia, Moravia, and Silesia, Pichon reiterated the order to Budapest to evacuate Slovakia—and this time included the demarcation line proposed by Beneš.[69] The Hungarian government protested but complied.

At about the same time, Czechoslovakia's military posture improved. On December 20, Masaryk returned to Prague from exile, via Italy, accompanied by the first elements of the Italian legion under Gen. Luigi Piccione. Together with new and better organized Czech troops, the legionnaires were at once sent to Slovakia. Moving swiftly along the strategic Bohumín (Oderberg)-Košice railway, they reached Košice on December 30, whereupon the Dvorčák republic collapsed. On January 1-2, 1919, another column occupied Bratislava. By January 20, the Czechoslovak government was in control of all of Slovakia.

THE TĚŠÍN CONFLICT

Another territorial problem that the Czechoslovak government had to face immediately upon its constitution, was that of the duchy of Těšín (Czieszyn, Teschen) in Silesia. The coal-rich district of Těšín, with the town of the same name, had an area of only about 350 square miles and a population (according to the last Austrian census of 1910) of 227,000, of whom 65 percent were Poles (many of them not indigenous to the area but recent arrivals from Austrian Galicia), 18.2 percent were Czechs, and 12.4 percent were Germans. The duchy had belonged to medieval Poland until the fourteenth century and from then until 1918 to the Bohemian crown. The new Polish Republic raised a claim to it on ethnic and distant historic grounds. Czechoslovakia claimed it partly on historic grounds, partly on ethnic grounds, but especially on economic grounds (it formed an integral part of the important Moravian-Silesian coal-and-steel complex). On November 5, 1918, the local Czech and Polish national councils divided the area pending its final disposition at the peace conference. The line of division was based on ethnic rather than economic considerations, and considerable friction soon developed. Apart

[69] Beneš, *Světová válka*, II, 497-99; Chaloupecký, *Zápas*, pp. 197-200; Pastor, "The Vix Mission," p. 489; Deak, *Hungary*, p. 13.

from depriving Czechoslovakia of coal, it cut across the Bohumín-Košice railway, which was one of only two railroads that linked the Czech provinces to Slovakia at that time.[70]

When the French government recognized Czechoslovakia's right to the "boundaries of Bohemia, Moravia, and *Austrian Silesia*" in its note to Austria of December 19, the Czechoslovak government thought that it had French support for its claim to Těšín. However, the French government gave that assurance only against German-Austrian claims, not Polish. It viewed both Czechoslovakia and Poland as potential allies against Germany, but regarded Poland as more important than Czechoslovakia. It refused to back the Czechoslovak claim. In January, 1919, the Czechoslovak government, pressed by its military men, decided to secure Těšín by force and present the peace conference with a *fait accompli*. President Masaryk had qualms about using force, but his objections were overruled.[71] On January 21, 1919, the Czechoslovak government sent a note to Warsaw, reviewing its claim to Těšín and summoning the Poles to evacuate it.[72] Two days later Czechoslovak troops moved into the Polish-held portion of Těšín. The Poles, who were involved in armed conflicts over boundaries with the Ukrainians, Russians, and Germans at that time, yielded. However, they brought the matter before the peace conference that had opened in Paris on January 18. On January 29, the Council of Ten summoned Beneš and the Polish delegate Roman Dmowski to explain the dispute, and on February 1 obliged them to sign an agreement redividing the area pending its final disposition by the peace conference.[73] Czechoslovakia thus failed to gain her objective in Těšín. With this exception, however, and that of Ruthenia, to which she had not yet raised a claim, she entered the peace conference in possession of essentially all the territory to which she aspired.

PARIS PEACE CONFERENCE

When the Paris Peace Conference opened on January 18, the Allied powers were faced with a series of *faits accomplis* in East Central Europe, which they neither wished nor could challenge. By their inactivity after the Padua armistice, they had let control of the development in the area of the former Habsburg empire slip out of their hands. Now all they

[70] Titus Komarnicki, *Rebirth of the Polish Republic, 1914-1920* (London, 1957), pp. 356-58; Peroutka, *Budování státu*, I, 229-40.

[71] Peroutka, *Budování státu*, II, 603.

[72] Ibid., 603-11; Komarnicki, *Rebirth*, pp. 358-59; for the text of the Czechoslovak note, see Kocman, *Boj o směr*, I, No. 35, pp. 48-53.

[73] *The Paris Peace Conference*, III, 819-21; Kocman, *Boj o směr*, I, No. 38, pp. 55-56; Dagmar Perman, *The Shaping of the Czechoslovak State: Diplomatic History of the Boundaries of Czechoslovakia, 1914-1920* (Leiden, 1962), pp. 97-120; Komarnicki, *Rebirth*, 359-60.

could do was to arbitrate boundary and other conflicts between the successor states. It was relatively easy for them to adjudicate conflicting claims between an Allied and an enemy nation; they generally decided in favor of the former. The greatest difficulties at the peace conference arose when the Allied peacemakers were called on to arbitrate territorial disputes between two Allied nations, for example the Polish-Czechoslovak dispute over Těšín.

The Czechoslovak delegation to the Paris Peace Conference was led by Kramář and Beneš. Because of this greater experience in dealing with the Allied powers, however, Beneš assumed the main burden of defending the Czechoslovak claims. Despite his youth (thirty-four years of age), Beneš was an accomplished diplomat.

The difficulty inherent in presenting the Czechoslovak claims to the peace conference was the impossibility of putting the claims of the Czechs, who considered themselves heirs of the historic kingdom of Bohemia, and those of the Slovaks, who had no historic state to claim as predecessor, on a uniform basis. On the other hand, Czechoslovakia had the advantage that—with the exception of Těšín, which it disputed with Allied Poland—all of its claims were to be realized at the expense of "enemy" countries: Austria, Hungary, and, to some extent, Germany. Beneš presented the Czechoslovak claims before the Council of Ten on February 5 with skill and restraint.[74] He based the Czechoslovak claim to Bohemia, Moravia, and Silesia on historic grounds, in order to preserve the centuries-old natural boundary of the kingdom of Bohemia, even though this entailed including a large (about 3.2 million) Sudeten German minority in Czechoslovakia. On the other hand, he based the Czechoslovak claims in Slovakia on a mixture of historic, economic, and strategic considerations. In the north, he sought to preserve the historic Polish-Hungarian boundary, in order to protect Slovakia against Polish encroachment. In the south, where no historic boundary existed, he demanded a "natural" boundary based on the Danube and Ipel' rivers, in order to make Slovakia economically viable and strategically defensible. This entailed, however, inclusion in Slovakia of a large (about 750,000) Hungarian minority.

In addition to these claims Beneš put out a cautious and not too insistent claim to Lusatia, on the ground that the Lusatian Sorbs were Slavs

---

[74] *The Paris Peace Conference*, III, 877-87; Perman, *The Shaping*, pp. 125-31. In addition to presenting the Czechoslovak claims orally, Beneš also presented them at the request of the Allied powers in the form of eleven memoranda. See Czechoslovak Delegation to the Peace Conference of 1919, *Mémoires* (Paris, 1919). The memoranda, which were printed privately for the use of the Peace Conference only, were later translated into German and published by Hermann Raschhofer (ed.), *Tschechoslowakischen Denkschriften für die Friedenskonferenz von Paris, 1919-1920* (Berlin, 1937).

and would prefer to live in Slavic Czechoslovakia and that Lusatia had been a province of the Bohemian crown until the Thirty Years' War. In the east, he put out a claim to Ruthenia (Subcarpathian Russia, Carpatho-Ukraine, Transcarpathian Ukraine), on the ground that the Slavic Ruthenians would be happier in Slavic Czechoslovakia than in Hungary, where they had been sorely oppressed and exploited,[75] and because possession of Ruthenia would give Czechoslovakia the strategic advantage of a common frontier with Rumania. On similar strategic grounds, he demanded the creation of a territorial corridor across western Hungary, in order to give Czechoslovakia a common boundary with Yugoslavia. After hearing the Czechoslovak claims, the Council of Ten created the Commission of Czechoslovak Affairs to advise them.

The Czechoslovak Commission, which consisted of experts of the major Allied powers, completed its recommendations early in March.[76] It rejected the Czechoslovak claims to Lusatia and a territorial corridor to Yugoslavia, but otherwise satisfied all their demands. It confirmed the historic Bohemian frontier and the historic Polish-Slovak boundary; it delimited the Slovak-Hungarian boundary substantially as Beneš had requested; and it approved the attribution of Ruthenia to Czechoslovakia, though with a provision for Ruthenian autonomy. On March 25, to expedite the work of the peace conference, the Council of Ten was divided into the Council of Four (The "Big Four") and the Council of Five (the foreign ministers). Early in April the two councils considered and approved the recommendations of the Czechoslovak commission without a change—with the exception of Těšín, which they referred to Poland and Czechoslovakia to settle in bilateral negotiations.[77]

The signing of the peace treaties with Austria and Hungary was delayed by the rise of the Hungarian Soviet Republic under Béla Kun and its attempt to recover Slovakia for Hungary. During the conflict (May 1-June 23, 1919), the Hungarian Red Army penetrated deep into central Slovakia and overran all of eastern Slovakia. On May 25, a Czech left-wing socialist and Béla Kun's associate, Antonín Janoušek, proclaimed

---

[75] The initiative toward the union of Ruthenia with Czechoslovakia came largely from Ruthenian immigrants in the United States. See Victor S. Mamatey, "The Slovaks and Carpatho-Ruthenians," in Joseph P. O'Grady (ed.), *The Immigrants' Influence on Wilson's Peace Policies* (Lexington, 1967), pp. 239-49.

[76] Perman, *The Shaping*, pp. 153-55.

[77] When the Polish-Czechoslovak negotiations failed, the Allied powers proposed plebiscites in the Těšín area and also in the border districts of Orava and Spiš in Slovakia to which the Poles had raised claims. In the end, however, no plebiscites were held. Instead, on July 28, 1920, during the Polish-Soviet war, the Conference of Ambassadors divided each of the three disputed areas between Poland and Czechoslovakia, leaving them both somewhat unhappy. See Perman, *The Shaping*, pp. 255-56 and 272; Komarnicki, *Rebirth*, p. 365.

a "Slovak Soviet Republic" at Prešov.[78] It allied itself with Soviet Hungary against the Czechoslovak Republic. However, when Béla Kun yielded to an ultimatum from the Allied powers and ordered his troops to evacuate Slovakia, the Slovak Soviet Republic collapsed.

The Peace of St. Germain with Austria was signed on September 10, 1919, and the Peace of Trianon with Hungary on June 4, 1920.[79] At the same time as the Treaty of St. Germain, Czechoslovakia was obliged to sign with the Allied powers a "minorities" treaty[80] placing her ethnic minorities under the protection of the League of Nations and a treaty providing for a financial settlement with the Allies.[81]

Together with the other successor states of Austria-Hungary, Czechoslovakia had to assume a share of the defunct empire's financial obligations. As "enemy" nations, Austria and Hungary also had to pay reparations. As "Allied" nations, Czechoslovakia, Poland, Yugoslavia, and Rumania could not be required to pay reparations, since reparations were tied to the "war guilt" thesis, according to which only the Central Powers were responsible for the outbreak of the war. However, the Allied powers felt that Czechoslovakia, Poland, Yugoslavia, and Rumania owed their national independence and/or national unity to the Allied victory and that they should pay something for it. They were assessed "liberation costs."

If the Allied powers showed partiality toward Czechoslovakia in the political settlement, they showed her none in the financial settlement. It was based solely on economic considerations, that is, ability to pay. The liberation costs assessed to Czechoslovakia, Poland, Rumania, and Yugoslavia were fixed at 1.5 billion gold francs. Of this amount, Czechoslovakia, as the most prosperous of them, was required to pay one half, or 750 million gold francs.[82] She began her national existence, therefore, burdened with a considerable foreign debt.

To sum up, Czechoslovak independence would not have been possible

---

[78] Peter A. Toma, "Slovak Soviet Republic of 1919," *The American Slavic and East European Review*, XVII (April, 1958), 203-15. For highly colored discussions of the Slovak Soviet Republic by the post-World War II Czech and Slovak communist historians, see Václav Král, *Intervenční válka čs. buržoazie proti maďarské sovětské republice r. 1919 [The Interventionist War of the Czechoslovak Bourgeoisie against the Hungarian Soviet Republic in 1919]* (Prague, 1954); Martin Vietor, *Slovenská sovietska republika [Slovak Soviet Republic]* (Bratislava, 1959); and Zdeněk Hoření, *Antonín Janoušek: Predseda revolučnej vlády Slovenskej republiky rád [Antonín Janoušek: Chairman of the Revolutionary Government of the Slovak Soviet Republic]* (Bratislava, 1964).

[79] For the texts of the Treaties of St.-Germain and Trianon, see H.W.V. Temperley (ed.), *A History of the Peace Conference of Paris* (6 vols.; London-1920-24), v, 173-304.

[80] Ibid., pp. 437-70.

[81] *The Paris Peace Conference*, XIII, 822-30.

[82] Ibid.; Kocman, *Boj o směr*, II, No. 31, pp. 33-36.

without the Allied victory over the Central Powers. However, the initiative toward Czechoslovak independence was taken by the Czechs and Slovaks themselves. President Wilson told Charles Pergler, the first Czechoslovak "diplomatic agent" accredited to the United States, when he received him on September 9, 1918: "By your conduct throughout the war, especially by your armies, you have demonstrated that you insist upon complete independence. We have merely recognized an accomplished fact."[83]

[83] Charles Pergler, *America in the Struggle for Czechoslovak Independence* (Philadelphia, 1926), pp. 55-56.

· 2 ·

CZECHOSLOVAK DEMOCRACY AND ITS PROBLEMS
1918-1920

Václav L. Beneš
Indiana University

THE LAND AND THE PEOPLE

Geographically, the Czechoslovak Republic represented a link between Western and Eastern Europe, its westernmost province of Bohemia being situated roughly in the center of the continent. Its shape was that of a rather narrow strip. With its area of 54,244 square miles Czechoslovakia was the thirteenth largest state in Europe. Its population of 13,613,172 (1921) secured for it the ninth place among European nations.

The founders of Czechoslovakia insisted on the idea that the new republic was a national state of the Czechoslovaks. This assumption could be upheld only insofar as it meant that the state resulted from the endeavors of the Czechs and Slovaks. In reality, however, Czechoslovakia had a large number of other nationalities.[1]

Despite their large numbers, the Germans were not united in one geographical area but split into larger groups mainly along the borders of Germany to which, however, they had never belonged. The northwestern districts of Bohemia and those of eastern Silesia had impressive German majorities, but elsewhere the German population was inextricably mixed with the Czechs. While more compact, especially in the area of the Great Rye Island (Velký Žitný Ostrov, Gross Schüttinsel) between two branches of the Danube, the Hungarian minority in Slovakia and Ruthenia, which was settled in a continuous strip along the Hungarian border, was intermingled with the Slovaks and the Ruthenes.[2] The Polish minority was relatively small but assumed special importance in the development of Polish-Czechoslovak relations.[3]

[1] See Table I, which indicates the distribution of nationalities living in the territory of Czechoslovakia as registered by the 1910, 1921, and 1930 census figures.

[2] Masaryk, who at first was prepared to make certain territorial concessions in favor of Hungary, in the end accepted the new boundaries because of economic and particularly strategic considerations, irrespective of the fact that the new state included a relatively large number of Magyars. See Ferdinand Peroutka, *Budování státu: Československá politika v letech popřevratových* [*The Building of the State: Czechoslovak Politics in the Postwar Years*] (2nd ed., 5 vols. in 6; Prague, 1936), II, 1105; C. A. Macartney, *Hungary and Her Successors: The Treaty of Trianon and Its Consequences, 1919-1937* (London, 1937), p. 109.

[3] There was a fundamental discrepancy between the Czech official census of

TABLE 1.

NATIONALITIES LIVING IN THE TERRITORIES OF CZECHOSLOVAKIA

Land	Total Number of Citizens									Percentage of total number of citizens						
	Czechoslovak Citizens	Aliens	Czechoslovaks	Ukrainians and Russians	Germans	Magyars	Poles	Jews	Others	Czechoslovaks	Russians and Ukrainians	Germans	Magyars	Poles	Jews	Others
Census of 1910[a] (conducted on the basis of language of daily use)																
Territories of Czechoslovakia	13,441,689		8,034,887	434,005	3,750,327	1,070,854	169,641	....	....	59.48	3.21	27.76	7.93	1.26	....	....
Census of 1921[b] (conducted on the basis of mother tongue)																
Bohemia	6,576,853	93,757	4,382,816	2,007	2,173,239	5,476	973	11,251	1,091	66.64	0.03	33.04	0.28	0.02	0.17	0.02
Moravia	2,616,436	46,448	2,048,426	976	547,604	534	2,080	15,335	1,481	78.29	0.04	20.93	0.02	0.08	0.58	0.06
Silesia	622,738	49,530	296,194	338	252,365	94	69,967	3,681	99	47.36	0.05	40.52	0.02	11.24	0.59	0.2
Slovakia	2,958,557	42,313	2,013,792	85,644	139,900	637,183	2,536	70,529	8,973	68.07	2.89	4.73	21.54	0.09	2.38	0.3
Ruthenia	599,808	6,760	19,737	372,884	10,460	102,144	297	80,059	14,227	3.29	62.7	1.74	17.03	0.05	13.35	2.37
Republic	13,374,364	238,808	8,760,937	461,849	3,123,568	745,431	75,853	180,855	25,871	65.31	3.45	23.36	5.57	0.57	1.35	0.19
Census of 1931[c] (conducted on the basis of mother tongue)																
Bohemia	7,041,559	94,817	4,713,366	7,162	2,270,993	7,603	1,195	12,735	1,555	67.19	0.10	32.32	0.11	0.02	0.18	
Moravia-Silesia[d]	3,501,688	63,322	2,295,534	4,012	799,995	4,012	79,450	17,267	2,570	74.12	0.11	22.85	0.08	2.27	0.49	0.08
Slovakia	3,254,189	75,604	2,345,909	91,079	147,501	571,988	933	65,385	31,394	72.09	2.80	4.53	17.58	0.03	2.01	0.96
Ruthenia	709,129	16,228	33,961	446,916	13,249	109,472	159	91,255	14,117	4.79	63.02	1.87	15.44	0.02	12.87	1.99
Republic	14,479,565	249,971	9,688,770	549,169	3,231,688	691,223	81,738	186,642	49,636	66.91	3.79	22.32	4.78	0.57	1.29	0.34

[a] *Manuel statistique de la république tchécoslovaque* (Prague, 1925) II, 362-63.
[b] *Statistická příručka Republiky československé* [The Statistical Handbook of the Czechoslovak Republic], (Prague, 1928), III, 275.
[c] *Statistická příručka Republiky československé* [The Statistical Handbook of the Czechoslovak Republic], (Prague, 1935), 7.
[d] After 1928 Silesia fused with Moravia constituting the Moravian-Silesian Province.

The 1921 census statistics recognized an independent Jewish nationality as an exception from the basic criterion of the census, which determined nationality on the basis of the mother tongue. Only the Jews were allowed to embrace either Jewish or any other nationality, regardless of their native tongue. Thus, in 1921, of the 354,000 persons of Jewish faith living on the Czechoslovak territory, 180,000 chose to embrace the Jewish nationality.[4]

Given the multiplicity of nationalities inhabiting its territory, it was only natural that Czechoslovakia was subjected at the Paris Peace Conference to the system for the protection of minorities. By the minorities treaty signed on September 10, 1919 at St. Germain, the Czechoslovak government willingly accepted an obligation to grant full protection to its minorities "without distinction of birth, nationality, language, race or religion." Also, it promised to constitute "the Ruthene territory south of the Carpathians . . . as an autonomous unit within the Czechoslovak state and accord to it the fullest degree of self-government compatible with the unity of the Czechoslovak state." These provisions were subsequently incorporated into the Czechoslovak constitution.

The occupational distribution of the Czechoslovak population, especially in the Czech provinces, likewise displayed a similar diversity. It resembled that of Western Europe. Throughout the existence of the First Republic (1918-38) Czechoslovak society could be described as industrial-agricultural. Equilibrium between industry and agriculture, while not realized in all parts of the country, gave it a peculiar balance and contributed to the emergence of a class structure characteristic of a modern society.[5]

1921 and the unofficial Polish claims as to the actual number of Poles living in the Czechoslovak part of the former Duchy of Těšín (Cieszyn, Teschen). While the former put the total Polish population to around 70,000, the latter referred to more than 150,000. This discrepancy was due largely to two factors. The first was the difficulty in establishing the nationality of the so-called Slonzaks (Slązaks), who spoke a dialect which was transitional between Czech and Polish, and who had a cultural background different from that of the Poles in former Austrian Poland (Galicia), let alone in former Russian Poland. The second, perhaps even more important, factor was the decision of Prague to deny Czechoslovak citizenship to those Poles who became residents of the area after 1914 or were settled there after 1908. See Patrz W. Sworakowski, *Polacy na Śląsku za Olzą* [*Silesian Poles Beyond the Olza*] (Warsaw, 1937), p. 172f, and Joseph Chmelář, *La minorité polonaise en Tschécoslovaquie* (Prague, 1935), pp. 36-56.

[4] The impetus toward the recognition of Jewish nationality came from Masaryk, who during and after the war established contacts with Jewish leaders and gave support to the Jewish national movement. See Tomáš G. Masaryk, *Cesta demokracie: Soubor projevů za republiky* [*The Way of Democracy: A Collection of Speeches under the Republic*] (2 vols.; Prague, 1933-1934), II, 46, 78-79, and 153. It is only fair to point out that Masaryk's views were welcomed by the great majority of the Czechoslovak political leadership as the recognition of Jewish nationality promised to decrease the number of Germans and Magyars.

[5] See Table II. It indicates the distribution of population according to occupation as recorded in the census statistics of 1921 and 1930.

TABLE 2.
DISTRIBUTION OF POPULATION ACCORDING TO CALLINGS AS REGISTERED IN THE 1921 AND 1930 CENSUS

The number of inhabitants engaged in

a) In absolute figures

Year, Census, Province	Agriculture, Forestry, and Fishery including			Industry and Handicrafts	Trade and Banking	Transport	Public administration and free professions	Army	Personal and household service	Other callings or persons without callings	Persons without indication of calling	
		In Agriculture	In Forestry and Fishery									
1	2	3	4	5	6	7	8	9	10	11	12	13
1921												
Bohemia	1,980,389	1,896,657	83,732	2,705,006	458,048	372,152	330,710	75,249	79,781	600,386	68,889	6,670,610
Moravia and Silesia	1,177,649	1,128,688	48,961	1,261,883	176,949	165,835	146,556	35,021	32,524	291,113	51,447	3,338,977
Slovakia	1,817,878	1,761,748	56,130	522,593	124,129	105,740	107,499	42,829	17,403	179,494	80,679	2,998,244
Ruthenia	408,871	377,401	31,470	62,916	28,167	14,956	19,517	6,771	2,545	36,609	24,241	604,593
Czechoslovak Republic	5,384,787	5,164,494	220,293	4,552,398	787,293	658,683	604,282	159,870	123,253	1,107,602	225,256	13,612,424
1930												
Bohemia	1,710,723	1,636,976	73,747	2,970,255	633,327	438,995	364,534	84,862	106,028	725,499	75,153	7,109,376
Moravia and Silesia	1,017,993	976,089	41,909	1,455,295	237,908	194,745	165,252	48,808	47,766	359,805	39,438	3,565,010
Slovakia	1,892,042	1,822,114	69,928	634,797	181,278	157,634	155,933	54,090	25,919	160,811	67,239	3,329,793
Ruthenia	480,856	424,048	56,808	86,590	41,550	23,094	30,072	7,703	4,101	26,056	25,335	725,357
Czechoslovak Republic	5,101,614	4,859,227	242,387	5,146,937	1,094,063	814,468	715,841	193,463	183,814	1,272,171	207,165	14,729,536

TABLE 2 Continued

b) In percentages (of every 1,000 inhabitants)

Year, Census, Province		Agriculture, Forestry, and Fishery including		Industry and Handicrafts	Trade and Banking	Transport	Public administration and free professions	Army	Personal and household service	Other callings or persons without callings	Persons without indication of calling	
		In Agri-culture	In Forestry and Fishery									
1	2	3	4	5	6	7	8	9	10	11	12	13
1921												
Bohemia	296.8	284.9	12.5	405.5	68.7	55.8	49.6	11.3	12.1	90.0	10.3	1,000.0
Moravia and Silesia	352.7	338.0	14.7	377.9	53.0	49.7	43.9	10.5	9.7	87.2	15.4	1,000.0
Slovakia	606.3	587.6	18.7	174.3	41.4	35.3	35.8	14.3	5.8	59.9	26.9	1,000.0
Ruthenia	676.3	624.2	52.1	104.1	46.6	24.7	32.3	11.2	4.2	60.5	40.1	1,000.0
Czechoslovak Republic	395.6	379.4	16.2	334.4	57.8	48.4	44.4	11.8	9.7	81.4	16.5	1,000.0
1930												
Bohemia	240.6	230.2	10.4	417.8	89.1	61.8	51.3	11.9	14.9	102.0	10.6	1,000.0
Moravia and Silesia	285.6	273.8	11.8	408.2	66.7	54.6	46.4	13.1	13.4	100.9	11.1	1,000.0
Slovakia	568.2	547.2	21.0	190.6	54.4	47.3	46.9	16.3	7.8	48.3	20.2	1,000.0
Ruthenia	662.9	584.6	78.3	119.4	57.3	31.8	41.5	10.6	5.7	35.9	34.9	1,000.0
Czechoslovak Republic	346.4	329.9	16.5	349.4	74.3	55.3	48.6	13.1	12.5	86.3	14.1	1,000.0

Source: Zprávy státního úřadu statistického Republiky československé [Reports of the State Statistical Office of the Czechoslovak Republic], xiv (1933), No. 104.

Despite the wide diversity of the population of the Czech provinces, they suffered relatively less than similar European areas from internal strife caused by social antagonisms or rigid isolation among different occupational groups. For a relatively long time after 1918, issues of the prewar period dominated the public life of the Czechs. Of these the most important was the national idea. Resistance against an alien dynasty and defense against German pressure, which endangered the continued existence of the nation, blurred and weakened social conflicts and generally acted as centripetal and leveling force in Czech society. In Slovakia this resistance was directed against the Magyars but was much weaker than the Czech resistance against the Germans. Among the Slovak peasant masses, resistance was basically social in character rather than national. Only the very small group of politically powerless Slovak intellectuals regarded the struggle against magyarization in terms of national antagonism. Thus, Slovak nationalism, unlike its Czech counterpart, did not play a socially integrative role in a society dominated by the semifeudal traditions of Hungary.

Another factor which contributed to the lessening of social tensions was the relatively short distance, both psychological and chronological, of the great majority of the Czechs and Slovaks from the village. Their modern societies resulted from a gradual process of differentiation of one class from another, the lowest basis of the social pyramid being the peasants. Even members of the Czech upper classes more often than not were little more than three generations removed from their rural origin. Until 1918 the Slovaks had no upper class and their middle class was very small, being composed of no more than several hundred families.[6] Consciousness of common social origin, which among the Slovaks was combined with familial paternalism, contributed to decreasing the sharpness of social differences stemming from the traditional urban-rural antagonism.

Of the Czechs it could be said that theirs was a classic society of the "little man" ("malý člověk"), whose main characteristic was his close association with the native land, ability to work hard and to take pride in his achievements, as well as to lead a frugal life marked by love for his family.[7] His personal and social ambitions could be measured in terms of short-run, limited, and unostentatious tasks rather than grandiose schemes. This pattern of social behavior resulted from the almost

[6] According to the highest estimate, namely that of *Národnie noviny* [*National Newspaper*], the Slovak middle class was composed almost entirely of intellectuals and included around one thousand families. See Anton Štefánek, "Novoslováci" ["The Neo-Slovaks"] in *Sociologicka revue*, VI, 272-73.

[7] Jan Hajda (ed.), *Czechoslovakia* (Human Relations Area Files, Inc.: New Haven, 1955). The volume includes an excellent survey of the sociological aspects of inter-war Czechoslovakia written by its editor, pp. 56-106.

two-hundred-year period of national decline which brought the Czech people to the brink of extinction in the eighteenth century. Not surprisingly, the first steps of the national revival were marked by tactics of compromise, caution, and moderation which refused to risk the still precarious existence of the Czech nation in a head-on conflict with its powerful German antagonist. At the same time a large part of the Czechs embraced the humanitarian ideals of František Palacký (1798-1876) and Tomáš Masaryk, who gave their nation a firm belief in a special historical mission to promote human progress against the forces of reaction and work for the realization of the ideals of human brotherhood and understanding. Such was the behavior not only of the lower classes but also of those who toward the end of the century achieved the stature of middle or even upper classes of society.

Another factor which tended to mitigate the differences between the individual classes of the Czech people was a relative lack of either excessive wealth or poverty. The transitions between classes were fluid and access to education lent to Czech society its fundamentally open character.[8] Availability of educational opportunities helped to overcome the handicap of the poor and had a leveling influence on the national community. It contributed to the emergence of a rather homogeneous society marked by similar aspirations, style of life, and, up to the outbreak of World War I, even a similar world outlook.

Of course, social modernization and growing economic prosperity brought about distinctions based on differences in wealth. Czech social stratification was marked by a peculiar dichotomy between rank consciousness and a definite tendency toward egalitarianism. The former was less developed and found its expression in the use of titles, especially among the members of the middle classes, along the lines of the Austro-German usage. The latter tendency was much stronger and permeated the entire society, deriving its origin from the belief in the fundamental equality of men which, the Czechs held, they were denied in the conditions of the Habsburg empire. Egalitarianism was further strengthened by the absence of a native Czech nobility, the indigenous nobility of the Bohemian kingdom having been dispossessed and expelled from the country by the Habsburgs following their defeat of a revolt of the Bohemian Protestant estates at the outset of the Thirty Years' War in the seventeenth century. Even after the recovery of national independence in 1918, Czech belief in the equality of men manifested itself by the readiness of the people to refuse to recognize authority and to criticize mer-

[8] Tomáš Masaryk was a son of a Slovak coachman and Edvard Beneš, Masaryk's successor in the office of President of Czechoslovakia, was a son of a poverty-stricken farmer who only gradually managed to improve his social and economic standing. Both men owed their leading positions to their educational backgrounds and scholarly achievement.

cilessly those who acquired prominence or leadership in the society.[9] A more positive aspect of Czech egalitarianism was the spirit of national solidarity which it engendered, giving rise to nationwide Czech organizations, such as the gymnastic and cultural association Sokol (The Falcon). Despite its beginnings, which were influenced by the model of the German Turnverein, Sokol soon acquired typically Czech characteristics and associated egalitarianism with the necessity of national self-discipline.

Social conditions in Slovakia differed from those in the Czech provinces markedly because of widespread poverty, lower educational achievements among the Slovak masses, and the heritage of the Magyar feudal-aristocratic traditions. With few exceptions, the Slovak population suffered from sociological retardation and underdevelopment prior to 1918. The agricultural masses were denied the right to take part in the Hungarian political life, while the Slovak elite often adopted the social habits and values of the Magyar gentry with which it became identified. Only a few members of the Slovak intelligentsia, many of them of Protestant faith, had a feeling of national consciousness. It was only natural that after so many centuries of common life in one state that part of Slovakia's relatively small middle class, which after 1918 chose to be Slovak, could not rid itself of the Hungarian world outlook and patterns of social life. They formed a more exclusive group, tied together by religious and political conservatism, and displayed a feeling of superiority over the country folk. Almost unconsciously, they admired the elegant social life of the Hungarian gentry and frequently subscribed to its elitist political concepts. Thus the nascent Slovak middle class had little understanding of the egalitarian attitudes of the Czechs and their aversion to high society. Despite their opposition to the Magyars, the members of the semifeudal world of Slovak peasants were to a large degree influenced by social conservatism which, in the case of the Catholic majority of the population, was inherited from the paternalistic concepts of the Magyar and pro-Magyar high clergy. The creation of Czechoslovakia liberated the Slovaks from foreign rule, but at the same time constituted a veritable revolution resulting from the confrontation of the more religious, traditional, and generally more conservative Slovaks with the rationalistic, progressive, and often agnostic Czechs.

While the German inhabitants of Czechoslovakia enjoyed a higher standard of living than the Czechs, the life styles of the two peoples, particularly their middle classes, were very similar. But the patterns of their social life were in many respects different. German social stratification, which was marked by a much higher proportion of industrial workers, was more rigid and possessed an upper class with much older traditions

[9] Hajda, *Czechoslovakia*, p. 87.

46

than its Czech counterpart. Also, the major part of the nobility even in purely Czech districts—while recognizing the concept of regional patriotism (*Landespatriotismus*)—regarded themselves as Germans and greatly contributed to the more elegant and sophisticated social life of the Germans.[10] The German-speaking population in the Czech provinces was more class- and rank-conscious and, having enjoyed a privileged position for several centuries, lacked the unifying element of national solidarity. This relative absence of national cohesion was due to the practice, common among all Germans, to distinguish carefully between those who were *völkisch* and those who, for instance the socialists, accepted more cosmopolitan views which set them apart from the German community.

The Hungarian minority in Czechoslovakia was predominantly agricultural, and in its great majority continued to subscribe to the social patterns of old Hungary. Its occupational differences from the Slovaks, however, were negligible, which tended to blur the national differences between them. The Magyars had a larger share in trade and commerce and lived in the more fertile southern plains of Slovakia, thus enjoying a somewhat higher standard of living than the Slovaks.[11] When Austria-Hungary collapsed, the majority of the Hungarian civil servants, teachers, and even members of free professions refused to serve the new Czechoslovak Republic, and could not easily rid themselves of the traditional Hungarian value system. Only the experiences of daily life gradually alleviated the antagonism between the Slovaks and the Magyars who perhaps unconsciously accepted the post-1918 democratic practices of Czechoslovakia.

The land of Czechoslovakia had most of the ingredients necessary for the achievement of a rather high degree of economic prosperity. Czechoslovakia inherited from the former Habsburg empire its main sources of coal in Silesia and huge lignite deposits in northwestern Bohemia. The new republic was somewhat deficient in metallic ores, notably iron ore, which it had to import. It had, however, considerable deposits of other minerals, such as salt, graphite, and even uranium. The exploitation of uranium, which is found at Jáchymov (Joachimsthal), did not begin un-

[10] Bohemian *Landespatriotismus* was a feeling of attachment to the historic provinces of the kingdom of Bohemia and their traditions. Its basis was geographic, and it was shared equally by the Czechs and Germans of Bohemia. After 1848 it gave way increasingly to Czech and German nationalism, the basis of which was ethnic and the respective aims of which were mutually exclusive. Cf. Karl Bosl (ed.), *Handbuch der Geschichte der böhmischen Länder* (4 vols.; Stuttgart, 1968-70), III, 18-21.

[11] Antonín Boháč, "Národnosti v Čsl. republice: Statistika a současný stav" ["The Nationalities in the Czechoslovak Republic: Statistics and the Present Status"] in Národní rada československá, *Idea československého státu* [*The Idea of the Czechoslovak State*], p. 116.

til after World War II, under Soviet supervision. Disposing of sources of cheap, even though limited, power energy, the fringe areas of the Czech provinces were among the first Habsburg possessions to become industrialized. After the dissolution of the Austro-Hungarian empire Czechoslovakia received the greatest share of the empire's industrial wealth, ranging from almost one hundred percent (china, glass industries, and sugar refineries) to well over forty percent (distilleries and breweries). Despite its backward economy, Slovakia contained around seventeen percent of all Hungarian industries. On the average, the new state, which had an area of only one fifth and a population of around one fourth of the Habsburg empire, inherited between seventy and eighty percent of its industries. Its industrial potential placed it among the first ten most industrialized states of the world.[12]

The existence of a highly developed industrial establishment became a source of both strength and weakness. It represented the foundation of its economic prosperity, enabling the Czech provinces to achieve a higher standard of living than most of Czechoslovakia's neighbors. The importance of Czechoslovak industry was enhanced by a high degree of balance between heavy, light, and consumer goods industries. The manufacturing of iron and steel gave rise to huge engineering enterprises, such as the famous Škoda Works in Plzeň (Pilsen), which produced not only armaments, but also other types of machinery, including locomotives, agricultural machines and implements, machine tools, and automobiles. Of special importance was the chemical industry concentrated in northern Bohemia. The great wealth of timber provided a basis for paper cellulose, and other types of wood-derivative industries, which represented a sizable part of Czech and Slovak exports. Since the second half of the nineteenth century, however, it had become necessary to supplement the insufficient domestic supplies of raw materials by imports, especially of iron ore and other metals, from other parts of the empire or even from abroad.

These imports were paid for by the exports of highly developed light industries such as textiles, china, glass, and leather goods, which became steady money-earners for the Czech provinces. On the other hand, agricultural production was not large enough to cover all the requirements of the country, making it necessary to import relatively large quantities of grain and, particularly, fodder. Yet industrial crops, such as malt, hops, and above all sugar, were of great economic significance. They gave rise to a highly profitable consumer goods industry—breweries, distilleries, and sugar refineries. In the middle of the twenties Czechoslovakia was the greatest exporter of sugar in Europe. Sugar, referred to as

[12] Československá akademie věd, *Přehled československých dějin* [*Survey of Czechoslovak History*] (3 vols. in 4; Prague, 1958-1960), III, 47. Hereafter *Přehled*.

"White Gold," helped to maintain a favorable balance of trade and to secure hard currencies for the purchase of raw materials.[13] As subsequent developments proved, the relatively large industrial potential of Czechoslovakia rendered it highly vulnerable to world trade fluctuations and business cycles.

Three additional factors played an important role in the economic and political life of Czechoslovakia. Its industry was almost entirely concentrated in the western provinces of Bohemia, Moravia, and Silesia, which were formerly Austrian. About 39 percent of their population depended on industrial pursuits, whereas little over 31.3 percent were employed in agriculture and forestry. In Slovakia the corresponding percentages were 17.1 and 60.4 percent, respectively. Thus, compared to the Czech provinces, Slovakia was an economically undeveloped country. Its backwardness was further increased by the nature of its agriculture, which was less advanced than that of the other parts of former Hungary. In terms of agricultural yields and the use of machinery it was well behind the Czech provinces.[14] Only about 5 percent of the industries located on Slovak territory were in the hands of Slovaks, the rest being owned by nonindigenous owners and as a rule administered from Budapest.[15] The Slovak share of ownership of banks and other financial institutions was likewise small, amounting to about 16 percent.[16] Thus the situation in Slovakia and to an even greater degree in Ruthenia represented a challenge to the new Czechoslovak Republic to bring about a more equitable balance between its eastern and western provinces.

Equally important, both economically and politically, was the fact that the most industrialized parts of the Czech provinces were in the predominantly German border areas of the country. They were the first to become industrialized, as early as the eighteenth century, and their light industry products, such as textiles, china, glass, paper, and chemical goods, represented the most lucrative part of the Austrian and later Czechoslovak exports. First held by individual German owners, they later came, at least to a certain extent, under the control of German banks. The same was true of the highly concentrated heavy industry, such as the mining, metallurgical, and even the armaments enterprises. While some were situated in almost purely Czech areas, practically all were controlled by the Viennese capital. On the other hand, consumer

[13] Jozef Faltus et al., *Stručný hospodářský vývoj Československa až do roku 1955* [*A Concise Survey of the Economic Development of Czechoslovakia until 1955*] (Prague, 1969), p. 116.

[14] Ibid., pp. 41-43 and 69-70.

[15] Jozef Faltus and Václav Průcha, *Prehľad hospodárskeho vývoja na Slovensku v rokoch 1918-1945* [*Survey of the Economic Development of Slovakia in the Period of 1918-1945*] (Bratislavia, 1967), p. 19.

[16] Faltus, *Stručný hospodářský vývoj*, p. 87.

goods, engineering, and even some textile industries were owned by the Czechs or, to a large degree, controlled by Czech banks. Before World War I the share of Czech-owned industry was estimated at between twenty to thirty percent of the total industrial capital in the Habsburg empire.[17]

The capital assets of the Czech banks and loan associations were higher than those of German banks in the Czech provinces. It was, however, difficult to determine the actual ownership of the overall capital assets belonging to Czech financial institutions as Czech banks operated not only in different parts of the monarchy but also in the Balkan states and even in Russia. In turn, the Viennese capital had considerable assets in the Czech provinces. Combined, German capital maintained its control over much of the economy of the Czech provinces.[18]

The third economic problem with far-reaching political repercussions stemmed from the nature of Czech and Slovak agriculture which, until 1918, suffered partially from the remnants of feudalism. Almost thirty percent of agricultural land and forests belonged to a few aristocratic landowners and the Roman Catholic Church.[19] In the Czech provinces, thirty-one predominantly aristocratic families owned one fifth of all land. In Slovakia and Ruthenia, the percentage of large landowners was even larger.[20] Further disequilibrium in land ownership was caused by the fact that the majority of the rural population had only dwarf holdings or no land at all. Dwarf lots of less than two hectares (4.54 acres) represented more than one half of all agricultural holdings but only 8.8 percent of all soil. While in the industrialized Czech provinces owners of such lots managed to supplement their revenue by industrial employment, in Slovakia and Ruthenia they did it by seasonal labor on larger farms and estates. In these areas chronic rural unemployment gave rise to a steady flow of emigration. Nevertheless, even before World War I, there existed a sizable group of economically independent farmers in the Czech provinces, while the same was true to a smaller degree in Slovakia.[21]

In many cases the owners of large estates had little interest in personal management of their property, preferring to rent a part of their land to large agricultural entrepreneurs, or even small farmers.[22] This absentee ownership exacerbated the land-hunger characteristic of the rural popu-

[17] Ibid., p. 59.   [18] Ibid., pp. 85-86.   [19] Přehled, III, 51.

[20] Rudolf Olšovský (ed.), Přehled hospodářského vývoje Československa v letech 1918-1945 [Survey of the Economic Development of Czechoslovakia in 1918-1945] (Prague, 1961), pp. 49-50.

[21] In 1902, around 15.5 percent of all land in the Czech provinces belonged to this category of farmers. See Milan Otáhal, Zápas o pozemkovou reformu v ČSR [The Struggle for Land Reform in the Czechoslovak Republic] (Prague, 1963), table on p. 243.

[22] Antonin Pavel, "Land Reform" in Josef Gruber, Czechoslovakia: A Survey of Economic and Social Conditions (London, 1924), pp. 47-48.

lation.[23] The practice of renting parts of their estates was strengthened by the existence of entailed, hereditary, and inalienable estates (the so-called *Fideikommis*) owned in most cases by the nobility, the Roman Catholic Church, monasteries, and foundations. Prevented by law from disposing of their land and unwilling to manage it personally, these few large landowners rented large tracts of land, frequently to persons who had no land of their own. In Slovakia and Ruthenia the greater part of all estates was leased to small farmers on a share-crop basis. The system often resulted in ruthless exploitation of the peasants.

Thus, the demand for more equitable distribution of land played a very important role in modern Czech and Slovak history. During World War I this demand was adopted by their political leaders at home, as well as by the leader of their liberation movement abroad, Tomáš Masaryk, who, in his Washington declaration, spoke of far-reaching social and economic reforms and foreshadowed the partitioning of the large estates. This action acquired great popularity for historical reasons also. To deprive the German and Hungarian aristocracy of their domains was regarded as an act of historic justice that would right the wrong done the Bohemian Protestant nobles, whose property was confiscated and distributed among foreign nobles by the Habsburgs after their defeat of the Bohemian Protestant cause in 1620.

THE FIRST STEPS

To forge a strong and stable state out of the conglomerate of different peoples located in a geographically exposed position between East and West and surrounded mostly by hostile nations, required not only great skill but also time. "We need fifty years of undisturbed peace and only then shall we have achieved what we would like to have today," President Masaryk stated.[24] It is in the light of this statement that both successes and failures of the Czechoslovak democracy should be judged.

The Prague National Committee, headed by Karel Kramář, acted for a little over two weeks as Czechoslovakia's provisional government. It was composed of the leaders of prewar Czech political parties, their representation being proportionate to their electional strength in the last Austrian election of 1911.[25] The acceptance of this criterion disregarded

[23] Otáhal, *Zápas o pozemkovou reformu*, p. 87.

[24] Karel Čapek, *Hovory s T. G. Masarykem* [*Talks with T. G. Masaryk*] (London, 1951), p. 312.

[25] The Prague National Committee, as originally constituted in July, 1918, consisted of 10 Social Democrats, 9 Agrarians, 9 members of the Democratic State Rights party, 4 Czech Socialists, 4 members of the Populist party, 1 member of the Old Czech party, and 1 representative of the Realist party. See František Soukup, *28. říjen 1918* [*October 28, 1918*] (2 vols.; Prague, 1929), II, 827.

the profound political and social changes brought about by the war, but there was no other solution that would be more objective.[26] The invitation extended to a few outstanding Czech national figures without pronounced political preference to join the National Committee was likewise based on party decision, and the members thus added were allotted to the quotas of the individual political parties. The way the National Committee was constituted clearly foreshadowed the future decisive role that political parties would play at the expense of independent personalities.

Party loyalty was traditionally paramount particularly in the Czech provinces. Political parties were relatively little influenced by shifts in public opinion and by events. A strong party discipline made the position of the party leadership almost invulnerable. Moreover, the existence of numerous Czech parties and the consequent necessity to reach a settlement by compromise strengthened a pragmatic and realistic appraisal of the given possibilities and prevented ideology from becoming the main criterion of Czech political life.

The National Committee, in which the agrarians and the National Democrats (State-Rights Democrats) predominated, was faced with a host of extremely difficult problems. Not only did it have to organize the administration and the armed forces of the new republic, but it was also called upon to give the country general political direction. By stressing the necessity of national unity, the committee managed to harmonize the radical demand of the socialist with the more conservative outlook of the nonsocialist parties. Despite its revolutionary nature, the National Committee laid great stress on the maintenance of public order, which was achieved to a large degree by establishing legal continuity with the defunct Austro-Hungarian empire. The first act promulgated by the National Committee on October 28, 1918, stipulated that all Austro-Hungarian laws and ordinances should remain provisionally in force and that state and local administrative and judicial organs inherited from the old monarchy should carry on their activities under the authority of the National Committee.[27]

The installation of the new power structure in Czechoslovakia did not represent any departure from the traditional model of Czech politics. The permanence of the Czech party system tended to reassure the Czech people, fevered with national enthusiasm and social unrest. Well aware that the formation of a legitimate government was the first step toward consolidation, the National Committee proceeded rapidly toward normalization of the situation in the country. It feared the consequences of

---

[26] Peroutka, *Budování státu*, I, 18.

[27] Alois Kocman *et al.* (eds.), *Boj o směr vývoje československého státu* [*Struggle for the Direction of the Development of the Czechoslovak State*] (2 vols.; Prague, 1965-69), I, 113.

a revolutionary climate in Europe, suspecting that many of the neighbor states might be willing to use the threat of Bolshevism to win territorial concessions from the Allied peacemakers in Paris at Czechoslovakia's expense. The founding of representative democratic institutions was viewed as a prerequisite to the successful conclusion of the future settlement of the boundaries. The National Committee also felt that its own security and authority required utmost stability and internal peace, for without public order it could hardly put up an effective fight against the increasingly virulent influence of the radicals.

In acting upon the country's most urgent problems, the National Committee showed affirmative, creative, and responsible leadership. On October 29, 1918, it took over the majority of the formerly Austrian civil servants and the police forces in the Czech provinces, which assured continued smooth functioning of the state administration and public order in those provinces. On November 9, 1918, to satisfy popular clamor for land reform, the National Committee issued a decree suspending the right of great landowners to dispose of their estates until the future Czechoslovak National Assembly decided the land question.[28]

Whatever their errors, it would be unfair to minimize the efforts of the leaders of the National Committee aiming at internal stabilization and economic prosperity within the framework of a democratic system of government. Despite their insistence on a centralized government, they recognized and respected the pluralistic way of life as the sole means by which unity out of diversity could be achieved.

The Provisional Constitution

The most effective demonstration of Czech national consensus was the adoption of a provisional constitution on November 13, 1918.[29] The document vested all power in a unicameral national assembly, which assumed undivided authority similar to that of revolutionary constituent assemblies. The prime minister and the cabinet were to be elected by the National Assembly and, in fact, were to be little more than its executive committee. The rights of the head of state (president) were strictly limited and subordinated to the National Assembly. He had no say in the selection of the members of the cabinet, could not dissolve the legislative, and was denied the right of legislative initiative. The curtailing of the powers of the president was due—apart from the principle of radical democracy which distrusted the individual and favored the collective— to two factors. The first was that Masaryk, who was the only candidate for the office of president, had not yet returned home from exile and,

[28] Otáhal, *Zápas o pozemkovou reformu*, pp. 145-46.
[29] Kocman, *Boj o směr*, I, 133-35.

consequently, could not appoint the cabinet. More important, however, was the second consideration, which derived from genuine fear on the part of the Czech party leaders that Masaryk might upset the delicate balance of power that they had succeeded in establishing between the political parties.[30]

Kramář expressed the hope that Masaryk would stay "above the clouds,"[31] that is, stay aloof from the rough and tumble of politics and content himself with a representative role as president. It would have been perfectly honorable for Masaryk to do so. More than any other Czech or Slovak he had contributed to the liberation of his people. The task was now completed. He was almost sixty-nine years old. To rest on his laurels, as it were, would have entailed no loss of prestige for him. It was not in Masaryk's temperament to be a figurehead, however. All his life he had been an activist, combining scholarship and politics in roughly equal proportions. Although liberated, Czechoslovakia still faced many domestic difficulties and foreign perils. During his exile Masaryk had acquired much valuable experience and was genuinely convinced that he still had much to contribute to his country's development. Upon his return to Prague on December 21, 1918, he expressed dissatisfaction with the inferior position allotted him in the provisional constitution. His demand for extension of his powers was eventually met, in May, 1919, albeit not without considerable opposition in the National Assembly.[32]

The provisional constitution, which had been largely prepared by a Social Democratic member of the National Committee, Alfred Meissner, was by no means a complete constitutional charter. It contained no provision for judicial power and had no list of rights and duties of citizens. Yet it included and fully set out all the principles which characterized the definitive constitution of 1920. While the provisional constitution represented an extension of Western constitutionalism into East Central Europe, its terms stemmed predominantly from the political and social realities that prevailed in the Czech provinces at the time.

From a democratic point of view the provisional constitution suffered from two shortcomings. First, it was not adopted by an elected body but was unilaterally imposed by the National Committee. In fact, with certain modifications, it provided for the organization of a provisional national assembly in the same manner as the National Committee. The Czech parties were represented in the National Assembly on the basis

[30] Peroutka, Budování státu, I, 255.
[31] Ibid., p. 253.
[32] See Act of May 23, 1919, No. 271, in Sbírka zákonů a nařízení [Collection of Acts and Ordinances]. For a discussion of the amendment, see Peroutka, Budování státu, II, 914-19, and Emil Sobota et al., Československý president Republiky [President of the Czechoslovak Republic] (Prague, 1934), p. 110.

of their electional strength in the last Reichsrat elections in 1911 and the Slovaks by forty (later fifty-four) members.[33] Czechoslovakia's national minorities were not represented in the National Assembly at all. As for the manner in which the members were selected, the Czech representatives were chosen by their respective party executive committees while the Slovaks were selected in a somewhat arbitrary manner which will be described later. This procedure for organizing the National Assembly was justified by the confused conditions then prevailing in parts of Czechoslovakia which precluded the holding of popular elections: the Hungarians held parts of Slovakia until January, 1919, and again from April to June, 1919, when the Hungarian Red Army invaded it; the Poles occupied a part of Silesia; and the Germans in the Czech provinces refused to recognize the authority of the Czechoslovak government and cooperate with it until the signing of the Peace of St. Germain in September, 1919. In these circumstances, the argument that the National Assembly, though not a product of a popular vote, was at least partly "based on elections in the executive committees of individual parties" carried some weight.[34]

The second shortcoming of the provisional constitution was that it endowed the provisional National Assembly with the prerogatives of a constituent assembly, that is, with the right to draft and adopt a permanent constitution. The only basis for this greatly extended competence of the National Assembly was the right of revolution. The motivation of the provisional ("revolutionary") National Assembly was best expressed by Ferdinand Peroutka, the foremost historian of Czechoslovakia's foundation, who wrote that "the Czech leaders were obviously determined to impose on all state institutions their political will which, they sincerely believed, was identical with that of the whole liberated nation."[35]

The provisional constitution went into effect on November 14, 1918, when the provisional National Assembly held its first meeting in Prague,

[33] In its final composition, the provisional National Assembly had 268 members, who were divided into seven parliamentary clubs. The Agrarian Club had 55 members and was the largest. It was closely followed by that of the Social Democrats, with 53 members, and of the State-Rights Democrats (later National Democrats), with 46 members. The Czech Socialists (later National Socialists) had 29, the Czechoslovak Populist party 24, and the Czech Progressive party 6 representatives. The Slovak Club had 53 members. The clubs of the Czech Socialists and of the Czech Progressives combined into one. See Karol Laco, *Ústava predmnichovskej ČSR a ústava ČSSR* [*The Constitutions of the pre-Munich Czechoslovak Republic and of the Czechoslovak Socialist Republic*] (Bratislava, 1965), p. 204.

[34] See *Národní shromáždění Československé Republiky v prvém roce Republiky* [*The National Assembly of the Czechoslovak Republic in the First Year of the Republic*] (Prague, 1919), p. 61.

[35] Peroutka, *Budování státu*, I, 247.

during the course of which it elected Masaryk first president of Czechoslovakia and invested the first Czechoslovak cabinet under Karel Kramář as prime minister.

THE SLOVAKS IN PRAGUE

While the transition from Austro-Hungarian to Czechoslovak rule in the Czech provinces was swift and orderly, in Slovakia it was slow and confused. On October 30, 1918, the Slovak National Council was established at Turčiansky Svätý Martin. During the first days of November, as Slovak soldiers of the disbanded Austro-Hungarian army straggled home from the fronts, Slovakia was swept by a great wave of social turbulence. Hungarian officials and gendarmes fled the area. Many local national councils sprang up that sought to preserve a modicum of order. On the model of Russian soviets, a number of workers' councils was also organized.[36] Unlike the Czech National Committee in Prague, which swiftly established its control over the larger part of the Czech provinces, the Slovak National Council failed to establish its authority over Slovakia. After the Belgrade armistice on November 13, the Hungarian government sent troops to reestablish its authority over Slovakia. On November 15, they occupied Turčiansky Svätý Martin and dispersed the Slovak National Council. Although the council was later reconstituted, it never played an important role in Slovak affairs. The fate of Slovakia was decided in Prague.

As early as October 26, sensing that the collapse of the Habsburg empire was approaching, Vavro Šrobár, the foremost Hlasist spokesman before the war, set out for Prague, where he arrived on the morning of the eventful October 28. He was at once co-opted by the Prague National Committee, and was the only Slovak who signed the proclamation of the Czechoslovak state on the same day. Although later Ivan Dérer, Milan Hodža, and other prominent Slovaks arrived in Prague, Šrobár remained Prague's man of confidence in Slovak affairs.[37] It was he whom

[36] Karol Medvecký, *Slovenský prevrat* [*The Slovak Revolution*] (4 vols.; Trnava, 1930-31), I, 334-57. For eyewitness accounts of the social upheaval in Slovakia after the armistice, see ibid., IV, 63ff. For Marxist interpretations of these events, see Michal Dzvoník, *Ohlas Veľkej októbrovej socialistickej revolucie na Slovensku, 1918-1919* [*Echoes of the Great October Socialist Revolution in Slovakia, 1918-1919*] (Bratislava, 1957), *passim*; Ľudovít Holotík, "Októbrová revolucia a revolučné hnutie na Slovensku koncom roku 1918" ["The October Revolution and the Revolutionary Movement in Slovakia at the end of 1918"], *Historický časopis*, XV (1967), 489-511. Both authors view the events in Slovakia as "echoes" of the Bolshevik Revolution in Russia.

[37] It was quite natural that Šrobár should look to Prague and that Prague should have confidence in him. After expulsion from a Hungarian *gymnasium* (high school) for Slovak national feeling, he completed his secondary school education in Moravia and medicine in Prague. See Vavro Šrobár, *Z môjho života*

the Prague National Committee sent to Slovakia on November 4 to establish the "Skalica government." Two days later he was recalled to Prague and entrusted with the delicate task of selecting forty Slovak deputies to represent the Slovak people in the provisional National Assembly. Šrobár was also the only Slovak appointed to the first Czechoslovak cabinet, apart from General Milan R. Štefánik, who, however, was in Siberia at the time and unable to take part in the work of the government. Šrobár was minister of public health and Štefánik minister of war.[38] Finally, on December 10, Šrobár was appointed head of the newly created ministry for the administration of Slovakia.

In choosing the Slovak deputies to the National Assembly, Šrobár drew heavily on those members of the diminutive Slovak intelligentsia, who were known as Slovak nationalists before the war. He chose only one worker and no peasant. As far as religion was concerned—which, it should not be forgotten, was an important consideration in Slovakia— he chose fully one half of the Slovak deputies from among the Protestants, although the Protestants constituted only 16.8 percent of the Slovak people and only about 12 percent of Slovakia's population. He included in the Slovak delegation seven Czechs who had won Slovak gratitude for their prewar Slovakophile activities. On the other hand, no representative of Slovakia's national minorities was included in the delegation. As far as political parties were concerned, Šrobár chose some representatives of all prewar Slovak political trends, but gave his (the Hlasist) trend by far the largest representation.[39]

It cannot be said, therefore, that the Slovak delegation constituted a representative cross section of the Slovak people, let alone of all of Slovakia. It should be pointed out, however, that when Šrobár composed the Slovak delegation he had no opportunity to consult with anyone in Slovakia, which was in a state of confusion and partly occupied by the

---

[Out of My Life] (Prague, 1946), pp. 126-61. Unlike Hodža and some other Slovak politicians who moved just as easily in Prague as they did in Budapest or Vienna, Šrobár felt at home in Prague alone.

[38] At the Geneva conference between the representatives of the Paris National Council and the Prague National Committee at the end of October, 1918, it was agreed to include in the first Czechoslovak cabinet three Slovaks, in addition to Štefánik: Šrobár, Hodža, and Milan Ivanka. See Edvard Beneš, Světová válka a naše revoluce [The World War and Our Revolution] (3 vols.; Prague, 1927-29), II, 394. In the end, however, because of the ambition of Czech politicians, room was found in the cabinet for Šrobár only. For the composition of all Czechoslovak cabinets under the First Republic, see Miroslav Buchválek et al. (eds.), Dějiny Československa v datech [History of Czechoslovakia in Dates] (Prague, 1968), pp. 444-51.

[39] For a detailed study of the origins, composition, and activity of the Slovak Club in the provisional National Assembly, see Ladislav Lipscher, "Klub slovenských poslancov v rokoch 1918-1920" ["The Club of the Slovak Deputies in 1918-1920"], Historický časopis, XVI (1968), 133-68.

Hungarians, and that it was quite uncertain at the time what the boundaries of Slovakia would be and whether they would include any national minorities or not.

POSTWAR DIFFICULTIES

As in other parts of the defunct Austro-Hungarian empire, postwar conditions in Czechoslovakia were highly confused. Until the winter of 1920-21 Czechoslovakia suffered from economic, social, and political disorders, which the first three cabinets were unable fully to resolve. Apart from the general effects of war and the demoralizing influence of the fighting in Slovakia, several specific factors worked against a smooth transition from monarchy to republic and from war to peace.

Immediately upon its establishment, Czechoslovakia had to cope with serious economic difficulties. The requirements of the Austro-Hungarian army and the Allied blockade had left the storehouses empty, the system of food requisitioning had broken down, and railway transportation was disrupted by division of the Habsburg empire. The summary, unselective mobilization of most able-bodied men into the Austro-Hungarian armies during the war had deprived industry and agriculture of essential labor. As food, fuel (especially coal), raw materials, and consumer goods had become scarce, inflation developed. The peasants became reluctant to sell their produce for the inflated currency, at government-fixed prices, and preferred to hoard it or dispose of it on the black market. In the fall of 1918 food was relatively plentiful in Hungary, because of its government's callous policy of hoarding the country's supplies, but in the Austrian half of the empire the urban population was on the verge of starvation.[40]

The choice of Karel Kramář, after Masaryk the most popular Czech politician, for the premiership was due to his leading position in the Viennese Reichsrat. During the war he had earned the respect of his compatriots by his stand against Austria, remaining undaunted by imprisonment and a death sentence, which the government dared not carry out. Kramář's appointment was a tribute to his person rather than recognition of the strength of his party (the State-Rights Democrats), which with the advent of national independence lost much of its appeal.[41]

[40] Peroutka, *Budování státu*, I, 241-44; Jan Opočenský, *The Collapse of the Austro-Hungarian Monarchy and the Rise of the Czechoslovak State* (Prague, 1928), pp. 28-35.

[41] Peroutka, *Budování státu*, II, 799-818. The party also suffered from Kramář's absence from Prague, from January to September, 1919 when, together with Beneš, he represented Czechoslovakia at the Paris Peace Conference. No full account of Kramář's career exists. Vladimír Sís (ed.), *Dr. Karel Kramář: život—dílo—práce vůdce národa [Dr. Karl Kramář: Life—Achievement—Work of the*

The Kramář government, which remained in office until July 8, 1919, had to take a number of highly unpopular economic measures. Fortunately, it had in Finance Minister Alois Rašín an able and energetic statesmen who did not hesitate to take unpopular measures if he thought he could thereby solve the financial and economic confusion created by the dissolution of the Habsburg empire.[42] Like Kramář whose close associate he was, Rašín had been arrested and condemned to death by the Austrian authorities during the war, and later pardoned by Emperor Charles. One of the cosigners of the Czechoslovak declaration of independence on October 28, 1918, he was a courageous patriot and a man with an unusual sense of public morality. The secret of his influence was not so much the originality of his financial policies as his honesty and determination, which enabled him to gain the support even of his leftist antagonists. Thanks to his moral qualities he acquired great power in the Kramář cabinet, becoming virtual financial and economic dictator. Under his stern guidance, the government not only continued but even tightened wartime economic controls and passed special legislation against black marketeering.

Rašín believed that the solution of Czechoslovakia's postwar economic difficulties required, first of all, the establishment of a stable currency. It should be noted that Czechoslovakia did not establish a currency of its own immediately upon declaring independence. Instead, it continued to use the old Austrian currency, which it shared with the other successor states. There was much to be said for maintaining the financial and economic unity of the fallen empire. However, this would have required close economic and political cooperation between the successor states. Unfortunately, this was very difficult to achieve because after being pitted against one another for centuries by the Habsburg policy of divide and rule their peoples were too distrustful of one another to cooperate wholeheartedly.

Rašín found it intolerable that his efforts to achieve Czechoslovak

---

Nation's Leader] (Prague, 1936), is an unsystematic collection of eulogistic articles, Kramář's memoir, Paměti (Prague, 1937), edited by Karel Hoch, is likewise of limited value. Stanley B. Winters, "Karel Kramář's Early Political Career," unpublished doctoral dissertation, Rutgers University, 1965, is scholarly and thorough, but reaches only to 1897. A brief but sharp portrait of Kramář may be found in R. H. Bruce Lockhart, Retreat from Glory (New York, 1934), pp. 77-79. Finally, see Robert W. Seton-Watson's obituary "Karel Kramář, 1860-1937," in The Slavonic and East European Review, XVI (1937), pp. 183-89.

[42] Like Kramář, Rašín has not yet found an adequate biography. Karel Hoch, Alois Rašín: Jeho život, dílo a doba [Alois Rašin: His Life, Accomplishment, and Times] (Prague, 1934), is laudatory and tentative. Rašín's memoir, Paměti (Prague, 1929), edited by his son Ladislav Rašín, does not go beyond the end of World War I. Peroutka, Budování státu, II, 754-71, gives a perceptive analysis of Rašín's policies and personality, and Lockhart, Retreat from Glory, pp. 76-77, an interesting portrait.

financial stability were largely annulled by the indiscriminate printing of bank bills in Vienna and Budapest, which unleashed a runaway inflation.[43] He proposed, therefore, to separate the Czechoslovak currency from those of the other successor states and to reform it. The essential features of his currency reform, which the National Assembly approved on February 25, 1919, was to stamp bank bills in Czechoslovakia in order to differentiate them from those in circulation in the other successor states, and to hold—as a forced loan to the state—one half of all personal and corporate cash holdings and savings in order to reduce the amount of currency in circulation.[44] Like a bitter but necessary medicine, Rašín's currency reform was unpopular but it worked. While the other successor states suffered further inflation and financial confusion, Czechoslovakia became an island of financial order and stability in East Central Europe. This image was of great benefit to it at the Paris Peace Conference.

Czechoslovakia's most menacing postwar problem, however, was not economic but political. It was the internal conflict within the large Czechoslovak Social Democratic party which, because of the party's hold on the Czechoslovak working class, cast a spell over all of Czechoslovak politics. The conflict was not singular; analogous conflicts were raging within nearly all European socialist parties at the time. They had their source in Europe's postwar social convulsions and ranged from the Russian Revolution to social turmoil in East Central Europe. As early as the first postwar congress of the Czechoslovak Social Democratic party in December, 1918, a dispute developed between the moderate leadership of the party which subscribed to evolutionary socialism within the framework of democratic Czechoslovakia, and the left-wing extremists in the party who were more or less prepared to emulate the example of the Bolshevik Revolution.[45] While the moderates retained the leadership of the party, the radical left-wingers were able to infiltrate the party apparatus and press, thus gradually acquiring the power to thwart the moderate policies of the party leadership and to spread their own concept of socialism among the broad masses of the population.

At the congress, however, Bohumír Šmeral, who had led the party until 1917 when he was removed from its leadership because of his op-

[43] Karel Engliš, "Outline of the Development of Czechoslovak Currency" in National Bank of Czechoslovakia, *Ten Years of the National Bank of Czechoslovakia* (Prague, 1937), p. 38.

[44] Peroutka, *Budování státu*, II, 701-24; Chapter V below.

[45] Only one month after liberation, Alois Muna, the founder of the Czechoslovak Communist party in Russia, and a member of the Red Guards appeared in Prague and immediately found a warm reception among the members of the left wing led by Bohumír Šmeral, Antonín Zapotocký, Josef Skalák, and Václav Šturc. Muna spoke openly in favor of the Bolshevik Revolution. See Peroutka, *Budování státu*, II, 561-80.

position to the Czechoslovak struggle for national independence, publicly admitted his past mistakes and subscribed to both the Czechoslovak Republic and the special conditions of the Czechoslovak proletariat.[46] Neither he nor his supporters—who later constituted the core of the leadership of the Communist Party of Czechoslovakia—intended to remain faithful to the promises made at the first postwar congress. They continued their membership in the Social Democratic party, aiming at achieving control over its organization and its not inconsiderable property.[47] Using radical slogans which were intended to incite the poverty-stricken and excitable workers, they pushed the moderate majority of the party leadership into a defensive position.[48]

Conscious of this danger and recognizing the relevance of social issues, the Kramář cabinet adopted, at the beginning of January, 1919, a declaration in which it announced its determination to punish all those who were guilty of profiteering and to work for the nationalization of coal mines and the expropriation of all estates above a certain acreage.[49] Even the representatives of the conservative parties declared themselves in favor of further nationalization, suggesting that it might cover iron and steel works and all enterprises which were monopolistic in nature.[50]

The actual moving force behind the socialization program, however, was the Socialist Council, which was composed of the Social Democrats and the (National) Socialists. The organization of the Socialist Council in September, 1918, represented an attempt to separate the revolutionary approach from the more cautious and legalistic approach of the moderate parties that looked to the Prague National Committee for leadership. During the course of 1919, however, the Social Democrats and National Socialists split and the drive for socialization lost momentum, ultimately ending in complete failure.

THE NEW GOVERNMENT

It was the pressure of the left-wing Social Democrats which caused the first crisis in the Kramář cabinet, in March, 1919. Accusing their partners of sabotaging the promised socialization and land reform, the Social Democratic ministers presented a virtual ultimatum to the government.

---

[46] Ibid., 517-24. Speaking of the mission of the Social Democratic party, Šmeral declared that "it has the power to give to Czech independence and the Czech republic a correct guidance." Adolf Mokrý (ed.), *Osemdesát let československé sociální demokracie* [*Eighty Years of Czechoslovak Social Democracy*] (London, 1958), p. 99. On Šmeral see also Zdeněk Kárnik, *Socialisté na rozcestí: Habsburg, Masaryk či Šmeral?* [*The Socialists at the Crossroads: Habsburg, Masaryk or Šmeral?*] (Prague, 1968); and Karel Gorovský, "Bohumír Šmeral," *Revue dějín socialismu*, IX (1969) 893-922, and X (1970), pp. 112-39.

[47] Peroutka, *Budování státu*, II, 853. [48] Mokrý, *Osemdesát let*, pp. 98-99.
[49] Kocman, *Boj o směr*, I, 167-68. [50] Peroutka, *Budování státu*, II, 545.

In the absence of Kramář, who was at the Paris Peace Conference, Deputy Premier Antonín Švehla negotiated with the Social Democrats.[51] An able politician, he managed to settle the conflict amicably, but only after the government promised to speed up the inauguration of the land reform and the holding of local elections.

In May, popular discontent—mostly because of the serious food shortage—filled the streets of many cities with demonstrators. In addition, impatience with what was considered to be leniency on the part of the authorities in rounding up black marketeers and in taking adequate steps against the rising prices was causing political repercussions in the government coalition. The National Democrats advocated taking stern measures against agitators and ignored the underlying causes of the radicalization of the masses. On the other hand, the socialist parties felt underrepresented in the government and thus unable to carry out a policy of social and economic reforms. Fearing that they might lose control of the popular movement, the moderate socialist leaders pressed for reorganization of the government. The dissension within the coalition resulted in the resignation of the National Democratic ministers from the cabinet.[52] Because of foreign policy considerations, President Masaryk refused to accept their resignation. However, the government could not further delay the holding of local elections—even though, because of Czechoslovakia's military conflict with Soviet Hungary, they could be held in the Czech provinces only.

The local elections were based on a new electoral law which introduced proportional representation and fixed lists of candidates as presented by the parties. The results of the voting, which took place on June 15-16, confirmed the popularity of the two socialist parties.[53] Among the Germans, who took part in the elections only very reluctantly, the German Social Democratic party secured well over 40 percent of all votes.[54] The clear swing of the electorate to the left which the elec-

[51] Švehla regarded the ultimatum as a vote of nonconfidence and submitted a secret resignation to Masaryk, who, however, refused to accept it. Thanks to Švehla's negotiating skill and also the conciliatory attitude of the Social Democrats, an agreement was reached and the crisis passed away. See Peroutka, *Budování státu*, II, 781-99.

[52] Kocman, *Boj o směr*, I, 220.

[53] Peroutka, *Budování státu*, II, 1022-26. The Social Democrats received 30.1, the agrarians 20.5, and the Czech Socialists 15.6 percent of all votes. The National Democrats with 8.2 percent occupied the fifth place after the Catholic Populist party which received 9.7 percent of all votes. See *Přehled*, III, 90.

[54] *Přehled*, III, 90. The German parties at first hesitated to take part in the communal elections because they were afraid that this might be interpreted as their recognition of the Czechoslovak state. In the end, however, they decided to participate. See Jaroslav César and Bohumil Černý, *Politika německých buržoázních stran v Československu v letech 1918-1938* [*The Politics of the German Bourgeois Parties in Czechoslovakia in 1918-1938*] (2 vols.; Prague, 1962), I, 154-56.

tions revealed caused the replacement on July 8 of Kramář's cabinet by that of the Social Democratic leader, Vlastimil Tusar (1880-1924). It was based on the cooperation of the Czechoslovak Social Democrats, the Czech (National) Socialists, the Czech agrarians, and the Slovak Club. The National Democrats and the Czech populists were not represented in it. The new coalition, which because of its composition was referred to as the "Red-Green coalition," enjoyed the confidence of President Masaryk.[55] The Czechoslovak political system, which was marked by strong social consciousness, called for rapid rectification of any past injustices against the poor and the working man. Stimulated by fear of the consequences of serious disorders because of misery and Bolshevik agitation, the coalition leaders strove feverishly to achieve a modicum of stability and to carry out the most essential internal reforms.

President Masaryk's decision to ask a socialist to head the government reflected his determination to solve the acute internal crisis in cooperation with the two main political forces in the country—the socialists and the agrarians. Eventually, the existence of the socialist-agrarian coalition depended largely on the success of Švehla's efforts.

To understand Antonín Švehla (1873-1933) it is essential to recognize him as a Czech peasant leader. Chairman of the Czech agrarian party since 1909, Švehla developed a national constituency as a champion of the countryside. He had more appeal to two constituencies—the small and middle-size farmers—than any of the other agrarians. A moderate, opting for change, not the status quo, Švehla leaned neither left nor right; he was simply reaching out to enlist support for a politics of trust. His genius lay in his putting together the self-interests of different groups. Accessible, shrewd, flexible, willing to listen and accommodate, he was one of the few major figures to have survived the years of turmoil without earning many enemies. Soon after Masaryk's return from abroad there developed a steady, close relationship of mutual confidence and friendship between the two most influential men on the Czech political scene. Masaryk admired Švehla's ability to visualize quickly the essentials of a problem, strip away the irrelevancies, and produce by laborious negotiations the workable compromise necessary to solve it.

Švehla was not so much a reformer as a man shrewd enough to know when to bend before the inevitable. Through patient negotiations he accommodated seemingly irreconcilable forces. He shunned the spotlight of publicity, living unobtrusively on his farm near Prague. He emerged from the crisis of 1919 as the most important political figure in Czechoslovakia, ideally suited to pacify the widespread waves of unrest within the framework of party and coalition politics. The basic principle of the

[55] Peroutka, *Budování státu*, II, 1140-61. For the text of Tusar's program, see Kocman, *Boj o směr*, II, 70-72.

Czechoslovak Land Reform was his. It was to strengthen the class of small and medium farmers by distributing the land of the partitioned estates among them. He aimed thus to retain the land in private ownership rather than to transfer it to the collective ownership of farm of cooperatives, as the socialists would have preferred to do. This gained the agrarian party the overwhelming support of the countryside in the 1920's and catapulted it, after the Social Democratic split in 1920-21, into the position of Czechoslovakia's strongest political party. Švehla's influence remained unequaled until the onset of his fatal illness in the late 1920's. At times even Masaryk submitted to the wise advice of this practical and independent-minded parliamentary leader who never failed to throw his influence behind the president. Švehla realized that the stability of Czechoslovakia, in which his own party played the leading role, depended to a large extent upon Masaryk.[56]

Karel Kramář had two successive careers, one before 1918 as the leading Czech representative in the Austrian Reichsrat, and one after 1918 as a Czechoslovak statesman. Paradoxically, his career in Austria, which he did his best to tear down, was more successful than his career in Czechoslovakia, which he strove to build up. World War I profoundly altered Czech society, and he was unwilling or unable to adjust to the new Czech outlook. Reluctant to face squarely the post-1918 shift in Czech public opinion from primarily national to primarily social issues, he left in January, 1919, to represent Czechoslovakia at the Paris Peace Conference, which he attended until after the signing of the Peace of St. Germain in September, 1919. He did not content himself at the peace conference with fighting for Czechoslovak interests but involved himself in Allied schemes to intervene in Russia to overthrow the Bolshevik government. Kramář believed—quite correctly, as the events of 1938-39 were to show—that Czechoslovakia could not survive German aggression without Russian support. Therefore, it was essential for Czechoslovakia to have a friendly government in Russia. Since the Bolsheviks had repudiated Panslavism and had postulated World Revolution as the basis of Soviet foreign policy, Kramář felt that it was not only Czechoslovakia's duty but also in its national interest to help to rescue Russia from the clutches of the Bolsheviks—in the hope that a post-Soviet government would resume the Tsarist government's role of protector of the Slavs.[57]

[56] For perceptive appraisals of Švehla's personality and policies, see Peroutka, *Budování státu*, II, 890-904, and Anthony Paleček, "Antonín Švehla: Czech Peasant Statesman," *Slavic Review*, XXI (December 1962), 699-708. For a highly critical communist view, see Eduard Kučera and Zdenka Kučerová, *O agrárnický stát [For an Agrarian State]* (Prague, 1955), pp. 25-42. Lockhart, *Retreat from Glory*, pp. 75-77, contains an engaging portrait of Švehla.

[57] Peroutka, *Budování státu*, II, 1318-30.

Kramář's relations with Masaryk were at times strained before the war. Yet in 1918 Kramář rallied wholeheartedly to the move to elect Masaryk the first president of Czechoslovakia. However, the two men had different personalities and backgrounds. After the downfall of his cabinet in June, 1919, Kramář believed—quite unjustly—that Masaryk had used his (Kramář's) absence from Prague to undermine his position. After that the two men were never able to accommodate their political and personal differences. Kramář declined all official functions offered him and sulked, obdurately refusing to accept the reality of social change in Czechoslovakia or the permanence of the Soviet government in Russia. Initially, he had a strong following among the Czech middle classes and he tried to stay clear of narrow party politics. Gradually, however, he became the chief spokesman of the Czech conservative and nationalist opposition to Masaryk's endeavors to reach a political settlement with the democratic left and the national minorities, and to Beneš's efforts to establish diplomatic relations with Soviet Russia. He sought to establish an independent center of power as a conservative alternate to Masaryk and Beneš. By the time of his death in 1937, however, his influence and following had dwindled to insignificance.

The survival of the center-left coalition established by Tusar in June, 1919, depended largely on the situation within the dissension-ridden Social Democratic party. Tusar was a respected moderate, who had served in Vienna during the war as the liaison man of the Czech Social Democratic party with other Social Democratic parties of the Habsburg empire. After the Russian Revolution in 1917 he cast his lot with the nationalist elements in the party leadership.[58] He naturally gravitated toward the pragmatic group of Rudolf Bechyně, Gustav Habrman, and Antonín Hampl, who in 1918 hastened to identify the Czech Social Democratic party with the new Czechoslovak state. As head of the cabinet, Tusar worked assiduously for a settlement of social issues. His program called for change in the organization and ownership of industry, but in fact proved to be moderate; it referred only vaguely to the socialization of the coal mines and mineral deposits. The main demand of Tusar's program concerned the preparation of the definitive constitution, which demonstrated again the conviction of the Red-Green coalition that the best hope for effective change lay in representative democracy and the ballot box rather than in the streets.[59]

Soon, however, troubles began to pile up for the Tusar government. In particular, the emergence of the pro-Leninist left as a new power cen-

[58] For a discussion of Tusar's personality and policies, see ibid., III, 1989-2008; Kárnik, *Socialisté na rozcestí, passim*; and Lockhart, *Retreat from Glory*, pp. 79-80.

[59] Kocman, *Boj o směr*, I, 70-72; and Peroutka, *Budování státu*, II, 1140-61.

:d him of much support from his own party. In the fall of 1919
vakia suffered a serious setback in its budgetary and monetary
he government felt compelled to introduce a sales tax to im-
financial situation, despite the fact that sales taxes were generally regarded as socially unjust. In the international money markets the
Czechoslovak crown (koruna) lost six sevenths of its prewar value. The
demands of the left-wing Social Democrats continued to increase. In October, the representatives of the left wing formally constituted themselves
a distinct body within the party, adopting the name the Marxist Left, and
endorsing the theoretical and practical theses of Bolshevism.[60]

POLITICAL PARTIES

The principal Czechoslovak political parties had their origins in the
Czech provinces in the decades prior to 1918. The same was true to a
somewhat lesser degree of the German political parties. The emergence
of organized parties as the real centers of power was a development that
came about gradually in the first two years of Czechoslovakia's existence.
In the course of 1919-20, the principal Czech parties extended their organizational net to Slovakia and Ruthenia. The Ruthenes were the most
handicapped of all nationalities of Czechoslovakia. They had practically
no political experience and were forced to organize—not without substantial Czech influence—their party life almost from scratch.

One of the main characteristics of Czechoslovakia's constitutional life
was the large number of political parties. Their proliferation was caused
by a number of factors: great diversity in social background and culture,
unequal political experience, and considerations of religion.[61] These factors found their expression in the adoption of proportional representation in the electoral system. The almost mathematical precision with
which proportional representation was applied made possible a host of
small parties.

The demand for proportional representation had long been a Czech
political demand in the Habsburg empire, because the Austrian electoral
system was based on the majority principle and often resulted in gross
distortion of the representation of the non-German nationalities in the
Reichsrat. The presence of relatively large minorities in Czechoslovakia

---

[60] The Marxist Left called for the seizure of power by the working class, the
socialization of means of production and distribution, and the creation of workers'
councils. It also expressed its agreement with the main principles of the Communist Third International (Comintern), rejecting all suggestions to resuscitate
the Socialist Second International. See Peroutka, *Budování státu*, III, 1975-76, and
Přehled, III, 94-96.

[61] Edward Taborsky, *Czechoslovak Democracy at Work* (London, 1945), pp.
40-41 and 83-84.

created a similar problem—only proportional representation appeared to be able to secure the minority rights of the Germans, Hungarians, Poles, and other national groups. The Czechoslovak legislators adopted it as a matter of basic justice, therefore, first in the law of January 31, 1919, providing for local elections, and then in the constitutional laws of February 29, 1920, providing for parliamentary elections. Its pitfalls were realized only later.

Viewed in retrospect, and in comparison with other East Central European countries, the political party system in Czechoslovakia—especially in so far as it concerned the major parties—remained remarkably stable. The decisive, fundamental changes on the political scene resulted from the appearance of two alien totalitarian forces: international communism and German National Socialism. If one excludes the German and Hungarian parties, the communists who were international, and the fascists who remained insignificant, seven major Czechoslovak parties figured in all four parliamentary elections. With the exception of the period between March, 1926, and November, 1929, five Czechoslovak parties represented the backbone of the coalition governments. The leading parties of democratic Czechoslovakia—unlike those of the neighboring states—were agreed as to the bases of political, economic, and social life of the country and also with regard to tactics. No doubt this characteristic was due largely to the almost subconscious realization of the ethnically Czechoslovak parties that their unity alone provided for the continued existence of the Czechoslovak Republic.

The most stable political force and one of the pillars of the Czechoslovak state was the agrarian party, which had emerged in the Czech provinces in the 1890's, still under Austrian rule.[62] In 1922, when the Czech agrarians fused with the Slovak agrarians (the Slovak National Republican and Peasant party), the common party assumed the name of Republican Party of Farmers and Peasants (Republikánská strana zemědělského a malorolnického lidu), but its members continued to be known popularly as the agrarians. With the exception of landless rural laborers, many of whom were attracted by communism, the agrarians became the principal political spokesmen of Czechoslovakia's large agricultural population. Because of Švehla's statesmanship, they managed to combine two ostensibly incompatible elements—the owners of large farms and the small holders, many of whom earned a precarious living on dwarf farms. Švehla consciously built up his party on the support of small and medium farmers, never allowing the owners of large estates to determine agrarian policies. It was only at the beginning of 1928, when

[62] See Table III in the appendix. For a succinct description of the agrarian party, see Josef Chmelař, *Political Parties in Czechoslovakia* (Prague, 1926), pp. 31-35; and a very critical view, Kučera and Kučerová. *O agrárnický stát*, pp. 93-103.

grave illness removed Švehla from the political scene, that the owners of large estates gradually acquired greater influence in the party, at times clashing with the interests of the small farmers. A small fraction of this group made an attempt in the middle thirties and again at the beginning of 1938 to replace the fundamental moderation of the agrarian party with ultra-rightist policies, toying with the idea of cooperating with the Nazi-controlled Sudeten German (Henlein) party and excluding the socialists from the government.[63] This attempt, however, foundered on the opposition of the majority of the agrarian leaders and that of the rank-and-file members, who refused to betray the democratic record of their party.

The power of the Agrarian party was based on its control of a variety of economic institutions rather than on an appeal to a special agrarian ideology. Because of the ascendancy of pragmatists typified by Švehla, who combined the principle of progressive social legislation with a genuinely democratic outlook and favored cooperation with the socialists, the agrarians assumed a position in the center of the Czechoslovak political spectrum. From 1922 until 1938 they were the core of all center-left or center-right coalitions, occupying the ministries of the interior and agriculture, and holding the office of prime minister.

Briefly, until the secession of the communists in 1920-21, the Czechoslovak Social Democratic Workers' party (Československá socialně-demokratická strana dělnická) was the largest force in the National Assembly. After the secession of the communists there remained about fifty Social Democrats in the National Assembly. The party had suffered a stunning blow. In the Czech provinces, especially central Bohemia, its membership fell well behind that of the communists, and in Slovakia the Social Democrats were almost wiped out.[64]

Gradually three factors helped the Social Democratic party to regain its strength. The first was the existence of a tough leadership and of a reliable hard core of party and labor union cadres. The party officials largely succeeded in cutting the party's losses and in keeping the local organizations going. In the 1920's they gradually regained support of the working class by their professionalism and skill in dealing with bread-and-butter issues. The second element was the party's success in obtaining passage of long-promised social legislation in the National Assembly and in achieving marked progress in the participation of organized labor in the political and administrative processes. The party thus won back the loyalty of many of the radicals to the Czechoslovak state.[65] The third

[63] Taborsky, *Czechoslovak Democracy*, p. 90.
[64] Peroutka, *Budování státu*, III, 1976, 1983-87. See also Chmelař, *Political Parties*, pp. 38-44.
[65] Kocman, *Boj o směr*, II, 162-64.

element which worked in favor of democratic socialism was the general decline of postwar radicalism, as well as the growing factional strife among the communists, which gradually undermined their strength. In the elections of 1925 the Social Democrats received only twenty-nine seats in the Chamber of Deputies as against the communists' forty-one, but only four years later, in the elections of 1929, the Social Democrats exceeded the communists in the lower house by eleven deputies.

In keeping with their official program the Social Democrats subscribed to the principles of scientific socialism (Marxism) and became associated with the Second International in The Hague. Their actual practice, however, was similiar to that of Western socialist parties. Moderation, repudiation of doctrinaire policies, and full understanding for the problem of the Czechoslovak state were their main characteristics. In its 1930 program, the party declared itself unconditionally in favor of the principles of parliamentary democracy.

With the exception of the four years between 1925 and 1929, the Social Democrats played an important role in all cabinets. The party's chairman, Antonín Hampl, was a leader of the metal workers' union who had risen from the ranks through the party's hierarchy. He was known as a strong disciplinarian and a supporter of cooperation among the main democratic political forces—a position that brought him into conflict with the radical Marxist Left in 1919-20. Having the apparatus of the party in hand and enjoying firm support among the skilled workers, he devoted his efforts to building up the party. Other leaders, including the most outstanding member of the party's parliamentary delegation, Rudolf Bechyně, the party boss of the important industrial city of Plzeň, Gustav Habrman, and the leader of the party's Slovak branch, Ivan Dérer, greatly contributed to maintaining a viable system of democracy. One might add, however, that moderation and reformism, which proved to be an asset in times of Czechoslovakia's internal and external stability, worked to the party's disadvantage in times of crisis.

The second socialist party in Czechoslovakia was the Czech Socialist party, which was renamed, in 1926, the Czechoslovak National Socialist party (Československá národně-socialistická strana).[66] It was founded before World War I by a group of men who broke off from the Social Democratic party, because they refused to accept Marxian doctrine, especially the notion of class struggle, and emphasized the idea of nationalism. In the radical atmosphere of the immediate postwar period the National Socialists adopted an almost revolutionary stand on social is-

[66] Chmelař, *Political Parties*, pp. 49-52; Peroutka, *Budování státu*, I, 488-96. The Czechoslovak National Socialist party must not be confused with the German National Socialist party. In aims and ideals, it approached much more the French Radical Socialist party.

sues and even contemplated joining the future socialist international.[67] Soon, however, reacting to the general swing to the right and the split in the Social Democratic party, they tended to abandon their radical socialist views. It was only in 1929, under the impression of the outbreak of the Great Depression, that they began again to cooperate with the Social Democrats, especially in practical policies designed to alleviate unemployment and suffering among the workers. Only a part of the following of the National Socialist party, however, were workers. The majority of its members was recruited from among the lower middle class, civil servants, and the intelligentsia.

The National Socialist party played an important role in the majority of Czechoslovak cabinets, being forced to go into opposition only between 1925 and 1929. The fact that one of its leading members, Edvard Beneš, held the position of foreign minister uninterruptedly from 1918 to 1935, when he was elected president, was due partly to his personal prestige but, above all, to the support given him by President Masaryk. The actual leader was Václav Klofáč (1868-1942), an astute, folksy politician, who served as Czechoslovakia's first minister of national defense, despite a lifelong antimilitarist record. Another of the party's leaders, Jiří Stříbrný, played an important role in the critical days of October, 1918 (he was cosigner of the Prague National Committee's declaration of independence). However, in 1926, after a serious internal crisis in the party, he was expelled from it and drifted into fascism.

Somewhat smaller than the National Socialist party was the Czechoslovak Populist party (Československá strana lidová).[68] It was formed gradually by the fusion of several Catholic political parties, groups, and labor unions, first in Bohemia in October, 1918, and then in Moravia in January, 1919. The Bohemian and Moravian wings remained autonomous until 1922, when they formed a common executive committee and chose the leader of the Moravian wing, Msgr. Jan Šrámek (1870-1956), as the party's chairman. The party's program was based on Christian moral principles and the social encyclicals of Pope Leo XIII. In the first years of Czechoslovakia the Czech populists were discounted as a political force, because of their close association with the Roman Catholic Church. Even before World War I Czech public opinion largely turned against the Catholic Church, because of its role in the Czech national disaster in the seventeenth century and its close identification with the Habsburg dynasty. The Church's aloofness from the Czechoslovak strug-

[67] Peroutka, pp. 32-37.

[68] Ibid., vol. II, 618-35; Chmelař, *Political Parties*, pp. 53-58; for more recent information about the Populist party, see Miloš Trapl, *Politika českého katolicismu na Moravě, 1918-1938* [*The Politics of the Czech Catholics in Moravia, 1918-1938*] (Prague, 1968); and Mořic Hruban, *Z času nedlouho zašlých* [*From the Recent Past*] (Rome-Los Angeles, 1967).

gle for national independence during the war further alienated Czech opinion from it. The Czech socialist parties were notably critical of the Church and suspicious of the aims of the Populist party.

The Czech populists were underrepresented in the Prague National Committee and the provisional National Assembly, because party representation in these two bodies was based on the results of the last Austrian elections, and the Austrian electoral system penalized splinter parties. The Czech populists were likewise slighted in the Kramář cabinet, and altogether excluded from Tusar's two Red-Green coalition cabinets. Gradually, however, by showing complete loyalty to the Czechoslovak Republic and a strong sense of social responsibility toward the Czech working class, they managed to dissipate the hostility and suspicions of the leftist parties and to disarm Czech anti-Catholicism generally. Much of the credit for this success was due to the able leadership of Msgr. Šrámek, whose meek priestly manner concealed a realistic, tenacious, and very astute politician. He combined Catholic faith with progressive social views and genuine patriotism. As a member of all political cabinets from 1921 to 1938, he succeeded in removing many initial obstacles to good church-state relations and in finding a comfortable place for the Czech Catholics in Czech national and political life.

The once powerful representative of the Czech bourgeoisie, the Young-Czech party, merged in February, 1918, with other right and center parties into the Czech State-Rights party, which was renamed the Czechoslovak National Democratic party[69] (Československá strana národně-demokratická) at its first postwar congress in March, 1919.[69] Its initially leading position in Czechoslovakia was due to the prestige of its two leaders, Karel Kramář and Alois Rašín, whose popularity was enhanced by the persecution they had suffered at the hands of the Austrian authorities during the war. The party increased its importance by attracting outstanding representatives from among high civil servants, liberal professions, and the intelligentsia. In the first days of Czechoslovakia the choice of Kramář for the premiership and of Rašín to the highly responsible function of finance minister was taken for granted.

After their decisive defeat in the local elections in June, 1919, the National Democrats fell to sixth, and later to the ninth, place among the Czechoslovak political parties. Their program was that of national radicalism, hostility to the Germans, and in the initial years a rather unrealistic concept of Slavism which was to be expressed by the future cooperation of Czechoslovakia with a Russia liberated from Bolshevik domination. The National Democrats were perhaps the most adamant enemies of the Soviet Union. Advocating the principles of orthodox eco-

[69] Peroutka, *Budování státu*, II, 799-819; Chmelař, *Political Parties*, pp. 20-27.

nomic liberalism, they became the party of big businessmen, bankers, industrialists, and the emerging Czech upper class generally.

The defeat of the National Democratic party in the 1920 parliamentary elections initiated the process of its gradual disintegration. On several occasions the National Democrats joined the government coalition, but their policies were marked by implacable opposition to Masaryk and Beneš. This attitude alienated from the party many of its most talented members. Its decline was strikingly revealed in the 1935 parliamentary elections, in which it combined with extreme chauvinistic groups and ran under the name[70] National Union (Národní sjednocení). Viewed in retrospect, the progressive decline and deterioration of the National Democrats worked to the disadvantage of the Czechoslovak system of democracy—it deprived it of a genuine conservative party necessary for the maintenance of internal political equilibrium.

Of the minor Czechoslovak parties, many of which were ephemeral, the most important was the Tradesmen's party (Živnostenská strana).[71] It originated in 1920 to represent the class and professional interests of small businessmen and tradesmen which were threatened, on the one hand, by the socialist parties representing labor and, on the other, by the National Democrats representing big business. The Tradesmen's party cooperated closely with the agrarians.

Most of the German parties were constituted in the course of 1919 on the basis of prewar political groupings.[72] Their new alignment paralleled that of the Czechoslovak parties, with a greater emphasis on the national issue. The Hungarian minority was originally divided into several parties based on class or religion, which originated before the war. Gradually, however, the Hungarian parties were united into a national coalition.[73] The Polish minority showed a similar trend.[74] Among the Ruthenes, who did not elect their first representatives into the Prague National Assembly until 1924, the Communist party established an ascendancy which it maintained (with the exception of the elections of 1929) to the end of the First Republic.[75]

The Communist Party of Czechoslovakia (Komunistická strana Československa—KSČ) stood apart from all the other parties and repre-

---

[70] Alena Gajánová, Dvojí tvář: Z historie předmnichovského fašismu [Two-Face: Out of the History of pre-Munich Fascism] (Prague, 1962), pp. 45-46 and 111-12.

[71] Chmelař, Political Parties, pp. 27-28.

[72] Ibid., pp. 65-77; J. W. Bruegel's chapter below.

[73] Chmelař, Political Parties, pp. 78-83; and Macartney, Hungary and her Successors, p. 118.

[74] Chmelař, Political Parties, pp. 83-85.

[75] Ibid., pp. 89-95; and Macartney, Hungary and her Successors, p. 240.

sented all the nationalities in the country.[76] Even before the communists formally constituted themselves a party in 1921, they existed as the Marxian left within the Social Democratic party. In the first National Assembly elected under the Constitution of 1920, eighteen leftist Social Democrats founded an independent club, the Left-Wing Social Democracy. This tactic was based on the hope of infiltrating the Social Democratic party and guiding it into the Communist (Third) International in Moscow. However, the tactic failed.The party split. Though much diminished, the Social Democrats continued.

The communists' intention to remain a mass party determined the nature of their policies. It enabled the party to pose as the main representative of the idea of social justice, thus attracting support not only from the masses but also from a relatively large group of the intelligentsia, including some of the leading Czech *literati*. At the same time insistence on remaining a large party resulted in lack of revolutionary élan and in doctrinal flabbiness, for which the party's leadership was regularly criticized at the Comintern congresses. This was a serious defect from the point of view of Soviet-type communism. Its seriousness was increased by the atmosphere of political freedom in Czechoslovakia, which was not propitious to the growth of revolutionary ardor. The party was allowed to pursue a totally antagonistic policy toward the Czechoslovak Republic, without fear of reprisals or suppression. More often than not, the party's fiery words were not accompanied by action.

PARTIES, MEN, AND POLITICS IN SLOVAKIA

Following the practice in the Austrian Reichsrat, parties in the Czechoslovak provisional National Assembly organized themselves into parliamentary "clubs" for the purpose of caucusing. Members of the clubs were subject to a rigorous discipline and voted *en bloc*. Since the Slovak National party was the only Slovak political party in the immediate postwar period, all Slovak deputies were organized into a single "Slovak Club" and subjected to a single discipline. The Hlasists provided the leadership of the club and entirely dominated its tactics.

In his opening address to the National Assembly on November 14, 1918, Prime Minister Kramář defined Czechoslovakia as a "Czech state" and welcomed the Slovaks as long lost sons who had "returned to the nation's fold, where they belong."[77] At first, the Slovaks in the National

---

[76] Chmelař, *Political Parties*, pp. 44-49; Paul Reimann *et al.*, *Dějiny Komunistické strany Československa* [*History of the Communist Party of Czechoslovakia*] (Prague, 1961), pp. 143-76.

[77] Soukup, *28. říjen 1918*, II, 1127.

Assembly accepted Kramář's view of the Czechoslovak relationship and the Hlasist leadership of the Slovak Club readily. The sharp division in Slovak opinion, between the centralists who supported the principle of Czechoslovak unity and the autonomists who supported the principle of Slovak distinctness, did not arise until later. At the time, all Slovak deputies in the National Assembly were centralists and supporters of Czechoslovak unity. Fearful of the Hungarians who were reoccupying Slovakia at the time and also of a threat of a Bolshevik-type social revolution in Slovakia; they nestled close to the Czechs. The first act of the Slovak Club was to "interpellate" (i.e., demand of) the government to send Czech troops to occupy Slovakia. Father Ľudovít Okánik expressed their innermost thought when he said in the ensuing debate that unless the Czechs cleared the Hungarians from Slovakia, "we Slovaks in Prague will not be deputies but only exiles of the Slovak people."[78] Surveying the chaotic Slovak scene from Skalica, Pavel Blaho wrote to Šrobár in Prague on November 30: "Vavro, only an iron centralism can save us."[79]

The composition of the Slovak Club did not long remain the same. In March, 1919, after the Slovaks complained that they were not proportionately represented in the National Assembly, the Slovak Club was allotted fourteen additional seats, which brought its membership to fifty-five. The new deputies were selected by the Hlasist leaders of the club.[80]

The early unanimity of the members of the Slovak Club did not last long, either. Soon party divisions reasserted themselves. New Slovak political parties were formed. The Slovak populists (ľudáks), who chafed most under the Hlasist dominance of the club, took the lead. As early as December 19, 1918, at a meeting in Žilina, the Slovak Populist party (Slovenská ľudová strana) was reestablished under its prewar leader, Andrej Hlinka.[81] The socialists were next in the field. On December 25, at a meeting in Liptovský Svätý Mikuláš, the Slovak branch of the Czechoslovak Social Democratic party was formed, likewise under its prewar leader Emanuel Lehocký.[82] In May, 1919, two prominent Hlasists, Ivan Dérer and Ivan Markovič, joined it and soon dominated

[78] Karol, Sidor, Slovenská politika na pôde pražského snemu [Slovak Politics in the Prague Parliament] (2 vols.; Bratislava, 1943), I, 43.

[79] Vavro Šrobár, Osvobodené Slovensko: Pamäti z rokov 1918-1920 [Liberated Slovakia: Recollections of the Years 1918-1920] (Bratislava, 1928), p. 336.

[80] Lipscher, "Klub," p. 135; Sidor, Slovenská politika, I, 52. Incidentally, Edvard Beneš was coopted by the Slovak Club and brought into the National Assembly. He was not an elected politician before the war. Therefore, he could not be easily brought into the National Assembly in the quotas of any of the Czech parties.

[81] Medvecký, Slovenský prevrat, III, 199; Karol Sidor, Andrej Hlinka, 1864-1926 (Bratislava, 1934), pp. 331-34.

[82] Miloš Gosiorovský, Dejiny slovenského robotníckeho hnutia, 1848-1918 [History of the Slovak Labor Movement, 1848-1918] (Bratislava, 1956), pp. 304-306.

it.[83] On May 26, 1919, the Slovak branch of the Czechoslovak Socialist party (later National Socialist party) was formed at Bratislava, and came under the leadership of another prominent Hlasist, Igor Hrušovský.[84] In September, 1919, the Slovak National party was reorganized on the initiative of Milan Hodža as the Slovak National Republican and Peasant party (Slovenská národná republikánska strana rol'nícka), Most of the Hlasists, including Šrobár, Blaho, and Anton Štefánek, joined it. However, some of the older members of the Slovak National party objected to giving the new party a class (agrarian) character and withdrew from it. The Slovak National Republican and Peasant party was not definitely constituted until January 11, 1920.[85]

With the exception of the Slovak Populist party, all the parties were dominated by the Hlasists. They insisted on maintaining a single Slovak Club, despite the different party affiliations of its members. The party affiliations of the club's members fluctuated at first, but by the fall of 1919 stabilized thus: 32 Agrarians, 10 Social Democrats, 9 Populists, and 3 National Socialists. The Slovak Club lasted until the dissolution of the provisional National Assembly in April, 1920.

In the Hungarian tradition, which was strikingly different from the Czech traditions, Slovak politics were highly personal. Political parties were regarded primarily as personal political machines, designed to elect the party leaders and keep them in power. Party doctrines and ideologies were less important. The Slovaks surrounded their party leaders with a cult of personality, which the Czechs reserved only for President Masaryk. In 1925, the Slovak Populist party formally renamed itself Hlinka's Slovak Populist party (Hlinkova slovenská l'udová strana— HSL'S).[86] The other Slovak parties did not go that far in venerating their leaders. Nevertheless, the agrarian party was popularly referred to as Hodža's party and the Social Democratic party as Dérer's party.

Undoubtedly, if he had lived, General Štefánik would have been the leading Slovak political personality. He perished tragically in an airplane accident on May 4, 1919, however, on his return home from exile, as he was about to land near Bratislava. He was virtually unknown in Slovakia at the time. As the story of his romantic career and wartime deeds became known, however, he was enshrined in national legend as the Slovaks' greatest hero. He was buried in an imposing mausoleum built on the Bradlo, a hill overlooking his native village. Since he had not had oc-

---

[83] Ivan Dérer, *Slovenský vývoj a luďácká zrada* [*The Slovak Development and the L'udák Betrayal*] (Prague, 1946), p. 246.

[84] Lipscher, "Klub," p. 147.

[85] Vladimír Zuberec, "Príspevok k dejinám vzniku agrárnej strany na Slovensku, 1918-1921" ["Contribution to the History of the Origins of the Agrarian Party in Slovakia, 1918-1921"], *Historický časopis,* xv (1967), 573-99.

[86] Sidor, *Slovenská politika,* I, 260-61.

casion to take part in Czechoslovak politics, little was known of his views. This made it possible for both the Slovak autonomists and centralists to claim his mantle.

In 1918-20, which was Czechoslovakia's formative period, the most influential Slovak politician was Šrobár. Immediately after his appointment as minister with special powers to administer Slovakia on December 10, 1918,[87] he left Prague and set up a Slovak "government," first at Žilina in northwestern Slovakia and then, after it was occupied by Czechoslovak troops in January, 1919, at Bratislava. Until 1918, Slovakia had no capital, whether administrative or cultural. It was Šrobár's decision to create one at Bratislava (or Prešporok, as it was then known from its German name, Pressburg). Its population was at the time largely German or Hungarian; only its working class was Slovak. However, it was the largest and most modern town in Slovakia, and had good railway connections to Budapest and Vienna as well as to Prague. Other Slovak towns were at the time devoid of modern facilities.

Temperamentally, Šrobár was well suited for his office, which conferred on him dictatorial powers.[88] A radical, Jacobin-like politician, he did not hestitate to use his powers ruthlessly to cleanse Slovakia of Hungarian influence, implant a Czechoslovak administration and institutions in it, and to suppress social unrest and disorder. Like most members of the Slovak intelligentsia at the time, he had little confidence in the wisdom and patriotism of the Slovak masses. He believed that they had been so warped by Hungarian rule that they did not know where their own self-interest lay. If given democratic freedoms too soon, they might follow the leadership of the magyarized Slovaks instead of genuine Slovak patriots like himself. Therefore, he and a few like-minded intellectuals would have to take matters into their hands and act for the masses of the Slovak people, until a new generation of Slovaks, educated entirely in Slovak schools, came to maturity. On January 8, 1919, he abolished the Slovak National Council and the various local national committees and workers' councils. On March 24, after the proclamation of the Hungarian Soviet Republic under Béla Kun, Šrobár put Slovakia under martial law, and on June 5, after the Hungarian Red Army overran all of eastern Slovakia, he placed it under a military dictatorship. A sincere democrat, Šrobár believed, like many an impatient reformer, that the end justified the means, and that it was legitimate to use undemocratic methods to establish democracy.

The tasks that Šrobár faced in Slovakia were formidable. He had to organize an entirely new administration. Hungarian officials had either

[87] Kocman, *Boj o směr*, I, 152-53.
[88] For a good appraisal of Šrobár's personality and politics, see Peroutka, *Budování státu*, I, 406-11.

fled from Slovakia or had been fired by him for lack of loyalty to the Czechoslovak government. There were few qualified Slovaks to take their place. Owing to the lack of educational opportunities under Hungarian rule, the Slovaks lacked not only experienced administrators but also skilled personnel of every kind necessary to operate a modern state.[89] Srobár was, therefore, obliged to appeal to the government in Prague for Czech personnel. Fortunately, the Czechs had a surplus of skilled administrators and technical personnel, having long provided a large proportion of the personnel of the Austrian administration.

Some of the Czech officials and technicians who arrived in Slovakia did so out of idealism to help their Slovak brothers. Others were less loftily motivated. Whatever their motivation, however, they brought with them the traditions of the Austrian bureaucracy that were superior to those of Hungarian officialdom. Thanks to the efforts of Czech officials and technicians, a new administration, courts, and public services were organized in Slovakia in a relatively short time. Generally speaking, the Czechoslovak administration was superior in standards of honesty and efficiency to that of the fallen Hungarian regime.

At first, the Slovaks welcomed the assistance of Czech officials and technicians. Speaking in the National Assembly on January 23, 1920, the Slovak populist deputy Father Ferdiš Juriga insisted, even while expatiating on the need of Slovak autonomy: "We need a million Czechs in Slovakia."[90] Later, however, when a new generation of Czech-trained Slovak officials and professionals arose, they saw in their Czech teachers obstacles to their own advancement and resented them.

In making appointments to responsible positions, especially the sensitive posts of county chiefs (*župani*) who had extensive police powers, Srobár chose more Protestants than Catholics, because, generally speaking, the Protestants had rallied to the Czechoslovak Republic with fewer reservations than the Catholics. Historically, the Protestants tended to be Czechophile. They had nothing to lose by leaving Hungary, in which they had been a religious as well as an ethnic minority. While it would be an oversimplification to say that all Slovak Protestants were Czechophiles and centralists and all Slovak Catholics anti-Czech and autonomists, there were fewer exceptions to this rule on the Protestant side than on the Catholic. For this reason, Srobár trusted the Protestants more than his fellow-Catholics. The Czechs likewise showed preference to the Protestants.

[89] Out of a total of 6,185 state, county, district, and municipal officials in Slovakia in 1910, only 154 were Slovaks. Out of a total of 1,879 lawyers in Slovakia in the same year only 150 were Slovaks. See Ladislav Lipscher, *K vývinu politickej správy na Slovensku v rokoch 1918-1938* [*On the Development of Political Administration in Slovakia in 1918-1938*] (Bratislava, 1966), pp. 66-70.

[90] Sidor, *Slovenská politika*, I, 68-69.

The Protestants were not slow to take advantage of the situation.[91] As long-aggrieved minorities are wont to do when they come out on top, they felt no compunction about claiming all important positions in Slovakia and those available to the Slovaks in the central government in Prague. The situation was aggravated by nepotism. Family ties were close and clannishness was pronounced in Slovakia. Because of class and religious prejudices, members of the small Protestant intelligentsia usually married only their own kind. As a result, virtually all of them were related. Family ties combined with the natural solidarity of a long-embattled minority to make of them an exceptionally cohesive group. They helped each other more than the Catholics did. With remarkable speed, the Protestant intelligentsia transformed themselves from a rather pitiful minority into an exclusive, self-serving ruling élite. Thereafter, the Protestant intelligentsia had a vested interest in supporting centralism, because they knew that in an autonomous Slovakia they would fare poorly at the hands of the Catholic majority.

Inevitably, the favor shown the Protestants by Šrobár and Prague incited Catholic jealousy. In the years immediately preceding World War I, Slovak nationalist feeling tended to override religious divisions between the Catholics and Protestants. Hlinka then admonished his followers: "In politics, a Lutheran with [Slovak] national feeling is a brother, a Catholic without it an enemy."[92] After the war Catholic-Protestant relations deteriorated. The Catholics were wont to expatiate invidiously about the "Lutheran aristocracy" and the "twenty [Lutheran] families" that ruled Slovakia.

The Catholics were also disgruntled over the nationalization of schools in Slovakia. After the establishment of Czechoslovakia in 1918, the entire school system in Slovakia, both state and church, was placed under government control. For the first time in history, a quota of schools proportionate to Slovak numbers was reserved for their education, and a really impressive effort was made to reduce the educational lag they had incurred under Hungarian rule. Instruction in Slovak schools was given at once in Slovak, despite a desperate shortage of Slovak teachers and an almost complete lack of Slovak textbooks.[93] Hungarian teachers and

---

[91] Peroutka, *Budování státu*, III, 1226-27.

[92] Sidor, *Slovenská politika*, I, 38.

[93] According to Anton Štefánek, *Základy sociografie Slovenska* [*Foundations of Sociology in Slovakia*] (Bratislava, 1944), p. 299, the Czechoslovak authorities took over from the Hungarians or opened 3,605 primary schools, with 376,604 pupils. There were only 276 primary schools, with 36,118 pupils and 390 teachers, in which instruction was partially given in Slovak. The need was for over 2,500 Slovak primary schools and over 3,000 Slovak teachers. The situation was even worse in secondary schools. Of the 59 secondary schools in Slovakia in 1918 none gave instruction in Slovak. There was a need for about 500 Slovak secondary school teachers. Instead, there were only about 20. See Medvecký, *Slovenský prevrat*, II, 360.

textbooks were replaced with Czech. The proximity of the Slovak and Czech languages (the Slovaks and Czechs can converse, each using their own language, and understand each other) made the replacement possible.

On June 6, 1919, the National Assembly voted the establishment of the first Slovak university at Bratislava. The Slovenská Matica[94] (Slovak Mother), the old Slovak cultural institution hallowed by martyrdom under Hungarian rule, was reestablished and served as a sort of Slovak academy. Thanks to these energetic steps, Slovak national consciousness and culture revived with remarkable speed. Unquestionably, the establishment of Slovak schools[95] was the First Republic's greatest contribution to Slovak national development. The Slovak Catholics did not, of course, object to the development of Slovak schools—in fact, they were duly appreciative of it—but to their secularization. The autonomists among them were also critical of the use of the schools to promote the ideology of Czechoslovak cultural and political unity.

Šrobár was a strong proponent of Czechoslovak cultural unity and political centralism. He did not use his powers to foster any Slovak particularism, but, on the contrary, to integrate Slovakia into a uniform Czechoslovak state as fast and as thoroughly as possible. He opposed the formation of new Slovak parties. He would have preferred the formation of a single Slovak government party. When this proved impossible, he joined the Slovak agrarian party, which was the government party *par excellence* in Slovakia, from its beginning in 1919 to its end in 1938. However, Šrobár had little taste for "playing politics." He made no attempt to court popularity and to build himself an independent political base in Slovakia. Instead, he continued to depend on Prague for support. Inevitably, Prague's confidence in him incited the jealousy of other Slovak politicians, who did their best to undermine his position during his absence from Prague to administer Slovakia. Besides, the government did not give him unlimited support. He had great difficulty getting funds from the government. Finance Minister Rašín pursued a deflationary policy, stressed economy in government, and begrudged expenditures in

---

[94] The original Slovak *Matica* was founded in 1863 on the model of the Serb *Matica* (1826) and the Czech *Matice* (1831) to develop the Slovak language and culture. It was abolished in 1875 by the iron-fisted Hungarian Prime Minister Kálmán Tisza (1875-90) on the ground that there was "no Slovak people." With cruel irony, the Hungarian government transferred the Slovak *Matica's* property to an association, the purpose of which was to magyarize the Slovaks. Cf. František Bokes, *Dejiny Slovenska a Slovákov od najstarších čias po oslobodenie* [*History of Slovakia and the Slovaks from the Oldest Times to the Present*] (Bratislava, 1946), pp. 238-39, 273-74.

[95] The number of secondary schools in Slovakia increased from 59 in 1918 to 65 in 1928. Of these 48 were Slovak in 1928. Štefánek, *Základy sociografie*, p. 300. Illiteracy was reduced from 34.9 percent in 1910 to 8.16 percent in 1930. See ibid., p. 295.

Slovakia. Generally speaking, with the exception of a handful of Czech Slovakophiles, Czech politicians took little interest in Slovakia. The Czechs were a resourceful and self-reliant people. They had pulled themselves up by their own bootstraps in the Habsburg empire in the nineteenth century, and felt that the Slovaks should be able to do the same in the much more propitious atmosphere of the Czechoslovak Republic.

Šrobár had little control over Slovakia's economy. This was exercised by appropriate ministries in Prague. Until 1921 the government continued the Austrian wartime controls over the economy, and extended them to Slovakia. During the war Slovakia had suffered less privation due to army requisitions and the Allied blockade than the Czech provinces, because the Hungarian government had hoarded food and supplies, even while the Austrian half of the empire was starving. After the war, to alleviate food shortages in the Czech provinces, the government instituted requisitions in Slovakia. The requisitions and the abrupt severance of Slovakia from Hungary, from which it received much of its food, caused food shortages in Slovakia, too. The break with Hungary also disorganized Slovakia's industrial production. Unemployment, an old scourge of the Slovak people, reappeared. Military operations from November, 1918, to January, 1919, and again from April to June, 1919, when the Hungarian Red Army invaded Slovakia, also contributed to the disruption of Slovakia's economy. By 1920 it showed little sign of recovery.[96] Although Šrobár was not primarily responsible for the economic difficulties, growing popular dissatisfaction over them was vented on him, as the government's principal representative in Slovakia.

On March 26, 1920, amidst the first Czechoslovak parliamentary electoral campaign, gendarmes fired into a crowd of striking farm workers in the village of Rumanová in Slovakia and killed two of them. Although Šrobár was not personally responsible for the tragedy, as responsible minister in Slovakia he had to take the blame for it. In the National Assembly, a Czech Social Democrat denounced him as a "bloody dog" and demanded his ouster. None of his cabinet colleagues or the Slovaks rose to defend him. He had become a political liability for the government.[97]

[96] Medvecký, Slovenský prevrat, III, 210-11; Peroutka, Budování státu, II, 1220-21; Faltus, Prehľad hospodárskeho vývoja, pp. 28-35; Macartney, Hungary and her Successors, pp. 127-28. In 1920 unemployment in Slovakia was estimated at 120,000. See Jan Mlynárik, Nezamestnanosť na Slovensku, 1918-1938 [Unemployment in Slovakia in 1918-1938] (Bratislava, 1964), p. 47. Emigration, which had been halted by the outbreak of the war, resumed soon after its conclusion. See František Bielik, "Príspevok k otázke vysťahovalectva zo Slovenska v rokoch 1919-1924" ["On the Question of Emigration from Slovakia in 1919-1924"], Historický časopis, I (1953), 505-20.

[97] Sidor, Slovenská politika, I, 121-22; Peroutka, Budování státu, III, 1771-72; Milan Filo, "Udalosti v Rumanovej r. 1920" ["Events in Rumanová in 1920"], Historický časopis, XI (1953), 106-16.

When the Slovak agrarian party did not fare as well as it had expected in the elections, he was blamed for it. After the elections, his influence in the government and the agrarian party declined. For better or for worse, however, he had affected Slovak development permanently.

In the meantime, the star of Milan Hodža had risen on the political horizon.[98] His ascendancy was somewhat surprising. To be sure, in the Geneva conference in October, 1918, he had been earmarked for a post in the first Czechoslovak cabinet. However, by the time he arrived in Prague on November 16 all posts were gone. Then his Budapest mission ended in a fiasco, the repercussions of which were to hound him for years. When he returned to Prague in January, 1919, to take his seat in the provisional National Assembly, he was surrounded with a cloud of suspicion.[99] What had he really been up to in Budapest? Was he not in reality a Magyarone or a Slovak autonomist? As a matter of fact, Hodža was a sincere Slovak nationalist; he might have been a Slovak autonomist if he had been a Catholic. Apart from being a Protestant, however, he had little taste for "the dry bread of opposition."[100] He loved political power and its trappings and spoils. From his days in Budapest he retained the grand manner of a Hungarian gentleman and a taste for sartorial elegance. Of all Slovak—or Czech, for that matter—politicians he cut the most statesmanlike figure. Polished, experienced, and worldly-wise, he took an interest in foreign affairs—unlike most Slovak politicians, whose horizons were rather narrow. He would have liked to be foreign minister, but that post was firmly held by Beneš. Hodža undoubtedly had the welfare of the Slovak people at heart, but he tended to identify it with his own political fortunes.

Casting about for a role and anxious to dispel the suspicions surrounding him, Hodža looked for an issue designed to appeal to the Czech and Slovak centralists. He found one in the legal disunity between the Czech provinces that operated under the Austrian code and Slovakia and Ruthenia that used the Hungarian code. New laws passed by the National Assembly were usually in harmony with the Austrian code but often violated the Hungarian code, with which the Czech legislators were not familiar. Much legal confusion resulted. To remedy the situation, Hodža and his supporters in the Slovak Club proposed and successfully steered through the assembly a law creating a new ministry for the unification

---

[98] For an appraisal of Milan Hodža, see Anton Štefánek, *Milan Hodža: Životopisný nástin [Milan Hodža: A Biographical Sketch]* (Bratislava, 1938), *passim*, and Jozef Rudinský, *Československý štát a Slovenská Republika [The Czechoslovak State and the Slovak Republic]* (Munich, 1969), pp. 234-57. An ordained Catholic priest, Rudinský was originally a Slovak populist and companion of Hlinka but later became an agrarian and attached himself to Hodža.

[99] Peroutka, *Budování státu*, II, 1238.

[100] Rudinský, *Československý štát*, p. 247.

of Czechoslovak laws and codes (July 22, 1919).[101] To no one's surprise, the first minister of unification, appointed on December 6, 1919, was Milan Hodža.

Unlike Šrobár, Hodža had a keen understanding of the reality of political power. He understood the necessity of having a solid political base in Slovakia and a well-organized party behind him. He took the lead in the organization of the Slovak agrarian party, and after its merger with the Czech Agrarian party in 1922 retained control of it. In the late 1920's and in the 1930's he became an indispensable intermediary between Prague and Slovakia. In 1919, however, his position was not yet assured.

In 1920 Hodža published a book on the "Czechoslovak Schism" in which he expressed regret over Štúr's linguistic reform and the belief that Czech and Slovak cultures would converge and their languages eventually merge.[102] As subsequent developments proved, however, his acceptance of the principle of Czechoslovak unity was by no means definite. With the passing of time and the growth of Slovak national consciousness, the subject of "Czechoslovakism" became increasingly controversial. Hodža did not return to it. Instead, he gradually began to speak in a manner that reassured the centralists and gave the autonomists the impression that, at heart, he was one of them. Later, in exile during World War II, he claimed to have believed in Slovak distinctness all along.[103]

Hodža's principal adversary in Slovakia was Andrej Hlinka.[104] To the uninitiated observer, Slovak politics must have often appeared as a duel between them. Hlinka had rallied to the Czechoslovak Republic with enthusiasm. He had taken a prominent part in the memorable meeting at Turčiansky Svätý Martin on October 30, 1918, and became a member of the Slovak National Council.[105] Gradually, however, he became disillusioned with the Czechoslovak government. Eventually, he denounced the Martin Declaration as "sinful and irresponsible"[106] and voiced a de-

[101] Peroutka, *Budování státu*, II, 1238; Kocman, *Boj o směr*, II, 75-76; Sidor, *Andrej Hlinka*, p. 362.

[102] Milan Hodža, *Československý rozkol: Príspevky k dejinám slovenčiny* [*The Czechoslovak Schism: Contributions to the History of the Slovak Language*] (Turčiansky Svätý Martin, 1920), pp. 14-15; Rudinský, *Československý štát*, pp. 244-46.

[103] Michal Mudry (ed.), *Milan Hodža v Amerike: Články, reči, štúdie* [*Milan Hodža in America: Articles, Speeches, Studies*] (Chicago, 1949), pp. 98-107.

[104] Karol Sidor, *Andrej Hlinka*, though not covering the whole span of Hlinka's career, remains the fullest biography of the Slovak leader. L. G. Fagula, *Andrej Hlinka* (Bratislava, 1943), is a panegyric without any historical value.

[105] Martin Grečo, *Martinská deklarácia* [*The Martin Declaration*] (2nd ed.; Turčiansky Svätý Martin, 1947), p. 110.

[106] Juraj Kramer, *Slovenské autonomistické hnutie v rokoch 1918-1929* [*The Slovak Autonomist Movement in 1918-1929*] (Bratislava, 1962), p. 81.

mand for Slovak autonomy. Several events contributed to his disenchantment.

From the first, Hlinka had personal and political disagreements with Šrobár. They were from the same town, Ružomberok. and had known each other from childhood. However, they had little liking for each other. They quarreled over politics before the war, and drifted farther apart afterwards. Hlinka was critical of Šrobár's reliance on the Protestants. What alienated Hlinka most, however, was the upsurge of anti-Catholic and anticlerical feeling among the Czech people after the war. The feeling was natural among the Czechs, since they held the Catholic Church largely responsible for the loss of their national independence in the seventeenth century. However, it had no parallel in Slovakia. Historically, priests and ministers had been the most important Slovak national leaders. Pious Slovak Catholics were shocked to hear about the toppling of the column of the Virgin Mary in the Old Town Square in Prague by an anti-Catholic crowd on November 4. Matters were not helped by the ostentatiously anti-Catholic behavior of some Czech soldiers, officials, and teachers in Slovakia.[107]

In January, 1919, in a speech to a Czech Catholic audience in Prague, Hlinka complained of the anti-Catholic behavior of Czech officials in Slovakia. For his speech he was taken to task in the National Assembly on January 23 by the Czech Social Democrat Bechyně. Hlinka was not present at the session. None of the members of the Slovak Club rose to defend him, the usual parliamentary practice. On the contrary, the Hlasist Andrej Devečka, a Lutheran minister, and other Hlasists joined in attacking him. However, they did not criticize him on the ground of clericalism, as Bechyně had, for the Slovaks had no quarrel with it. Instead, they impugned his loyalty to Czechoslovakia and the Slovak people ("Hlinka betrayed Slovakia"). The attack set a pattern for most subsequent Slovak political quarrels. They rarely touched on issues at hand, but usually consisted of attempts at character assassination, of impugning one's adversary's motives, and of hints of betrayal or corruption. The only deputy who rose to defend Hlinka was Msgr. Šrámek, the leader of the Czech Populist party.[108] A few days later, Hlinka defended himself in the National Assembly by recounting his prewar battles with the Hungarian government and Church hierarchy, his trials, and his imprisonment (he had spent three and a half years in Hungarian jails).[109] The episode was soon forgotten, but it marked a break between Hlinka and the Hlasists in the Slovak Club and his rapprochement with the Czech populists.

---

[107] Peroutka, *Budování státu*, II, 1227.   [108] Sidor, *Slovenská politika*, I, 60-61.
[109] Ibid., pp. 61-63.

What drew the Czech and Slovak populists together was, of course, Catholicism. They also held similar views on provincial autonomy. The bastion of the Czech populists was Moravia and that of the Slovak populists Slovakia. Provincial autonomy would concentrate their strength, while a centralized state would diffuse it. The first to raise the question of provincial autonomy in the National Assembly was Šrámek, in a speech on July 11, 1919.[110] Hlinka followed suit in August.

By then Hlinka knew of the "Czecho-Slovak Agreement" of May 30, 1918, which Masaryk had drafted in Pittsburgh, Pa., as a program for the Czech and Slovak emigrant organizations in the United States to follow. Like most wartime Czechoslovak programs, it was designed, in part, to influence Allied, especially American, opinion. It envisaged autonomy for Slovakia analogous to that enjoyed by the states of the American union. It stipulated that Slovakia should have its diet, courts, and administration, and that Slovak should be its official language. However, it left the detailed provisions for Slovak autonomy to the decision of the elected representatives of the Czech and Slovak peoples after the war.[111] When Hlinka found out about the Pittsburgh agreement,[112] he eagerly seized on it, making it the cornerstone of his policy until his death in 1938.

In June, 1919, the Allied peacemakers announced their decision on Hungary's boundaries and served an ultimatum on Béla Kun to comply with it and evacuate the part of Slovakia overrun by the Hungarian Red Army. He complied. With the fear of Hungarian occupation and Bolshevik revolution gone, Hlinka's relative moderation was also gone.

Hlinka was a natural-born leader, but was not a skillful politician. He could declaim, but could not debate. In practical politics, he always depended on the advice of others. Of peasant origin, he had the peasant's respect for book-learning and was easily influenced by intellectuals with a better formal education than his (he had been trained in parochial schools and a diocesan seminary). After the war he came under the influence of Dr. František Jehlička (1879-1938), a Catholic priest and erudite professor of theology in Budapest. An ambitious schemer, Jehlička had been elected to the Hungarian parliament in 1906 as a Slovak deputy but then forsook the Slovak cause. In 1918 he returned to the

---

[110] Ibid., pp. 65-67.

[111] Victor S. Mamatey, *The United States and East Central Europe, 1914-1918: A Study in Wilsonian Diplomacy and Propaganda* (Princeton, 1957), pp. 282-84; Konstantin Čulen, *Pittsburghská dohoda* [*The Pittsburgh Agreement*] (Bratislava, 1937), pp. 142-56; for an English translation of the Pittsburgh agreement, see Jozef Lettrich, *History of the Modern Slovakia* (New York, 1955), pp. 289-90.

[112] According to Čulen, *Pittsburghská dohoda*, p. 240, Jozef Hušek, an American Slovak newspaperman, gave Hlinka a photostatic copy of the Pittsburgh agreement in April, 1919. According to Rudinský, *Československý štát*, p. 89, it was Father František Jehlička who gave it to him in August, 1919.

Slovak fold, was forgiven, and was appointed to the National Assembly in March, 1919. He attached himself to Hlinka, whose ambition he excited with visions of becoming the first Slovak archbishop.

Since the Hlasist-dominated Slovak Club was not likely to recommend and the National Assembly to approve Slovak autonomy, Jehlička advised Hlinka to take the matter before the lofty forum of the Paris Peace Conference. On August 27, 1919, Hlinka, Jehlička, and two other companions secretly set out through Poland to Paris. There they submitted a memorandum drafted by Jehlička to the Allied delegations, demanding an international guarantee of Slovak autonomy in Czechoslovakia, similar to the one given Ruthenia in the Treaty of St. Germain. However, even before the signing of the Peace of St. Germain on September 10, the Allied powers drifted apart, and the chances of their revising the treaty to include a guarantee of Slovak autonomy were nil. Hlinka's mission to Paris was a complete failure.[113]

When the news of his action reached Prague it produced an uproar in the Slovak Club. The Hlasists were frightened beyond all reason by his attempt to expose them and overreacted. By September the peace conference was quite impotent. But they did not know that. Šrobár returned to Prague from Slovakia to direct the counterattack. The Slovak Club voted and sent to Paris a disavowal of Hlinka's action, proposed to deprive him and Jehlička of their mandates and parliamentary immunity, and demanded their trial for treason.[114]

When Hlinka's companions heard of the uproar in Prague they scattered like a flock of sparrows at the throw of a rock. Some went to America. Jehlička fled to Budapest, where he became a paid agent of Hungarian revisionist propaganda for the rest of his life. Hlinka, however, whatever his faults, was no coward. He returned home at once, breathing defiance and courting martyrdom.[115] Tusar had misgivings about punishing him. After all, the government did not propose to prosecute the Sudeten German leaders, who returned from Vienna about the same time,

---

[113] Sidor, *Hlinka*, 372-75; Kramer, *Slovenské autonomistické hnutie*, pp. 71-78; Rudinský, *Československý stát*, pp. 71-82. Rudinský accompanied Hlinka on his trip to Paris. The account of Hlinka's Paris mission in Stephen Bonsal, *Suitors and Suppliants: Little Nations at Versailles* (New York, 1946), pp. 157-66, partakes of the nature of fiction; it is full of factual errors and completely unreliable. For the text of Hlinka's memorandum to the Paris Peace Conference, see Joseph A. Mikus, *Slovakia: A Political History, 1918-1950* (Milwaukee, 1963), pp. 331-40.

[114] Sidor, *Slovenská politika*, I, 75-81; Kramer, *Slovenské autonomistické hnutie*, pp. 78-79.

[115] Kramer, *Slovenské autonomistické hnutie*, pp. 80-82; Sidor, *Hlinka*, pp. 380-82; Peroutka, *Budování státu*, II, 1251.

after embarrassing Prague for a year by innundating the peace conference with memoranda denouncing Czechoslovakia. On October 8, without giving Hlinka a hearing, the Slovak Club revoked his and Jehlička's mandates. Three days later, Hlinka was arrested and interned in Moravia.[116]

Once it arrested Hlinka, the government did not know what to do with him. The charge of treason was absurd. He had not demanded Slovak *independence* but only *autonomy*, that is, he did not aim at the integrity of the Czechoslovak state but only sought a particular form of its internal organization. The Czechoslovak constitution had not been drafted yet. It was, therefore, perfectly legitimate to propose Slovak autonomy, or, for that matter, any other form of government, although it was extremely indiscreet to do so in a foreign forum. In this instance, it was also naive and futile. Tusar conceded to a Slovak populist delegation that Hlinka had not violated any law, only passport regulations. Eventually, the government recognized that his arrest had been a blunder. After the adoption of the constitution in February, 1920, it ordered his release without trial.[117] However, in order to keep him from participating in the parliamentary electoral campaign that followed, he was temporarily kept in Prague. Nevertheless, he was resoundingly elected to the National Assembly and returned triumphantly to Slovakia in May.

The Hlinka affair caused the government to lose prestige in Slovakia. To the martyr's halo for suffering imprisonment under the Hungarian government, he now added one for suffering imprisonment under the Czechoslovak government. The Slovaks tended to be politically passive, because under the Hungarian rule any political action on their part could partake only of the nature of a *beau geste*; it seldom brought positive results and usually provoked harsh Hungarian retribution. However, for that very reason, the Slovaks greatly admired the rare man who had the courage to act according to his conviction, with the knowledge that he would accomplish nothing thereby except incur punishment. Hlinka had lived up to their image of a hero. Henceforth, his position in Slovakia was unassailable. Even his critics treated him with respect. When this became apparent from the electoral results, Šrobár's colleagues blamed him for mishandling the Hlinka affair. It contributed to Šrobár's downfall. On the other hand, the affair alienated Hlinka from his old companions in the National Assembly, who—he felt—had not defended him and his program (in the constitution) resolutely enough. Presently, he came under the influence of another dubious intellectual, Prof. Béla (Vojtech) Tuka.

[116] Kramer, *Slovenské autonomistické hnutie*, pp. 83-84; Sidor, *Hlinka*, p. 384.
[117] Peroutka, *Budování státu*, II, 1254-57.

Tomáš G. Masaryk and the Idea of
Humanitarian Democracy

In its philosopher-president, Tomáš G. Masaryk, the Czechoslovak Republic found a man remarkably well suited to deal with new responsibilities arising from national independence. His prestige and authority among his compatriots were immense. Realizing the importance of his authority in a nation whose independence lacked strong traditions and which tended to think of freedom more in terms of rights than responsibilities, Masaryk conceived of his presidential duties in a very broad manner. Resolutely rejecting the suggestion of some political leaders that he stay above politics, he took a vigorous part in shaping his country's destiny from the outset.[118]

The political and diplomatic struggle for national liberation brought about important changes in Masaryk's outlook. Before the war, he played an outstanding role as a philosopher and sociologist in the public life of his people and whole of Austria. His influence stemmed from his critical and analytical mind, which he applied uncompromisingly. He became involved—in most cases involuntarily—in practically all important issues of Czech political and cultural life. His views more often than not brought him into conflict with the official representatives of the nation and the beliefs of the people. It was this quality of mind, as well as the systematic endeavor to introduce into Czech politics criteria of morality and individual responsibility, that helped him to draw the Czech people closer to the West.

Yet, as he himself later admitted, many of his prewar views, being based on abstract theory and lofty moralizing, made little allowance for the weaknesses and complexities of human nature. His voice was always listened to, but his didactic manner, his impatience with human ignorance, and his beliefs caused him to be regarded only as the "influential outsider of Czech political life."

During and after the war Masaryk was faced with the most difficult test of his life: he had to reconcile the abstract nature of his Western-oriented philosophy of humanism with the mundane requirements of political life, the seamy side of which he almost instinctively tried to avoid. He passed this test with flying colors, revealing another aspect of his versatile personality. He proved to be a philosopher who was able to act and rule. Only thus was it possible that a man who regarded revolutionary methods with utmost suspicion himself became a leader of a national liberation movement. He subordinated his original antimilitarism, which bordered on pacifism, to his firm belief in the necessity of defense against

[118] Čapek, *Hovory*, p. 291.

evil and violence. As president, Masaryk paid special attention to building up the Czechoslovak army, a difficult task because, before an army could be created, he had to overcome the antimilitaristic tradition deeply embedded in the Czech and Slovak outlook. The president realized that, despite his lifelong insistence on the persuasive strength of peaceful arguments, he could not overlook the fact that this was not the way to recover national independence. It was no accident that the only time that he presided over the meeting of the council of ministers was when he wanted to push through his proposal to invite a French military mission to organize the Czechoslovak army.[119]

Masaryk did not hesitate to deal with the petty struggles among parties and leaders, nor did he avoid using his personal prestige in the solution of personal differences.[120] Above all, he realized the importance of compromise—the salt and catalyst of democracy—and at the same time he remained faithful to his humanistic principles. He was in constant touch with the government and party leaders, and in the first years of Czechoslovakia he exerted a direct influence, literally living through all the problems and crises of the new state. In the appointments of cabinets, he insisted on filling certain sensitive posts with experts rather than politicians, the ministry of foreign affairs with Beneš, for instance, or the ministry of finance with Karel Engliš, a distinguished economist.

Masaryk did not support nationalism; he believed in the supreme value of the human being as the sole criterion of political activities. Basically socialistic in his economic and social philosophy, Masaryk responded to acute social problems with deeply felt concern. An ardent champion of broadening the rights of individuals as an effective way of solving social problems, he contributed much to shaping the humanistic traditions that became a distinctive feature of Czechoslovak democracy.

At the beginning of his presidency, Masaryk's position appeared unassailable. Later, however, when the initial enthusiasm over independence wore off, he encountered opposition to his person, his policies, and his entire concept of humanitarian democracy. As early as 1920, some of the prewar feuds revived, such as Masaryk's old feud with Kramář, and new conflicts arose, such as the quarrel between Kramář and Beneš over the orientation of Czechoslovak foreign policy or the rather sterile debate over the respective merits and contributions to Czechoslovak independence of the home resistance led by Kramář and the independence movement abroad led by Masaryk.[121] Thus, fairly early in the existence of Czechoslovakia, a generally weak, but vocal, countercurrent gradually

[119] Peroutka, *Budování státu*, II, 1069.   [120] Ibid., 1069-70.

[121] Jan Herben, *T. G. Masaryk: Život a dílo Presidenta Osvoboditele* [*T. G. Masaryk: Life and Accomplishment of the President-Liberator*] (5th ed.; Prague, 1946), p. 383.

developed that attacked Masaryk, Beneš, and their associates—or, as they were generically referred to, the Hrad (Castle), after Masaryk's residence—alleging that they pursued unpatriotic, cosmopolitan, or even pro-German policies.[122]

The Hrad group was not a distinctive political faction or a secret society, as some of its opponents alleged. It developed from the cooperation of those who were followers of Masaryk's policies. Hence one could find adherents of the Hrad practically in all parties, including the National Democrats. That such a group came into existence was another indication of Masaryk's active participation in the political life of the country. As time passed, however, the opponents of the Hrad changed both in their composition and aims. At first, the anti-Hrad campaign to some extent represented an attempt on the part of some of Masaryk's prewar foes to settle accounts with their old adversary. Later it became the rallying point of different right-wing groups and other disgruntled elements.

Less visible and articulate, but at the same time less expected, was the opposition which Masaryk at times encountered even within those political parties which came to be regarded as the mainstay of democracy. Indeed, there was a fundamental incompatibility between Masaryk and some professional politicians, who resented his criticism of their practices and inability to resist the temptations of power. In relations with the members of this group, Masaryk maintained a reserve bordering on iciness, cool imperviousness, and professional aloofness.

Masaryk's ultimate strength was his hold over the people. Traveling extensively through the country, especially at the outset of his tenure, he established direct contacts with the people. Curiously, he was no orator in the usual sense of the word: his style was terse and at times seemed almost inadequate to express the wealth of his ideas. Yet his unemotional and reassuring manner of speech, his candor, and his profound humanity found their way to the hearts of his audiences. When he died in September, 1937, he became in the minds of the Czechs and Slovaks a symbol of their national existence.[123]

THE LAND REFORM

The priority accorded to the land reform reflected a democratic trend accentuated by the sheer pressure of postwar social and national circum-

---

[122] The name of the group was derived from the Hradčany Castle in Prague, the official residence of the president of the republic.

[123] There is no adequate biography of President Masaryk. For information, see studies by Herben; Čapek; Peroutka; Emil Ludwig, *Defender of Democracy: Masaryk of Czechoslovakia* (London, 1936); Paul Selver, *Masaryk: A Biography* (London, 1940); Edward P. Newman, *Masaryk* (London, 1960); and Milan Machovec, *Tomáš G. Masaryk* (Prague, 1968).

stances. The initial program was subject to modifications, some of which coincided with changes in the balance of power between the various parties in the Kramář cabinet. The pressures caused by a long war, rising expectations of the rural population, urgent demands of landless rural workers, an all-pervading black market, a dramatic rise in the cost of living, the need to convert the existing great estates of the nobility and the Church into national property—all contributed to make the reform ever more urgent. The land reform itself consisted of a large number of acts and ordinances which provided for a minutely detailed plan of land redistribution.[124] Its actual realization continued to be a subject of a serious conflict between the socialists and the agrarians. The latter insisted that the land, which was to be bought and confiscated, should be transferred to the direct ownership of small and medium farmers. The socialist parties proposed that the estates be taken over without compensation and then changed either into state or cooperative farms. The hunger for soil was such that the agrarian point of view, which promised a speedy distribution of the land, prevailed.[125]

The Land Control Act of April 16, 1919, empowered the government to expropriate all large estates exceeding 150 hectares (370 acres) of arable land or 250 hectares (618 acres) of land in general.[126] In special cases (where the land served agricultural industry) the original owner was allowed to retain as much as 500 hectares (1,235 acres). The law accepted the principle of compensation which in 1920 was fixed at the prewar price level of the estates.[127] The execution of the reform was entrusted to the Land Office. One of the main characteristics of the reform was its graduality, which foresaw changes in agricultural ownership taking place within a protracted period of time. While theoretically all estates above a certain acreage were subjected to expropriation, before this right was exercised by the government the owner remained in possession of the estate and retained its profits.

Viewed in retrospect, the reform could be hailed as an act of great political wisdom, which "brought our state nearer to the West."[128] When it was adopted by the provisional National Assembly it was billed as an

[124] By 1928 the number of acts, ordinances, and government regulations reached the figure of 117. See *Deset let Republiky Československé* [*Ten Years of the Czechoslovak Republic*] (3 vols.; Prague, 1928), III, 419-23.

[125] Otáhal, *Zápas o pozemkovou reformu*, p. 160.

[126] Elisabeth Textor, *Land Reform in Czechoslovakia* (London, 1923), p. 29.

[127] Compensation was based on the average price during the years 1913-1915. In most cases only a small amount was paid in cash, the rest was provided in bonds. The issue of compensation, which amounted approximately to 25 percent of the actual postwar price, was a subject of heated debate in the country. See Textor, *Land Reform*, pp. 92-109.

[128] Peroutka, *Budování státu*, II, 889.

exceptional measure that would remedy ancient social and economic wrongs. It suffered, however, from a number of shortcomings.

While the land reform did away with the huge aristocratic estates, the major part of the allotments was too small and economically inexpedient. The following table illustrates the fact that the reform did not eliminate the problem of dwarf holdings:

TABLE NO. 3*

Individual categories by size in hectares	The number of recipients	
	before allotment	after allotment
Landless persons	65,169	—
0—1	139,269	112,258
1—2	59,612	89,729
2—5	65,934	114,309
5—10	14,430	27,609
10–20	9,851	12,694
20–50	50	354
20–100	21	604
over 100	7	350

* Quoted from Otáhal, *Zápas o pozemkovou reformu*, p. 200.

It may well be that the number of dwarf holdings up to one hectare had diminished, but the equally unsatisfactory holdings of up to five hectares still represented the majority of farms. In the Czech provinces, where holders of small lots in many cases found employment in industry, the disequilibrium presented no special hardships. In Slovakia and Ruthenia, however, where there was no or very little opportunity to supplement farming with industrial employment, the economic situation of this lower group of landowners continued to be highly unsatisfactory. Another alleged shortcoming of the reform was its slow tempo, so that it was not terminated by the time of the 1938 destruction of Czechoslovakia. What was even more criticized was the fact that 56 percent of all land and 34 percent of agricultural soil was returned to its original owners.[129] The complaint of the members of the German[130] and Hungarian minorities that an unconcealed purpose of the land reform in ethnically mixed areas was to strengthen the material position of the Czechs and Slovaks was likewise not altogether without foundation.

Last but not least, the land reform allowed the creation of perhaps too

[129] Faltus, *Stručný hospodářský vývoj*, p. 166; and Olšovský, *Přehled hospodářského vývoje*, p. 194.

[130] For the German opposition to the land reform, see Textor, *Land Reform*, pp. 116-34; Otáhal, *Zápas o pozemkovou reformu*, pp. 142-44; and J. W. Brügel's chapter below.

many so-called "residual estates" (*zbytkové velkostatky*). These were relatively large farms left after the partition of the great estates, which could have been subdivided but were not—allegedly for economic reasons. The disposition of the residual estates was in the hands of the Land Office and through it of the Agrarian party, which used their sale to promote its political interests.

Still, all in all, the post-World War I Czechoslovak land reform was—for its period—a progressive and enlightened measure, which benefited a very large number of persons and harmed the interests of only very few.

THE CONSTITUTION OF 1920

The most important action of the provisional National Assembly based on the "law of revolution" was the adoption of the definitive constitution of 1920. It expressed the political will of the Czechs and Slovaks alone. What the constitution would have been if it had been adopted by a constituent assembly representative of all national elements in the country is difficult to say. One might argue that the Czechoslovak majority would have been forced to make a number of concessions to the individual nationalities by adopting a less centralistic basic law. However, the chasm between the Czechs and the Germans was such that there existed "no bridge associating the constitutional draft with those autonomist plans which fired every German politician and every German newspaper."[131] Adoption of the constitution, the last act of the revolutionary period, offered the Czechoslovak political parties the last opportunity to confirm their unity and to demonstrate their determination to build a strong state.

The main virtue of the constitutional charter was its moderation, largely achieved through the balancing of political forces which secured support of representatives both of the right and the left.[132] The text of the constitution gave rise to few fundamental conflicts. Its main features were agreed upon in the first days of national independence and applied in the framing of the provisional constitution and its amendments. Its single most important model was the constitution of the French Third Republic, but its authors took full account of the main democratic constitutions of the world.[133] They were too sophisticated, however, to believe

[131] Peroutka, *Budování státu*, II, 1307. [132] Ibid., III, 1443.

[133] The opening words of the Constitution "We, the Czechoslovak nation . . ." were suggestive of the preamble of the United States constitution. However, in the text, there was no direct evidence of American influence. The preamble was suggested by Masaryk's closest co-worker, Jan Herben. See Peroutka, *Budování státu*, III, 1448.

that Czechoslovak constitutionalism could be based on mere transplantation of ideas and forms developed under different political circumstance and in different cultures. Thus the final product was greatly influenced by the past political experiences of the Czechs, especially the experience of the Czech politicians in the Vienna Reichsrat.

While most Czech and Slovak political leaders were agreed that Czechoslovakia should be a democratic parliamentary republic, they were divided in opinion, by party interest and ideology, on just how this was to be achieved.

Historically, the conservative parties in the Habsburg empire favored a restricted suffrage and identified themselves with provincial autonomy, which derived from the empire's feudal past. On the other hand, the liberal and progressive parties favored a broad suffrage and centralism, which derived from the rationalist traditions of the French Revolution. With certain modifications, the political parties in the Czechoslovak provisional National Assembly reflected the same tendency. All Czech parties rallied to the principle of universal, direct, and secret suffrage, with proportional representation, although with greater fervor on the left than on the right.

On the Slovak side of the National Assembly there was less agreement about suffrage. The agrarian faction of the Slovak Club was strenuously opposed to universal suffrage, because its Hlasist leaders had no confidence that the Slovak people would follow them. The populists were more confident of their ability to influence the people, through the network of Catholic priests, and insisted particularly on giving women the right to vote. The socialist favored universal suffrage, both because of party principle and because the rising popular discontent over economic difficulties in Slovakia favored them at the time. In the end, it was thanks to an unlikely alliance between the populists and socialists that the Slovak Club voted for universal suffrage.[134]

The question of provincial autonomy naturally excited more interest among the Slovaks than the Czechs. The Slovak agrarians recognized that provincial autonomy was desirable in one form or another, but felt that the Slovak people were not ready for it. Consequently, the agrarians wished to postpone the question to the indefinite future.[135] The Slovak populists wished to secure both administrative and legislative autonomy for Slovakia, but recognized that the time was not ripe for it yet. They were willing to postpone the question—provided firm guarantees of Slovak autonomy in the future were inserted in the constitution.[136] The

---

[134] Lipscher, "Klub," pp. 158-60.
[135] See Slovak agrarian electoral program in 1920 in Kocman, *Boj o směr*, II, 129-30.
[136] See the Slovak populist reservation concerning the constitution, below.

Slovak socialists were opposed to autonomy in any form and at any time.[137]

The lack of confidence of so many of the Slovak leaders in the patriotism of the Slovak masses and their assumption that if Slovakia were given autonomy it would inevitably slide back into the arms of Hungary, were probably not warranted. The common Slovak people were not given to nationalist flag-waving, because in Royal Hungary, the ethos of which was aristocratic, the working folk (*misera plebs contribuens*), whether Slovak, Magyar, or other, were discouraged from expressing political sentiment, even one favorable to Hungary. To borrow Tennyson's phrase, it was not for them to reason why, it was for them to do and die. However, this did not mean that the Slovak masses had no nationalistic feeling, although it was dormant in eastern Slovakia. Moreover, whether in western or eastern Slovakia, they had a keen social consciousness. Under the Hungarian government they had been not only nationally oppressed but also socially exploited. They shed no tears when the Hungarian regime collapsed in 1918, therefore, whatever they thought of the new Czechoslovak government. It is conceivable that if Soviet Hungary had lasted it might have developed an attraction for them. However, with its downfall and the rise of Horthy's counterrevolutionary regime, any prospect that the Hungarians might win back the allegiance of the Slovak people was definitely buried. Despite its persistence and stridency, Hungarian revisionist propaganda never succeeded in eliciting any response from the broad strata of the Slovak people. Only a handful of intellectuals responded to it. On close examination, most of them were found to be men who had been disappointed in their personal ambitions in Czechoslovakia.[138]

Any prospect that provincial autonomy might be provided for in the constitution was buried in the furor aroused in the National Assembly over Hlinka's secret trip to Paris. It stiffened the Slovak centralists' opposition to autonomy, and aroused the suspicions of the Czech party leaders that the Slovaks could not be trusted with autonomy. In a message to the American Slovaks on February 6, 1920, the Slovak Club thanked them for their efforts in behalf of Slovak freedom during the war, but declined to accept the Pittsburgh agreement on the ground that Slovak rights would be amply protected in the Czechoslovak constitution, the adoption of which was then pending.[139] President Masaryk

---

[137] Lipscher, *K vývinu*, pp. 93-94.

[138] For a thorough discussion of Hungarian revisionism and its Slovak agents, Jehlička, Tuka, and others, see Juraj Kramer, *Iredenta a separatizmus v slovenskej politike* [*Irredentism and Separatism in Slovak Politics*] (Bratislava, 1957), *passim*. This study is based on research in Hungarian archives.

[139] Čulen, *Pittsburghská dohoda*, pp. 291-94. The declaration bore the signa-

likewise felt that in the circumstances Slovak autonomy would be inopportune, and declined to press for the adoption of the Pittsburgh agreement.[140]

Slovakia (and Ruthenia) had inherited from Hungary the system of counties (*župy*), which had extensive self-government. The Czech provinces did not have it. Švehla, who more than any other member of the provisional National Assembly could claim to be the father of the Czechoslovak constitution, perceived in this institution the means to reconcile the divergent party views on the political and administrative organization of Czechoslovakia. He offered a compromise, the object of which was— according to Peroutka—"to dissolve Slovakia like a lump of sugar in a glass of water."[141] He proposed to abolish the historic provinces and to extend the Slovak (Hungarian) system of counties throughout the country. To mollify the supporters of the provinces, it was further agreed that the counties could form provincial unions, that is, when province-wide interests were at issue the county assemblies could meet in joint sessions, thus forming sort of *ad hoc* provincial assemblies.[142]

On February 24, 1920, the National Assembly's constitutional committee submitted to it the draft constitution and bills of five constitutional laws. On February 27, when the National Assembly began to debate the draft constitution and constitutional laws, a preamble to the constitution expressing the principles and ideals that animated its makers was adopted.[143] The preamble identified the "Czechoslovak nation" as the creator and principal carrier of the Czechoslovak state, thus making it clear that the constitution-makers conceived of Czechoslovakia as a national state.

The constitution, which was divided into six parts, defined Czechoslovakia simply as a "democratic republic at whose head there stands an elected president" (part one). It entrusted the legislative powers to the National Assembly consisting of a 300-member chamber of deputies and 150-member senate, to be elected both on the basis of universal suffrage and by a direct and secret ballot (part two); the executive powers to the president and the cabinet of ministers, whose respective competence it carefully defined (part three); and judicial powers to an independent judiciary (part four). Following Western models, the constitution provided for the protection of fundamental civil and political rights of all

---

tures of all members of the Slovak Club. However, when the Slovak populist deputies learned of it from the American Slovak press (it was not published in Czechoslovakia) they denied having signed it and denounced it as a forgery.

[140] Masaryk, *Cesta demokracie*, I, 249-50.

[141] Peroutka, *Budování státu*, III, 1588.

[142] Ibid., 1588-89.

[143] Ibid., 1448.

citizens on a completely equal basis (part five) and for special protection of the rights of national and religious minorities (part six).[144]

Compared with the provisional constitution, the definite constitution marked a retreat from the radical tendencies which prevailed in the first months of Czechoslovakia's existence. By specifying the powers of the National Assembly in detail and by defining the competence of the executive and judicial branches carefully, the definite constitution provided for a better balanced system of government. Still, on the whole, it favored the legislative branch. Thus, the National Assembly reserved to itself the right to elect the head of the state every seven years. On paper, the presidential powers seemed impressive; in reality, they hardly changed from what they had been under the provisional constitution, as amended in May, 1919. Their clearcut enumeration pointed to the intention of the authors of the constitution to create a weak head of state.[145] Of the two bearers of executive powers, the president and the cabinet, the latter was by far more important.

Among the constitutional laws, the Language Law designated "Czechoslovak" as the country's official language. Since in reality no single Czechoslovak language existed, this meant that Czech and Slovak were to enjoy the status of official languages. The law, however, assured the national minorities full freedom in the use of their languages in everyday life and in schools, as well as in dealing with authorities in districts in which they constituted at least 20 percent of the population.[146] The constitutional Law of Counties and Districts provided for Czechoslovakia's political and administrative organization on the basis of Švehla's compromise, except that it did not include any provision for the provincial unions.[147]

By identifying the Slovaks with the Czechs under the label "Czechoslovaks," the constitution allotted the Slovaks the status of Czechoslovakia's "state people" (*Staatsvolk*) rather than that of a national minority. Nevertheless, the Slovak populists were deeply disappointed with the constitution, because it provided for a unitary Czechoslovak state and ignored Slovakia's identity. It was only after considerable pressure on the part of the agrarian and socialist wings of the Slovak Club

[144] Masarykova akademie práce, *Československá vlastivěda* [*A Study of Czechoslovakia*] (10 vols. in 12; Prague, 1929-1936), v, 121.

[145] That the problems were considered by the authors of the constitution is apparent from the following statement of Prof. Jiří Hoetzl: "If the constitution could have been made to apply solely to the first president, the National Assembly would have been more generous in defining the powers it gave him. However, a constitution has to be framed on a permanent basis and must be applicable to average presidents. We endeavored to remove from it everything reminiscent of the monarchy." *Slovník národohospodářský, sociální a politicky* [*Economic, Social, and Political Encyclopedia*], p. 432.

[146] *Československá vlastivěda*, v, 163-68.   [147] Ibid., 146-48.

that the Slovak populists agreed to vote for the constitution, and then only after registering a reservation that their vote should "in no way prejudice their demand for Slovakia's autonomy with a legislative diet" in the future.[148] In accepting the Law of Counties and Districts for the Slovak Club as a whole, Ivan Markovič described it as an expedient made necessary "for the moment" (*nateraz*) by the lack of political education on the part of the Slovak people.[149] On the other hand, the agrarian and socialist factions of the Slovak Club rallied to the support of the populists, both Slovak and Czech, who strenuously opposed the inclusion in the constitution of a provision for the separation of state and church. Masaryk had put it in the Washington declaration in October, 1918, and then, as president, pressed for its adoption in the constitution. The supporters of the measure had the necessary votes to secure its passage in the National Assembly. However, out of deference to the unanimity of the Slovak opposition to it, they dropped the proposal.[150] On February 29, 1920, the constitution was unanimously approved by the National Assembly.

Subsequent power-political realities in Czechoslovakia differed in several important respects from the ideals set forth in the constitution. Thanks to the strength of their personalities and the prestige they enjoyed as the country's liberators, Masaryk and Beneš managed to build up the presidency, despite the meager grant of constitutional powers, so that it checked, *de facto* if not *de jure*, the parliament and the cabinet. The president rather than the parliament came to be the representative and symbol of the sovereignty and independence of the Czechoslovak state.

Another fundamental difference between constitutional ideal and practice was created by the political parties. Although the constitution mentioned them only indirectly, the political parties arrogated to themselves *de facto* powers that transcended those of the National Assembly and the cabinet. Before any important political measure could be taken by the cabinet or enacted by the National Assembly, it had to be agreed upon by the coalition committee consisting of representatives of the coalition parties. Another shortcoming of constitutional practice was the atrophy of the principle of judicial review. Although the constitution provided for the creation of a constitutional court that was supposed to decide on the validity of laws, it was never given an opportunity to function. So this part of the constitution was obsolete from the beginning.

---

[148] Sidor, *Slovenská politika*, I, 100-101; Lipscher, "Klub," p. 158; Peroutka, *Budování státu*, III, 1590.

[149] Peroutka, *Budování státu*, III, 1590-91; Lipscher, *K vývinu*, pp. 94-95; Sidor, *Slovenská politika*, I, 105-107.

[150] Peroutka, *Budování státu*, III, 1468-70.

Finally, a discrepancy between the constitutional ideal and practice developed when the electoral court provided for by the constitution extended its powers beyond the original intent of the constitution-makers. The purpose of the electoral court was to verify results of elections. However, because of the composition of its membership, in which lay assessors elected by the Chamber of Deputies predominated, it acquired the characteristics of a political court. In practice, it became an instrument for the enforcement of party discipline. It could deprive a member of the National Assembly of his seat "if for base and dishonest reasons he ceased to be a member of the party on whose list he was elected."[151] It was the broad interpretation of this provision that changed the court into a political tribunal. Despite these and other deficiencies, however, the Czechoslovak constitutional-democratic system functioned well until the end of the First Republic—which, it should not be forgotten, did not break up *from within* as a result of constitutional or other internal deficiencies, but was broken up *from without* by foreign intervention.

The drafting and adoption of the permanent constitution completed the task of the provisional National Assembly. It was dissolved on April 15, 1920, and elections to the regular National Assembly were held a few days later. Czechoslovakia's "revolutionary" (i.e., formative) period had come to an end.

[151] *Československá vlastivěda*, v, 128.

· 3 ·

THE DEVELOPMENT OF CZECHOSLOVAK DEMOCRACY
1920–1938

Victor S. Mamatey
University of Georgia

CONSTITUTIONAL GOVERNMENT

The first parliamentary elections held under the permanent constitution in April, 1920, marked the beginning of regular constitutional government in Czechoslovakia.[1] Altogether twenty-three parties, including—for the first time—the parties of the national minorities, entered the electoral contest. The former Slovak Club in the provisional National Assembly was dissolved, and its factions—agrarian, populist, and Social Democratic—entered into electoral compacts or merged with their Czech counterparts. Suffrage under the Constitution of 1920 was universal and the voting direct and secret, which for the Slovaks, at least, was an entirely new experience. The results of the elections were therefore awaited with considerable curiosity. They confirmed the swing to the left already indicated in the local elections in the Czech provinces in June, 1919.[2]

The Czechoslovak Social Democratic party scored 25.7 percent of the vote and received 74 seats in the Chamber of Deputies, becoming by far the largest party in the National Assembly. The German Social Democrats were likewise successful, gaining 31 seats in the lower house. The Czech (National) Socialists gained 24, the Progressive Socialists 3, and the Hungarian Social Democrats 4 seats. Altogether, the socialist parties won 136 out of the 281 seats contested.

---

[1] The election into the Chamber of Deputies was held on April 18 and the election into the Senate on April 25. No election was held in Ruthenia, which was not yet fully under Czechoslovak control; in the Polish-Czechoslovak plebiscite areas in Těšín, Spiš, and Orava; or in three small enclaves ceded to Czechoslovakia by Germany and Austria. Therefore, only 281 seats out of 300 in the Chamber of Deputies and 142 seats out of 150 in the Senate were contested. See Československá akademie věd, *Přehled československých dějin* [*Survey of Czechoslovak History*] (3 vols. in 4; Prague, 1958-60), III, 104 (hereafter *Přehled*).

[2] For the results of the elections, see ibid., 104-105; Předsednictvo poslanecké sněmovny a předsednictvo senátu, *Národní shromáždění republiky československé v prvém desítiletí* [*The National Assembly of the Czechoslovak Republic in the First Decade*] (Prague, 1928), pp. 188-89 (hereafter *Národní shromáždění, 1918-1928*); Masarykova akademie práce, *Československá vlastivěda* [*A Study of Czechoslovakia*] (10 vols. in 12; Prague, 1929-36), V, 548-60 (hereafter *Československá vlastivěda*); Miroslav Buchválek et al. (eds.), *Dějiny Československa v datech* [*History of Czechoslovakia in Dates*] (Prague, 1968), pp. 466-68.

On the other hand, the parties of the center or the right either lost ground or, at best, held their own. The Czech agrarians fell from the eminence of being the largest party in the provisional National Assembly (55 seats) to third place in the new one (28 seats). Their loss was partially concealed thanks to their electoral compact with the Slovak agrarians. Together, the Czech and Slovak agrarians held 40 seats in the Chamber of Deputies. The National Democrats were likewise greatly reduced (19 seats), while the Czech populists just about held their own (21 seats). The German nonsocialist parties gained together 41 seats.

In Slovakia the swing to the left was even more pronounced than in the Czech provinces.[3] The Social Democratic faction of the Slovak Club in the provisional National Assembly had only nine members. Now, the Social Democrats garnered about 38 percent of the vote and received 23 seats in the Chamber of Deputies, emerging as the largest party in Slovakia. The agrarians, who received about 18 percent of the vote in Slovakia and 12 seats, suffered a severe setback. The Slovak populists improved their position, but not as much as they had hoped—17.8 percent of the vote and 12 seats. The (National) Socialists received 2.2 percent of the vote, principally from Czechs living in Slovakia, and were awarded one seat in the Chamber of Deputies. The Hungarian Christian Socials and agrarians received 12.3 percent of the vote in Slovakia and six seats in the Chamber of Deputies.

Following the elections, the Czech and Slovak agrarians perpetuated their electoral agreement by forming a common parliamentary club, but remained separate parties. The Czech and Slovak populists followed the same course. The German nonsocialist parties likewise formed a common parliamentary club to coordinate their policies. On May 25, 1920, Prime Minister Vlastimil Tusar recast his cabinet to comport with the results of the elections. He did not alter its base, the "Red-Green" (socialist-agrarian) coalition, but the Social Democrats claimed one-third of the posts in it.[4] On President Masaryk's insistence and much to the displeasure of party leaders, two sensitive posts were entrusted to nonparty experts. Edvard Beneš, who did not yet belong to any party, continued as foreign minister, and Prof. Karel Engliš, a famous economist, was appointed minister of finance.[5] The Slovak agrarian leader Milan Hodža

---

[3] For the results of the parliamentary elections in Slovakia, see C. A. Macartney, *Hungary and her Successors: The Treaty of Trianon and its Consequences, 1919-1937* (London, 1937), p. 118.

[4] Ferdinand Peroutka, *Budování státu: Československá politika v letech popřevratových* [*The Building of the State: Czechoslovak Politics in the Postwar Years*] (5 vols. in 6; Prague, 1936), III, 1746-50; *Přehled*, III, 106; *Národní shromáždění 1918-1928*, pp. 207-208; Buchválek, *Dějiny*, p. 445.

[5] Though a member of the National Democratic party, Engliš was not a professional politician. He entered the cabinet as an expert, not a respresentative of a

was dropped from the cabinet. His fellow agrarian Vavro Šrobár was shifted from the post of minister for the administration of Slovakia, in which he had incurred much unpopularity, to the less exposed post of minister of unification. His place as minister for the administration of Slovakia was taken by the Slovak Social Democrat Ivan Dérer.

The opening session of the new National Assembly on May 27, in which for the first time there appeared representatives of the national minorities, was devoted to the reelection of President Masaryk.[6] The German nonsocialist parties put up the only other candidate for the presidency, Prof. August Naegel. They staged a demonstration of their hostility to Masaryk personally and to Czechoslovakia generally that was reminiscent of the rowdy scenes in the old Austrian Reichsrat in Vienna. Although the German Social Democrats did not take part in the demonstration, they too registered their protest against Czechoslovakia, which had been organized—they said—without the consent of the national minorities and thus violated the principle of national self-determination. Spokesmen of the Hungarian parties registered an analogous protest.[7]

Although Masaryk was easily reelected, the protests of the national minorities augured ill for their cooperation with the Czechs and Slovaks in the National Assembly. For the moment, however, the greatest difficulty for the Tusar government was not occasioned by the opposition of the national minorities but by that of the radical Marxist Left in his own (Social Democratic) party.

THE SOCIAL DEMOCRATIC SCHISM

The great socialist victory in the elections of 1920 did not heal the growing rift between the right and left wings of the Czechoslovak Social Democratic party and the Social Democratic parties of the national minorities. On the contrary, it tended to widen it.[8] The Marxist Left insisted that the

---

party. See Jan Kolařík, *Peníze a politika: Karel Engliš—bojovník o stabilisaci* [*Money and Politics: Karel Engliš—Fighter for Stabilization*] (Prague, 1937), pp. 205-206.

[6] Masaryk was reelected by 284 votes out of a possible 423; Prof. Naegel received 61 votes; 6 votes went to two Radical Socialists, who were not formally candidates. See *Národní shromáždění, 1918-1928*, p. 193; *Přehled*, III, 106; Buchválek, *Dějiny*, p. 301; Peroutka, *Budování státu*, III, 1732-34; Jan Herben, *T. G. Masaryk: Život a dílo presidenta osvoboditele* [*T. G. Masaryk: Life and Work of the President-Liberator*] (5th ed.; Prague, 1946), p. 364.

[7] *Národní shromáždění, 1918-1928*, pp. 217-25; J. W. Brügel, *Tschechen und Deutsche, 1918-1938* (Munich, 1967), pp. 150-51; Jaroslav César and Bohumil Černý, *Politika německých buržoazních stran v Československu v letech 1918-1938* [*The Politics of the German Bourgeois Parties in Czechoslovakia in 1918-1938*] (2 vols.; Prague, 1962), I, 214-16.

[8] For a discussion of the growing rift between the right and the left wings of the Social Democratic party, see herein, Chapter II.

101

Czechoslovak government should be based on the class principle rather than on the ethnic, that is, that it should be based on a coalition of the Czechoslovak socialist parties and the socialist parties of the national minorities instead of on a coalition of the Czechoslovak socialist and "bourgeois" parties. The radical left-wingers hoped that in this way Czechoslovakia would become a socialist state. However, the moderate right-wing leaders of the Czechoslovak Social Democratic party feared that an attempt to form an alliance with the "proletariat" of the national minorities would not lead to Czechoslovakia's socialization but to its dissolution. The hostility shown Czechoslovakia even by the socialist representatives of the national minorities in the National Assembly gave substance to these fears.

In the summer of 1920 the working class of all nationalities in Czechoslovakia was swept by a great wave of restlessness. Strikes and riots were widespread and demands for reform or revolution were commonly voiced. The phenomenon was not unique to Czechoslovakia but was widespread in Europe. Undoubtedly, it represented an outpouring of the social discontent of the working class that had built up during the war and the immediate postwar period, but had been stifled by the emergency measures then in force in most European countries. A catharsis of this pent-up feeling may have been precipitated by the triumphant advance of the Red Army toward Warsaw in July, 1920, during the Polish-Soviet War, and the militant propaganda emanating from the second Comintern congress in Moscow in July and August. At that congress, Lenin laid down his famous twenty-one conditions for the admission of the world socialist parties to the Communist International. Under the impression of these events, socialist parties all over Europe began to split up between the radical left wing and the moderate right wing. The radical left-wingers appeared to believe that a millennium—the World Revolution heralded by socialist prophets since the nineteenth century—was at last at hand. The moderate right-wingers appeared to be dispirited and disoriented.

On July 5, railroad workers on the Košice-Bohumín line struck to prevent transshipment of French munitions for the Polish army. The Tusar government was prevented from disciplining them by massive defections of workers to the Marxist Left.[9] On August 9, despite the frowns of France and Britain, the government declared Czechoslovak neutrality in the Polish-Soviet conflict,[10] which was to embitter Polish-Czechoslovak relations till the end of the First Republic. A week later Jozef Piłsudski dramatically reversed the tide in the Polish-Soviet War by intercepting and hurling back the Red Army (the "miracle on the Vistula"). In

[9] Peroutka, *Budování státu*, III, 1870.
[10] Ibid., 1864-65.

Czechoslovakia, however, the Marxist Left appeared to be carried on by the momentum of earlier Soviet successes.

On September 5, at a conference in Prague, the Marxist Left summoned the leadership of the Social Democratic party to accept Lenin's twenty-one conditions and join the Communist International or face ouster at the party's congress, which was scheduled to meet in Prague later in the month.[11] Tusar and the moderate right-wing leaders of the party appeared not to know what to do until President Masaryk came to their rescue. Since his last stay in Russia in 1917-18, where he witnessed the Bolshevik Revolution, Masaryk held the Russian communists in rather low esteem. On the other hand, he tended to overestimate the political sophistication of the Czech working class and its imperviousness to Bolshevik propaganda. Now, however, aroused by the belligerence of the Marxist Left, he exerted himself to contain it. He addressed workers, held conferences with socialist leaders, and wrote anonymous articles to try to influence left-leaning intellectuals. In conferences with Tusar and other leaders on September 8 and 12, it was decided that the cabinet would resign and that President Masaryk would appoint a cabinet of nonparty officials, which would be unhampered by political considerations in dealing with the situation.[12] On September 14 Tusar and his cabinet resigned, and on the following day President Masaryk appointed a cabinet of officials under Jan Černý, the provincial president (highest administrative official) of Moravia.[13] The only well-known figures in the cabinet were Beneš and Engliš, both of whom were holdovers from the Tusar cabinet.

On September 14 the executive committee of the Social Democratic party, which was controlled by the moderates, approved Tusar's resignation and postponed the party congress until December. The Marxist Left countered this move by holding a rump congress on September 25-28, as originally scheduled. The left-wingers claimed that their congress was attended by 67.7 percent of the whole party's delegates. The left-wing congress ousted the old right-wing leaders and chose a new executive committee under Bohumír Šmeral to replace them.[14] For the moment, however, the Marxist Left did not join the Comintern or rename the party communist, undoubtedly because the Social Democratic party had

[11] *Přehled*, III, 118; Paul Reimann *et al.*, *Dějiny Komunistické strany Československa* [*History of the Communist Party of Czechoslovakia*] (Prague, 1961), pp. 156-57 (hereafter *Dějiny KSČ*).

[12] František Nečásek *et al.* (eds.), *Dokumenty o protilidové a protinárodní politice T. G. Masaryka* [*Documents on the Antipopular and Antinational Policies of T. G. Masaryk*] (Prague, 1953), pp. 67-70; *Dějiny KSČ*, p. 155; *Přehled*, III, 120.

[13] *Přehled*, 120-21; *Národní shromáždění, 1918-1928*, pp. 239-40; Buchválek, *Dějiny*, p. 445; Peroutka, *Budování státu*, III, 1940-42.

[14] *Dějiny KSČ*, pp. 156-57; *Přehled*, III, 122-23.

an old tradition and its name held a strong emotional appeal to the Czech working class, and because the party owned quite a bit of property, which the left-wingers wanted to keep. Indeed, they succeeded in gaining control of the party's large center in Prague, Lidový dům (the People's House), which housed the party secretariat and printing plant. The right-wingers brought suit in a court of law to recover the property. Under a court decision, the left-wingers were forbidden to use the name of the party's organ, *Právo lidu* (*The People's Right*), as their own. Thereupon, on September 21, they began to publish *Rudé právo* (*The Red Right*), which remains the Czechoslovak Communist party organ to this day.[15] Another court verdict decided the dispute over the People's House in favor of the right-wingers.

After reforming their ranks at a rump congress of their own on November 27-29, the right-wingers launched a counteroffensive. When the left-wingers ignored their demand to return the People's House, the right-wingers called in the police to enforce the court decision—despite the odium of breaking "proletarian solidarity" that this incurred. On December 9, after a brief scuffle, the police evicted the left-wingers from the center. This action caused great excitement among the left-wingers. Taking it as a direct challenge by the government, the Marxist Left called for a general strike in the whole country. Widespread strikes, riots, and seizures of factories, churches, and public buildings by the workers followed,[16] which inspired the middle-class belief that the Marxist Left planned a *coup d'état*. General tension was heightened by a recent outbreak of Czech-German conflicts in Teplice (Teplitz), Cheb (Eger), and Prague (October 28-November 16), in which troops had to intervene.[17]

Actually, the Marxist Left had no plans for revolution. It had rashly called for the strike, without making any preparations for it or formulating any political program. It obviously expected the government to give in at once before the threat of the strike and comply with the workers' demands, which were of an economic rather than a political nature. However, unlike the Tusar government which quaked before the wrath of the workers, the Černý government felt no compunction about ordering the police to fire into the rioting workers. Moreover, the strike was far from general. The Marxist Left had overestimated its influence on the workers and the workers' revolutionary élan. In fact, the Czech workers had little tradition of revolutionary violence. Only one worker was killed in a clash with the police in Prague. The Slovak workers likewise had no revolutionary tradition, properly speaking, although—being still close

---

[15] *Přehled*, III, 121; *Dějiny KSČ*, p. 156.

[16] *Dějiny KSČ*, pp. 158-61; *Přehled*, III, 127-37; Peroutka, *Budování státu*, III, 2094-2108.

[17] Peroutka, *Budování státu*, III, 2020-2022; César and Černý, *Politika*, I, 228-30.

to the soil—they had a fading memory of peasant *jacquerie*; social conflicts in Slovakia were more often marred by violence than in the Czech provinces. Three workers were shot by the police in a riot at Vráble in Slovakia.[18] The bloodiest incident occurred at Most (Brüx) in the Sudeten German area, where nine persons were killed in a riot.[19] Undoubtedly, the difference in nationality between the German workers and the Czech police in part accounted for the severity of the clash and the extent of the tragedy.

The general strike collapsed by December 15. About 3,000 persons were arrested by the authorities during and after the strike. A somewhat smaller number was tried—without the benefit of jury in parts of Bohemia and in Slovakia and Ruthenia where martial law had been declared.[20] However, in no instance did the government action assume the form of mass reprisals, let alone terror. Indeed, as early as June 1921 an amnesty was offered to those who would ask for it. However, revolutionary pride prevented the left-wing leaders from appealing for the government's clemency. So they had to wait until February, 1922, when President Masaryk proclaimed a general amnesty for all offenders in the December, 1920, events.[21]

It is also worth noting that the government did not exploit the December, 1920, events to suppress the Marxist Left. The left-wingers remained free to pursue their activities. Indeed, they now realized their inability to capture the Social Democratic party and proceeded openly to organize a communist movement. In January, 1921, delegates of the Marxist Left in Slovakia and Ruthenia held a meeting at Lubochňa, at which they accepted the twenty-one conditions of admission to the Comintern and constituted themselves a communist party.[22] In March the left wing of the German Social Democratic party followed suit at a meeting at Liberec (Reichenberg).[23] Finally, at a constituent congress in Prague on May 14-16, delegates of the Czech Marxist Left and the Marxist Left in Slovakia and Ruthenia constituted the Communist Party of Czechoslovakia (KSČ).[24] Šmeral had reservations about accepting the Germans into the party, for which he was criticized at the third Comintern congress in Moscow in the summer of 1921. The Comintern denied the KSČ admission until it corrected the error, which the party did at a unification

---

[18] *Přehled*, III, 134.   [19] Ibid., 135.

[20] Peroutka, *Budování státu*, III, 2108-2109; Věra Olivová, *Politika československé buržoazie v letech 1921-1923* [*The Politics of the Czechoslovak Bourgeoisie in 1921-1923*] (Prague, 1961), pp. 13-16.

[21] Peroutka, *Budování státu*, III, 2114.

[22] *Dějiny KSČ*, p. 165; *Přehled*, III, 161-62.

[23] *Přehled*, III, 162-63; *Dějiny KSČ*, p. 167; Peroutka, *Budování státu*, III, 2213-14.

[24] Peroutka, *Budování státu*, pp. 2214-23; *Dějiny KSČ*, pp. 169-71; *Přehled*, III, 163-64.

congress in Prague in October 1921.[25] The KSČ became the only Czechoslovak political party in which all the nationalities in the country were represented. Because of its persistent hostility to the Czechoslovak "bourgeois state" until 1935, however, the Communist party was placed "beyond the pale" of Czechoslovak politics. Until the end of the First Republic it could exercise only an indirect influence.

Post-World War II Czechoslovak Marxist historians have built up the December, 1920, strike into a great revolutionary epic, which supposedly failed only because of the treachery of the right-wing socialists and the brutality of the organs of the Czechoslovak bourgeois state. The reality was much less dramatic. Nevertheless, the December, 1920, strike and its suppression represented an important turning-point in the history of the First Republic. It marked the high point of postwar social and political radicalism and a return to law and order. The authority of the government, previously often wavering, was firmly established, and the continuation of parliamentary democracy—with freedom for all political groups, including the communists—was assured.

Though checked by the Černý government's resolute action, the communists were by no means finished. They had entrenched themselves in the labor movement—often by the use of strong-arm tactics—and fought hard to preserve their positions. Particularly fierce was their struggle with the Social Democrats for the control of the labor unions. The labor unions had traditionally been the principal source of Social Democratic strength. To help the Social Democrats preserve the control of the unions, the Černý cabinet introduced and the National Assembly passed a law on July 19, 1921, adopting the so-called Ghent system of unemployment insurance. Under the Ghent system, which was based on the guild principle, the government surrendered the administration of unemployment insurance to the labor unions. Union members were required to pay premiums into special funds, to which the government contributed. Out of the funds benefits were paid to unemployed members. To allow time for the funds to build up, the application of the law was delayed until 1925.[26] It worked well enough with old and well established craft unions which were usually Social Democratic, but not so well with new and poor industrial and agricultural unions which were often communist. Nonunionized labor, of course, received no unemployment benefits at all. This was often the case with the agricultural labor in Slovakia and Ruthenia.[27]

To warn communists and other political groups with a penchant for

[25] Přehled, III, 164; Dějiny KSČ, pp. 174-75; Peroutka, Budování státu, III, 2228-32.

[26] Přehled, III, 167.

[27] Ján Mlynárik, Nezamestnanosť na Slovensku, 1918-1938 [Unemployment in Slovakia, 1918-1938] (Bratislava, 1964), pp. 89-95.

violence, the National Assembly passed on August 6, 1921, the Law against Terror, which provided stiff penalties against the use of force as a method of political action.[28] A few days later, on August 12, the National Assembly passed the Law on Workers' Committees, which authorized workers in enterprises with thirty or more employees to elect workers' committees.[29] The law was billed as a radical socialist measure. Actually, workers' committees had come into existence in larger factories spontaneously, without the sanction of any law, as early as November, 1918. Invariably, they were dominated by radical left-wing Social Democrats (future communists). By carefully prescribing the mode of the workers' committees' election, the new law sought to prevent their monopolization by the communists.

If the Law on Workers' Committees was meant to be a socialist measure, then it represented a swan song of the once powerful movement for socialization in Czechoslovakia. By 1921 the nonsocialist parties had become dominant and they were firmly opposed to any further socialization. Important also was the cautious stand taken by President Masaryk, who pointed out that it was impossible for a state so dependent on foreign trade as Czechoslovakia was "to put into effect an economic revolution against the will of foreign countries."[30] The Law on Workers' Committees failed to live up to its billings as a starting point in the building up of economic democracy in Czechoslovakia.

Finally, in August, 1921, the Černý cabinet introduced a bill in the National Assembly to raise the tariff on the import of automobiles into Czechoslovakia, which was to have important economic and political consequences. Approved and supplemented by later tariff modifications in the National Assembly, it tended to strengthen Czechoslovakia's heavy industry, the principal markets for which were—initially, at least—at home. On the other hand, it tended to weaken the country's light industry, which was geared heavily to export.[31] Since heavy industry was centered in the Czech-inhabited cities in central Bohemia and Moravia and the light industry in the German-inhabited periphery of the provinces, the new tariff policy added to the political discontent of the German minority.

[28] Peroutka, *Budování státu*, IV, 2353-54; *Přehled*, III, 168.

[29] Peroutka, *Budování státu*, IV, 2336-38; *Přehled*, III, 168-69.

[30] Tomáš G. Masaryk, *Cesta demokracie: Soubor projevů za republiky* [*The Path of Democracy: A Collection of Speeches under the Republic*] (2 vols.; Prague, 1933), II, 20.

[31] *Přehled*, III, 158; *Deset let Československé Republiky* [*Ten Years of the Czechoslovak Republic*] (3 vols.; Prague, 1928), II, 198. In consequence, the ratio of heavy industry to light industry shifted (in percentages) from 38.2:61.8 in 1921 to 46.0:54.0 in 1929, and to 48.8:51.2 in 1937. See Jozef Faltus *et al.*, *Stručný hospodářský vývoj Československa do roku 1945* [*Concise Economic Survey of Czechoslovakia to 1945*] (Prague, 1969), p. 119.

POLITICAL CONSOLIDATION

Czechoslovakia's speedy political consolidation after the December, 1920, strike was in no small measure due to that peculiarly Czechoslovak political institution—the committee of "Five" (Pětka).[32] The origin of the committee was fortuitous. The nonparty Černý cabinet resembled a ventriloquist's dummy: it had no political will or voice of its own. To give it political direction and to provide it with parliamentary support, representatives of the five major parties or parliamentary blocs— Antonín Švehla (agrarian), Alois Rašín (National Democrat), Rudolf Bechyně (Social Democrat), Jiří Stříbrný (National Socialist), and Jan Šrámek (populist)—began to meet informally and discuss and decide political measures for the Černý cabinet to take, which their parties supported in the National Assembly. The *spiritus movens* of the Pětka was Švehla. His influence was all the greater because early in 1921 President Masaryk fell seriously ill and was unable to take part in the affairs of the government for some time. Even after he recovered, he was content to leave matters largely in Švehla's competent hands, for he had confidence in the judgment and integrity of the agrarian leader. It was not until the later 1920's when illness removed Švehla permanently from active politics that the president began to play a direct and personal part in the affairs of government again.

Originally, it was assumed that when the emergency created by the split in the Social Democratic party passed and a political cabinet was created again, the "Five" would cease to function. However, in politics *ce n'est que le provisoire qui dure*—the provisional often proves lasting. With some interruptions and changes in name, the committee lasted to the end of the First Republic.

The Pětka was often criticized for being unconstitutional and undemocratic and for supposedly reducing the National Assembly to a rubber stamp. However, its continued existence indicated that it filled a useful— perhaps an indispensable—function. The parliaments of Vienna and Budapest, in which most Czech and Slovak politicians had learned their trade, were not the best schools of parliamentary democracy: the Czech and Slovak parliamentarians had retained many bad habits, notably a tendency toward carping, unconstructive criticism, and a penchant for obstructionism, from them. They rid themselves of these habits only gradually. By its power to discipline members of the National Assembly and to impose on them compromises without which Czechoslovak politics might have come to a halt, the Pětka probably saved Czechoslovakia from the fate of its neighbors, whose parliaments' inability to agree paved the way to dictatorship.

[32] Peroutka, *Budování státu*, IV, 2161-73.

The Černý cabinet lingered on until September, 1921—months after the end of the socialist crisis. The reason for the delay in returning to a political cabinet was that the party leaders were unable to agree on the composition of one. According to the European parliamentary practice which was followed in Czechoslovakia, the largest party in the National Assembly was supposed to take the lead in forming the cabinet and providing the premier. However, the Social Democrats, who were the largest party—even after the communist defections—were too disoriented by their recent crisis and declined the honor. Next in line for the responsibility was the agrarian bloc. However, the agrarian leader Švehla likewise turned down the honor, because he thought that the situation was still too unsettled and public opinion still too agitated for his cabinet to have a long and successful life. In the end, President Masaryk asked his closest collaborator, Edvard Beneš, to form a cabinet.

The Beneš cabinet, which was appointed on September 26, 1921, and lasted until October 7, 1922, was a semi-political one.[33] The five major Czechoslovak political parties or blocs were all represented in it, although not by their first-rank leaders. Of the members of the Pětka only Šrámek, the populist leader, accepted a post in it. On the other hand, Beneš retained two nonparty ministers from the previous cabinet—Prime Minister Černý, who agreed to serve as minister of interior in Beneš's cabinet, and Martin Mičura, who continued as minister for the administration of Slovakia. Beneš himself was not yet a member of any party.

The principal reason why Masaryk offered the premiership to the perennial foreign minister was that the international situation at the time made it desirable to have an experienced diplomat at the helm. Indeed, Beneš' government was primarily preoccupied with foreign affairs. The attempt of the former Emperor Charles to recover his throne by landing in Hungary in October, 1921, threatened the entire fabric of peace treaties in East Central Europe.[34] Czechoslovakia and Yugoslavia mobilized their armies, and the attempt at Habsburg restoration collapsed. The crisis had one side-effect at home—some Sudeten German recruits refused to obey the mobilization orders, which set off another round of Czech-German rioting.[35] Thanks to Beneš's diplomatic skill, however, Czechoslovakia's international position was so strengthened by the time he left office that some Sudeten Germans came to the reluctant conclusion that the republic was there to stay. The solid front of German opposition to Czechoslovakia began to crumble. In November, 1922, the German parliamentary club was dissolved, and the moderate German parties

[33] Ibid., 2366-69; *Národní shromáždění, 1918-1928*, pp. 268-69; Buchválek, *Dějiny*, pp. 445-46.

[34] Peroutka, *Budování státu*, IV, 2406-24.

[35] Ibid., 2426-30; César and Černý, *Politika*, I, 261-62; *Přehled*, III, 174-75.

indicated their readiness to take an active part in Czechoslovak political life.[36]

By the fall of 1922 Švehla deemed Czechoslovakia's foreign and domestic situation to be sufficiently consolidated for him to assume the premiership. On October 7, he formed a prestigious ministry comprising all the members of the Pětka[37]: the redoubtable Rašín resumed the post of finance minister, Bechyně took education, Stříbrný the railroads, and Šrámek public health. The Pětka decided that Beneš, who continued in foreign affairs, should be a political minister rather than a nonparty expert. Therefore, he formally joined the (National) Socialist party and thenceforth represented it in the cabinet. The only nonparty member in the Švehla cabinet was Jozef Kallay, a civil servant, who served as minister for the administration of Slovakia. Like the Beneš government, the Švehla cabinet was based on the "all-national" principle, that is, it was supported by a coalition of the five major Czechoslovak parties or blocs (except the Slovak populists, who had withdrawn from the populist bloc in 1921). The Švehla cabinet lasted until November 11, 1925, which was longer than any other cabinet endured under the First Republic.

ECONOMIC CONSOLIDATION

The sudden separation of Czechoslovakia from the Habsburg empire in 1918 caused many dislocations in the Czechoslovak economy. The large industries of the Czech provinces, which had been the industrial center of the empire, lost many profitable markets. Czechoslovakia's economy had to make many painful adjustments and inevitably underwent basic structural changes.

Czechoslovak economic policy at home was based on the principle of *laissez-faire*, somewhat modified by the concept of *Kriegssozialismus*—the wartime government economic controls, which however were regarded as emergency measures that should be abolished when economic conditions returned to normal. Abroad, Czechoslovak economic policy was largely based on the last Austro-Hungarian tariff (1906), which was designed to protect Austro-Hungarian industry from industrial competition, principally of the empire's powerful German ally, and was one of the highest in Europe.

In the immediate postwar period, however, the Czechoslovak government was not much concerned with broad questions of economic policy, but rather addressed itself to the pressing task of trying to solve practical economic problems, such as finding supplies of food, fuel, and raw ma-

[36] Ibid., 175; César and Černý, *Politika*, I, 290; Olivová, *Politika*, p. 42.

[37] *Národní shromáždění, 1918-1928*, pp. 287-88; Peroutka, *Budování státu*, V, 2542-43; *Přehled*, III, 181-83; Olivová, *Politika*, pp. 63-64; Buchválek, *Dějiny*. p. 446.

terials, restoring transportation, and—above all—halting the inflation. As already seen, it was largely successful in containing inflation through Rašín's currency reform in February, 1919.

Rašín's approach to finance and business was essentially moralistic.[38] He abhorred inflation, for it appeared to rob the thrifty and reward the profligate, in other words, punish virtue and reward vice. His economic concepts were somewhat simplistic. He attached too much importance to the "strength" of the Czechoslovak crown (*koruna*), as measured by its exchange rate in the international money markets. It was his ambition to drive the Czechoslovak crown to the level of the Austrian crown in 1914, which would have done justice to the hard-working, thrifty Czech middle-class people (like himself), who had seen their savings eaten away by the war-induced inflation. Before Rašín could fully deploy his deflationary policies, however, he was forced out of office by the fall of the Kramář cabinet in July, 1919.

Rašín's successors in the first Tusar cabinet (July, 1919-May, 1920) —Cyril Horáček and Kuneš Sonntag—were agrarians with civil service backgrounds. Both were competent administrators but not influential politicians. The most important achievement of the Tusar cabinet in the economic realm was to steer through the National Assembly the Law of Nostrification on December 12, 1919,[39] the purpose of which was to free Czechoslovakia from foreign economic domination, especially from the stranglehold of Viennese banks on business and industry in the country. Foreign-owned commercial and industrial enterprises in Czechoslovakia were obliged to establish headquarters in the country and register as Czechoslovak companies. Larger industrial and commercial enterprises, with branches in Czechoslovakia and other parts of the former empire, were required to separate their establishments in Czechoslovakia and set them up as autonomous companies. The practical effect of the law was to force foreign owners either to form partnerships with Czechoslovak firms or to sell out. The Law of Nostrification, which was applied gradually, was largely successful in its purpose. By the end of the First Republic in 1938, 231 foreign-owned companies had been "nostrificated." The principal beneficiaries of the law were the great banks in Prague, especially the famous Živnostenská banka (Živnobanka), which experienced phenomenal growth.

Rašín fully approved of the Law of Nostrification, in the preparation of which he had in fact taken a hand. He was less approving when his successors let the crown slip in the foreign money markets, and was positively alarmed by the policies of Prof. Karel Engliš, who became minister of finance in the second Tusar cabinet (May-September, 1920) and tem-

[38] On Rašín and his financial reform, see herein, Chapters II and V.
[39] Faltus, *Stručný hospodářský vývoj*, pp. 136-37; *Přehled*, III, 49-50.

porarily also in the Černý cabinet. A fellow-National Democrat, Engliš shared most of Rašín's middle-class views and virtues, including his devotion to hard work and thrift. However, he was perhaps the foremost theoretical economist in Czechoslovakia at the time, and had much more sophisticated economic views than Rašín, who was a lawyer by training. Czechoslovakia was a trading nation. Its prosperity and solvency depended largely on an active balance of trade. Engliš feared that a precipitously deflationary policy might result in "overpricing" the crown, which would tend to discourage exports and encourage imports. Therefore, he sought to stabilize the crown.

During the turbulent year of 1920, laborers managed to obtain considerable wage raises and benefits. This inevitably led to the demand of government employees that they be given a raise, too. When, at the end of 1920, Engliš presented the budget for 1921, he recommended a raise for government employees. The proposed budget was—for the first time —in balance. To pay for the additional expenses and to keep the budget in balance, Engliš proposed a fiscal reform, which envisaged introduction of some new taxes. Rašín regarded this plan as a proposal for squandering, and used his influence as a member of the Pětka to veto it. In January, 1921, Engliš resigned. His successor, Vladimír Hanáčík, was Rašín's close collaborator.

By 1921, the shortages of food and consumer goods, which had characterized the Czechoslovak economy since the war, began to disappear. On July 1, under the pressure of the agrarian party, the government abandoned wartime economic controls. Contrary to the fears of the socialist parties, no serious rise in prices resulted. The economy appeared to be returning to normal again. The euphoric feeling that went with it, however, proved shortlived, for by the end of the year there were signs of an economic recession. By 1922, the country experienced a sharp depression. The index of industrial production dropped from 60.1 in 1921 to 54.7 in 1922 (1929=100).[40] The ranks of the unemployed rose to 441,000 or about 22 percent of the labor force.[41] Encouraged by the abundance of labor, the employers made a determined effort to drive down the wage level again. Inevitably, this produced dangerous new social tensions.

In the meantime, the government steadfastly pursued a deflationary policy. The mobilization of the Czechoslovak army during the Habsburg restoration crisis in October, 1921, threw the government's budget out of kilter. However, rather than permit a deficit and inflation, Augustín Novák, the finance minister in the Beneš cabinet, proposed in January, 1922, to cut the salaries of government employees and solicited a loan

[40] Buchválek, *Dějiny*, p. 305.
[41] *Přehled*, III, 186-87.

abroad. Partly because of these measures and partly because of the great German inflation and the ensuing flight from the German mark, the Czechoslovak crown rose 323 percent in Zürich from November, 1921, to October, 1922.[42] This was gratifying to Czechoslovak pride, but did not contribute to the solution of the country's economic difficulties.

Rašín, who returned to the office of finance minister in the Švehla cabinet in October, 1922, was made a scapegoat for the difficulties. He was vilified in the leftist press, which blamed the suffering of the common people on his deflationary policy. On January 5, 1923, a mentally disturbed youth, who had been a communist, shot him. He died of his wounds in February. This act of violence shocked the country, for political assassinations were not common in Czechoslovakia.[43] It stirred the National Assembly into passing the "Law for the Protection of the Republic" on March 3, 1923.[44] Modeled on a similar law in Weimar Germany, the law treated as crimes against the state a great variety of acts, without differentiating between deeds accomplished and deeds intended. It was aimed against the communists, the Czech fascists who had made a recent appearance, and other violence-prone groups. However, because of its all-inclusive nature, in irresponsible hands it could become a weapon against any party or group. It was denounced by the communists, the national minorities, and the Slovak autonomists, but it caused uneasiness even among some members of the socialist parties, which had voted for it. It caused a schism in the (National) Socialist party. A group of former Czech anarchists led by Bohuslav Vrbenský, who had joined the party in 1918, seceded from it because of the law and eventually passed into the communist ranks.

In the latter part of 1923, the depression began to abate, and in 1924 it gave way to a growing wave of prosperity. This was perhaps due less to any specific policies of the Czechoslovak government than to the general amelioration of the European economy after the end of the Ruhr crisis and adoption of the Dawes Plan in 1924. Thanks to the hopeful mood that attended the conclusion of the Locarno treaties in 1925 (the "spirit of Locarno"), even skeptics began to believe that Czechoslovakia was in Europe to stay. It appeared solid and stable. This is not to say, of course, that it had succeeded in solving all of its problems. Slovakia and Ruthenia, notably, failed to share in the broad prosperity of the country.

[42] Ibid., 158; Jozef Faltus, *Povojnová hospodárska kriza v Československu v rokoch 1921-1923* [*The Postwar Economic Crisis in Czechoslovakia in 1921-1923*] (Bratislava, 1966), p. 193.

[43] Peroutka, *Budování státu*, v, 2701-02. On January 18, 1919, an attempt was made on Kramář's life, likewise by a radical left-wing socialist. Kramář was unharmed. Both acts were out of Czechoslovak political tradition.

[44] *Národní shromáždění, 1918-1928*, pp. 299-300; *Přehled*, III, 192-95; Peroutka, *Budování státu*, v, 2731-39; Olivová, *Politika*, pp. 82-84.

SLOVAKIA'S ECONOMIC DEVELOPMENT

In 1918, Slovakia's economic development lagged far behind that of the Czech provinces. Generally speaking, while the Czech provinces had a well-balanced industrial-agrarian economy, Slovakia's economy was predominantly agrarian.[45] Nevertheless, Slovakia was not completely devoid of modern industry. From the end of the nineteenth century, the Hungarian government had sought to stimulate Hungary's industrialization by giving industry tax exemptions, preferential railroad rates, government orders, and outright subsidies. Slovakia's share of Hungary's new industry was relatively high. In 1913, there were altogether 817 industrial plants in Slovakia employing more than twenty workers.[46] Slovakia's share of Hungary's population was 16.8 percent, but its share of Hungary's industrial enterprises was 17.3 and its share of Hungary's industrial labor force 20.8 percent.[47]

After 1918, Slovakia's hopeful industrial development came to a halt. The sudden separation of Czechoslovakia's economy from that of the rest of the Habsburg empire in 1918 produced economic dislocations throughout the country. However, for a variety of reasons, the shock of separation was felt more keenly in Slovakia (and Ruthenia) than in the Czech provinces. Slovak industry lost its natural markets in Hungary. The Czech provinces could scarcely provide it with alternate markets, because they also suffered from loss of their markets in other parts of the former empire. As a matter of fact, they looked to Slovakia and Ruthenia as their only sheltered domestic markets left.

Slovakia's industry was not in a good position to compete with the industries in the Czech provinces. Technological standards, managerial skills, and labor productivity were all lower in Slovakia than in the Czech provinces.[48] Despite a substantially lower wage level in Slovakia, the cost of the products of Slovak industry was relatively high. Slovak industry found it also hard to support the high costs of transportation to

[45] In 1910, 62.6 percent of the population in Slovakia was in agriculture and 18.4 percent in industry, while in the Czech provinces 34.4 percent of the population was in agriculture and 39.5 percent in industry. See Buchválek, *Dějiny*, p. 482.

[46] *Přehled*, II-2, 844.

[47] Milan Strhan, *Kríza priemyslu na Slovensku v rokoch 1921-1923: Počiatky odbúravania slovenského priemyslu* [*The Crisis of Industry in Slovakia in 1921-1923: The Beginning of the Liquidation of Slovak Industry*] (Bratislava, 1960), p. 19. For surveys of industry in Slovakia before 1914, see *Přehled*, II-2, 840-47; Faltus, *Stručný hospodářský vývoj*, pp. 70-80; Pavel Rapoš, *Priemysel na Slovensku za kapitalizmu* [*Industry in Slovakia under Capitalism*] (Bratislava, 1957), pp. 14-20.

[48] Faltus, *Stručný hospodářský vývoj*, pp. 140-41; Strhan, *Kríza priemyslu*, pp. 37-41; see also Chapter V, herein.

the Czech provinces. Because of Czechoslovakia's elongated shape, Slovakia was farther from most points in the Czech provinces than from most points in Hungary. Because of Hungarian railway policy and Slovakia's topography (the Slovak rivers flow south into the Hungarian plain), Slovakia had numerous railway connections with Hungary but only two with the Czech provinces, and they followed rather circuitous routes. The fact also that a large part of Slovakia's railroads was privately owned added to the costs of transportation.[49]

The credit shortage that accompanied Rašín's deflationary policy affected Slovak industrial development more adversely than the Czech, because Slovakia's capital resources were smaller. Before 1918 the Czechs had a well-developed banking system, while the few existing Slovak banks were little better than one-room savings banks. After 1918 Slovak banks experienced considerable growth, but it remained small compared with that of the Czech banks. Before 1918 virtually all of Slovakia's larger business and industry was owned by Budapest and Viennese banks. After the war, because of the Law of Nostrification, most of it passed under domestic ownership. However, the Slovak share of this ownership remained small. Most commerce and industry in Slovakia, including the banks, passed under the control of the great banks in Prague.[50]

For the most part, the older, better capitalized, and more efficient Czech industries weathered the postwar crisis of industry. In place of the lost markets in other parts of the former Habsburg empire they found new markets in Western Europe and overseas. Partly as a result of the different requirements of these new markets and partly of deliberate policy, the emphasis in Czechoslovak exports shifted from light consumer

[49] The question of railroad tariffs in Czechoslovakia was a very complicated one. Before 1918, railroad tariffs in Hungary were considerably higher than in the Austrian half of the empire. Moreover, while a large share of Hungary's railroads was privately owned, Austria's railroads were mostly state-owned. Beginning in 1921, Czechoslovakia progressively adopted a uniform railroad tariff, under which—as was general European practice—the rates per ton/per mile dropped in proportion to the distance over which the goods were transported. However, this advantage was offset in Slovakia and Ruthenia by the fact that a large part (1,151 miles out of a total of 2,360 miles of railroads in Slovakia in 1921) was still privately owned. Rates on private railroads were higher and separately computed. The government progressively bought out the private railroads, but the process was not completed by 1938. See Jozef Faltus and Václav Průcha, Prehľad hospodárskeho vývoja na Slovensku v rokoch 1918-1945 [Survey of the Economic Development of Slovakia from 1918-1945] (Bratislava, 1967), pp. 84-90; Strhan, Kríza priemyslu, pp. 61-65.

[50] Strhan, Kríza priemyslu, pp. 43-60; and the same author's study "Živnostenská Banka na Slovensku, 1918-1938" ["Živnostenská Bank in Slovakia, 1918-1938"], Historický časopis, xv (1967), 177-218; Faltus and Průcha, Prehľad hospodárskeho vývoja, pp. 226-27.

goods to heavy industrial goods. Generally, the shift in markets and the nature of Czechoslovak exports worked to the detriment of Slovakia's industries and also those of the Sudeten German area.

When Czechoslovakia was forced to curtail industrial production because of the loss of markets and for other reasons, the Czech banks shut down the less profitable and less efficient factories in Slovakia first. The phenomenon did not remain a limited one, but developed into a broad movement resulting in large-scale deindustrialization of Slovakia.[51] From 1918 to 1923 over 200 plants in Slovakia were shut down. Their equipment was dismantled and sold, mostly to Hungary. Slovakia was relentlessly forced back to the status of an agrarian province exclusively, the function of which was to raise food and provide a market for the industrial products of the Czech provinces. Ruthenia, which however had not had even the modest industrial development of Slovakia, likewise remained an agrarian province.

After 1918 the Slovaks and Ruthenians briefly placed great hopes in the promised land reform. After a slow start, the land reform got under way intensively in the years from 1923 to 1926 and then continued at a diminishing pace until 1938. The deliberate pace of the land reform and its relatively limited scope soon dissipated the hopes placed in it.[52] Even if it had been instant and drastic, however, it could not have satisfied the land-hunger of the Slovak peasantry. There simply was not enough land to go around in Slovakia, especially in the light of the backward character of Slovak agriculture and the consequent low yield per acre.

The essentially mercantilist division of economic functions between the industrial west and agrarian east in Czechoslovakia was unfortunate. By their mountainous character, Slovakia and Ruthenia were not naturally suited for it. It is true that the best farmland in Czechoslovakia was found along the Danube River and its tributaries in southwestern Slovakia and along the Tisza River and its tributaries in eastern Slovakia and southwestern Ruthenia. However, only two fifths of Slovakia's area were cultivable. The rest was covered with mountains and forests. The land reform alone could not, therefore, solve Slovakia's economic prob-

---

[51] Ibid., pp. 33-35 and 38-40; Ľubomír Lipták, *Slovensko v 20. storočí* [*Slovakia in the 20th Century*] (Bratislava, 1968), p. 11; Macartney, *Hungary*, pp. 130-31. For a detailed, industry by industry, account of the liquidation of Slovakia's industries, see Strhan, *Kríza priemyslu*, pp. 80-192. Employment in both industry and agriculture in Slovakia declined, from 14.9 percent in industry and 60.4 percent in agriculture in 1921 to 14.6 percent in industry and 56.7 percent in agriculture in 1930. See Buchválek, *Dějiny*, p. 482. This reflected partly the growth of the third or service sector of the economy, but mainly persistently high levels of unemployment and the growth of a horde of flotsam labor without any regular trades.

[52] Lipták, *Slovensko*, pp. 114-15; Macartney, *Hungary*, pp. 122-24.

lems. Only the development of a balanced industrial-agrarian economy, the same as the Czech provinces had, could solve the problem.

Traditionally, the population in Slovakia's mountainous areas had to earn a part or the whole of its income by labor in the forests, as seasonal agricultural laborers in the flat lands of Hungary, or in industry. Slovakia's separation from Hungary limited the opportunity for seasonal agricultural labor and Slovakia's deindustrialization the opportunity for work in industry. The Czech provinces were unable to absorb Slovakia's surplus labor. Their agriculture was more modern and mechanized than in Hungary, and needed only little additional seasonal labor. Their industries found ample labor locally. Only the construction business in the Czech provinces, especially in Prague, which experienced a great construction boom in the 1920's, found a larger need for imported labor, but by no means enough to dry up the pool of available Slovak labor.

The social consequences of Slovakia's deindustrialization were, therefore, quite unhappy. Rural overpopulation and unemployment or under-employment were intensified.[53] Emigration abroad, which had been interrupted by the outbreak of World War I, resumed shortly after its conclusion. The adoption of immigration restrictions in the United States in 1921 and 1924 did not halt the stream of Slovak emigration but only diverted it to less desirable countries—Canada, some Latin American countries (Argentina), and also European countries (France and Belgium). While emigration from the Czech provinces remained small, emigration from Slovakia and Ruthenia steadily increased,[54] even during the period of relative prosperity, from 1924 to 1929, when Slovakia's industry experienced a partial and temporary revival.[55]

Dearth of indigenous capital and general weakness of private enterprise in Slovakia hampered the development of its resources. Only state intervention in the economic process in Slovakia could halt and reverse its deindustrialization and develop its resources. Unfortunately, the Czechoslovak government adopted a *laissez-faire* attitude and let nature take its course in Slovakia. The result of this policy was Slovakia's continued economic stagnation. Post-World War II Czech and Slovak Marxist historians have given the phenomenon a good deal of attention. They have blamed it on "Czech bourgeois policy," which supposedly sought "Slovakia's economic domination and its adaptation to the interests of the Czech capital."[56] This characteristically Marxist view attributes to Czechoslovak economic policy in Slovakia a class and national motiva-

---

[53] Mlynárik, *Nezamestnanosť*, pp. 29-41.

[54] *Přehled*, III, 187; *Československá vlastivěda*, v, 452-53.

[55] Faltus and Průcha, *Prehľad hospodárskeho vývoja*, pp. 40-46.

[56] Zdeněk Šolle and Alena Gajanová, *Po stopě dějin: Češi a Slováci v letech 1848-1938* [*On the Trail of History: The Czechs and Slovaks from 1848 to 1938*] (Prague, 1969), p. 275.

tion and a clearer purpose than it actually had. In reality, a narrowly conceived profit motive on the part of Czech business leaders and a lack of interest and purpose on the part of government leaders would appear to characterize Czechoslovak economic policy in Slovakia better. The Prague banks did not close down factories in Slovakia because they were Slovak, but because they were often unprofitable. Similarly, the government in Prague did not neglect business interests in Slovakia because they were Slovak, but because they lacked political influence.

It cannot be gainsaid that the Czech politicians, whether bourgeois or socialist, took little interest in Slovakia's economic development. Slovakia's welfare was not primarily their responsibility, however, but that of the Slovak politicians. Generally speaking, the Slovak politicians took the fatalistic view that Slovakia had always been poor and always would be. Yet, as the example of Switzerland—among others—shows, a small mountainous country need not necessarily be poor. As a matter of fact, Slovakia had the natural endowment for a reasonably prosperous economy. It is true that its mineral wealth was not outstanding—some low-grade iron ore (in the Ore Mountains in central Slovakia), a small quantity of soft coal (at Handlová), and a trickle of oil (at Gbely). However, Slovakia had ample waterpower to generate electricity; large timberlands to provide the raw material for the production of lumber, paper, matches, and cellulose; mountain pastures (*hole*) to serve as a basis for a Swiss-type dairy industry; great scenic beauty to support a tourist business; and sufficient farmland not only to feed its population but to provide small surpluses for export. None of these resources was fully developed under the First Republic.

Until about 1930, when the Great Depression first affected Czechoslovakia, the Slovak politicians showed commendable energy in promoting the cultural and educational development of the Slovak people, but they grossly neglected Slovak social and economic progress. They made no concerted effort to pressure the government in Prague to save Slovakia's industries and to develop its resources. To understand why, one must examine the character of Slovak political leadership and the structure of Slovak political parties.

For the most part, the Slovak politicians belonged to the Slovak intelligentsia, which for all practical purposes constituted the Slovak middle class. Before 1918, because of Hungary's peculiar social structure, educated Slovaks were virtually excluded from commercial and industrial enterprise. They found employment only in the free professions (the ministry, teaching, law, and medicine). Hungarian education had a class basis: higher education was designed to produce gentlemen. To some extent, the Slovak intelligentsia reflected the Hungarian gentry's disdain for economic activity as sordid money-grubbing that was best left to the

Jews and the Germans. After 1918, Slovak society did not change much. The Slovak intelligentsia expanded in numbers but did not change much in outlook or character. In addition to the professions, educated Slovaks now found employment in government service. By and large, however, they neither sought nor were readily admitted to business and industry, the control of which in Slovakia remained in nonindigenous hands. Consequently, as a class, the Slovak intelligentsia did not feel that they had a stake in commerce and industry and remained woefully ignorant of Slovakia's social and economic problems.

The Slovak political parties reflected the structure of the Slovak society. Since there was no substantial class of Slovak bankers, industrialists, and big businessmen, there was no Slovak political party to represent them. The attempt of the Czech National Democrats to groom the Slovak National party, which was reestablished in 1921, as a conservative party of business was a complete failure. The agrarian party, which appealed to the Slovak peasantry and intelligentsia for support, did creditable work in improving agriculture and in promoting the organization of peasant cooperatives, both producer and consumer, and a network of peasant savings banks. It did not believe, however, that it had an interest in promoting industry, except that engaged in processing farm products (flour, sugar, alcohol, etc.).

The Slovak populist party appealed to the same electoral clientèle as the agrarian party. It did not hesitate to exploit the adverse social consequences of Slovakia's deindustrialization to promote its program of Slovak political autonomy, but had little interest in promoting industry. As a clerical party, it was also inhibited in its attitude toward business and industry by the knowledge that when Slovak peasants were transformed into industrial workers they usually came under the influence of socialist propaganda and tended to "lose God," that is, become irreligious and escape the influence of the Catholic Church.

The results of the 1920 elections showed that the Slovak working class looked to the Social Democrats to relieve the poverty that oppressed them. The Czechoslovak Social Democratic party, of which the Slovak Social Democrats were a branch, could claim major credit for Czechoslovakia's advanced social legislation. Apart from being more important to the urban working class in the Czech provinces than to the predominantly rural working class in Slovakia, however, Czechoslovak social legislation was not designed to solve the problem of poverty in Slovakia, but only to mitigate its effects. In attacking the source of poverty in Slovakia, namely, the absence of a well developed and balanced industrial-agrarian economy, the Social Democrats showed no more initiative than their bourgeois competitors. Since Czechoslovakia was a capitalist country, to promote business and industry inevitably meant promoting the interests of their capitalist owners. As a Marxist workers' party, the Social Democrats did not feel that that was their responsibility.

The Communist party vehemently criticized the dismantling of Slovakia's industry as an example of the failure of the capitalist system to solve the country's economic problems. The communist solution of the problem of Slovakia's poverty was to abolish the capitalist system and establish a socialist state. Such a solution was, of course, unacceptable to the other parties. Because of the communist hostility to the "bourgeois" Czechoslovak Republic, their influence in Czechoslovak politics was slight. In Slovakia, where they received a large part of their support from the Hungarian minority, their influence was at first hampered by a lack of Slovak leaders. The party leaders in Slovakia, who were either Hungarian or Czech communists, lacked an intimate knowledge of Slovak psychology and conditions. It was not until the late 1920's and in the 1930's that there appeared a group of young Slovak communist intellectuals, known, after their review *Dav* (*The Masses*), as the Davisti,[57] who were rooted in the country. However, the Davists did not rise to influence in the party until World War II or after.

SLOVAK POLITICAL DEVELOPMENT

While the struggle between the political right and left was the basic feature of Czech politics, the fundamental issue of Slovak politics was centralism versus autonomy and its cultural concomitant, Czechoslovak unity versus Slovak distinctness ("one nation or two?").

The Slovak populist leader Andrej Hlinka was outraged by the obliteration of Slovakia's identity in the constitution of 1920, and regarded the county system provided for by the constitution as a poor substitute for it. He refused to be bound by the vote of his party in the constituent assembly (taken during his imprisonment), and demanded the revision of the constitution. Slovak autonomy on the basis of the Pittsburgh agreement became the alpha and omega of his policy to the end of the First Republic.

After the elections in 1920, the Slovak and Czech populist parties formed a joint parliamentary club in the National Assembly. Catholicism and their common hostility to centralism formed the principal bonds between them. However, personal and political differences between Šrámek

---

[57] Viera Rybárová (ed.), *Dav: Spomienky a štúdie* [*Dav: Recollections and Studies*] (Bratislava, 1965), *passim*. The best known of the Davists was Vladimír Clementis (1902-52), who was elected to the National Assembly in 1935. After World War II he served as foreign minister (1948-50). During the witch-hunt against the Titoists (nationalist communists), he was arrested, tried for "bourgeois nationalism," and hanged in 1952. A very junior member of the Davist group was Gustáv Husák, the present Secretary-General of the Czechoslovak Communist party.

and Hlinka soon strained the relations between the two parties. Šrámek would have been content with a moderate administrative autonomy in the provinces. Hlinka insisted on legislative autonomy. In September, 1921, when Beneš formed a cabinet he invited the Catholic bloc to participate in it. Šrámek felt that he could protect Catholic interests better inside the government than in the opposition, and eagerly accepted Beneš's offer. Hlinka went along reluctantly and supported the government. On November 26, however, after Šrobár who was minister of education in the Beneš cabinet went back on a promise of his predecessor in the Černý cabinet to restore three gymnasia in Slovakia to the Catholics, Hlinka angrily pulled his party out of the joint populist club and went into the opposition. His break with Šrámek was quite acrimonious, and was never healed.[58] In January, 1922, the Slovak populists introduced their first bill for Slovak autonomy on the basis of the Pittsburgh agreement in the National Assembly.[59] It was overwhelmingly defeated, but Hlinka was undaunted.

The most centralist of the Czechoslovak parties was the Social Democratic party. In Slovakia it subordinated its social and economic goals to its political goals of promoting centralism and the principle of Czechoslovak unity. "There is no Slovak question," declared *Robotnické noviny*, the organ of the party's Slovak branch, in 1922. "It was solved once for all at the moment when Austria-Hungary was broken up and the Czechoslovak Republic established. . . . The problems of the Slovak people are completely identical with those of the Czech people. There is no difference between them, whether socially or economically."[60] Actually, owing to a thousand years of different history and the unenlightened Hungarian rule over the Slovaks, there were profound, social, economic, and cultural differences between them and the Czechs. The party's refusal to recognize this manifest fact prevented it from playing a constructive role in Slovak affairs.

Ivan Dérer (1884-), the leader of the Slovak branch of the Social Democratic party, not only dominated the party's tactics in Slovakia but also played an important role in its national leadership. A blunt, ener-

---

[58] *Národní shromáždění, 1918-1928*, p. 1138; Miloš Trapl, *Politika českého katolicismu na Moravě, 1918-1938* [*The Politics of the Czech Catholics in Moravia, 1918-1938*] (Prague, 1968), p. 24; Karol Sidor, *Slovenská politika na pôde pražského snemu* [*Slovak Politics in the Prague Parliament*] (2 vols.; Bratislava, 1943), I, 178-83. Šrámek's parting words to Hlinka were a threat: "We shall return to Slovakia!" Indeed, the Czech populists put up candidates in Slovakia in the parliamentary elections in 1925, and succeeded in electing one, Martin Mičura, the former minister for the administration of Slovakia. He was reelected to the National Assembly until 1938.

[59] Sidor, *Slovenská politika*, pp. 186-87.

[60] Quoted in Zdenka Holotíková, "Niektoré problémy slovenskej politiky v rokoch 1921-1925" ["Some Problems of Slovak Politics in 1921-1925"], *Historický časopis*, XIV (1966), 440.

getic, and courageous man, he was usually one of the Social Democratic ministers in the cabinet. A Budapest-trained lawyer, he retained from his student days a deep and abiding dislike for the Hungarian gentry and everything they stood for. Fear of Hungarian revisionism was the master motive of his policy. Paradoxically, he never quite lost the imprint of his Hungarian education, whether in his manner or narrow social outlook. A Hlasist before the war, he joined the party only in 1919, because it supported the principle of Czechoslovak unity most uncompromisingly. He was not a Marxist, and never took an interest in the party's social and economic goals. In 1920, when the party split and the left wing formed the Czechoslovak Communist party, he fought the communists. However, he regarded them as a smaller threat to Czechoslovakia than the Slovak autonomists, whom he took to be witting or unwitting tools of Hungarian revisionism. Like Šrobár, he had little confidence in the wisdom and patriotism of the Slovak people[61] and believed that only their total merger with the Czechs could save them. Appointed minister for the administration of Slovakia in the second Tusar cabinet, he exceeded even Šrobár in the zeal with which he combated the remnant of Hungarian influence in Slovakia and promoted Czechoslovak unity. However, it apparently never occurred to him that the best way to bind the Slovak people to the Czechoslovak Republic might have been to try to solve their social and economic grievances. His party's calamitous defeat in Slovakia in 1925 did not change his views one whit. Doctrinaire and inflexible, Dérer was the most consistent of the major Slovak politicians—and also the most inept.[62]

The attitude of the Slovak agrarian party toward the issue of centralism or autonomy was at first ambiguous. Šrobár opposed Slovak auton-

[61] In 1924, Dérer wrote that "when the World War broke out the broad masses of the Slovak people . . . lacked not only all national, but even general human consciousness." See Ivan Dérer, *Slovensko v prevate a po ňom* [*Slovakia during and after the Revolution*] (Bratislava, 1924), p. 2. Dérer's opinion of the Slovak people after the war was scarcely better. Speaking in the National Assembly on November 21, 1922, he declared: "All Slovak classes are at present inferior to Czech classes. It is impossible to conceal the fact that the present Slovak generation is inferior to the present Czech generation . . . in no civilized state are there so many incompetent people in positions of importance as in Slovakia." See Sidor, *Slovenská politika*, I, 219. Apart from being impolitic, such statements were inherently unjust. The Slovaks were only too painfully aware of their inferiority in relations to the Czechs. However, there were good historical reasons for it. To have their inferiority flung in their faces by one of their own, without explaining the reason for it, offended Slovak nationalist opinion past forgiveness. Dérer was unquestionably the most unpopular of the major Slovak politicians. By his tactlessness, he largely defeated his political purpose.

[62] During the Czechoslovak "springtime" in 1968, Dérer, who was by then a venerable octogenarian, completely unknown to the younger generation of Czechs and Slovaks, emerged from retirement like a ghost out of the past to denounce Czechoslovakia's projected federalization, which was among the reforms discussed and adopted in that hectic year.

omy in any form. However, his influence in the party began to decline after the elections of 1920. Hodža, whose influence in the party increased, wavered on the issue in rhythm with the ebb and flow of politics. The Slovak agrarians were disappointed with the results of the 1920 elections, which reduced them to parity with the Slovak populists. Each now had 12 seats in the Chamber of Deputies, while the Social Democrats had 23. After the elections the Slovak and Czech agrarian parties formed a joint parliamentary club. Švehla urged the Slovaks to merge the two parties into one. Combined, the party would have 40 seats in the Chamber of Deputies, and might exceed the Social Democratic party in size if the developing split in the latter materialized. This would give Švehla a chance at the premiership. However, Hodža resisted the suggestion, because in a combined party he would have been reduced to the position of a leader of a small regional section of the party (12 seats out 40). Instead of merger with the Czech agrarians, he toyed with the idea of forming a Slovak agrarian-populist bloc, which would have been the strongest Slovak group (24 seats). Tusar had excluded Hodža from his second cabinet. As the leader of the strongest Slovak group (Hodža assumed—perhaps over optimistically—that Hlinka would yield the group's leadership to him), Hodža could not be kept out of the government for very long.

In the constituent assembly, Hodža had strongly supported the passage of the county law.[63] After the 1920 elections, however, he came out in favor of Slovak administrative autonomy and the formation of a Slovak county union, which would have partially restored Slovakia's identity.[64] Hlinka, however, insisted on a firm commitment to Slovak political autonomy (i.e., one with a provincial legislative diet), which Hodža was neither willing nor able to make. It would have taken the Slovak agrarian-populist bloc into the opposition. Hodža was determined to prevent this, because his whole purpose was to get into the cabinet, not stay out of it. As a government party, the Slovak agrarian party was the principal beneficiary of government largess in Slovakia, which was an advantage that Hodža was not prepared to forsake. In January, 1921, the agrarian-populist negotiations to form a bloc ended in failure.[65]

Some of the old leaders of the former Slovak National party, who favored Slovak autonomy and disliked the agrarian principle pushed by Hodža, then withdrew from the agrarian party. In March, 1921, they reestablished the Slovak National party. Consisting of conservative Protestants for the most part, the new Slovak National party was averse to

[63] Sidor, *Slovenská politika*, I, 146-47 and 153-54.

[64] Ibid., pp. 158-59.

[65] Vladimír Zuberec, "Príspevok k dejinám vzniku agrárnej strany na Slovensku, 1918-1921" ["A Contribution to the History of the Origin of the Agrarian Party in Slovakia, 1918-1921"], *Historický časopis*, XV (1967), 597.

combining with the Slovak Populist party (because of the latter's Catholicism) and too small to stand alone. Therefore, it joined the parliamentary club of the Czech National Democrats.[66]

When Beneš failed to include Hodža in his cabinet in September, 1921, Hodža became amenable to Švehla's proposal for the merger of the Czech and Slovak agrarian parties. It was carried out in June, 1922. The new party assumed the name Czechoslovak Republican Party of Farmers and Peasants. The merger committed the Slovak agrarians to support centralism, which some of them did sincerely and others opportunistically. In October, when Švehla formed his first cabinet, he included Hodža in it as minister of agriculture. Hodža, however, who retained control of the Slovak contingent in the new party, never quite discarded the possibility of coming to an understanding with Hlinka. A very pragmatic politician, he liked to keep many options open.

The Švehla cabinet took the initiative in implementing the constitutional Law of Counties and Districts, which had been left in abeyance since its adoption in February, 1920. The law was only a *loi-cadre*, the content of which it remained to spell out in appropriate government decrees. Fear lest the national minorities, and also the Slovaks and Ruthenians, abuse self-government to undermine the unity of the Czechoslovak state led the government to circumscribe the jurisdiction of the county and district assemblies rather strictly and to put them under close bureaucratic controls. Moreover, for a period of twenty years, until 1940, the government reserved to itself the right to appoint one third of their members and also the right to appoint the county and district chiefs, who had large police powers. To prevent the border counties from becoming bastions of the national minorities, the government tried to gerrymander their boundaries in such a manner as to combine in each some Czech population with German in the Czech provinces and Slovak or Ruthenian population with Hungarian in Slovakia and Ruthenia.[67] Unlike the old Hungarian counties in Slovakia and Ruthenia which were small, natural geographic units, the new counties were rather large and unwieldy units.

Nevertheless, if gradually liberalized, the county system might have provided a manageable outlet for the cultural particularism and special educational needs of the national minorities, as well as the Slovaks and Ruthenians. However, the system encountered the opposition of nationalistic Czechs, who objected to the fact that two of the counties

[66] Natalia Krajčovičová, "Slovenská národná strana pod vedením Dr. Emila Stodolu, 1921-1922" ["The Slovak National Party under the Leadership of Dr. Emil Stodola"], *Historický časopis*, XVIII (1970), 17-38.

[67] Ladislav Lipscher, *K vývinu politickej správy na Slovensku, 1918-1938* [*The Development of Political Administration in Slovakia, 1918-1938*] (Bratislava, 1966), pp. 101-10; Peroutka, *Budování státu*, III, 1596-97.

would have German majorities. The National Democrats interposed their veto in the Pětka against the application of the county system in the Czech provinces. Consequently, it was introduced in October, 1922, in Slovakia and Ruthenia only.[68] This created a dualism in the Czechoslovak administration, which was exactly what Švehla had tried to prevent in the constitution. The county system thus failed to satisfy anyone and was discarded before long.

In March, 1922, Hlinka appointed Prof. Béla (Vojtech) Tuka (1880-1947) editor-in-chief of his party's organ, *Slovák*. Tuka, formerly a professor in the Hungarian Law Academy in Bratislava, was born in Slovakia of Hungarian parents and was a Hungarian by education. In 1919, when Czechoslovak forces occupied Bratislava the faculty of the law school left for Hungary. However, Tuka stayed behind—apparently at the suggestion of Prof. František Jehlička, whom Šrobár had appointed commissioner of the Law Academy. Jehlička held before Tuka the prospect of receiving an important position in the projected new Slovak university at Bratislava. When Tuka failed to get an appointment, he became a paid agent of Hungarian revisionist propaganda in Slovakia.[69] Under his direction *l'udák* propaganda acquired a venomous anti-Czech, anti-Protestant, and increasingly also anti-democratic edge. Many Slovaks, even within the Slovak Populist party, began to suspect Tuka's true allegiance. However, out of misguided loyalty, Hlinka defended him through thick and thin. Dérer was so upset by Tuka's activity and Hlinka's defense of him that he came to regard the Slovak Populist party as a tool of Hungarian revisionism. Tuka became his *bête noire* and the destruction of the Slovak Populist party his *idée fixe*. Actually, despite the shelter offered in the Slovak Populist party by Hlinka to men like Jehlička and Tuka, it was an authentic Slovak nationalist party. What was more suspect than its Slovak nationalism was its devotion to democratic principles. An ominous portent of its future course was the appearance of black-shirted guards, the Rodobrana (Home Defense), at party rallies in 1923, to protect the speakers and silence hecklers. Organized by Tuka, the Rodobrana was unpleasantly similar to the Italian fascist *squadristi*.[70]

From the beginning of the Czechoslovak Republic, the Slovak centralists and autonomists engaged in ardent polemics over the issue of "one nation or two," often with the aid of elaborate historical and philological

[68] Peroutka, *Budování státu*, III, 1595.

[69] Juraj Kramer, *Iredenta a separatizmus v slovenskej politike, 1919-1938* [*Irredentism and Separatism in Slovak Politics, 1919-1938*] (Bratislava, 1957), pp. 62-72; Ivan Dérer, *Slovenský vývoj a luďácká zrada* [*The Slovak Development and the Luďák Betrayal*] (Prague, 1946), pp. 19-57.

[70] Juraj Kramer, *Slovenské autonomistické hnutie v rokoch 1918-1929* [*The Slovak Autonomist Movement in 1918-1929*] (Bratislava, 1962), pp. 312-18.

arguments. Above all, there was the "battle of the hyphen," that is, arguments over whether Czechoslovakia should be spelled with a hyphen, Czecho-Slovakia, as in the wartime documents and the peace treaties, or without it, as in the constitution. In December, 1923, when Kramář chided the Slovak populists in the National Assembly for straying away from the principle of Czechoslovak unity to which Hlinka had subscribed in the Martin Declaration, they replied by reading a solemn declaration formally repudiating the principle of Czechoslovak unity and affirming that of Slovak distinctness.[71]

By then the Slovak autonomists and centralists were scarcely on speaking terms. Any proposal by one would produce, as if by conditioned reflex, a repudiation by the other. Essentially, they denied each other the character of Slovaks. The Czech politicians, incidentally, maintained a prudent reserve toward the conflict. Although largely products of Austrian training, they never tried to emulate Habsburg practice by playing the Slovak factions off against each other. Instead, sincerely believing that the centralists alone represented authentic Slovak opinion, the Czech politicians steadfastly backed them. They themselves, however, rarely interfered in the conflict. Direct Czech-Slovak confrontations, whether in the press or the parliament, were rare. Contrary to an impression widely spread abroad, the supposed Czecho-Slovak conflict was largely one between two Slovak political factions, not between Czech and Slovak politicians, let alone the Czech and Slovak peoples as a whole.

BREAKUP OF THE ALL-NATIONAL COALITION

In 1919, when the first local elections were held, the National Assembly set the term of city and communal councils at three years. Therefore, the second local elections were due in 1922. Because of the social restlessness that attended the economic crisis of 1922-23, however, the government parties feared to face the electoral contest. The Social Democrats, notably, were apprehensive about their first confrontation with the communists, who demagogically fanned popular discontent over the difficult economic situation. While the Pětka endlessly discussed the situation, the government delayed the elections until September 16, 1923. Unlike the first local elections in 1919 which were held only in the Czech provinces, the second local elections were held throughout the country. Two weeks later, on September 30, elections into the county assemblies were also held, but these were limited to Slovakia and Ruthenia.

The apprehensions of the Social Democrats proved well warranted. Although the government permitted publication of only partial results

[71] Sidor, *Slovenská politika*, I, 238.

of the local elections, they could not conceal the seriousness of the Social Democratic defeat.[72] The communists made deep inroads into former Social Democratic territory. On the other hand, the (National) Socialists appeared to hold their own, and the Czech populists gained considerable strength. In Slovakia, where the complete results of the county elections were published, the Slovak populists likewise made impressive gains.[73] The agrarians merely held their own, in both the Czech provinces and Slovakia. Nevertheless, as a result of the division of the Social Democratic party, the agrarians became the largest party.

The government stated that the results of the local and county elections would not affect the relationship of the parties in the National Assembly. Inevitably, however, by providing clues as to where the parties stood in the graces of the electorate, these results affected the parties' standing on the national level, too. The agrarians, whose self-assurance was strengthened by the knowledge that they were the largest party, began to press for the adoption of high tariffs on the imports of farm products. They justified their demand by the fact that the farmers were beginning to suffer acutely from the slump in the world prices of farm products. On the other hand, the Social Democrats began to press for the adoption of a comprehensive social security legislation to recover grace with their electorate. They were supported in this demand by the (National) Socialists. On October 30, 1924, after tortuous negotiations in the Pětka, the National Assembly passed the Social Insurance Law, which associated the Czechoslovak health insurance system with the invalidity and old-age insurance.[74] The law, which went into effect in 1926, provided for a social welfare system which was at the time among the most progressive in the world.

The agrarians had backed the passage of the Social Insurance Law and expected that, in return, the Social Democrats and (National) Socialists would back their demand for a protective farm tariff. However, a protective farm tariff would result in the rise of food prices. The Social Democrats and (National) Socialists, who considered themselves protectors of the consumer classes, declined to support it. The agrarians felt that they had been duped. In June, 1925, they secured—against socialist opposition—adoption of a government decree which provided for a tariff with a sliding scale on imports of farm products. The tariff fluctuated according to the prices of farm products on the domestic market.[75] The agrarian decision to impose the measure without the consent of the

[72] Peroutka, *Budování státu*, v, 2839-44; for the results of the communal elections in the principal Czech and Slovak cities, see Olivová, *Politika*, pp. 105-106.
[73] For the results of the county elections in Slovakia, see Lipscher, *K vývinu*, p. 114.
[74] *Národní shromáždění, 1918-1928*, p. 314; *Přehled*, III, 228-29.
[75] *Přehled*, III, 230; *Národní shromáždění, 1918-1928*, p. 315.

socialist parties shattered the all-national coalition and made the holding of parliamentary elections inevitable.

Another factor that contributed to the dissolution of the all-national coalition was the disapproval of the Czech Populist party of the official participation of President Masaryk and the majority of the cabinet at the July 6, 1925, commemoration of the burning of John Hus at the stake. This tribute to a "heretic" in a predominantly Catholic country caused the papal nuncio, Francesco Marmaggi, to leave Prague demonstratively. The Czechoslovak government answered the gesture by breaking off diplomatic relations with the Vatican.[76] The Catholic parties in Czechoslovakia naturally disapproved. Believing that it would come out of an electoral contest strengthened, the Czech Populist party asked for the holding of parliamentary elections.

The results of the parliamentary elections, which were held on November 15, 1925, confirmed the trend indicated in the local and county elections in 1923.[77] The Social Democrats dropped from the first to the fourth place among the parties, receiving only 8.9 percent of the vote (compared with 25.7 percent in 1920) and only 29 seats in the Chamber of Deputies (compared with 74 in 1920). The agrarians became the largest party, although their gain in votes was small (0.5 percent). They received 13.7 percent of the vote and 46 seats in the lower house. The communists emerged as the second largest party, with 13.2 percent of the vote and 41 seats in the Chamber of Deputies. Because of deep internal dissension, however, their victory was not as great as they had hoped or their opponents had feared. The real winners were the Czech populists, who moved up from 7.5 percent of the vote in 1920 to 9.7 percent and received 31 seats in the lower house. The (National) Socialists slightly improved their position (8.6 percent of the vote and 28 seats). The decay of the National Democrats moved apace; they dropped to seventh place among the parties, with only 5 percent of the vote and 14 seats.

Among the German parties the same trend as among the Czechoslovak parties was evident. The agrarians replaced the Social Democrats as the largest German party; the Catholic Christian Socials improved their position; and the nationalist parties held their own. In Slovakia the Slovak populists swept to a great victory, receiving 34.3 percent of the vote and 23 seats and emerging as the largest Slovak party. The Social Demo-

---

[76] *Národní shromáždění, 1918-1928*, pp. 315-19; Trapl, *Politika*, pp. 34-35; Šolle and Gajanová, *Po stopě dějin*, pp. 256-57.

[77] *Národní shromáždění, 1918-1928*, pp. 337-38; *Přehled*, III, 233-34; Buchválek, *Dějiny*, pp. 466-68; *Československá vlastivěda*, V, 458-60; for electoral results in Slovakia, see Macartney, *Hungary*, p. 118.

crats were all but wiped out (4.3 percent of the vote and 2 seats). The agrarians held their own (19.9 percent of the vote and 12 seats). The communists did about as well in Slovakia (13.2 percent of the vote) as in the Czech provinces, and in Ruthenia became the largest party (30.8 percent of the vote). The Hungarian Social Democratic party disappeared in Slovakia, most of its former members being absorbed into the Communist party and a small remainder of moderates into the Czechoslovak Social Democratic party. The Hungarian and German national, agrarian, and Catholic parties in Slovakia scored together 16.1 percent of the vote and received 9 seats in the Chamber of Deputies.

As a result principally of the Social Democratic losses, the all-national coalition failed to secure a majority in the new National Assembly. Švehla, therefore, broadened it by including in it the Tradesmen's party, and on December 12 recast his cabinet to reflect the new distribution of party strength.[78] He was unable to appease the growing quarrel between the parties in the coalition, however. Reassured by the electoral results, the agrarians raised a demand for high and fixed tariffs on grain and other farm products. Emboldened by their electoral victory, the Czech populists presented a demand for government salaries (*congrua*) to the clergy. To both of these demands, the socialist parties were adamantly opposed. Ill health and his inability to break the impasse between the parties in the coalition led Švehla to resign on March 18, 1926. The all-national coalition, and temporarily also the Pětka, came to an end.

THE ČERNÝ INTERREGNUM

To replace the Švehla cabinet, President Masaryk asked Jan Černý again to form a nonparty cabinet of officials, which was to serve as a stopgap until a new coalition was formed.[79] Engliš reappeared in it as finance minister, and Beneš continued in it as foreign minister—despite the fact that he had been a political minister since 1923. The Černý cabinet remained in office until October 12, 1926.

In the meantime, a search for a new coalition went on. Since 1918 all the government coalitions had been based on the "national" principle, that is, they comprised Czech and Slovak parties only. This reflected the initial fears of the Czech and Slovak political leaders that unless they banded together, the national minorities might destroy the Czechoslovak state. By 1926, however, the consolidation of Czechoslovakia had pro-

---

[78] *Národní shromáždění, 1918-1928*, pp. 337-38; *Přehled*, III, 235; Buchválek, *Dějiny*, pp. 446-47.

[79] Buchválek, *Dějiny*, p. 447; *Národní shromáždění, 1918-1928*, p. 367; *Přehled*, III, 236.

gressed so far that the Czech and Slovak politicians began to view the possibility of including the parties of some of the national minorities in the government without fear.

Hodža made himself the spokesman of a move to form a center-right coalition, which would comprise—in addition to the agrarians, the Czech populists, and the National Democrats—representatives of the Slovak populists and the German agrarians (*Bund der Landwirte*) and the German Christian Socials.[80] The proposal reminded some of Count Edward Taaffe's celebrated "Iron Ring" in the 1880's, which was also a coalition of conservative and clerical parties and the parties of the national minorities in old Austria.

Not unnaturally, the Social Democrats and the (National) Socialists, who had been members of every government coalition since 1918, deeply resented the proposal to form a government without them. What was worse, President Masaryk was opposed to it. He believed that the most stable cabinet was one based on a balance of right and left parties. He did not oppose the inclusion of German or other minority parties in the government. As a matter of fact, he had advocated it for some time. However, he felt that the inclusion of the German agrarians and clericals should be balanced by the inclusion of the German Social Democrats in the coalition.

Švehla, who had originally proposed the right-center coalition, favored it for practical reasons: he thought that it could secure the passage of the farm tariffs and the *congrua* in the National Assembly. However, he hesitated to press for it, because of the opposition of President Masaryk and the socialist leaders to it.[81] Although the illness which he gave as the reason for his resignation was unfortunately genuine, he resigned also because he did not wish to break with the president and the socialists, who were his old friends. After his resignation he went to Italy to rest, which left the affairs of the agrarian party largely in Hodža's hands. In the next few months, Hodža was perhaps the most influential and certainly the most active Czechoslovak politician. By ruthless power plays, rather than by the patient bargaining practiced by Švehla, he secured the passage of the farm tariffs and the *congrua* in the National Assembly in June, 1926.[82] The socialist parties, which had opposed these acts, were embittered.

With the end of the Pětka, the discipline that it imposed on the mem-

---

[80] Dušan Uhlíř, "Republikánská strana lidu zemědělského a malorolnického ve vládě panské koalice" ["The Republican Party of Farmers and Peasants in the Government of the Gentlemen's Coalition"], *Československý časopis historický*, XVIII (1970), 200-204.

[81] Ibid.

[82] *Národní shromáždění, 1918-1928*, p. 372; Trapl, *Politika*, p. 51; *Přehled*, III, 237.

bers of the former coalition also ended. Moreover, with their fear for the future of Czechoslovakia dissipated, Czech and Slovak politicians began to feel that they could afford the luxury of family quarrels again. Conflicts between, as well as within, the parties of the former all-national coalition, long suppressed out of national solidarity, came into the open. Even President Masaryk and Beneš did not escape criticism. Anti-Hrad[83] politicians, who were most numerous in the National Democratic and agrarian parties, cited the formation of the nonparty Černý cabinet as proof that Masaryk wanted to be an autocrat, ruling through disciplined appointed officials instead of through independent, elected representatives of the people. Those who did not dare to attack the president directly often made Beneš their whipping boy. Illogically, he was criticized at one and the same time for depending too much on the Western powers and the League of Nations for Czechoslovakia's security and for seeking friendly relations with the Soviet Union. Beneš's critics insisted that Czechoslovakia could establish relations with Moscow only when Russia became "Slavic" (i.e., noncommunist) again.[84] How and when Russia was going to purge itself of the sin of communist internationalism and become Slavic and nationalist again, they did not say.

The most intemperate in their attacks against the Hrad were the Czech fascists. In the spring of 1926 the leftist press reported that the fascists intended to overthrow the democratic constitution and establish a fascist dictatorship. The dictator was supposed to be the Chief of Staff of the Czechoslovak army, General Rudolf Gajda (Geidl) (1892-1945). Gajda had won fame as a colorful and adventurous commander in the Czechoslovak Legion in Russia during World War I, and was the darling of the extreme rightist and chauvinist Czech elements. The fascist coup was supposed to be carried out during the quadrennial congress of the "Falcon" (Sokol) gymnastic organization in Prague in July, which was expected to attract hundreds of thousands of people to the capital. On July 2, on Masaryk's insistence, General Gajda was relieved of his duties and retired from active service.[85] The Sokol congress, which opened a few days later, passed without any untoward event. The reports of the fascist plot had been greatly exaggerated. Apart from much loose talk on Gajda's part, no concrete evidence of fascist plans for a coup d'etat was ever disclosed.

With his military career ended, Gajda turned to politics. In January, 1927, the National Fascist Community (Národní obec fašistická) was

[83] For an explanation of the terms *Hrad* and anti-*Hrad*, see herein, Chapter II.
[84] Herben, *T. G. Masaryk*, pp. 382-84; Alena Gajanová, *Dvojí tvář: Z historie předmnichovského fašismu* [*Two-Face: History of Fascism before Munich*] (Prague, 1962), pp. 45-46.
[85] Šolle and Gajanová, *Po stopě dějin*, p. 263; Peroutka, *Budování státu*, v, 2821-24.

reorganized into a political party, and Gajda became its "leader" (*vůdce*). Czech fascism, however, lacked roots in the country; it was a grotesque imitation of foreign models.[86] Generally speaking, what made European fascist movements dynamic was offended or frustrated nationalism. Outrage or disappointment over the Paris peace settlement made Germany and Italy fascist breeding grounds. There was a close connection between fascism and the movement for the revision of the Paris peace treaties. However, Czechoslovakia was well satisfied with the Paris peace settlement. Czech fascism, therefore, had no *raison d'être*. It was an artificial creation, the main purpose of which was to serve the anti-Hrad politicians (who secretly subsidized it) as a mouthpiece—to say things against the Hrad which they themselves did not dare to say. However, socialist politicians also found it to be a convenient scarecrow —to create images of fascist plots and threats to the republic, from which supposedly only they, good republicans and democrats, could save the country.

Fascism found perhaps a more fertile soil in Slovakia and Ruthenia than in the Czech provinces. Slovak and Ruthenian nationalism had been deliberately and systematically outraged by the Magyars and was still occasionally unwittingly offended by the Czechs. Most Slovak elements that inclined toward fascism had been absorbed into the Slovak Populist party, in which they clustered around the person of Prof. Tuka. In the 1920's, however, the Slovak Populist party was still predominantly a conservative clerical party, not a radical fascist one.

The most dangerous attack against Beneš and his pro-Western policy, however, did not come from the fascists or their patrons in the National Democratic or agrarian parties, but from the anti-Hrad faction in his own party led by Jiří Stříbrný. In June, 1926, while Beneš was on a diplomatic mission abroad, the executive committee of the (National) Socialist party ordered him to resign from the cabinet, because the party was going to vote against the government bills for farm tariffs and the *congrua* in the National Assembly. The party could not very well remain represented in the government and vote against bills sponsored by it. On Masaryk's instructions, however, Beneš did not resign from the cabinet but from the party. Meanwhile, the pro-Hrad faction of the party led by Václav Klofáč mounted a counter-offensive. At the party's congress in Brno in September, the anti-Hrad faction was defeated. Stříbrný was expelled from the party and Beneš reentered it.[87] The party was reorganized and renamed *National* Socialist. Stříbrný, who was one of the re-

---

[86] On the origins of Czech fascism, see Peroutka, *Budování státu*, v, 2790-96; Gajanová, *Dvojí tvář*, pp. 30-34.

[87] *Národní shromáždění, 1918-1928*, p. 373 and pp. 1175-76; Šolle and Gajanová, *Po stopě dejin*, pp. 262-63.

spected "men of October 28" (i.e., cosigners of the declaration of independence), did not take his humiliation meekly. An influential publisher of two popular newspapers in Prague, he spent the rest of his career inspiring malicious intrigues and attacks against the Hrad.

THE GENTLEMEN'S COALITION

In September, 1926, Švehla returned to political activity. Hodža then began to promote a scheme to elect Švehla to the presidency in May, 1927, when Masaryk's term would expire.[88] Beneš, who was Masaryk's closest collaborator and heir-designate, was to be excluded from the candidacy and public life generally. The scheme, if successful, would permit Hodža to pick up the premiership or the foreign ministry or both. Švehla was personally loyal to Masaryk, however. He resolutely crushed Hodža's plan. According to one report, he threatened personally to "box the ears"[89] of any agrarian who would lend his support to it. On October 10 he formed a cabinet—his third—essentially along lines suggested by Hodža, except that it did not comprise the National Democrats and Slovak populists. Hodža was forced to content himself with the post of minister of education in Švehla's cabinet, which lasted until February 1, 1929.[90]

The inclusion of German parties in the government lessened tensions between the Czechs and the Germans. On the other hand, the exclusion of the Czechoslovak socialist parties from it created tensions between the political right and left in the Czechoslovak camp. The Social Democrats and the National Socialists were deeply incensed at being cut off from the spoils of power, to which they had become accustomed since 1918. They dubbed the new coalition a "gentlemen's coalition" (*panská koalice*), and subjected Hodža, whom they blamed for it (Švehla curiously escaped their anger almost completely), to an unprecedented campaign of vilification in the parliament and the press. They succeeded in enlisting the help in the campaign not only of the Slovak socialists Dérer and Hrušovský but also of Hodža's fellow-agrarian Šrobár. Hodža was accused of corruption; the aims of his Budapest mission in 1918 were raked over; and he was found to be a "camouflaged autonomist" masquerading as a centralist.[91]

[88] Uhlíř,."Republikánská strana," pp. 206-207.

[89] Šolle and Gajanová, *Po stopě dejin*, p. 266; Mořic Hruban, *Z časů nedlouho zašlých [Out of the Recent Past]* (Rome-Los Angeles, 1967), p. 223.

[90] *Národní shromáždění, 1918-1928*, pp. 375-76; Uhlíř, "Republikánská strana," pp. 210-11; Buchválek, *Dějiny*, p. 447.

[91] Uhlíř, "Republikánská strana," pp. 212-15. The publication of Šrobár's recollections, *Osvobodené Slovensko [Liberated Slovakia]* in 1928, in which he accused Hodža of dealing with the Hungarian politicians in Budapest and with the Czech

When Švehla formed his third cabinet, he invited the Slovak populists to join it. Hlinka agreed on condition that the constitutional law of the counties be repealed and the provinces be restored. Until this was assured, he delayed sending his representatives into the cabinet. It was not until January, 1927, that the Slovak populists, Father Jozef Tiso (1887-1947) and Marek Gažík, were appointed to the cabinet as minister of public health and minister of unification, respectively.[92]

On July 14, 1927, over the objections of the Social Democrats and the National Socialists, the National Assembly approved a government bill to amend the county law.[93] The counties were abolished and their functions were transferred to four provinces (Bohemia, Moravia-Silesia, Slovakia, and Ruthenia). The districts were retained. Like the counties earlier, the provinces had assemblies, two thirds of whose members were elected and one third appointed by the government. Their jurisdiction was much more restricted than that of the county assemblies, however. The provinces were presided over by "presidents," who were not elected but—as the county chiefs had been—appointed by the government from the ranks of the bureaucracy. At the same time, the office of minister for the administration of Slovakia, which had become a purely bureaucratic post as early as the formation of the first Černý cabinet in 1920, was abolished.

Hlinka rejoiced over the provincial law as a "first flash of autonomy."[94] Reflecting about it later, however, Beneš thought that it represented a "step backward." It introduced, he wrote, "powerless provincial assemblies that were supposed to create the impression that the administration was being decentralized when in fact it was being further centralized."[95]

Another measure designed partly to satisfy the populists, both Czech and Slovak, was the *modus vivendi* with the Vatican. Concluded by Beneš on January 20, 1928, it stipulated that in no part of Czechoslovakia were Catholics to be subject to the jurisdiction of Catholic bishops abroad. By making Catholic ecclesiastical boundaries coincide with those of Czechoslovakia, it removed the old grievance of the Slovak Catholics against being subordinated to the jurisdiction of the archbishop of

politicians in Vienna during the war, was a part of the campaign to discredit Hodža. Later Prof. Václav Chaloupecký fortified the charges against Hodža in his scholarly volume *Zápas o Slovensko* [*Struggle for Slovakia*] (1930).

[92] *Národní shromáždění, 1918-1928*, p. 380; Uhlíř, "Republikánská strana," p. 215; Sidor, *Slovenská politika*, I, 300.

[93] *Národní shromáždění, 1918-1928*, pp. 496-97; Lipscher, K vývinu, pp. 145-71; *Přehled*, III, 250-51; *Československá vlastivěda*, V, 146-48; Trapl, *Politika*, p. 54.

[94] Sidor, *Slovenská politika*, I, 309.

[95] Edvard Beneš, *Mnichovské dny: Paměti* [*The Days of Munich: Recollections*] (Prague, 1968), p. 10.

Esztergom in Hungary.[96] It also wound up Czechoslovakia's conflict with the Vatican over the official celebration of the John Hus anniversary in 1925.

On May 27, 1927, Masaryk was easily reelected president. He received 274 out of the 434 ballots cast. His only opponent, the communist candidate Václav Šturc, received 54 votes. The rest of the ballots were empty.[97] The Czech National Democrats, German nationalists, and Slovak populists abstained from voting. On the other hand, the German government parties, as well as the German Social Democrats, voted for Masaryk.

It is interesting that the go-between in the negotiations to bring the Slovak populists into the government coalition was not Hodža, who had originally suggested it. Hlinka did not trust him. Instead, it was Kramář, even though the National Democrats themselves were not in the government at the time. Kramář approved heartily of forming a coalition without the socialist parties. However, he had reservations about including the German parties in it, and delayed entering it until he was satisfied that the Germans behaved loyally and responsibly. It was not, therefore, until April, 1928, that the National Democrats sent their representative, Ladislav Novák, into the cabinet. By then the coalition was in an eclipse.

DECLINE OF THE GENTLEMEN'S COALITION

In October, 1927, Švehla suffered a heart attack and in March, 1928, another one. The second attack incapacitated him completely and—as events were to show—permanently.[98] The Czech populist leader Šrámek assumed the duties of premier *pro tempore* during his illness. Without Švehla's genius for conciliation and compromise, the coalition began to break up. President Masaryk disapproved of the center-right coalition, but had confidence in Švehla. He was content to leave matters in the premier's competent hands. After the breakdown of Švehla's health, however, the president began to take a more active part in Czechoslovak politics.

Slovak matters contributed in no small degree to the coalition's decline. The provincial law did not contribute to the appeasement of the quarrel between the Slovak centralists and autonomists. The former thought that it had gone too far and the latter that it had not gone far enough. Dérer and Igor Hrušovský, the leaders of the Slovak branches of the Social Democratic and National Socialist parties, respectively,

---

[96] *Československá vlastivěda*, v, 341; Trapl, *Politika*, pp. 52-53; Sidor, *Slovenská politika*, I, 352-54.

[97] *Národní shromáždění, 1918-1928*, p. 331; Herben, *T. G. Masaryk*, pp. 391-92; *Přehled*, III, 261; Buchválek, *Dějiny*, p. 311.

[98] Uhlíř, "Republikánská strana," p. 218.

were also outraged to see the despised *ľudáks* (populists) ensconce themselves in the government and gain access to the spoils of power, while they, good Czechoslovak centralists, were left out in the cold. They did their best to discredit the government coalition.[99] On the other hand, the populists did not noticeably tone down their autonomist propaganda after entering the coalition. Partly, it was because the communists tried to steal this aim from them. In 1926, when the populists indicated their readiness to join the government, the communists made themselves loud champions of "revolutionary" autonomy in Slovakia and Ruthenia.[100]

On New Year's Day, 1928, Tuka published an article in *Slovák* entitled "Ten Years after the Martin Declaration," in which he alleged that the declaration contained a secret clause limiting Czechoslovak sovereignty in Slovakia to ten years, and, consequently, that there would be what he designated a *"vacuum juris"* in Slovakia after October 30, 1928.[101] The article, which was based on a distorted version of discussions in the Slovak National Council on the morrow of the issuance of the Martin Declaration,[102] caused a sensation in Slovakia and much jubilation in the Hungarian revisionist press. It increased Slovak apprehen-

[99] Dérer, *Slovenský vývoj*, pp. 125-26; Sidor, *Slovenská politika*, I, 319.

[100] See Bohumír Šmeral's speech in the National Assembly on December 18, *Slovenská politika*, I, p. 284. For recent discussions of communist policy toward the Slovaks, see Lipták, *Slovensko*, pp. 140-42, and Miloš Gosiorovsky, "K niektorým otázkam vzťahu Čechov a Slovákov v politike Komunistickej strany Československa" ["Some Aspects of the relations of the Czechs and Slovaks in the Politics of the Communist Party of Czechoslovakia"], *Historický časopis*, XVI (1968), 359-65.

[101] Dérer, *Slovenský vývoj*, pp. 130-31; Sidor, *Slovenská politika*, I, 320-22; Kramer, *Slovenské autonomistické hnutie*, pp. 411-15.

[102] On October 31, 1918, on the morrow of issuing the Martin Declaration, the executive committee of the Slovak National Council met to discuss Slovakia's future status in the Czechoslovak state. Most of the participants in the discussion felt that Slovak autonomy was desirable, but all agreed that the Slovaks were not yet ready for it. There would have to be, they felt, a transitional period during which Slovakia should be ruled in a "dictatorial" manner. At the end of the discussion an obscure resolution was passed: ". . . after a transitional period of no longer than ten years, the legal status [*štátoprávny pomer*] of the branch of our nation now living in Hungary will be settled by the legal representatives of Slovakia, on one hand, and of Bohemia, Moravia, and Silesia, on the other. This resolution is to be spread among the people." See Martin Grečo, *Martinská deklarácia* [*The Martin Declaration*] (2nd ed.; Turčiansky Svätý Martin, 1947), p. 168, and Natalia Krajčovičova, "Slovenská národná rada roku 1918" ["The Slovak National Council in 1918"], *Historický časopis*, XVII (1969), 180-81. The resolution, however, was not immediately published, because the Slovak National Council was dispersed by the Hungarian authorities in November, 1918, and abolished altogether by Šrobár in January, 1919. As minister for the administration of Slovakia, Šrobár tended to treat the Slovak National Council, of which he was formally a member, as some sort of aberration, and drew a veil of official secrecy over its activities. The council's resolution was not published until August 21, 1929, in the Slovak populist organ *Slovák*. Until then it was known only by rumor.

sion aroused in 1927 by the campaign of the English press magnate Lord Rothermere to revise the Trianon treaty. The falsehood of Tuka's allegations could have been easily exposed by opening the records of the Slovak National Council, which Šrobár had impounded in 1919 when he abolished the council, to public scrutiny. However, whether out of bureaucratic inertia or through political design, this was not done.

Dérer and Hrušovský accused Tuka of treason in the National Assembly, and demanded the lifting of his parliamentary immunity (he had been elected deputy in 1925) so that he might stand trial.[103] However, since the Slovak populists were members of the government coalition the government hesitated to move against him—until the elections into the provincial assemblies on December 2, 1928, revealed a sharp drop in Slovak populist strength. The party lost about 168,000 votes, compared with the results of the parliamentary elections in 1925.[104] The other government parties did not do too well, either. The agrarians lost in Bohemia and Moravia and gained in Slovakia and Ruthenia, coming out of the elections with a very slight net gain. The Czech populists remained the strongest party in Moravia but suffered a net loss. Altogether, the government parties won only 47.7 percent of the vote. On the other hand, the opposition National Socialists considerably improved their position and the Social Democrats made a remarkable comeback.[105] Inevitably, the socialist parties raised the cry that the government had lost the confidence of the electorate and should resign, after providing for general elections. However, acting Premier Šrámek declared that the results of the provincial elections had no bearing on the standing of the parties in the National Assembly, and that the government had no intention of resigning and holding parliamentary elections.[106] Despite his bland disclaimer, however, the provincial elections did affect national politics.

The results of the provincial elections convinced President Masaryk that the government coalition had outlived its usefulness and should be replaced with one that would include the socialist parties. This was not a simple matter to arrange. In December, 1928, and the next few months Masaryk and his supporters became very active. By coincidence, on the

[103] Kramer, *Slovenské autonomistické hnutie*, pp. 417-19; Sidor, *Slovenská politika*, I, 320.

[104] Sidor, *Slovenská politika*, 343; Lipscher, *K vývinu*, p. 169.

[105] Předsednictvo poslanecké sněmovny a Předsednictvo senátu, *Národní shromáždění Republiky československé v druhém desitiletí, 1928-1938* [*The National Assembly of the Czechoslovak Republic in the Second Decade, 1928-1938*] (Prague, 1938), pp. 58-59 (hereafter *Národní shromáždění, 1928-1938*); *Přehled*, III, 261-62.

[106] *Národní shromáždění, 1928-1938*, p. 59; Uhlíř, "Republikánská strana," p. 229.

day of the provincial elections, a sharp conflict broke out again between Beneš and the right-wing agrarians and National Democrats.[107] Masaryk tried to take Švehla's place as the great conciliator and mediate the conflict—a task for which he had little talent. He was by nature a fighter, not a conciliator.

Since the agrarians remained the largest party and would be the kingpin in the future coalition, it was necessary to find a successor to Švehla, to lead the party and serve as prime minister. The latest *passe d'armes* between Beneš and his right-wing critics had strong anti-Hrad overtones and underscored the necessity of finding a man in whom the president could have confidence and with whom he could cooperate. In the end, Masaryk's choice fell on František Udržal, the minister of national defense in Beneš's cabinet and in Švehla's first and third cabinets.[108] A gentleman farmer like Švehla, Udržal was an experienced politician and an able administrator, who had done a very good job in building up the Czechoslovak army. He was not a creative statesman. However, Masaryk did not want an idea man as premier but a man loyal to him—one who would execute his will faithfully. For such a role Udržal was admirably suited. His attitude toward the president was one of soldierly obedience.[109]

The anti-Hrad right-wing agrarians accepted Udržal reluctantly, largely because they resented Šrámek's occupying the office of premier and were anxious to recover it for the agrarians as soon as possible. They helped to persuade Švehla to resign. On February 1, President Masaryk appointed Udržal to succeed him. Udržal retained Švehla's cabinet without a change.[110] He himself retained the post of minister of national defense. The Slovak populists remained in the cabinet. However, on February 20, Hodža was abruptly dismissed from it by a presidential decree, for interfering in foreign affairs.[111] By his ambition and ruthlessness, he had an-

---

[107] Uhlíř, "Republikánská strana," pp. 230-32.

[108] Dušan Uhlíř, "Konec vlády panské koalice a Republikánská strana v roce 1929" ["The End of the Gentlemen's Coalition Government and the Republican Party in 1929"], *Československý časopis historický*, XVIII (1970), 553.

[109] Ibid., 554-55.

[110] Ibid., 582n.; *Národní shromáždění, 1928-1938*, pp. 61 and 63; Buchválek, *Dějiny*, pp. 447-48.

[111] As a part of building up the Peasant or "Green" International (the organization of agrarian parties of East Central Europe with headquarters in Prague), Hodža subsidized Radič's Croat Peasant party in Yugoslavia and Stambulisky's Peasant party in Bulgaria. Since both parties were in opposition, Hodža's action complicated Beneš's task of maintaining friendly relations with the Yugoslav and Bulgarian governments. The immediate reason for Hodža's dismissal was the protest of the Yugoslav government against his arranging a meeting between Ramsay MacDonald, the former British prime minister, and the Croat Peasant party leaders in Prague in October, 1928. See Uhlíř, "Konec vlády," pp. 556-59; Jozef F. Rudinský, *Československý štát a Slovenská Republika* [*The Czechoslovak State and the Slovak Republic*] (Munich, 1969), p. 150.

tagonized not only President Masaryk and Beneš and the socialist parties but also the left wing of his own party. He took his disgrace without protest and bided his time. He still controlled the Slovak wing of the party, without which the party would have lost its place as the largest party and the right to the premiership. With Šrobár's aid, the pro-Hrad agrarians tried to wrest control of the Slovak wing from Hodža, but he easily outmaneuvered Šrobár and remained the undisputed leader of the Slovak agrarians.

In the meantime, President Masaryk and his advisers decided to stage political trials of Tuka and Gajda—the former as a way of discrediting the Slovak populists and the latter as a way of discrediting the National Democrats and the right-wingers in the agrarian party. This would likely bring about the downfall of the gentlemen's coalition and pave the way for the return of a balanced left-right coalition, which Masaryk preferred.[112] On December 20, 1928, the National Assembly lifted Tuka's immunity and early in January, 1929, he was arrested on charges of treason and military espionage. His trial began on May 28 and lasted into the autumn. Hlinka, who was completely convinced of Tuka's innocence, professed to welcome the trial. When Hlinka's old companions, the Catholic priests Ferdiš Juriga and Florian Tománek, who believed in Tuka's guilt, insisted that the party wash its hands of him, Hlinka had them summarily expelled from the party.[113] At about the time of Tuka's arrest Gajda was also indicted for military espionage. On June 19 he was convicted—implausibly—of selling French military secrets to Soviet Russia. He was cashiered from the army and sentenced to two months of imprisonment.

The division between the agrarian right and left wings was widened at the party's congress in Prague on May 7 and 8. Švehla, around whom there had grown up a strong personality cult, was reelected party chairman—despite the evident fact that he was too ill to fill the function. Owing to his disability, the chairman's policy-making powers tended to devolve on the party secretary, whose function was originally mainly administrative. The party secretary was Rudolf Beran, an anti-Hrad right-winger.[114] However, the importance of this development did not become apparent until later.

On September 19, Udržal relinquished the post of minister of national defense to another agrarian, which provoked a sharp quarrel between the agrarians and the Czech populists. Šrámek protested that it upset the "party balance" in the cabinet. On September 25, after the failure of the

---

[112] Uhlíř, "Konec vlády," pp. 571, 575-76.

[113] Sidor, *Slovenská politika*, I, 345; *Národní shromáždění, 1928-1938*, pp. 68-69.

[114] *Národní shromáždění, 1928-1938*, p. 830; Uhlíř, "Konec vlády," pp. 564-70.

parties to agree, Udržal dissolved the National Assembly and called for new elections.[115]

The third parliamentary elections, which were held on October 27, 1929, confirmed the trends indicated in the provincial elections in December, 1928.[116] The agrarian party remained the largest party, winning 15 percent of the vote and 46 seats in the Chamber of Deputies. The most remarkable shift in party strength was represented by the comeback of the Social Democratic party, which won 13.0 percent of the vote and 39 seats. The National Socialists likewise made a stronger showing than in 1925 (10.4 percent of the vote, 32 seats). On the other hand, the Communist party, which had been the second largest party in 1925, dropped to fourth place (10.2 percent and 30 seats). The Czech populists suffered a setback (8.4 percent of the vote, 25 seats). The National Democrats made a mild recovery (4.9 percent, 15 seats); they might have done a little better had not the fascists and rightists entered the electoral contest and drawn votes from them. In April, Stříbrný formed a party of his own (the Slavic Socialists), and just before the elections in October he and Gajda formed an electoral bloc (the "National League Against Fixed-Order Lists"), which won a little less than 1 percent of the vote and received 3 seats in the Chamber of Deputies.

The German parties showed roughly the same evolution as the Czechoslovak parties. The German Social Democratic party recovered first place among German parties (21 seats). Unlike their Czechoslovak counterparts, however, the German agrarian party lost some strength (16 seats) and the Christian Social party gained some (14 seats). The German nationalist parties declined in combined strength (15 seats), but the German National Socialist (Nazi) party gained strength (7 seats). The ominous significance of the latter was not realized until later.

In Slovakia the elections were affected to a considerable extent by the outcome of Tuka's trial, which had been purposely spun out until the eve of the elections. On October 5 he was found guilty of both charges (treason and espionage) and sentenced to fifteen years of imprisonment.[117] Three days later, in protest, Hlinka recalled the Slovak populist ministers from the cabinet and the party went into opposition again. Against the advice of his associates, Hlinka insisted on putting Tuka up for reelec-

[115] Uhlíř, pp. 573-75; *Národní shromáždění, 1928-1938*, p. 67.

[116] *Národní shromáždění, 1928-1938*, pp. 79-86; *Československá vlastivěda*, v, 458-60; *Přehled*, iii, 236; Buchválek, *Dějiny*, pp. 466-68; Macartney, *Hungary*, p. 118.

[117] *Národní shromáždění, 1928-1938*, pp. 66-69; Dérer, *Slovenský vývoj*, pp. 134-35; Sidor, *Slovenská politika*, i, 347. The evidence presented in court against Tuka was rather flimsy (see Sidor ii, 208-13). However, after World War II, the historian Kramer proved irrefutably Tuka's treason, with the aid of official documents which he had found in Hungarian archives. See Kramer, *Iredenta*, pp. 131-51.

tion.[118] He believed that Tuka would be reelected and vindicated, as he himself had been in 1920 when he was in confinement. The decision proved to be an error. No one, not even his opponents, doubted the sincerity of Hlinka's Slovak nationalism. Many Slovaks, however, even within the ranks of the Slovak Populist party, doubted Tuka's innocence. He was not reelected and the party's identification with his cause contributed to its setback in the elections. It received only about 28 percent of the vote in Slovakia and was allotted 18 seats in the Chamber of Deputies. The communists likewise lost votes in Slovakia (they received 10 percent of the vote and 5 seats) and their place as the strongest party in Ruthenia. The agrarians held their own (19 percent, 12 seats), and the Social Democrats made a modest comeback (9 percent, 5 seats). The Hungarian and German minority parties in Slovakia remained stable (9 seats).

Even before the elections, President Masaryk gave Udržal precise instructions for the formation of a new government coalition. It was to include the National Democrats ("on condition that they let Beneš and the Hrad alone") on the right; the Czech populists, agrarians, and the Tradesmen's party in the center; and the National Socialists and Social Democrats on the left.[119] Of the minority parties, the German agrarians were to be included again in the new coalition, but were to be balanced by the inclusion—for the first time—of the German Social Democrats. On the other hand, the German Christian Socials, as well as the Slovak populists, were to be dropped from the new coalition.

During the ensuing negotiations between the parties, there was some talk (not initiated by Masaryk) of bringing the German and Slovak Catholic parties into the new coalition through the back door, as it were, that is, not on their own but in a Catholic bloc under Šrámek's leadership. The Slovak populists were willing to join the bloc, because they had tasted the sweets of power and wanted to stay in the governing coalition. However, the Czech leader was not anxious to lead it. By the 1930's, Czech anti-Catholicism had considerably abated. The Czech Catholics had found a modest but comfortable niche in Czech political and social life, and were loath to jeopardize it by forming a new political partnership with their disreputable (in Czech eyes) Slovak coreligionists.[120] Conceivably, if Hlinka had been willing to "go to Canossa," as it were, that is, to repudiate Tuka, abjure Slovak autonomy as his goal, and ask Šrámek's forgiveness, the Czech leader might have taken him in. However, there was no chance that the fiery old Slovak tribune would

---

[118] Sidor, *Slovenská politika*, II, 10-11; Dérer, *Slovenský vývoj*, pp. 136-39.

[119] Nečásek, *Dokumenty*, pp. 213-15.

[120] Trapl, *Politika*, pp. 65-66; Sidor, *Slovenska politika*, II, 35-36; Šolle and Gajanová, *Po stopě dějin*, p. 276; *Národní shromáždění, 1928-1938*, pp. 857-58.

do that. In any event, Udržal dismissed him lightly: "There was a time when Hlinka meant something in Slovakia, but now he does not mean a thing."[121] Udržal's belief was based on a somewhat exaggerated estimate of the impact of Tuka's conviction on Slovak opinion. Although the Slovak populists had suffered an electoral setback, they remained the largest Slovak party. Therefore, they could not be easily dismissed.

Even without the Slovak populists and German clericals, the new coalition was a very broad one. Not surprisingly, the negotiations to form a cabinet, whose members were chosen by President Masaryk, were long and complicated. It was not until December 7, 1929, that Udržal's second cabinet was officially appointed.[122] It lasted until October 24, 1932, and marked the height of Masaryk's influence in Czechoslovak politics. He appointed and dismissed ministers at will.

On March 7, 1930, the president reached eighty years of age. The National Assembly paid him tribute by passing a law—"T. G. Masaryk has benefited the state"—the terseness of which was inspired by his own.[123] The parliament also voted a fund of 20 million crowns for him to draw on, to support causes that were close to his heart. In the same year he made his last tour of the country, and attended the army maneuvers. He was acclaimed everywhere. The occasion marked his apotheosis. His remaining years were anti-climactic.

THE GREAT DEPRESSION

Like President Hoover in the United States, Udržal expected to preside over a prosperous country. Indeed, Czechoslovakia reached the peak of its postwar prosperity in 1929. On November 7, one month before Udržal's appointment, the government realized Rašín's dream: it adopted the gold standard for Czechoslovak currency. During the course of 1930, however, the Great Depression spread over the country. The Udržal government was unprepared for it, and slow to cope with its effects. The depression reached its lowest point in 1933, and then gradually—very gradually—eased off.[124] By 1937, which was the last full year before the Munich agreement disrupted the country, its economy had not yet returned to normal.

Czechoslovakia was eminently a trading nation. At the height of its postwar prosperity as much as one third of its industrial production was destined for exports. Therefore, the effect on the country's economy of

---

[121] Sidor, *Slovenská politika*, II, 83.

[122] *Národní shromáždění, 1928-1938*, pp. 89-90; Uhlíř, "Konec vlády," pp. 584-89; Buchválek, *Dějiny*, pp. 448-49.

[123] Herben, *T. G. Masaryk*, pp. 403-404; *Národní shromáždění, 1928-1938*, p. 18.

[124] Faltus, *Stručný hospodářský vývoj*, pp. 145-54.

the collapse of international trade and the general rush toward autarky in the 1930's was little short of disastrous. By 1933, Czechoslovakia's exports declined to 28 percent (1929 = 100 percent).[125] Although its imports also declined, it was at a slower rate. Consequently, in 1932 Czechoslovakia suffered an unfavorable balance of trade. The decline of foreign trade slowed down the country's production. By 1933 industrial production declined to 60.2 percent and agricultural production to about 61 percent of their 1929 levels.[126] The result of this unfortunate development was widespread unemployment and misery. Unemployment reached a peak in the winter of 1932-33. The labor exchanges then reported 920,000 unemployed; however, it is estimated that the actual number was perhaps as high as 1,300,000 throughout the country.[127]

While all parts of the country suffered from the depression, Slovakia and Ruthenia suffered worst, because their economies were precarious in the extreme even in the best of times. In the years from 1924 to 1929, Slovakia's industries experienced a brief and partial revival.[128] The level of industrial production, however, did not quite reach the level of 1913. With the onset of the depression, it came to a virtual standstill. At the same time, emigration—the old safety valve of social discontent in Slovakia—was virtually choked off.[129] It is estimated that in the winter of 1932-33 about 300,000 were out of work in Slovakia. Together with their families, this meant that about one third of Slovakia's population had no regular income.[130]

As in other countries, the Great Depression created great social tensions in Czechoslovakia. Strikes, lockouts, and resistance to public auctions of property to collect debts and taxes often resulted in bloody clashes between the unemployed workers and the police or the gendarmerie. From 1930 to 1933, 29 persons were killed and 101 wounded in such unfortunate clashes.[131] Because of greater population pressure and higher unemployment, the incidence of violence was more common in Slovakia and Ruthenia than in the Czech provinces.

Under the impression of unemployment the attention of Slovak public opinion focused once again on the vexatious question of Czech government employees in Slovakia. Actually, by the 1930's this question was well on the way toward solution, at least on the professional level. Since 1918 the number of educated Slovaks in government service had steadily increased, though never fast enough to satisfy the young Slovak national-

[125] Přehled, III, 320.   [126] Ibid., 312, 317.

[127] Ibid., 321; Buchválek, Dějiny, p. 318.

[128] Faltus and Průcha, Prehľad hospodárskeho vývoja, pp. 40-66.

[129] Přehled, III, 325.

[130] Lipták, Slovensko, p. 117; Mlynárik, Nezamestnanosť, pp. 53-55.

[131] Buchválek, Dějiny, p. 319; Věra Olivová, Československo v rozrušené Evropě [Czechoslovakia in a Disturbed Europe], (Prague, 1968), pp. 175-77.

ists.[132] They found it intolerable that by right of seniority many higher posts in the administration were still held by Czechs. While the spectacular careers made by the handful of educated Slovaks in 1918 were no longer possible, however, educated young Slovaks continued to find employment appropriate to their training. Unlike some of its neighbors, Czechoslovakia did not suffer the socially dangerous condition of being unable to find suitable employment for its educated class. Slovak manual laborers were not in such a happy position. Not unnaturally, they looked hungrily at the large number of petty posts in government service in Slovakia held by Czechs, for which no other qualification than a primary-school education was required. This question was much less publicly discussed, however, because the intelligentsia which largely formulated Slovak public opinion was not interested in such positions.

As the depression deepened, however, the attitude of the Slovak intelligentsia toward social and economic questions began to change. On June 25-26, 1932, a "Congress of the Young Slovak Generation" was held at Trenčianske Teplice, the program of which was devoted to the study of Slovakia's economic and social problems.[133] Although the political parties engaged in their usual jousting at the congress, the remarkable thing about it was that for the first time since 1918 an important Slovak gathering (it was attended by about 500 young Slovak intellectuals) found the problem of Slovakia's poverty important enough to study. The congress was a harbinger of a new awareness on the part of the Slovak intellectuals that Slovakia's problems were not only political and cultural, as they had generally assumed in 1918, but social and economic as well.[134] There is no doubt that if the First Republic had lasted longer the Slovaks would have found within its democratic framework a solution to Slovakia's age-old problem of poverty.

After 1933 Czechoslovakia's economic situation gradually improved, thanks partly to economic measures adopted by the government and partly to the improvement of world economic conditions. Not the least

---

[132] Lipták, *Slovensko*, p. 129; Macartney, *Hungary*, pp. 133-34; Konštantin Čulen, *Češi a Slováci v štátnych službách ČSR* [*The Czechs and Slovaks in State Service in Czechoslovakia*] (Bratislava, 1944), pp. 149-50.

[133] Sidor, *Slovenská politika*, ii, 58; Šolle and Gajanová, *Po stopě dějin*, p. 238; *Přehled*, iii, 334.

[134] A pioneering study was Imrich Karvaš, *Sjednocení výrobních podmínek v zemích českých a na Slovensku* [*Unifying Conditions of Production in the Czech Provinces and in Slovakia*] (Prague, 1933), which first documented the economic inequality between the Czech provinces and Slovakia and pleaded for its removal. The political parties, however, were slow in grasping the importance of the issue. In 1936 the Slovak Populist party adopted the demand for Slovakia's reindustrialization into its program. The Communist party followed suit in the following year. The centralist parties failed to take a stand on the issue before the end of the First Republic.

important cause of the economic revival was rearmament, necessitated by the growing threat of Nazi Germany; by 1937 it absorbed 37.9 percent of the state budget. On the insistence of the Ministry of Defense some armament industries were transferred from the exposed Czech provinces to Slovakia, giving industry in that province a new lease on life. For strategic reasons also new east-west railroads were hastily completed. By 1937 the level of industrial production in the country as a whole almost reached that of 1929. In Slovakia, however, it not only passed the level of 1929 but—at last—even that of 1913.[135]

Udržal and Malypetr

Czechoslovakia's economic difficulties during the depression were naturally reflected in its politics. The tensions between the political right and left increased. The agrarian party, which stood at the center of the political spectrum, was in danger of being pulled apart. Its polarization between the right and the left wings, already manifest at its congress in 1929, deepened in 1930. The right-wingers showed increasing dissatisfaction with Udržal's policy. They felt that the prime minister was too subservient to President Masaryk and that he neglected economic interests generally and those of the agrarian party particularly.[136] The National League, which the agrarian right-wingers secretly subsidized, became virulent in its attacks against the Hrad.

In 1931, goaded by the League's sniping, the Hrad determined to purge its parliamentary triumvirate—Gajda, Stříbrný, and Charles Pergler. Pergler was found to have claimed Czechoslovak citizenship falsely and to be in reality an American citizen. He was deprived of his Czechoslovak citizen rights and his parliamentary seat and forced to leave the country. Gajda was tried, sentenced, and imprisoned for libeling a minor functionary and also deprived of his parliamentary seat. Stříbrný was indicted for corruption.[137] He was an experienced politician who had been in the thick of Czech politics since the turn of the century, however, and knew many a secret. He defended himself by threatening to expose some of his adversaries in his newspapers. The court failed to convict him.

Meanwhile, Hodža, who was one of the most aggressive anti-Hrad agrarians before his downfall, underwent a great conversion. During his

---

[135] Faltus and Průcha, *Prehľad hospodárskeho vývoja*, pp. 48-54.

[136] Uhlíř, "Konec vlády," p. 555; Tomáš Pasák, "K politickému pozadí krize vlády Františka Udržala roku 1932" ["The Political Background of the Crisis of František Udržal's Government in 1932"], *Československý časopis historický*, XI (1963), 176-77.

[137] *Národní shromáždění, 1928-1938*, pp. 105-109; Šolle and Gajanová, *Po stopě dějin*, p. 280.

"exile" from power he worked to mend his political fences, especially to effect a reconciliation with President Masaryk and Beneš. On their part, Masaryk and Beneš were inclined to forgive him, because of their uneasiness over the growing polarization between the left and the right wings of the agrarian party. In the event of a showdown between the two wings, Hodža, who controlled the Slovak agrarians, might be a decisive factor. In September, 1931, President Masaryk received him, after which Hodža confided to his associates: "They need me."[138] But they did not need him —not yet, anyhow. In October, 1932, the National Socialists, Social Democrats, and Czech populists withdrew their support from Udržal's government because of its inactivity on the economic front, which obliged Udržal to resign. As his successor, the leaders of the agrarians party proposed a compromise candidate, Jan Malypetr (1873-1947), the chairman (speaker) of the Chamber of Deputies, who was acceptable to Masaryk.[139]

Malypetr's first cabinet, which was appointed on October 29, 1932, and lasted until February 14, 1934, represented no radical departure from Udržal's cabinet.[140] It was based on the same coalition and included twelve of Udržal's fifteen ministers. Most of them retained their former posts. Among the newcomers, the most important was Hodža, who had lobbied intensively to become Udržal's successor, but was forced to content himself with his old post of minister of agriculture in Malypetr's cabinet.

Like Švehla and Udržal, Malypetr was a prosperous farmer who had considerable political and administrative experience (he had served as minister of interior in Švehla's first cabinet). Although he was a singularly lackluster politician, he understood economic problems well and attended to them conscientiously. In his programmatic statement as prime minister, he repudiated the "once efficacious and enlightening principle of 'laissez-faire, laissez-passer,'" and warned that "if private enterprise is not to sink into . . . anarchy it must accept regulation of production, as well as of markets."[141] Malypetr did not propose to abolish the capitalist system in Czechoslovakia, but, on the contrary, to save it, by adopting a variety of pragmatic measures, somewhat in the manner

[138] Rudinský, *Československý štát*, p. 152; Pasák, "K politickému pozadí," p. 188.

[139] Pasák, pp. 188-89; *Národní shromáždění, 1928-1938*, pp. 109-10.

[140] *Národní shromáždění, 1928-1938*, pp. 116-17; *Přehled*, III, 352; Buchválek, *Dějiny*, pp. 448-49. The only notable personal change in the cabinet was the removal of the minister of interior, Juraj Slávik, a Slovak agrarian, who was held responsible for the government's harsh repression of the unemployed and strikers.

[141] Olivová, *Československo v rozrušené Evropě*, p. 183; Šolle and Gajanová, *Po stopě dějin*, p. 285.

of the New Deal in the United States. On June 6, 1933, the National Assembly approved a government bill to broaden the government's authority to regulate the economy.[142] Thanks to this authority, the government issued over 240 decrees designed to prime the pump of the stalled economy. Earlier, on March 23, it floated a "Work Loan" (*Půjčka práce*) to raise money for public work projects.

On February 17, 1934, over the protests of the National Democrats, the government devalued the Czechoslovak currency to stimulate exports. When their protests proved of no avail, the National Democrats withdrew from the government coalition.[143] This obliged Malypetr to reshuffle his cabinet, but not to change the basis of the coalition or the course of his policy. On March 14, 1934, the National Assembly passed a government bill to create a Rediscount and Deposit Institute (Reeskontní a lombardní ústav), the purpose of which was to serve as a reserve bank for private banks. Finally, on July 13, 1934, the National Assembly voted to create the Czechoslovak Grain Company (Československá obilní společnost), a government corporation, which was given a monopoly of sale and purchase and of export and import of all grain, fodder, and flour products in the country.[144] The Grain Monopoly, as it was commonly called, proved to be the most controversial creation of Czechoslovakia's New Deal. It succeeded in its purpose of stabilizing the prices of grain—at some cost to the Czechoslovak taxpayer. This was beneficial to medium and large farmers who produced surpluses of grain for sale, but harmful to consumers by causing a rise in the cost of food. Cattle and hog farmers, who were buyers rather than producers of feed, likewise found the Grain Monopoly detrimental to their interests.

There is no doubt that Malypetr's economic policy contained inequities, since he approached economic problems from a frankly class (agrarian) point of view. On the other hand, it must be said that, unlike Udržal, he tried to get the stalled wheels of Czechoslovakia's economy turning again, and that, to some extent, he succeeded.

Malypetr proved less successful in dealing with political problems. Like everywhere else, the economic depression stimulated the growth of radical political movements in Czechoslovakia. The communists tirelessly sought to exploit the social unrest of the working class to undermine Czechoslovakia's democratic system. The Czech fascists likewise continued to be active. On the night of January 21-22, 1933, a band of Czech fascists led by a former army lieutenant, Ladislav Kobzínek, and Gajda's brother, Duchoslav Geidl, attacked the army barracks at Žide-

---

[142] *Přehled*, III, 356; *Národní shromáždění, 1928-1938*, p. 135.
[143] *Národní shromáždění, 1928-1938*, pp. 151-54; *Přehled*, III, 362.
[144] *Přehled*, III, pp. 373-74.

nice in Brno. Allegedly, they wanted to overthrow democracy and establish a fascist dictatorship in Czechoslovakia. The attempt, which smacked of the lunatic, was a complete failure.[145]

More dangerous to democracy in Czechoslovakia and the Czechoslovak Republic itself than communist social demagogy or the quixotic capers of the fascists was Hitler's rise to power in Germany in January, 1933. This dramatic event had far-reaching repercussions, not only among the German minority in Czechoslovakia but on all the ethnic minorities in Czechoslovakia, as well as the Slovak autonomists. In dealing with this menace Malypetr proved indecisive. The government hesitated between repression and accommodation of the national minorities. In the end, it contented itself with a series of legalistic pin-pricks, which neither hurt nor deterred but only irritated the minorities.

On July 10, 1933, the National Assembly passed a law authorizing the government to suspend or suppress newspapers that were "dangerous to the state," and another law expanding the provisions of the 1923 Law for the Protection of the Republic. On October 25 it passed a law authorizing the government to suppress subversive political parties.[146] Earlier, on October 4, the government suspended the activities of the German National Socialist and the German National parties, and in November dissolved them. However, on October 2, Konrad Henlein had already issued a proclamation to the German minority to form a single "Sudeten German Home Front" (*Sudetendeutsche Heimatsfront*), the objectives of which were indistinguishable from those of the dissolved German National Socialist party.[147]

The Malypetr government showed little initiative in trying to solve the question of ethnic minorities in Czechoslovakia. In fairness to it, however, it must be said that a solution to this question was not easy to find. It was as much a foreign-policy problem as it was one of domestic policy. Its solution depended as much on the good will of foreign governments, especially the powerful government of Hitlerite Germany, as on the initiative of the Czechoslovak government.

THE SLOVAK PROBLEM

Unlike the question of ethnic minorities, the Slovak question—the problem of adjusting satisfactorily the relations between the Czech and Slovak peoples—was a purely domestic one. Though less immediately dan-

---

[145] *Národní shromáždění, 1928-1938*, pp. 139-42; Šolle and Gajanová, *Po stopě dějin*, p. 289.

[146] *Národní shromáždění, 1928-1938*, pp. 142-43; *Přehled*, III, 357 and 360.

[147] Radomír Luža, *The Transfer of the Sudeten Germans: A Study of Czech-German Relations, 1933-1962* (New York, 1964), pp. 71-75; César and Černý, *Politika*, II, 219-20.

gerous, it was nevertheless important, for in the long run the existence of Czechoslovakia depended on the mutual trust and voluntary cooperation of the Czech and Slovak peoples, who were the Czechoslovak state's main carriers.

Like Udržal, Malypetr tended to underestimate the influence of the Slovak populists. He did not invite them into his cabinet. Left in the opposition, they grew more radical in the 1930's. Their growing radicalism reflected partly the radical temper of the period, partly the growing national self-assurance of the Slovaks as a whole, and partly a change in the leadership of the Slovak Populist party. The expulsion of Juriga and Tománek from the party in 1929, as well as death, thinned the ranks of the old pre-1918 populists, and made room for the rise of younger men in the party leadership. Hlinka remained the absolute master of the party, but because of his advancing age and declining health he gave a freer hand to younger leaders. Tuka's place as editor of the *Slovák* and the party's principal ideologist was taken by Karol Sidor (1901-53), an ardent Polonophile, who was regarded as a firebrand. Jozef Tiso, a shrewd parliamentary tactician, became the principal party strategist. He was regarded as a moderate at that time. Below Sidor and Tiso there emerged in the 1930's a still younger generation of future leaders, who were known as the Nástupisti (after their review *Nástup—Step Forward!*).[148] Too young to have experienced the oppression and humiliation of Hungarian rule personally, the Nástupists took for granted the freedoms that Czechoslovakia had brought the Slovaks and looked admiringly at the "virile" and "dynamic" totalitarian regimes.

On May 8, 1930, the Slovak populists had introduced their second bill for Slovak autonomy in the National Assembly.[149] It met with the same fate as their first proposal for autonomy in 1922. However, they went on doggedly pursuing their objective. Hodža's comfortable belief that it would always be possible to buy the Slovak populists off with a ministerial post or two was no longer true, for his basic concept of Slovak politics as a game to be played by the political leaders, with the masses passively looking on, was no longer valid. By the 1930's Slovak politics had acquired a broader mass basis and firmer ideological orientation.

On October 16, 1932, at a large mass meeting at Zvolen, Hlinka and Martin Rázus (1888-1937), the leader of the Slovak National party, agreed on the programmatic cooperation of their parties.[150] The Slovak National party broke with the Czech National Democrats and became

---

[148] The most prominent of the radical Nástupists were the brothers Ján and Ferdinand Durčanský, who were the editors of *Nástup*, Karol Murgaš, Alexander (Šaňo) Mach, and Štefan Polakovič. See Jörg K. Hoensch, *Die Slowakei und Hitlers Ostpolitik, 1938-1939* (Cologne, 1965), p. 8 note.

[149] Sidor, *Slovenská politika*, II, 35-36.   [150] Ibid., p. 59.

a second Slovak autonomist party, which showed that the demand for Slovak autonomy was gaining ground among the Slovak Protestants, too. At a working meeting of the two parties at Trenčín on December 28-29, 1932, Hlinka first made the fateful statement, "I shall defend the nation even *at the cost of the republic*,"[151] which revealed a dangerous progression in his and his followers' thought; henceforth they did not exclude the possibility of seeking a solution of the Slovak question outside the Czechoslovak Republic.

Dérer had an inkling of the new character of the Slovak autonomist movement and was resolved to combat it. However, his bull-in-a-china-shop methods defeated his purposes. As minister of education from 1929 to 1934, he made a creditable effort to build Slovak schools and improve education generally. His aim, however, was not only to educate but also to indoctrinate. This had been the aim of state-supported Slovak schools all along, but Dérer infused it with a crusading fervor. His *Kulturkampf* culminated in 1932 in an attempt to reform the Slovak language. Since 1918 the Slovak language had experienced a remarkable evolution, and the need to reform its grammar and orthography was generally recognized. The arbiter of the Slovak language was the Slovenská Matica. On Dérer's instructions its grammarians, with the assistance of members of the Czech Academy in Prague, prepared a new grammar that reflected a conscious effort to render the Slovak language as close to Czech as possible. As a people long deprived of free use of their language, the Slovaks were very sensitive to any tampering with it, especially by outsiders. The reform provoked deep resentment. At the Matica's annual meeting on May 12, 1932, the opponents of the new grammar prevailed. The Czechophile grammarians were ousted from its linguistic committee, and a new committee was entrusted with preparing a new grammar, pending whose completion the old usage was to continue.[152] Dérer retaliated against the Matica "*putsch*" (as the press styled it) by suspending the Matica's government subsidy and ordering school authorities to use the grammar prepared with the assistance of the Czech academicians. The episode was not important except as an indication that Slovak particularism had not waned since 1918, but, on the contrary, had increased.

Another indication of this trend was provided a year later, on August 13, 1933, at the celebration of the 1100th anniversary of the consecration of the first Christian church on the territory of Czechoslovakia at Nitra in Slovakia. Planned originally as a simple church observance, the celebration was turned into a test of strength between the Slovak cen-

---

[151] *Národní shromáždění, 1928-1938*, p. 863; Dérer, *Slovenský vývoj*, p. 146. Italics this author's.

[152] Tomáš Winkler, *Matica Slovenská v rokoch 1919-1945* [*The Slovak Matica in 1919-1945*] (Turčiansky Svätý Martin, 1971), pp. 26-28.

tralists and autonomists by the decision to make it an official state observance, presided over by Prime Minister Malypetr and attended by high government and church dignitaries, as well as foreign guests. Hlinka and his followers managed to steal the show and turn the observance into a wild anti-government demonstration.[153]

Dérer was so upset by the event and the gleeful comment on it in the Hungarian revisionist press that he demanded that the government dissolve the Slovak Populist party at once and stage a political trial of Hlinka and his associates. Hodža, however, counseled against such a course, and Malypetr thought it would distract the parties from the coming negotiations over the price of sugar beet. No action was taken against Hlinka. However, as a warning, the organs of the Slovak Populist and Slovak National parties were briefly suspended. The police investigated the demonstration at Nitra and charged about 150 persons with anti-government rioting. Dérer was furious over his cabinet colleagues' complacency about the Nitra affair, and decided to act alone. As minister of education, he instituted disciplinary action against school teachers who had participated in the demonstration. Later, on the occasion of a government amnesty of political offenders in 1935, action against all participants in the Nitra demonstration was dropped.[154] Their harassment had only created a few cut-rate martyrs and had provided grist for the autonomist propaganda mills.

Nevertheless, Malypetr was nettled by the insults proferred him at Nitra. He decided to abandon the reserve with which Czech politicians usually treated Slovak matters and to answer the Slovak autonomists. In a speech in the National Assembly on October 20, 1933, which was officially placarded in every Slovak town and village, he argued that Slovak autonomy was not feasible, because Slovakia could not pay its way. As proof, he cited the fact that the government disbursements in Slovakia from 1919 to 1932 had been 15.6 billion crowns while tax receipts from Slovakia in the same period had amounted to only 14 billion crowns. The press reduced his speech to a rather crude slogan: "We are losing money in Slovakia" ("Na Slovensko se dopláci")—words which he had actually not used.[155]

Economics was perhaps not the best ground on which to attack the Slovak autonomists. They answered Malypetr that his figures were misleading because, among other things, most firms doing business in Slovakia had their central offices in Prague and paid their taxes there, and went on to rehearse the old Slovak grievances that industry in Slovakia

[153] Sidor, *Slovenská politika*, II, pp. 75-83; *Národní shromáždění, 1928-1938*, pp. 146-47; Dérer, *Slovenský vývoj*, pp. 148-56.

[154] Dérer, pp. 160-66; Sidor, *Slovenská politika*, II, 83.

[155] Sidor, II, 86-88; *Národní shromáždění, 1928-1938*, pp. 148-51.

was handicapped by a discriminatory railroad tariff and that it did not receive a fair share of government orders. Even Hodža, who was Malypetr's rival for leadership in the agrarian party and the government, tried to refute his arguments, in a speech at Liptovský Svätý Mikuláš.[156] The Slovak autonomists gleefully noted the polemic between Malypetr and Hodža, who were members of the same party and cabinet, and demanded that the government publish a detailed account of its tax receipts and its expenses by province. Malypetr promised to provide the information, but never did. It is interesting that when Hodža became prime minister, he, too, refused to reveal it. Their decision to treat the information as *arcana imperii* was unfortunate, for without it no objective analysis of the problem could be made. Consequently, the Czechs continued to feel that they were required to pay an unfair share of the taxes, and the Slovaks that they did not receive a fair share of the government's disbursements.

PRESIDENTIAL AND PARLIAMENTARY ELECTIONS

On May 1, 1934, as his term of office was about to expire, President Masaryk suffered a stroke, which paralyzed his left side and impaired his eyesight. For this reason, he did not wish to run for reelection. In the end, he agreed to become a candidate again only because he was uncertain whether the National Assembly would heed his recommendation to elect Beneš as his successor. On May 24, the National Assembly elected Masaryk president for the fourth time, with a larger majority than ever before: out of the 418 votes cast, he received 327. His only opponent, the communist candidate Klement Gottwald, received 38 votes. The National Democrats, the Slovak populists, and the Hungarian nationalists cast blank ballots. The German government parties voted for Masaryk, while the German opposition parties abstained altogether from voting.[157]

The fourth and final parliamentary elections under the First Republic took place a year later, on May 19, 1935. On the eve of the elections some minor party realignments took place. On April 25, 1935, a new political grouping, the National Union (Národní sjednocení), was formed under Kramář's chairmanship. It comprised, in addition to Kramář's National Democrats, Stříbrný's National League and Prof. František Mareš' National Front. By entering the National Union, Kramář hoped to recover a mass following for his party, which had become by 1935 a big-business Czech upper-middle-class party. Originally, Gajda belonged to the National Front, but later broke with Prof. Mareš. For

---

[156] Sidor, *Slovenská politika*, II, 91-92; Dérer, *Slovenský vývoj*, p. 172.
[157] *Národní shromáždění, 1928-1938*, pp. 24-25; Herben, *T. G. Masaryk*, p. 440; Buchválek, *Dějiny*, p. 320.

the first time, the fascists decided to run on their own in the elections of 1935. Another new electoral grouping was the "Autonomist Bloc" formed by the Slovak populists. Since 1932, the Slovak Populist and the Slovak National parties had worked closely together. Now they were joined in the Autonomist Bloc by the Polish party in Silesia (Těšín) and the Ruthenian Autonomist Agrarian Union. On April 30, Henlein transformed his "Sudeten German Home Front" into the "Sudeten German party" (Sudetendeutsche Partei), with a branch in Slovakia called "Carpathian German party" (Karpathendeutsche Partei). However, his negotiations with the German agrarians to form a bloc failed, because both parties made a bid for the vote of the dissolved German National and German National Socialist parties. The Hungarian National party, the Hungarian Christian Social party, and the German ethnic group in the Spiš district of Slovakia formed a bloc, as they had done in 1929.

On the eve of the elections, the Communist party effected a drastic change in its tactics, the reason for which was the conclusion of the Soviet-Czechoslovak alliance treaty on May 16, 1935, and the general reorientation of Soviet foreign policy at that time, from xenophobic isolationism to cooperation with the Western democracies against the totalitarian powers. As a directive for the world Communist parties, Moscow's new dispensation was translated into the formula "popular front of all antifascist forces" at the Seventh Comintern Congress held in Moscow from July 25 to August 8, 1935.

Moderation was not a communist virtue. They tended to follow the new line to its logical extreme. Until 1935 the Communist party had been hostile to the "bourgeois" Czechoslovak Republic. It was critical of Czech nationalism and stood up for the national minorities and Slovak and Ruthenian autonomy. Now, however, it adopted a stance of fervent Czechoslovak patriotism, treated the national minorities with scarcely veiled suspicion as alien fifth columns, and espoused a most extreme centralism.

The results of the elections, which passed without incident, did not basically alter the balance of Czechoslovak parties.[158] All the government parties lost a little ground, but not disastrously so. The agrarians received 14.3 percent of the vote and 45 seats in the Chamber of Deputies; the Social Democrats garnered 12.6 percent of the vote and received 38 seats; the National Socialists slipped a little, to 9.2 percent of the vote and 28 seats; and the Czech populists lost a little more (7.5 percent of the vote and 22 seats). The National Union achieved no more than its components had done in 1929 (5.6 percent and 17 seats). Later, in April, 1937, the National Union was dissolved. On the other hand, the

[158] *Národní shromáždění, 1928-1938*, pp. 179-85; *Přehled*, III, 385-86; Macartney, *Hungary*, p. 118.

Czech fascists made a surprisingly good showing (2 percent of the vote and 6 seats). The communists held their own (10.3 percent of the vote and 30 seats), but the areas of their support had significantly changed: their support in the areas inhabited by the national minorities sharply declined, while it rose considerably in the areas inhabited by Czechs and Slovaks. In Ruthenia they recovered their former primacy.

The electoral results in Slovakia did not differ markedly from those in the Czech provinces. The Autonomist Bloc received 30 percent of the vote in Slovakia and received 22 seats. Of these the Slovak populists retained 19 and gave their partners in the bloc a seat each. The Slovak National party and the Ruthenian Autonomist Agrarian Union complained that this fell short of their electoral strength, and refused to join the Slovak populist parliamentary club in the new parliament. The Hungarian electoral bloc improved its position a little, largely at the expense of the communists. It won 14.5 percent of the vote in Slovakia and received 9 seats in the lower house. The Hungarian parties continued the bloc after the elections, and in 1937 were merged into a single party.

The great electoral upset in 1935 was the landslide victory of the Sudeten German party. It polled 15.2 percent of the total vote and 66 percent of the German vote in Czechoslovakia, and was awarded 44 seats in the Chamber of Deputies. It was only by engaging in some rapid-action parliamentary arithmetic that the agrarians, who had fallen behind the Sudeten German party in voting strength, came out one seat ahead of them. On the other hand, the Sudeten German government parties suffered severe losses. The German Social Democratic party was reduced almost to half of its 1929 strength (from 21 seats in 1929 to 11 in 1935) and the German agrarians were cut to less than one third of their former strength (16 seats in 1929, 5 in 1935). The opposition German Christian Socials were likewise much reduced (14 seats in 1929, 6 in 1935).

The electoral losses of the government parties reduced the ruling coalition to a minority in the National Assembly. Malypetr was therefore obliged to broaden the base of his government. There was talk again of forming a Catholic bloc under the aegis of the Czech populists. Malypetr actually sounded the Slovak populists out on joining his cabinet, and they showed interest. As the price of their support, they did not demand Slovak autonomy, but—knowing of his predilection for economics—presented him with a list of thirty-two economic and administrative demands. After taking one look at their shopping list, however, Malypetr postponed negotiations with them indefinitely.[159] Instead, he secured the return of the Tradesmen's party to the government coalition. Malypetr's

---

[159] Sidor, *Slovenská politika*, II, 164-67; *Národní shromáždění*, p. 196.

third cabinet, which was appointed on June 6 and which lasted until November 5, did not differ substantially from his previous cabinets.[160]

Early in November when the chairman (speaker) of the Chamber of Deputies, the agrarian Bohumil Bradáč, died, the agrarian leaders asked Malypetr to resume this important post. Hodža's hour had at last arrived. On November 5, President Masaryk appointed him prime minister. A few days later, on November 21, Masaryk, whose health continued to decline, announced his intention to resign from the presidency and expressed the wish that Beneš succeed him. Because of the proximity of the two events, it was widely believed that Masaryk had appointed Hodža prime minister in order to arrange Beneš's succession. Whether this was true or not Hodža backed Beneš's candidacy.

At first, it appeared that Beneš's election would be a mere formality.[161] There was no other candidate for the office. Masaryk's announcement had caught the anti-Hrad politicians unprepared. At first, they tried to dissuade Masaryk from abdicating. When he refused to change his decision, they produced, on December 7, another candidate, Bohumil Němec, a respectable but obscure university professor. A real electoral contest then developed. The socialist parties, the Czech populists, and the German socialists and clericals backed Beneš. The communists, who had put up a candidate of their own in previous presidential elections, now likewise backed Beneš. The Czechoslovak and German agrarian parties, the National Union, the Tradesmen's party, and the fascists backed Němec. Neither candidate had a majority of votes. The matter could have been decided by the large Sudeten German party. However, both candidates refused to solicit the support of this Nazi-tainted party, which would put an albatross around the winner's neck. The Sudeten German party, therefore, abstained from voting. The attitude of the Slovaks then became crucial.

The election precipitated a showdown between the right and the left wings of the agrarian party. Paradoxically, the left wing was now led by Hodža, while Beran emerged as the leader of the right wing. On November 19, as compensation for Hodža's promotion to the premiership, Beran was appointed to the office of chairman of the party that had been left vacant since Švehla's death in 1933. Beran committed the party to support Němec's candidacy. This put Hodža in a difficult position. He tried to get out of it by offering his resignation as premier on Decem-

---

[160] *Národní shromáždění, 1928-1938*, pp. 197-98; Buchválek, *Dějiny*, p. 449.

[161] *Národní shromáždění, 1928-1938*, pp. 49-54; Gajanová *Dvojí tvář*, pp. 154-78; Šolle and Gajanová, *Po stopě dějin*, pp. 294-97; Olivová, *Československo v rozrušené Evropě*, pp. 192-93; Herben, *T. G. Masaryk*, pp. 445-47; Trapl, *Politika*, pp. 72-73; Sidor, *Slovenská politika*, II, 155-59.

ber 11. However, President Masaryk refused to accept it, and on December 14 he formally abdicated. Hodža then decided to go against his party and to throw the support of the Slovak agrarians behind Beneš. Briefly, the attitude of the Slovak populists then became decisive. Hlinka found himself the center of unwonted attention; he was courted by emissaries of both candidates. In the end, prompted by the Vatican and persuaded by Tiso,[162] he decided to support Beneš. When the Slovak populist decision became known the opposition to Beneš's election collapsed. There was an undignified rush to rescue the victor. On December 18, Beneš was elected president by a comfortable majority (340 out of the 440 votes cast).

THE REPUBLIC'S END

The emergence of Henlein's large Sudeten German party at home and the growing menace of Hitler's revisionist policy abroad cast deep shadows over the remaining years of the First Republic.

When Hodža took over the premiership from Malypetr in November, he effected no changes in his cabinet and announced no changes in his policy. The first change in the cabinet came in December, 1935, when Beneš gave up the foreign ministry to assume the presidency. As president, he intended to retain control of foreign policy in his own hands. Therefore, he recommended as his successor a distinguished Czech historian, Kamil Krofta (1876-1945), who was his trusted collaborator and could be relied upon to execute his policy. He was not in a position to insist on Krofta's appointment at the time of the election, however. Hodža, who had always aspired to playing the role of a great European statesman, insisted on taking over the foreign ministry himself. At the same time, he relinquished the ministry of agriculture to another agrarian.

Hodža was intent on launching a grand foreign policy, the basic aim of which was to form a bloc of Danubian nations to thwart Hitler's *Drang nach Südosten*.[163] *Per se*, the plan was not without merit. However, it was extremely difficult to realize in view of the intense ill will prevailing among the Danubian peoples. Their reconciliation, which was the prerequisite of the plan's success, would have taken years to achieve —and Hitler was not likely to allow them a long period of peace. On February 29, 1936, after getting the reins of his new office firmly in

[162] Konštantin Čulen, *Po Svätoplukovi druhá naša hlava: Život Dr. Jozefa Tisu* [*Our First Head of State since Svätopluk: The Life of Dr. Jozef Tiso*] (Cleveland, 1947), pp. 167-75.

[163] Milan Hodža, *Federation in Central Europe* (London, 1942), pp. 126-39; Alena Gajanová, *ČSR a středoevropská politika velmocí, 1918-1938* [*The Czechoslovak Republic and the Central European Policy of the Great Powers, 1918-1938*] (Prague, 1967), pp. 343-47.

hand, President Beneš obliged Hodža to relinquish the foreign ministry to Krofta. This ended Hodža's initiative, if not always his interference, in foreign affairs.

Hodža was the first and only Slovak prime minister under the First Republic. His Czech colleagues thought that he would be in a better position than they to deal with Slovakia. He exploited this belief to strengthen his position in Prague, but was probably less able to deal with the Slovaks than a Czech prime minister would be. Like the appointment of a *Landsmannminister* in old Austria, his appointment to the premiership was regarded in Slovakia as his personal, not a national Slovak, success, because he had not identified himself with specifically Slovak aspirations and had made his career in the national political arena in Prague, not in Slovakia.

In an autonomous Slovakia Hodža's influence would be very small, if any. He had no reason, therefore, to come to an agreement with the Slovak autonomists. Nor could he very well have made them substantial concessions without destroying his position in Prague. Nevertheless, since it was generally expected of him, he opened discussions with the Slovak populists on January 21, 1936. While they had demanded only economic and administrative concessions of Malypetr, they made the same demands on Hodža and, in addition, sought political concessions. Specifically, they demanded constitutional revisions to recognize the distinctness of the Slovak people and of the Slovak language, creation of a Slovak diet as provided in the Pittsburgh agreement, and restoration of the office of minister with full powers to administer Slovakia.

Hodža rejected both the economic and political demands of the Slovak populists, justifying his rejection partly by rehearsing Malypetr's argument that an autonomous Slovakia would not be economically viable and partly by arguing that the rising threat of war made decentralization untimely. The Slovak populists conceded that the times were difficult and declared that they would be content with a firm government promise to grant their demands at a later, more peaceful, time. Hodža, however, refused to make even such a promise, and by March 27 his negotiations with the Slovak populists ended in complete failure.[164]

Hodža thought it more pressing for the government to try to conciliate

---

[164] *Národní shromáždění, 1928-1938*, pp. 242-44; Dérer, *Slovenský vývoj*, pp. 173-75; Čulen, *Po Svätoplukovi*, pp. 163-65. As a part of Hodža's efforts to secure the support of the Slovak populists for his coalition, Dérer, who was minister of justice in his cabinet, reviewed Tuka's case and recommended him for an amnesty. On June 3, 1937, President Beneš amnestied Tuka, on condition that he abstain from all political activity and that he reside at Plzeň in Bohemia, where he was kept under police surveillance. See *Mnichov v dokumentech [Munich in Documents]* (2 vols.; Prague, 1959), II, 21. Tuka's amnesty was typical of Hodža's belief that it was possible to buy off the Slovak populists with personal concessions.

the national minorities, because of the support they received from their kinsmen abroad. The Sudeten Germans, who were the largest and most important of Czechoslovakia's national minorities, were less suspicious of Hodža than of most Czech politicians and he was completely free of any emotional handicap in dealing with them. Indeed, initially he had some success in dealing with, at least, the German "activist" (i.e., pro-government) parties. On July 2, 1936, the German Christian Socials entered the government coalition and their leader, Erwin Zajiček, joined Hodža's cabinet. On February 18, 1937, the German activist parties formulated demands, which—if granted—would have gone far toward removing the legitimate grievances and satisfying the reasonable aspirations of the Sudeten German minority.[165] The government responded favorably to the activists' demands. However, Hitler's notorious speech of February 20, 1938, in which he declared himself protector of the ten million Germans living outside of Germany (i.e., in Austria and Czechoslovakia) frightened the activists. After the Austrian *Anschluss* in March, the German Christian Socials and the agrarians panicked, dissolved their organizations, and joined Henlein's party. The German Social Democrats likewise withdrew from the government, but did not disband their party. On the other hand, impressed by the German threat, the Czech National Democrats, who had left the government in 1934, returned to it on March 19, 1938. Kramář had died in 1937, as had President Masaryk. The National Democrats therefore delegated František Ježek to represent them in the Hodža cabinet.

On New Year's Day, 1938, Beran startled Czech public opinion by publishing an article in the agrarian party organ *Venkov*, urging the government to bring Henlein's Sudeten German party and Hlinka's Slovak Populist party into the government coalition and to seek an agreement with the German government.[166] Indeed, Hodža had been in touch with Henlein since September, 1937. Their contacts bore no fruit, however, because the ultimate aim of Henlein's party was not an agreement with the Czechoslovak government but its destruction. "We must always demand so much that we can never be satisfied," Henlein said in explaining his tactics to Hitler in Berlin on March 28, 1938.[167] By coincidence, on the same day, Hodža announced the government's intention to codify all measures relating to the national minorities in a "minority statute," which would provide them with a single standard of their rights.[168] How-

[165] Brügel, *Tschechen und Deutsche*, pp. 308-12; Beneš, *Mnichovské dny*, pp. 349-51; *Národní, shromáždění, 1928-1938*, pp. 244-50.

[166] César and Černý, *Politika*, II, 423-24.

[167] *Documents on German Foreign Policy*, Series D, Vol. II, 197-202.

[168] Beneš, *Mnichovské dny*, pp. 33-34. Hodža's statement may be found in Royal Institute of International Affairs, *Documents on International Affairs 1938* (2 vols.; London, 1943), II, 123-26.

ever, on April 24, at his party's rally at Karlovy Vary (Karlsbad), Henlein formulated an eight-point program that went far beyond the existing minority rights.[169] In fact, it challenged the basic concept of Czechoslovakia as a national state of the Czechs (he did not concede the Slovaks the status of a *Staatsvolk* but treated them as a minority) and proposed to transform the country into a loose confederation of nationalities, somewhat in the nature of the German Confederation in the early nineteenth century.

Official negotiations between the Czechoslovak government and the Sudeten German party began in May and were spun out until September. In the light of Henlein's tactic agreed upon with Hitler in March they became a grotesque charade. It would be superfluous to review them here. Their principal purpose was not to reach an agreement but to impress the British government with the good faith and reasonableness of the Sudeten German party. By September, Hitler had grown impatient with them, because the deadline he had set for taking over the Sudeten German areas in Czechoslovakia—October 1—was approaching. Consequently, after Hitler's speech on September 12 at the Nazi party rally in Nuremberg, Henlein and his associates broke off the negotiations and vanished from the scene, leaving the Czechoslovak government face to face with the German government. The Sudeten German crisis passed from the domestic to the international stage.[170]

Meanwhile, the Slovak and Ruthenian autonomists, as well as the Hungarian and Polish minorities, intensified their pressure on the Czechoslovak government to obtain autonomy. Pursuing its objective of disrupting Czechoslovakia, the Sudeten German party endeavored to build up a "minorities front" against the Czechoslovak government. As early as February 8, 1938, a delegation of the Sudeten German party called on Hlinka in his home in Ružomberok to offer the party's cooperation. Hlinka received the delegation cordially and promised to appoint a liaison man with the Sudeten German party. However, because of Nazi hostility to the Catholic Church, he remained suspicious of the Sudeten German leaders and loath to cooperate with them.[171] On the other hand, the

---

[169] For Henlein's Karlsbad speech and program, see Royal Institute, *Documents . . . 1938*, 130-42.

[170] The great international crisis over Czechoslovakia in 1938, which led to the Munich conference, is discussed in Chapter VII. Here only its domestic political aspects are reviewed.

[171] See the report of Franz Künzel, who was one of the Sudeten German emissaries to Hlinka, in *Documents on German Foreign Policy*, Series D, Vol. II, 124-25. On the basis of Künzel's report, the exiled Slovak leader Jozef Lettrich, *History of Modern Slovakia* (New York, 1955), p. 88; the Czech Communist historian Imrich Stanek, *Zrada a pád: Hlinkovští separatisté a tak zvaný Slovenský stát* [*Betrayal and Downfall: The Hlinka Separatists and the So-called Slovak State*] (Prague, 1958), pp. 101-102; as well as other Czech and Slovak com-

young Nástupists felt no compunction about dealing with the Sudeten German party, but their influence in the Slovak Populist party did not become decisive until after the Munich conference.

Early in 1938, President Beneš opened discussions with the Slovak populists, but was adamant in his refusal to consider Slovak autonomy, nor did his attitude change even after the Austrian *Anschluss*.[172] However, the Slovak populists were encouraged to press their demands by the increasing pressure put on the Czechoslovak government by the great powers to accommodate the national minorities. In May, 1938, the Slovak populists made elaborate preparations to observe the twentieth anniversary of the Pittsburgh agreement, the original copy of which was brought to Slovakia at that time by a delegation of American Slovaks. On Whitsunday, June 5, Hlinka exhibited it at a huge populist rally in Bratislava and announced a new populist program for Slovak autonomy.[173] On the following day, the agrarians and socialists staged a vast counterrally in Bratislava, at which Hodža and Dérer publicly embraced, in token of their reconciliation and common resolve to fight the autonomists.[174] On August 19, the Slovak populists introduced the "Whitsun program" (*svätodušný program*) as their third bill for Slovak autonomy in the National Assembly, where it was left to languish in committee.

Meanwhile, on August 16, Hlinka died without designating a successor, which precipitated a conflict between Tiso and Sidor for Hlinka's mantle. Reflecting about Slovakia later, in exile, Beneš paid Hlinka a reluctant tribute: "We made a mistake. Slovakia became the property of twenty families. Everyone chased after money and careers, and in this atmosphere Hlinka found a fertile soil. Whatever his faults, however, he was still a personality among them [the Slovak leaders] and always remained consistent."[175] On August 31 Tiso was chosen acting chairman

---

munist historians have jumped to the conclusion that Hlinka and the Sudeten German emissaries had reached an "agreement" on cooperation of their parties. A careful reading of the report, however, does not permit that conclusion. On this point, see also the opinions of Hoentsch, *Die Slowakei*, pp. 56-57; and Brügel, *Tschechen und Deutsche*, p. 391.

[172] Sidor, *Slovenská politika*, II, 201-202; Čulen, *Po Svätoplukovi*, p. 193.

[173] *Národní shromáždění, 1928-1938*, pp. 867-68; Sidor, *Slovenská politika*, II, 248; Dérer, *Slovenský vývoj*, pp. 188-89; Peter P. Hletko, "Na prahu velʹkých událostí roku 1938" ["On the Threshold of Great Events in 1938"] in Mikuláš Šprinc (ed.), *Slovenská Republika, 1939-1949* [*The Slovak Republic, 1939-1949*] (Scranton, 1949), pp. 36-41. Hletko was the leader of the American Slovak delegation. For the text of the Whitsun program, see Robert Nowak, *Der künstliche Staat* (Berlin, 1938), the Slovak original on pp. 312-19, and the German translation on pp. 302-11.

[174] Dérer, *Slovenský vývoj*, pp. 189-90; Hletko, "Na prahu," p. 39.

[175] Libuše Otahalová and Milada Červínková (eds.), *Dokumenty z historie československé politiky, 1939-1943* [*Documents on the History of Czechoslovak Politics, 1939-1943*] (2 vols.; Prague, 1966), II, 719.

of the party, but the rivalry between him and Sidor continued until after the collapse of Czechoslovakia in March, 1939.

On September 8 Tiso represented his party at a meeting of the parties of Czechoslovakia's national minorities called by the Sudeten German party, which raised Czech fears of collusion between the Slovak populists and the Henleinists. On the same day, President Beneš invited Tiso to discuss the Slovak populist demands with him. Although they reached no immediate agreement, their talk marked a resumption of a dialogue between them. In September, the Slovak populists moderated their course, because Poland and Hungary joined Germany in raising territorial claims on Czechoslovakia. In addition to the Těšín district in Silesia, the Polish demand included Slovak territory in the border districts of Orava and Spiš, and the Hungarian demand the whole of southern Slovakia. On September 19, the executive committee of the Slovak Populist party met in Bratislava to decide on its course. The communique issued after the meeting reiterated the Slovak populist demand for Slovak autonomy on the basis of the Pittsburgh agreement and the Whitsun program. It denied having made a deal with "non-Slavic parties" (i.e., with the Sudeten German and Hungarian parties), and spoke out against a "bloody and forceful" solution of Czechoslovakia's internal problems, that is, against armed resistance to Hitler's demands.[176]

On the same day, September 19, the French and British envoys in Prague handed President Beneš Hitler's demand for the Sudeten German areas of Czechoslovakia, with their own recommendation that Czechoslovakia comply. The Czechoslovak government agonized over the reply to the Anglo-French note on September 19 and 20. President Beneš gave vent to his bitterness against the Western powers:

This is a betrayal. France betrayed us. I could have made a deal with Hitler's representatives, which would have required smaller sacrifices than this [the Anglo-French note]. But I did not do it. I did not do it, because it would have meant sacrificing our pact with France. I remained faithful to her, and now they throw us overboard.

Paradoxically, the representatives of the most anticommunist parties, the Czech populist Msgr. Šrámek and the National Democrat Ježek, were the most vehement in advocating the rejection of the Anglo-French note and relying, if necessary, on the Soviet Union alone. In the end, the government decided to decline the Anglo-French note and to appeal for the arbitration of the German-Czechoslovak conflict under the German-Czechoslovak arbitration treaty of 1925.[177] Foreign Minister Krofta

[176] Sidor, Slovenská politika, II, 251.
[177] The Anglo-French note and the Czechoslovak reply to it were discussed in the Political Cabinet (a successor of the Pětka, consisting of the heads or dele-

handed the reply to the French and British ministers at 7:45 P.M., September 20. Less than seven hours later, at 2:15 A.M., September 21, the French and British envoys were back in the Hradčany to present President Beneš with the notorious Anglo-French ultimatum, demanding unconditional Czechoslovak acceptance of the Anglo-French note of September 19 and threatening that otherwise France and Britain would wash their hands of Czechoslovakia.

Even before the night was over, President Beneš summoned the party leaders to the Hradčany to consider the Anglo-French ultimatum. The discussion of it continued through the morning and ended that afternoon. Although the ultimatum was not altogether unexpected, it nevertheless shocked the Czech and Slovak political leaders deeply. Once again the National Democratic and Czech populist spokesmen, Ježek and Šrámek, took the most intransigent stand. They insisted that the government did not have authority under the constitution to alienate Czechoslovak territory, and that, consequently, it should either reject the ultimatum or refer it to the National Assembly for action. President Beneš, however, maintained that there was no time for the National Assembly to act on it, and that, therefore, the government had to do it alone. The agrarians Hodža and Josef Černý favored acceptance of the ultimatum, but tried to evade the responsibility of suggesting it first. The Social Democratic spokesman Bechyně was almost hysterical and argued for submission to it. The representative of the Tradesmen's party, Rudolf Mlčoch, was likewise highly emotional in his pleas for compliance. The National Socialist Emil Franke deferred to the judgment of President Beneš in the matter.[178]

---

gates of the coalition parties) and in the full cabinet. Although the discussions in the Political Cabinet were informal (no vote was taken and no minutes were kept), it was the decision-making body. See František Ježek, "Z pamětí o mnichovské krizi roku 1938" ["Recollections of the Munich Crisis in 1938"], *Historie a vojenství* (1969), 4, 683-90; and Beneš, *Mnichovské dny*, pp. 249-55. Ježek's story is particularly valuable, because it contains an account of the informal discussion in the Political Cabinet, with the reactions of the political leaders to the Anglo-French note. Beneš's account puts in relief the international significance of the Anglo-French note and the Czechoslovak reply, but sheds no light on the attitude of the Czechoslovak party leaders to them or to the Munich crisis generally.

[178] Ježek, "Z pamětí," 690-700, provides the only overall account of the reaction of the coalition party leaders toward the Anglo-French ultimatum. Beneš's account in *Mnichovské dny*, pp. 262-73, is important for the international crisis, but adds little light on the domestic crisis. Despite its title, the collection *Mnichov a politické strany: Dokumenty* [*Munich and the Political Parties: Documents*] (Prague, 1961), edited by Václav Král, documents the attitude of only one party —the National Socialist—toward Munich. Some additional light on the attitude of the Czech populists toward Munich is thrown in Trapl, *Politika*, p. 76, and Hruban, *Z časů*, pp. 241-42. For the minutes of the full cabinet meeting on September 21, in which the Czechoslovak reply to the Anglo-French ultimatum was formally approved, see *Mnichov v dokumentech*, II, 215-24. Outside the gov-

Indeed, in the end, it was the president, whose authority remained supreme throughout the crisis, who decided the issue. He, too, was swept by emotion, but kept his feelings under control and viewed the situation from a coldly realistic point of view throughout the crisis. He condemned bitterly the "betrayal of France and the singularly obtuse policy of Chamberlain," who was concerned only with saving a momentary peace for England. But the British were mistaken, Beneš said. They would not prevent war but only delay it until later, when they would have to fight under more difficult circumstances, because Germany's strength was growing faster than theirs. By sacrificing Czechoslovakia, they only deprived themselves of potential help, which could be not inconsiderable. Beneš showed a fear of Germany's power, verging on panic. On the other hand, he tended to rate Soviet military power low. He was doubtful whether Russia would fight without France and, if it did, whether its help would be timely and effective. Moreover, Soviet help—if it came—would have the political disadvantage of tainting Czechoslovakia with Bolshevism in Western eyes. The president took a dim view of Czechoslovakia's ability to resist alone. In fact, he equated fighting alone with national suicide. In these circumstances, he saw no other course but to submit to the Anglo-French ultimatum, on condition that Britain and France guarantee the remainder of Czechoslovakia. Some cabinet members wondered about the value of an Anglo-French guarantee of rump Czechoslovakia, since France and Britain had betrayed the country once and they might do it again. Beneš pointed out, however, that only France had a contractual obligation to Czechoslovakia, and professed to believe that if Britain gave Czechoslovakia a guarantee it would honor it.[179] In the end, the Czech and Slovak political leaders heeded the president's advice. At 5 P.M., September 21, Krofta informed the French and British

---

ernment, the Communist party resolutely opposed capitulating to the Anglo-French ultimatum, but not being one of the coalition parties it was able to influence the government only indirectly.

[179] Ježek, "Z pamětí," 691-700. Beneš was unbendingly opposed to Czechoslovakia's fighting alone, which was probably the only alternative to capitulation the country had—given the determination of Britain and France not to go to war in 1938 and of the Soviet Union not to be caught in an isolated war with Germany. Beneš explained his reasons against fighting alone most clearly in an account of a conference he had on September 28 with the commanders of the Czechoslovak army, who had come to plead for resistance at all cost: "It would be irresponsible of me to lead the nation to the slaughterhouse in an isolated war at this time." Beneš, *Mnichovské dny*, pp. 340-42. A recent account of Beneš' Munich policy—Mila Lvová, *Mnichov a Edvard Beneš* [*Munich and Edvard Beneš*] (Prague, 1968)—obscures the subject rather than elucidates it. Another recent communist account of the Munich crisis—Václav Král, *Zářijové dny* [*September Days*] (Prague, 1971)—covers the familiar ground of Czech complaints against France and Britain and praise for the Soviet Union, but likewise sheds little light on the domestic aspects of the crisis.

ministers of Czechoslovakia's compliance with the Anglo-French ultimatum.

President Beneš had shown a remarkable grasp of the international situation, both current and future, but tended to discount psychological factors in the crisis, especially the impact of the government's surrender on his own people. The reaction of the Czech people to the government's action was one of deep indignation. On the same night, September 21, as the news of the government's capitulation spread, crowds poured out into the streets of Prague to protest against it. On the following day, an estimated quarter of a million people milled through the streets of the capital, frenziedly crying: "We want to fight!" Hodža and his cabinet, greatly shaken by the popular outburst, hastened to resign. On the same day, President Beneš appointed a nonpolitical cabinet of experts under General Jan Syrový.

The government's capitulation also deeply shocked the Slovaks. They had always taken it for granted that the government in Prague had the means not only to compel their obedience but also to protect them and the country, as a whole, from German, Hungarian, and Polish revisionism through Beneš's ingenious system of alliances. When, instead of being a means of protection, the alliances turned out to be a means of coercion and the government surrendered to the Anglo-French ultimatum, it and President Beneš lost face in Slovak eyes. If the government would not fight to save the Sudeten German areas which were so vital for the Czech provinces, then surely it would not fight to save southern Slovakia —possibly all of Slovakia—from the Hungarians. The Slovaks might have to fend for themselves. The question was no longer of Slovak autonomy but of Czechoslovakia's survival.

Briefly, Czechoslovakia's disintegration was arrested by the disagreement between Chamberlain and Hitler at the Godesberg conference on September 22, which caused a shortlived revival of the British, French, and Czechoslovak governments' will to resist Germany. On the night of September 23, with French and British approval, the Syrový government decreed general mobilization, which appeased the Czechs and reassured the Slovaks. On September 22 and 23, President Beneš received Tiso to discuss the Slovak populist demands. Although he rejected the Whitsun program, he made a counterproposal, which the Slovak populists accepted as a partial basis for further discussions. They agreed to send their representatives into the Syrový cabinet.[180] Immediately before the issuance of the mobilization decree, Sidor joined representatives of all Slovak parties in an appeal to the Slovak people broadcast over Radio Brati-

---

[180] Sidor, *Slovenská politika*, II, 254. For Beneš's proposals to the Slovak populists, see his book, *Úvahy o slovanství* [*Reflections about the Slavs*] (Prague, 1947), pp. 317-22, or its French translation, *Où vont les Slaves?* (Paris, 1948), pp. 277-81.

slava to rally around the government in defense of the fatherland. On September 25, the Slovak populist organ *Slovák* published an appeal to the same effect.[181] Whether in response to the party leaders' exhortations or not, Slovak soldiers responded to the mobilization orders quietly but willingly. If they had been called on to fight for Czechoslovakia they would undoubtedly have done so with their usual quiet, fatalistic courage.

Hitler's belligerent Sportspalast speech in Berlin on September 26, in which he demanded self-determination not only for the Sudeten Germans but also for the other national minorities and the Slovaks, reversed the whole situation, however. The British, French, and Czechoslovak governments' will to resist Germany faltered again. As October 1, the deadline set by Hitler to meet his demands, approached, German, Hungarian, and Polish invasions of Czechoslovakia were expected. On September 28, Sidor and Tiso presented themselves at the Polish embassy in Prague with a resolution of the Slovak populist executive committee proposing, in the event of Czechoslovakia's destruction, a Polish-Slovak union to forestall Hungarian occupation of Slovakia.[182] On the same day Hitler agreed to a four-power conference at Munich.

On September 29—the day of the Munich conference—the Syrový cabinet held a meeting with the Slovak autonomist parties to discuss the Slovak demands. It was decided that the Slovak parties, both centralist and autonomist, should first agree on common demands.[183] The Munich conference awarded the Sudeten German areas to Germany. In principle, it also recognized the Polish and Hungarian territorial claims on Czechoslovakia, but deferred their adjustment until later. The four-power Munich *Diktat* was communicated to the Czechoslovak government at 6:15 A.M., September 30. By noon of the same day the Czechoslovak government surrendered to it, with scarcely a demurrer.[184] Once a pattern of capitulation was established on September 21, it was easy to repeat it on September 30. The population likewise reacted to the government's second surrender with resignation. The hour of the Czech right-wingers and the Slovak populist radicals, who had advised the government to try to deal with Hitler directly, instead of relying on France and Britain alone, had arrived. Now they were in a position to crow: "We told you so!"

There were rumors that the radical Slovak populists would try to dissociate the Slovaks from the Czechs when the great powers adjudicated

---

[181] Hubert Ripka, *Munich: Before and After* (London, 1939), p. 142.
[182] Pal'o Čarnogurský, "Deklarácia unii Slovenska s Pol'skom z 28. septembra 1938" ["The Declaration of the Union of Slovakia and Poland on September 28, 1938"], *Historický časopis*, XVI (1968), 407-23.
[183] Sidor, *Slovenská politika*, II, 258.
[184] *Mnichov v dokumentech*, II, 254-60.

ungarian and Polish claims, in order to gain more lenient terms. in this atmosphere of *sauve qui peut* that the representatives of the list parties met in Bratislava on October 5, in order to agree on a ion stand prior to meeting with the representatives of the autono- mist parties at Žilina on the following day. Dérer was still full of fight. However, the agrarians, who had only a short time before sworn to fight the l'udáks to their last breath, were now ready to surrender to them, in the hope of saving something of their influence in Slovakia.[185] At the same time, Tiso's counsel against dissociating the Slovaks from the Czechs and for standing on the Whitsun program prevailed among the Slovak autonomists meeting at Žilina.

On October 6, the representatives of the Slovak centralist and autono- mist parties met at Žilina. The centralists (the agrarians and three splin- ter parties) accepted the Slovak populist Whitsun program as their own. The "Žilina agreement" thus concluded was communicated to the Syrový government in Prague as representing the aspirations of all the Slovak parties.[186] The Prague government confirmed it on the same day with- out debate. The centralist First Czechoslovak Republic gave way to the federalist Second *Czecho-Slovak* Republic.

Despite its many limitations, the First Republic had brought political freedom and human dignity not only to the Czech and Slovak peoples but also to its German, Hungarian, Polish, and Ruthenian minorities, which their kinsmen in Germany, Austria, Hungary, Poland, and the Soviet Union had either never known or had enjoyed only fleetingly. The First Republic had been the most successful and enduring European democracy east of the Rhine, and as such had won an honorable and permanent place in European history.

[185] Dérer, *Slovenský vývoj*, pp. 304-306; František Lukeš, *Podivný mír* [*Strange Peace*]. (Prague, 1968), p. 79.
[186] Lukeš, pp. 79-80; Sidor, *Slovenská politika*, ii, 259; Čulen, *Po Svätoplukovi*, p. 391. For the text of the Žilina Declaration, see Lettrich, *History*, pp. 296-97.

· 4 ·

THE GERMANS IN PRE-WAR CZECHOSLOVAKIA

J. W. Bruegel
London

From the first moment when Tomáš G. Masaryk decided to abandon his former belief in the possibility of reforming Austria-Hungary and to embark on propagating the idea of creating a separate Czechoslovak state, there was no doubt in his mind that he wanted to include in this state the border districts of Bohemia, Moravia, and Silesia that were mainly inhabited by Germans. In October, 1914, when he discussed his plans in Rotterdam with his English friend Professor Robert W. Seton-Watson, he envisaged the unification of the "Czech lands" (Bohemia, Moravia, and Silesia) with Slovakia. He was willing to make certain territorial concessions in Silesia, but insisted on retaining northern Bohemia as indispensable for the new Czechoslovak state.[1] After returning again to Prague from Holland, Masaryk left his country for good in December, 1914. In May, 1915, after reaching London, he handed a memorandum to British Foreign Secretary Sir Edward Grey, in which he again insisted on the inclusion of the German population living in the border regions of Bohemia, Moravia, and Silesia into the new Czechoslovak state he had in mind. Referring to the contradiction between the idea of self-determination which he put forward and the desire to incorporate in the new state Germans who in his scheme would not have the right to self-determination, he said:

> Though we advocate the principle of nationality, we wish to retain our German minority. It seems to be a paradox, but it is on the principle of nationality that we retain our German minority. Bohemia is a quite unique example of a mixed country; in no country are two nationalities so intermixed and interwoven, so to say, as in Bohemia. Between the Germans and Italians, for instance, the ethnographical frontier is simple, sharply cut; it is not so in Bohemia—in a great many places and in almost all the cities we have Bohemian (or German) minorities.[2]

In his book *The New Europe* Masaryk reduced the problem to the simple question of whether it would be fairer to keep more than nine million Czechs and Slovaks under German rule or three million Germans

[1] Robert W. Seton-Watson, *Masaryk in England* (Cambridge, 1943), p. 128.
[2] Ibid.

167

under Czech rule.[3] The answer to this question is obvious enough, but Masaryk's ideal was after all that no people should rule over another. He may have felt misgivings, for he explained the same idea in his memoirs in a less objectionable form: "The question arises whether it is fairer that a fragment of the German people should remain in a non-German State or that the whole Czechoslovak people should live in a German State."[4] From this point of view official Czech policy, represented in those days mainly by Masaryk and Beneš, never deviated. The same idea was expressed in the so-called "Mémoire III" which the Czechoslovak delegation submitted to the Paris Peace Conference in February, 1919. This was a hurriedly concocted propaganda pamphlet which consequently contained some incorrect statements of minor importance, although the contents were in general unobjectionable. Referring to some estimates made by the "Czech National Council" (a private, non-official organization), the Mémoire grossly overestimated the Czech minorities living in the German districts of Bohemia and underrated the number of Germans in the country. This discrepancy arose because of the Czechs' distrust of the Austrian census of 1910; later, the Czechoslovak census of 1920 showed that this distrust was exaggerated. There had, however, been no intention of misleading the Peace Conference, which based its decisions on the assumption arising from the old Austrian census of 1910 that within the frontiers allotted to Czechoslovakia by the peace treaties she had 3,747,000 German inhabitants.[5]

THE QUESTION OF SELF-DETERMINATION FOR THE GERMANS

On the other hand, the Germans or at least the German members of the Austrian parliament, elected in 1911 for constituencies in Bohemia, Moravia, and Silesia, insisted on self-determination for themselves. From a democratic point of view there could be no objection to that: the dissolution of Austria-Hungary had set all the nationalities free to make their own decisions about their futures. In this respect all German political parties were of one mind, but they were not of one mind about the way how self-determination should be exercised in case it was granted. Some were dreaming of a direct *Anschluss* to Germany of the western and northern regions of Bohemia, Moravia, and Silesia bordering on Germany. Most of them were thinking of somehow maintaining the unity of the territories which formerly had made up the Austro-Hungarian

[3] Tomáš G. Masaryk, *The New Europe: The Slav Standpoint* (London, 1918), p. 53.

[4] Tomáš G. Masaryk, *The Making of a State: Memories and Observations 1914-1918* (London, 1927), p. 389.

[5] Harold W. V. Temperley, *History of the Peace Conference in Paris* (5 vols., London, 1925), v, 155.

Monarchy through a certain collaboration between the new national states and these German-inhabited regions becoming or remaining parts of "German-Austria," the name which the Republic of Austria chose at the end of 1918. Others, mainly the German Social Democrats, demanded self-determination only in order to be able to decide freely whether, under certain conditions, to join with the Czechs in one state or to join with German-Austria and then, perhaps, to become part of the Weimar Republic through the *Anschluss* of German-Austria.

In contrast to their representatives, elected in 1911 under absolutely different circumstances, the German population as a whole, though naturally unhappy over the loss of the privileged position they had enjoyed in old Austria, were by no means in a furiously nationalistic or anti-Czech mood at the end of 1918. The German industrialists feared that an incorporation into Germany might result in a decline and extinction of their industries, which were unable to compete with the much more advanced industries of Germany. Instinctively, the German population disliked the idea of being cut off from their Czech hinterland and brought into a combination which would have been new and untried. Here was a possibility for the Czechs to win over large parts, and perhaps the majority, of the German population to the idea of remaining together within the newly built Czechoslovak state. Masaryk urged his countrymen to follow such a course, and though there were some Czech attempts to win German good will, in general the mistake was made to rely more on the peace conference which would certainly fulfill the Czechoslovak demands, and to ignore German wishes and aspirations. How mistaken this reliance was becomes obvious from a secret letter written by Karl Renner, the chancellor of German-Austria, to Otto Bauer, the foreign minister in his government, in December, 1918: "Jokl [a German Social Democrat Deputy from Austrian Silesia] thinks that if the Czechs offered autonomy to the Germans, 99 percent of them, including the workers, would opt for annexation to Czechoslovakia. Since similar views reach us from German-Bohemia in large numbers, I am always worried that we may suffer shipwreck," i.e., with their territorial demands.[6]

Karl Renner asked the peace conference for the inclusion of the German-speaking parts of Bohemia, Moravia, and Silesia into Austria, but he was a realist, and in his posthumously published memoirs he explained that he had not really believed in the feasibility of this proposal, but had only hoped thereby to strengthen the position of the Germans in Czechoslovakia.[7] (The name "Sudeten Germans" came into use only later in the twenties and referred merely to the Germans living in the

[6] Karl Renner to Otto Bauer, December 12, 1918, Personal files of State Secretary Dr. Otto Bauer, Vol. 8 "Czechoslovakia," Austrian State Archives, Vienna.
[7] Karl Renner, *Von der Ersten zur Zweiten Republik* (Vienna, 1953), pp. 24, 30, 34, 211-12.

predominantly German border districts of Bohemia, Moravia, and Silesia. Later, this name was used for all the Germans of Czechoslovakia.)

THE DECISION OF THE PEACE CONFERENCE

Edvard Beneš, as Czechoslovak representative at the peace conference, was prepared to cede some salients of Bohemia to Germany. The peace conference, however, decided in favor of maintaining the unity of the "Czech lands," without holding a plebiscite which the Austrian Delegation had demanded. The separate administrations organized by the Germans at the end of 1918 for the German parts of Bohemia, for northern Moravia and Silesia, for southern Bohemia, and for southern Moravia had collapsed after a few days or weeks. Only the *Landesregierung* (provincial government) of German Bohemia had developed an administrative activity for a short time, trying mainly to solve the question of securing food supplies for the starving population. Some towns under German administration had even called in Czech troops out of fear of riots. The whole area was occupied by the Czechoslovak army before the end of 1918, in accordance with the armistice provisions. No military or other resistance of any size had to be overcome. Although the Germans naturally disliked this new situation, they had no burning desire to escape from the new state.

Even before the Peace of St. Germain was signed in September, 1919, many Germans proved their readiness to collaborate under the new conditions. In April, 1919, the vice-chancellor of the German university and the head of the German institute of technology in Prague, without being asked by anybody to do so, swore allegiance to the Czechoslovak Republic. On June 15, 1919, the first municipal elections were held in Czechoslovakia and all German political groups took part in it; the system of newly introduced proportional representation secured a fair and just representation of the Germans in local administration. For the first time in decades Germans were elected to Prague's city council. Impressed by the outcome of these elections, which gave a great majority to the German non-nationalistic parties—in Bohemia the German Social Democrats obtained 44 percent of all German votes—the organ of the Czechoslovak Social Democratic Party wrote: "We must not be content with winning the Germans' passive loyalty but must establish a cordial relationship with them, so that they will readily and enthusiastically cooperate in the building of our new State which is also to be theirs."[8]

In August, 1919, the German Social Democrats in Czechoslovakia organized an independent party, breaking their links with the Austrian Social Democratic party. Their leader, Josef Seliger, protested against

[8] *Právo Lidu* (Prague), June 21, 1919.

the denial of self-determination to the Germans in Czechoslovakia, but at the same time proclaimed the readiness of his party to conduct its policy within the framework of the new Czechoslovak state.[9] With a few insignificant exceptions, not even the German nationalists attempted to carry out a policy of *irredenta*—except in words.

In theory, the German population of old Austria unquestionably had the right to self-determination, as did all the other nationalities. In practice, however, the Germans in that part of the Austrian empire which became Czechoslovakia could not expect that they would be able to use this right in a way which would endanger the self-determination of another people, namely the Czechs and Slovaks, whose natural desire had been to build up a politically and economically viable state. The Commission on Czechoslovak Questions at the Paris Peace Conference accepted Beneš's plausible arguments:

... However desirable it appeared to give the greatest possible ethnic unity to the new Czechoslovak State, it was equally obvious that the new state must be placed in a position where it could satisfy its economic requirements. For this reason it appeared *important* on the one hand *not to disrupt the existing economic life* and on the other hand to give to the Czechs the means of communication essential for their economic development, together with a frontier which provides them with the necessary quarantees for their national security. . . .

The Commission was *unanimous* in its recommendation that the Czechoslovak frontier in this area (with Germany) should basically be identical with *the old frontier* between Austria and the German Reich. . . .

The Commission was *unanimous* in its recommendation that the Czechoslovak frontier in this area (with Austria) should basically be identical with the administrative border separating Bohemia and Moravia from the Austrian provinces. . . .

The Commission fully acknowledged the fact that the incorporation of so large a number of Germans into Czechoslovakia may involve certain disadvantages for the future of the new state.

The Commission was at the same time unanimous in its recommendation that the separation of all areas inhabited by German-Bohemians would not only expose Czechoslovakia to great dangers but equally create *great difficulties for the Germans themselves. The only practicable solution was to incorporate these Germans into Czechoslovakia.*[10]

[9] Josef Hofbauer and Emil Strauss, *Josef Seliger* (Prague, 1930), p. 167.

[10] David Hunter Miller, *My Diary at the Conference in Paris* (21 vols., New York, 1924), XVI, 11-16. My italics. *La Paix de Versailles* (Paris, 1939), IX, 142-52.

This point of view was accepted by the "Big Four"—Clemenceau, Orlando, Lloyd George, and Colonel E. M. House, acting as President Wilson's substitute—on April 4, 1919.[11]

DR. BENEŠ'S PROMISES

After the territorial question had been settled by the Peace Conference, the safeguards for the application of equal rights to the minorities in the newly created states were studied and minorities' treaties guaranteeing basic rights to "racial, religious and linguistic minorities" were signed, one of them by Czechoslovakia. A memorandum by Beneš dated May 20, 1919, submitted to the Peace Conference's Committee on New States and outlining his ideas about the internal settlement, was later the source of the repeated charges that a promise to create Czechoslovakia as a second Switzerland had been violated. But Beneš had spoken only about an intention "to make the Czechoslovak Republic a sort of Switzerland [*une sorte de Suisse*], taking into consideration, of course, the special conditions in Bohemia."[12]

By this Beneš clearly meant that the liberal ideas of Switzerland should be taken over by Czechoslovakia, not Swiss institutions copied. In the memorandum he set out in detail how he imagined the application of Swiss principles to the thoroughly different Czechoslovak conditions. What he had promised on May 20, 1919, tallied in general with the internal regime of Czechoslovakia until 1938.

After studying Beneš's memorandum the Committee on New States was convinced that the question of the Germans in Czechoslovakia went beyond the sphere of merely protecting a small and perhaps helpless minority, and summarized its conclusions:

The position of the Germans in Bohemia is, of course, completely different [i.e. from the situation of the Hungarians and the Ruthenians]; they had until recent years been the dominating influence in the State, they form a highly developed, very capable element, and, in the past, have been a very aggressive population. *It is clear that the prospects and perhaps almost the existence of the new State will depend on the success with which it incorporates the Germans as willing citizens.* The very magnitude of this task makes it one quite different in character from the mere protection of the other minorities with which the Committee has had to deal; it is one which goes so deeply into the heart of

---

[11] Paul Mantoux (ed.), *Les Délibérations du Conseil des Quatre* (2 vols., Paris, 1955), I, 148.
[12] Miller, *My Diary*, XIII, 69-70. *La Paix de Versailles*, X, 53-54.

all the institutions that the solution of it is probably be[s
Czechs themselves.

The Committee has received a communication from D
in which he has informed them that it is the intention o
Government to treat the Germans with the greatest liber[
proposals go far beyond anything which the Committee ~~~~ ~~
felt justified in putting forward. Under the circumstances, therefore,
they consider that it would be wiser not to make any specific reference
to the Germans.[13]

This remarkable document, which first became known through an
American publication in 1924, was, strangely enough, never published
in Czechoslovakia; had it been, it would have strengthened the hands of
those Czechs striving for greater justice for the minorities against the
more nationalistic followers of Karel Kramář, the first premier.

THE CZECHOSLOVAK CONSTITUTION

The Czechoslovak Constitution of 1920, which remained unchanged
until 1938 and was theoretically in force until 1948, was drafted and
adopted in February, 1920, by Czechoslovakia's "revolutionary" National Assembly, consisting of Czechs and Slovaks only. It was definitely
a tactical mistake not to give at least those Germans, Hungarians, Poles,
and Ukrainians in Czechoslovakia who were prepared to accept the
framework of the new state an opportunity to cooperate in the
task of providing the country with a constitution. The failure of
the Czechs to do so led to the charge that the constitution had
been imposed on the minorities, not accepted by them in the democratic
way. In spite of this fact, however, it was a thoroughly liberal constitution following Western models and guaranteeing not only the usual political rights of the citizens, but incorporating also the special provisions
of the Minorities' Treaty for the national and other minorities.

The hint of the peace conference that the problem of the Germans in
Czechoslovakia was "quite different . . . from the mere protection of
other minorities" was, however, not acted upon. The most important
constitutional safeguard was embodied in Article 128, sub-section 2:

Differences of religion or language do not form an obstacle to any citizen of the Czechoslovak Republic within the general body of the law
and in particular do not debar him from admission to the public service, or from the practice of any trade or profession.

[13] Miller, *My Diary*, XIII, 78-80, also 162-63. My italics. *La Paix de Versailles*,
X, 61-62, also 122.

173

FIRST ATTEMPTS TO GIVE THE GERMANS A PLACE
IN THE GOVERNMENT

When the first elected parliament met at the end of May, 1920, all German parties were in opposition. The attempts of the Social-Democratic premier Vlastimil Tusar to organize a government composed of the Czechoslovak and German socialist and agrarian parties came to nothing, because the German Social Democrats insisted that national autonomy or home rule must first be granted to the German-inhabited territories. The constitution was a product of a difficult compromise between the Czech Social Democrats and National Democrats. Tusar did not dare, at that moment, to make a concession to the Germans and reopen the debate over the constitution, all the more so because he was at the same time threatened by a revolt of the communist wing inside his own party. In the end, the revolt led to the establishment of an independent communist party and to the downfall of Tusar and his government a few months later. Thus, even if a compromise with the Germans could have been arranged at that time, important as it would have been as a precedent, it could not have been of long duration.

THE QUESTION OF NATIONAL AUTONOMY

With the exception of the German nationalists who did not want to have anything to do with the new state and refused to think about securing the position of the Germans inside Czechoslovakia, all German parties insisted, at first, on national autonomy. But, again, the ideas which should form the basis of such an arrangement were very varied, ranging from demands for a cultural autonomy with the minorities administering their schools themselves to a far more radical demand for building up something which would have been a "state within the state." The Czechs were certainly right in refusing to accept such a radical solution, for a separate existence of the Germans within, but ignoring the political reality of, Czechoslovakia would not only have sapped the vitality of the latter, but would even have reacted unfavorably on the economic structure of the German-inhabited parts which, to a large extent, were dependent on the Czech-inhabited regions of the country. What Czechoslovakia, however, should have set out to do at that time was to try to remove the stigma of political inferiority from the minority concept and to restore its original simple numerical meaning.

In the beginning, however, even President Masaryk bluntly declared territorial autonomy for the minorities out of the question: "There will be no discussion about territorial autonomy."[14] The statement reflected

[14] Tomáš G. Masaryk, "Message on the Occasion of the Tenth Anniversary of October 28, 1918," *Lidové Noviny* (Brno), October 30, 1928.

the fear of the Czechs that any concession in this respect could lead to a secession to Germany of the German areas vitally important for the economy and wellbeing of the state. Those fears were certainly exaggerated, because at that time the German democratic parties, which were ready to collaborate with the Czechoslovak government, would have had a decisive majority in all elections for organs of territorial self-government, and Weimar Germany would have rejected all ideas of incorporating territories from other states. Masaryk later revised his originally negative attitude and stated:

> In a democracy . . . the desire for local self-government is natural: if the population of a country is such that, although numerous, its natural and cultural development is not uniform, and yet the whole people is to cooperate in the administration, then political power must also be divided according to the natural differences among the population. . . . Therefore, I have always quite deliberately advocated territorial autonomy and a degree of corporate independence; I am not unaware of the fact that a state, and particularly a modern state, cannot do without a centralized organization, but it is the task of a modern democratic state to harmonize central government and local government.[15]

CULTURAL AUTONOMY PREPARED

There were also some attempts from the Government side to prepare the foundations for a cultural autonomy for the minorities. In 1926, the Minister of Education, Milan Hodža, announced that he was going to introduce legislation to strengthen the existing district and provincial educational authorities, which were already split up into a Czech and German group, by including lay representatives. But unanimity could not be reached in the cabinet, and eventually the matter was dropped when Hodža left the government at the beginning of 1929.

The question became topical again when the Czechoslovak Social Democrats included the demand for cultural autonomy for the national minorities in their party program in 1930.[16] The resolution was not intended to remain a dead letter: the Slovak Social Democrat, Ivan Dérer who had become Minister of Education in December, 1929, took action; by the end of 1932 he was able to submit a draft law[17] providing for lo-

[15] Tomáš G. Masaryk, *Cesta demokracie* [*The Way of Democracy*] (2 vols., Prague, 1934), II, 206-19.
[16] *Programm der Tschechoslowakischen sozialdemokratischen Arbeiterpartei,* beschlossen vom Parteitag [*Program of the Czechoslovak Social Democratic Labor Party* adopted by the Party Convention], September 27-29, 1930 (Prague, 1930), p. 13.
[17] *Prager Tagblatt*, December 24, 1932.

cal, district, and provincial education councils (wherever they did not already exist) in the form of linguistically separate groups independent of other authorities. In practice, this would have meant that a Hungarian educational authority would have been created in Slovakia, in addition to the German ones which already existed in Bohemia and Moravia. Appropriate representation was also envisaged for the Poles in Moravia-Silesia and the Germans in Slovakia. Two thirds of the councils were supposed to consist of lay members of the public and one-third of teachers, "so that within the framework of the law each nation administered its own schools." In recommending the proposal in a parliamentary committee Dérer said: "In the question of minorities we must start from a point of mutual confidence. We [the Czechoslovaks] as the national majority, primarily entrusted with the task of preserving the state which we have founded, will have to show a certain amount of confidence in the minorities."[18] But a few days after his statement Hitler came to power in Germany and the repercussions of this tragic event were immediately felt in Czechoslovakia, so that any hopes for a full national reconciliation along this road were dashed for the moment and in fact buried for good.

"NATIONAL STATE" OR "STATE OF NATIONALITIES"

Was Czechoslovakia, until October, 1938, a "national state" or a "state of nationalities"? This question has long been a bone of contention. The constitution nowhere proclaimed Czechoslovakia a "national state" nor did it concede any special privileges to the Czechs and Slovaks (regarded at that time as two branches of one nation). Beneš is now frequently considered to have been the leading exponent of the "intransigent national state." In reality, however, he never had anything to do with this slogan. Neither was his political activity up to 1938 in line with the view that Czechoslovakia was or ought to be a national state: on the contrary, there are countless utterances of his on record which clearly show that during those years Beneš was a partisan of absolute equality of all citizens without consideration of the language they spoke. Only once before 1938 did he mention the concept of a "national state," and that was in his (very first) report in the National Assembly on September 30, 1919, on his activity at the Paris Peace Conference. The peace conference, he explained, considered the successor states of Austria-Hungary to be "national states" representing the fulfilment of national aspirations; nevertheless the peacemakers realized that "it was not possible from the international point of view to form these national states as if they were really

[18] *Lidové Noviny*, January 26, 1933.

national states; it was not possible to draw their frontiers in such a way as to exclude from them all minorities."[19]

Thus, when Beneš spoke of "national states," he interpreted not his own views but those of the peace conference, with the implication that none of the successor states was really a "national state." Nineteen years later—on August 17, 1938—Beneš explained to Henlein's delegates that "the expression *les Etats nationaux* was used during the peace negotiations not in the sense of national States, but merely to contrast them with Austria-Hungary."

Not content with correcting a factual misunderstanding, Beneš went farther in 1938 by pointing out that "during the parliamentary negotiations over the Constitution [he] sounded a warning note against designating Czechoslovakia as a National State [according to Herbert Kier this is historically correct]. . . . He [Beneš] considered the theory of the National State to be mistaken."[20] The Sudeten German deputy Ernst Kundt had confirmation of this information from Kier, a Henlein party expert.

In a discussion which took place a few days later, on August 25, 1938, Beneš related, according to the notes made by his interlocutors, that Kramář had opposed him, because "he [Beneš] had already, in the Revolutionary National Assembly, stood against the idea of a State language and the plan to designate Czechoslovakia in the Constitution as a National State."[21] Here Beneš may well have had in mind his Paris encounter with Kramář, who had refused to sign a minorities treaty, and his subsequent quarrel with him about the expression "state language" in the constitution.

Before 1938, there was only one consistent advocate of the theory of the "national state" in Czechoslovakia, Kramář and his ever-diminishing party of National Democrats. None of the other political parties used the term. The bureaucracy, however, did frequently behave as if the state had been created for the *Staatsvolk* only and that the others were to get what was left over. It would, however, be rash to condemn Czechoslovakia on this count alone: to reconcile the needs of the Czechs and Slovaks who felt especially responsible for their state with the basic rights of the other nationalities was no simple matter. The process could be eased by admonitions from above which Masaryk and later Beneš did not fail to offer; a satisfactory state of affairs needed more time than merely twenty years and was bound to depend on the degree of

[19] Ferdinand Peroutka, *Budování státu* [*Building the State*] (5 vols. in 6, Prague, 1934), II, 1293.

[20] *Documents on German Foreign Policy*, Series D (1937-45), vol. II: *Germany and Czechoslovakia (1937-1938)* (Washington, 1949), No. 378.

[21] Ibid., No. 398.

allegiance to the state felt by members of those ethnic groups which for one reason or another were absent when the republic was founded in 1918.

The position was explained by Jaroslav Stranský, who declared, in a German newspaper in 1920, that Czechoslovakia was a state "whose purpose it is to create and to protect the political independence of the Czechs and Slovaks in their entirety."[22] No German could quarrel with this definition. President Masaryk, in his message on the tenth anniversary of Czechoslovakia in 1928, decisively rejected the idea that Czechoslovakia was a "national state" with special rights for Czechs and Slovaks by declaring:

> . . . It is of supreme importance that we are an *ethnically and linguistically mixed state* and although it is true that other states, in fact all other states, have national minorities, *ours are in a different category.* There is no universally applicable solution to the minority problem: each minority represents its own particular problem. What concerns us most is the relationship between the Czechoslovak majority and our German fellow-citizens. Once this problem has been solved, all other linguistic and national problems can be dealt with easily. It has so happened that for many years past, side by side with Czechs and Slovaks, considerable numbers of Germans have lived in our state. Our German fellow-citizens, moreover, are highly civilized. . . . *Any sort of chauvinism must be excluded; on both sides, of course.*
>
> Not only our Germans but all others, likewise, are now our fellow-citizens and will therefore enjoy democratic equality. . . . In a democracy the representation of the minorities is a necessity. In every case it is the task of the majority which must imprint its own characteristics on society to win the minorities' confidence for the state.[23]

Unfortunately, Masaryk's well-meant advice was not always heeded by the far too powerful bureaucracy of the state.

Until 1935 the Majority of Germans were in the Democratic Camp

While up to 1926 all German political parties were in opposition, only the German Nationalists and German National Socialists, who were not numerically very important at that time, were in opposition to the Czechoslovak state as such. The German Social Democrats, who emerged from the first elections of 1920 as the strongest German party (and the second strongest in the country after the Czechoslovak Social Democrats) and held that position until 1935, were advocates of national autonomy but

---

[22] *Prager Tagblatt*, November 30, 1920.
[23] *Lidové Noviny*, October 30, 1928.

stood ready to collaborate within the framework of the Czechoslovak Republic. The other German parties started copying the example of the Czechs in the old Austrian Reichsrat by setting up a joint parliamentary club, but this foundered soon afterward over the unbridgeable divergencies between the extremists and the moderates. As early as 1922, the German agrarians started an "activist policy," which aimed at integrating the Germans into the Czechoslovak Republic and bringing them into the government. Until 1926, however, the government was composed solely of parties comprising Czechs and Slovaks. The German Christian Socials followed suit, together with some smaller groups. While there was always a vociferous and extremist minority among the German population of the country that followed the idea of pangermanism, German nationalism became a real threat to Czechoslovak democracy only after Hitler's rise to power in Germany in 1933. In the parliamentary elections of 1920, 1925, and 1929, the moderate German parties, which rejected any irredentist ideas, polled between 74 and 83 percent of the German votes, leaving the two groups of irreconcilables, the German Nationalists and the German National Socialists, in a hopeless minority. Using the customary terms "activist" and "negativist" for the moderates and extremists, respectively, we come to the following picture:

	1920	1925	1929
German Activists	1,249,341	1,297,568	1,252,281
German Negativists	328,351	409,272	393,297[24]

In 1920 the divergencies between those willing to cooperate with the Czechoslovak Republic and those who rejected it had not yet become apparent. However, the electoral battle for the German vote in 1925 was fought, and won, over the issue of coming to terms with the Czechoslovak Republic. When the elections of 1929 took place, two German parties had been in the government for three years. Apparently, however, the German electorate did not reject the idea, for the elections of 1929 registered a further decline of the nationalist vote.

In 1929, the German Social Democrats replaced the Christian Socials in the government and were responsible for the measures taken by the government to combat the economic crisis and mass unemployment. To overcome a catastrophe of the magnitude of the Great Depression was, however, beyond the capacities of a small state in Central Europe and, for obvious reasons, unemployment was much higher in German-inhabited, highly industrialized regions than in the less industrialized

[24] *Statistical Yearbook of the Czechoslovak Republic, 1920, 1925, and 1929* (Prague, 1921, 1926, and 1930, respectively).

districts. The logical consequence of the misery and hunger ex-
:ed by hundreds of thousands of unemployed Germans should
een the annihilation of the German government parties in the next
ns. As a matter of fact—mainly because of the success of Hitler
in Germany—the party of Konrad Henlein, which was from the beginning a thinly camouflaged Nazi party, now won an overwhelming victory
and became by far the strongest German party. However, the German
democratic parties, which cooperated with the government, were by no
means annihilated. They won about 33 percent of the German vote.
Needless to say, Henlein's victory meant a defeat for Czechoslovakia's
democracy and democracy in general. The radicalization of the German
electorate in Czechoslovakia has to be seen in connection with the plebiscite held a few months earlier in the Saar, however. The democratic
parties of the Saarland, the Christian Democrats and Social Democrats,
who were free of any government responsibility, had urged the electorate
to vote for the *status quo* of an autonomous Saar Territory, but only 8.83
percent heeded this appeal while over 90 percent voted for an immediate
return to Germany. In comparison with this result, the fact that 33 percent of the German voters expressed confidence in the feasibility of a
successful Czech-German cooperation was by no means a disheartening
outcome.

German Representation in the Government

Czechoslovakia was the only country on the continent of Europe in
which a national minority was represented in the government. In 1926
two German parties, the German agrarians and the German Christian
Socials, entered the government. Franz Spina (1868-1938), the leader
of the agrarians, became minister of public works and Robert Mayr-
Harting (1874-1947), the leader of the Christian Socials, minister of
justice. The ministries held by Germans were by no means insignificant,
but they did not offer much scope for concessions to the German demand
to participate in the administration. The situation changed in 1929 when
the German Christian Socials were replaced by the German Social Democrats, whose leading representative, Ludwig Czech (1870-1942), became the holder of a key ministry, the Ministry of Social Welfare. The
importance of this office increased during the depression when Czech was
able to introduce the principle of full ethnic justice, not only in
the sphere of help for the unemployed but in the whole field of social
welfare and labor relations. This principle was upheld by his Czech successors in office when he moved to the Ministry of Public Works in 1934
and to the Ministry of Health in 1935, which he administered until 1938.

Spina had been minister of health from 1929 to 1935. From 1935, when the German agrarians lost much support to the Henlein party, until 1938, he stayed on in the government as a minister without portfolio. In 1929 the German Christian Socials had quite unnecessarily been driven into opposition, but in all matters of importance to the Czechoslovak Republic, for instance in the re-election of Masaryk as president in 1934 and in the election of Beneš to the presidency in the following year, they voted with the government parties. In 1936, when all German democratic forces rallied around the government to stave off the growing danger coming from the Third Reich and its followers within Czechoslovakia, they joined the government again and one of the Christian Social deputies, Erwin Zajiček, became minister without portfolio. Until March, 1938, the German democrats were represented by three members in the government. The occupation of Austria by Germany in March, 1938, led to a panic in their ranks; many lost faith in the future of democratic cooperation, while others intensified, out of courage or despair, their determination to defend freedom and democracy to the last alongside the Czechs. Through an illegal *Putsch* of some of its functionaries, the agrarian party was taken over by the Henlein party. The official leadership of the Christian Social party no longer believed in the possibility of a further independent existence and followed suit, a step deplored by many ordinary members of both parties. Their representatives in the government, Spina and Zajiček, resigned but remained active in the democratic camp. In the summer of 1938, Zajiček declared to Lord Runciman that by no means all Germans in Czechoslovakia followed Henlein and Hitler.

The only remaining German government party, the German Social Democratic party, likewise relinquished its representation in the government. Only the secret files of the German foreign ministry revealed the reason for it after the War: the Henlein party had made the discontinuation of German democratic representation in the government a pre-condition for the talks the government was forced to hold with them, because of pressure from London and Paris. Thus, ironically, it was a veto from Berlin which put an end to German representation in the Prague government.

The time after 1933 might not have been propitious for large-scale reforms, and the previous demands for local self-government were shelved by the German government parties after Hitler's accession to power in 1933. Nevertheless, German cooperation with the government was by no means a story of failures alone. Perhaps their many-sided achievements could best be evaluated by reviewing the results of twenty years of Czechoslovak internal policy in the various fields, which we shall try to do later on. However, the strongest testimonial for a fair Czechoslovak nationality policy and for Czechoslovak democracy in general remains the fact that in September, 1938, tens of thousands of German democrats were ready to fight, together with the Czechs, for Czechoslovak independence.

THE RISE OF HENLEIN

It was certainly an extraordinary occurrence that a party founded by an obscure gymnastics teacher, absolutely unknown until 1933, could poll 1,200,000 votes in 1935. This was not due to any magic qualities in Konrad Henlein, but to the natural repercussions of the upsurge of National Socialism in Germany. Whether and how far mistakes and omissions in the official Czechoslovak nationality policy may have helped the rise of Henlein is an open question, but the decisive factor was that Hitler's success unleashed a wave of national fanaticism among the Germans outside Germany. Henlein had come to the fore at the moment when the Czechoslovak government dissolved the German National Socialist party and removed the German Nationalist party from the scene, steps which were necessitated by the fact that those two parties had obviously been agencies of the Berlin government in Czechoslovakia. At that moment Henlein appealed to the whole German population for assistance in setting up a new movement distinct from the old party configuration. He professed loyalty to the Czechoslovak Republic and readiness to come to terms with the Czechs. Many realized from the beginning that this was only a subterfuge to give the members of the dissolved parties a new and safer platform, but the warnings of German democrats that Henlein was simply the executor of Hitler's policy on Czechoslovak soil was not generally believed.

After further declarations of loyalty to Czechoslovakia, which should not have been taken at face value, Henlein's movement was admitted to the elections in 1935 under the suggestive name of "Sudeten German party." Some reactionary Czech elements saw in Henlein a possible partner for them in a post-election attempt to oust Foreign Minister Beneš and to replace the Czechoslovak-German coalition of the left- and right-wing parties by a right-wing combination.

But Henlein enjoyed other influential help, too. He had gone to London, where he repeated his story of readiness to work loyally inside Czechoslovakia to Sir Robert Vansittart, the Permanent Under-Secretary in the Foreign Office. Vansittart believed him and gave him every assistance, because he saw in Henlein an antidote to Hitler. With the growing aggressiveness of Hitler's foreign policy, Henlein gradually abandoned one democratic pretense after another until—after the Austrian *Anschluss*—he openly declared that his movement was national socialist. Until the last possible moment, however, he denied striving for union of the German-inhabited parts of Czechoslovakia to Germany. Instead, he proclaimed as his only goal autonomy for the Sudeten Germans, though it was a form of autonomy which had no resemblance to democratic self-government. If adopted, it would have been an authoritarian regime which, as a preliminary step toward union with Germany, would have introduced the undemocratic one-party system in the Sudeten German areas of Czechoslovakia. The British and French statesmen believed Henlein when he professed to demand merely home rule, and supported him to the hilt.

The German democratic parties in Czechoslovakia, although they represented the great majority of the German population in the country until 1935, had always had a much more difficult life; they did not enjoy any support from abroad and in their own country they often met with a lack of understanding, although Masaryk as president and Beneš as foreign minister and later as president supported them and fought for a democratic understanding between Czechs and Germans. The slogan "equals among equals," coined by Antonín Švehla when he presented the first multi-national government to parliament in 1926, was not always totally implemented.

The Civil Service

When one looks back on the various features of the Czechoslovak nationality policy between 1918 and 1938, the question of the representation of the country's national minorities in the civil service immediately springs to mind. One of the most frequently criticized aspects of the nationality policy was that neither the Germans nor the Hungarians or Poles were represented in the civil service according to their numerical strength in the country. Until 1918, the top echelons in the civil and juridical service in Bohemia, Moravia, and Silesia had been almost exclusively German, a state of affairs which was neither just nor tenable; but there was no rigidly automatic replacement of German officials by new Czech ones. When the new ministries were formed in Prague after 1918 the Germans were, however, largely ignored and the general reduction of the number of civil servants during the mid-twenties affected the Germans much more than the Czechs, because German officials often knew only German while Czechs were usually bilingual (even though perfect command of Czech was by no means immediately expected from all German officials).

The ideal solution of the problem in a multi-national state would have been the proportional representation of all the nationalities in the public service. In Czechoslovakia the retirement of older officials, the creation of new offices staffed mainly by Czechs, and, to a lesser extent, staff re-

183

ductions had in the course of the years reversed the former German pre-
ponderance in government service. The process was again halted after
the German activists joined the government and gained political influence. Germans were newly employed in all branches of the civil service,
and those who had been taken over from the old Austrian administration
were promoted. The German parties in the Czechoslovak government
achieved a notable success in their efforts for an increased share in the
Czechoslovak administration by an agreement with the government in
1937.

In the beginning of 1938 the principle of proportional representation
in the civil service was officially adopted as a guideline by the government, but this decision could no longer be implemented, because of the
dismemberment of Czechoslovakia.[25]

EDUCATIONAL AND CULTURAL OPPORTUNITIES
FOR GERMANS

One of the most important questions in evaluating the record of the
Czechoslovak Republic is whether the Germans in the country had
enough schools and other educational requirements of their own. After
1918 many German schools, mainly grammar schools with a poor at-
tendance, many of them in purely Czech towns, were closed down; but
new German schools were opened in Slovakia, where there had been no
German school system at all before 1918. The three million Sudeten
Germans had one university and two institutes of technology, while in
Germany there was only one technological institute for every six million
inhabitants.[26] The Germans received 25.46 percent of Czechoslovakia's
expenditure on higher education, which was more than their proportion
of the population (23.32 percent) warranted.

The most striking results are obtained when we compare German with
Czech schools in Czechoslovakia and with German schools in Germany
within her old frontiers:[27]

	Average number of pupils per elementary school form	Number of pupils per teacher
Germany	40.3	42.4
Czechoslovakia		
German schools	34.3	34.2
Czech/Slovak schools	37.0	37.0

[25] *Prager Presse*, March 19, 1938.
[26] Antoine Karlgren, *Henlein, Hitler et les Tchèques: La Question Allemande des Sudètes* (Paris, 1939), pp. 83-84.
[27] *Statistical Yearbook of the Czechoslovak Republic 1938* (Prague, 1938).

This was the situation before Hitler "liberated" the Sudeten Germans. After that, the equilibrium was altered even more in favor of the former Czechoslovak system.[28]

	Pupils per elementary school form	Pupils per teacher
"Altreich" (Germany within her 1937 frontiers)	40	42.1
"Reichsgau Sudetenland"	34	28

In the institutions of higher secondary education the Germans were not deprived either:[29]

	Average number of pupils per form in		
	Gymnasia (Humanistic high schools)	Technical high schools	Teacher-training institutes
German	34.5	34.0	41.2
Czech or Slovak	38.0	38.1	41.3

THE LAND REFORM

One post-war action aimed at bringing about a more socially just distribution of the land and breaking up the large estates, the so-called Land Reform, naturally had many repercussions on the national minorities. The Prague authorities were often accused of using the Land Reform, which gave to landless peasants land taken over from estate holders against compensation, to strengthen the Czech element at the expense of the Germans. Czech applicants were allegedly given land in German districts while local German applicants were ignored, which resulted in a change of the ethnic composition of those districts. It is undeniable that there was not full ethnic justice in this field and that Czech applicants were obviously favored by the authorities. It must, however, be borne in mind that there were proportionately more Czech applicants than German ones, as the German population in Czechoslovakia was industrialized to a much higher degree than the Czechs, although the manner in which the land reform was carried out is certainly open to criticism. Yet one witness who cannot be suspected of pro-Czech sympathies testified in a secret memorandum that Czech neglect of German interests in this field was far less blatant than was publicly stated. Guido Klieber, a dep-

[28] *Münchner Neueste Nachrichten*, January 4, 1941.
[29] "Der Proporz im Schulwesen" *Prager Presse*, August 18, 1938.

uty of Henlein's party in the Prague parliament, at the end of 1938 compiled a memorandum[30] for Henlein about the alleged deprivation of the Germans through the Czechoslovak Land Reform in order to prepare "reparation claims" against post-Munich Czechoslovakia. But his conclusions proved the exact opposite:

> That the double acreage (in the German area) was allotted to German small-holders can be explained as follows: this allotment was to German small lease holders who for generations had been cultivating small plots in large German holdings as so-called hereditary tenants. Of 55,206 hectares, [1 hectare = 2.47 acres], 31,172 went to German tenants. Of the confiscated large Czech holdings in German territory the Germans (mainly hereditary tenants) received 5,527 hectares, and the Czech 2,937.

No Ethnical Discrimination in Social Policy

It has already been mentioned that the Czechoslovak authorities showed full ethnic justice in combating the consequences of the world depression. This was not because of any "benevolence" on the part of the Czech bureaucracy, but because of the participation of German parties in the government. It shows, incidentally, that the German members of the government were not simply yes-men.

Unemployment benefits in Czechoslovakia were paid by trade unions with the help of government subsidies. During the years 1930-35, the Czechoslovak government paid 704 million Czechoslovak crowns, to German trade unions for unemployment relief, compared with 958 million crowns to Czech and Slovak trade unions and 135 million crowns to "mixed" (i.e., communist) trade unions.[31] The disproportionate amount paid out to the Germans was a highly undesirable privilege, and was due to the special social structure of the German area. Equally meticulous attention was paid to the equitable alleviation of distress by means of the various extra-statutory aid for those out of work. Between 1930 and 1935, 576 million crowns was spent on relief in kind to predominantly German areas and 576 million crowns to mainly Czech ones.

Neither Heaven nor Hell

This short survey of the practical aspects of Czechoslovak nationality policy in the years before 1938 seems to bring out two points: *there can be no question of a suppression of the rights of the non-Slav population;*

---

[30] Dr. Guido Klieber Memorandum, December 1, 1938. *German Foreign Office Film 2367*, Frames 489672-84.

[31] Czechoslovak Sources and Documents, *Czechoslovak Cabinet Ministers on the Complaints of the Sudeten German Party* (Prague, 1937), pp. 67-70.

on the other hand, there was *never any systematic attempt* [to] *existing difficulties*. There was no precise government plan fo[r] the subject, and much was left to chance and the policies purs[ued by] various government coalitions. Pre-Munich Czechoslovakia wa[s not] the heaven on earth it seems in the memories of the older Czech genera-tion nor the hell conjured up by the biased nationalist German historians. Until October 28, 1918, the Germans had been masters in Bohemia, which was two-thirds Czech, and in Moravia, where the Czech majority was three-quarters; this state of affairs could not reasonably be expected to last, although German influence was too deeply entrenched economi-cally to be dislodged. Changes were not always carried out in Masaryk's humane and liberal spirit. However, it is perhaps inevitable that the ful-filment of justified ethnic aspirations by one group will always result in a more or less justified feeling of injustice for another.

Otto Lechner, formerly a Prague banker who, during his British exile during World War II, became a political writer, described the situation succinctly when, in the course of a fictitious political conversation, he let his Czech interlocutor say in one of his books:[32] "The treatment of the minorities in our country was good—it could have been better."

In his broadcast appeal of September 10, 1938, Beneš painted a fasci-nating picture of Czechoslovakia's achievements and failures in the years up to 1938:

> For fully twenty years the development of our Republic has been peaceful and progressive. Her liberal democratic policy, her advance in economic and cultural spheres, in religious toleration and in social justice have been achieved step by step by means of peaceful evolu-tion and without crises, *putsches*, or revolts. Situations which else-where have caused dangerous disturbances, and indeed revolutions, have been dealt with in this country in a reasonably practical manner without blind passion. We have had, and still have, one problem: a problem fraught with difficulty, now as for centuries past on our terri-tory, a problem which calls for ever new forms of solution—the prob-lem of the nationalities.[33]

It can never be proved that in a hypothetical situation this problem could have been solved satisfactorily, but all indications lead to the con-clusion that the difficulties besetting Czechoslovakia because of her multi-national structure could have been largely overcome in a demo-cratic way if the country had been allowed a peaceful development of some decades.

[32] Dr. Otto Lechner, *As We Saw It in Prague* (London, 1942), p. 116.
[33] Royal Institute of International Affairs, *Documents on International Affairs 1938* (2 vols., London, 1943), II, 184.

· 5 ·

CZECHOSLOVAK ECONOMIC DEVELOPMENT
IN THE INTERWAR PERIOD

Zora P. Pryor
Swarthmore College

This survey of the economic development of Czechoslovakia begins with the foundation of the republic in 1918 and ends with its dismemberment after the Munich Agreement in 1938. These twenty years represented a period of territorial, political, and economic integrity for the country during which Czechoslovakia remained essentially a free market economy closely interrelated with the European and world trade network. Within the limited space of this essay it is possible to focus only upon the most important economic problems of the nation.

In the first section of this essay problems arising from the economic heritage of Czechoslovakia—especially relating to the dissolution of the Austro-Hungarian empire and the effects of war inflation—are presented with the view of analyzing the policy choices facing the nation for the achievement of monetary stabilization and economic consolidation. Subsequent sections deal with Czechoslovak dependence on foreign trade and the impact of commercial policies on the development of the domestic economy, the growth, or lack of growth, in some of the major economic sectors, and finally the impact and problems arising from the regional disparities in the level of economic development.

THE FIRST THREE YEARS

The Heritage From the Austro-Hungarian Monarchy

The dissolution of the Habsburg Empire at the end of World War I and the emergence in East Central Europe of new states raised countless new economic and political issues, many of which, however, did not originate purely in the political and geographic reorganization of European frontiers. Rather they were latent long before 1914 and appeared more clearly after the war only because of the destruction of those institutions that had long veiled these deep-seated problems.

One major set of latent difficulties stemmed from the unequal distribution of income and development of resources in the various regions of Austria-Hungary that were sealed by the new frontier boundaries. These inequities created tensions between those nations embarking on indus-

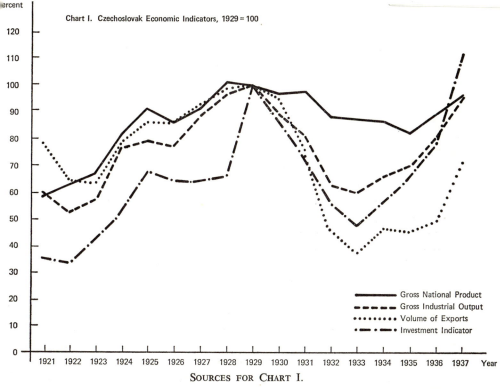

Chart I. Czechoslovak Economic Indicators, 1929 = 100

Gross National Product
Gross Industrial Output
Volume of Exports
Investment Indicator

SOURCES FOR CHART I.

Gross National Product: 1929-37: Jaroslav Krejčí, *Intertemporal Comparability of National Income in Czechoslovakia*, unpublished manuscript, Prague: 1967, p. 8. 1926-29: Index of gross physical output of goods and services, *ibid.*, p. 9; 1921-26: rough estimate by the author.

Gross Industrial Output: Státní úřad statistický, *Statistická ročenka Republiky československé* [*Statistical Yearbook of the Czechoslovak Republic*], 1935, p. 73; Ústřední statistický úřad v Praze, *Statistická ročenka Protektorátu Čechy a Morava* [*Statistical Yearbook of the Protectorate of Bohemia and Moravia*], 1941, Prague, 1941, p. 185.

Volume of Exports: 1929-37; Státní úřad statistický Republiky československé, *Zprávy*, XIX (1938), No. 97-100, deflated by index of wholesale prices; 1923-1929: Quantum index of foreign trade in League of Nations, *Memorandum on Balances of Payments and Foreign Trade, 1910-1924*, I, Geneva, 1924, p. 98, and later volumes; 1921-23, *Zprávy*, XIX, *loc. cit.*, deflated by index of wholesale prices.

Investment Indicator: Based on an unweighted geometric mean of steel and cement consumption used by Svennilson. See Ingvar Svennilson, *Growth and Stagnation in the European Economy*, United Nations Economic Commission for Europe, Geneva, 1954, Appendix to Chapter X and Appendix Tables A-41 and A-46. For the years 1929-37 the investment indicator calculated in this manner was remarkably close to an index of gross domestic fixed capital formation in constant prices given in Krejčí, *op. cit.*, p. 8.

189

trialization and the more advanced successor states that had to seek new channels of trade. Czechoslovakia reflected this regional imbalance within her new territory, which incorporated two areas with wide differences in historical tradition, economic development, and administrative system. The three western provinces, the Czech lands, which belonged to the Austrian part of the Habsburg empire, were relatively more urbanized and industrialized, and their national income per capita was not very far below that of Germany. They were interrelated through many centuries of common history and formed the nucleus of the country. The two eastern provinces, Slovakia and Ruthenia,[1] which for over a thousand years had belonged to the Hungarian dominion, were predominantly rural, and their industrial development was in its infancy. Their per capita income was estimated at less than two-thirds of that of the Czech lands.

A second set of difficulties arose from the heritage of the monarchy's traditionally protectionist commercial policy, and this tradition could not easily be shaken off. The dissolution of the Austro-Hungarian customs union radically changed the locational and market factors for many industries in the successor states, and Czechoslovakia faced a particularly painful adjustment. Her industrial heritage was considerable: 43 percent of the total industrial labor force of Austria-Hungary was employed on Czechoslovak territory inhabited by only 27 percent of the total population.[2] In some industries the concentration was much larger. For instance, Czechoslovakia employed almost three-quarters of the total textile labor force of the empire, and more than half of the mining and primary metal workers. These branches sent over half of their exports to other parts of the empire, and since they had also enjoyed considerable tariff protection they were less competitive than industries in other advanced countries and were more adversely affected after the war by rising barriers to trade in their former markets and by foreign competition.

The situation was not completely bleak, however. In a few specialized branches of industry, such as sugar refining, glass, and porcelain, the Czech lands concentrated almost the entire prewar Austrian labor force engaged in these industries. But these industries were exporting mostly

---

[1] Ruthenia, a tiny mountainous territory that had been part of the Hungarian dominion, was assigned to Czechoslovakia by the Treaty of Trianon in 1920. Originally it was to be administered as an autonomous region, but its extreme backwardness and unsettled political relations with Hungary made administration from the center more expedient. After World War II this area was annexed by the Soviet Union as the Transcarpathian Oblast of the Ukrainian Soviet Socialist Republic.

[2] Calculated on the basis of the 1910 census of the economically active population, adjusted to exclude persons living on independent income (such as pensioners and persons receiving rents, interest, and dividends), inmates of institutions, and students. Adjusted for postwar boundary changes.

TABLE 1.1.

TOTAL AND ECONOMICALLY ACTIVE POPULATION IN AUSTRIA-HUNGARY
AND IN CZECHOSLOVAKIA

Census of December 31, 1910
(Figures have been rounded to the nearest thousand)

Country and region	Total population	Economically Active Population[a]				
		All sectors	Agriculture Forestry Fishing	Mining Industry Construction	Trade Transports Communications	Services and other branches
Austria-Hungary[b]	49,457	23,702	14,107	4,920	1,937	2,738
Czechoslovakia[c]	13,595	6,438	3,038	2,118	557	725
Prewar Austria	28,571	14,951	8,506	3,538	1,321	1,585
Czech Lands[c]	10,071	5,010	2,174	1,890	462	530
Prewar Hungary	20,886	8,751	5,601[d]	1,381	617	1,153
Slovakia and Ruthenia[c]	3,524	1,429	910[d]	228	96	195

[a] The economically active population enumerated in the Austro-Hungarian census includes all gainfully occupied persons, unpaid family workers, persons unemployed at the time of the census, armed forces, and persons living on independent income. This latter category (such as pensioners, annuitants, stockholders, other property owners, and persons living on relief subsidies) as well as students and inmates of institutions were excluded in the above data. Regional differences in census classifications between Austria and Hungary, the Czech Lands and the eastern provinces were adjusted to make the data comparable. Domestic servants, excluded from the economically active population in the Austrian census, were included in the service sectors.

[b] Excluding Bosnia and Herzegovina, which had a population of 1,932,000 according to the census of October 10, 1910.

[c] Data have been adjusted to reflect postwar boundary changes.

[d] In the Hungarian census the reporting procedure for women active in agriculture differed from that in the Austrian census, and, by comparison, reflects a considerable undercount of women. If we adjust the Hungarian data on the basis of the Austrian participation rate of women in agriculture, we obtain the following number of economically active persons in agriculture: Prewar Hungary 8,380,000; Slovakia and Ruthenia 1,362,000.

Source: K.K. Statistische Zentralkommission, Österriechische Statistik, Vol. 3, No. 1, 119-28; Office central de statistique du Royaume de Hongrie, Annuaire statistique hongrois, Nouveau cours, 1914, pp. 23 and 117; Státní úřad statistický, Statistická příručka Republiky československé, II, pp. 99, 100-104, 146-48; Manuel statistique de la République tchécoslovaque, III, 300.

to other European countries and were therefore less affected by the partition of the monarchy.

Czechoslovakia's third important heritage was a heavy dependence on trade with East Central Europe.[3] The traditional pattern of trade within

[3] Germany, Austria, Poland, Hungary, Rumania, Yugoslavia, and Bulgaria. Trade with Russia, the Baltic republics, Greece, and European Turkey was insignificant at that time.

TABLE 1.2.

ECONOMICALLY ACTIVE POPULATION IN INDUSTRY AND CONSTRUCTION
IN AUSTRIA-HUNGARY AND IN CZECHOSLOVAKIA, DECEMBER 31, 1910
(Figures have been rounded to the nearest thousand)

Branch of Industry	Austria-Hungary	Czecho-slovakia	Percent of Czechoslovakia in economically active part of Austria-Hungary
Industry	4,287	1,858	43.3
Mining, primary metals	268	143	53.3
Metalworking	505	187	37.0
Machinebuilding and transport equipment	304	102	33.4
Chemicals	79	29	37.3
Power, gas, water[a]	22	5	24.8
Building materials[b]	294	166	56.6
Printing	77	21	27.1
Pulp and paper	51	28	53.7
Leather	95	28	29.7
Wood	421	153	36.4
Food processing	526	213	40.6
Textiles	571	411	71.9
Clothing and footwear	970	341	35.2
Other branches	105	30	28.9
Construction	633	235	37.2

[a] According to the Hungarian census classification, employment in power, gas, and water was included in machinebuilding and transport equipment and in part under chemicals. These two branches were adjusted to exclude this category.
[b] Includes glass.

Source: The same as of Table 1.1.

the Austro-Hungarian Empire and with Southeastern Europe was a simple exchange of manufactured against agricultural products. After the war, the increasing protection of developing industries in the new nations and the introduction of agricultural protection in many of the industrialized countries began to upset these traditional channels of trade and contributed to economic instability from which Czechoslovakia could not always easily disentangle herself.

Legacy of the War

When Czechoslovakia became an independent state in October, 1918, the difficulties the new nation faced were enormous. The frontiers were still uncertain, and the government had no control over the eastern parts

TABLE 2.1.

REGIONAL DISTRIBUTION OF EXPORTS AND IMPORTS,
SELECTED YEARS 1921 TO 1937

in millions of crowns
(Figures have been rounded to the nearest million)

Year	Total Imports[a]	East Central Europe[b]	Rest of Europe	Rest of the World[c]
1921	23,685	11,273	5,012	7,400
1924	15,855	9,469	5,092	1,293
1929	19,988	9,467	4,530	5,991
1933	5,831	2,321	1,715	2,089
1937	10,980	3,636	3,517	3,827

Year	Total Exports[a]	East Central Europe[b]	Rest of Europe	Rest of the World[c]
1921	29,458	20,592	7,244	1,622
1924	17,035	10,272	5,140	1,623
1929	20,499	11,288	5,964	3,247
1933	5,923	2,560	2,249	1,144
1937	11,983	4,398	4,476	3,098

[a] Includes merchandise trade and nonmonetary gold, reimports, and re-exports.

[b] Germany, Austria, Poland, Hungary, Rumania, Yugoslavia, and Bulgaria. In 1921 all reimports and re-exports were assumed to be with Eastern and Central Europe.

[c] Includes unspecified countries and returned merchandise. For 1921 it includes all nonmonetary gold.

Source: Státní úřad statistický, Statistická příručka Republiky československé, II, 174; Manuel statistique de la République tchécoslovaque, III, 126; Statistická příručka Republiky československé, IV, 200, 216; Statistická ročenka Republiky československé, 1935, p. 128; Zprávy, Vol. XIX (1938), No. 97-100; Ústřední statistický úřad, Statistická ročenka Protektorátu Čechy a Morava, pp. 198, 199.

of the territory until early in 1919. Furthermore, in 1918 industrial employment had dropped to about two thirds of its prewar level, and productivity per worker had declined. In those branches not essential for the war effort, employment conditions were even worse. Foodstuffs were in short supply, since the output of the main crops and potatoes declined to less than half the average prewar level. Livestock declined by almost one third in terms of head of cattle and by more than half of pigs.[4] War losses, both human and capital, created many urgent problems.

Against these shortages of supply the demand was swollen by a for-

[4] See Státní úřad statistický, Statistická příručka Republiky československé [Statistical Handbook of the Czechoslovak Republic] (Prague, 1920), I, 46, 48, and 51; Statistická příručka Republiky československé (Prague, 1925), II, 96-108.

TABLE 2.2.

COMPOSITION OF EXPORTS BY MAJOR COMMODITY, SELECTED YEARS 1921 TO 1937

(In percent of the total value of exports)

Commodity category[a]	1921	1924	1929	1937
Textiles	32.1	31.0	31.0	20.8
Sugar	13.7	14.3	5.2	2.1
Glass and glass products	7.6	7.3	6.7	6.6
Coal and manufactured fuels	7.4	6.2	4.5	5.2
Metals and manufactured metal products	6.5	7.8	11.6	18.8
Machinery, electrical machinery and appliances, and transport equipment	4.1	3.6	3.8	6.0
Leather and leather manufactures, including footwear	3.2	2.2	6.9	5.3
Chemicals and allied products[b]	2.7	1.7	3.0	2.6
Pulp, paper, and paper products	2.4	1.6	2.3	3.7
Wearing apparel and other made-up textile goods	2.9	2.1	3.4	4.2
Timber	2.9	3.9	2.2	3.3

[a] Commodity categories have been aggregated from the Czechoslovak tariff classifications.

[b] Excluding explosives.

Source: *Statistická příručka Republiky československé*, ɪɪ, p. 163; *Statistická příručka Republiky československé*, ɪᴠ, p. 207; *Manuel statistique de la République tchécoslovaque*, p. 116; *Zprávy*, Vol. xɪx, 742-44.

midable inflation of the currency in circulation, and as a result prices rose. During the war the soaring public expenditures were financed through successive war loans and by direct government borrowing from the Bank of Austria-Hungary, which in turn printed new bank notes. Between the end of 1914 and October, 1918, the public debt of Austria-Hungary increased eightfold, bank notes in circulation almost fifteen times, and prices more than fifteen times, but wages and salaries lagged far behind. The distribution of income was therefore shifted in favor of those segments of the population that were in a position to reap the windfall profits—businessmen, speculators, and farmers. The external value of the crown (*koruna*, K), however, depreciated only slightly because of the severe foreign trade and exchange controls and was quite artificial.

Czechoslovakia's most urgent task after the end of the hostilities was to curb inflation in order to restore conditions for normal economic activity. The first minister of finance was Alois Rašín, an economic conservative and a forceful leader, who gave the new nation a solid monetary and financial foundation. In the first months of 1919 he enacted a monetary reform that had three major aspects. First, it separated the bank notes circulating on Czechoslovak territory from those in the other parts of the former monarchy, by differentiating them with a stamp.[5] The new monetary unit, the Czechoslovak crown, was defined as being equivalent to the prewar Austro-Hungarian crown depreciated to a level that had not been officially determined and that was, at the beginning, essentially a currency unit with a floating exchange rate. Moreover, in creating the Czechoslovak crown Rašín reduced the currency in circulation by approximately 20 percent (50 percent of the notes presented by the holders above a certain minimum and half of the private accounts at the branch offices of the Bank of Austria-Hungary were withheld as a forced loan). Second, a ceiling was set on the note issue in order to restore some limitations on the creation of money.[6] Henceforth, new notes could be issued only against a rediscount of approved bills and loans on securities —a measure reflecting the ideas of the real bills doctrine. Third, a tax on property and war property increases was planned to remove gradually the stamped notes, for which the government assumed responsibility, from circulation. This triple reform was a compromise solution. Rašín, inspired by the quantity theory of money, misled by the relatively high exchange rate of the crown immediately after the war and the depressed level of wages, and counting on a substantial flexibility of prices, originally wanted to reduce the money supply by 80 percent and restore the prewar parity of the crown with the support of a dollar loan. He was not the only European leader to have severely underestimated the disruptive consequences of war inflation. He had to abandon this radical plan, however, because he faced strong opposition in the parliament, and because it was impossible at that time to obtain a loan from the United States.

Monetary Stabilization

Although the reform itself did not stabilize the currency, it gave Czechoslovakia a basis for an independent economic and monetary policy, created confidence within the country in the government's ability to maintain order, and provided a framework for recovery. During the subsequent two years the economy of the country recovered very rapidly.

[5] It was not possible to have new notes printed at the time; the large American firms gave six months as the shortest period for such printing. For more details on the monetary reform, see Alois Rašín, *Financial Policy of Czechoslovakia During the First Year of its History* (Oxford, 1923).

[6] Because of the limited role of commercial bank checking accounts and the general practice of payments by checks in most continental European countries, the concept of "payments media" was usually restricted to bank notes and demand deposits at the central bank. An additional reason for this definition was political, since the statements of the central bank showed most conspicuously the fluctuating state of the currency liabilities against banking coverage and hence the relative stability of the country's monetary foundation.

Industrial employment returned to almost prewar levels, many tight controls of the economy were relaxed, foreign trade flourished, and the balance of trade showed a substantial export surplus. These euphoric conditions were supported by a considerable credit expansion in the economy, which was difficult to control because of the great liquidity of the market. Between 1919 and 1921 loans and deposits of the commercial banks more than doubled. Although budget deficits in 1919 and 1920 contributed somewhat to inflationary pressure, the government borrowed from individuals and financial institutions, and these securities, rediscounted at the Central Banking Office, amounted only to a small fraction of the increase in the total money supply.[7]

Although government expenditures during these years increased considerably because of heavy social, economic, and military outlays, taxes were increased so that revenues increased faster and the actual deficit was much smaller than estimated. Whereas in 1919 the deficit amounted to 64 percent of total revenues, in 1920 it had fallen to 6 percent, and in 1921 the accounts closed with a budget surplus.

From the end of 1918 the exchange rate had steadily depreciated from its artificially high level and during 1920 and 1921 had stabilized around the rate of 8 Swiss centimes per crown (the prewar parity of the Austro-Hungarian crown was 105 Swiss centimes),[8] which represented a depreciation corresponding more closely to the rise in domestic prices. Financial stabilization proceeded at such a pace, however, that by 1921 certain liberal leaders were advocating an official stabilization of the currency at the quoted rate.

Economic stabilization was accompanied by social stabilization. During the first three years wages and salaries rose at a considerable pace so that the distribution of income was brought within the prewar mold. Social unrest was quieted by a series of remarkable legislative measures, including the eight-hour day, land reform, unemployment benefits, aid to war widows and orphans, education measures, raises in government salaries, and many other measures. The socialist parties that achieved these measures acted in a much more cooperative spirit than prevailed in neighboring states, where there was considerable social turbulence.

Because of these favorable domestic conditions, the world crisis of 1920-21 was substantially bypassed in the country. This maintenance of domestic economic order by a new nation was a considerable achieve-

---

[7] See *Statistická příručka*, II, 214-37. The banking office was attached to the Ministry of Finance and performed all the functions of a central bank until the foundation of the National Bank in 1925.

[8] Swiss quotations are used because the Swiss franc maintained its prewar parity; the Czechoslovak crown was not quoted in New York in the immediate postwar years.

ment, especially in view of the increasingly chaotic conditions in neighboring countries. In the middle of 1921 the final ruin of the German mark began. Its path was followed by the Austrian crown and most of the other East European currencies. Thus, the Czechoslovak crown showed that it had acquired autonomy in relation to neighboring currencies.

At this juncture, the conservative Rašín assumed his second term as minister of finance. Ever since the compromise solution he had adopted for his earlier monetary reform, he had never given up the idea of revaluing the currency. In his mind, the lower the degree of devaluation of a currency with respect to its prewar parity, the higher the prestige and respectability a country would enjoy. Therefore, at the turn of 1922, when the Czechoslovak crown became a refuge for funds fleeing the hyper-inflated neighboring countries and the heavy demand shot the freely floating exchange rate to an unprecedented level, Rašín misread this situation as a permanent sign of confidence in the Czechoslovak crown. He did not let the exchange rate fall back to the level at which it had stabilized during 1920 and 1921 but supported it at double that level, using for this purpose the foreign exchange reserves accumulated by the Central Banking Office and the proceeds of a foreign loan. This sudden revaluation provoked an unnecessary deflationary crisis, since all wages and prices had to be adjusted downward. Bank failures, bankruptcies, and soaring unemployment during the year were the result.[9] A drastic fall in exports was mitigated somewhat by the French and Belgian occupation of the Ruhr and the passive resistance of German industrialists, who diverted their orders of crude iron and products to Czechoslovakia. On the whole, the Czechoslovak currency remained relatively overvalued during the entire period, serving as a drawback for the export trade so important to the domestic economy. After the stabilization of the German and Austrian currencies in 1924, when those funds placed in Czechoslovakia during the inflationary period were again withdrawn, it was not always easy to maintain the high exchange rate of the crown.[10] Control of foreign exchange transactions had to be reimposed in 1924 and was not lifted again until 1928.

[9] Karel Engliš, Minister of Finance in 1920 and on several occasions during the interwar period, criticized Rašín bitterly for his revaluation measures. The exchange rate was raised by only about 5 percent of its prewar parity and instead of adding to the prestige of the country weakened its economy. See his "Nástin vývoje československé měny" in *Deset let Národní banky československé* [*Ten Years of the Czechoslovak National Bank*] (Prague, 1937), pp. 33-51.

[10] From the end of 1923 the exchange rate was stabilized around 15.3 Swiss centimes and 2.96 U. S. cents per crown. The crown was defined, in terms of gold content in 1929, equivalent to 44.58 milligrams of fine gold.

FOREIGN TRADE AND COMMERCIAL POLICY
DURING THE INTERWAR PERIOD

Foreign Trade

With the breakup of the Austro-Hungarian customs union, the Czechoslovak economy became greatly dependent on foreign trade and as a result sensitive to shocks from abroad. Commodity trade was the major source of foreign exchange earnings, to provide for the necessary imports, on the one hand, and for the accumulation of gold and foreign exchange reserves to secure the increased stability of the currency on the other.

Exports of goods and services were a substantial component of the total demand for gross national product and a factor influencing domestic output and employment. In 1929 sales of goods and services abroad represented 25 percent of gross national product, and sales of merchandise alone, 22 percent. Almost three-fourths of merchandise exports were manufactured products. In some industries, such as textiles, glass, wood, and leather products, as much as 40 to 80 percent of gross output was exported. With vanishing hopes of recreating a large preferential trading area similar to the former customs union, Czechoslovak industry was threatened with idle capacity and chronic unemployment, especially in the branches in which there were heavy concentrations of labor. The effort to reconquer the former markets was made difficult by the postwar turmoil in these countries and their depressed volume of trade. It was estimated that by 1924, Czechoslovak industries recovered 80 percent of their prewar markets in Western and Northern Europe, but only 30 to 40 percent of their traditional markets in East Central Europe.[11]

Two basic solutions were possible in these circumstances: to change the structure of domestic industrial production toward emphasis on those commodities in rising world demand, or to change the geographic distribution of trade. The first would be a long and slow process. With a large available skilled labor force in the traditional industries, a more practical short-run policy would be to find new markets in Western Europe and overseas. During the 1920's, therefore, while fundamentally maintaining her old composition of exports, Czechoslovakia redirected some of her trade away from East Central Europe.[12] This was achieved against many unfavorable factors, not the least of which were the price handicap of domestic products resulting from the devaluation of the crown in

[11] *Obzor Národohospodářský*, XXXI (1926), 69-79. See also W. T. Layton and Charles Rist, *The Economic Situation of Austria* (Geneva, 1925), pp. 27-28.

[12] For an extensive analysis of the composition and geographic distribution of Czechoslovak interwar trade see Zora Procházka, "Foreign Trade and Economic Development of Czechoslovakia, 1919-1937" (unpublished Ph.D. dissertation, Radcliffe College, 1960).

1922-23 and a vigorous German export offensive after the stabilization of the mark in 1924. Czechoslovakia was a relative newcomer to Western markets and many of her products were similar to German exports. But her industry made a great effort toward improving technology and the quality of goods and services in order to gain a competitive advantage. In this respect banks played an important role through their strong and traditional influence on industry by encouraging modernization and technological progress.

The foothold gained in the West for the exports of manufactured products in the 1920's played a positive role during the world economic depression after 1929. Czechoslovakia then suffered her greatest losses in her traditional markets, partly because of the tremendous decline in the national income of the East Central European agricultural countries and partly because of the autarkic policies that reduced her commercial relations within this region to bilateral bargaining. Within three years, between 1929 and 1932, the value of Czechoslovak exports to East Central Europe declined by more than two thirds. But her trade with Western Europe remained at about half its predepression value and declined by less than one third with the rest of the world.

In this geographical redistribution of trade, exports and imports acted in a somewhat different manner. Czechoslovakia began the period with a large export surplus with East Central Europe. During the 1920's about half of her imports came from this region, but its share in exports declined from more than two thirds in 1921 to about one half in 1929, as the direction of exports changed toward the West. Czechoslovakia's trade surplus with East Central Europe declined until exports almost reached the level of imports. Thereafter, they moved together. Czechoslovakia remained a creditor to this region but on a much smaller scale in the 1930's than during previous years.

Czechoslovakia also had an export surplus with other European countries and a deficit in her trade with the rest of the world. But over the entire period there was an overall surplus in the merchandise balance of trade in all but three of the interwar years: 1919, 1932, and 1933. The net outflow of capital was used in great part for industrial investment abroad to acquire new sources of income, as rising tariffs were reducing export trade.

The soundness of Czechoslovakia's balance of payments and of her economy depended to a great extent on a well-functioning world trade and payments network. The breakdown of this network in the 1930's severely damaged the country's ability to maintain a free economy with a minimum of restrictions. The volume of exports, which rose during the 1920's to reach its prewar level by 1929, fell drastically thereafter, and in 1933 was less than 40 percent of the 1929 volume. Even after the rest of the economy had recovered from the depression by 1937, exports recovered scarcely two thirds of the 1929 level. This in turn had two implications: first, the ability to control imports was crucial in maintaining a balance of trade surplus; second, foreign demand played a less important role in economic recovery in the period between 1934 and 1937 than during the preceding decade.

Commercial Policy

In the early postwar years the economy's need for large export possibilities and wide markets abroad was overshadowed by instability and unsettled monetary problems. During this period the major policy effort was oriented toward currency rehabilitation. Commercial policy was reduced to measures of expediency, with no broad and unified direction or long-run perspective. There was a lack of tradition in foreign economic policy. Before the war, commercial policy had been decided in Vienna, and the policy of Austria-Hungary aimed mainly at furthering the development of the empire into a self-supporting territory. Even though the war brought a radical transformation of the basic conditions underlying such a policy, a core of protectionist sentiment remained in Czechoslovakia, generating considerable heat in the debate to liberalize trade policies.

The favorable development of domestic production in 1920 and 1921 permitted the liquidation of many of the stringent economic controls. An important crack in the authoritarian system of trading appeared with the introduction of general trade agreements, the first of which was concluded with Germany in 1920. But the liberalization of trade was soon slowed by monetary disorders in the neighboring countries.

With the gradual reduction of direct trade controls, the tariff question became important. Czechoslovakia took over the old Austro-Hungarian tariff of 1906 and adjusted it to the depreciation of the currency by multiplying the specific tariffs by certain "coefficients of increase." On the whole, however, industrial tariffs during this period were lower than before the war vis-à-vis the value of goods, and agricultural tariffs that had been suspended during the war were not restored. As the depreciation of neighboring currencies made Czechoslovak competition more difficult, industrial interests began to demand increased protection. The existing tariff structure was therefore revised at the end of 1921, increasing industrial protection by about 30 to 50 percent above the prewar level. However, most agricultural products were excepted. But when the new tariff came into force in 1922, the crown was in the process of rapid appreciation, so that foreign goods became cheaper in crowns. Therefore the appreciation offset part or all of the protective effect of the measure. At this point the tariff debate became even more complicated, because the fall in the price of foreign foodstuffs alarmed the agricultural interests. Therefore, discussion of a revision of industrial tariffs began to be linked with changes in agricultural tariffs.

The revaluation depressed many of the export industries, and it became clear that these industries had to be aided in some manner. Czechoslovak policymakers chose the negotiation of trade and tariff agreements and the granting of reciprocal concessions, a type of measure that would stimulate exports while at the same time putting pressure on domestic import-competing industries to lower prices. In the middle of 1923 the first such agreement on a broad scale was negotiated with France, and contractual tariff reductions were granted on a considerable number of items, from 25 to 75 percent; other agreements followed. Czechoslovak policy was committed to the unconditional most-favored-nation clause, so that any concession would benefit all other countries with whom she concluded a most-favored-nation agreement. This step represented a major change in Czechoslovakia's attitude toward foreign trade relations and mitigated some of the effect of her high autonomous tariffs. Except for the introduction of agricultural duties in 1925, the tariff policy remained the same until the world economic crisis.

During the entire interwar period there was never any considered direction of economic policies to coordinate the growth of domestic production and foreign trade. As commercial policy moved in the direction of freer trade, and as foreign demand for exports increased, internal conditions acted to discourage domestic investment. That is, until the very end of the 1920's, domestic interest rates were relatively high, investment costs were rising faster than other prices,[13] and the balance of payments showed a considerable export of capital.

With the onset of the world depression, the lack of coordination between domestic and foreign policies became even more apparent. Exports fell off rapidly and the official commitment to the maintenance of the external value of the currency worsened the domestic economic contraction. The money supply shrank because of the withdrawal of foreign balances, private hoarding, and government borrowing from the private sector—all of which acted to maintain high interest rates. In addition there was credit rationing, since the liquidity of the banks was further reduced by many frozen credits granted previously to industry and by a moratorium on farm indebtedness. The reduction of the official rate of interest did not, and could not, lead to a reduction of commercial interest rates. As discussed below, certain emergency fiscal policy measures were taken that did counteract the deflationary spiral.

[13] After 1926 the index of construction costs increased faster than the index of wholesale or industrial prices, up to 1929. See Ústřední úřad statistický, Statistická ročenka Protektorátu Čechy a Morava, 1941, p. 206.

The difficulties in coordinating domestic and foreign economic policy were overcome in the depth of the depression when the severity of the situation became apparent to all. A devaluation measure was considered early in 1934. Unfortunately, strong conservative opposition to any tampering with the currency forced the adoption of a too mild devaluation —only 16.66 percent—in contrast to the earlier devaluations by 30 to 40 percent carried out in the sterling area countries. Although the main purpose of the devaluation was to adjust domestic to world prices, this policy measure provided a narrow margin for any increase in the internal price level and required a continuance of cautious monetary policies. The devaluation therefore was not followed by any monetary and credit expansion, and although exports rose slightly, there were no signs of any marked improvement in economic conditions in 1934. In contrast, in the United Kingdom, Sweden, and some of the other countries of the sterling group, devaluation was accompanied by an increase of effective monetary supply and a lowering of the long- and short-term interest rate. Thus, after 1933, building activity in both the United Kingdom and Sweden rose far above the 1929 level, and by 1936 their industrial production surpassed the 1929 level. In Czechoslovakia, however, recovery finally responded to rising domestic investment and rearmament, which were unrelated to trade.

PRODUCTION

Overall View of the Economy, 1921-1937

Reliable estimates of gross national product have not been made for Czechoslovakia prior to 1929,[14] and to trace the development of the economy during the decade after World War I, rough estimates and other indicators such as gross industrial production, construction activity, employment, agricultural output, or the volume of foreign trade have to be used. Chart I shows a graph of some of these indices from 1921 to 1937. The pattern reveals a more pronounced cyclical fluctuation in the 1930's than during the 1920's. The first postwar decade was influenced by the overall ascending trend in most sectors of the economy, from the early postwar low—which was prolonged by the recession following the revaluation of the currency in 1922—to a peak in 1928-29, interrupted only by a brief slowdown in 1926. During this period, the gross industrial

---

[14] The first detailed national income estimates in current prices were published by Miloš Stadník, *Národní důchod a jeho rozdělení* [*National Income and its Distribution*] (Prague, 1946), pp. 180-81. The gross national product in constant prices was estimated by Jaroslav Krejčí, "Intertemporal comparability of National Income in Czechoslovakia" (Prague, 1967, unpublished manuscript). The Krejčí calculations leave something to be desired and an American group is attempting a completely new set of estimates.

TABLE 3.

GROSS INDUSTRIAL PRODUCTION BY BRANCH OF INDUSTRY, 1921-1937
(Index numbers 1929 = 100)

Year	All Branches	Mining	Metals	Glass	Porcelain	Building Materials	Chemicals
1921	60.1	78.0	37.5	73.4	74.6	62.8	35.7
1922	54.7	66.8	31.2	67.6	65.7	40.9	34.3
1923	57.6	69.8	47.7	48.1	42.7	44.6	53.4
1924	76.0	86.8	59.3	84.9	86.1	62.6	71.9
1925	79.0	78.7	66.3	83.7	89.2	69.6	72.4
1926	76.7	84.5	61.4	81.8	86.2	77.5	72.5
1927	89.0	87.2	76.7	84.0	91.9	86.5	78.5
1928	95.8	90.5	94.4	91.7	98.1	107.7	86.7
1929	100.0	100.0	100.0	100.0	100.0	100.0	100.0
1930	89.2	85.9	85.4	83.4	83.6	91.4	91.8
1931	80.7	78.8	72.0	75.1	64.4	79.6	89.9
1932	63.5	66.5	40.0	54.3	45.8	69.5	80.9
1933	60.2	64.4	41.4	48.6	41.4	53.1	85.8
1934	66.5	64.9	48.5	51.8	40.0	46.8	90.2
1935	70.1	66.9	61.0	54.3	44.6	46.3	93.6
1936	80.1	76.5	75.9	56.9	43.9	60.1	97.2
1937	96.3	91.6	105.8	60.8	56.3	69.8	124.3

Year	Wood	Paper	Printing	Textiles	Leather	Clothing, Footwear	Food-stuffs	Power
1921	50.0[a]	47.7	77.0[a]	69.5	38.9[a]	72.0	87.9	46.0
1922	51.6[a]	44.4	72.9[a]	67.1	53.2	69.0	88.4	44.7
1923	66.0[a]	44.0	81.1[a]	56.6	51.1	68.2	99.6	48.9
1924	93.2	63.1	69.2[a]	81.4	75.4	73.9	106.3	57.7
1925	92.0	70.5	77.1[a]	88.9	81.0	78.8	96.1	64.5
1926	77.7	80.9	82.8[a]	80.7	78.6	82.8	94.8	69.1
1927	88.5	91.3	84.8[a]	106.0	84.7	90.1	91.9	78.4
1928	112.7	92.2	88.1	101.1	87.7	96.2	93.7	90.2
1929	100.0	100.0	100.0	100.0	100.0	100.0	100.0	100.0
1930	84.6	96.6	96.8	90.8	84.2	93.3	96.1	99.3
1931	66.6	92.9	93.9	82.5	79.3	98.1	95.8	94.5
1932	49.7	80.5	91.6	67.9	68.1	79.3	99.4	85.5
1933	48.5	74.0	90.3	63.3	70.3	71.6	88.4	87.2
1934	52.0	80.5	95.4	75.9	87.8	77.9	94.5	95.3
1935	53.3	87.3	113.4	73.9	66.8	78.0	99.4	101.9
1936	57.8	95.8	109.6	91.3	90.9	82.3	95.1	116.4
1937	69.1	114.4	122.7	102.3	96.6	91.7	89.1	139.3

[a] Estimated on the basis of data in Karel Maiwald, "Pokus o provisorní index průmyslové výroby ČSR," *Statistický obzor*, XII, No. 9-10 (December 1931), 602-39.

Source: Statistická ročenka Republiky československé, 1935, p. 73; *Statistická ročenka Protektorátu Čechy a Morava*, 1941, p. 185.

output, the volume of foreign trade, and the gross national product moved together. The investment indicator, however, shows the inhibited nature of the domestic capital formation. Investment activity lagged behind the growth in other sectors until the very last years of the decade, when it was again cut back by the onset of the world depression.

After 1929 the graph shows a clear separation in the growth path of gross national product and development in these other sectors. While the volume of foreign trade and industrial output fell sharply, and investment activity exhibited typical features of an acceleration model, gross national product declined comparatively less.

In the early depression years, the government followed a deflationary monetary policy that aggravated the crisis, but the emergency fiscal measures that had to be taken in response to the distressed conditions and political pressures were in contradiction to the deflationary monetary principles and brought some relief. Among such factors was the persistent budget deficit. As the depression gained momentum, budget revenues fell more sharply than expenditures, because of the increase in transfer payments. Although employment outside of agriculture declined by about 25 percent at the lowest point of the depression in 1934,[15] unemployment benefits increased more than 20 times by 1933. In addition, other benefits accrued to the unemployed, such as the free distribution of food, Christmas bonuses, and care of their children,[16] all of which increased aggregate demand.

Other important countercyclical policy measures were taken in the field of agriculture. Under the pressure of falling agricultural prices and the rising burden of farm indebtedness, and in response to political pressures of the well-organized Agrarian party, various measures were introduced to support agricultural prices, such as increased customs duties and import restrictions. With the continuing distress of the farm population, especially in grain farming, these piecemeal measures finally culminated in 1934 in the centralization of all purchasing and distribution of grain products within a state grain monopoly agency, which provided the small farmers with a guaranteed sale of their harvest at relatively stable prices.[17] These measures prevented the income of the sizable farm population from falling to a much lower level and, in addition, increased domestic aggregate demand for agricultural commodities by import substitution.

Thus for both urban and rural workers, public policy measures acted

[15] "Trh práce na rozhraní 1937-38" ["The Labor Market at the End of 1937 and Beginning of 1938"], *Obzor Národohospodářský*, XLIII (1938), 142-46. The estimates of employment are based on the statistics of compulsory medical insurance and refer to workers and employees. According to statistics of social security encompassing about 72 percent of the nonagricultural labor force, the fall in employment was only about 15 percent between 1930 and 1934. See Ludmila Jeřábková and Miluše Salcmanová, *Vývoj důchodového zabezpečení v ČSSR (1930-1956)* [*The Development of Assuring Income in Czechoslovakia 1930-1956*] (Prague, 1965), p. 25.

[16] Ibid. See also *Statistická ročenka Protektorátu Čechy a Morava*, 1944, p. 253.

[17] These measures are described in more detail in Eduard Reich, *Die Tschechoslowakische Landwirtschaft. Ihre Grundlage und Ihre Organisation* (Berlin, 1935), pp. 142ff; also L. Feierabend, *Obilní monopol, jeho stav a dnešní úkoly* [*The Grain Monopoly: its State and Present-day Tasks*] (Prague, 1937).

to cushion the fall in domestic consumption and offset in part the much greater fall in investment. This can be seen in the increased share of public and private consumption in the gross national product.

Industry

Among the most complete sets of indices available for the interwar years are those for gross industrial output, by branch, from 1921 to 1937.[18] During the 1920's total industrial production rose 80 percent from the early postwar low to 1919. With the onset of the depression, it declined to about 60 percent of its 1929 level in 1933 and still had not quite reached its predepression level in 1937. In most branches the rate of growth was faster up to 1925. But in those industries—such as mining, machine building, clothing, and shoe manufacture—that had greatly increased their production to meet wartime needs, production was not so depressed in the early part of the period, and they began to expand faster only in the latter part of the 1920's. The fastest growing industries were those embodying relatively recent technologies, such as chemicals, machinery, pulp and paper, and power production, the outputs of which were in rising demand. These were also the ones that, except for machinery, suffered the least setback during the depression years and recovered above their 1929 output in 1937. The greatest contraction in the 1930's was suffered by those branches depending heavily on exports, such as glass, porcelain, wood, and textiles, or those industries depending on investment activity, such as primary metals and building materials.

Between 1921 and 1930 the structure of industry as reflected in labor force statistics[19] remained fundamentally unchanged. The most significant changes occurred during World War I, with a shift away from textiles and toward metals and machine building. These changes were maintained in the 1920's. A structural change, however, occurred during the depression years and the subsequent recovery that favored the dynamic industries and those serving the domestic market over those dependent

[18] Státní úřad statistický, *Statistická ročenka Republiky československé*, 1935 (Prague, 1936), p. 73, and *Statistická ročenka Protektorátu Čechy a Morava, 1941*, p. 185. For a description of the manner in which the indices were constructed see Karel Maiwald, "Pokus o provisorní sestavení indexu průmyslové výroby ČSR" ["Attempt at a Provisional Organization of an Index of Industrial Production in Czechoslovakia"], *Statistický obzor*, XII, no. 9-10, 602-39 and "Index průmyslové výroby v Československu" ["Index of Industrial Production in Czechoslovakia"], *Obzor národohospodářský*, XXXIX, 331-48. These indices have been criticized in recent years by Czechoslovak economists, but so far more adequate estimates have not been substituted.

[19] Only two population censuses were taken during the interwar period, in 1921 and in 1930, which also give detailed data on the economically active population. For later years changes of industrial structure are inferred from different growth rates in various branches of industry as reflected in the index of gross industrial production.

TABLE 4.

ECONOMICALLY ACTIVE POPULATION BY BRANCH OF THE ECONOMY AND REGION

Census of December 31, 1910, February 15, 1921, and December 1, 1930

(Figures have been rounded to the nearest thousand)

Branch of the Economy	Czechoslovakia			Czech Lands			Slovakia and Ruthenia		
	1910a	1921	1930	1910a	1921	1930	1910a	1921	1930
All branches[b]	6,438	6,103	6,993	5,010	4,561	5,278	1,429	1,452	1,716
Agriculture, forestry, and fishing	3,038	2,425c	2,675	2,127	1,522e	1,612	910d	903	1,063
Nonagricultural branches	3,401	3,589	4,319	2,882	3,040	3,666	519	549	653
Industry	1,858	1,914	2,124	1,655	1,695	1,899	203	219	226
Mining	116	150	109	100	137	99	16	13	10
Primary metals	27	10	34	26	9	32	1	1	2
Metalworking	187	275	284	157	237	250	30	39	35
Machinebuilding and transport equipment	102	165	189	92	148	174	10	17	15
Chemicals	29	37	33	23	32	29	4	5	4
Power, gas, water	5	10	16	5	9	15	1	1	2
Building materials	109	89	126	98	81	113	11	8	13
Glass	58	58	63	54	55	61	3	3	2
Printing	21	25	37	19	23	34	2	2	3
Pulp and paper	28	31	36	23	26	31	4	5	5
Leather	28	31	32	24	26	28	4	5	4
Wood	153	169	211	133	141	175	20	28	36
Food processing	213	209	242	183	179	206	31	29	36
Textiles	411	280	351	401	268	336	10	11	15
Clothing	214	210	242	195	190	219	20	21	23
Footwear	127	151	112	103	122	91	24	29	21
Other branches	30	14	8	18	12	7	13	2	1

Branch of the Economy	Czechoslovakia			Czech Lands			Slovakia and Ruthenia		
	1910[a]	1921	1930	1910[a]	1921	1930	1910[a]	1921	1930
Construction	260	270	400	235	241	349	25	29	51
Trade, finance, insurance	364	361	559	302	305	475	62	56	84
Transports, communications	194	243	290	160	198	238	34	45	52
Public service and liberal professions	231	279	337	188	224	261	43	55	76
Armed services	79	140	164	56	94	109	23	47	55
Personal services	37	28	48	32	25	42	5	3	5
Domestic service	215	197	203	149	150	152	65	48	51
Laborers	138	103	86	91	75	72	47	28	14
Other branches	26	52	107	14	33	69	12	19	38

[a] Data have been adjusted to reflect postwar border changes and postwar classification categories.

[b] Economically active population as defined in Table 1.

[c] For the agricultural labor force in the Czech lands 1921 data are not comparable with data in 1910 or 1930 because of a considerable undercount of economically active women; this is apparent from the following data:

Economically active women as percent of the total agricultural labor force, 1910, 1921, and 1930

	1910	1921	1930
Slovakia and Ruthenia	26.1	22.2	34.0
Czech lands	53.6	36.7	45.5

[d] Data for Slovakia and Ruthenia are not adjusted for the undercount of women in agriculture compared with the Czech lands. If adjusted to reflect the same participation rate as in the Czech lands, the number of economically active in agriculture in Slovakia and Ruthenia would be 1,362,000 compared with 910,000 of those actually reported. The share of agriculture in the total economically active would thus rise to 74.7 percent if the adjusted figure is used compared with 63.7 percent if calculated on the basis of unadjusted data. The higher proportion should be used in comparing the structure of employment between the eastern provinces and the Czech lands, where the share of agriculture in the total economically active was 42.5 percent in 1910.

Source: Státní úřad statistický, Statistická příručka Republiky československé, II, 99-104, 146-48; Manuel statistique de la République tchécoslovaque, III, 303-306; Statistická ročenka Republiky československé, 1934, pp. 15-19.

on foreign demand. The textile industry benefited most from the maintenance of a relatively favorable level of domestic consumption. Although the volume of textile exports was only half the 1929 level in 1937, gross domestic production was higher than in any predepression year except 1927.

Agriculture

In contrast to industry, agriculture was in a chronic state of maladjustment during the interwar years, although its production suffered less from cyclical fluctuations.

As Czechoslovak agriculture recovered from the war it began to face severe competition from Southeastern Europe and overseas; in the domestic market, agriculture remained essentially unprotected and imports rose. Prices of agricultural products began to decline after 1920, and although they remained higher than before the war, industrial prices rose much more and the internal terms of trade turned against agriculture. The land reform in Czechoslovakia created many new small farms, which remained heavily indebted. Farm indebtedness became especially burdensome after the revaluation of the crown in 1922 and a further fall in prices. Thus, toward 1925 rising pressure in favor of restoring agricultural protection led to the introduction of tariffs on grain products in 1925 and 1926.

At this juncture a decline in foreign demand for sugar caused further difficulties. Czechoslovakia was one of the largest refined-sugar exporters in the world[20] and sugar beet farming flourished up to the mid-1920's. The domestic market absorbed only about one-third of sugar output, so that any change in foreign demand would strongly affect sugar beet farmers. The encouragement after 1925 of sugar beet production in other countries and the introduction of tariffs on refined-sugar imports reduced Czechoslovak sugar exports by more than one-half in value and by over one-third in volume between 1925 and 1929. These unfavorable conditions, combined with the introduction of tariffs on grain imports, encouraged a switch from sugar beet to grain acreage and created stronger pressure against grain imports. Such developments naturally strained Czechoslovakia's commercial relations with her East European neighbors. The support of grain and fodder prices made animal husbandry less profitable for those farms that had to purchase supplementary feedstuffs. This led to rising imports of farm animals. Thus, agriculture was already facing multiple difficulties when the world crisis and the collapse of

---

[20] In Europe, Czechoslovakia was the most important among the three largest beet sugar exporters, preceding Poland and Germany. The problems of Czechoslovak sugar exports are described in Erich Dittrich, "Die Tschechoslowakei in der Weltwirtschaft," *Weltwirtschaftliches Archiv*, XL, 535-36.

prices compounded the problems. To relieve the distress of the farmers the government intervened with various price supporting measures and import substitution policies. As a result, total agricultural output fell only slightly during the 1930's and Czechoslovakia became almost self-supporting in grain production.

Investment

Domestic investment was discouraged during most of the interwar years. In the early postwar years, persistent deficits and government borrowing kept interest rates high, especially since government debt was monetized only to a very limited degree by discounting such debt with the Central Banking Office. Although the official discount rate, which moved between 5 and 7 percent, was not much higher than that in most other European countries at the time, it was not representative of the real cost of credit. Market rates were as high as 10 to 16 percent and acted as a deterrent to private borrowing.[21] After the revaluation of the crown in 1922, the industrial recession worsened the liquidity position of industries and squeezed profits between falling prices and the sustained weight of wages, unemployment benefits paid by enterprises, high taxes, and interest rates. Many industrial losses were shifted to the banks, and "transitory" working credits were transformed into "permanent" loans, which put industry into chronic dependence on the banks and further burdened the cost of production. Some efforts to improve the export competitive position of industry were made by modernizing production techniques and equipment during the subsequent years, and by resisting wage increases.

After 1925, interest rates were reduced, but it was primarily the abstention of the government from any major domestic borrowing for several years that restored liquidity to the capital market. Tax relief on private construction encouraged building activity, but although gross national product rose after the slight recession in 1926, investment activity did not show any appreciable increase until 1928—too short a respite for any sustained growth before the onset of the world crisis. Part of the explanation for the slow start of the investment boom after 1926 lies in rising investment costs during this period, compared with other industrial prices,[22] and in considerable capital export.[23] After 1929 investment fell

[21] A. Chanal, *Monnaie et économie nationale en Tchécoslovaquie* (Ph.D. dissertation, University of Montpellier, Montpellier, 1929), pp. 239-40.

[22] See footnote 13. Detailed price indices are given in Státní úřad statistický *Československá statistika, CXL; Velkoobchodní ceny a velkoobchodní indexy v letech 1922-1936 [Wholesale Prices and Whole Indices in the Years of 1922-1936]* (Prague, 1937).

[23] Between 1925 and 1929 the balance of payments showed long-term private capital exports rising from 58 million crowns in 1925 to 875 million in 1929.

off sharply compared with a much slower decline in the gross national product, in terms of what one would expect from a model acceleration; in contrast to the 1920's, however, investment in 1933 began to rise very steeply, propelled by an increasing demand for investment goods, of which rearmament became an important component after 1935-36.

PROBLEMS ARISING FROM REGIONAL DISPARITIES

Differences in Development

Only a brief outline of regional economic disparities is possible within the limitations of this essay. At the time of the birth of the Czechoslovak Republic in 1918, the economic consequences of joining two areas of very different level of development were not understood and, as a result, were underestimated. The differences were considerable, both in the level of educational attainment and labor skills and in the structure of the economy.

According to the 1910 census, the illiteracy rate of the population in the eastern provinces was ten times as high as that in the Czech lands. Only 0.3 percent among the Slovaks and Ruthenes had any education above the elementary level, whereas among the other nationalities—the Magyars, Germans, and others—the proportion was twenty times higher. The differences were also reflected in the per capita national income, which in Slovakia and Ruthenia was less than two-thirds of that in the Czech lands in 1911-13.[24] Slovakia and Ruthenia had 28 percent of the total population but only 18 percent of the national income produced on the territory of Czechoslovakia, 29 percent of value added in agriculture, and only 10 percent of value added in industry. These provinces had a predominantly rural and agricultural economy while in the Czech provinces urbanization was much greater and industry was much more important.

Net purchase of foreign securities rose from 150 million to 1,460 million crowns between 1925 and 1927 and then declined to 860 million in 1928 and to 439 million in 1929. Short-term capital exports and balances held in foreign currencies abroad also declined in the last two years of the decade, when domestic investment began to grow more rapidly. See Státní úřad statistický, *Statistická ročenka Republiky československé*, 1934, pp. 306-307.

[24] The 1911-13 estimates of national income for Austria-Hungary and its division among the succession states by Waizner and Fellner have been adjusted by the author for missing branches of the economy and other incomparables. See Ernst Waizner, "Volkseinkommen Alt-Oesterreichs und seine Verteilung auf die Nachfolgestaaten," *Metron*, VII, No. 4 97-183; Friedrich von Fellner, "Die Verteilung des Volksvermoegens und Volkseinkommens der Länder der Ungarischen Heiligen Krone zwischen dem heutigen Ungarn und den Successions-Staaten," *Metron*, III, No. 2.

1. Tomáš G. Masaryk (1850-1937), first president (1918-1935) of the Czechoslovak Republic

2. Edvard Beneš (1884-1948), Czechoslovakia's second president (1935-1938)

3. General Milan R. Štefánik (1880-1918), the Slovak member of Czechoslovakia's liberating triumvirate, Masaryk-Beneš-Stefánik

4. Beneš and Masaryk

5. Karel Kramář (1860-1937), Czechoslovakia's first prime minister

6. (*Above*) Four Czechoslovak prime ministers: (l. to r.) Jan Malypetr, 1932-35; Antonín Švehla, 1922-26, 1926-29; František Udržal, 1929-32; Milan Hodža, 1935-38

7. (*Opposite*) The Castle of Prague (Hradčany), residence of Bohemia's kings and Czechoslovakia's presidents; behind it is the Cathedral of St. Vitus and in the foreground is the Charles Bridge

8. Bratislava, the capital of Slovakia, from across the Danube

9. Brno, the capital of Moravia

10. The Škoda works at Plzeň, one of the largest armament factories in the world

11. Sheep-raising at the foot of the High Tatras, Slovakia

12. Mass calisthenics in the stadium at Prague, 1938. The congress of the Sokols, a Czech gymnastic and patriotic organization

13. A Greek Catholic church in a Ruthenian village

The problem of Slovak development during the interwar period was therefore one of rising from a very low level in the face of acute competition from a much more developed region and in a period of generally slow overall economic growth.

Industry

Before the war, Slovakia and Ruthenia were part of the Hungarian dominion. Industrial development was encouraged through subsidies, state orders, tax alleviations, and favorable transport rates. Thus, Slovak industry never faced a challenging competition because it remained effectively shielded from the more advanced Czech provinces, both by such protective advantages and by the difficulty in east-west communications. Most roads and railroads as well as waterways converged southward to Budapest, so that these two provinces traded primarily with central Hungary. Most of the capital in industry came from Hungary, as the capital market and banking in these provinces were little developed.

After the war, when Slovakia and Ruthenia were joined politically with the more advanced Czech lands, the sudden severance of traditional ties with Hungary presented the Slovak economy with tremendous problems of adjustment. Other problems resulted from the sudden exposure of Slovak industries, hitherto protected by various forms of subsidies, to the much more advanced and productive competition in the Czech provinces, which forced many Slovak enterprises out of business.

On the whole, therefore, industry in these two eastern provinces stagnated, and even during the relatively prosperous 1920's the growth in the Czech provinces was faster in most economic sectors. A number of factors were responsible for the lagging development in the eastern provinces. One set stemmed from a lower endowment in natural resources, especially fuels. Competition was also made more difficult by the unfavorable geographical formation of the country and the great distance of markets. This handicap was aggravated by the transportation rates, which were relatively high over longer distances. Because of the many privately owned railroad lines in the eastern part of the country compared with a practically state-owned railroad network in the west, it took many years before transportation rates could be unified and reduced. A further burden was the relatively higher tax rates in the east. Slovakia and Ruthenia remained under the Hungarian tax system until the countrywide overhaul of the tax system in 1929. Finally, a more restricted access to credit was an additional handicap to Slovak industries in competition with the Czech lands.

The stagnation of Slovak and Ruthenian industry is clearly reflected in the available statistics. In most industries employment in 1930 was lower than in 1921 and in some branches lower than in 1910.[25] It did rise, however, in those branches that were oriented to the local market or that had a good local raw material base and were encouraged; for example, construction materials, power and gasworks, printing, textiles, woodworking, and food processing. Those branches that faced the keenest competition suffered most, such as metals and machine building, the chemical industry, leather, and footwear manufacture. These developments stand in contrast to the Czech lands where in almost all industries the labor force increased in 1930 with respect to 1921 and 1910 (with isolated exceptions, such as textiles, mining, and footwear).

The picture does not appear entirely unfavorable for the eastern provinces if we look at employment in large-scale factory establishments for which comparable data were compiled by the Slovak Statistical Office.[26] From these data it appears that overall industrial employment of blue-collar workers in Slovakia in large-scale industries increased somewhat faster over the period 1926-37 than in the Czech lands and did not fall as low in the trough of the depression, because these enterprises had a better competitive position than industry as a whole and did not depend as much on exports. Even in 1937, however, employment in large-scale industry in Slovakia represented only 8 percent of the country total. Another instance is provided by power production. In the years between 1923 and 1928, power outputs in the eastern provinces tripled, but it still represented only 8 percent of the total production. By 1932 fewer than 20 percent of the communities in Slovakia and less than 11 percent in Ruthenia had electricity, compared with 60 percent in the Czech provinces.

Agriculture

Almost 75 percent of the labor force was engaged in agriculture in the eastern provinces in 1910 compared with 42 percent in the Czech provinces.[27] Agriculture had initially a good prospect for development as a result of the union, since the Czech lands were considerable importers of agricultural commodities. But at the beginning of the republic, Slovak farms were backward in techniques and had little tradition in producing for the market. Agriculture in Slovakia, however, benefited considerably

---

[25] According to census data on the economically active population, in 1921 and 1930. For 1910, census data for the Czech lands and for Slovak and Ruthene counties were adjusted for postwar border changes.

[26] See *Zprávy Státného plánovacého a štatistického úradu*, I, Nos. 5-6 (1946), 128-33, and III (1949), 16-17 (cited in Jozef Faltus, *K niektorým otázkam hospodárskeho vývoja Slovenska v období 1918-1938* [*About Some Questions of Economic Development in Slovakia in the Years 1918-1938*], Bratislava, 1965). Data exclude Ruthenia.

[27] Data on the agricultural labor force in 1910 for the Czech lands and the eastern provinces were adjusted for comparability.

over the two interwar decades, in organization and cooperative movement as well as in improvement of farming methods. Acreage and yields rose, and for some crops sizable markets were found in the western provinces.

In the Czech provinces the share of labor engaged in agriculture declined between 1910 and 1930, but in Slovakia and Ruthenia it increased.[28] Although employment outside of agriculture increased in both regions, in the eastern provinces the rise was insufficient to absorb the rapid rising working-age population and its increasing participation in the labor force. One of the most serious problems was the underemployment of the labor force in Slovakia and Ruthenia. In the past it had been relieved by considerable migration overseas—between 1900 and 1910, 77 persons per 1,000 in Slovakia emigrated—and by seasonal migration of agricultural workers to Hungary, Austria, and Germany. After the war both seasonal and overseas migration declined and the underemployment problems became more severe, since migration to the Czech provinces exposed migrants from the east to the competition of a more highly skilled labor. Furthermore, after 1929, the western provinces also suffered from a sizable unemployment crisis, which made competition in the labor market even more unfavorable.

Overall Results

The overall picture of a relatively more favorable development in the Czech provinces during the interwar period than in Slovakia and Ruthenia is also borne out by the comparison of national income estimates for 1911-13, 1929, and 1937.[29] Of the combined national income produced on the territory of Czechoslovakia in 1911-13, 18.2 percent originated in the eastern provinces. By 1929, their share in the national income was estimated roughly at about 15 percent. It rose somewhat during the depression years as income fell to a much lower level in the western provinces, but in 1937 was again about 15 percent. In per capita income there was a relative regression in Slovakia and Ruthenia to less than one half of the level in the Czech provinces in 1929, and, after the recovery in 1937, to under two-thirds of 1911-13 levels.

However pervasive the picture of stagnation in the interwar development of Slovakia and Ruthenia, both provinces also benefited from great

[28] Due to some methodological differences concerning the economically active population in agriculture, the 1921 census is not entirely comparable with the censuses of 1910 and 1930.

[29] For 1911-13 national income estimates see footnote 24. National income estimates for 1929-37 were published in Stádník, *Národní důchod*, pp. 180-81 and 231. The comparison between the prewar and postwar national income must be considered only as approximate, since these estimates were made by different methods and at widely separated time intervals.

expansion in other sectors of the economy. During the years following World War I there was a rapid rise in the educational attainment of the population and in the service sectors, such as transportation and communications, financial institutions, social and medical services, and social security. Many of the Slovak complaints against the central government for neglecting to direct special consideration toward the development of the eastern provinces were justified. But it must be borne in mind that the peculiarly persistent problems of regional underdevelopment have not been adequately understood until recent years. One need only examine the abundant literature on the regional development problems of Italy since World War II.

CONCLUSION

The interwar years between 1919 and 1937 represented for Czechoslovakia a solid achievement in economic consolidation and political stability, especially in the light of the severe difficulties experienced by the neighboring countries.

At the dissolution of the Austro-Hungarian empire, Czechoslovakia was a fortunate heir with respect to an endowment of natural resources, industries, and the technical skills of her labor force. The heritage, however, also included a close dependence on trade with East Central Europe—a region of which she formed an integral part throughout past history. This part of Europe suffered heavily under the impact of World War I, and the resulting intensification of protectionism and autarkic policies prevented a renewal of the past scope of trade regulations. Czechoslovakia therefore strove to reorient her foreign trade pattern toward Western Europe and overseas countries. She succeeded to a considerable extent. The need to overcome acute competition from these countries encouraged continued improvement of the quality of industrial production and technological progress.

The general trend in Czechoslovak domestic policy was to maintain a firm stand in matters of public finance and a willingness to build up the entire economic system without undue recourse to foreign borrowing. In the immediate postwar years a sound policy of monetary stabilization was pursued in the midst of regional inflationary chaos. But the fetish of a high external value for the currency carried monetary restoration too far, at the expense of internal prosperity. A relative stringency in the credit market delayed a more rapid growth of investment. Nevertheless, compared with other European countries, the first postwar decade in Czechoslovakia showed a favorable trend in the growth of industrial production and foreign trade.

With the onset of the world depression, the Czechoslovak economy

214

suffered a setback from which it had barely recovered by 1937. During this period economic policies were not directly aimed at internal economic expansion. Rather, goals were formulated in terms of the classical view: maintenance of stable exchange relations and an adjustment of domestic prices and wage levels to this effect. The deflationary policy pursued undoubtedly contributed to the severity and length of the depression in Czechoslovakia.

During the interwar period little was changed in the great disparity of development between the western and the eastern parts of the country, which gave rise to considerable political dissatisfaction in the less-developed provinces. The major reasons were due in part to a lack of understanding of the nature of regional underdevelopment and in part to the pressure of other postwar issues, which focussed attention on international, rather than domestic, problems.

The year 1937 was the last full year of normal development for Czechoslovakia. In the fall of 1938, vital industrial regions were separated from the nation and annexed to the German Reich as a result of the Munich Agreement. Five and a half months later, Germany occupied the western provinces and created a protectorate of Bohemia and Moravia with an apparent economic independence. Slovakia was established as a vassal puppet state and Hungary occupied Ruthenia. The territorial dismemberment of the Czechoslovak Republic and her subsequent absorption into the German sphere put an end to the achievement of economic independence of the interwar years.

· 6 ·

THE FOREIGN POLICY OF EDVARD BENEŠ, 1918-1938

Piotr S. Wandycz
Yale University

On October 14, 1918, the provisional Czechoslovak government abroad notified the Allied powers of its formation. The note was signed by Dr. Edvard Beneš, minister of foreign affairs. With the dispatch of this document the thirty-four-year-old Beneš began a career as the head of his country's foreign ministry, a position he occupied uninterruptedly until 1935. Even after his election to the presidency of Czechoslovakia he continued to determine foreign policy until the catastrophe of Munich. Rarely in the annals of diplomacy was a man able to achieve such a continuity of his policy and practically identify the country's conduct of external affairs with his personal diplomacy.[1]

The foreign policy of any state is comprised of many factors: geographic location, economic structure, national composition, and political regime, as well as such less easily measurable elements as national outlook and characteristics, historical heritage, and a way of thinking about foreign matters. A successful minister of foreign affairs must take all of these into account and translate them into practical terms. If he is a man of strong personality, he can impose his own interpretation and vision on the country within the limits imposed by national interests and the political nature of the state.

Edvard Beneš was exceptionally well qualified to attempt a synthesis between his own ideas and the country's interests. A disciple of Tomáš G. Masaryk and his closest collaborator, free from the dictates of a political party—he joined the National Socialists in 1923 largely for reasons of convenience—Beneš in many respects personified Czech traditions and aspirations. His achievements stemmed both from his undoubted talents and the Czechoslovak position in Europe. Still, Beneš was not merely a typical representative of his nation, and his personality, outlook, and approach to people and ideas were in many ways unique. Brought up in a hard school of life, he was a selfmade man. All that he had learned from books and travel came through his own energy, privations, and an amazing capacity for hard work. He disciplined his mind and body, eliminated emotions and sentimentality, and thus learned to

---

[1] One must remember, however, that until the early 1930's Beneš's foreign policy was formed largely under Masaryk's guidance.

use his head, not his heart. Beneš did not smoke or drink and was hardly a charmer in a salon. He impressed his listeners by the logic of his argument rather than by the warmth of his personality. His biographers emphasize the shell he built around himself.[2] Except for the constant support of Masaryk, he owed little to other people. He did not seek sympathy and had few intimate friends.

In politics he was sometimes compared to a salesman, tirelessly representing Czechoslovak interests, and he impressed his contemporaries by the fifty important trips that he took abroad between 1920 and 1928. Clearly he preferred to do things by himself.

Although shy by nature, Beneš knew how to talk to people. Harold Nicolson, who was not generous with compliments, found Beneš in 1919 "an intelligent, young, plausible, little man with broad views."[3] Others praised him in more glowing terms. Beneš was a master tactician, and, as one biographer put it, his quick mind seized opportunities and sometimes even anticipated them.[4] A historian who compares his writings and public statements with more confidential utterings can easily notice discrepancies between the two. Nor would Beneš shrink from occasional half-truths and different presentations of the same problem to different people. These, however, are traditionally the characteristics of a skillful diplomat.

While Beneš had to fight in the political arena all his life, he was not a fighter in the usual meaning of the word. Largely responsible for the creation of a modern Czechoslovak army, he faced conflicts not as a soldier but as a politician and an intellectual. This unusual combination seemed to blend with his personality. Although some of his mental habits and ideas appeared rigid, he was by temperament and reason opposed to extremism. He was no gambler in politics. His onetime secretary, Edward Taborsky, called him the grand master of compromise: a tireless negotiator for whom compromise became an "integral part of his per-

---

[2] There are many biographies of Edvard Beneš. They include: Pierre Crabitès, *Beneš* (New York, 1936); Louis Eisenmann, *Un Grand Européen: Édouard Beneš* (Paris, 1934); Radim N. Foustka, *Život, dílo a příklad Dr. Edvarda Beneše* [*Life, Work, and the Example of Dr. Edvard Beneš*] (Prague, 1946); Edward B. Hitchcock, *"I Built a Temple for Peace": The Life of Eduard Beneš* (New York and London, 1940); František M. Hník, *Edvard Beneš: filosof demokracie* (Prague, 1943); E. Lennhoff, *In Defense of Dr. Beneš and Czechoslovak Foreign Policy* (London, 1938); Compton Mackenzie, *Dr. Beneš* (London, 1946); Jan Opočenský, ed., *Edward Beneš: Essays and Reflections Presented On the Occasion of his Sixtieth Birthday* (London, 1945); Jaroslav Papoušek, *Dr. Edvard Beneš. Sein Leben* (Prague, 1937); C. H. Roberts, *Dr. Eduard Beneš* (London, n.d.); and Fritz Weil, *Édouard Beneš ou la renaissance d'un peuple* (Paris, 1934). They vary from journalistic efforts to valuable semischolarly publications, but there is as yet no scholarly study, critical and based on unpublished material.

[3] Harold Nicolson, *Peacemaking* (London, 1945), p. 196.

[4] Mackenzie, *Dr. Beneš*, p. 130.

sonality." According to Taborsky, Beneš combined "the traditional Cartesian rationalism" with "the practical approach of a hard-bargaining, down-to-earth Czech peasant." The influence of the League of Nations' "wordy legalism" also could be traced in his diplomatic technique.[5]

Beneš was a democrat and a European who looked to the West and not to the East for inspiration. He belonged to the mainstream of Czech tradition formed by great thinkers and historical circumstances. Hus and Komenský had stood for rationalism, universal moral values, and equality. After the defeat at the White Mountain, the Czechs had to rebuild their nation along egalitarian lines. Czech thinkers used universal moral terms to deplore the national oppression of their people. Aware that lack of strength precluded policies of *farà da se*, Czech political leaders tried to link national destinies with wider conceptions—Austro-Slavism, Neo-Slavism, or European cooperation. When Beneš identified the Czechoslovak cause with democracy, humanitarianism, and Europe, he followed a well-trodden path in which convictions mingled with national interests. Thus he was never cosmopolitan but profoundly Czech, a patriot if not a nationalist.

Edvard Beneš claimed that all his ideas formed a rational system at which he had arrived through reasoning and experience. While his tactics changed, his fundamental approach remained constant. He elevated his diplomacy to a science, which he applied with tenacity and shrewdness. Strongly believing in his system, he had a feeling of intellectual superiority over other diplomats. A historian called him "a critical optimist,"[6] and this optimism at times approached complete self-confidence. Such predictions as that Mussolini would fall as a result of the Ethiopian venture, that Hitler's regime would be unstable, that the German-Polish non-aggression pact would not be achieved, sounded like wishful thinking. But Beneš was not a naive politician, and in spite of his ingrained optimism he often simply made *bonne mine à mauvais jeu*. This was not always appreciated by others. Clement Attlee, who visited Beneš in 1934 and 1936, felt that the Czechoslovak statesman seemed "too ready to think that his diplomatic skill would get his country through all the danger which faced it." The Englishman commented that Beneš, in dealing with the Germans, displayed "too much confidence in his cleverness. He did not seem to realise how long a spoon was needed to sup with the devil."[7]

Beneš expounded his views in an almost professorial manner on nu-

[5] Edward Taborsky, "The Triumph and Disaster of Eduard Beneš," *Foreign Affairs*, xxxvi (1958), 669-70.

[6] Felix Weltsch, "A Critical Optimist: An Essay on Edward Beneš as Philosopher," in Opočenský, *Edward Beneš*, pp. 118-56.

[7] Clement Attlee, *As It Happened* (London, 1954), pp. 90, 93.

merous occasions, and his parliamentary addresses are less revealing for his tactics than for his general views on diplomacy.[8] He was impatient of public opinion, and in an important speech he remarked that "there is nothing worse than when the press and public opinion criticizes foreign matters which it does not know and understand." He then gave his credo of diplomacy: politics, he said, is a science, and the politician must look for and study "the constant, the regularly-occurring." He must be versed in history, geography, and economics, especially in sociology, psychology, and biology. He must mentally vivisect society. According to Beneš, the diplomat must be trained like a scientist. To be "calm, prudent, scientifically reserved, especially today in a democracy, is a categorical imperative of every politician." But politics is also an art—"for some creators the greatest art that exists." Hence, the politician should not only analyze reality, and through observation establish a basis for action, but he must also be a good psychologist, a tactful person, and possess the spirit, feeling, and intuition of an artist. Thus defined, diplomacy becomes almost a mystery revealed only to the initiated. Beneš recognized the need for democratic control and open diplomacy, but he underlined the need to educate the public to approach diplomatic matters "with greater reserve and caution than problems of internal policy." As he put it: "The more mature and developed the democracy, the more open can be the diplomacy."

Beneš explained that Czechoslovak relations with other countries were based on almost mathematically calculated foundations derived from moral-philosophical premises. Defining politics as a "struggle to appraise properly today's realities and the possible realities of tomorrow," he rejected policies based on prestige and insincerity, and said that "we created a political system supported by a philosophical approach and scientifically proved."[9]

[8] Beneš's speeches and writings are too numerous to be listed here. A collection of his speeches prior to 1924 appeared in *Problémy nové Evropy a zahraniční politika Československa* [*Problems of New Europe and the Foreign Policy of Czechoslovakia*] (Prague, 1924); those during the decade after in *Boj o mír a bezpečnost státu* [*Struggle for Peace and Security of the State*] (Prague, 1934). Major statements of policy were published by the Orbis publishing house in Prague in Czech and Western languages. There are numerous articles scattered in such periodicals as *Foreign Affairs*, *Le Monde Slave*, or *Nineteenth Century and After*. Then there are Beneš's multivolume memoirs and such studies as *Où vont les Slaves?* (Paris, 1948), *Democracy Today and Tomorrow* (London, 1940), and many others.

[9] All the quotations come from a speech at Brno on March 23, 1923, printed as "Zahraniční politika a demokracie: problémy a metody naši zahraniční politiky" ["Foreign Policy and Democracy: Problems and Methods of our Foreign Policy"], *Zahraniční Politika*, I, 1923. For recent treatment of the origins of Czechoslovak diplomacy see Radko Břach, "To the Origin and the Beginnings of Czechoslovak Foreign Policy," *Problems of Contemporary History*, I, 1968; Alena Gajanová, "Entstehung und Entwicklung der Internationalen Beziehungen der ČSR," *Die*

These statements were made in 1923, when independent Czechoslovakia had existed for barely five years. Beneš, however, seemingly felt that wartime experiences and the developments at the Paris Peace Conference were sufficient proof of the correctness of his system. Thus it was largely on the foundations of the immediate postwar European situation that he constructed his diplomatic edifice, even if later experiences at Geneva and the changing international situation brought corrections and modifications. Two fundamental assumptions seemed to lie at the bottom of the system: first, that Czechoslovakia was a small state whose fate was inextricably linked with European developments, and second, that among the great powers she had no implacable enemy. The peace conference had indicated this. The victorious powers had shown sympathy for Czechoslovak democracy, understanding for its aspirations. Defeated Germany did not act as an irreconcilable foe. As for Russia, there was hope that relations might be correct if not friendly.

Proceeding from these assumptions and linking them to an ideological basis, Beneš sought to avoid entangling alliances with any great power that could expose Czechoslovakia to risks and tried to retain a maneuverability in European politics. As long as a certain amount of stability prevailed, Czechoslovakia, occupying a central position on the Continent, would be safe. Hence collective security was a canon of Beneš's diplomacy, and he became one of the staunchest supporters of the League of Nations. Given the importance of Franco-British cooperation in the league, he did his best to foster it. Czechoslovakia signed an alliance with France in 1924 only when the chance of a broader system based on agreement between Paris and London did not materialize. Even so, Beneš insisted that his country belong to no bloc directed against a great power. Paris was Prague's closest partner, but no more.

The only great power considered inimical almost by definition was Austria-Hungary, which disappeared in 1918. However, among the successor states there was the small Austrian republic and the more ominous-sounding kingdom of Hungary. To counter Hungarian revisionism and Habsburg restoration, Beneš devised the Little Entente. Useful as a counterargument against the alleged "balkanization" of Central Europe, and a working alternative to schemes of Danubian confederation, the Little Entente became a handy diplomatic tool. Elevated to semi-great-power status within the League of Nations, it greatly enhanced the position of its three member states—Czechoslovakia, Yugoslavia, and Rumania—and gave Prague, the *spiritus movens* of the group, a privi-

Entstehung der Tschechoslowakischen Republik und ihre International-Politische Stellung (Prague, 1968); as well as the *Mezinárodní konference k 50. výročí Československé Republiky, Praha 11-15 X. 1968* [*International Conference on the Occasion of the Fiftieth Anniversary of the Czechoslovak Republic, Prague, October 11-15, 1968*].

leged role in international counsels. Ensuring tranquility in the Danubian region, not overtaxing the strength of its members, opposed to no great power, the Little Entente appeared as an ideal organization with limited interests.

With the League and the French alliance operating on the European level and the Little Entente on the regional level, Beneš's system was practically complete by the mid-1920's. Relations with Germany were correct, and Beneš hoped that they might improve in time, provided Germany and France arrived at some workable settlement. As for Russia, the Czechoslovak statesman hoped for her reentry into European politics, though for the time being he had to exercise a cautious attitude toward Moscow, given domestic and international anti-Soviet feelings.

The main lines of Beneš's system imposed certain rules governing Czechoslovak relations with other states. Policy toward Italy, insofar as that country was France's competitor in East Central Europe, was characterized by correctness mingled with caution. Poland raised more complex issues. A country in latent conflict with both Germany and Russia, whose diplomacy appeared adventuresome to Czechoslovakia, Poland could become a trouble spot, the "northern Balkans."[10] In view of the Franco-Polish alliance, and to neutralize the long common border between Poland and Czechoslovakia, correct and even friendly relations were in order; but there was to be no alliance or genuine involvement. Furthermore, Warsaw entertained good relations with Budapest, and the bitter and revisionist Hungary was a major enemy. While it was in the Czechoslovak interest that Austria function as an independent state, and Prague favored economic aid to prevent an *Anschluss* or a Danubian union, policy toward Hungary was more negative. A certain anti-Hungarian and anti-Habsburg complex gave an emotional touch to Beneš's otherwise calculated diplomacy.[11]

Creation of the Little Entente represented the first important political achievement of Czechoslovak diplomacy. Hungarian revisionism, which derived new hope from secret Franco-Hungarian exchanges, and the tense situation in Central Europe in the summer of 1920 made Beneš

[10] Beneš allegedly called Poland the "Northern Balkans" in the late 1920's. See Jerzy Kozeński, *Czechosłowacja w polskiej polityce zagranicznej w latach 1932-38* [*Czechoslovakia in Polish Foreign Policy in the Years 1932-38*] (Poznan, 1964), p. 32, quoting from the controversial F. Kahánek, *Beneš contra Beck* [*Beneš versus Beck*] (Prague, 1938), p. 172. The German envoy Koch also heard of Beneš's alleged remark and reported it to Berlin. See F. Gregory Campbell, "Czechoslovak-German Relations during the Weimar Republic 1918-1933" (unpublished Ph.D. dissertation, Yale University), p. 149.

[11] Even as late as March, 1934, Beneš said that the return of the Habsburgs to Central Europe "means there will never be peace and quiet." Cited in Mackenzie, *Dr. Beneš*, p. 143.

conclude a defensive alliance with Yugoslavia on August 14. The pact stressed the need to maintain the Treaty of Trianon and singled out Hungary as a potential aggressor. Negotiations with Rumania led first to a vague agreement on cooperation, Bucharest being more interested in a wider and more all-embracing alliance in Eastern Europe. However, events in the Danubian area played into the hands of Czechoslovak diplomacy. The abortive attempts in April and October, 1921, by ex-Emperor Charles to regain the throne of Hungary made Rumania a full-fledged partner, and the three states were able to force Charles out of Hungary. So, the Little Entente was born, and the French who originally had opposed this grouping were forced to recognize it, thus vindicating Beneš's policy.[12] Prague's international position became strong, and within a short time it could claim two other successes. On November 6, 1921, Beneš signed a political agreement with the new Polish foreign minister, Konstanty Skirmunt, marking a detente in the hitherto strained relations between the two countries. On December 15, the Treaty of Lány with Austria brought Vienna's engagement against a Habsburg restoration. Such events showed that Prague was becoming the center of a diplomatic constellation in East Central Europe.[13]

Beneš attempted to represent the Little Entente as an element in the struggle between democracy and reaction, economically important, and making a positive and lasting contribution to European reconstruction.[14] By attributing to it such general significance, he was overestimating if not misinterpreting its nature. The Czechoslovak foreign minister was not interested in making the Little Entente the beginning of a wider regional alliance system in East Central Europe that could protect the area against a great power. During the brief period of Czechoslovak-Polish cooperation—reaching its height at Genoa—the accepted formula was

[12] Earlier studies of the Little Entente do not reveal that the initiative to form the group went against the then-current policy of the Quai d'Orsay. For newer French interpretations see Pierre Renouvin, *Les Crises du XXe siècle*, première partie (Paris, 1957), pp. 280-83; also Piotr S. Wandycz, *France and Her Eastern Allies 1919-1925* (Minneapolis, 1962), pp. 193-201; and a recent Hungarian article about the origins of the Little Entente, Ferenc Boros, "Adalékok a kisantant létrejöttének történetéhez és jellegéhez" ["Contribution to the History of the Origins and Character of the Little Entente"], *Századok*, nos. 4-5 (1966), 816-46. (I am indebted for its summary to Miss Eva Balogh.) For Czechoslovak diplomacy see the well-documented work by Věra Olivová, "Československá zahraniční politika a pokus o restauraci Habsburků v roce 1921" ["Czechoslovak Foreign Policy and the Attempt at Habsburg Restoration in 1921"], *Československý časopis historický*, VII (1959).

[13] See Věra Olivová, "K historii československo-rakouské smlouvy z roku 1921" ["About the History of Czechoslovak-Austrian Agreement of 1921"], ibid., IX (1961).

[14] See Beneš's analysis in *Five Years of Czechoslovak Foreign Policy* (Prague, 1924).

the Little Entente *and* Poland; nothing more vast was contemplated. Such a policy prevented the appearance of a bloc that might have antagonized Berlin, Rome, or Moscow, and gave Prague freedom of action in the international field. While a secret military convention concluded in 1923 foresaw Czechoslovak aid in military materials to Rumania and Yugoslavia (when in war with a third power), common action was contemplated only in case of a struggle against Hungary.[15]

Having achieved greater stability in the Danubian basin and enhanced his prestige as a European statesman, Beneš sought to safeguard the Czechoslovak position through collective security. Careful to avoid identification with any great power, the foreign minister tried to bring France closer to Britain and to mediate between France and Germany. This was an ambitious policy, which reflected Beneš's belief that greater security in Europe would automatically increase the security of his country.

While unable to achieve his goals, Beneš could claim several successes and, what was more important, make his diplomacy respected in the capitals of the great powers and in Geneva. There was little he could do to prevent the failure of a working security system based on cooperation between London and Paris—London being determined to make no commitments in Eastern Europe—or avert the fiasco of the Genoa conference, whose only by-product was the ominous treaty of Rapallo. But at least he could claim that Czechoslovak diplomacy had played a positive part in all these developments, and that he brought home from Genoa an economic rapprochement with Soviet Russia that resulted in a trade agreement signed in Prague on June 5, 1922.

The skillful policy of maneuvering between the great powers without becoming anyone's pawn was put to a test in early 1923 when France, under the premiership of Raymond Poincaré, adopted a hard line vis-à-vis Germany and occupied the Ruhr.[16] This placed Prague in an awkward position. Her economic ties with Germany were affected, and the course of events could involve Czechoslovakia in a struggle with Germany. Masaryk and Beneš privately offered strong criticism of the adventurous French policy and publicly insisted that "only an entente between France and Germany can bring about international cooperation and assure lasting peace in Europe."[17] Beneš indicated his willingness to

---

[15] See Henryk Batowski, "Sojusze wojskowe Czechosłowacji, 1919-1938" ["Military Agreements of Czechoslovakia of 1919-1938"], *Przegląd Zachodni*, XVII, 2 (1961), 291. See also the study by Rudolf Kiszling, *Die Militärische Vereinbarungen der Kleinen Entente, 1929-1937* (München, 1959).

[16] An excellent discussion of Prague's policy is Olivová, "Československá diplomacie v době rurské krise roku 1923" ["Czechoslovak Diplomacy during the Ruhr Crisis of 1923"], *Československý časopis historický*, VI (1958).

[17] Cited in Wandycz, *France and her Eastern Allies*, p. 274.

mediate between Paris and Berlin, and his stand gained the appreciation of Britian and Germany. Nor could the new French cabinet of Edouard Herriot hold it against him.

Czechoslovak policy at Geneva sought the same objectives as it held during the Ruhr crisis: a relaxation of tensions and the strengthening of a system of collective security. Beneš found the atmosphere at Geneva especially conducive to a display of his talents as a negotiator and master of compromise. Six times chairman of the council and once president of the assembly, not to count his chairmanships of important committees and his work as rapporteur, Beneš became the man of the League of Nations. In September, 1923, he was primarily responsible for the drafting of the Treaty of Mutual Assistance, which linked disarmament with general security and general security with regional pacts and arrangements. The treaty, which represented an ingenious reconciliation of divergent British and French proposals, received the unanimous approval of the League Assembly. But in spite of being an almost perfect formula, it stood little chance of acceptance by the British government. The attempt to bring Paris and London closer to each other was unsuccessful.

Czechoslovakia drew a lesson from this state of affairs and decided for a rapprochement with France. Ever since the Paris Peace Conference, relations between the two states had been close but not formalized through any treaty. Sure of French support in essential matters, Beneš saw no need to assume written commitments. Practical military matters were arranged through the French military mission in Prague; political and economic affairs, through diplomatic and private channels. But in the spring of 1923 Paris made suggestions for an alliance, and in the autumn Masaryk and Beneš paid a state visit to France.[18] In the course of protracted negotiations the two statesmen indicated they were interested in a flexible alliance that would not oblige them to follow French foreign policy blindly.

The treaty of January 25, 1924, largely satisfied these objectives. It provided for the maintenance of the status quo and for the prevention of Habsburg and Hohenzollern restoration, and included a provision against the *Anschluss* of Austria. There was no military convention but merely an exchange of letters between foreign ministers that reaffirmed existing cooperation in the military sphere. Thus Beneš could truthfully deny that his country had joined a bloc or bound herself to any automatic action. To emphasize Czechoslovak diplomatic freedom, Prague pro-

[18] Characteristically, Masaryk and Beneš did not limit their visit to Paris but went also to London and Brussels. For Prague's relations with France during this period see the interesting contribution of Radko Břach, "Francouzský alianční systém a Československo na počátku roku 1924" ["The French Alliance System and Czechoslovakia at the beginning of 1924"], *Historie a vojenství*, I, 1968.

ceeded to conclude a treaty with Italy, even though such an arrangement was devoid of any real importance. There was no rapprochement with France's ally, Poland, although Paris had indicated its interest in Czechoslovak-Polish military cooperation. In fact, relations between Warsaw and Prague cooled considerably.

The international sequel to the Ruhr episode was a gradual abandonment by France of a tough policy toward Germany. Acting under pressure from the Anglo-Saxon powers, Paris agreed to the Dawes plan, which restricted its freedom of action vis-à-vis Berlin. The acceptance of the plan and the failure of yet another attempt to strengthen the League—the Geneva Protocol, largely Beneš's brainchild—facilitated a new approach to the problem of international security: the pacts of Locarno.

The Locarno settlement of October, 1925, dealt a blow to the French alliance system in Eastern Europe. By drawing a distinction between Germany's borders in the west, which were officially confirmed and internationally guaranteed, and the eastern frontiers that were not, Locarno opened possibilities for German revisionism in the east. By immobilizing France on the Rhine, the treaties rendered any future French military aid to Czechoslovakia or Poland highly problematic. True, on October 16, 1925, France negotiated new treaties of alliance with Prague and Warsaw that contained assurances of help in case of German aggression. But the wording of the alliances, which clearly linked assistance with Articles 15 and 16 of the covenant, cast doubt on the effectiveness of the guarantees.

In spite of Gustav Stresemann's ironic remarks about Beneš at Locarno, and the insinuations of the Czechoslovak opposition that the foreign minister had merely picked up "the crumbs which fell from the Great Powers' table," Beneš described the pacts as "a tremendous advance on anything that has yet been accomplished."[19] He could claim that Locarno meant a French-German reconciliation, which lay in the Czechoslovak interest, especially as Britain was also a party to the new system, and that Germany had been contained by agreements rather than by war. The new French alliance and a German-Czechoslovak arbitra-

---

[19] See Zygmunt J. Gasiorowski, "Beneš and Locarno: Some Unpublished Documents," *Review of Politics*, xx, 223. For a similarly favorable appraisal of Locarno see Kamil Krofta, *Z dob naši první republiky* [*In the Times of our First Republic*] (Prague, 1939), pp. 81-86. Stresemann's oft-quoted remarks included the phrase about Beneš and the Polish foreign minister, Aleksander Skrzynski, having to sit at Locarno "in a neighboring room until we let them in," and the malicious boast that "such was the situation of states which had been so pampered until then, because they were the servants of others, but were dropped the moment it seemed possible to come to an understanding with Germany." Gustav Stresemann, *Vermächtnis* (3 vols.; Berlin 1932), ii, 243.

tion treaty signed at Locarno were surely important achievements. As for possible eastern German expansion, it seemed to threaten Poland, not Czechoslovakia, and Czechoslovak diplomats had gone out of their way to stress the different positions of Warsaw and Prague.[20] Discounting the importance of the recently concluded conciliation and arbitration treaties with Poland, Beneš had worked for direct exchanges with Berlin, distancing himself from Warsaw. Both he and Masaryk dropped disparaging remarks about the Franco-Polish alliance and expressed belief that the Danzig Corridor was "an absurdity" that in time Poland would abandon to the Germans.[21]

Germany's entry into the League of Nations in 1926 and Stresemann's rise to a prominent position in Europe made Beneš doubly eager to cultivate "friendly relations"—the new term that replaced "correct relations"—with Berlin. The Czechoslovak minister made pro-German gestures in Geneva and sought to smooth over possible friction in the matter of the Sudeten Germans. However, the large issue was a German-Austrian union, and Czechoslovak diplomacy at once showed great nervousness at the prospect. When rumors of an impending union began to circulate in 1927 and 1928, Prague reacted by trying to divert German interest from Vienna toward Danzig. According to Stresemann, he learned from Czechoslovak leaders that they had disregarded recent Polish feelers for cooperation because they had no intention of pulling Poland's chestnuts out of the fire in case of a German-Polish conflict. Allegedly, both Masaryk and Beneš expressed hopes for a speedy German solution of the Danzig problem.[22] Czechoslovak diplomats also dropped hints about the desirability of a nonaggression treaty between Prague and Berlin. The fear of an *Anschluss* seemed overpowering, and when the question became an open issue in 1931, Beneš indicated that Czechoslovakia would oppose it even "to the point of self-destruction."[23]

The brief period of illusory fulfillment and the "Locarno spirit" came to an abrupt end with Stresemann's death in 1929. The same year the American Wall Street crash shook the foundations of European and world security. The effects of the Great Depression were felt in Czechoslovakia by 1932, and Prague's diplomacy began to operate in far more difficult domestic and international conditions. The Manchurian crisis

[20] Wandycz, *France and her Eastern Allies*, pp. 336-37.

[21] Report of the American envoy in Prague, cited in Gasiorowski, *Review of Politics*, xx, 220.

[22] Stresemann's memorandum of March 13, 1927, on a conversation with Tomáš G. Masaryk, cited in Campbell, *Czechoslovak-German Relations*, p. 147. An entire chapter in Campbell's study is significantly entitled "Vienna or Danzig?" The most detailed and extensive study of interwar Czechoslovak-German relations is Johann Wolfgang Brügel, *Tschechen und Deutsche, 1918-1938* (Munich, 1967).

[23] Koch's report cited in Campbell, *Czechoslovak-German Relations*.

beginning in 1931 had shown the weakness of the League of Nations: the breakdown of the disarmament conference of 1932-34—at which Beneš acted as secretary-general—indicated the impossibility of resolving crucial issues through international agreements.

The time had now come for a reappraisal of accepted canons of foreign policy. To cope with the economic situation in the Danubian basin, France came forth with the Tardieu plan. Seeking a rapprochement of the Little Entente countries with Austria and Hungary, the plan envisaged a preferential tariff agreement among the five states. No great power was to be involved, France remaining in the background as the *spiritus movens*. Beneš approved it, but he felt that the Little Entente ought to be the center and basis of the proposed reorganization.

Neither Germany nor Italy, Austria nor Hungary found the Tardieu plan attractive. Beneš realized the gravity of the situation. He thought that Italy was siding with Germany in the then German-Polish conflict (a tariff war and a revisionist war of nerves), and that Mussolini was striving for a division of spheres of influence in East Central Europe, trying to bring Austria and Hungary under his wing. Czechoslovakia was to be left in the German sphere, and Yugoslavia to be isolated. The Little Entente could become paralyzed. Acting on this analysis, Beneš proposed at the extraordinary meeting of the Little Entente in December, 1932, measures for strengthening this organization. The Little Entente was to establish a permanent council, a secretariat with a section in Geneva, and an economic council. The object was to bring a permanent unification of foreign policies of the three countries, to prevent attempts to undermine the Little Entente from within, to establish foundations for a definitive organization of East Central Europe, and to give the Little Entente a proper place in European politics. These were ambitious aims, and Beneš asserted that the Little Entente so reorganized would "have great political importance and influence on international politics." The Czechoslovak statesman was against a broadening of the basis of cooperation—Titulescu's project to oppose in the preamble a revision of *all* treaties—and, while advocating closer military cooperation, was unwilling to accept new commitments.[24]

The chief weakness of the Little Entente remained in the economic field. Czechoslovak agricultural circles protested against Rumanian and Yugoslav imports, which opened the field to German expansion into the Balkans. As a remedy, the Czech agrarians suggested closer cooperation

[24] See Robert Kvaček, *Nad Evropou zataženo* [*Clouds over Europe*] (Prague, 1966), pp. 46-49. Compare the less reliable *O československé zahraniční politice, 1918-1939: Sborník statí* [*Czechoslovak Foreign Policy, 1918-1939: A Collection of Studies*], edited by Vladimír Soják (Prague, 1956), pp. 196-99. According to the latter, Beneš proposed to call the strengthened Little Entente the Ligue Centrale Européenne.

with Poland, and indeed in early 1933 there was a chance of winning the Poles to a pro-Little Entente policy. German-Polish relations were tense. Close cooperation with Poland might have cemented the Little Entente but at the same time would have drawn the group into an anti-German and possibly anti-Russian camp. This Beneš was not prepared to do. Exchanges between Prague and Warsaw centered around a somewhat meaningless pact of friendship instead of an alliance in which both the Czechoslovak and Polish chiefs of staff showed interest.[25]

Hitler's rise to power and Mussolini's proposal of a four-power pact heralded a new offensive by the revisionist powers and provided a new chance for a closing of the ranks among East Central European states. However, after a brief period, during which Warsaw and the capitals of the Little Entente took a strong line against the four-power pact, divergencies began to appear. Having received assurances that the pact would be of little significance and that stiff opposition would only render the French position more difficult, Beneš made the Little Entente abandon its intransigent line.[26] The Poles continued to voice opposition. A proposed visit by Jozef Beck to Prague was cancelled.[27] The Czechoslovak foreign minister had little sympathy for the "new look" of Polish diplomacy, and he took no notice of rumors about Polish plans for a preventive war with Germany. At the same time he showed no interest in German soundings for a nonaggression treaty with Prague.[28]

In January, 1934, Poland and Germany exploded a diplomatic bomb by signing a declaration of nonaggression. The paths of Czechoslovak and Polish diplomacy parted for good.

If the nonaggression agreement was a blow to Prague's diplomacy, Czechoslovak attempts to strengthen her position through an economic or political rapprochement with Austria and Hungary also suffered a defeat. A mistrust of Chancellor Engelbert Dollfuss and contacts with the socialist opposition did not assist Beneš's diplomacy. Nor did Yugoslavia and Rumania view the Austrian question with the same eye as Czechoslovakia. In March, 1934, Italy, Austria, and Hungary concluded the Rome Protocols, which represented a new danger to the Little Entente.

[25] A very detailed analysis of Czechoslovak-Polish exchanges in 1932 and 1933 is in Kozeński, *Czechosłowacja w polskiej polityce*, pp. 47-73. Compare Kvaček, *Nad Evropou zataženo*, pp. 29-30.

[26] It is also likely that Beneš, who in June, 1933, advocated a French-Italian agreement guaranteeing Austrian neutrality, did not wish to antagonize Rome. See Koloman Gajan, "Die Rolle der Tschechoslowakei in Mitteleuropa 1918-1945," *Österreichische Osthefte*, Jahrgang 8 (May, 1966), 188.

[27] For Beck's account see his *Dernier rapport: politique polonaise, 1926-1939* (Neuchâtel, 1951), p. 41.

[28] For the German proposals of a nonaggression agreement with Czechoslovakia see Kvaček, *Nad Evropou zataženo*, pp. 38-42; *O československé zahraniční politice*, pp. 221-22; and Kozeński, *Czechosłowacja w polskiej polityce*, p. 67.

Nor was the appearance of the Balkan Pact, a regional grouping seemingly complementing the Little Entente in Southeastern Europe, a net gain. By diverting Rumanian and Yugoslav attention to Balkan problems, the new pact weakened the cohesion of the Little Entente.

No wonder Beneš, feeling it increasingly necessary to strengthen Czechoslovak security, turned to the East. Together with Masaryk, Beneš had opposed intervention in Russia, concluded a commercial agreement with Moscow in 1922, promoted a recognition of the Soviet regime in 1924 and 1926, and in 1925 spoken of an eastern Locarno. In 1933 he again advocated a *de jure* recognition of Soviet Russia, to which he encountered opposition at home and among the Little Entente partners.

When in the spring of 1933 the Soviet ambassador in Paris, Valeriian Dovgalevskii, mentioned Russian readiness to conclude a pact with the Little Entente and France, Paris and Prague showed interest. Then there were second thoughts in France about a link with Soviet Russia. But by early 1934, worried by the German-Polish agreement, French Foreign Minister Louis Barthou came forth with his plan for an Eastern pact, and Beneš became one of its staunchest supporters. True to his preference for multilateral treaties, the Czechoslovak statesman advocated a collective arrangement—at least a tripartite French-Soviet-Czechoslovak pact —hoping that it might in time become even more all-embracing. He considered that France must not "create the smallest doubt in Russia as to her intentions regarding an Eastern pact" and use the Russian trump to impress Italy and make her collaborate with Paris.[29] In accord with Moscow, Beneš promoted a collective approach to the problem of security in contrast to Berlin's policy of bilateral treaties. The death of Barthou shattered Czechoslovak hopes. The new foreign minister, Pierre Laval, had doubts about an alliance with Russia and preferred closer links with Italy. Eventually only two bilateral treaties—a Franco-Russian and a Czechoslovak-Russian—were signed in 1935.

The treaty between Prague and Moscow of May 16, 1935, made Russian aid to Czechoslovakia conditional on the working of the French alliance of 1925. There were many reasons for that arrangement. In instructions to the Czechoslovak envoy in Berlin, Prague emphasized that it did not want an alliance that could be interpreted as contrary to Locarno: "Being conscious of belonging to Western Europe, we do not want to tie ourselves one-sidedly to Russia."[30] But there was more to it. In the connection between the Czechoslovak-Russian and French-Russian treaties, Beneš saw a substitute for the tripartite treaty that Laval had been unwilling to accept. Although no military convention had been

[29] Cited in *O československé zahraniční politice*, p. 247.
[30] Ibid., p. 255.

signed, the Czechoslovak statesman sought to achieve a working collaboration between Soviet and Czechoslovak armies, making the alliance with Russia similar in essence to that with France.[31]

The Franco-Czechoslovak-Soviet plan of building a dam to contain Hitler's expansion made sense, provided the great powers showed solidarity and determination vis-à-vis Germany. This did not prove to be the case. Britain signed a bilateral naval agreement with Hitler behind the back of the French, and the Italian aggression against Ethiopia placed the Western powers and Czechoslovakia in a quandary. Should they stand by the League, condemn Italy, and risk an Italian rapprochement with Germany, or keep Italy friendly at the cost of trampling upon the covenant and collective security? Britain and France chose a middle road, combining sanctimonious speeches in Geneva with underhand deals (the Hoare-Laval agreement) and indecision.

As president of the Assembly of the League, Beneš strongly condemned Italian aggression. Apart from moral reasons, Czechoslovakia could not tolerate an open breach of the covenant: a dangerous precedent. At the same time Beneš could not afford to antagonize Italy, whose policy in the Danubian area was of paramount importance for Prague. A certain uneasiness surrounded the moves of Czechoslovak diplomacy; there was restricted room for maneuver and danger inherent in any move. In spite of the French and Czechoslovak alliances with Russia, neither Paris nor Prague wished to burn their bridges to Berlin. Hints were dropped about a nonaggression pact with Germany that met a cool reception.

There was need for a more imaginative policy on Czechoslovakia's side, and the Hodža plan was born. Milan Hodža became prime minister on Beneš's election to the presidency of the republic, and he took over the Ministry of Foreign Affairs. Facing up to the growing German problem in international politics and at home—Konrad Henlein's Sudeten German party marched to victory in 1935 carrying seventy percent of Sudeten German votes—Hodža sought to improve relations with Germany. Realizing Czechoslovak weakness, he strove after a consolidation of the whole of East Central Europe so as to negotiate with Germany from a position of greater strength. His plan involved an economic and political rapprochement between the states of the Little Entente and of the Rome Protocols, and closer ties to England. He also took an interest in Poland. Hodža's belief that "with such a big organism as Germany, small and medium-sized states can only deal on the basis of a Central

---

[31] For the most recent and detailed treatment see Olivová, "Československo-sovětská smlouva z roku 1935" ["Czechoslovak-Soviet Treaty of 1935"], Československý časopis historický, XIII (1965).

European regional entente" was eminently sound.[32] However, the practical possibilities of realizing the plan were dim by 1935-36. Britain was indifferent; Italy insisted on the cessation of sanctions as a *conditio sine qua non* of rapprochement with the Little Entente. Rumania and Yugoslavia could ill afford to antagonize Germany, which had already acquired hold over their economies. Nor was Warsaw likely to jeopardize her position vis-à-vis Berlin by lending support to Hodža's plan, even if Colonel Beck clearly preferred him to Beneš. Hungary opposed, and while Austria proved more receptive, the old problem of the Habsburg restoration as well as poor communications between Prague and Vienna did not smooth the way to an understanding. In late February, 1936, Hodža handed over the foreign ministry to Kamil Krofta, a strict adherent of the Beneš line of diplomacy. The attempt to build a united Central Europe, coming as it did after the Ethiopian venture and the Polish-German pact, was condemned to failure.

German reoccupation of the Rhineland on March 7, 1936, provided perhaps the last occasion to stop Hitler's expansionist policies. French allies in Eastern Europe—Czechoslovakia, Poland, and even Soviet Russia—signaled their willingness to stand by France. Paris, however, looked only in the direction of London and was unwilling to take the initiative. Aware of French hesitations, Prague, not unlike Warsaw, showed a certain caution in its official pronouncements. At the same time, increasingly conscious of a direct German menace to Czechoslovakia, Beneš proposed during the summer and autumn of 1936 a military pact of the Little Entente directed against *any* aggressor. This was a considerable departure from his previous idea of the Little Entente and a greatly belated move. Rumania looked up to Yugoslavia, and Belgrade was not willing to take a stand against Berlin. The Yugoslav diplomat Božidar Purić brutally disposed of the Little Entente by calling it *"une blague politique"*, for "none of the Little Entente states can seriously assume that Hungary would on its own begin an attack against any one of them."[33] And by 1936 Belgrade and Bucharest were not interested in reorganizing the Little Entente to assist Czechoslovakia, whose position seemed more vulnerable than their own.

Under these circumstances Beneš, who in early 1936 had been reluctant to contemplate a nonaggression pact with Germany, now began to consider it seriously. The Czechoslovak position had weakened considerably. Domestic German pressure was on the increase, and inimical

[32] Cited in *O československé zahraniční politice*, p. 278. For a discussion of Hodža's plan see his *Federation in Central Europe* (London, 1942), pp. 126-39, and Alena Gajanová, *ČSR a středoevropská politika velmocí, 1918-1938* [Czechoslovakia and the Central European Policy of the Great Powers, 1918-1938] (Prague, 1967), pp. 345-47.

[33] Cited in Kvaček, *Nad Evropou zataženo*, p. 331.

propaganda accused Prague of being an outpost of Soviet Bolshevism. The right wing of the Agrarian party was talking again of Hodža's plan and of a detente with Germany. The Czechoslovak minister in Berlin attempted to improve relations and assured the Germans that "the 7th of March changed all the bases of Czech policy" and might lead to a reappraisal of commitments to France and Soviet Russia.[34] Foreign Minister Krofta was preparing the diplomatic missions abroad for the possibility of talks with Germany concerning a nonaggression pact, which, however, would be negotiated in agreement with Rumania and Yugoslavia and conform to the existing international obligations.

The secret talks of two German envoys—acting outside of the Wilhelmstrasse—with Beneš and Krofta lasted through November and December, 1936.[35] The German side was at first interested in a nonaggression pact, full economic and cultural equality for the Germans in Czechoslovakia, increased trade exchanges, a press truce, and eventually a common anti-Habsburg front. Beneš skilfully avoided talking about the Sudeten Germans. He dwelt on genuine and lasting agreement constructed on the basis of the 1925 German-Czechoslovak arbitration treaty. He contrasted his approach with that of Beck in 1934 and indulged in bitter remarks against Poland. He also protested his alleged dependence on Soviet diplomacy.

Kept *au courant* of the secret talks, Hitler showed that he was not keen on a genuine nonaggression pact. The points of a future agreement that mattered to him related to trade, the position of the Germans in Czechoslovakia, a press truce including restraints on the activity of German exiles in Prague, and a neutralization of Czechoslovakia in case of a German-Soviet conflict. The exchanges broke down when Konstantin von Neurath voiced stern opposition to a policy of detente with the Czechoslovaks, but it is likely that Berlin never intended to go beyond soundings, being bent on discrediting and isolating Czechoslovakia diplomatically. Prague's assurances that "Czechoslovakia would not join in any preventive war against Germany" were unlikely to impress Hitler.[36]

By late 1936, Berlin, Rome, Budapest, and Warsaw began to gain the

---

[34] Cited in Gerhard L. Weinberg, "Secret Hitler-Beneš Negotiations in 1936-1937," *Journal of Central European Affairs*, XIX (1960), 368.

[35] The negotiations are extensively analyzed by the above-mentioned Weinberg; Kvaček, "Československo-německá jednání v roce 1936" ["Czechoslovak-German Negotiations in 1936"], *Historie a vojenství*, XIII (1965); Michał Pułaski, "Tajne rokowania czechosłowacko-niemieckie o pakt nieagresji w latach 1936-1937" ["Czechoslovak-German Secret Negotiations for a Non-aggression Pact in 1936-1937"], *Przegląd Zachodni*, XX (1964); and A. Šnejdárek, "Tajné rozhovory Beneše s Německem v letech 1936-1937" ["Beneš's Secret Peace Talks with Germany in 1936-1937"], *Československý časopis historický*, XI (1961).

[36] Weinberg in *Journal of Central European Affairs*, XIX, 369.

conviction that the days of the Czechoslovak Republic were numbered. Prague's situation was undoubtedly difficult, and there was something pathetic about the still optimistic-sounding statements of Beneš on foreign policy. The Rome-Berlin Axis and the Austro-German agreement precluded the possibility of meaningful policies in the Danubian area. Most of the diplomatic weapons in Beneš's arsenal were blunted. The Little Entente was hardly operative even as a tool of diplomacy, and the new leaders of Rumania and Yugoslavia merely paid lip-service to the organization. Renewed attempts to effect a rapprochement with Austria and Hungary were becoming ever more hopeless. Nor did the final agreement to lift restrictions on Hungarian armaments—at the Little Entente meeting at Bled in 1938—pay any political dividends in the form of a desired nonaggression pact with Hungary. The French alliance, the cornerstone of Czechoslovak foreign policy, was losing its importance, and Yvon Delbos refused formal written guarantees to Czechoslovakia, merely stating at the congress of his Radical Socialist party that France would be faithful to all her commitments.

With the breakdown of Soviet-Rumanian exchanges concerning the passage of the Red Army through Rumania, there was no way in which Russia could assist Czechoslovakia physically. Prague modeled its attitude toward the Soviet alliance on the Franco-Russian pact, and as Stalin said to Gen. Charles de Gaulle in 1944, "the pact was lost through mutual mistrust."[37] No wonder that in early 1938 Beneš could tell the German envoy that the Soviet-Czechoslovak alliance "was a relic of a former epoch," but he added that "he could not just throw it into the wastepaper basket."[38]

The *Anschluss* of Austria, which Czechoslovak diplomacy could do nothing to prevent, made the country's strategic position almost indefensible. In case of an armed showdown with Germany, Prague could either capitulate or engage in a desperate gamble that a local war might transform itself into a European conflict. The entire foreign policy of Beneš, and his belief that war could wipe out the Czech nation, militated against a policy of gamble.[39] The president could not conceive that his rationally constructed foreign policy might collapse, and during the months between the *Anschluss* and the September crisis he still assured his people that he had plans for every contingency.[40] Yet neither plans, formulas, nor hopes for a cabinet change in France could alter the realities of the day. Abandoned by the West, isolated by the enmity of

[37] Cited in Kvaček, *Nad Evropou zataženo*, p. 128.

[38] See *Documents on German Foreign Policy*, Series C, ii, 56.

[39] As Taborsky put it, "the supreme aim of his [Beneš's] foreign policy was to prevent war from ever involving his country." *Foreign Affairs*, xxxvi, 672.

[40] See especially the speech on September 22, 1938, in Hubert Ripka, *Munich: Before and After* (London, 1939), pp. 111-12.

neighboring states, powerless, Beneš and Czechoslovakia bowed to the diplomatic formula of Munich, which meant the end of the first Czechoslovak Republic.

Czechoslovak foreign policy from 1918 to 1938 may well be described, to borrow Taborsky's title, as the triumph and disaster of Edvard Beneš. While not an entirely free agent, Beneš was the creator and executor of a diplomatic system that registered many successes but failed to meet the ultimate test of Munich.

What was the reason for Beneš's failure? Observing the international scene in the 1930's one cannot help feeling that in contrast to the "revolutionary" methods of fascist and Nazi diplomacy, Czechoslovak policy looked like a traditional game of chess. Prague could not play the new games of its adversaries. The Beneš system was too well-established, its author too certain of its efficacy, to permit radical departures. It was hard for him to imagine that the West, which for so long had considered him "the cleverest, the best informed, and for many years the most successful of European ministers,"[41] would abandon him in the hour of need. Nor was the Czechoslovak nation, which in 1919 had thought of itself as "the darling of the Entente," prepared for the part of a "far away nation" about which the British knew nothing.[42]

Paradoxically, one of the flaws of Czechoslovak foreign policy stemmed from Beneš's belief in peace. "I built a temple for peace," the president said wistfully in 1940.[43] Although preparing the country for war in a technical sense—large army and modern equipment—Beneš probably never intended to use the Czechoslovak troops except in the event of a general war.[44] The existing system of alliances looked formidable only on paper and it was quite true, as Gen. S. Bláha commented, that "without a military cooperation with Poland, Czechoslovakia could not devise any operational plans."[45] When in the 1920's a major war in Europe seemed unlikely, the system based on the Little Entente, the flexible French alliance, and the League of Nations worked admirably. But when the threat of war became a trump card of the diplomacy of the dic-

[41] F. P. Walters, *A History of the League of Nations* (2 vols.; London, 1952), II, 116.

[42] For the optimistic mood of the Czechs in 1919 see Ferdinand Peroutka, *Budování státu* [*Building the State*] (4 vols. in 5; Prague, 1934-36), I, 223. The latter phrase is Chamberlain's.

[43] Hitchcock, *"I Built a Temple for Peace": The Life of Eduard Beneš*, xi.

[44] A.J.P. Taylor, *The Origins of the Second World War* (New York, 1962), p. 154.

[45] Jaroslav Valenta, "Nebezpečí fašistické agrese a boj za kolektívní bezpečnost 1933-1937" ["The Danger of Fascist Aggression and the Struggle for Collective Security in 1933-1937"], in *Češi a Poláci a minulosti* (2 vols.; Prague, 1964-67), II, 547.

tators, the old diplomacy lost much of its usefulness. Speaking of Munich, a student of Beneš's diplomacy remarked that "confronted with this crisis, Beneš did not seem to be in full possession of his diplomatic skill."[46] This is an understatement, for by that time Beneš's diplomacy had no means of averting a threat of war. Events had gone beyond his control.

Strange as it may seem, some of the successes of the 1920's contained the seeds of failure in the 1930's.[47] The Little Entente, a useful stopgap arrangement as long as European stability prevailed, was of little use in the 1930's and its strengthening in 1934 was illusory. It could neither satisfy Rumanian and Yugoslav economic needs nor prevent German economic expansion into the Balkans. But it did prevent new departures in Czechoslovak diplomacy. After the failure of the Treaty of Mutual Assistance and of the Geneva Protocol, the League of Nations ceased to offer chances for building a security system in Europe. Yet the Beneš-inspired Organizational Pact of the Little Entente still centered on Geneva.

Beneš's genuine belief in the League was connected with his preference for multilateral arrangements. As compared with bilateral treaties, the value of the former often lies in less precise commitments. In the Czechoslovak alliances with France and with Russia, Beneš would have preferred to have a collective arrangement, because two-sided agreements may carry automatic clauses and involve a country in conflicts. Opposed to the risk of involvement with any single power, Beneš unwittingly increased the risk of Czechoslovak isolation in case of a showdown, for numerous friends are a poor substitute for one determined ally.

Czechoslovak statesmen also generally underestimated Poland as a factor in international relations—a feeling that the Poles reciprocated—and Beneš made no real effort to overcome Polish prejudices and bring Warsaw closer to Prague. Then there was a certain rivalry, which became more evident when Beck took over the foreign ministry in Poland. Collaboration with Poland, a possibility in the 1920's, meant collaboration with a country occupying an exposed position in Europe, which might adversely affect the Czechoslovak position. As we have mentioned, Masaryk and Beneš not only opposed real involvement with Poland but also tended to weaken the latter's position vis-à-vis Germany. The last

[46] Paul E. Zinner, "Czechoslovakia: The Diplomacy of Eduard Beneš," in Gordon A. Craig and Felix Gilbert, eds., *The Diplomats 1919-1939* (Princeton, 1953), p. 122. This article is superior to the solid but dated monograph by Felix J. Vondracek, *The Foreign Policy of Czechoslovakia 1918-1935* (New York, 1937).

[47] For a brief presentation of Czechoslovak policy in the 1930's see Kvaček, "Situation de la Tchécoslovaquie dans la politique internationale des années trente du 20e siècle," *Historica*, XI (1965).

chance of an alliance existed in 1933, but it could only have been accomplished through a radical reorientation of the policies of both countries.[48] In the mid-1930's, when the anti-Czechoslovak policy of Beck reached its zenith, Prague had lost all chances of working out a *modus vivendi* with Warsaw.

The policy of good relations with Germany was sound economically— Germany and Austria took nearly fifty percent of Czechoslovak exports —and valid also for domestic political reasons. However, even during the Stresemann era, Germany treated Czechoslovakia as a second-rate power. Despite all Beneš's efforts to mediate between Paris and Berlin, the latter never invited him for an official visit. Hitler's rise to power constituted a threat to Czechoslovakia, but the means used by Prague to cope with it proved inadequate. Collective security in the 1930's was an illusion; the Czechoslovak-Russian alliance exasperated Germany. In his dealings with Berlin, Beneš could only negotiate from a position of increasing weakness.

A Czechoslovak diplomat criticized Beneš for neglecting Italy, and indeed a rapprochement with Rome might have helped increase the chances of Austrian survival and smooth the differences with Hungary.[49] But, apart from ideological reasons, it is unlikely that Czechoslovakia could have acted differently vis-à-vis Rome. The Ethiopian venture created insurmountable difficulties for Prague as it did for the Western powers. Relations with Italy entered a dead-end street.

The question of Russia remained another unresolved issue. A policy of cooperation corresponded to the old pro-Russian feeling in the country but was complicated by the anti-Soviet attitudes of the traditional Russophiles. Prague recognized the Soviet Union only in 1934, and, though working in accord with it for the Eastern pact, could not and did

---

[48] For recent discussiens of the problem see Kozeński, *Czechosłowacja w polskiej polityce*, and his "Rokowania polsko-czechosłowackie na tle niebezpieczeństwa niemieckiego w latach 1932-1934" ["Polish-Czechoslovak Discussions Concerning the German Danger in 1932-1934"], *Przegląd Zachodni*, no. 2 (1962), 253-77. See also remarks in Michał Pułaski, *Stosunki dyplomatyczne polsko-czechosłowacko-niemieckie* [*Polish-Czechoslovak-German Diplomatic Relations*] (Poznan, 1967). The most up-to-date though less detailed presentation of the problem is by Valenta in *Češi a Poláci v minulosti*, II, 544ff. Documentary evidence does not completely bear out Beneš's later statement that he had thrice offered a pact to Poland, unless he meant a vague "pact of friendship." In a talk with a British diplomat in Geneva in March, 1933, the Czechoslovak minister denied any intention of concluding an alliance with Poland. See *Documents on British Foreign Policy*, Ser. 2, IV, Doc. 298; also V, Doc. 43; Valenta cites Krofta's remark that Czechoslovakia did not intend "to take upon herself the risk of Polish foreign policy," ibid., II, 545.

[49] See Vlastimil Kybal, "Czechoslovakia and Italy: My Negotiations with Mussolini, 1922-1923," *Journal of Central European Affairs*, XIII (Jan. 1954), 352-68, and XIV (April, 1954), 65-76.

not want to divorce the Russo-Czechoslovak alliance from a larger security scheme. Since she was playing a cautious game, Prague was unable to make full use of the pact with Moscow. Thus, subordinated to the working of the French alliance, the treaty with Russia did not prove to be the trump card to be used in an emergency. But the alliance did prove a propagandistic handicap, exploited by Nazi Germany, British appeasers, and East Central European neighbors.

Through the twenty years of its existence, the Czechoslovak Republic pursued a middle-of-the-road policy in international relations. Given the size, the geographic location, and the strength of the country, this may have been the only feasible policy. None of the East Central European countries was in a position to determine the course of European diplomatic events. Seen within this context, Beneš's diplomacy had many merits. Czechoslovakia played a disproportionately large role in international affairs. Prague stood for peace, the League of Nations, and collective security. Desirous of establishing a rational basis for Czechoslovak diplomacy, Beneš followed in the steps of the universalist, humanist, and very Czech, tradition of Hus, Komenský, Palacký, and Masaryk. In speeches and writings he made his policy appear so rational that at times one could suspect that he was mistaking logic for reality. In spite of domestic criticisms by agrarians, National Democrats, and communists, he weathered all the storms simply because there was no alternative policy attractive to the nation. As the socialist Bechyně put it retrospectively: "It is true that Dr. Edvard Beneš created the system of Czechoslovak foreign policy. But it is equally true that behind him stood the majority of the National Assembly and that all the governments that were in the Republic agreed with him."[50]

Beneš's diplomacy reflected national interests and predilections. A feeling of security and well-being in Czechoslovakia militated against taking risks and gambles. The policy was consciously Western, and as Beneš explained himself: "East differs from the West in that it always had and always will have great romantic political conceptions. It imagines that to make policy signifies to create great, unexpected things, to 'make history' . . . instead of performing difficult, daily, and in their majority small tasks."[51] Beneš excelled in making policy in accord with his definition. But Czechoslovakia, though Western in outlook, lay on the crossroads between East and West. The security of this area, as the events of World War II demonstrated, is indivisible. A "Western" policy often had as its corollaries: economic selfishness, a tendency not to an-

[50] Rudolf Bechyně, *Pero mi zůstalo* [*I have Kept My Pen*] (Prague, 1947), p. 34.
[51] Beneš on January 31, 1920. See Beneš, *Problémy nové Evropy*, p. 45.

tagonize the mighty, and excessive cautiousness. Looking from a fifty-year perspective, one cannot help wondering if a more "Eastern" policy accompanied by greater risks but inspired by a bolder vision might not have helped to avert the Munich disaster that befell the Czechoslovak Republic.

2. German areas of settlement, 1918-1938

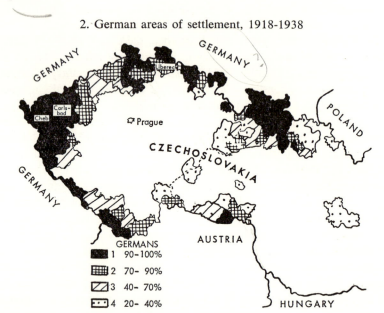

The map is based on census of 1930. J. Chmelař, Le problème allemand en Tchécoslovaquie.

Czechoslovakia after Munich

· 7 ·

MUNICH

Keith Eubank
Queens College of The City University
of New York

Czechoslovakia was not yet twenty years old when the nation suffered an international crisis ending in the Munich Agreement, which weakened national security and ultimately destroyed all freedom.[1] Fomented by the Sudeten German minority problem, the crisis was exploited by Adolf Hitler as the means to thrust German forces into the vacuum of East Central Europe created by the collapse of the Hohenzollern and Habsburg empires.

Hitler realized that once Czechoslovakia was overcome, German troops could debouch into East Central Europe, outflanking Poland, menacing Austria, and overawing Hungary and Rumania. Then he could seize the *Lebensraum* that he insisted was rightfully Germany's. But a direct attack had to be avoided lest Germany appear the aggressor and arouse opposition. A more subtle method of defeating Czechoslovakia had to be devised, one that gave Germany a less aggressive role. It was found by exploiting the existing Sudeten German minority problem in Czechoslovakia.

Hitler did not create this problem; it already existed when he came to

[1] For the history of the Munich crisis consult Boris Čelovský, *Das Münchener Abkommen von 1938* (Stuttgart, 1959); Keith Eubank, *Munich* (Norman, 1963); Radomír Luža, *The Transfer of the Sudeten Germans: A Study of Czech-German Relations, 1933-1962* (New York, 1964); Henri Noguères, *Munich: "Peace For Our Time"* (New York, 1965); Hubert Ripka, *Munich: Before and After* (London, 1939); Keith Robbins, *Munich 1938* (London, 1968); Helmuth K. G. Rönnefarth, *Die Sudetenkrise in der internationalen Politik: Entstehung-Verlauf-Auswirkung* (2 vols.; Wiesbaden, 1961); Laurence Thompson, *The Greatest Treason: Untold Story of Munich* (New York, 1968); Geneviève Vallette, *Munich, 1938* (Paris, 1964); John W. Wheeler-Bennett, *Munich: Prologue to Tragedy* (New York, 1948); and R.G.D. Laffan, *Survey of International Affairs, 1938* (London, 1951). The most important collections of documents can be found in *Documents on German Foreign Policy, 1918-1945*, Series D, Vol. II: *Germany and Czechoslovakia, 1937-1938* (Washington, 1955); Václav Král, ed., *Das Abkommen von München 1938: Tschechoslowakische Dokumente, 1937-1939* (Prague, 1968); V. F. Kločko et al., eds., *New Documents on the History of Munich* (Prague, 1958); *Nazi Conspiracy and Aggression* (8 vols.; Washington, 1946); and *The Trials of the Major War Criminals before the International Military Tribunal* (42 vols.; Nuremberg, 1947-49). There is an excellent collection of pertinent documents in Francis L. Loewenhein, ed., *Peace or Appeasement? Hitler, Chamberlain, and the Munich Crisis* (Boston, 1965).

power. He only exploited it for his own purposes, without having any genuine interest in the grievances of the Sudeten Germans. They resented their position within the Czechoslovak Republic, longing for the old days when the Habsburgs dominated Bohemia and Moravia. But the Austro-Hungarian defeat in 1918 had destroyed the empire and thrust the Sudetens into the new republic for which they had little love. They had not lost their citizenship and there was a place for them in the new nation if they would forget the past and work for the future. However, dreams of the old life died hard. Many Sudetens looked to Berlin for help, but they received little encouragement from the Weimar government.[2] With the accession of the Nazis to power in Germany and the formation of the Sudeten German party, agitation for autonomy became more aggressive. Berlin subsidized the party, which subordinated its policies to the wishes of the Reich Foreign Ministry and the Nazi party.[3] In the elections held during the spring of 1935, over 60 percent of the Germans in Czechoslovakia voted for the Sudeten German party.[4] The success of the party, dominated by Nazis, offered Hitler a welcome opportunity for achieving his goals.

The Führer had not hidden his plans from his associates, reminding them on more than one occasion that, after rearming, he would use the weapons to acquire territory. On February 3, 1933, he informed his audience that the "rebuilding of the armed forces is the most important prerequisite for attaining the goal: Reconquest of political power." After he had restored universal military training and completed his conquest of the German nation, the new power would be used for the "conquest of new living space in the east and ruthless Germanization of the latter."[5]

In 1935 Hitler ended all restrictions on rearmament and introduced universal military training. In March, 1936, German troops occupied the Rhineland, a necessary step before Hitler turned to the East. Until armaments had been increased, however, there was little more that could be done.

In August, 1936, Hitler issued secret instructions for a crash economic program to prepare Germany for war within four years.[6] He was preparing the nation for a "blitzkrieg" war—short, ruthless, and with limited objectives. By making war in this way, he hoped to win quick victories and avoid the mistakes that had produced the stalemate in the war years

[2] J. W. Bruegel, "German Diplomacy and the Sudeten Question before 1938," *International Affairs*, XXXVII (July, 1961), 323-31.

[3] Luža, *The Transfer*, pp. 74-75.

[4] Ibid., p. 80.

[5] *Documents on German Foreign Policy*, hereafter cited as *DGFP* (Washington, 1957), Series C, I, fn. 7, 37.

[6] Memorandum, August, 1936, ibid., v, 853-62.

from 1914 to 1918. At the same time, the threat of blitzkrieg could be used to blackmail weaker nations into surrendering.[7] This type of warfare was designed to be used, if necessary, against Czechoslovakia in order to reach his goals.

Hitler discussed his plans in general terms until a conference held on November 5, 1937, in the Reichschancellery, called because his generals and admirals were quarreling over the allocation of raw materials. He repeated his old arguments about the need for living space, which had to be obtained through force. Because the rearming of Germany's opponents would decrease the advantage of German armaments, it was necessary to act before 1943. If Germany became embroiled in war, he said, the first objective would be to "overthrow Czechoslovakia and Austria simultaneously in order to remove the threat to our flank in any possible operation against the west."[8]

If Czechoslovakia could be overthrown, Hitler foresaw a more neutral attitude on the part of Poland. He believed that Britain and France had already "written off the Czechs and were reconciled to the fact that this question would be cleared up in due course by Germany." Annexation of Czechoslovakia and Austria would mean acquiring an additional five to six million people and additional raw materials for the German armaments industries. Frontiers would be improved, and there would be manpower for additional army divisions. War between France and Italy appeared very probable to Hitler; he would use that war to "settle the Czech and Austrian question." When the time came to attack the Czechs, he wanted the attack "carried out with 'lightning speed.' "[9] In short, he was proposing to exploit whatever opportunity appeared to wipe out Czechoslovakia.

Hitler was serious in his remarks. There is little reason to imagine that he would trick the men whose support and professional advice he would need in conquering Czechoslovakia. The meaning of the conference for Czechoslovakia was revealed in the directive of December 21, 1937, approved by Hitler on December 7. Originally it had been planned that in case of a two-front war, German forces would move toward the West, but this plan was altered: "When Germany has achieved complete preparedness for war in all fields, then the military conditions will have been created for carrying out an offensive war against Czechoslovakia, so that the solution of the German problem of living space can be carried to a victorious end even if one or other of the great powers intervene against us." If a favorable situation developed before Germany was fully pre-

---

[7] Alan S. Milward, *The German Economy at War* (London, 1965), pp. 1-27.
[8] Memorandum, November 10, 1937, *DGFP*, Series D, I, 35.
[9] Ibid., 38.

pared for war, then the attack on Czechoslovakia would begin "with speed, surprise and the greatest impetus."[10] The bulk of the Luftwaffe and the army would be committed against Czechoslovakia, with only covering forces remaining in the West. Czechoslovakia had replaced other nations as Hitler's target for the offensive that would open up East Central Europe to German forces. The Sudeten Germans, however, had to provide the excuse for this attack.

Speaking on February 20, 1938, Hitler pledged protection for "those fellow Germans who live beyond our frontiers and are unable to insure for themselves the right to a general freedom, personal, political, and ideological." If the Sudeten troubles were not solved, he hinted at the use of force.[11] The *Anschluss* on March 11, 1938, gave his words a frightening meaning.

German troops now ringed western Czechoslovakia on three sides. When Hitler's soldiers marched into Austria they violated the Czechoslovak-Austrian frontier in several places. German diplomats rushed to assure the Prague government that the *Anschluss* was not aimed at Czechoslovakia. Field Marshal Hermann Goering gave his own and Hitler's word in promising that Czechoslovak-German relations would not be altered by the *Anschluss*.[12] Consequently, Czechoslovak troops were not mobilized, and the government took no action against Germany. The Czechoslovak people had no wish to die for Austria, for whom no one else was prepared to fight. France intended only a mild protest, and Britain objected only to the manner in which the *Anschluss* occurred; but they both sensed that Czechoslovakia and the Sudeten minority question would now tempt Hitler.

Hitler had not considered settling the Austrian problem so soon, because Czechoslovakia had been the greater danger for his dreams of dominating East Central Europe. Now he had to devise a fresh policy to suit the opportunity presented by the successful *Anschluss*. The Sudeten minority problem offered the key. It could now be fully exploited through the Sudeten German party.

Konrad Henlein, the Sudeten German party leader, offered his party as the agent for Hitler's campaign against the security of the Czechoslovak state. The party, Henlein vowed, "desired nothing more ardently than the incorporation of Sudeten German territory, nay of the whole Bohemian, Moravian, and Silesian area within the Reich."[13] His wish

[10] Wehrmacht Directive, December 21, 1937, ibid., VII, 635-36.

[11] Norman Baynes, ed., *The Speeches of Adolf Hitler, April 1922-August 1939* (2 vols.; London, 1942), II, 1404-1406.

[12] Eisenlohr to the German Foreign Ministry, March 13, 1938, *DGFP*, Series D, II, 158-60; Mastný to the Czechoslovak Foreign Ministry, March 12, 1938, Král, *Das Abkommen*, pp. 86-87.

[13] Henlein to Neurath, November 19, 1937, *DGFP*, Series D, II, 57.

meant the incorporation within German frontiers of the areas in which lay the fortifications necessary to protect Czechoslovakia against German invasion. He received his instructions on March 28, 1938, from Hitler in a conference in Berlin: As Hitler's "viceroy," he must raise demands unacceptable to the Czech government; he must demand more than Prague could satisfy. Berlin would not intervene for its own sake but would cooperate closely with Henlein, who would seek to destroy Czechoslovakia under the cover of negotiating with Prague over self-determination.[14]

Following instructions, Henlein announced the Sudeten demands publicly on April 24 at Karlovy Vary (Carlsbad). They were broad but specific enough to reveal their intent: a special German state with complete self-government and freedom to profess Nazi ideology.[15] If Henlein's demands were granted, the Sudeten state would have enough autonomy to align itself with Nazi Germany. Of course the demands were impossible for Prague to accept, but Hitler was counting on those in Britain and France who were conscience-stricken over the Versailles Treaty to pressure the Czechoslovak government into granting concessions.

Frightened by the *Anschluss* and alarmed at Hitler's public statements, Britain and France swallowed the bait. Czechoslovakia must concede lest an angry Hitler be goaded into action on behalf of the suffering Sudetens. This was the policy of appeasement that had been practiced in one form or another since 1919, with only one lapse in 1923. Then, French and Belgian troops had occupied the Ruhr when Germany had been declared in default of her reparations payments. Because this action had met with strong foreign opposition and was not an immediate success, the troops had been withdrawn. Enforcement of the Versailles Treaty had failed; the policy of appeasement prevailed.

In 1938 neither French Premier Edouard Daladier nor British Prime Minister Neville Chamberlain wished to ignite a European war over the Sudeten question. Daladier sensed the aggressive intentions in Hitler's policies, but he failed to convert Chamberlain to his views because his heart was never in the struggle. He wanted Britain to help him evade French promises made to Czechoslovakia in 1925 in a mutual defense pact.

Chamberlain, a former businessman with a good record as a cabinet officer, saw war only as a destroyer of the reviving British economy. He considered Sudeten German grievances just and Hitler's intentions limited and beneficial but not aggressive. An opinionated man, often ruthless with political opponents, he now chose to do everything possible to

[14] Memorandum, March 28, 1938, ibid., 197-202; Ribbentrop to Eisenlohr, March 29, 1938, ibid., 203-205.
[15] Memorandum, April 24, 1938, ibid., 242.

force Czechoslovak concessions to Henlein's demands. Chamberlain led a campaign to settle the Sudeten question before it set off war by forcing Prague to make concessions to the Sudeten Germans in order to appease Hitler. The prime minister and Foreign Secretary Lord Halifax believed that Czechoslovakia was indefensible and not worth another great, bloody war. Daladier and French Foreign Minister Georges Bonnet, dreading another 1914-1918 bloodbath, adopted Chamberlain's policies.

The governments of Britain and France demanded in May, 1938, that the Czechoslovak government settle the minority problem with the Sudeten German party in "a comprehensive and lasting settlement." Berlin soon learned of the request for "a supreme effort to reach a settlement . . . in the interest of Czechoslovakia's survival, as well as European peace."[16] The Anglo-French insistence on a settlement at any price presented Edvard Beneš and Milan Hodža, the Czechoslovak prime minister, with the very real danger that substantial concessions to the Sudetens would be followed by equivalent demands from other minorities, thus spelling the end of Czechoslovakia as a viable state. Beneš resisted pressure to move toward minority autonomy or federalism lest the German drive for domination be aided.

Suddenly the question of the Sudeten German minority became a crisis on May 20, when rumors spread that German troops were moving toward the Czechoslovak frontiers. In Prague the Czechoslovak cabinet wrestled with the question of mobilizing troops against the rumored invasion. The ministers decided on a partial mobilization to prevent an *Anschluss*, but the German authorities denied that there had been any hostile troop movements. Apparently they were telling the truth. An increase in troop movements to and from Austria had panicked Prague.[17]

Although the crisis was over by May 23, its effects were detrimental to the security of Czechoslovakia. Because London and Paris had been obliged to pledge help (indirect for Britain) if German troops had marched, both governments were unhappy with Czechoslovakia, not Germany, fearing that similar crises could precipitate war. They insisted on a more conciliatory attitude on the part of the Czechoslovak government.

The May crisis showed the German high command how swiftly and efficiently Czechoslovak troops could be mobilized. Any repetition would enable the Czechoslovak general staff to iron out problems and prepare

[16] Halifax to Newton, May 4, 1938, *Documents on British Foreign Policy*, hereafter cited as *DBFP*, Third Series (London, 1919), I, 241-43.

[17] For the story of the May crisis consult Gerhard L. Weinberg, "The May Crisis, 1938," *Journal of Modern History*, XXIX (Sept., 1957), 213-25; W. V. Wallace, "The Making of the May Crisis of 1938," *Slavonic and East European Review*, XLI (June, 1963), 368-90; D. C. Watt, "The May Crisis of 1938. A Rejoinder to Mr. Wallace," ibid., XLIV (July, 1966), 475-86.

a more rapid mobilization. This opportunity had to be denied if Hitlers' blitzkrieg technique was to succeed. Delay would only help the Czechoslovak generals prepare counter-measures that could stall the invasion. With this in mind, Hitler conferred with his military leaders on May 28 and stressed the danger from Czechoslovakia if Germany were engaged in war in Western Europe, seeking to conquer Belgium and Holland. He declared that it was his "unshakable will that Czechoslovakia shall disappear from the map," not because he wished to help the Sudeten Germans but in order "to clear the rear for advancing against the west, England and France."[18]

Two days later Hitler signed a directive for war against Czechoslovakia. To the politicians he left the task of creating the favorable moment for putting the plan into operation. Hitler emphasized the need for surprise and speed in the conquest of Czechoslovakia, with the entire might of the army and Luftwaffe being thrown into the affray. The attack must be ready for launching no later than October 1.[19] In a directive issued on June 18 he pointed out that if the French actually intervened in sufficient strength, he would have to revise his plans, because only a light force would be left along the French frontier. However, he was certain that there would not be any intervention.[20]

Because the Sudeten question would be used to manufacture the opportunity for aggression, negotiations between the Sudeten Germans and the Czechoslovak government did not prosper. Whatever Prague proposed, the Sudeten spokesmen always found cause for rejecting. Compromise was possible for the government provided national unity was not imperiled, but the Sudetens insisted on dividing the nation into separate national units. Because these units would have a high degree of autonomy, Czechoslovakia would be wrecked in the cause of self-determination. Negotiations were slow, because any proposal of the government had to be scrutinized and discussed carefully by the Czechoslovak parliament and cabinet according to the democratic process. The resulting delays helped Hitler and alarmed London and Paris.

By summer, reports of military preparations increased as well as rumors of an impending war over Czechoslovakia in the autumn.[21] London and Paris needed a device to increase the pressure on the Czechoslovaks. The idea of a mediator was considered in London and mentioned in Paris. At last the rumor of another crisis in July, similar to the May crisis, forced action on London. Suddenly the British government

---

[18] Wiedemann memorandum, *DGFP*, Series D, VII, 632.
[19] Directive for Operation Green, May 30, 1938, ibid., II, 357-62.
[20] Directive, June 18, 1938, ibid., 473-77.
[21] Osuský to the Czechoslovak Foreign Ministry, July 4, 1938, Král, *Das Abkommen*, p. 149; Strang to Henderson, July 21, 1938, *DBFP*, Third Series, I, 610-12.

demanded that Beneš request a mediator. If he refused, the story would be leaked to the papers and he would bear the responsibility. To keep his nation's ties with London and Paris, Beneš reluctantly accepted as mediator Walter Runciman, millionaire shipowner and politician, who was without experience in such matters.[22] Publicly, Chamberlain and Halifax declared that Runciman was independent of the government, but the truth was otherwise, because he was instructed by Halifax and expected to force solutions on Beneš that would be acceptable to the Sudeten Germans.

After his arrival in Prague on August 3, Runciman was inundated with memoranda, articles, documents, and tales of Czech persecution of the Sudetens in a massive effort to prove that all responsibility lay with the Czechs for disturbing the peace of Europe. They were "in no way prepared to make concessions of a kind that would lead to a real pacification of the state."[23] "Spontaneous" demonstrations were staged by the Sudeten Germans for the benefit of Runciman and his staff. He and his associates considered Henlein "an absolutely honest fellow"; they accepted the Sudeten demands as truthful while trying to extract concessions from Beneš.

Beneš could stand up to Runciman and risk losing the support of Britain and France or seek to keep their friendship by agreeing to concessions that endangered the security of the nation. He did not want to isolate Czechoslovakia from the West, for he remembered the fate of Austria. At last Beneš gave way under Anglo-French pressure.

On September 2 he called in the Sudeten leaders and informed them that he would satisfy their demands as much as he could. He drafted the so-called Fourth Plan, which he submitted to them on September 7. The astonished Sudeten Germans learned that Beneš had granted virtually all of Henlein's Carlsbad demands, which were never intended to be obtained. If the plan was accepted, the Sudeten Germans would have full autonomy and the means to weaken Czechoslovakia from within. If the Sudeten Germans rejected the offer, Beneš would win the sympathy of Britain and France.[24] An incident was staged at Moravská Ostrava on September 7, when Czechoslovak police were goaded into arresting

[22] Eubank, *Munich*, pp. 78-91. Jan Masaryk, the Czechoslovak ambassador in London, regarded Runciman as "cunning, obstinate, non-conformist, clerical, a teetotaler, and rich." See Masaryk to the Czechoslovak Foreign Ministry, July 26, 1938, Král, *Das Abkommen*, p. 161.

[23] Henlein to the German Foreign Ministry, August 17, 1938, *DGFP*, Series D, II, 578.

[24] Krofta to the Czechoslovak ambassadors in Paris, London, and Berlin, September 3, 1938, Král, *Das Abkommen*, p. 211; Krofta to the Czechoslovak ambassadors in Paris, London, and Moscow, September 6, 1938, ibid., 215-16; Hencke to the German Foreign Ministry, September 7, 1938, *DGFP*, Series D, II, 711-12; September 8, 1938, 714-19.

Sudeten demonstrators who were ostensibly protesting the jailing of gun-runners. The Sudeten negotiators seized on the incident as an excuse to break off negotiations until September 13, a day after Hitler was scheduled to deliver an important speech at the Nuremberg party rally. By September 10 planned violence had erupted in the Sudetenland, adding to the tension.

When Hitler spoke on September 12, he did not declare war, as many had feared, but denounced Beneš and the Czechs for oppressing the Sudeten Germans. Hitler said he would not "look on calmly forever at a further oppression of German fellow countrymen in Czechoslovakia." He demanded that the oppression of the Sudeten Germans be ended and replaced by the right of self-determination: "The Germans in Czechoslovakia are neither defenseless nor are they deserted, and people should take notice of that fact."[25] Before Hitler finished his speech, disorders began in the Sudetenland, necessitating the dispatch of Czechoslovak troops to restore law and order. Henlein's agents broke off negotiations with the Czechoslovak government, and he fled across the frontier into Germany. From the safety of the Reich, on September 15 he issued a proclamation demanding the return of the Sudetenland to Germany.[26]

The fighting in the Sudetenland frightened London and Paris, since it gave Hitler an excuse for intervention. Daladier and Bonnet looked to Chamberlain for salvation, and he did not fail them. Realizing that a new device was imperative because the Runciman mission had failed, he decided that the moment had come for a face-to-face meeting with Hitler in order to make the British position clear. Chamberlain sought to avoid the mistakes he believed had been made during the summer of 1914. Had the British intention to intervene on the side of Belgium then been made clear, Chamberlain was certain that Germany would have held back. This reading of history led him on September 13 to propose a meeting with the Führer. Although dumbfounded at the request, Hitler agreed to receive Chamberlain on September 15. Beneš was not invited nor was his approval of the mission solicited.[27]

At the Berchtesgaden conference, Hitler demanded the swift return of the Sudetenland to the Reich under threat of a world war. Areas where the Sudeten Germans were in the majority should be ceded quickly to Germany on the basis of self-determination, because the Czechs were slaughtering the Sudeten Germans. Convinced that his visit had

[25] Baynes, *The Speeches of Adolf Hitler*, II, 1488-97.
[26] Henlein's proclamation, September 15, 1938, *DGFP*, Series D, II, 801-802.
[27] Regarding Chamberlain's trip, Masaryk commented: "I am very much afraid that the senile ambition of Chamberlain to be the peacemaker of Europe will drive him to success at any price, and that will be possible only at our expense." (Masaryk to the Czechoslovak Foreign Ministry, September 15, 1938), Král, *Das Abkommen*, pp. 223-24.

saved the peace of Europe, Chamberlain gladly accepted Hitler's demands for consideration by the British cabinet and the French government.[28]

After discussions with his cabinet on September 17 and a meeting in London with Daladier and Bonnet the next day, Chamberlain's proposal was accepted. It called for a direct transfer to Germany of those areas in Czechoslovakia with more than a 50 percent Sudeten German population. After the transfer had been arranged, new frontiers would be determined by an international commission on which Britain and France would be represented. Then Britain would join in an international guarantee of these frontiers against unprovoked aggression. The Czechoslovak government, however, rejected the proposal because it would ruin the nation's economy and ultimately lead to German control; it would not solve the minority question. Instead, the government appealed for arbitration based on the 1925 treaty with Germany.

The British and French governments countered the Czechoslovak rejection with an ultimatum. Unless Czechoslovakia accepted the Anglo-French proposals, France would not stand by her pledge to Czechoslovakia, and if war broke out Britain would not aid France. As Hitler had hoped, Czechoslovakia was now isolated, for upon French help depended the Soviet-Czechoslovak alliance, signed in 1935, that required France to help Czechoslovakia before the Soviet Union had to send aid. The Russians maintained a correct position, promising to abide by the terms of the alliance but risking little because the French government preferred to evade its obligations. Thus the French defection resulted in isolation for Czechoslovakia and capitulation to the ultimatum on September 21.[29]

Satisfied by the results of his efforts to achieve peace, Chamberlain reported to Hitler at Godesberg on September 22. But his joy turned to despair when Hitler announced that he wanted more. The claims of Poland and Hungary for their minorities within Czechoslovakia must also be satisfied. Because so many refugees were streaming across the German frontiers, Hitler announced that occupation of the Sudetenland must take place no later than October 1. Then the plebiscite could be held to determine which areas would be returned to Germany and the frontiers could be delimited.[30]

[28] Chamberlain's notes, September 15, 1938, *DBFP*, Third Series, II, 338-41; memorandum on the Hitler-Chamberlain conversation, September 15, 1938, *DGFP*, Series D, II, 786-98.

[29] Eubank, *Munich*, pp. 144-54, 301-303; Lacroix to Beneš, September 21, 1938, Král, *Abkommen*, p. 242; Krofta's circular dispatch, September 21, 1938, ibid., pp. 242-43.

[30] Minutes of conversation between Chamberlain and Hitler, September 22, 1938, *DGFP*, Series D, II, 870-79; *DBFP*, Third Series, II, 462-73; Chamberlain

Shaken by Hitler's demands, an unhappy Chamberlain returned to London for more consultations with the cabinet and with the French. Chamberlain and Halifax tried without success to extract from Daladier a renunciation of the French pledge to Czechoslovakia. Then, reluctantly, Chamberlain promised his government's support if France went to the aid of Czechoslovakia.

Already Czechoslovak troops had begun to mobilize, French troops manned the Maginot Line, and Britain called up reserve units. Despite the mobilizing of these troops, there was no concerted plan to wage war. Czechoslovakia would remain on the defensive, leaving the initiative to the German armies; British and French forces would await the German offensive. Czechoslovak forces would be divided, because the Polish frontier could not be left unguarded. At Hitler's urging, the Polish government demanded that Czechoslovakia immediately cede Těšín (Teschen), an area that Poland coveted but Czechoslovakia had controlled since 1920. Consequently, if war came, Czechoslovak forces would feel the strain of defending both the German and Polish frontiers.

Hitler seemed bent on a war over the Sudetenland, even though he was warned on September 27 that Britain would support France.[31] His Western opponents, however, were resolved to give him no cause for battle, because the French cabinet knew that members of the British Commonwealth opposed the war. It was not surprising then that on September 28 Chamberlain and Bonnet, each acting independently, sent messages to Hitler begging him to negotiate. Both men promised to satisfy his demands and compel the Czechs to accept whatever he wished. Not satisfied with this, Chamberlain informed Hitler of his readiness to come to Germany for another meeting with representatives from Italy, Czechoslovakia, and France.[32] On the same day, through the British ambassador in Rome, Chamberlain asked Mussolini to use his influence with Hitler. The Italian dictator, frightened at the prospect of a war that might involve Italy, whose army was unprepared, implored Hitler to postpone the attack on Czechoslovakia for twenty-four hours.[33]

In one way or another, three governments were begging Hitler not to

to Hitler, September 23, 1938, *DGFP*, Series D, ii, 887-88, 892; Hitler to Chamberlain, September 23, 1938, ibid., 889-91; notes of conversation between Hitler and Chamberlain, September 23-24, 1938, ibid., 989-98, *DBFP*, Third Series, ii, 499-508.

[31] Notes of conversation between Hitler and Horace Wilson, September 27, 1938, ibid., 564-67; *DGFP*, ii, 963-65.

[32] Weizsäcker minute, September 28, 1938, ibid., 988-89; Halifax to Henderson, September 28, 1938, *DBFP*, Third Series, ii, 587; Georges Bonnet, *Défense de la Paix* (2 vols.; Geneva, 1946), i, 283-84.

[33] Mackensen to the German Foreign Ministry, September 28, 1938, *DGFP*, Series D, ii, 993-94; Wilson to Hull, October 21, 1938, *Foreign Relations of the United States: Diplomatic Papers, 1938* (Washington, 1955), i, 727-29.

go to war and promising to fulfill his desires. If he were to accept the proposal of Chamberlain for another conference, the results seemed guaranteed in advance. Czechoslovakia was isolated, but if she would not agree to Hitler's demands, which would be supported by Britain, France, and Italy, blame for the war would belong to her. On September 28, when Hitler agreed to a conference and invited Mussolini, Daladier, and Chamberlain to come to Munich for a conference over Czechoslovakia, there was no reason for going to war.

The four leaders assembled in the Führerhaus in Munich about noon-time on September 29 to decide the fate of Czechoslovakia, a nation that had not been defeated in battle and would be unrepresented at the conference. None of the principals wanted Czechoslovak representatives there lest they raise objections. Soviet Russia was not invited either.

The German Foreign Ministry provided a draft plan for discussion, which Mussolini put before the conference, and it was accepted by the others. Hitler was in an ugly mood, complaining because of the delay and savagely rejecting the few technical points raised by Chamberlain. Daladier, who looked ill, concurred in Hitler's demands. The conference was held amid great confusion, with people wandering in to watch the heads of government at work. In the early morning hours of September 30 the agreement was completed, corrected, and signed. It now had to be handed over to the Czechoslovak representatives, Hubert Masařík and Vojtěch Mastný, Czechoslovak minister in Berlin, who were summoned before a sleepy Chamberlain and a dour Daladier to learn the sentence passed on their country.[34]

According to the terms of the Munich Agreement, Czechoslovakia must cede territory to Germany. The latter would begin the occupation on October 1 and complete it by October 10 in five stages. All existing installations within the ceded area had to be left untouched. An international commission, with representatives from Germany, Britain, France, Italy, and Czechoslovakia, would determine the conditions governing the evacuation of the territory, decide where plebiscites would be held, and fix the final frontier. A transfer of population within six months would be permitted. Sudeten prisoners serving sentences for political offenses must be released by the Czechoslovak government, and Sudeten Germans in the Czechoslovak army and in the police force must be released if they so desired. Britain and France promised to join in the international guarantee of the new frontiers against unprovoked aggression. Germany and Italy, however, would not join in this guarantee until after the Polish and Hungarian minorities' problems had been solved.[35]

[34] Hubert Masařík's memorandum on the Munich conference, September 30, 1938, Král, *Das Abkommen*, pp. 271-72.
[35] Munich agreement, September 29, 1938, *DGFP*, Series D, II, 1014-16. For

After hours of agony, the Czechoslovak government surrendered at 12:30 P.M. on September 30. Kamil Krofta, the foreign minister, called in the representatives of the victorious powers—Britain, France, and Italy—and announced his government's decision:

> I do not intend to criticize but this is for us a disaster which we have not merited. We surrender, and shall endeavor to secure for our nation a peaceful existence. I do not know whether your countries will benefit by these decisions which have been made at Munich, but we are certainly not the last: after us, there are others who will be affected and who will suffer from those decisions.[36]

Surrender for Beneš had not been easy, but he would not take the nation into war alone, without an ally, and bear the responsibility for a war when the Czechoslovak cause seemed hopeless. The war, he believed, would come some day, but Czechoslovakia could escape the destruction that was later suffered by Poland. It was for this reason that he rejected the pleas of his generals to fight without allies. No nation would aid Czechoslovakia. France had deserted the alliance, and Britain would hold Czechoslovakia responsible for provoking Hitler into war. Poland gave every indication of joining in the war as a German ally. The Soviet Union could not be relied on, despite the brave words of Maxim Litvinov, words that were intended to lead others to fight—but not Soviet Russia. The French desertion of Czechoslovakia absolved the Russians from any burden of aiding Czechoslovakia. The isolation of Czechoslovakia forced Beneš to accept the onerous terms signed at Munich.

By this agreement an independent nation was torn asunder by nations that had previously recognized her independence. They did not even give the victim an opportunity to present a defense. No nation had suffered such treatment since the partitioning of Poland in the eighteenth century. Even Germany had been allowed to discuss the terms of the Versailles Treaty by note before signing. The manner of the capitulation indicated the depth of Western fear that a European war could erupt over Czechoslovakia. However, it did not prevent war, because the Munich Conference tricked Hitler into believing that there could be a repetition for Poland.

The Munich Agreement was a death blow for Beneš's policy of aligning Czechoslovakia with Britain and France, who had now revealed their weakness and duplicity. By betraying Czechoslovakia into opening her

---

the minutes of the meetings consult *DBFP*, Third Series, II, 630-35; *DGFP*, Series D, II, 1003-1008. Bullitt to Hull, October 3, 1938, *Foreign Relations of the United States, 1938*, I, 711-12, contains Daladier's impressions of the conference.
[36] Ripka, *Munich*, pp. 230-31.

frontiers to an invader, they were forcing on future Czechoslovak governments a policy of alignment with whatever power dominated Eastern Europe. The shadow of 1948 was foretold in the meaning of the Munich Agreement for Czechoslovakia.

· PART TWO ·

Occupation, War, and Liberation
1938 to 1945

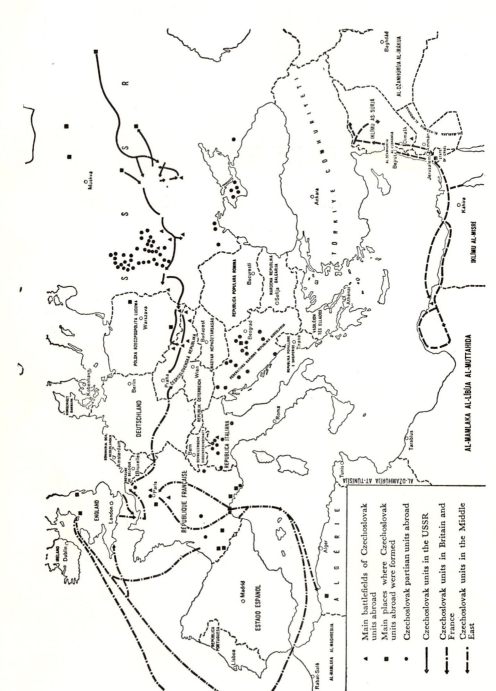

3. Czech and Slovak involvement at the various fronts of World War II

Main battlefields of Czechoslovak units abroad

Main places where Czechoslovak units abroad were formed

Czechoslovak partisan units abroad

Czechoslovak units in the USSR

Czechoslovak units in Britain and France

Czechoslovak units in the Middle East

· 8 ·

THE SECOND REPUBLIC, 1938-1939

Theodor Prochazka
Washington, D. C.

The Munich Agreement was a momentous divide in European history between the two world wars as well as in the history of Czechoslovakia. For Prague it meant a negation of the last twenty years of evolution, which had been distinguished by a remarkable growth in all fields of national life. The impact of the big totalitarian neighbor was a negation of the democratic spirit bequeathed to the nation by its founder, T. G. Masaryk. The upsurge of the will to defend the country was now followed by a period of despondency and disorientation. On the larger scene, in Europe, the atmosphere was not dissimilar. The feeling of uncertainty was all-pervading.

"This is the end," said President Beneš when he read the Munich document on September 30. "This is a betrayal which will produce its own punishment."[1] Later that day the president accused the two western countries, France and Britain, of cowardice.[2]

On October 5, President Beneš resigned. His departure came under pressure from Berlin, which depicted his person as the chief obstacle to the normalization of relations between the two countries. Even his resignation did not, however, change the hostile attitude of Berlin toward Prague, as was demonstrated in the course of negotiations about the new border. Before resigning, Beneš appointed a new government less burdened with the past, though headed again by General Jan Syrový. The most conspicuous change was in the head of the Ministry of Foreign Affairs. To succeed Kamil Krofta, Beneš chose Dr. František Chvalkovský, the minister in Rome, who was a man of a more conservative outlook

[1] Míla Lvová, *Mnichov a Edvard Beneš* [*Munich and Edvard Beneš*] (Prague, 1968), p. 176. For a general survey of Czechoslovakia's history in this period see also Henryk Batowski, *Kryzys dyplomatyczny w Europie: Jesień 1938-Wiosna 1939* [*The Diplomatic Crisis in Europe: Autumn 1938-Spring 1939*] (Warsaw, 1962); Miloš Hájek, *Od Mnichova k 15. březnu* [*From Munich to the 15th of March*] (Prague, 1959); George F. Kennan, *From Prague after Munich: Diplomatic Papers, 1939-1940* (Princeton, 1968); R.G.D. Laffan *et al.*, *Survey of International Affairs 1938*, vol. III (London, 1953), edited by V. M. Toynbee; František Lukeš, *Podivný mír* [*A Strange Peace*] (Prague, 1968); and Theodore Prochazka, "La Tchécoslovaquie de Munich au 15 mars 1939," Unpublished doctoral dissertation, University of Paris, 1954.

[2] Lukeš, *Podivný mír*, p. 28.

and critical of several aspects of the general line of Beneš's foreign policy.

Czechoslovakia was now facing difficult negotiations with her three neighbors, Germany, Hungary and Poland, all of whom had come with farreaching demands for the rectification of frontiers. This rush for Czechoslovak territories was so great that at times the personnel of the foreign ministry in Prague were so busy they could not produce delegates and negotiators in sufficient numbers.[3]

Most important, of course, were negotiations with Germany, the initiator of the territorial upheaval in East Central Europe. The Munich Agreement ruled that the evacuation of the areas inhabited by Germans was to take place between October 1 and 10; the four zones marked on the map attached to the agreement were occupied by German troops between October 1 and 7. The choice of the remaining territory to be ceded was to be made by an international commission deliberating in Berlin and consisting of representatives of the powers that had signed the Munich Agreement and of Czechoslovakia. It was the demarcation of this territory, the so-called fifth zone, which gave rise to a sharp dispute and in a general way indicated the spirit of things to come. On Sunday, October 2, Hitler called the German members of the international commission to brief them on the stand to take. According to his instructions the new frontier line had in principle to coincide with the Godesberg line. Only "some small revisions" in favor of the Czechs could be admitted.[4] Hitler's views prevailed and on October 5, almost at the same moment as Syrový announced over the Prague radio the resignation of President Beneš, the Czechoslovak representatives in Berlin were presented with the map of the new frontiers, which cut deeply into the body of the Czech lands. The next day, the Czechoslovak minister in Berlin, Mastný, declared that his government accepted the new line, with sorrow.[5]

One of the most painful losses for Czechoslovakia was a salient of German territory occupying the German-language enclave of Svitavy between Bohemia and Moravia. This area severed the vital railroad connection between the western and eastern parts of the state. Hitler manifested a special interest in this territory and stubbornly stuck to the new line. Czechoslovak protests proved to be of no avail. On the contrary, Germany responded with new demands and the final delimitation came as a German *Diktat* in November. The final line only accentuated the bizarre sinuosities of the border which had been fixed on October 5.

Bohemia and Moravia lost about 11,600 square miles, which was

---

[3] *Documents on German Foreign Policy, 1918-1945*, Series D, Vol. IV: *The Aftermath of Munich, 1938-1939* (Washington, 1951), No. 28. Hereafter this collection will be cited as *DGFP*.

[4] Ibid., No. 12.   [5] Ibid., No. 41.

about 38 percent of their combined area. They lost 3,869,000 inhabitants (approximately 34 percent of the whole population). Some 2,806,000 Germans went to Germany (along with about 720,000 to 750,000 Czechs).[6]

In addition, on November 19 Prague was forced to sign an agreement allowing the construction of an extraterritorial German *Autobahn* across Moravia, which was designed to increase German control of the country.[7] Because of the war, however, its construction was never undertaken.

Germany thus realized the maximum of her territorial demands, and Hitler, by pushing the nationality principle to the utmost, undermined the viability of post-Munich Czechoslovakia. By so doing, he had removed the potential threat to Germany's right wing in case of future operations in the East. On the whole, the two western powers represented on the international commission in Berlin followed the dissection of the Czechoslovak Republic as passive onlookers. Under these circumstances Mastný was perhaps right when he declared that it would have been almost better if Czechoslovakia had not been represented on the commission at all.[8]

The negotiations with Hungary appeared much simpler. To strengthen its position, on October 1 the Hungarian government asked Germany for her diplomatic support.[9] This secured, the Hungarians increased their pressure on Prague. Czechoslovakia, occupied with other negotiations and aware of the military weakness of Hungary, tried to postpone the opening of the talks until the middle of the month. Finally, however, it was agreed to begin them in the border town of Komárno on October 9. Their beginning brought the first satisfaction to Hungary. At the outset of the negotiations, the Czechoslovak delegation agreed, as a token of its good will, to cede to Hungary one railroad station and a border town (Ipol'ské Šahy). This was the only point on which the two sides agreed. The Hungarians proposed a line which would have deprived Slovakia and adjacent Ruthenia (Subcarpathian Russia) of their most important towns, fertile soil, and vital railroad connections. They rejected the Czechoslovak counterproposal, which would have preserved most of these towns in Czechoslovakia but offered Hungary an area of 2,234 square miles with 400,000 inhabitants (of whom 320,000 were Hungarians), and on October 13 broke off the negotiations.[10]

[6] Theodor Prochazka, "The Delimitation of Czechoslovak-German Frontiers after Munich," *Journal of Central European Affairs*, XXI, No. 2 (July, 1961), 216.
[7] *DGFP*, No. 123.
[8] Ladislav Feierabend, *Ve vládách druhé republiky* [*In the Governments of the Second Republic*] (New York, 1961), p. 42.
[9] *DGFP*, No. 9, n. 6.
[10] Microfilmed German documents in the National Archives, Washington, D. C. 281/210154-5, 210200, 210157. See also the telephonic report from Komárno

Budapest then proceeded to a partial mobilization and tried to create an atmosphere of unrest and insecurity in the border regions of Czechoslovakia by sending into them irredentist bands. In the diplomatic sphere, Hungary sought the support and approval of Germany and Italy. Two prominent Hungarian emissaries went to the Axis capitals to sound out their opinions about Hungarian military measures and the whole of Budapest's demands. Former Prime Minister Kálmán Darányi visited Munich, while Count István Csáky, a foreign ministry official, went to Rome.

Darányi met with Hitler's old aversion to the Hungarian nation, which the wavering Hungarian attitude in the period immediately preceding the Munich Agreement had increased.[11] While the results in Munich were meager, Hungary had complete success in Rome. Mussolini approved of the Hungarian military measures and of the suggestion to submit the controversy to a conference of the four Munich signatories.[12] After some diplomatic exchanges in the second half of October, the Czechoslovaks and Hungarians agreed to submit the dispute to the arbitration of the two Axis powers.

The meeting took place in Vienna on November 2. The border of eastern Czechoslovakia was pushed northward. Virtually not a mile of the former frontier remained unchanged. In all, the Vienna Award deprived Czechoslovakia of 4,570 square miles of territory with 972,092 inhabitants (census of 1930) of whom 53.9 percent were Magyars. Hungary's territory increased by 13 percent, her population by 11.7 percent. Czechoslovakia retained Bratislava, but lost several towns in the southern areas, the biggest of them being Košice (70,000 inhabitants) and Užhorod (27,000).[13]

Ruthenia, which Hungary claimed but Germany wished to keep in reserve for future eventualities (not yet definitely fixed in Hitler's mind), remained in Czechoslovakia. The failure to recover Ruthenia was a disappointment to Hungary. It was not only a setback in her efforts to break the chains of the Trianon Treaty of 1920, but also hampered her effort to establish a common border with Poland. For her part, Poland firmly supported the Hungarian claims to Czechoslovak territory. In the first place, the Poles were afraid that the autonomy granted to Ruthenia after Munich by the Prague government and the victory of the Ukrainian nationalists in the province (see below, p. 261) might increase the agita-

---

quoted by Ferdinand Vávra and Jan Eibel, *Viedenská arbitráž—dôsledok Mnichova* [*The Vienna Arbitration—A Consequence of Munich*] (Bratislava, 1963), p. 71; and Jörg K. Hoensch, *Der ungarische Revisionismus und die Zerschlagung der Tschechoslowakei* (Tübingen, 1967), pp. 130-42.

[11] *DGFP*, No. 62.   [12] Ibid., No. 60.
[13] Vávra and Eibel, *Viedenská arbitráž*, pp. 112-13.

tion among the numerous Ukrainian population in eastern Poland. In the second place, they hoped by establishing a common frontier with Hungary to erect a barrier against German penetration eastward. At the same time, the Poles pretended in Berlin that they wanted a common frontier with Hungary to raise a barrier against the spread of Bolshevism westward. At the end of the year, however, Germany was still undecided as to what course to take with regard to Ruthenia (or Carpathian Ukraine as it was now called; see p. 261), and preferred, for the moment, to keep it in Czechoslovakia. The arbitration in Vienna reflected this standpoint. A somewhat precipitous Hungarian attempt toward the end of November to seize Ruthenia and put before Germany a *fait accompli* was energetically rebuffed by Berlin.[14]

Simultaneously with her negotiations with Hungary, Czechoslovakia held talks with Poland. However, the psychological climate of the Polish-Czechoslovak negotiations was somewhat different. An important factor in the Polish attitude toward Prague was the Polish insistence on being treated as a great power and determination to proceed independently of the Reich. The Polish Foreign Minister Jozef Beck regarded it as offensive to relegate the Polish demands on Czechoslovakia to an annex to the Munich Agreement, to put them on the same level as the claims of Hungary, friendly ally though Hungary was, and to postpone their implementation for three months. He determined to secure Czechoslovak compliance by his own efforts, not as a gift from Hitler's hands.[15]

On the very day of the Munich Agreement, it was decided in Warsaw to present the Polish demands to Prague "in the categorical form of an ultimatum."[16] Czechoslovakia had to yield again. On October 2, the evacuation of the disputed zone of the Těšín (Teschen) area, the long-standing apple of discord between the two countries, began. To forestall any complications from the German side stemming from the unclarified status of the vitally important railroad junction of Bohumín (Oderberg), Polish troops occupied it two days earlier than originally planned.

Warsaw thus acquired two districts, 56 percent of whose 227,000 inhabitants were according to the Czechoslovak census of 1930 Czechs and 35 percent Poles. The districts were important industrial areas. Czecho-

---

[14] *DGFP*, Nos. 118, 122, 127-34. See also Hoensch, *Der ungarische Revisionismus*, pp. 216-45, and M. Lvová, "Československá otázka v diplomatických spisoch horthyovského Mad'arska" ["The Czechoslovak Question in the Diplomatic Documents of Horthy's Hungary"], *Historický časopis*, XV (1967), Nos. 1, 2.

[15] For negotiations between Czechoslovakia and Poland see Joseph Beck, *Dernier Rapport: Politique polonaise 1926-1939* (Neuchâtel-Paris, 1951); Anna M. Cienciala, *Poland and the Western Powers, 1938-1939* (New York, 1968); Jean Szembek, *Journal 1933-1939* (Paris, 1952).

[16] Szembek, *Journal*, p. 342.

slovakia lost eight coal mines, providing 45 percent of her total coal production. In addition, Poland acquired important iron and steel works.[17] Two minor border areas in northern Slovakia also went to Poland, which offended the Slovak autonomists who had regarded Warsaw as an ally in their political struggle.

The territorial and international changes resulting from the Munich Agreement created numerous internal problems for Czechoslovakia. Thus, immediately after Munich, the urgent problem of Slovak autonomy appeared, and also, though less pressingly, that of Ruthenia. Another set of problems concerned the adaptation of economic life to the diminished size of the state. A new president had to be elected and foreign policy realigned according to the changed power balance.

Hlinka's Slovak People's party (Hlinkova slovenská ľudová strana— HSĽS) laid down its demands for autonomy in June, 1938, and presented them to the parliament on August 17. They asked for recognition of the individuality of the Slovak people, exclusive use of the Slovak language in Slovakia, creation of an autonomous Slovak diet, and the immediate transfer of executive power to the representatives of the HSĽS.

Until Munich, Prague's negotiations with the Slovak Populists brought no concrete results. After Munich, however, the weakened position of Prague encouraged the Slovak autonomists to renew their demands. This change in the balance of forces became immediately apparent when the executive committee of the HSĽS met in Žilina on October 5. The deliberations led to an agreement between the Populists and other Slovak parties (with the exception of the Social Democrats) about autonomy as conceived by the Populists. The executive power was to be transferred immediately to a Slovak autonomous government consisting of five ministers, who were to be appointed by the vice-president of the party, Mgr. Jozef Tiso. Foreign affairs, defense, and public debt and loans for the common needs of the state were to be excluded from the competence of the Slovak government.[18]

The Prague government, still unsettled by the loss of the Fifth Zone to Germany and assailed by Polish and Hungarian demands, was forced to yield. On October 6 Tiso was appointed minister for the administration of Slovakia. In November, the House of Deputies and the Senate passed a law on autonomy. The change became apparent with the gradual introduction of a new spelling of the name of the State: the former Czechoslovakia now became Czecho-Slovakia.

[17] Vladimír Soják et al., eds., Mnichov v dokumentech [Munich in the Documents] (2 vols.; Prague, 1958), II, 355.

[18] For the Slovak developments see Jörg K. Hoensch, Die Slowakei und Hitlers Ostpolitik (Köln-Graz, 1965), pp. 98-115 and passim.

Democracy in Slovakia gave way to a single-party system. During the elections in December only one list of candidates was submitted, that of HSĽS, and it was made impossible to present any opposing list. The Slovak autonomous government thus won almost 97 percent of the vote.

Farther in the east, in Ruthenia, the evolution was similar. At the beginning of October representatives of the two traditional factions of the Ruthenian people, the Russophiles and the Ukrainophiles, reached an agreement to establish an autonomous government in the province. This was constituted on October 11. At its head was Andrej Bródy, a deputy to the parliament in Prague who represented the Russophile trend. The Ukrainian orientation was represented by the deputy Julian Révay. A few weeks after Bródy's appointment, however, it turned out that he was a paid agent of Budapest, and he was deposed. The appointment of Mgr. Augustin Vološin as his successor marked a victory for the Ukrainian orientation. Ruthenia, previously officially designated "Subcarpathian Russia," now assumed the name of "Carpathian Ukraine."

After the geographic surgery of October and November, 1938, Czechoslovakia lost one third of her territory and a good third of her population. Her area shrank from about 54,200 to about 38,200 square miles, and her population from about 14 million to about 10 million. The ratio of nationalities, which had given Hitler the pretext for his moves, had changed radically: the German minority fell to less than 4.5 percent (about 444,000); the Hungarian minority was considerably diminished; the Poles became practically nonexistent.[19]

Czechoslovakia lost not only her natural frontiers but also a chain of the most modern and costly fortifications. From the military point of view she was at the mercy of Germany, whose frontier at one point approached Prague to within 25 miles.

Czechoslovakia emerged from the Munich crisis with a seriously weakened economy. She lost about 40 percent of her industrial potential. Especially great were the losses of light industry, located in the borderlands ceded to Germany. Czechoslovakia lost 54.7 percent of her coal, 93.2 percent of lignite, and 35.3 percent of her coke production.[20]

Another disquieting phenomenon was increasing unemployment. In the course of the winter it more than doubled (77,000 in October, 148,000 in December, 1938, 172,000 in February, 1939).[21] About 140,000 persons fled from the occupied border areas, among them 116,000 Czechs and 12,000 anti-Nazi Germans.[22]

[19] Soják, *Mnichov v dokumentech*, II, 355.

[20] R. Olšovský *et al.*, *Přehled hospodářského vývoje Československa 1918-1945* [*Survey of the Economic Development of Czechoslovakia 1918-1945*] (Prague, 1961), pp. 474-75.

[21] Hájek, *Od Mnichova*, p. 118.

[22] *Sociální revue* [*Social Review*], Prague, January, 1939.

The deteriorated economic situation and the problem of the refugees forced Prague to seek financial aid abroad to help her bridge the most critical period of transition. Immediately after Munich, Prague turned to London and Paris. At first the Czech demands were received favorably, but with the lapse of time, when it became obvious that Czechoslovakia was becoming a mere toy in the hands of Berlin, the initial readiness to aid her began to evaporate. In the end, the financial assistance given by Great Britain and France amounted to only about £16 million. Of this a large proportion was to be used to finance the emigration of Germans and Jews from Czechoslovakia. Thus the contribution to the economic reconstruction of the country was minimal.

Several minor symptoms indicated a change of the political climate even in the western part of the state. The portraits of the first two presidents, Masaryk and Beneš, were to be removed from the schools and sent to the archives or storage rooms. Only toward the end of the year did the authorities decide that the portrait of Masaryk could be placed among those of the great Czech historical figures on the walls of the schools.

At the same time, some small fascist or semi-fascist groups, which before Munich vegetated on the periphery of the political scene, began to stir. In general, however, the Germans did not trust them because of their ultranationalistic past.[23]

Berlin naturally attempted to streamline the Czech press, from which any anti-German propaganda had to disappear. In October, six Masonic lodges were dissolved.

The party system had to be simplified. Eventually two large parties emerged: the National Unity party comprising mostly former rightist groups, and the National Labor party composed of leftist elements. The former dominated the political scene and the latter was condemned to a timid and ineffectual opposition during the short existence of the Second Republic. The activities of the Communist party were prohibited in Slovakia on October 9, in the Czech provinces on October 20. On December 27, the party was dissolved.[24] The chairman of the party, Klement Gottwald, left for Moscow in November and his deputy, Rudolf Slánský, followed some months later.

Only in November, when the frontiers of Czechoslovakia had been clearly defined, did Prague proceed to the election of the president of the republic. The choice fell on Dr. Emil Hácha, the first president of the Supreme Administrative Court, a distinguished jurist and a conservative without any marked political profile, a man whose health at the age of 66 was already declining. After the presidential election, the Syrový government resigned, and on December 1 a new government was formed

[23] German documents, microfilm 916/387198-9, 387131-2, 387153-4, 387159-60.
[24] Lukeš, *Podivný mír*, pp. 51, 205.

with the chairman of the Agrarian party, Rudolf Beran, as prime minister. The Slovak autonomist Karol Sidor was appointed vice-premier and minister for Slovakia. Until Munich Beran had directed his party from behind the scenes. Like some contemporary European statesmen of much greater stature than himself, Beran believed in pacific coexistence with National Socialist Germany, and hoped that a conciliatory attitude would be more profitable to his country than the former unyielding line of Beneš. With Beran at the helm of the government and under the pressure of circumstances, appeasement became the dominant theme in Czechoslovakia, too.

The international treaty system, which had failed to guarantee the security of Czechoslovakia, belonged to the past. The Little Entente was mere ashes. The relations between Prague and Moscow cooled off. According to the Czechoslovak minister in Moscow, Zdeněk Fierlinger, the Soviet minister in Prague, Sergei Alexandrovsky, complained toward the end of January, 1939, that Chvalkovský the new foreign minister, avoided all contact with him.[25]

France began to evacuate her positions in Czechoslovakia. In November, her military mission in Prague was recalled. The great armament concern, the Škoda Works, which had been under French control since 1919, was sold to a Czechoslovak consortium and later passed under the control of the Hermann-Göring Werke.

Czechoslovak foreign policy was dominated by two problems: improving relations with Germany and obtaining the international guarantee promised by the Munich Agreement. In his valedictory statement Beneš advised his countrymen to adapt themselves to the new situation, but said that this did not mean they should give up their former friends: "We will look around us for new friends quietly, objectively, with loyalty toward all." This was good advice, but it proved hard to apply. Czechoslovakia's former friends showed increasing reluctance to exert themselves in her behalf at Berlin, and new friends were hard to find.

Chvalkovský deluded himself that he could use the friendly relations that he had built up in Rome to resist the pressures of Berlin. But there is no evidence that the Italians ever tried to help Czechoslovakia. Immediately after his appointment, Chvalkovský sought interviews with the German leaders. He was received by Foreign Minister Ribbentrop on October 13 and on the following day, at Munich, by the Führer himself.[26] He assured the German leaders of "a complete *volte-face* of the Czechoslovak policy," but Hitler was not easily convinced; he warned

---

[25] Microfilmed documents of the Czechoslovak Ministry of Foreign Affairs in German translation, National Archives, Washington, D. C. 1039/412075 (hereafter cited as Czechoslovak documents).

[26] *DGFP*, Nos. 55, 61.

Chvalkovský ominously that if Czechoslovakia showed any indication of returning to the "Beneš policy," he would settle her fate in eight hours.[27]

The promise of international guarantees contained in the Franco-British proposals of September 19 had played a decisive role in persuading Czechoslovakia to accept them. In the annex to the Munich Agreement Britain and France declared that they were standing by their offer. Germany and Italy likewise promised guarantees to Czechoslovakia when the questions of the Polish and Hungarian minorities had been settled. In the general euphoria after Munich, Paris and London thought that the promised guarantees would be a sufficient compensation to Czechoslovakia for the destruction of her treaty system.

Chvalkovský immediately seized the possibilities thus opened and sought the implementation of the promise of guarantees without delay. However, when he raised the issue during his first visit to Germany in October, Hitler's reaction was vague: Czechoslovakia should realize that the British and French guarantees were as worthless as her treaty of alliance with France or the pact with Russia had been during the September crisis, and that "the only really effective guarantee was that by Germany."[28] In November Ribbentrop declared that the guarantees depended on further political developments in general.[29] The French likewise became evasive. On November 21, the Secretary General at the Quai d'Orsay, Alexis Leger, declared that things should not be hurried, unless there was an immediate danger.[30]

On November 23, when the chapter of territorial changes seemed definitely terminated by the protocol just signed in Berlin, Chvalkovský informed the representatives of the four Powers in writing that the question of the guarantees was now in order.[31]

The German answer was negative. On Ribbentrop's instructions the German chargé d'affaires in Prague replied that there was no direct connection between the two questions, the guarantees being a separate matter. France and Britain took up the question at the meeting of Chamberlain and Halifax with Daladier and Bonnet in Paris on November 24. The four statesmen had met to undertake a diplomatic *tour d'horizon* on the eve of the signature of the Franco-German declaration. The results were inconclusive. According to the British, the guarantees should only come into force as a result of a decision by three of the four powers. Lord Halifax pointed out that "there was perhaps some danger in establishing a position where a future Czechoslovak government might look

[27] Feierabend, *Ve vládách*, p. 53. Cf. dispatch of the American minister in Prague, Wilbur J. Carr, of October 21, 1938 (Dept. of State files, 760F.62/1751).
[28] *DGFP*, No. 61.   [29] Ibid., No. 116.
[30] Czechoslovak documents, 1039/412107-8; 1040/412969-70.
[31] *DGFP*, No. 136.

to France and Great Britain for support in pursuing a policy not entirely in conformity with German wishes."[32]

When Ribbentrop came to Paris on December 6 to sign the Franco-German declaration, he tried to raise doubts about the guarantees. He urged Bonnet to give up French interests in East Central Europe, including Czechoslovakia, and to abandon the area to German influence. A four-power guarantee, he intimated, might tempt Czechoslovakia to follow once more the paths of the Beneš policy. Later he repeated that Germany regarded a French guarantee of Czechoslovakia "as a form of interference in our sphere of influence," and added that the idea of such a guarantee would not be auspicious for the course of Franco-German understanding just embarked upon.[33] Thus the result of the Paris talks, when they touched this point, was not satisfactory. Ribbentrop promised only to reexamine the problem after his return to Berlin.[34]

Shortly before Christmas, however, Britain suggested to France a joint approach to the German and Italian governments to ask them about their opinion regarding the fulfilment of the promise given in Munich.[35] The two notes raising this question were not delivered in Berlin until February 8, 1939, by which time Hitler had already made up his mind to liquidate Czechoslovakia.[36]

The Munich Agreement had deprived Hitler of the opportunity to settle the fate of Czechoslovakia by a quick war. The Franco-British capitulation in Munich made it difficult for him to start hostilities. However, Hitler was convinced that "the solution of Munich could be only temporary," and that Germany could not tolerate on her flank "an abcess" of an independent, though smaller, Czechoslovakia.[37] The tension thus continued, and the attitude of Berlin toward Prague continuously hardened. On October 21, Hitler issued a directive to the Wehrmacht for the liquidation of the remainder of Czechoslovakia, in which he declared: "It must be possible to smash at any time the remainder of the Czech State, should it pursue an anti-German policy."[38]

Nevertheless, about the same time, the German Foreign Office prepared a draft of a "treaty of amity" between Germany and Czechoslovakia, by which Prague would have been forced into the same degree of dependence on Germany as Berlin had intended for Belgium during

[32] *Documents on British Foreign Policy 1919-1939*. Third Series, Vol. III, 1938-39 (London, 1950), No. 325, pp. 300-306. Hereafter quoted as *DBFP*.

[33] *DGFP*, No. 370, pp. 471-77.

[34] *Le Livre jaune français* (Paris, 1939), No. 32; Georges Bonnet, *Fin d'une Europe* (Geneva, 1948), p. 27.

[35] *DBFP*, No. 446.

[36] *Le Livre jaune français*, No. 47; *Documents on British Foreign Policy 1919-1939*. Third Series, Vol. IV, 1939 (London, 1951), Nos. 90, 91.

[37] Martin Bormann, *Le Testament politique de Hitler* (Paris, 1959), pp. 118-19.

[38] *DGFP*, No. 81.

World War I. Later, however, this draft disappeared in Ribbentrop's files, and proposals for a more radical solution appeared.[39] The October directive was amended, probably under the influence of the Franco-German exchanges in Paris in December and the particularly advantageous position acquired by Germany in Prague. Whereas the first instructions envisaged military action, the second directive, issued on December 17, proposed only police action: "Outwardly it must be quite clear that it is only a peaceful action and not a warlike undertaking."[40]

This period of German policy, marked by a certain hesitation and uncertainty, closed toward the end of January when Hitler's plans concerning Poland crystallized. At that time, Ribbentrop brought from Warsaw the news that the Polish attitude toward the German proposals concerning Danzig and the solution of the Corridor problem was negative. Hitler decided to settle the dispute by force. Accordingly, it became necessary to remove from his right flank the potential danger represented by Czechoslovakia. To this end, he resolved to use the ambitions of the Slovak radicals.

In these circumstances, the results of the visit which Chvalkovský made in Berlin toward the end of January were bound to be disappointing for Prague. Ribbentrop complained that Czechoslovakia did not seem stabilized, and that she showed symptoms of a reawakening of her earlier tendencies to pursue a disguised "Beneš policy." Hitler, who also received Chvalkovský, rehearsed the same grievances. The Germans formulated a series of new demands on Czechoslovakia: reorientation of her foreign policy to Berlin, her immediate withdrawal from the League of Nations, drastic reduction of her armed forces, promulgation of anti-Semitic laws, etc.[41]

A few days after Chvalkovský's visit, Hitler summoned several members of the German secret service, and ordered them to continue their previous contacts with the Slovak extremists with a view to inducing them to declare an independent Slovak State about the middle of March.[42] In the middle of February he declared to Generals Keitel and Brauchitsch that he was ready to launch a military operation for the "pacification" of Czechoslovakia.[43]

The Slovak question thus assumed an international character. The radical elements of the HSĽS considered the ample autonomy accorded

[39] Ernst von Weizsäcker, *Erinnerungen* (Munich, 1950), p. 212; *Trials of War Criminals Before the Nuremberg Military Tribunals*, XII (Washington, 1951), Woermann, Doc. No. 116.

[40] *DGFP*, No. 152.

[41] Ibid., Nos. 158, 159; *Le Livre jaune français*, No. 48.

[42] Walter Hagen, *Die geheime Front* (Stuttgart, 1952), p. 174.

[43] Walter Görlitz, ed., *Generalfeldmarschall Keitel* (Göttingen, 1961), p. 199.

Slovakia in October, 1938, as insufficient. Unlike Sidor and Tiso, who wished to attain independence in a slow, evolutionary way, they pressed for radical moves and quick action, and relied on German assistance to realize their plans. The young Slovak radicals (D'určanský, Černák, Mach, and Murgaš), who were without any practical political experience, were hostile to any cooperation with Prague even before Munich. They found an apt leader and organizer in Professor Vojtech Tuka.

On February 12, in the presence of Ribbentrop, Hitler received Tuka. This was one of the first indications of the decisions Hitler had made in the preceding weeks. Tuka addressed Hitler in the German style as "Mein Führer" and declared, "I lay the destiny of my people in your hands, my people await their complete liberation by you." Hitler indicated that he saw dark days for Slovakia if the Czechs persisted in their old ways. Tuka replied that he knew that the Czech future was dark, and that was all the more reason why the Slovaks should free themselves from Czechoslovakia.[44]

About two weeks later, on February 28, Germany at last answered the British and French note on guarantees. The response was negative. Germany declared herself against the "prematurely given" guarantees. In the German opinion this area fell "first and foremost within the sphere of the most important interests of the German Reich." Therefore, it was imperative to await first the clarification of the internal development of Czechoslovakia, and the improvement of her relations with the surrounding states.[45]

The German note sounded the knell of the Second Republic. It came amid the rumors circulating in Berlin about the uncertain fate of post-Munich Czechoslovakia. Within a few days, Hitler seized developments in the eastern part of the state as a pretext for the final blow.

In the meantime, a Slovak delegation was sent to Berlin without the knowledge of the central government. Its official mission was to talk about economic questions; its real aim was to sound out the possibilities of separation from Bohemia. Göring told the Slovaks that Germany wished to aid Slovakia, but only on condition of a total separation, that they separate themselves completely from the Czechs and the common state.[46]

Prague soon learned about the visit, and, as a precautionary measure, strengthened the garrisons in Slovakia. During the first days of March, as the deadline set by Hitler was approaching, Germany increased her activity. On March 7 an assistant of the Austrian Governor Seyss-

[44] *DGFP*, No. 168.   [45] Ibid., No. 175.
[46] Karol Sidor, *O vzniku slovenského štátu* [*On the Origins of the Slovak State*] (Bratislava, 1945), p. 9.

Inquart visited Slovakia to stress to Sidor and Tiso the absolute necessity of proclaiming Slovak independence.[47] In the evening of the same day Seyss-Inquart himself arrived in Bratislava to discuss the problem.

Prague, though perhaps not fully informed about the details of these contacts and the situation in Bratislava, lost her confidence in Tiso. Late in the evening of March 9, Hácha signed a decree, dated the next day, dismissing the Slovak government. Police reinforcements were sent to Bratislava, and at dawn Czechoslovak troops had public buildings all over Slovakia under their control. Tuka, Mach, and Černák were apprehended and interned in Moravia. Ďurčanský fled to Austria and over Radio Vienna called upon the Slovaks to rise against the Czechs.

On Saturday, March 11, Sidor, who as a member of the central government was not affected by Hácha's decree, was appointed prime minister of Slovakia, a move which represented a compromise and a certain retreat by Prague. At the same time, however, the influence of the radical separatists was weakened. The appointment of the vacillating Sidor as Slovak prime minister was a setback for Hitler's plans, and the Germans renewed their pressure. In the early hours of Sunday, March 12, a special adviser to Hitler, State Secretary Wilhelm Keppler, and Gauleiter Josef Bürckel, arrived in Bratislava. They found that Sidor, though not opposing the radical separatists, refused to go along with the immediate radical solution urged by the Germans.[48]

The Germans therefore approached Tiso, who was invited by Hitler to visit Berlin. Tiso accepted the invitation, arriving in the German capital in the late afternoon of March 13. Hitler put the problem bluntly to him: "The question is whether Slovakia wishes independence or not. It is a question not of days but of hours." If Slovakia wished to become independent, he would support her and even guarantee her efforts. If she hesitated or refused to be separated from Prague, he would abandon her to her fate. Tiso assured Hitler that he could trust Slovakia, and from Berlin summoned a meeting of the Slovak Diet for the following day.[49] At noon, on March 14, the Slovak Diet unanimously declared Slovak independence. Sidor resigned, and Tiso became prime minister. Ďurčanský was appointed minister of foreign affairs.

These changes also affected the fate of Ruthenia. On the same day that he was awaiting the visit of Tiso in Berlin, Hitler gave Hungary permission to occupy the province.[50] Prime Minister Vološin attempted in vain to save his country from Hungarian occupation by proclaiming it an independent state and placing it under German protection. Hitler, how-

[47] Lukeš, *Podivný mír*, pp. 260-61; Hoensch, *Die Slowakei*, p. 249.
[48] Karol Murgaš, *Národ medzi Dunajom a Karpatmi* [*The Nation between the Danube and the Carpathians*] (Bratislava, 1940), p. 143.
[49] *DGFP*, No. 202. Hoensch, *Die Slowakei*, pp. 289-303.
[50] *DGFP*, No. 198.

ever, had lost interest in the area. The Germans advised Vološin to offer no resistance.[51] Hungarian troops crossed the border on March 14 and completed the occupation on the 17th. The common Polish-Hungarian frontier became a reality, but under the circumstances it was deprived of any political or strategic value.

Hitler made the final decision about the Czech provinces, Bohemia and Moravia, on March 12, the same day that he invited Tiso to Berlin. On that day a preliminary order was given to the army and the air force to be ready for a possible invasion (*Einmarsch*) on March 15 at 6:00 A.M.[52] In accordance with the order German troops started moving toward the Czechoslovak frontier. At the same time the German press resumed its strident attacks on Czechoslovakia.

In the meantime, in Prague, Chvalkovský conceived the idea of an exploratory journey to Berlin. As he stated later,[53] he at first wanted to go alone to Berlin to discover the German intentions regarding Slovakia and Ruthenia. Since Tiso had gone to Berlin, however, it was decided in Prague that President Hácha himself should head the mission to Berlin. The German government delayed answering his request for an interview with Hitler until after the Slovak declaration of independence and the Hungarian invasion of Ruthenia, when these moves could be presented to him as accomplished facts. It was not until the afternoon of March 14 that the train with Hácha and Chvalkovský left for Berlin. By that time, of course, it was no longer the fate of Slovakia or Ruthenia that was in question but that of Bohemia and Moravia.

In Berlin, Hácha was immediately received by Hitler. The talks began at 1:15 A.M., on March 15, and lasted about three hours. Hitler informed Hácha that he had given the order for the German army to enter Bohemia and Moravia. The Czechs were presented with a document exacting the capitulation of their army. In the course of the conversation, Göring threatened Hácha that if the Czechoslovak army offered resistance to the Germans, he would order the Luftwaffe to destroy Prague.[54] Hácha yielded to these threats and telephoned orders to Prague for the army not to resist the German invasion. However, that did not exhaust the catalog of humiliations that Hitler had in store for him. The Germans also exacted from him that he sign a declaration by which "he confidently placed the fate of the Czech people in the hands of the Führer and of the German Reich."[55]

---

[51] Ibid., Nos. 210, 237. [52] Görlitz, *Keitel*, p. 100.
[53] To the author of this article.
[54] For the verbatim text of Göring's statement see Hácha's report on his fateful mission to Berlin in Soják, *Mnichov v dokumentech*, II, 392-95.
[55] *DGFP*, Nos. 228, 229; Soják, *Mnichov v dokumentech*, II, 392.

The German army crossed the Czechoslovak frontier in the early morning of March 15, according to Hitler's schedule.[56] During the evening of the same day Hitler himself arrived in Prague with his retinue, preceding Hácha, whose special train was deliberately detained on its way by the Germans under the pretext of snowdrifts. The Führer settled without delay in the castle of Hradčany, the ancient seat of the kings of Bohemia and later of Czechoslovak presidents. On March 16 he proclaimed Bohemia and Moravia a German protectorate and integral part of Greater Germany. The ill-fated Second Czechoslovak Republic had come to an end.

[56] To prevent the repetition of the incident of the previous October when Poland prematurely occupied Bohumín (see p. 289), the Germans entered the important town of Moravská Ostrava in the early evening of March 14, while the train with President Hácha was still on its way to Berlin. Cf. Tomáš Pasák, "Vstup německých vojsk na české území v roce 1939" ["The Entry of the German Forces into Czech territory in the year 1939"], *Československý časopis historický*, XVII, No. 2 (1969), 166.

· 9 ·

THE SLOVAK REPUBLIC, 1939-1945

Jörg K. Hoensch
University of Tübingen

On September 29, 1938, as a result of the notorious Munich Agreement, the First Czechoslovak Republic came to an end. Most Europeans welcomed the agreement with relief, because it exorcised the danger of war that had seemed imminent. Absorbed in the international aspects of the crisis, few were concerned with its repercussions on domestic Czechoslovak politics. The declaration of an independent Slovak state on March 14, 1939, and the establishment of the Protectorate of Bohemia and Moravia on the following day, came as a general surprise. Yet these events were the logical outcome of Hitler's East European policy and the Munich Agreement.

On October 6, 1938, the government of Gen. Jan Syrový, frightened not only by Hitler's action but also by a Polish ultimatum, exorbitant Hungarian revisionist demands, and the resignation of President Edvard Beneš, and fearful of a Slovak separatist movement, yielded to the demands of Hlinka's Slovak People's party (Hlinkova slovenská ľudová strana—HSĽS) for far-reaching concessions in the autonomous administration of Slovakia. The HSĽS, which was founded on December 19, 1918, by Father Andrej Hlinka, originally to represent the interests of the lower Catholic clergy, had agitated for twenty years for the recognition of "Slovak national individuality," cultural autonomy, and self-administration within the framework of the Czechoslovak republic. The conservative wing of the party, led by Father Jozef Tiso, who became party chairman on the death of Hlinka on August 16, 1938, recognized that Slovakia could not maintain an unlimited sovereignty, owing to its economic weakness, administrative inexperience, and relative cultural backwardness. However, as early as the 1920's—impressed by the success of the fascist and National Socialist movements in Italy and Germany—there emerged around the person of Dr. Vojtech Tuka, a law professor before 1918 and subsequently a party journalist, a small, radical, right-wing faction that hoped for the immediate establishment of a Slovak national state along authoritarian lines. In 1929, when Tuka was arrested and convicted of high treason, the right-radicals were temporarily checked. However, after Hitler's advent to power they steadily gained in strength until by 1938 they represented an important factor within the party.

The conservative-clerical majority of the HSĽS was largely anti-German, because of Hitler's policy toward the Catholic Church and the party's reservations concerning National Socialist ideology. In spite of their failure to gain Slovak autonomy and the promptings of the right-radicals, the conservative party leaders declined to cooperate closely with Konrad Henlein's Sudeten German party. They preferred to pursue a parallel but separate course. On September 23, 1938, when President Beneš gave in to the threats and ultimatum of the HSĽS and eased Czechoslovak domestic tensions by granting broad territorial autonomy to Slovakia,[1] the party leaders appeared to feel that the party's program had been achieved and took a positive stand in favor of the continuation of the Czechoslovak Republic within its 1919 boundaries. However, after the Munich Agreement, which revealed the complete helplessness of the Prague government, they increased their demands. At a meeting in Žilina on October 6, 1938, all Slovak parties, except the Social Democrats and the communists, formed a common program with the HSĽS. The program was no longer based on Beneš's proposals of September 23 but on the HSĽS's own June 4 and August 19 drafts of autonomy bills that envisaged a federal organization for Czechoslovakia. Under the effects of the Munich catastrophe and intensive Polish and Hungarian propaganda to bring about the secession of Slovakia from the Czechoslovak Republic, the Syrový government bowed before the Slovaks and accepted the "Žilina agreement." On the following day it appointed a coalition government for the state of Slovakia under the premiership of Tiso.[2] The Prague parliament implemented the Žilina agreement after much political haggling on November 23, when it passed laws that transformed the unitary First Czechoslovak Republic into the federalized Second "Czecho-Slovak" Republic.

The laws, however, failed to define the jurisdiction of the provincial governments of Slovakia and Ruthenia (Subcarpathian Russia, Carpathian Ukraine) with sufficient clarity. Further friction developed between Prague and Bratislava. Instead of providing a true inner consolidation of the country, federalization accelerated its decomposition.

Among the several factors that led to the liquidation of the Czechoslovak state, the Slovak right-radicals were a primary element. They were

[1] For the text of the agreement see Edvard Beneš, *Où vont les Slaves?* (Paris, 1948), p. 277; Joseph A. Mikuš, *Slovakia: A Political History, 1918-1950* (Milwaukee, 1963), pp. 340ff.

[2] The period before and after the "Žilina agreement" has been dealt with in great detail by Jörg K. Hoensch, *Die Slowakei und Hitlers Ostpolitik. Hlinkas Slowakische Volkspartei zwischen Autonomie und Separation, 1938/39* (Köln-Graz, 1965). This study contains a full bibliography. See also František Vnuk, "Slovakia's Six Eventful Months," *Slovak Studies*, 4 (1964), 7-164; Milan D'urica, *La Slovacchia e le sue relazione politiche con la Germania 1938-1945* (2 vols.; Padua, 1964), I.

dependent on German support and became tools of Hitler's expansionist policies. Their demand for the immediate declaration of full Slovak sovereignty placed the conservative leaders of the party in a difficult position. The final aim of the conservatives likewise was unlimited Slovak independence, but they planned to realize it gradually, through evolutionary methods, after strengthening the Slovak economy and bureaucracy and accumulating adequate financial reserves. Their efforts to prop up the feeble Slovak economy were dealt a severe blow by the First Vienna Arbitration Treaty of November 2, 1938,[3] under which, because of inadequate German diplomatic support, Slovakia was obliged to cede to Hungary its most fertile areas in the south (some 4,000 square miles and a population of 859,885). Thereafter, the conservatives had to yield the political initiative to the radicals.

The ambitious radical politicians—Karol Sidor, Alexander ("Šaňo") Mach, Dr. Ferdinand D'určanský, and the recently amnestied Tuka—exploited the general lack of Slovak experience in practical politics and gained control of totalitarian, anti-Czech, and anti-Semitic movements. Their main support was provided by the Hlinka Guards (Hlinkova garda —HG), a paramilitary organization with a mixed ideology drawn from fascist, National Socialist, and corporative concepts. The HG was founded in October, 1938, and built up with great speed thereafter. The radicals were encouraged and subsidized by various German agencies. In return, by their uncritically displayed Germanophilia, they provided Hitler with a convenient *point d'appui* to press successfully on the Prague government every German wish. Single-party rule enforced by the HSĽS on November 8, the suppression of the leftist parties and of "Czechoslovak" organizations, the elections to the Slovak Diet on December 18 that were carried out with thoroughly contestable methods, the demonstrations for independence during the festive opening of the Diet on January 18, 1939, and the authoritarian procedure adopted during its first session on February 21-23 all testified to the breakdown of democratic traditions and the growth of totalitarian methods in Slovakia.

The election of the respectable, willing, but politically inexperienced Dr. Emil Hácha, on November 30, 1938, to succeed Beneš as president of Czecho-Slovakia, and the formation of a weak central government under Rudolf Beran, chairman of the agrarian party, on December 1, could not conceal the Prague government's inner disintegration and loss of power.[4] The forced coordination of Czecho-Slovak foreign and do-

---

[3] For a detailed analysis see Jörg K. Hoensch, *Der ungarische Revisionismus und die Zerschlagung der Tschechoslowakei* (Tübingen, 1967).

[4] Most of its aspects were covered by Heinrich Bodensieck, in *Die Politik der Prager Regierung Beran der Zweiten Tschechoslowakischen Republik* (Kiel, 1956), unpublished Ph.D. diss. A summary of his findings may be found in his article "Die Politik der Zweiten Tschechoslowakischen Republik," *Zeitschrift*

mestic policies with those of the Third Reich and the inadequate diplomatic support received from the French and British governments further undermined the prestige of the Prague government and encouraged the Slovak radicals. The Slovak conservatives, after a few feeble attempts to stem the rising tide of German influence, opportunistically adjusted themselves to the German course.

In October, 1938, Hitler determined to liquidate the rest of "Czechia" by disintegration from within. From February, 1939 on, there were increasing indications that further German moves against Czechoslovakia were imminent, a fact that stimulated the basic readiness of the leaders of the HSĽS to use German help to gain full sovereignty for Slovakia. Without the moral and material support of Germany and of the leadership of the German ethnic minority in Slovakia (*Karpatendeutsche*), the radicals in the HSĽS would not have succeeded in accomplishing this change in the party's aims. On the other hand, the influence of the Slovak radicals on Hitler should not be minimized. There is no question that their blatant Germanophilia and their demands for full independence—which they expressed to various German agents and to Hitler himself—influenced the tactics he employed to bring about the liquidation of Czechoslovakia in March, 1939.

Under the Munich Agreement, Germany was pledged to guarantee the new boundaries, sovereignty, and independence of Czecho-Slovakia, but it delayed in extending this guarantee on the grounds that the Prague government had failed to enforce law and order. To remove this excuse and prevent German interference, the Prague government asked the Slovak government to declare its loyalty to Czecho-Slovakia and renounce its separatist policy. Evasive Slovak reaction to this request on March 1 and 6, and the absence of Prime Minister Tiso from a cabinet meeting on March 9, caused Hácha and Beran to take vigorous action in line with the constitution. During the night of March 9-10, Tiso and three other members of the Slovak government were dismissed from office and some army units, together with a small police force, were ordered into Slovakia. D'určanský, who was one of the dismissed ministers, escaped to Vienna. From there he sent a telegram to Berlin, denouncing the action of the Prague government and asking for German help, thus providing

---

für Ostforschung, 6 (1957), 54-71. See also Hans Schiefer, *Deutschland und die Tschechoslowakei vom September 1938 bis März 1939* (Göttingen, 1953), unpublished Ph.D. diss., and his article in *Zeitschrift für Ostforschung*, 4 (1955), 48-66; and the final chapter in Helmuth K. G. Rönnefarth, *Die Sudetenkrise in der internationalen Politik: Entstehung, Verlauf, Auswirkung* (2 vols.; Wiesbaden, 1961), I, 697-754. See also Ľubomír Lipták, *Slovensko v 20. storočí* [*Slovakia in the 20th Century*] (Bratislava, 1968), pp. 160-175, and František Lukeš, *Podivný mír* [*A Strange Peace*] (Prague, 1968), *passim*.

Hitler with a convenient excuse to intervene in the internal affairs of Czecho-Slovakia.

Meanwhile, on March 11, Hácha asked Sidor, the Slovak representative in the Prague government, to form a new Slovak cabinet. Although Sidor was a radical, he had "mellowed" somewhat in the Prague atmosphere and had had second thoughts on the wisdom and propriety of the Germanophile course of his associates. He formed a Slovak government under a mandate from Prague and managed to consolidate the situation in Bratislava. Despite crass German interference, he settled the unrest produced in Slovakia by the HG and the German minority. Hitler was therefore obliged to modify his tactics slightly. Tiso was summoned to Berlin, where he arrived on March 13. In his interview with Tiso, the Führer threatened to partition Slovakia among Germany, Hungary, and Poland, but indicated a way out for the Slovaks: to declare their independence. Tiso did not fail to accept Hitler's advice. On March 14 the Slovaks duly declared Slovak independence.

Meanwhile, incidents were manufactured by German agents in Bohemia and Moravia that were blown up by the Goebbels press into brutal acts of oppression against the few Sudeten Germans remaining in the provinces. These intolerable "acts of provocation" and the Slovak declaration of independence furnished Hitler with an excuse to repudiate the Munich Agreement and liquidate Czecho-Slovakia. President Hácha, who was confused by the speed and the course of the events, asked to see Hitler. He was received by the Führer on the night of March 14-15 and forced with uncompromising brutality to sign the capitulation of his country. On March 15 Bohemia and Moravia were occupied by the German army and annexed to Germany with the status of "protectorate" (*Protektorat*). For some time the Hungarian government had sought to annex Ruthenia, but Hitler vetoed its plans on November 20, 1938, and again on February 12, 1939. On March 12, however, the Hungarians received word from Berlin to go ahead with the annexation of Ruthenia. They proceeded to occupy the area, together with some eastern Slovak districts, on March 15.[5] The Czechoslovak state had come to an end.

The declaration of a "sovereign" Slovak state on March 14, 1939, represented a development for which the radical wing of the HSĽS had hoped since 1919 and had actively worked for since the Žilina agreement. Without putting in doubt the awareness of their "national individuality" among Slovak patriots or their desire to mold their future in their own national state, it must be said unequivocally that it was Hitler's di-

[5] The Ruthenian question was dealt with by George Stercho in *Carpatho-Ukraine in International Affairs, 1938-1939* (Notre Dame, 1959), unpublished Ph.D. diss.

rectives alone that brought about the Slovak declaration of independence at the time and in the form that it took place. From the beginning, Slovak statehood received the unanimous support of the Catholic clergy and at least the acquiescence, if not the support, of the majority of the Slovak population. On March 15 the country was hastily and partially occupied by the German army. Eight days later (March 23), the Slovak government was obliged to sign with Germany a "treaty of protection" (*Schutzvertrag*) and a "confidential economic protocol" that made Slovakia a "protected state" (*Schutzstaat*) of the Third Reich.[6]

These agreements severely curtailed the internal and external independence of the country. Responsible Slovak politicians may very well have wondered whether the Slovaks had not been better off under the federalized Czecho-Slovak Republic, in which they were equals of the Czechs in rights, than under the "sovereign" Slovak state. On the other hand, the Slovak state undoubtedly protected Slovak interests better and offered more chances for intellectual and material development than would have obtained in any other format conceivable at the time: occupation and partition among Hungary, Poland, and Germany; reunion with Hungary, with cultural and political autonomy; or incorporation of Slovakia into the Third Reich as a protectorate, like Bohemia and Moravia.

The new government under Jozef Tiso, which was dominated by the Hitlerites Tuka, D'určanský, and Mach, was faced with nearly unsolva-

---

[6] The text is printed in *Documents on German Foreign Policy*, Series D, vol. VI, No. 40, hereafter cited as *DGFP*. In return for the "protection of the political independence of the Slovak State and integrity of its territory," Slovakia committed itself to organize its military forces and to conduct its foreign policy "in close agreement" with the German government and to let the German army have a "protective zone" (*Schutzzone*) in western Slovakia for the construction of military installations and garrisons. The treaty, which reduced Slovakia to a status similar to that of protectorate, euphemistically apostrophized by the Reich authorities as "protective friendship" (*Schutzfreundschaft*), was merely the wrapping for the real German-Slovak agreement, the "Confidential Protocol concerning the Economic and Financial Cooperation between the German Reich and Slovakia," which was signed on the same day. Under the pretext of a program for the economic development of Slovakia, the protocol laid down the guiding principles for the exploitation of the Slovak industrial and agricultural resources in the interest of the German war economy. In exchange for manufactured goods, Slovakia had to export her agrarian and forestry products and her mineral wealth to Germany. Since 75 percent of the Slovak exports went to the Third Reich, the oft-repeated formula that the development of the domestic Slovak production was limited "by consideration of the market situation in Germany," reduced the Slovak economy to the status of a supplier of complementary goods. The tight German control of the Slovak foreign trade with other countries and the German veto power in exchange, credit, and budget matters completed a sophisticated machinery for the permanent German mastery of the Slovak economic potential. For a detailed interpretation and comparison with the protectorate treaty for Bohemia and Moravia, see Hoensch, *Die Slowakei und Hitlers Ostpolitik*, pp. 334-50.

ble problems. It had to carry out a complete reconstruction of a small, impoverished, mountainous country without an adequately trained civil service and with only a small nationally conscious and active intelligentsia.[7] It was encouraged by Germany only insofar as its efforts promised to contribute to the German war effort. For some time the very existence of the Slovak republic remained in doubt. Although Hitler's veto stopped the Hungarian advance in eastern Slovakia, he was prepared to cede northern Slovakia to Poland in exchange for Polish concessions on Danzig and a freeway through the Corridor. It was only when he discarded any idea of agreement with Poland and decided definitely on war with her that the survival of Slovakia was assured.[8]

Outwardly, Slovakia enjoyed the attributes of a sovereign, independent state. It had its own diplomatic service. Twenty-seven governments, among them those of the Soviet Union, France, and Britain (but not of the United States),[9] extended de facto, and in some instances de jure, recognition to the Slovak government. This outward recognition of Slovak independence, however, did not prevent German government agencies from assigning large "advisory missions" to all Slovak ministries to assure complete coordination of policy between Slovakia and Germany. Furthermore, German army units stationed in the Váh valley, outside Bratislava, and across the Danube in former Austria; the leadership of the German minority under the eager Franz Karmasin; and the German legation in Bratislava, successively under Hans Bernard, Manfred von Killinger, and Hans Elard Ludin; together with the Hitlerites (Tuka, D'určanský, and Mach) in the Slovak government and the HG assured that every German order was executed punctually. Tuka replaced Sidor, who had fallen out of Hitler's favor because of his stand during the March crisis, as minister of interior on March 16, 1939. The gifted and unscrupulous D'určanský became foreign minister. The fickle and unreliable Mach became the head of the office of propaganda and of the HG. Together, these Hitlerites lost no time in organizing the young state on the model of Fascist Italy and National Socialist Germany.

[7] On December 31, 1938, Slovakia had a population of 2,690,002 (185 persons per square mile). After the territorial losses to Hungary on April 4, 1939, the area of Slovakia was 14,615 square miles. On December 15, 1940, her population was 2,655,964. Bratislava was the largest city, with a population of 138,000 (as against 124,000 in 1938). There were only thirteen large settlements with a population of between 10,000 and 25,000. In June, 1939, 56 percent of the population was engaged in agriculture and forestry. About 1,000 factories and workshops employed about 100,000 workers: 15,000 were in iron works, 12,000 in the lumber business, and some 11,000 in the textile industry.

[8] It was as late as June, 1939, that Hitler came to the conclusion that war with Poland was inevitable and Slovakia worth preserving, for strategic reasons.

[9] For further details see Joseph M. Kirschbaum, Slovakia: Nation at the Crossroads of Central Europe (New York, 1960), pp. 130-44; Mikuš, Slovakia, pp. 90-91, 116-32.

At first, Berlin and Bratislava appeared to be on a very friendly footing. The German government was concerned with the impression its treatment of Slovakia would make on the Danubian and southeastern countries of Europe, on which it depended for wheat, oil, and other supplies for its rearmament program and, after the outbreak of war in September, 1939, its war effort. Therefore, it made a great show of respect for Slovak sovereignty and independence. Slovakia was designed as Germany's "calling card" (*Visitenkarte*) in Southeastern Europe and a showpiece of the German "New Order" in Europe. In the beginning the German government contented itself with a tight control of the Slovak army and administration, but did not unduly interfere in Slovak internal affairs.[10] On July 19, 1939, the Tiso government had to promise "to continue directing domestic political development in Slovakia in a spirit unqualifiedly positive and friendly towards Germany."[11] But for tactical reasons, the German government did not at first insist on ideological coordination of Slovakia, that is, on her outright adoption of National Socialist ideology.

The Slovak constitution, which the Diet passed on July 21, 1939, was influenced by elements of the papal social encyclicals, the corporative teachings of the Austrian political writer Othmar Spann, the Austrian Dollfuss-Schuschnigg system of government, and the authoritarian constitution of Portugal, as well as by Italian and German political practices. Even its political critics had to admit that "the Nazi model was not shamelessly imposed" and that "the new Slovak state was launched with all the paraphernalia of a national ideology apparently corporative and Christian."[12] The constitution, which consisted of 103 short paragraphs, put the real power in the country under the firm control of the HSĽS and its organizations. The Diet, the membership of which was enlarged through appointments from sixty-three to eighty, was unable to maintain its voice in political affairs, because the government was given the power to issue "decrees with the validity of laws" in cases that could brook no delay.[13] A newly created Council of State—consisting of six members

---

[10] *DGFP*, D, x, 17.

[11] Ibid., 205, note by Bernard of July 22, 1940.

[12] Alexander Kunoši, *The Basis of Czechoslovak Unity* (London, 1944), p. 60. For an interpretation of the constitution from the viewpoint of former HSĽS members see Anton Peltzner, *The Slovak Constitution and Modern Political Theory* (Montreal, 1957), unpublished M.A. thesis MS; Mikuš, *Slovakia*, pp. 91-94; Kirschbaum, *Slovakia*, pp. 145-64. For a critical view see Jozef Lettrich, *History of Modern Slovakia* (London, 1956), pp. 147-48.

[13] In the old Diet, 48 out of 63 deputies were members of the HSĽS even though the party had gained only 30 percent of the Slovak vote in the last free parliamentary elections in May, 1935. Four of the deputies represented the ethnic minorities (two Germans, one Magyar and one Ruthene). The Slovak Protestants, who numbered about 18 percent of the Slovak people, were represented by only 5 deputies of their faith. Nearly one fifth of the members of the Diet belonged

appointed by the elected president of the state, ten members chosen by the HSLS, one member to represent each of the minority nationalities and the six social estates, the prime minister, and the speaker of the Diet —became a sort of upper house of parliament with powers to impeach the president and ministers, draw up the list of candidates for elections to the Diet, and initiate laws.[14] The interests of the Churches and the ethnic minorities were well protected.

In the beginning the influence of the tightly organized HSLS and its shock troops, the HG, grew uniformly and without friction. At its peak in 1943, the HSLS had some 280,000 members. The HG was modeled on the Italian *Fasci di Combattimento* and the German storm troop detachments (SA, *Sturm Abteilung*). A government decree on September 5, 1939, put all male Slovaks between the ages of six and sixty under obligation to serve either in the "Hlinka Youth" (Hlinkova mládež— HM) or in the various formations of the HG. However, the many objections raised to the decree obliged the government to define anew the aims and duties of the HG on December 21, 1939. The new decree stated that the Hlinka Guards were "a corps organized according to military principles within the framework of the Hlinka Slovak People's Party," whose duty it was to "provide pre-military training, submit reports and proposals to appropriate authorities, and to assist the authorities in defending the state as well as in maintaining public order and security."[15] Before the HG could exert a strong influence in daily political affairs, however, the opposition of the conservatives limited their sphere of activity.

A change of positions in the HSLS gradually took place and by the end of 1939 began to affect German-Slovak relations. The tutelage exercised by the German government and its advisory outposts in Bratislava, which was grudgingly borne during the early weeks of "independence," exasperated the young Slovak nationalists as well as the conservatives. They began to demand a wider sphere of affairs free from German interference, especially when they realized the strategic and economic importance of Slovakia to the Third Reich in the coming German aggression

---

to the Catholic clergy. The newly appointed parliamentarians helped to increase the influence of the old People's Party still further. There was, of course, no possibility of an organized opposition in the Diet.

[14] The members of the Council of State were nominated before August 2, 1940. On July 9, 1943, Tiso pressed through a reduction in the membership of the Council from 26 to 12. This strengthened his position considerably, because he was granted the privilege of appointing ten of them for three-year terms. The prime minister and the speaker of the Diet were represented in the Council of State ex officio. Among the newly appointed members on August 30, 1943, was the President's cousin, Štefan Tiso, who later became prime minister. The German ethnic minority always held one seat in the council.

[15] *Code of Slovakia*. Statutory Decree No. 310/1939.

against Poland. Lengthy negotiations were necessary before the German army was granted permission to use Slovakia (outside the "protected zone") as a deployment area against Poland in August, 1939.[16] The participation of the Slovak army, which had been organized on the German pattern and drilled by German officers, in the Polish campaign brought Slovakia the award by Hitler of territory in the Javorina, Orava, and Spiš regions that Slovakia had lost to Poland in 1920, 1924, and 1938.[17] Tiso was honored by Hitler with the Grand Cross of the Order of the Black Eagle.

Tiso eagerly defended the German orientation at the congress of the HSĽS in Trenčín on October 1, 1939, but his remarks on ideological and administrative affairs must have caused some raised eyebrows among the German observers present.[18] On October 26, Tiso was elected president. However, the German government did not believe that it had cause to fear ideological estrangement at the time, because on November 2, Tuka, who was a firm adherent of Nazism, was appointed prime minister. The portfolio of interior, which he relinquished, was taken over by D'určanský, who was already foreign minister. D'určanský thus combined the two most important posts in the cabinet.

D'určanský was believed to be pro-German. It was he, it will be recalled, who had fled to Vienna on March 10 and called for German intervention against the Prague government. However, since then he appeared to have had a change of heart. He joined the conservatives in trying to secure the country on a Catholic-conservative basis, with the help of certain circles in industry, the bureaucracy, and the party as well as the army and the police, who jealously guarded their powers against any encroachment by the HG. In foreign affairs he had an inflated opinion of the importance of Slovakia (the "turnplate of Europe").[19] He believed that in the coming struggle in the West, Germany might be defeated by the Western powers. In the eventuality of Germany's defeat and Hitler's downfall, he tried cautiously to extricate Slovakia from Ger-

[16] The particulars of the German-Slovak negotiations are given in *DGFP*, D, VII, Nos. 100, 165, 187, 214, 222, 237, 250, 362, 401, 468, 488. The thrust of the German army group under General List over the Carpathian Mountains into the ill-protected southern flank of Poland and the German air raids from the nearby Slovak bases contributed considerably to the swift defeat of Poland. For details of Slovak participation *Armáda v obrane a práci* [*The Army in Defense and Work*] (Bratislava, 1944), pp. 26-32. A rather critical evaluation is in Lettrich, *History of Modern Slovakia*, pp. 159-61.

[17] *DGFP*, D, VIII, Nos. 360-81. Only 300 square miles with 33,576 inhabitants in 35 villages were affected.

[18] Tiso asked for the education of a new Slovak people, whose ideals would have to be a strong faith in God, the spiritual values of a Catholic philosophy of life, and the belief in the inseparable unity of the Slovak family.

[19] *DGFP*, D, IX, No. 2, report of the State Secretary for Special Duties, Wilhelm Keppler, of March 18, 1940.

many's grip under the guise of neutralism, which the countries of South-eastern Europe pursued at the time. He addressed proposals for neutrality to France and Britain, and maintained contacts with the Soviet Union, which had recognized the Tiso government on September 16, 1939. The Soviet Union maintained an overstaffed legation under G. M. Pushkin at Bratislava. The exact nature of D'určanský's contacts with the Soviet government has not yet been clarified, but undoubtedly they were designed, like his proposals to France and Britain, to assure Slovakia's independence in the event of Germany's defeat as well as to prevent Hungarian aggression, which the Slovaks feared would follow immediately upon Germany's disintegration as a power.

At home, D'určanský pursued analogous tactics. With all the tricks of the shrewd lawyer that he was, he sought to delay the German advance in the economic system and the administration. His ostentatious collaboration with pro-Czech and Jewish circles against the Hitlerites in the HG especially served that purpose. The relative indulgence shown the Jews was designed to repel German competition and also to dissociate Slovakia from Germany's anti-Semitic policies and enhance the Tiso government in the eyes of the Western powers. On December 1, 1939, Karmasin, leader of the German party (DP), who held the post of state-secretary for German affairs in the Slovak government, complained to Joachim von Ribbentrop, the German foreign minister, that "Communist, Czech, and other anti-German influences were making themselves felt very strongly in Slovakia." The German government reacted by proposing to place further German "advisers" in all Slovak administrative and industrial branches, to assure their cooperation.[20]

In December, 1939, when the Slovak government took steps to implement the constitution by introducing a corporative order,[21] the German minister Bernard protested that "the spiritual foundations of [this] legislation, so discredited from the political point of view, were openly directed against the guiding principles of public life as advocated by the Reich." This "Schuschniggiade," as it was called disapprovingly by the Nazis, and D'určanský's resistance in Jewish affairs, both of which touched on Slovak-German economic arrangements, led the German government to seize control of the Slovak armaments industry. Under the "treaty for the Organization for Total War" (*Wehrwirtschaftsvertrag*) of January 30, 1940, the entire Slovak armaments industry—

---

[20] Ibid., D, VIII, No. 409.

[21] The constitution of July 21, 1939, provided that the population had to be organized in one of six social estates: (1) agriculture, (2) industry, (3) trade and commerce, (4) banking and insurance, (5) professions, and (6) public employees and artists. It was planned to grant the social estates, which were to be responsible for the social, economic, and cultural interests of their members, wide autonomy.

which consisted of twenty-six large enterprises, among which were export branches of former Czech munitions factories in the Váh valley—was placed at the direct disposal and control of the German army, in the same manner as the armaments industry in Germany.[22]

In a countermove, the Tiso regime took measures against the HG, its right-radical wing, which was, because of its ideological affinity with the Nazis, in high favor with the Reich agencies in Slovakia. Šaňo Mach, the leader of the Hlinka Guards, perceived in the anti-German character of this move a possibility of recovering his diminished influence by demonstrating his loyalty toward the Reich. On February 21, 1940, the eve of his departure for a visit in Berlin, he submitted his resignation, undoubtedly hoping that he would be triumphantly returned to power with German backing. Tiso, however, refused to fall into the trap. He declined to accept Mach's resignation. On his return from Berlin, Mach, acting on the advice of German government circles, intensified his agitation against the Jews, freemasons, and "Czechoslovaks" (pro-Czech Slovaks) and for the establishment of an "authoritarian system." He tried also to exploit the rise in the cost of living against D'určanský and his group in demagogic fashion. The conflict reached a climax on May 19 when the HG addressed on ultimatum to the government. Tiso was forced into fast action. On May 21, exploiting the absorption of the Germans in the drama of their campaign in France, he dismissed Mach from all his duties and placed the Guards under the strict control of the party and the police.[23]

The exact motives for Tiso's action are still unknown. Did he expect a long war? Did he count on an early defeat of Hitler? Either way, the spectacular German victory in France ended all such calculations and put the Reich in a position to discipline its obstreperous Slovak protegé.

---

[22] It is one-sided to interpret the mastery of National Socialism over Europe as solely a product of ideology. The outrageous German race-hatred, as exemplified by the destruction of the Jews or the enslaving of the East European peoples, certainly suggests such a conclusion. However, little notice is taken of the fact that even the war of extermination in the East was aimed in the last analysis at securing German economic self-sufficiency by obtaining unhampered access to supplies of grain, oil, and minerals. On closer examination, germanizing tendencies, apparently motivated by racial ideology, proved to be in fact a function or even a correlation of imperialistic economic concepts. The "Treaty for the Organization for Total War" is a good case in point. It was motivated by the needs of the German war economy, and might be characterized better as an example of colonial, rather than racial, policy. Products of Slovak industries, which operated under orders of the German army, were preempted for exclusive and duty-free export to the Reich. Special permission of the German army command was necessary to use such products to satisfy Slovak needs. German officers were assigned to inspect such factories, which they could enter at any time and without restriction, to check the decisions of the management and alter them if they saw fit. See Lipták, *Slovensko*, pp. 191-205.

[23] For the German reaction, see *DGFP*, D, ix, Nos. 309, 336, 407.

The road seemed clear to bring the Slovak political apparatus under the same tight German control as already existed in the Slovak economic system, and, as Bernard noted on June 25, "to make it perfectly plain again, particularly with reference to the countries in Southeastern Europe, that Slovakia is in our *Lebensraum*, that is, that our wishes alone count."[24]

After the fall of France and the British withdrawal from the Continent, the German government expected the early conclusion of peace and began to make plans for the postwar era. It was suggested that the German-Slovak "protective friendship" be given a new form in the framework of the greater European economic sphere that the German government planned for after the war. A meeting of leading German economists concluded that Slovakia should be included in the German customs and monetary union after the war. If this plan had been realized, it would have put an end to the relics of Slovak sovereignty and would have reduced Slovakia to a status similar to that of Bohemia and Moravia. Martin Bormann's suggestion to replace the German minister in Bratislava with a resident general was similar in intent. Such projects, however, presupposed a freedom of action that Germany would have only after a victorious war.[25]

When Hitler found time to attend to the Slovak internal crisis, which did not hold a high priority in his concerns, German hopes for an early peace had already vanished. The British rejection of Hitler's peace proposal of July 16 opened the prospect of a prolonged war. The Soviet occupation and annexation of Bessarabia on June 28 created a threat to German interests in the Balkans. Therefore, Hitler found himself obliged to continue his policy of courting the governments of Southeastern Europe. That may explain why, instead of pronouncing a dictatorial solution of the Slovak crisis, as would have been appropriate in the heady days of June, he contented himself with a compromise at Salzburg, to which he summoned the Slovak politicians on July 28.

At the Salzburg conference the plan for a German-Slovak customs and monetary union was postponed for the time being. The German-Slovak "protective friendship" was continued in its existing form. However, the Germans were not prepared simply to return to the *status quo ante*. Tiso's position remained unchanged. Hitler appeared to respect this jovial, cunning, and stubborn country parson as a guarantor of order and stability in Slovakia. But D'určanský, who had been the most powerful minister in the Slovak government, had lost the Germans' confidence and was dismissed. His post as minister of foreign affairs was given to Tuka, and that of minister of the interior to Mach. The memoranda recording the proceedings of the Salzburg conference do not give a clear indication

[24] Ibid., D, x, No. 17.   [25] Ibid., D, x, No. 143.

of German motivation behind these personnel changes.[26] Presumably, Germany's aim was to polarize power in Slovakia between the conservatives (Tiso and the HSĽS) and the radicals (Tuka, Mach, and the HG), and to provide the latter with a firmer basis from which to gain exclusive power by evolutionary means and recast Slovakia completely in the image of National Socialist Germany. Tuka's proclamation of Slovak National Socialism on July 30,[27] presumably on Hitler's instructions, would indicate that that was in the Führer's mind at the time.

The outlook for the complete Nazification and Germanization of Slovakia, however, proved dim. Because of the lack of cadres and the continued German need of Slovakia as a propaganda showpiece in Southeastern Europe, Hitlerites were appointed only in some parts of the administrative apparatus. However, the army, Church, economy, parliament, and party, which constituted the real basis of power of the Tiso regime, were almost completely exempted from personal changes. Against this phalanx the HG could accomplish little. Despite the upgrading of Tuka and Mach, the prestige of the Guards had suffered as a result of German interference, which annoyed Slovak nationalists. The dual command between the HSĽS and the HG, imposed by the Germans at Salzburg, was based on an incorrect understanding of the real structure of power in Slovakia. It survived only so long as the Germans were willing and able to use their power and influence to offset the essential weakness of the HG.[28]

[26] For the German side of the conference see *DGFP*, D, x, No. 205 (note by Bernard of July 22, 1940, written in preparation for the Salzburg meeting) and No. 248 (record of the talks between Hitler and Tiso on July 28 at the Berghof). Slovak historiography provides only one full but rather polemical account of the event, namely Ľubomír Lipták, "Príprava a priebeh salzburských rokovaní roku 1940 medzi prestaviteľmi Nemecka a slovenského štátu" ["The Preparations and Course of the Salzburg Negotiations between Representatives of Germany and the Slovak State"], *Historický časopis*, XIII (1965), 329-65.

[27] As especially urgent duties to be carried out by the new government, Tuka mentioned a change in the constitution, the complete suppression of Jewish influence in economy and politics, a battle against corruption within the administration, and the improvement of the social status of farmers, workers, and employees.

[28] Yeshayahu Jelinek, in his balanced Ph.D. dissertation, *Hlinka's Slovak People's Party: A Small Totalitarian Party in a Small Totalitarian State* (Indiana University, Bloomington, 1966), has written the best account of the power struggle within the HSĽS to date. For the ideological opposition between Tuka, with his program of Slovak National Socialism, and Tiso's conservative-Catholic-corporative thinking, see Vojtech Tuka, *Slovenský národný socializmus* [*Slovak National Socialism*] (Bratislava, 1941), and *Slovenský štát* [*The Slovak State*] (Bratislava, 1944); Jozef Tiso, *Ideológia slovenskej ľudovej strany* [*Ideology of the Slovak People's Party*] (Bratislava, 1930); Štefan Polakovič, *Tisova náuka* [*Tiso's Teaching*] (Bratislava, 1941); *Z Tisovho boja* [*Out of Tiso's Struggle*] (Bratislava, 1941), and *K základom slovenského štátu* [*About the Foundations of the Slovak State*] (Turčiansky Svätý Martin, 1939). The only modern Slovak

The appointment of Manfred von Killinger, an ill-famed SA leader, as German minister in Bratislava after the Salzburg conference, and the further installation of "advisers" in all important government agencies and institutions of Slovakia, left no doubt that the German government was determined to enforce the dual distribution of power, albeit with evolutionary means. Killinger arrived at Bratislava with instructions to assure the new government of the unlimited support of the Reich. "In doing so," he added, "I shall not shrink from the utmost." His hand was strengthened when, in addition to his diplomatic duties, he formally assumed the role of special "adviser" to Prime Minister Tuka. Karmasin, state-secretary for German affairs, found a receptive ear in Mach for all his suggestions. Under these circumstances, only a façade appeared to be left of the sovereignty of the "protected state."

The new system of control was designed to assure the smooth incorporation of Slovakia into the German war economy and to avoid personal abuses of any kind. "I am determined, and shall carry it through," Killinger wrote to Berlin on October 27, 1940, "to govern Slovakia in such a way that during the war she will be economically 100 percent at our disposal and that she will be led politically in such a way that there cannot be the slightest doubt that she is absolutely keeping the line." It soon appeared, however, that Killinger's policy was based on a miscalculation of the real balance of power in Slovakia, and that Prime Minister Tuka's proclamation of National Socialism as the new Slovak ideology was a severe blunder. Tiso was prepared to collaborate with Germany in the economic and diplomatic spheres, but as a priest and a patriot he was dead set against the nazification and germanization of Slovak life. He mobilized the clergy and the party in defense of the clerical-conservative traditions of the Populist movement. In his struggle he was favored by Mussolini's misadventure in Greece in the fall of 1940, which diverted German attention. Tiso was able not only to reject Tuka's proposals for changes in the government and the Diet on the German model but also to launch a counteroffensive against Tuka by the end of the year and restructure the party in harmony with corporative principles.

After its failure to gain power by peaceful means, the HG determined to carry out a *coup d'état*. It is difficult to decide today whether this plan, which went counter to official German policy, was initiated by the Slovak radicals or by the members of the German legation and advisory corps. The behavior of Killinger and the German advisers, who were mostly fanatical members of the SS, as well as parallel developments in Rumania, would seem to indicate German initiative in the matter. In the fall

---

study, which is still full of polemics and hatred, is the book of Andrej Širácky, *Klerofašistická ideológia ľudáctva* [*The Clerico-fascist Ideology of the Ľudáks*] (Bratislava, 1955).

of 1940 the Hlinka Guards began to be trained on the pattern of the SS as a nucleus of a Nationalist Socialist, and later germanized, Slovakia, and in this way were being prepared to seize power. Examinations of "racial usefulness," disguised as physical fitness tests, were designed to select the racially outstanding and, consequently, it was believed, unconditionally loyal leaders of the Guards. However, in January, 1941, the amateurish plans for a *coup* were prematurely disclosed by army circles, which understandably disapproved of them, and nipped in the bud. As in the summer of 1940, considerations for their grand European strategy obliged the Germans to acquiesce in Tiso's action.

In the winter and spring of 1941, Germany and Soviet Russia engaged in a diplomatic duel for the allegiance of the Balkan states, preliminary to the German invasion of Russia in the summer. In these circumstances, the German government did not favor a violent struggle for power between the Guards and the Tiso regime in Slovakia, any more than an analogous conflict between the Iron Guards and the regime of Gen. Ion Antonescu in Rumania at the same time. In January, 1941, with Hitler's full approval, Antonescu bloodily suppressed the Iron Guards. In Slovakia also the German government sacrificed ideological conformity for the sake of political and economic stability. The transfer of Killinger to Bucharest, which was planned and announced before the disclosure of the HG plot as a routine reassignment, facilitated the shift in German policy. It permitted Germany to abandon the plan for a *coup* without disavowing its inceptor.

The new German minister, Hans Elard Ludin, arrived in Bratislava on January 13, 1941, and assured Tiso that "in the future he would have the sympathies and the confidence of the Führer and the Reich Foreign Minister." Ludin also warned Tuka against aggravating the situation.[29] Mainly for the sake of saving face, Ludin repeated the demand that the reconstruction of Slovakia along National Socialist principles be continued. After only a short stay in Bratislava, however, he recognized that as long as the majority of the Slovak population retained its Catholic conservative convictions, the nazification of Slovakia could be accomplished only by the application of brutal force. Therefore, he replaced Killinger's concept of indoctrination and political pressure with a program of continuous propaganda and education. Essentially, he trusted more to the results of a German military victory than to the attractions

[29] Tuka's speech on January 21, 1941, in Trenčianske Teplice, where he developed his program of a "Guardist Slovakia," gives the impression of a swan song. He asked for a reform of parliament and for the inclusion of the principle of personal responsibility in the constitution; for the legislative power to be entrusted to the government; and, instead of the democratic administration of justice, for new legal maxims to be adopted to take care of the interests of the people as a whole and provide social justice to every single person.

of National Socialism. Until victory, German interests would best be served by a properly functioning Slovak economy. Ludin therefore transformed the corps of German advisers from an instrument of ideological indoctrination into a team of economic experts that sought to increase Slovak war production through the modernization and reorganization of Slovak industry. Gradually, German advisers were withdrawn from such spheres as party organization and the cultural and educational fields, in which their presence particularly irritated Slovak opinion. Ludin's policy had the desired results. In the spring of 1944 his closest associate, Hans Gmelin, noted that Slovakia "was meeting her delivery commitments and her war contributions even more willingly since the Reich abstained from influencing the above mentioned sectors."[30]

Considering the limited economic potential of Slovakia, the backwardness of her means of production, and the lack of skilled personnel, the willingness and capacity of the Tiso regime to contribute to the German war effort proved truly astonishing. An export share of over 70 percent, cartel agreements, and the fixing of quotas guaranteed that the production of goods in all fields could be directed by the needs of the German markets. Only agriculture, the productivity of which was smaller than that of industry, was for some time permitted a wider margin of independence. To allow a sufficient food supply for the Slovak population was in the political interest of the Reich. However, by the end of 1941 the growing German need of food led to the sequestering of 80 percent of the Slovak agricultural surplus for the German market.

The description of Slovak economic development would be incomplete without mentioning the acquisition of controlling interests in all Slovak industries by German capital. With the assistance of two German banks, which had secured the lion's share during the forced concentration of Slovak banking, and aided by the German monopoly of political influence, a process took place that brought some 70 percent of Slovak share capital under direct or indirect control of German owners within a few years. In 1938, before the annexation of Austria, German ownership in Slovak industry was below 10 percent. In 1942, 99.6 percent of the mining and metallurgical industry and 76.5 percent of the chemical industry, to mention only two examples, were held by Germans. In the early war years this process caused no obvious friction, because for political reasons German acquisitions were limited to foreign stocks, mainly of Czech origin. Slovak competitors, who in any event had little capital, were allowed to compensate themselves from confiscated Jewish property.

The complex of Slovak economic expansion can be judged similarly. The largely unused Slovak economic potential was developed with the

[30] The best Slovak expert in this field, Ľubomír Lipták, gave a convincing picture of the tactics and tendencies involved in his *Slovensko*, pp. 175-255.

help of German investments and technical advice to satisfy the growing demand for military supplies, public construction, and the markets opened by private enterprise. German help, however, was neither whole-hearted nor disinterested. There existed an understanding between Germany and Slovakia that the latter's industrial development was "to be accomplished only by agreement with the Reich and by observing the possibility of reciprocal completion." Under this principle the establishment of new enterprises in Slovakia required advance permission from the Reich Ministry for Economy. In practice, it meant that the Germans could stop Slovak industrial expansion whenever it threatened German export interests.

The war stimulated a considerable economic boom in Slovakia. Between 1939 and 1943 the overall Slovak index of production rose some 30 percent and that of armament production about 50 percent. The drawbacks of this development were a distortion in the Slovak economic structure and an excessive dependence on German markets, which promised to cause trouble after the war. The extent of the Slovak contribution to the German war effort may be judged by the German debt to Slovakia, which steadily mounted during the war. As early as the spring of 1941 the German clearing debt to Slovakia reached 120 million Reichsmarks or more than 1.3 billion Slovak crowns (*koruny*, Ks). The cost of Slovak deliveries to the German army alone rose from 189 million Ks in 1942 (a rather low figure, because the demands of the Slovak army on the Eastern front likewise had to be met) to over 738 million Ks in 1942 and to 2.2 billion Ks in 1944.[31]

This sum, however, represented only a small fraction of the Slovak contribution to the German war effort. Other factors that helped to raise the German debt to Slovakia were the payments made by the Slovak government to the families of some 120,000 Slovak workers who were sent, not always voluntarily, to work in German war industries; to support

[31] The most important contributions on the Slovak economy during the war were written by Ľubomír Lipták, *Ovládnutie slovenského priemyslu nemeckým kapitálom, 1939-1945* [*Seizure of Control of Slovak Industry by German Capital, 1939-1945*] (Bratislava, 1960), and "Podrobenie slovenského priemyslu nemeckým kapitálom v čase fašistického pánstva" ["Control of Slovak Industry by German Capital during Fascist Rule"], *Historický časopis*, III (1955), 3-23. See also Radoslav Selucký, *Ekonomické vyrovnání Slovenska s českými kraji* [*Economic Leveling between Slovakia and the Czech Provinces*] (Prague, 1960), and Pavel Turčan, *Socialistická industrializácia Slovenska* [*Socialist Industrialization of Slovakia*] (Bratislava, 1960). Little has been published in Western languages. The outdated book by Adolf Bernhardt, *Die Wirtschaft der Slowakei* (Prague, 1941), contains useful statistical material. Of some value are Harriet Wanklyn's *Czechoslovakia* (London, 1954), and the article of Kurt Wessely, "Wirtschaftliche und soziale Probleme der Slowakei seit dem Ersten Weltkriege," in *Die Slowakei als mitteleuropäisches Problem in Geschichte und Gegenwart* (Munich, 1965), pp. 199-237.

children evacuated from the bombed German cities to Slovakia (*Kinderlandverschickung*); to provide maintenance allowances to the families of German minority members serving in the SS; and to found, improve, or move armament works to the strategically secure Váh valley. The German-Slovak balance of payments had risen to 6.5 billion Ks in Slovakia's favor by the time of the Slovak National Uprising in 1944, and to 8 billion Ks by the time of the German capitulation in 1945. The last sum was more than twice the amount of the average Slovak annual budget.[32]

The priority of economic contributions did not protect Slovakia or other countries of Southeastern Europe from having to make a military contribution after the German invasion of Russia. Slovak participation in the fighting on the Eastern Front was limited to two divisions, comprising altogether 50,689 men. The relative moderation shown by Germany in exacting a military contribution was due primarily to the German fear, which was not unfounded, that Slovak soldiers were not politically reliable,[33] and secondly to the lack of materiel with which to equip the satellite armies. Diplomatically, Slovakia committed herself to fight on the side of the Axis powers by adhering to the German-Italian-Japanese Tripartite Pact on November 24, 1940, and the Anti-Comintern Pact on November 25, 1941. Slovak participation in the Axis war reached a ridiculous point on December 12, 1941, when Tuka declared war on the United States and Britain. More meaningful than such paper declarations of war were Slovak plans to reestablish, together with Rumania and Croatia, the Little Entente against possible aggression by their "ally," Hungary. Berlin, however, firmly vetoed these plans as well as continuous Slovak importuning to allow a revision of the Slovak-Hungarian boundary in Slovakia's favor.[34]

[32] With the exception of Denmark, the economy of which does not offer a good parallel to that of Slovakia because of the higher level of Danish economic development, no other country under German domination contributed as much per capita to the German war effort as Slovakia. The Reich Ministry for Economy defeated suggestions of radical economist and SS circles to solve the mounting balance-of-payments difficulties with Slovakia through the introduction of a customs and monetary union, by pointing out that the Reich was in a position to break any fiscally motivated resistance of the Slovaks by threatening politically dire consequences.

[33] After the early success of Soviet psychological warfare, which brought about the desertion of complete Slovak units with their officers at the Caucasus front, the Slovak army was reorganized. Only 16,303 Slovak soldiers participated in the later stages of the war against the U.S.S.R. Some 10,000 Slovaks in a technical division were put into action on the Italian front.

[34] The Hungarian treatment of the Slovaks in the districts of southern Slovakia lost to Hungary under the Vienna Award of November 2, 1938, as well as unconcealed Hungarian hopes to annex the remainder of Slovakia, created a rising antagonism between the Slovak and Hungarian governments. See Ľubomír Lipták, "Maď'arsko v politike slovenského štátu v rokoch 1939-1943" ["Hungary in the

The relative readiness of Germany to allow the Slovaks a free hand in their domestic affairs, especially before the Salzburg conference, came to an end when it touched on the central aim of Hitler's absurd ideas: the Jewish question. Of the 130,000 Jews in Slovakia, according to the census of 1930—constituting 4.11 percent of the population; many in the professions, business, and industry—less than a third survived the German "special treatment" (*Sonderbehandlung*).

Anti-Semitism had a long tradition in Slovakia. The HSĽS subscribed to it from its beginning. As early as October 12, 1938, D'určanský had tried to gain German support for his separatist program by promising to introduce anti-Semitic legislation analogous to the Nuremberg laws in independent Slovakia. After the establishment of the Slovak state, Tiso agreed only to measures designed to oust the Jews from business, industry, and the administration.[35] Gradually, however, Slovakia adopted laws and decrees under which the Jewish population lost its constitutional rights and its economic basis. Yet the speed with which Bratislava acted against the Jews did not satisfy the Germans. The original Slovak criterion for determining who was a Jew was religious belief, not race (i.e. a converted Jew was treated as an Aryan). This violated the sacrosanct dogma of blood in Nazi ideology. Berlin was even more annoyed by the fact that the Slovak government, out of fear that the Germans would take the place of the Jews, did not sufficiently press the "Aryanization" of Jewish property.[36]

After the Salzburg conference a change took place in Slovak policy toward the Jews, partly because of the enhanced powers of Tuka and Mach, who wholeheartedly embraced the Nazi racist views, but also because of Tiso's misguided Slovak chauvinism and the general Slovak

---

Politics of the Slovak State in 1938-1943"], *Historický časopis*, xv (1967), pp. 1-35; and Martin Vietor, *Dejiny okupácie južného Slovenska, 1938-1945* [*History of the Occupation of Southern Slovakia, 1938-1945*] (Bratislava, 1968), which is a detailed account, based on all available source material.

[35] In 1942, after such outspoken anti-Semites as Ctibor Pokorný, *Židovstvo na Slovensku* [*The Jewry in Slovakia*] (Turčiansky Svätý Martin, 1940), and Augustín Morávek, *Príručka pre dôverníkov, dočasných správcov a arizátorov* [*Handbook for Trustees, Temporary Managers, and Aryanizers*] (Bratislava, 1940), among others, broke the ground, the notorious Anton Vašek, who was head of the XIV department in Slovak Ministry of Interior, proposed in his book *Die Lösung der Judenfrage in der Slowakei* the total liquidation of the Slovak Jews. In 1939 Tiso argued that the Jews, who amounted to 4 percent of the Slovak population, controlled 38 percent of the Slovak economy while the rest of the population controlled only 62 percent. Yet in July, when the government tried to reduce the Jews to 4 percent in all professions, the medical services, for instance, threatened to break down. Therefore, the Jews in essential professions, such as doctors, veterinarians, pharmacists, and engineers, were protected by presidential exemptions after September 1941. Most of these Jews in Slovakia survived the war, many with the active help of the Slovak population.

[36] *DGFP*, D, x, No. 205.

greed for Jewish property. In August, 1940, the Slovak government agreed with unseemly haste to the German demand for a "resettlement program" for the Slovak Jews in Poland. This handed Hitler an excellent propaganda argument. He could now trumpet that Slovakia, led by a Catholic priest, was the first European state that had agreed to the deportation of its Jewish population. On September 10, 1941, Tuka and Mach pushed through the Diet the approval of a Jewish code, in 270 paragraphs in true German fashion, which provided the legal foundation for the property expropriation, outlawing, internment, and, finally, extermination of 56,000 Jews between March and August of 1942 alone. Under the methodical guidance of high-ranking SS officer Dieter Wisliczeny, German "Adviser in Jewish Affairs" to the Slovak government and formerly a close aide to Adolf Eichmann, the 14th department of the Slovak Ministry of Interior prepared, with Tiso's full approval, the details of the deportation. The removal of the Jews offered a last field of action to the Guards, who were otherwise without a function, in which they were able to vent their fury over their loss of power on helpless people. The Slovak government even paid the German authorities a bounty of 500 Reichsmarks for every "resettled" Jew.

The deportations were halted only when the Vatican repeatedly protested against them and pointed out that the question was not of "resettlement" but of *extermination* of the Jews in Auschwitz, Majdanek, and Lublin. For two years Tiso steadfastly resisted the pressures of Tuka, Mach, and the Germans to resume the deportations. On May 15, 1944, when the fortunes of war were already inclining toward the Allies, the Diet passed a law to stop the transports and to confine the remaining Jews in relatively "humane" Slovak concentration camps. Unfortunately, in September, 1944, when the German army occupied all of Slovakia to suppress the Slovak National Uprising, the SS seized many Jews, most of whom did not survive the German "special treatment."[37]

[37] So far, no extensive monograph on the fate of the Slovak Jews, based on archival material, has been produced, though Prof. Ladislav Lipscher has nearly completed a manuscript on the topic. Much material, mainly testimonies, reports of experiences, and diaries, was used in the book of Andrew Rothstein, *The Fate of Slovak Jewry* (Tel-Aviv, 1961), in Hebrew. Important documents have been collected in the Wiener Library in London. No longer up to date are chapters dealing with Slovakia in the books of Gerald Reitlinger, *The Final Solution: The Attempts to Exterminate the Jews of Europe, 1939-1945* (London, 1953), of Raul Hilberg, *The Destruction of the European Jews* (New York, 1961), and of Hannah Arendt, *Eichmann in Jerusalem: Ein Bericht von der Banalität des Bösen* (Munich, 1964), also available in English. See also the short alibistic article of Milan St. D'urica, "Dr. Joseph Tiso and the Jewish Problem in Slovakia," in *Slovakia* (September-December, 1957), pp. 1-22, and the section on anti-Semitism in Lettrich, *History of Modern Slovakia*, pp. 174-91, both of which are rather biased. The books of Friedrich Steiner, *The Tragedy of Slovak Jewry* (Bratislava, 1949), and of Louis Mandel, *The Tragedy of Slovak Jewry* (New York, n.d.),

After Salzburg, with the exception of collaboration in the Jewish question, hardly any point of contact existed between the conservatives and radicals. The dualism of the regime became a source of constant friction and crisis, during which the overthrow of Tuka and Mach was prevented only by repeated German intervention. Unable to defeat his rivals by a frontal attack, Tiso adopted a policy of gradual erosion of their power. On October 23, 1942, in imitation of the German model, he had himself proclaimed by the Diet the "leader" (*Vôdca*) of the state and the party —a combination of functions that enabled him gradually to bring the administration under party control. The rights of intervention in all affairs of state and of appointment of personnel completed the armory of his weapons. Under Tuka, the executive branch of government increasingly lost its independence. On January 12, 1943, Tuka was obliged to resign from the vice-presidency of the HSĽS, which marked a victory for Tiso. Tiso's attempt to deprive Mach of effective powers, however, by transferring the constabulary and the police force from the jurisdiction of the Ministry of Interior to that of the army command, was frustrated by German intervention.

The Guards, upon whom Tiso looked with undisguised mistrust since their abortive attempt at a coup, fared worse. Their leaders were deprived of their positions or transferred, and their functions abolished. By the winter of 1943-44 the Guards had been brought under strict control of the party, in whose shadow they barely managed to survive. During the hunt against the Guards, the party, army, and parliament coalesced into a new "syndicate of power," which stood aloof from the legal executive under Tuka and the German "advisers." All attempts by the German ethnic group, which itself became an influential and privileged "state within a state,"[38] and of the SS agencies to check this development proved of no avail.

---

include heartbreaking pictures but not sufficient factual information. It is interesting that in communist Slovakia the subject of Jewish persecution appears to be tabu. Only one rather poor Ph.D. dissertation on it has been written so far: Jozef Dzugas, Ľudácke riešenie "Židovskej otázky" za tzv. Slovenského štátu [*The Ľudák Solution of the "Jewish Question" under the so-called Slovak State*] (Bratislava, 1965), unpublished. Its author was not permitted to make unlimited use of the vast material available in the Slovenská archívna správa (Slovak Archives administration) in Bratislava. Ľudovít Holotík, "The Jewish Problem in Slovakia," *East European Quarterly*, I (1967), pp. 31-37, is a concise summary of the problem by a leading Slovak Marxist historian. One major aspect of the question is dealt with by Ivan Kamenec, "Snem Slovenskej republiky a jeho postoj k problému židovského obyvateľstva na Slovensku v rokoch 1939-1945" ["The Diet of the Slovak Republic and its Attitude toward the Problem of Jewish Population in Slovakia in 1939-1945"], *Historický časopis*, XVII (1969), pp. 329-60.

[38] Apart from some polemical passages and omissions, the most authentic interpretation of the policy of the leadership of the German ethnic group in Slovakia to this day has been written by Ľubomír Lipták, "The Role of the Ger-

So long as the military success of the German army seemed to guarantee victory, the German authority in the "protected state" was not challenged. After the German defeat at Stalingrad and especially after the Allied landing in Sicily, Slovakia was swept by a mood of *sauve qui peut*. By the fall of 1943, drinking bouts on the occasion of Italy's defection from the Axis, dubious speeches by Tiso, and mass desertions of Slovak troops on the Eastern front alerted Berlin to the dangers of the situation and caused it to reconsider its old plans for a German-Slovak customs and monetary union, and, in the spring of 1944 when the German army occupied Hungary, to consider the occupation of Slovakia as well. These projects were put off for the moment on the advice of the unsuspecting Ludin, and also because the advance of the Red Army, the slowdown of the Allied drive in Italy, and the German occupation of Hungary appeared to sober the Tiso government and incline it to closer collaboration with Berlin.

The Germans and the Tiso government—and, for that matter, the majority of the Slovak population—were unaware of the revival of activity on the part of the prohibited former "Czechoslovak" parties, whose leaders were in secret touch with the Czechoslovak government in exile in London. The Slovak communists pursued a "separatist" Slovak course for some time, but later they submitted to the "centralist" leadership of Klement Gottwald in Moscow. At Christmas, 1943, the leaders of the democratic and communist clandestine political organizations reached an agreement to form an underground Slovak national council to launch a struggle for "the removal of the Nazi German dictatorship" and the restoration of a democratic Czechoslovak republic in which the Slovaks and the Czechs would be equal partners and all fascist and totalitarian movements would be rigorously suppressed.

Several high-ranking officers of the Slovak army, who were involved in this activity, began to plot an insurrection of the army against the Tiso regime. They hoped to secure the approval and support of the Western Allies as well as the Soviet Union through the emigrés in London and Moscow. Independently, Minister of Defense Gen. Ferdinand Čatloš also contemplated defecting with the army, at an appropriate time, from the camp of the defeated Germans to that of the victorious Allies.

The plans for the Slovak National Uprising were poorly coordinated. The army plotters managed, probably with Čatloš's tacit approval, inconspicuously to concentrate army units and supplies in the highlands of central Slovakia. The two best-equipped Slovak divisions were deployed in eastern Slovakia with a view to opening a corridor at an appropriate time for the Soviet advance into and occupation of Slovakia. The prepa-

man Minority in Slovakia in the Years of the Second World War," *Historica Slovacca*, I (1964), pp. 150-84.

rations for the uprising were complicated by the outbreak of partisan warfare, led in part by Soviet soldiers, which threatened to bring on the German occupation of Slovakia before the uprising was ready. The mission sent by the plotters to Moscow on August 4, 1944, failed to secure a binding pledge of Soviet support. Nor did the exiles in London secure a promise of support from the Western Allies, who tacitly recognized Slovakia to be in the Red Army's sphere of operations and were reluctant to arouse the suspicions of Moscow by a commitment to the Slovaks.

The defection of Rumania to the Soviet side on August 23 caused nervousness in Bratislava and ferment in the country. The inopportune capture and execution of the German military mission under General Paul von Otto on its return from Rumania on August 26 by Slovak partisans and fear of imminent German occupation forced the Slovak National Council prematurely to proclaim the Slovak National Insurrection at Banská Bystrica on August 29.[39] Apart from one Czechoslovak brigade under Col. Vladimír Přikryl flown in belatedly from Russia and some supplies and medicines flown in from Italy, no Allied help arrived. On the other hand, German counteraction proved swift and effective. In the very first days of the insurrection the Germans surrounded and disarmed the two Slovak divisions in the east and secured the strategic Váh valley in the west. Bitter fighting continued in central Slovakia for two months, but on October 27 Banská Bystrica fell to the Germans. The national uprising collapsed. However, remnants of the insurrectionists retreated into the mountains. There they continued guerrilla warfare until the occupation of Slovakia by Soviet armies, one under General Petrov coming across the Carpathian Mountains in the north and another under Marshal Malinovsky coming from the Hungarian plain in the south, in the spring of 1945.

The new Slovak government under Štefan Tiso, appointed on September 5, 1944, was a mere puppet of, and executioner for, the German occupation force. The distrust of the disillusioned Germans and the relentless advance of the Soviet army prevented it from developing any political initiative. The decision on the future of the Slovak state and the loss of independence was made by the Slovak National Council and the exiled government. The Slovak National Council was based on the uneasy collaboration of, on one hand, the communists supported by the Social Democrats and, on the other, a new political combination of bourgeois-democratic opponents of the HSĽS, the Slovak Democrats. Although the two groups were distrustful of each other and divided on the political and social organization of postwar Czechoslovakia, they agreed that Slovakia should have a large measure of cultural and political auton-

[39] For a discussion of the Slovak National Uprising see Anna Josko's chapter herein, "The Slovak Resistance Movement."

omy in the new state. Confronted with their solidarity on this matter, President Beneš yielded to their demands in negotiations in London, in Moscow, and finally in Košice. The "Košice program" of April 5, 1945, postulated the existence of a distinct Slovak people and envisioned a large degree of administrative autonomy for Slovakia.

On April 4, one day before the adoption of the Košice program, Bratislava fell to the Red Army. Tiso and his government retreated under the protection of the German army to Kremsmünster in Upper Austria. Here, on May 8, 1945, Tiso signed a formal document of capitulation to the Allies, represented by Gen. W. A. Collier of the United States army. The experiment of Slovak independent statehood failed after six years in the wake of Hitler's defeat.

In looking for reasons why Hitler's conception of a "protective friendship" and the HSĽS program of "Slovak independence" failed, one may find them in, on the one hand, the divergence of the German military-economic interests and political motives, and, on the other, in the friction between the conservative and radical wings of the HSĽS which paralyzed all efforts to consolidate the Slovak state. The experiment was doomed to failure also because the larger part of the Slovak intelligentsia and the bulk of the Slovak nation believed that their social interests and political rights would be better safeguarded in a reestablished Czechoslovak state than in the Slovak state, which had been a wartime chimera and promised only continued enslavement in the future.

· 10 ·

THE PROTECTORATE OF BOHEMIA AND MORAVIA*
1939-1945

Gotthold Rhode
Johannes Gutenberg University at Mainz

When German troops invaded the territory of the Second Czechoslovak Republic on March 15, 1939, and its president, Emil Hácha, was compelled to announce that he had placed the destiny of the Czech people "trustfully into the hands of the Führer," the Czechoslovak state lost its independence and sovereignty. In the days that followed, Ruthenia was forcibly annexed to Hungary, Slovakia was reorganized into an independent state with limited sovereignty, and the remnants of Bohemia and Moravia, which had constituted the heartland of the fallen republic, entered upon an unparalleled destiny.[1]

* A slightly different version of this article has been published in Eugen Lemberg and Gotthold Rhode, eds., *Das deutsch-tschechische Verhältnis seit 1918* (Stuttgart: W. Kohlhammer, 1969). It should be noted also that the article was written before the books of Vojtech Mastny, *The Czechs under Nazi Rule, 1939-1942* (New York, 1971), and of Detlef Brandes, *Die Tschechen unter deutschem Protektorat*, vol. I: *1939-1942* (Munich, 1969), were published, and that, consequently, the author was not able to draw on them.

[1] The literature available to date on the overall development of the Protectorate of Bohemia and Moravia is unsatisfactory. There exist two books apparently dealing with the entire territory: Eugene V. Erdely, *Germany's First European Protectorate: the Fate of the Czechs and Slovaks* (London, 1941), and Sheila Grant Duff, *A German Protectorate: the Czechs under Nazi Rule* (London, 1942). Both books naturally deal only with the first two or three years of the Protectorate and are based on the limited material then available. In the case of Duff, the sources are rounded out with information provided her by exiled Czech politicians in London. The books of Václav Král, *Otázky hospodářského a sociálního vývoje v českých zemích v letech 1938-1945* [*Questions of Economic and Social Development of the Czech Provinces in 1938-1945*] (3 vols.; Prague, 1957-1959), and *Pravda o okupaci* [*The Truth about the Occupation*] (Prague, 1961), deal mainly with the economic involvement of the Protectorate with the Reich or are aimed at discrediting the non-communist resistance forces. Other accounts concentrate wholly on the Czech resistance, the assassination of Heydrich, and the destruction of Lidice, while making no effort at an overall appraisal. The essay of the present writer ("Das Protektorat Boehmen und Maehren," in *Aus Politik und Zeitgeschichte*, 11 [1964], 3-15) is only a brief initial study. In the short account by Joerg K. Hoensch (*Geschichte der tschechoslowakischen Republik, 1918-1965* [Stuttgart, 1966]), the author deals with the Protectorate only on pp. 108-14.

The number of source publications is not large either. Important legal source material is contained in the bulletins of the Reich Protector in Bohemia and Moravia (*Věstník nařízení*) and the collection of laws and regulations (*Sbírka*

Bohemia and Moravia were not placed under a German military and civilian administration and treated as objects of exploitation in the same manner as the East European countries conquered in World War II. Unlike the occupied countries of western and northern Europe, they were not regarded as a national entity that would regain its sovereignty after the war, either. Their special status of "protectorate" had elements of both systems. While their territorial integrity was to be preserved, they were to be completely subordinate to the political, economic, and military interests of the Third Reich. A minimum of German personnel was to be tied up in their supervision and control, and a maximum of Czech manpower was to be exploited for the German war effort.

Hitler's long-range goal was undoubtedly to germanize all of Bohemia and Moravia, and to incorporate them directly into the Reich, after expulsion or extermination of those parts of the Czech population that were not suitable for germanization.[2] This long-range objective, of course, could have been achieved only after a completely victorious war. When Germany suffered massive defeats in the winter of 1942-43, the plan was gradually relegated to the remote future, although State Secretary Karl Hermann Frank referred to it several times in later speeches.

If Hitler's actual policy in the Protectorate, notwithstanding its harshness and cruelty in some ways, was generally more restrained compared with his policy in Poland and the Soviet Union, it was surely less a matter of more sober judgment or greater sympathy for the Czechs than a result of very pragmatic considerations. During the few months remaining between March 15, 1939, and the beginning of the war, the German gov-

---

zákonů a nařízení). However, these collections can tell us nothing about the execution of the laws.

From the archives of the Reich protector and other German authorities, Václav Král has published a small selection in Die Vergangenheit warnt. Dokumente über die Germanisierungs -und Austilgungspolitik der Naziokkupanten in der Tschechoslowakei (Prague, 1960). Of the memoirs, Edvard Beneš's From Munich to New War and Victory (London, 1954), deals mostly with the writer's activities in exile, and the very valuable recollections of Ladislav K. Feierabend, Ve vládě Protektorátu [In the Government of the Protectorate] (New York, 1962), naturally reach only to his flight abroad in January, 1940. The diary-like notes of the German official Wilhelm Dennler, Die boehmische Passion (Freiburg, 1953), are sporadic and not accurate, and give the impression in some parts of having been written at a later date.

[2] Plans of this kind were made especially in the summer of 1940, after the fall of France and during the preparations to invade Britain, when the Third Reich seemed to stand at the apex of its powers. See the memorandum of State Secretary K. H. Frank of August 28, 1940, in Král, Die Vergangenheit warnt, pp. 59-72, and the notes of the Wehrmacht plenipotentiary General Friderici of October 15, 1940, ibid., pp. 95-96. Even more harsh was the first speech of R. Heydrich after assuming office on October 2, 1941 (ibid., pp. 121-32). The reaction among the German civil servants is reported by Dennler (Die boehmische Passion, pp. 61-63), but erroneously placed in November.

ernment found it useful to be able to point out to its neighbors that there was a certain degree of self-administration and prosperity in the Protectorate and that National Socialist rule was not as bad as they had feared.

After the war began, however, it was useful for Germany to possess in Bohemia and Moravia an area of agricultural supply and industrial production, whose people could be made to work as much as possible and cowed into obedience, without, however, being driven by brutal terror to extreme resistance, sabotage, and strikes. Despite much inconsistency by the German authorities in individual cases, Hitler's intention was to exploit the material and human resources of the country to the greatest degree, without driving the Czech people to acts of desperation and provoking guerrilla warfare in the rear of the German army.[3] Nevertheless, even at a time of relative restraint, Hitler said that "by firmly leading the Protectorate, it ought to be possible to push the Czech language in about twenty years back to the importance of a dialect."[4]

In view of the overwhelmingly superior German forces and the lack of hope for quick help from the outside, the only chance for the Czech people in the Protectorate lay in refraining from an unequal struggle that would have cost rivers of blood, to preserve or even strengthen their material position, and collaborating just enough to give the Germans no cause for harsh repression and compulsory measures, while providing the lowest possible degree of effective aid to the German war machine.

As long as the war lasted, neither side had reason to want an open conflict; relative quiet served the interests of both. While the German administration was interested in exploiting the working capacity of the Czech population to the utmost, and for this reason in keeping it relatively content materially, it wanted to lull or kill off its political and intellectual life as completely as possible. The Czech leaders, for their part, saw that their interest lay in keeping the political awareness of their people as alert as possible, holding collaboration to a minimum, "throwing sand into the cogwheels," and resisting all efforts and inducements at germanization.

If we consider these aspects, the political attitudes of both sides and the relative tranquility that prevailed during the six years of the Protec-

---

[3] During his "table conversations" on May 16 and 20 and July 4, 1942, Hitler discussed the treatment of the Czechs. He emphasized that the threat of deportation (expulsion) of the Czech population was a useful means of exerting pressure on the Protectorate government. At the same time he declared that the Czech population must not be permitted to take part in the war, because it could then raise demands, but that it should be induced to work hard with "double rations" and "good treatment." Gerhard Ritter, ed., *Hitlers Tischgespräche im Führerhauptquartier, 1941/1942* (Bonn, 1951), pp. 85, 91, 176-77, 288; (second edition; Stuttgart, 1963), pp. 349, 359, 363, 434-35.

[4] Ritter, *Hitlers Tischgespräche*, p. 91 (May 20, 1942; second edition), p. 363.

torate (compared with conditions in other occupied countries, such as Poland, Yugoslavia, or Greece) become easier to understand. This also explains the motives of most members of the Protectorate government and of numerous Czech civil servants, who remained at their posts not out of opportunism or selfishness but to serve the national cause and then, perforce, slipped into collaboration. The great majority of them believed that they could serve the future of the Czech nation best by remaining in their places. However, they often found themselves facing the painful dilemma of deciding at what point collaboration with the Germans ceased to serve the national cause and became treasonable. Like other peoples under German occupation, they never found a satisfactory solution to the dilemma.

The following periods may be discerned in the development of Czech-German relations during the Protectorate's history:

1. From March to November 17, 1939: a period during which both sides made efforts to accommodate themselves to the new situation.

2. From November 17, 1939, until the appointment of Reinhard Heydrich in September, 1941: a period of harsh German measures against the Czech intelligentsia but of relative quiet under the moderating influences of Baron Konstantin von Neurath.

3. From September, 1941, to May, 1942: a period of unrestrained rule by Reinhard Heydrich and of increasing terror against the entire Czech leadership, with simultaneous German efforts to divide the Czech people by the carrot-and-stick method.

4. From June, 1942, to May, 1945: a period first of terror and then of efforts to perpetuate the existing situation, while the war fronts increasingly hardened.

SPRING AND SUMMER 1939

The theoretical basis of the relationship between the Reich and the Protectorate was established in the "Decree of the Führer about the Protectorate of Bohemia and Moravia,"[5] which was published on March 16, 1939. The decree made the remnants of the provinces of Bohemia and Moravia part of Reich territory without giving them legal parity with the *Länder* and *Gaue* of the Reich. All the important attributes of sovereignty—foreign affairs, military authority and defense, customs and monetary affairs—went to the Reich, which also assumed control of the mails and telecommunication (Arts. 6-9). Although the new Protectorate was to have autonomy and self-administration (Art. 3), its president and

[5] *Reichsgesetzblatt 1939*, Part 1, No. 47, pp. 485-88. *Verordnungsblatt des Reichsprotektors*, No. 2, 1939. *Sbírka zákonů a nařízení 1939*, No. 28. English translation in Duff, *Protectorate*, n. 1, pp. 53-57.

government were left with little power. The "Reich Protector," an office to which the former German foreign minister, Baron von Neurath,[6] was appointed on March 18, 1939, could countermand "in the interest of the Reich" any measures of the government of the Protectorate (Art. 5). The Reich could issue regulations valid for the Protectorate (Art. 11). In this way it could abrogate in practice the laws of the Czechoslovak Republic that were still valid in the Protectorate (Art. 12). The Reich protector could in effect appoint and dismiss the members of the government (Arts. 5, 3). Although the president of the Protectorate was to enjoy the prerogatives of a head of state, he needed to retain the confidence of the Reich chancellor (Art. 4). Hitler could, if he so chose, dismiss and replace him with someone else. In actual fact, he never considered the step. The Protectorate was to be represented in Berlin by an envoy to the Reich government (Art. 6), but it was deprived of all other foreign representation.

The provisions of the decree of March 16, 1939, restricted the formally maintained Czech national independence from the beginning, and the subsequent German rule in its practical application restricted Czech autonomy even further. Under Article 2 of the decree the inhabitants of the Protectorate were divided into Germans and non-Germans. Only the first could become citizens of the Reich, while the others, as citizens of the Protectorate, held a lower legal status. This status entailed one advantage for the Czechs during the war: they could not be drafted for service in the German army. In the summer of 1939 a small corps of Protectorate "government troops" (280 officers and 7,000 men) was formed. It was meant only to "preserve internal security and order" (Arts. 7, 2) and never saw combat service.

There was symbolic significance for the future of the Protectorate in the fact that Hitler, after reaching Prague on the evening of March 15, spent the night in the castle of Prague, and that he received President Hácha there, after Reich Foreign Minister Joachim von Ribbentrop had given the latter the decree on the establishment of the Protectorate. This was an unmistakable assertion of who was really master in the house. On the other hand, this gesture by Hitler produced not only the intended mood of Czech resignation but also gave rise to a strong feeling of aversion and will to resist. The Reich Protector took up residence in the Czernin Palace, near the Hradčany castle, until then and again after 1945 the office of the Czechoslovak foreign minister.

[6] Baron von Neurath was born on February 2, 1873. He was Reich Foreign Minister from June 2 to November 17, 1932, and from January 30, 1933, to February 5, 1938. On September 27, 1941, he was relieved of his office "for reasons of health" and did not return. On August 25, 1943, he was definitely dismissed. He was condemned to 15 years at the Nuremberg Trials, released ahead of time in 1954, and died on August 14, 1956.

On March 21, before the Reich Protector took office, General von Blaskowitz, the German commander-in-chief, acting in Hitler's name, ordered that the official languages in the Protectorate should be German and Czech. On March 18 the Reich government set the ratio for the exchange of Reichsmarks and Czech crowns at 1:10, although a ratio of about 1:5 would have reflected more accurately their respective purchasing power.[7] Another step of German financial exploitation that was taken soon afterward was to have six million pounds sterling, held in the Bank of International Settlements at Basle by the Czechoslovak National Bank, transferred to the account of the Reichsbank.[8] The Swiss bank raised no objection to the transfer.

In the spring and summer months of 1939 a threefold process took place in the life of the Protectorate:

1. German rule was officially established by the German Wehrmacht, the Reich Protector, and the authorities subordinate to him, who initially stressed the principle of Czech-German cooperation.

2. The public life of the Czech population and of the Czech administration was reorganized.

3. The Gestapo and its subsidiary organizations were built up. Without regard for the official line of German policy, the Gestapo undertook large-scale arrests, turning first mainly against German political emigrés and the Jews but later increasingly against Czech politicians.

The occupation of Bohemia and Moravia by the German forces took place without friction. Neither the Czech army units, any of the national organizations, nor the formerly strong Communist party, which had been officially dissolved in the fall of 1938, offered any real resistance. A rich booty, consisting of armament and equipment for twenty infantry divisions, nearly 1,600 aircraft, and 2,175 artillery pieces, fell into the hands of the Wehrmacht, which proceeded to stage a show of strength with a parade in Prague's Venceslas Square on March 19. As a conciliatory gesture, General von Blaskowitz placed a wreath on the Tomb of the Unknown Soldier in Prague on March 26. To the indignation of many Czech patriots, he was accompanied to this ceremony by Gen. Jan Syrový, who still held the post of minister of defense. After a period of military government headed by Generals von Blaskowitz (Bohemia) and List (Moravia), the Reich Protector took over on April 16.

The former deputy leader of the Sudeten German party, Karl Hermann Frank, became secretary of state under the Reich Protector. Speaking Czech and having a good knowledge of Czech politics, Frank soon wielded far more power than the personally retiring Württemberg baron, von Neurath. A German civil servant, Kurt von Burgsdorff, became undersecretary of state.

[7] Ladislav K. Feierabend, *Ve vládě*, p. 14.   [8] Ibid., p. 24.

301

In the office of the Reich Protector, departments corresponding to the Czech ministries were established. Endowed with the requisite authority under the Führer's decree, they often encroached on the decisions of their Czech counterparts. Locally, only small German control offices were set up. They were headed by district governors (*Kreishauptleute*), each of whom was responsible for from three to five Czech districts. In the summer of 1939 they were replaced by nineteen regional governors (*Oberlandräte*), who were first to see to the affairs of the Reich citizens in the Protectorate and next to supervise the Czech district authorities in matters of passports and communications, but who soon extended their functions to yet other fields. The region governed by an *Oberlandrat* also corresponded to from three to five Czech districts.[9]

In the political development of the Protectorate there arose a possibility that the leader of the Czech fascists, Gen. Rudolf (Radola) Gajda, who had commanded the Czechoslovak Legion in Siberia at the end of World War I and then served as chief of the Czechoslovak general staff until 1926, would offer his services as head of government, and that his small following, aided by the occupation authorities, would dominate the life of the Czech nation. To forestall this, and to take the wind out of the sails of a Czech National Committee (Český Národní Výbor) formed by Gajda, President Hácha dissolved the parliament on March 21 and prohibited the activity of all political parties. They announced their dissolution in early April. Their place was taken by a collective movement, the Národní Souručenství (National Assemblage). It was headed by a fifty-member committee, the Národní Výbor (National Committee), whose members were appointed by Hácha from all parties, including the fascists but excluding the communists. Hácha was the nominal leader of the National Assemblage. Its actual leadership was assumed by Adolf Hrubý, a member of the former Agrarian party, and Šimon Drgač became its secretary general. This collective party, the first proclamation of which denounced the Freemasons and the Jews, soon enjoyed great growth. By May 3, 1939, it had more than two million members, or 98 percent of all adults qualified to join.[10]

The local leadership of the Assemblage was formed according to the "Führer principle," i.e. not by election from among the membership but by appointment by the higher leaders. Despite its authoritarian trappings, it presented quite a number of former party politicians with a field of action. Although the agrarians were by far the most numerous, former

[9] Alfred Bohmann, "Die Stellung der Oberlandräte-Inspekteure; zur deutschen Verwaltungsreform im ehemaligen Protektorat Böhmen und Mähren," *Zeitschrift für Ostforschung*, 15 (1966), 118-27.

[10] Membership in the National Assemblage was restricted to the male population. The wags soon compared it to a cemetery: "Everybody ends up in it."

members of the Social Democratic party, the Catholic People's party, and the bourgeois National Union were represented in the assemblage, while the fascists of Gajda played a relatively minor role.[11]

The program of the Národní Souručenství was a melange of anti-Semitism, national solidarity, and an "organic" national structure, poorly defined and stated in generalities, so that it resulted in a multiform and quite inconsistent conglomerate. The Assemblage received very little support from the Germans, since a Czech sister party associated with the German National Socialist party would have placed the German claim to leadership in Bohemia and Moravia in doubt and made the subordination of the Protectorate's own interests to those of the Reich more difficult.

As late as May, the Czech fascists still called for a stronger representation in the Národní Výbor, and for the extension of the "Nuremberg Laws" to the Protectorate.[12] This was evidently instigated by the German authorities, who wanted to show Hácha and the Assemblage that they could cooperate also with other, more radical, forces. When Hácha did not comply with the fascist demands, but instead dissolved the National Committee on May 17 and appointed a new one with seventy members,[13] in which all parties and occupational groups were again represented, Gajda and the fascists withdrew from it on May 20.[14] The Fascist party was nevertheless recognized on June 27, when seven new fascist representatives were appointed to the Národní Výbor. Hácha made this concession to them under pressure from the Reich Protector as the lesser of two evils, for at the same time he denied them the Ministry of Interior, which Gajda had also demanded. Gajda then announced the reentry of his party into the Assemblage.[15] The Fascist party was thereby dissolved, and thenceforth made no effort to play a role in the political life of the Protectorate.

The role of the Fascist party was next assumed by a small right-radical group that called itself Vlajka (the Flag).[16] This group had originally been an organization of Czech students led by a certain Jan Rys.[17] He

[11] Král (Pravda, p. 191) asserts that of the 326 leading personalities in the National Assemblage on the regional and district levels, 145 had come from the Agrarian party, 35 from the Social Democratic party, 35 from the National Union, 29 from the People's party, 22 from the Tradesmen's party, and only 18 from the Fascist party. A similar proportion prevailed among the 285 local secretaries. These figures evidently apply to the summer of 1939.

[12] Feierabend, Ve vládě, p. 42.

[13] Expanded to 80 persons just 10 days later.

[14] Archiv der Gegenwart, 1939, p. 4047 C.

[15] After the proclamation of the party on July 14, 1939, the dissolution took place that summer. See Archiv der Gegenwart, 1939, p. 4137 C. Feierabend (Ve vládě, p. 97) places it in September.

[16] This was also the name of its magazine.

[17] Later, Rys had difficulties with the National Socialists and was even placed

tried to expand it into a political party, which, at least at first, could count on the support and probably the financing of the German authorities, but which was to play no major role.

An important change took place in the National Assemblage on June 24, 1939, when Adolf Hrubý, who had compromised himself in an attempt at bribery, was replaced by Josef Nebeský,[18] likewise a member of the Agrarian party. He held the presidency of the Národní Výbor and the National Assemblage until their forced dissolution in the spring of 1942. The Národní Výbor, the composition of which changed, played the role merely of a shadow parliament. However, it was significant that in the Výbor, at least, the vitality and cultural awareness of the Czech people found an expression.

More important than the National Assemblage, however, was the Protectorate government, whose members had to confront daily the demands of the Reich protector and the Wehrmacht. The government of Beran resigned on March 14, but continued in office *ad interim*. General Syrový was obliged to dissolve the Ministry of Defense. Foreign Minister František Chvalkovský could not dissolve his ministry himself: he was appointed envoy to the Reich government, with which, however, he had to deal, anomalously, through Hans Heinrich Lammers, head of the Reich chancellery, rather than Reich Foreign Minister von Ribbentrop.

A new government was formed after long consultation with former ministers by Gen. Alois Eliáš, who had been minister of transport in Beran's cabinet. Eliáš had become personally acquainted with von Neurath at the Geneva disarmament conferences,[19] and it was hoped that this fact might facilitate relations between his government and the Reich protector. Eliáš also assumed the post of minister of interior. Former Minister of State Jiří Havelka became his deputy and also took over the Ministry of Transport. All other cabinet members, among them Minister of Justice Dr. Jaroslav Krejčí, Minister of Agriculture Ladislav Feierabend, and Minister of Education Dr. Jan Kapras, were held over from the Beran government. The new cabinet was sworn in by the president of the Protectorate on April 28. It was essentially a continuation of the Beran government, which did not in the least accord with the wishes of the fascists, nor, for that matter, the ideas of the National Assemblage.[20] Never-

---

in a concentration camp. In 1945, he was nevertheless extradited to Czechoslovakia and condemned to death.

[18] Feierabend (*Ve vládě*, p. 62) confirms German press reports about a bribery attempt by Hrubý. Nebeský was Secretary-General of the Union of Beet Growers (Řepařská Jednota).

[19] Král, *Pravda*, p. 186.

[20] Feierabend (*Ve vládě*, p. 37) emphasizes that five of the nine government members were Freemasons: Eliáš, Kapras, Klumpar, and Šádek, in addition to himself.

theless, it tried to establish a good working relationship with these groups by appointing representatives to them who were ready to cooperate. Another attempt of the fascists to gain control of the Ministry of Interior was forestalled by the nomination of General of the Gendarmerie Josef Ježek, who was sworn in on July 3.

The fascists' drive to apply the German anti-Jewish laws to the Protectorate was prevented by the Reich Protector himself, who issued a directive concerning Jewish property.[21] Jewish civil servants, however, had already been dismissed from their posts. This harmonized with the anti-Semitism that had already manifested itself in the Second Republic, and which was clearly expressed in the program of the National Assemblage.

A special problem for the government was to find employment for about 120,000 persons who had lost their jobs after March 15. The largest group among them were the commissioned and noncommissioned officers of the former Czechoslovak army, which was being disbanded. Then there were the officials of the dissolved ministries, especially the Foreign Ministry. Incidentally, most of the officials on foreign missions, e.g. in Washington, Paris, and London, refused to obey the government's summons to return home and to hand over their missions to the Germans.[22] The new "Government army" (Vládní vojsko) that had been formed in August 1939 and was destined merely for representative duties was too small to absorb the officers. Moreover, service in it was not considered honorable. A government directive on June 6, 1939,[23] provided for the transfer of army personnel to the civil service or for continuance of pay while they sought civilian employment. Finding jobs in business and industry presented no insuperable difficulties, because the hiring of Czech workers for employment in Germany had already begun in the spring, and Czech industry was soon fully occupied with orders from the Reich.[24]

Unemployment dropped rapidly, from not quite 93,000 in March to 57,000 in May and to less than 17,000 in June. By July there was a manpower shortage. As early as August the number of Czech workers in the Reich was estimated at 80,000. They were not yet forced laborers, but regular contract workers.[25] On July 25 the government issued a directive for the establishment of a one-year general labor service.[26] This, how-

---

[21] *Bulletin*, No. 6, pp. 45-49. Feierabend (*Ve vládě*, pp. 44-45) describes the pressure exerted on this occasion, in vain, by State Secretary Frank.

[22] *Documents of German Foreign Policy*, Series D, Vol. VI, Nos. 102 and 106.

[23] *Sbírka zákonů*, 1939, No. 52 (June 9, 1939).

[24] *Feierabend, Ve vládě*, p. 65.

[25] Ibid., p. 65; *Archiv der Gegenwart*, 1939, p. 4097.

[26] *Sbírka zákonů*, 1939, No. 69 (August 22, 1939); see also Ausführungsverordnung of August 24, 1939, ibid., No. 72 (August 28, 1939).

ever, had nothing to do with the elimination of unemployment or pro-
curement of labor, but copied the German system and established the
first preconditions for the recruitment of forced labor.

The relatively favorable economic development, though vitiated by
a rapid increase in prices, could not conceal the fact that the Protectorate
government's freedom to act was considerably restricted, even at this
early, relatively accommodating stage in Czech-German relations. As
early as June 7 the Reich Protector was empowered by Hitler to "change
the autonomous law" by means of directives,[27] of which he and especially
K. H. Frank made ample use. The death of a German policeman in
Kladno on July 7-8 was made the occasion for harsh repression against
the town and excesses against Czech officials.[28]

The declaration of war on Germany by Britain and France on September 3 first awakened hopes among the Czech people for an early end
to their subjugation. These hopes were somewhat dampened by the unexpectedly rapid defeat of the Polish army. On the other hand, the
Czechs showed some satisfaction, for Poland's collapse and the suffering
of the Polish people seemed to justify the Czech attitude of nonresist-
ance, by which freedom might have been lost but the country was left un-
damaged. At the same time, the hope of an ultimate victory by the Allies
induced even members of the Protectorate government to join the resistance and enter the "Political Center" (Politické Ústředí) of the resistance movement.[29] The population manifested its national feelings clearly and publicly. For example, on St. Laurentius' day (August 21), an
anniversary of defeat of German crusaders by Czech Hussites in 1431
at Domažlice and on the first anniversary of the Munich agreement (September 30), the people boycotted the streetcars in Prague.[30] The manifestation on the anniversary of Czechoslovak independence (October
28) went much farther: bilingual Czech-German street signs were torn
down and State Secretary Frank was derisively whistled at. The police
opened fire on the demonstrating crowds. One worker was killed and a
medical student, Jan Opletal, was gravely wounded.

It is not clear whether certain outrages against German schools and
German inscriptions arose out of the excitement of the demonstrating
masses, who had at first quietly shown the national colors, or whether
they had been deliberately provoked by the German police to justify the

---

[27] *Bulletin*, No. 6 (July 7, 1939). Feierabend (*Ve vládě*, p. 61) erroneously
dates this document June 27.

[28] Duff, *Protectorate*, pp. 84-85; Feierabend, *Ve vládě*, pp. 57-58.

[29] Aside from Minister of Agriculture Feierabend, who represented the Agrarian
party, Jaromír Nečas, chief of the national price-control office, spoke for the
Social Democrats, Feierabend, *Ve vládě*, pp. 71-72, 87-89.

[30] *Dějiny Prahy* [*History of Prague*] (Prague, 1964), p. 613.

use of arms.[31] During the following days, when the German University in Prague was declared a "Reich University" (November 4) and Jan Opletal died of his wounds (November 12), the resentment of the Czech students naturally increased. Hácha and von Neurath tried to calm the heated emotions, despite objections from Frank. The funeral of Opletal took place on November 15 in an atmosphere that, though ceremoniously demonstrative,[32] was quiet. However, in the absence of von Neurath, the comportment of a few students, who sang the national anthem, "Kde domov můj?," at the funeral and who demonstrated against the German police on their way home, supplied Frank with the occasion for an unexpectedly harsh and brutal action. On the night of November 16-17, four Prague student dormitories were occupied, more than 1,800 Czech university students and teachers were arrested, and nine of them, accused as "ringleaders," were summarily shot. Among the executed was Josef Matoušek, chairman of the academic youth in the National Assemblage. Some of those arrested were freed the next day, while more than 1,000 were taken to the Oranienburg concentration camp in Germany, from which they were released a few at a time and permitted to return home.

Even harsher than this terror was the action of Hitler, who on the same day (November 17) personally and without the knowledge of von Neurath ordered the closing of all Czech universities and colleges for three years, on the ground that they were centers of resistance and were connected with the activities of former President Edvard Beneš.[33] The colleges and universities were not reopened after the three years had elapsed, and their buildings were either assigned to the German University in Prague or used by the German authorities. The building of the college of law in Prague was made into a *Schutzstaffel* (SS) barracks. The professors—with the exception of those in the schools of medicine who were permitted to continue to work in their clinics—were suspended, university assistants were sent to teach in secondary schools, and students were put to work.

[31] This is alleged by Duff, *Protectorate*, pp. 87-88. However, she offers no evidence. Feierabend (*Ve vládě*, p. 109) who was not an eyewitness but was well informed, states that communist leaflets called for use of force, and that Frank was personally responsible for the trouble by his actions.

[32] Jan Havránek, *Stručné dějiny university Karlovy* [*A Short History of Charles University*] (Prague, 1964), p. 290ff.

[33] Feierabend (*Ve vládě*, pp. 113-15) describes the events in the government. Witnesses at the Nuremberg Trials testified that von Neurath was surprised by these measures, taken while he was in Berlin. International Military Tribunal, *Trial of the Major War Criminals before the International Military Tribunal, Nuremberg, 1945-46.* 42 vols. (Nuremberg, 1947-49), XIX, 333; hereafter to be quoted as *IMT*.

With this stroke,[34] which was partially explained by an attempt against the life of Hitler in Munich on November 9, it had become clear that the intellectual community of the Czech nation, already decimated and weakened by arrests and worsened working conditions for journalists, lawyers, and teachers, was to be mercilessly exterminated. There was to be no new generation of intellectuals. The hope that a more lenient policy might be adopted toward the Protectorate had now been definitely crushed.

During these months of the intensive drive against the Czech intellectuals, a number of concessions were made to the general Czech population. Food rationing cards, for example, were introduced by special directives of the government on October 1, five weeks later than in the Reich, and the rations were more generous than those in the Reich and adjusted to the Czech diet.[35] Textile ration coupons, in use in the Reich since the beginning of the war, became effective in the Protectorate one year later, on October 1, 1940.

The eight months from March 15 to November 17, 1939, had shown that efforts toward trustful cooperation between the Protectorate and the German Reich had largely failed. Distrust had continued on both sides, and the attitude of being the "masters in the house," frequently shown by the men in the Reich Protector's office, had damaged the self-respect of exactly those Czech civil servants who might have been disposed to loyal cooperation.

The feeling among the people of having been deprived of their rights, of being exposed to arbitrary treatment, was reinforced by the behavior of the Gestapo in the Protectorate. Although in the early weeks of the Protectorate the Gestapo was not organized effectively enough to prevent the flight of many members of the imperiled Jewish community and influential politicians abroad,[36] it began mass arrests of German emigrés and Czech politicians even in the early days of the military regime under Generals von Blaskowitz[37] and List. New waves of arrests followed in times of international tension, e.g., right after the beginning of the war in September, 1939. However, the farmers, the great mass of the workers, and the small artisans who had not been politically active were largely spared the attentions of the Gestapo. This was designed to create a division among the Czech people.

[34] The German public was not told about these steps. The German News Service DNB issued a denial on November 19 that hinted that there might be "some possible necessary steps by the Czech government [!] against certain circles."

[35] *Sbírka zákonů*, 1939, No. 77 (September 29, 1939).

[36] They included the later Prime Minister in exile Msgr. Jan Šrámek, the socialist Rudolf Bechyně, the Czech National Socialist Jaroslav Stránský, and the leader of the Sudeten German Social Democrats, Wenzel Jaksch.

[37] Feierabend (*Ve vládě*, p. 23) estimates the number in the first two weeks at 18,000.

The Jewish population, whose fate will be discussed in detail below, was placed in an extralegal position by a decree of June 21, 1939, that forbade them to dispose of their property and to buy land. The German population, which constituted about 3.5 percent of the total population of 7.4 million,[38] was by contrast clearly favored by the opportunity to acquire Reich citizenship, by immunity from Czech courts of justice, and by assignment to the jurisdiction of the Oberlandräte. In the administration of the greater towns—Prague,[39] Brno (Brünn), Jihlava (Iglau), Moravská Ostrava (Mährisch-Ostrau), Olomouc (Olmütz), and České Budějovice (Budweis)[40]—the Germans were far more heavily represented than their share in the population warranted. Among other things, this caused the Czech population to identify their German fellow citizens with the Reich rulers. A division into four classes had already begun in the first four months: (1) the privileged Germans; (2) the Czech workers, minor officials, and farmers, who were permitted to live in modest comfort; (3) the intellectuals, who were marked for humiliation and deprivation of their social status; and (4) the Jews, who at this early stage were not yet faced with extermination but suffered a farreaching loss of their rights.

NOVEMBER 1939 TO SEPTEMBER 1941: TWO YEARS OF RELATIVE CALM

In the years between the bloody events of November, 1939, and the arrest of Prime Minister Eliáš in September, 1941, the Protectorate stood, in a manner of speaking, in the shadow of the rapidly changing developments of the war. The Czech population no longer openly demonstrated its patriotism but adopted a cautious wait-and-see attitude. The Reich Protector and his administration tried to exploit the working capacity of the Czech people as much as possible. They integrated the Protectorate economy completely into the German war economy and tried to make it function with as little friction as possible. Under the impression of a surprisingly easy German victory in the West, plans for the deportation of the Czechs were developed.[41]

In January, 1940, a first shock occurred when Minister of Agriculture Ladislav K. Feierabend and Jaromír Nečas, head of the main price con-

[38] In October, 1940, 262,000. See Alfred Bohmann, *Das Sudetendeutschtum in Zahlen* (Munich, 1959), p. 194.

[39] In Prague, in addition to the Czech Lord Mayor, Dr. Otokar Klapka, the German historian, Professor Dr. Josef Pfitzner, was made vice mayor, on March 15, 1939.

[40] On July 10, 1939, the town assemblies of these cities were disbanded and replaced with government commissioners. On June 4, Frank declared in a speech at České Budějovice that this city had to become German again.

[41] See footnote 3.

trol office, whose adherence to the Politické Ústředí had become known to the Gestapo,[42] fled to Britain with the knowledge and approval of Prime Minister Eliáš. Officially, only the dismissal of Feierabend, together with that of Minister of Commerce Vlastimil Šádek, was announced on February 3.[43] To succeed the escapees, Count Mikuláš Bubna-Litic was appointed minister of agriculture, Dr. Jaroslav Kratochvíl became minister of commerce, and Minister of Justice J. Krejčí was made deputy prime minister in place of Havelka.[44] Both sides were trying to avoid an open break. In other ways as well, the authorities moved slowly. The incorporation of the Protectorate into the German customs zone, provided for in Hitler's decree of March 16, 1939, which according to an announcement in February, 1940, was to become effective on April 1, was postponed until October 1, 1940.

In the summer of 1940, when evidence of Prime Minister Eliáš's ties to the resistance organization abroad was discovered in Paris, Frank and Himmler persuaded Hitler to order his arrest, but von Neurath managed to convince the Führer to revoke the order.[45] The trial of the members of the resistance organization Obrana Národa (Defense of the Nation),[46] who had been arrested in the winter of 1939-40, was likewise postponed. Later, when proceedings were instituted against them, it was with the express instruction from Hitler that death sentences were "not desired."[47]

The general line of German policy toward the Protectorate at this time was further to strengthen the authority of the administration in taking measures against the Czech population, but, for the moment, to make little or no use of it. Thus, the emergency-service regulation that had been effective in the Reich since October 15, 1938, was extended to the Protectorate on December 1, 1939,[48] but no Czechs were drafted for such service outside the Protectorate.[49] The economic position of the Jewish population in this period was further aggravated by a number of restrictive measures, but no interference with Jewish religious services or de-

[42] Feierabend, *Ve vládě*, pp. 128-45.

[43] Feierabend's flight became known when ministerial directives were no longer signed in his name but in that of Krejčí, as commissioner in charge of the ministry.

[44] Havelka retained the Ministry of Transport until the spring of 1941 when he was replaced by Dr. Jindřich Kamenický, who had been minister of transport in the first Syrový government.

[45] IMT, XIX, 335. The exact date of the intervention is not given.

[46] Compare Radomír Luža, *The Transfer of the Sudeten Germans: A Study of Czech-German Relations, 1933-1962* (New York, 1964), chapters dealing with the Ustředí.

[47] Helmut Heiber, "Zur Justiz im Dritten Reich: der Fall Eliáš," *Vierteljahrshefte für Zeitgeschichte*, 5 (1955), 278, on the basis of unprinted sources.

[48] *Verordnungsblatt*, 1939, Nos. 41 and 42.

[49] IMT, XIX, 335.

struction of synagogues, such as had been frequent in the Reich since November 8, 1938, took place as yet. This restraint was probably due to the influence of von Neurath, who managed to convince Hitler that a "soft" policy toward the Protectorate was better for the German war effort than a "hard" one. Although Hitler occasionally expressed similar ideas,[50] he was also exposed to entirely different influences and was equally ready to order harsh and brutal measures.

THE RULE OF HEYDRICH:
SEPTEMBER 27, 1941 TO MAY 27, 1942

In September, 1941, probably stimulated by German successes in the war against the Soviet Union, perhaps also affected by reports of sabotage by the Czech population,[51] and certainly under the influence of Reinhard Heydrich, head of the Reich Security Office (*Reichssicherheitshauptamt*), Hitler decided on a radical change in policy toward the Protectorate. Von Neurath was called by telephone to report to Hitler and told that he had been too mild and that harsher measures were now in order. When his objections went unheeded, he asked to be relieved of his duties. This request, however, was refused.[52] Instead, he was given a leave of absence "for reasons of illness" on September 27, and Heydrich was appointed his deputy. Heydrich arrived in Prague on the same day and began his rule without bothering to contact the Reich Protector, who withdrew to his estate in Württemberg. State Secretary K. H. Frank, long the spokesman of the "hard line," did not profit from the sudden change. His position remained that of a state secretary, but he was now under a very energetic boss who took everything into his own hands.

On the same evening, Heydrich issued a directive declaring martial law. It was extended over the greater part of the Protectorate, namely, the Oberlandräte regions of Prague, Brno, Moravská Ostrava, Hradec Králové (Königgrätz), and Kladno.[53] At the same time, after he had assured himself of the support of Otto Thierack,[54] president of the German Volksgerichtshof in Berlin, he ordered the arrest of Prime Minister Eliáš. Although the evidence against Eliáš, which showed that he had sent in-

---

[50] See footnote 3.

[51] The communists were relatively quiet from September 1939 to June 22, 1941. On the morning of that day mass arrests of Czech communists began. They, in turn, started acts of sabotage and resistance.

[52] See the testimony of von Neurath in IMT, XVII, 23-24.

[53] *Verordnungsblatt*, 1940, No. 47. An English translation may be found in the memorandum of the Czechoslovak government in exile, *On the Reign of Terror under the Regime of Reinhard Heydrich* (London, 1942), pp. 18-20. The area under martial law was enlarged a few days later.

[54] Detailed background information by Helmut Heiber (see footnote 47).

formation abroad and had tacitly tolerated a few acts of resistance, was rather thin for a capital case, he was condemned to death for attempted high treason on October 1, 1941, in a special session of the Volksgerichtshof in Prague. His execution was postponed,[55] but during the same week 150 to 200 persons were sentenced to death by summary courts and executed. By the end of November the number of victims increased to 400. In this way Heydrich initiated a pitiless policy of suppressing all impulses of Czech national life, while, at the same time, he put on a show of joviality toward the Czech farmers and workers.

While the Czech cultural and sports organizations were compelled to stop their activities and all efforts to have the universities reopened came to nothing, the workers were promised and given higher and better rations. When the customs barriers between the Protectorate and the Reich were removed on October 1, 1940, differences in prices and wages between the two areas disappeared. Czech workers were therefore less willing to go to work in the Reich, and the new incentives were meant to make them work harder at home. "Peace and Quiet," plus material advantages, were designed to make the working population forget their loss of freedom and, at the same time, turn them against a spirit of resistance that could imperil these benefits.

Martial law was ended on December 1, 1941,[56] after the cruel trials that had claimed as victims even some who had been arrested earlier but had not been tried, such as the Lord Mayor of Prague, Otokar Klapka. The cessation of martial law relaxed tensions to a certain extent. The Protectorate government, however, had been reduced to ineffectiveness. After the arrest of Eliáš, Jaroslav Krejčí presided over the government, *ad interim*, until it was reformed on January 19, 1942. In this cabinet reorganization only Prime Minister and Minister of Justice Krejčí, Minister of Finance Josef Kalfus, and Minister of Transport Jindřich Kamenický were taken from the old government into the new. Richard Bienert became minister of interior. The Ministry of Education and the new Office for Public Enlightenment went to Col. Emanuel Moravec,[57] once a member of the Czechoslovak Legion and a strong Czech nationalist who had become a propagandist for the Third Reich. The compromised (in 1939) Adolf Hrubý became minister of agriculture, and the three ministries for Industry and Commerce, Social Administration, and Public Works were combined and placed under a German, Walter Bertsch,

[55] Eliáš survived Heydrich by fifteen days. He was executed on June 19, 1942. On this point Heiber (footnote 47) is misinformed.

[56] *Verordnungsblatt*, 1941, No. 62.

[57] Moravec authored a number of booklets: *Das Ende der Benesch-Republik* (five editions), and *Tatsachen und Irrtuemer. Der Weg ins neue Europa* (Prague, 1942), among others. He committed suicide on May 5, 1945.

theretofore the head of the economic department in the Office of the Reich Protector.[58]

With the new government, there could no longer be any talk of independence or of justified protection of Czech interests. It was merely the executive organ of the deputy Reich Protector. Heydrich's speech at the new government's reception, given by Hácha, left no doubt about this. In the context of the new policy of terror and suppression of the intellectuals, coupled with material concessions to the peasants and workers, there was no longer any room for the National Assemblage either. This organization had gone through a crisis in 1940, when the Vlajka fascists tried to seize leadership by a *coup*. After the attempt failed, a campaign of lectures was launched in the fall and winter of 1940 to propagate the "cultivation of the concept of the Reich," but this failed also. In the spring of 1942 the Národní Výbor was dissolved under pressure from Heydrich, and the National Assemblage itself, though formally still in existence, was no longer visible. With these developments, the "shadow parliament" and attempts to "reeducate" the Czech people had come to an end.

The Assassination of Reinhard Heydrich and its Immediate Consequences

The new direction of German policy toward the Protectorate, with its great harshness and cruelty against the intellectuals and blatant attempts to win the masses for uninterrupted production through material concessions, gave rise to concern among the Czechs in exile. In contrast to the developments in Poland or Yugoslavia, there was no news of open resistance in the Protectorate, which made it easy for the Allies to believe that the Czech people in their great majority collaborated willingly.[59] Therefore, the Czechoslovak army in exile in Britain sent several teams of men, who were well trained in hand-to-hand combat and sabotage, into the Protectorate in 1941 to prepare major acts of resistance as well as to assassinate Heydrich. Although a few members of these teams, which were parachuted into the country, were betrayed into the hands of the Gestapo, most of them found shelter and support in the Czech underground and managed to hide for several months while preparing to kill the man who more than anyone else symbolized the German regime.

---

[58] Wilhelm Dennler became his deputy. See Dennler, *Boehmische Passion*, pp. 67ff. Bertsch died in prison in Brno in 1952.

[59] B. Hutak, *With Blood and with Iron: The Lidice Story* (London, 1957), p. 51, describes the attempt to seduce the workers: "This effort to buy out the spirit

The plans to assassinate Heydrich were received with skepticism by some members of the underground, including Vaněk (*nom-de-guerre* Jindra),[60] leader of the dissolved but still secretly active Sokol organization, because the great number of victims to be expected in case of a successful assassination did not seem to be justifiable. On May 4, 1942, Vaněk-Jindra sent a message to Beneš, in which he demanded that the assassination order be rescinded. Beneš, however, insisted on May 15 that under the given circumstances "an act of force, a direct action" was necessary. Internationally, he thought, it would mean, "the recovery of the destiny of the nation even if it should entail great sacrifices."[61]

On the morning of May 27, 1942, the assassination was successfully carried out by Jan Kubiš and Jozef Gabčík, two members of the parachutist team, at a skillfully selected point on the road along which Heydrich traveled every day. The assassins and their accomplices escaped. Heydrich died on June 4 from the bomb-splinter injuries that he had suffered.[62]

On Hitler's orders, the assassination was immediately followed by the appointment of Police Col.-Gen. Kurt Daluege as deputy to the Reich Protector. Martial law was proclaimed (it lasted until July 3), heavy-handed repressions were ordered, and summary courts sentenced to death and ordered the immediate execution of anyone who was denounced as having knowledge of, or "having approved of," the assassination. Himmler ordered the arrest of 10,000 hostages. The most harsh and cruel measure, however, was ordered by Hitler himself and by K. H. Frank: the destruction of the village of Lidice near Kladno on the night of June 9-10, in which some parachutists had allegedly been sheltered.

---

of national resistance was more dangerous than all the massacres of Heydrich." He affirms the necessity of an act of resistance by parachutists.

[60] The former Sokol leader, Dr. Augustin Pechlát, was shot on September 30, 1941, after a trial by a summary court. Compare Hutak, *With Blood*, p. 50, and *On the Reign of Terror*, p. 97.

[61] Král, *Otázky*, III, 242-43, reproduces the messages. According to these messages, the underground leaders suggested the assassination of Moravec instead of Heydrich, if an assassination were deemed necessary for reasons of foreign policy. Beneš (*Memoirs*) does not mention the whole assassination. Compare chapter by Luža in this volume.

[62] The Czech literature about Heydrich's assassination is less voluminous than might be expected, because the communists had no part in its planning or execution. For instance, the collection of Jiří Doležal and Jan Křen, *Die kaempfende Tschechoslowakei* (Prague, 1964), ignores the assassination and only mentions the repressions. The collective work *Lidice* (Prague, 1963) identifies neither the assassins nor the date. Aside from the book of Hutak, the following may be mentioned: Allen Burgess, *Seven Men at Daybreak* (London, 1962); Čestmír Amort, *Heydrichiáda* [*Heydrich's Rule*] (Prague, 1964); and "Ze zákulisí Heydrichiády" ["Secrets of Heydrich's Rule"], *Slovanský Přehled*, 48 (1962); Dušan Hamšík and Jiří Pražák, *Bomba pro Heydricha* [*A Bomb for Heydrich*] (Prague, 1963).

(This was later found to have been untrue.) The entire male population of the village (according to a Prague Gestapo report on June 24, 1942, a total of 199 persons) was shot, the women were taken to concentration camps where some of them lost their lives, and 105 children were sent to homes from which most of them did not return.[63] Then the entire village was razed to the ground. On the same day (June 10), the gruesome massacre of innocents was officially announced in Prague. A similar fate was met by the small hamlet of Ležáky, where a radio transmitter had been found. Thirty-three persons were shot there. This cruel act of revenge and deterrence, which, unlike similar acts of terror in Poland and the Soviet Union, was officially admitted, assured the Czech people of the sympathy of the entire world. "Lidice" became a symbol of the National Socialist rule of terror and of innocent suffering.

Under the pressure of terror—at times deliberate rumors were planted by the German authorities that 200,000 persons, or even that every tenth Czech, would be shot—and under the temptation of the high reward of 10 million Czech crowns[64] that was offered, the assassins and their closest accomplices—altogether seven men—were betrayed, and found in their hiding place, the Orthodox Carl-Borromaeus church (also called Cyril-Methodius church) in Prague. They resisted arrest. Some died in the fight and the rest took their own lives when resistance proved hopeless. The abettors of the deed, who were later executed, included the pastor of the church, its elders, and the bishop of the Czech Orthodox Church, Gorazd (Matthias Pavlík).

The Last Phase: June 1942 to May 5, 1945

The final and longest phase of the six-year history of the Protectorate, comprising nearly one-half of the entire period, was without substantive and outstanding developments. After the abrogation of martial law on July 3, 1942, conditions became "normalized" insofar as the policy of suppressing all symptoms of Czech national awareness, the degradation of the intellectuals, and the exploitation of the peasants and workers was concerned. On the Czech side, after the repressions and murders of June, 1942, in the course of which more than 1,000 persons were executed (442 of them in Prague), there were no more attempts at assassination or major acts of sabotage.[65]

---

[63] Amort, *Heydrichiáda*, pp. 212-15, 247.

[64] According to Dennler (*Die boehmische Passion*, p. 78) there were too many denunciations for all to be followed up.

[65] Reporting about the period from May 8 to August 1942, Daluege wrote Hitler: "The development of the current political line—i.e. the hard grip, the various political measures taken, the public mood artificially created by us, and

The provisional arrangements for German control of the Protectorate, made at the time of Heydrich's death, were continued for over a year. On August 20, 1943, it was announced that von Neurath's leave of absence had been terminated and that he had resigned as Reich Protector of Bohemia and Moravia. In his place, Wilhelm Frick, until then Reich minister of the interior, was appointed Reich Protector. Frick was unable to give the office the same respectability as von Neurath, who was an experienced diplomat and had treated the Czech ministers and staff with courtesy. Neither Frick nor Kurt Daluege, could compete with K. H. Frank, who was the real winner in the reshuffle of the German command structure in the Protectorate.

At this time a German Ministry of State for Bohemia and Moravia was created. According to Hitler's decree, the minister of state was to conduct "government business involving the maintenance of the Reich's interests in the Protectorate." Now Frank was promoted to minister of state for Bohemia and Moravia, a rank equivalent to that of a Reich minister. With his promotion, the real executive power in the Protectorate passed to him. The Reich Protector became merely the symbol of Reich authority.

Under the pressure of Germany's deteriorating war conditions, Frank had to concentrate his energies on harnessing the population of the Protectorate to the German total war effort. In the fall of 1943, on the requisition of Fritz Sauckel, Reich plenipotentiary for the utilization of manpower, 30,000 Czech workers were compelled to go to work in the Reich.[66] In the spring of 1944, Göring demanded and received 10,000 young Czechs to work in aircraft production for six months. At the end of the six months (October 1944), they were permitted to return home.[67]

A comprehensive administrative reform, already planned and prepared by Heydrich,[68] was put into effect on June 15, 1942. It created new administrative inspectors in the Oberlandräte districts of Prague, České Budějovice, Plzeň, Hradec Králové, Brno, Jihlava, and Moravská Ostrava. The Oberlandräte-Inspekteure, who were all Germans, were under Frank's ministry of state. It was their duty to use the smallest possible German staff for supervisory and control functions. The existing German offices also had their staffs reduced to a minimum by transfers to the army. The Czech administration continued alongside the German offices, except for a number of German district governors.

The streamlining of the German administration assured the smooth

---

the nervous tension of the Czechs, the things which led to an escalation of fear circulating as rumors of an impending decimation of the whole nation—has proved correct." Cited in Král, *Otázky*, III, 244.

[66] Dennler, *Boehmische Passion*, pp. 112-14.

[67] Ibid., pp. 116-25.

[68] Bohmann, "Die Stellung der Oberlandräte-Inspekteure." Compare footnote 9.

functioning of the Protectorate economy in the framework of the German war economy. Its proper functioning was all the more important to Germany at this time because the Allied air forces, which were in a position to bomb the Protectorate intensively from bases in Italy from late 1943 and from bases in France from mid-1944, spared it until late 1944 out of consideration for the Czech population. The first time Prague was bombed was on October 4, 1944, but no great damage was done. Only near the end of the war, when the Protectorate was the last intact industrial area at the command of the Reich, was Prague subjected to heavy air raids on February 12 and March 25, 1945.

In an effort to please the Czech population, on June 4, 1944, Frank marked the "Protectorate's Shield of Honor" by creating the order of the "Eagle of Duke Venceslas" in three classes for "citizens of the Protectorate who had distinguished themselves by their attitude, fulfillment of duty, and preparedness."[69] This fatuous gesture, the announcement of which roughly coincided with the news of the Allied invasion of France on June 6, could not but be met with skepticism or concealed derision by the Czechs. In August there followed a number of directives that extended to the Protectorate the "total war effort" already in effect in the Reich. In consequence, all work not directly contributing to the war effort was prohibited.

Although the directives caused hardships in the lives of the individual Czechs, the uprising that broke out in the final days of August in Slovakia had no counterpart in Bohemia and Moravia. Nor did any demonstrations or acts of sabotage take place earlier, when the exiled President Beneš concluded the Soviet-Czechoslovak alliance in Moscow on December 12, 1943. President Hácha and the six Czech ministers felt compelled to issue a declaration of protest on December 17, 1943, and two days later founded a "Czech League against Bolshevism." The Protectorate government, which was again reshuffled on January 19, 1945, with the erstwhile Minister of Interior Bienert becoming prime minister and Krejčí reduced to being his deputy, took this occasion to reaffirm its loyalty to the Reich.[70] All these gestures tended to be discounted at home and abroad as German-dictated. Yet the population of Bohemia and Moravia—areas that by this time were about the only territory at the command of the Reich in which the economy and communications functioned normally—remained quiet. Even the formation of a new Czechoslovak government under Zdeněk Fierlinger at Košice in eastern Slovakia, on April 5, 1945, and proclamation of the "Košice program" on the same day did not provoke an uprising in Bohemia and Moravia, which might have speeded up the collapse of the German front.

[69] *Archiv der Gegenwart*, 1944, p. 6412.
[70] Ibid., 1944/1945, p. 6670.

This attitude, perhaps difficult to understand, of quietly waiting into the final days before the German capitulation, was probably based on two considerations: the sober realization that any uprising even against a retreating German force would have resulted in bloody losses that a few days later would no longer be necessary, and the quiet hope that in this way the race between the American Third Army under General Patton and the Soviet armies under Marshals Konev and Malinovsky might perhaps be won by the Americans. The Czechs, of course, had no way of knowing that General Eisenhower had agreed with General Antonov, acting chief of the Soviet general staff, to halt the Americans along the Karlovy Vary-České Budějovice (Karlsbad-Budweis) line, and that Eisenhower meant to respect this agreement.

While the territory governed by the Reich Protector became steadily smaller during April, 1945, an eerie atmosphere prevailed in the Ministry of State,[71] where Frank and Bienert suffered the delusion that they could surrender the Protectorate directly to the United States army, while ignoring the Red Army, Beneš, and the Košice government. A delegation empowered to effect this surrender, led by Bienert, actually reached General Patton's headquarters, but was not received by him and had to return to Prague emptyhanded.

Despite all the losses and reverses, the waiting attitude of the Czech people not only succeeded in keeping the substance of the Czech nation intact, but also resulted in a substantial population increase. This surprising phenomenon was due to a favorable birthrate, which rose from 15 per thousand in 1938 to 16.7 in 1940 and to 20.7 in 1943. The death-rate also rose slightly, from a low of 1.82 per thousand in 1936 to 3.3 in 1940, 4.3 in 1942, and 7.1 in 1943.[72] The increased rate was considerably higher in the Protectorate than in the Reichsgau Sudetenland,[73] and allowed for a net population increase of about 236,000 by the end of the war.[74] This generally favorable biological development became evident also from the fact that the postwar female surplus in 1947 for all of Czechoslovakia, notwithstanding the loss of male population due to mili-

[71] Dennler, *Boehmische Passion*, pp. 139-40.

[72] "Fünf Jahre Protektorat Böhmen und Mähren," *Wirtschaft und Statistik*, 24 (1944), 17-40. The figures are probably correct. They are confirmed for the years until 1940 and in the comparative figures for the years from 1928 by a table in the *Statistisches Jahrbuch für das Protektorat Böhmen und Mähren* (German and Czech; Prague, 1942), II, 10. They are further confirmed by an investigation of Waller Wynne, Jr., *The Population of Czechoslovakia* (Washington: Bureau of Census, 1953), p. 44, table 3.

[73] See Alfred Bohman, *Bevölkerungsbewegungen in Böhmen, 1847-1947, mit besonderer Berücksichtigung der Entwicklung der nationalen Verhältnisse* (phil. diss., Mainz, 1958; Munich, 1958), p. 239; and *Wirtschaft und Statistik*, 22 (1942) and 23 (1943).

[74] Albin Eissner, "Die tschechoslowakische Bevölkerung im Zweiten Weltkrieg," *Aussenpolitik*, 13 (1962), 328-34.

tary action and the uprising in Slovakia, amounted to only 1,060 women for each 1,000 men, which was nearly normal.[75]

The favorable population figures were used by the Protectorate government to justify itself in the eyes of the Czech people. Speaking in the town of Vsetín on November 2, 1944, Prime Minister Krejčí pointed out that the Czech nation had lost 200,000 soldiers in World War I, but had sustained no losses in World War II, and that the population had even increased by 180,000.[76]

This biological growth, remarkable when compared with the last years of a free Czechoslovakia, was surely not only a consequence of the conditions of life and work in the Protectorate but also of a special kind of resistance: the Czechs met the foreign subjugation and the threatened loss of national identity by increasing the number of nationally conscious compatriots.

In view of the population increase, the losses suffered by the Czech people in the Protectorate from political persecution and in concentration camps, estimated at no less than 36,000 and no more than 55,000,[77] were of course terribly high in terms of the human suffering and degradation they represented but relatively low when compared with the losses sustained from war and occupation by other nations. It is not intended here to minimize the inhumanity of death by summary courts and concentration camps,[78] but it is still true that despite all the heavy losses, wide circles of the Czech population did not even have distant relatives among the victims.[79] This statement, however, applies in no way to the Jews.

JEWISH POPULATION

Some of the Jews of Bohemia and Moravia counted themselves part of the German population and others regarded themselves as Czechs. The

[75] The United Nations, *Demographic Yearbook*, 2 (1949-1950). In Hungary (1949) and Rumania (1948) the ratios were 1,082:1,000 and 1,069:1,000 respectively. *Demographic Yearbook*, 4 (1952), 181, 183.

[76] *Archiv der Gegenwart*, 1944, p. 6581 C.

[77] Gregory Frumkin, *Population Changes in Europe since 1939* (New York, 1951), p. 50. Frumkin bases his calculations on the Statistical Bulletin of the Central Statistical Office in Prague of December, 1946, January, 1948, and May/ June, 1949. The losses were not compiled on the basis of a bookkeeping action but through the addition of the known deaths plus a very high uncertainty factor of 50 percent.

[78] The number of Czechs who are known for certain to have died in concentration camps is given by Frumkin at 20,000. In the total figures, another 10,000 victims of the camps are listed as probable.

[79] The official report in the *Přehled československých dějin* [*Survey of Czechoslovak History*] (3 vols.; Prague, 1960), III, 490, gives no figures, and says only that the workers and progressive intelligentsia had furnished the greatest number of victims.

special laws promulgated for the Jews reduced them to the position of outcasts in both groups, without any rights at all. The Czechoslovak census of 1930 registered 118,000 Jews in the historic provinces of Bohemia, Moravia, and Silesia. The gradual elimination of the Jews from the economic life of the Protectorate was much more rapid than in the Reich, although it was based in both areas on the same laws.

Until October 1, 1941, the Jewish population was permitted to live in freedom. In November, 1941, the fortress-town of Terezín (Theresienstadt) near Litoměřice (Leitmeritz) was turned into a ghetto for Jewish families from the Protectorate as well as for German Jews who, as soldiers in World War I or for other national merits, were to enjoy preferential treatment. In January, 1942, the first Jewish families from Prague and Brno were brought to Terezín, which soon became hopelessly overcrowded. During 1942 nearly 40,000 Jews from the Protectorate and 37,000 from the Reich and Austria were transported there, to live in a town with a normal population of 7,000.

In the following years Terezín did indeed enjoy a privileged position compared with other ghettos and camps, inasmuch as there were no guards inside the town and no outrages were committed. Nevertheless, the "self-administered" Jewish community did represent a cruel irony, since the chief task of the self-administration was the selection of candidates for "resettlement lists," i.e., for transport to the death camps, and the least unfair allocation of the starvation rations[80] to those inhabitants unable to work. These rations were so small that the inmates of the "old people's home" died en masse of exhaustion. These victims included Dr. Ludwig Czech, former chairman of the German Social Democratic party of Czechoslovakia and several times minister.[81]

The many transports going out to the different extermination camps, from which very few returned after the war, and incoming transports from the different parts of Europe caused the population of Terezín to fluctuate rapidly. At all times only a part of its inhabitants were Jews who originated in the Protectorate. The total number of Jews sent from the Protectorate to Terezín was 50,000. For many of them it was simply a way-station on the road to extermination. From December, 1941, to the end of 1942, nearly 20,000 Jews from the Protectorate were sent di-

[80] According to Gerald R. Reitlinger, *Die Endlösung; Hitlers Versuch der Ausrottung der Juden Europas, 1939-1945* (Berlin, 1961), p. 168, the rations were 225 grams of bread, 60 grams of potatoes, and a bowl of soup. The story of Terezín is told in detail by H. G. Adler, *Theresienstadt, 1941-1945; das Antlitz einer Zwangsgemeinschaft* (Tübingen, 1965). In the three and a half years of the existence of Terezín as a concentration camp, about 155,000 Jews lived and suffered there.

[81] The story of Czech's final months (he died on August 20, 1942) is told by his wife, Lili Czech, who survived the internment, in J. W. Brügel, ed., *Dr. Ludwig Czech; Arbeiterführer und Staatsmann* (Vienna, 1960), pp. 156-57.

rectly to the death camps or into East European ghettos,[82] several thousand managed to live in freedom until the end of the war, and a few thousand more survived in hiding or managed to emigrate after 1939. When Terezín was surrendered to the Soviet army on May 7, 1945, some 8,000 Jews out of the 50,000 from the Protectorate were still alive. Most of those who had remained free also survived. Altogether, the total loss suffered by the Jewish population amounted to more than 70,000 persons, or more than three-quarters of the Jews who had fallen into the power of the Third Reich in March, 1939.[83]

During the last days of April and the beginning of May, the eastern and southeastern parts of the Protectorate became a war zone. Moravia especially suffered damage in the fighting. Western Bohemia, on the other hand, was taken by the Americans without a struggle and suffered no damage. On the whole, the damages were slight in comparison with those suffered in neighboring countries.

The rising in Prague, which broke out on May 5 and took a terrible form, affected the rest of the country only slightly. Upon the departure of the German forces, citizen committees took over the administration. With the capitulation of the German Wehrmacht on May 8, 1945, and the complete collapse of the German Reich, the six-year history of the Protectorate came to an end. A new chapter in the history of the lands of Bohemia and Moravia began. Frank, Daluege, and many other representatives of the inhuman Protectorate regime were punished. Acts of revenge were also perpetrated against many who were innocent, however.

President Hácha, who was for many Czechs and foreign observers the personification of treason, subservience, and egotism, and for others the model of a man who took the road of self-abasement in order to assure the continued existence of his people and a bearable condition for his country, survived the Protectorate associated with his name by only a few weeks. He died in prison on June 1, 1945, an old and gravely ill (diabetic) man, to whom no one showed any pity.

[82] Josef Tenenbaum, *Race and Reich* (New York, 1956), p. 336.

[83] Reitlinger (*Endlösung*, p. 562) estimates the victims at 63,000; Frumkin (*Population Changes*, p. 50) puts the figure at 71,000; and Tenenbaum (*Race and Reich*, p. 336) also at 71,000. This includes the cases of natural death, insofar as death by slow starvation may be called "natural." The tablets on the walls of the Pinkas Synagogue in Prague list the names of 77,297 Jewish victims.

· 11 ·

POLITICS IN EXILE, 1939-1945

Edward Taborsky
University of Texas at Austin

A discussion of Czechoslovak politics in exile during World War II must inevitably center upon, and revolve around, the personality and the activities of Edvard Beneš. As president of pre-Munich Czechoslovakia, he ranked highest among the Czechoslovak statesmen and politicians who found refuge abroad. Having been Tomáš Masaryk's main collaborator in the Czechoslovak liberation movement in World War I and having stood, as his country's perennial foreign minister and then president, at the helm of Czechoslovakia's foreign policy from 1918 until the Munich tragedy, he had experience that none of his political rivals could match. The fiasco of the Anglo-French appeasement policy, demonstrated so tragically by the outbreak of the war, vindicated Dr. Beneš's consistent anti-appeasement and anti-Hitler stand and proved right his hitherto unheeded predictions and warnings. As the men responsible for Munich and its consequences were falling one after the other from power and were vanishing into a political limbo, Beneš's international prestige and influence kept rising. Reports from back home continued, from the very beginning of the war, to bear unfailing testimony to the fact that Beneš, and he alone, was looked upon as their chosen leader by the overwhelming majority of the Czechoslovak people.

Thus Beneš prevailed with ease over his few challengers among the exiled statesmen, such as the former Czechoslovak premier, Milan Hodža, and Czechoslovakia's envoy to Paris, Štefan Osuský, and emerged as supreme chief of the Czechoslovak liberation movement, first as head of the Czechoslovak National Committee and, from 1940 to 1945, again as president of Czechoslovakia, so recognized by Britain, the United States, Soviet Russia, De Gaulle's Free French, and others. Indeed, his position became virtually that of a benevolent absolutist ruler, for he was not accountable to any other organ. Members of the three bodies that, together with the presidency of the republic, made up the Czechoslovak government machinery in exile—the cabinet, the state council, and the juridical council—were chosen by the president himself. Moreover, all three acted merely in an advisory capacity or handled matters of routine administration. Actual decision-making in all major policy matters, and even some minor ones, remained in Beneš's hands. That was so not only in the field of external relations, where the president actually combined his own presidential function with those of premier, foreign minister, and at times even ambassador, but also in all important matters of internal politics, such as contacts with the Czech and Slovak undergound, relations with Emil Hácha's Protectorate government, and plans for postwar political and economic reforms.

This does not mean that Beneš behaved as a self-appointed dictator or that he abused his authority. Having served as his personal secretary through those crucial years from 1939 to 1945, I can testify to the fact that the president did not attempt to impose his will on others. Rather, he consulted with his advisers on all major matters, was eager to listen to their arguments, always sought to persuade them of the correctness of his course, and upon occasion even modified his actions to meet their objections and criticisms. Nonetheless, from 1939 until at least late in 1944, when the Moscow-backed Czechoslovak communists began their power play, nothing of political importance, insofar as it depended on the Czechoslovak government in exile, could be decided without Beneš, let alone against him. In this sense, the substance of Czechoslovak politics in exile during World War II is inextricably linked with Beneš as its central figure. Therefore, the Czechoslovak president has to appear as its leading character.

The Czechoslovak Exile and the Munich Legacy

The story of Czechoslovak politics in exile must necessarily begin with the legacy of Munich. Not only was Munich the very *raison d'être* of Beneš's political exile, but the ghost and the burden of Munich went with him. Although the shock of those tragic days gradually wore off, the bitter lesson was never forgotten. The undoing of Munich and all its consequences became the dominant factor in Beneš's political thinking, the most important determinant of his entire policy, and the supreme task upon which he concentrated his boundless energy. "Ever since September, 1938, I kept thinking of it literally day in and day out, I lived by it and suffered from it, and all of my political actions were directed toward it," he confided in his *Memoirs*. "It was indeed the sole purpose of my life."[1] Beneš's preoccupation with Munich has been noted by all those who had frequent contact with him during the war.[2] Nor did these en-

[1] Edvard Beneš, *Paměti. Od Mnichova k nové válce a k novému vítězství* (Prague, 1947), p. 294, hereafter cited as *Paměti*. An English translation by Godfrey Lias was published as *Memoirs of Dr. Eduard Beneš. From Munich to New War and New Victory* (Boston, 1954); cited hereafter as *Memoirs*.

[2] See, for instance, Dr. Ladislav K. Feierabend, *Beneš mezi Washingtonem a Moskvou* [*Beneš Between Washington and Moscow*] (Washington, 1966), pp. 128-29; the same author's *Ve vládě v exilu* [*In the Government in Exile*] (2 vols.; Washington, 1965-1966), I, 121-23, and II, 131-33.

deavors aim solely at a correction of the wrongs perpetrated against Czechoslovakia at Munich and later. They strove as well to secure the country against a possible recurrence of such a dire menace in the future.

Thus, the "undoing of Munich" comprised several major and mutually interconnected objectives:

1. to gain official recognition of a Czechoslovak government in exile that could represent Czechoslovakia on the international forum;

2. to prevail upon Britain, the protagonist of the Munich tragedy, to repudiate fully and unequivocally Munich and all its consequences detrimental to Czechoslovakia;

3. to solve the problem of the German minority in Czechoslovakia so that the Sudeten Germans could never again become a tool of, or a pretext for, pan-German expansionism;

4. to guarantee the safety of postwar Czechoslovakia by a close association with Poland and a firm alliance with the Soviet Union while maintaining simultaneously friendly relations with the West; and

5. to reach a mutually acceptable *modus vivendi* with Czechoslovakia's communists, considered essential to minimize the danger of extremist tours de force during the chaotic conditions that were bound to develop in Czechoslovakia and throughout all of Eastern Europe in the wake of the Nazi collapse.

Gaining Recognition for a Czechoslovak Government in Exile

The foremost need of a political exile movement is, of course, to attain for itself recognition as the rightful spokesman for its country. Hence, when Beneš resumed his political work after Hitler had liquidated what was left of post-Munich Czechoslovakia on March 15, 1939, his efforts were aimed, first of all, at organizing a unified Czechoslovak liberation movement abroad with a central organ that would seek, at the proper time, official recognition as a government in exile.

Beneš harbored no illusions that this would be easy. First of all, he quickly realized that it would prove impossible to provide the Czech and Slovak politicians, diplomats, generals, and other prominent personalities who went into exile with functions that they would consider commensurate with their ambitions and their real or imagined prestige. Dissatisfaction was thus bound to arise and push some of the disgruntled into opposition, as had in fact occurred in the case of Osuský, Hodža, General Lev Prchala, and a few others.[3] Moreover, the Sudeten German So-

---

[3] See Beneš, *Paměti, passim*; Feierabend's works mentioned in the preceding note; and Jaromír Smutný, "Edvard Beneš a Československý odboj za druhé světové války" ["Edvard Beneš and the Czechoslovak Resistance in World War II"], *Svědectví*, VI, No. 21 (Summer 1963), 50ff.

cial Democrats, by far the strongest group among anti-Nazi German exiles from Czechoslovakia, were not ready in 1939 to join the Czechoslovak liberation movement as they flirted with the idea of joining perhaps some hoped-for future greater German federation.[4] Hence the attainment of complete unity was beyond Beneš's reach, and he knew that this was likely to impede his efforts to gain recognition.

Second, and more important, since men responsible for Munich continued to hold the reins of power in both France and Britain during 1939 and 1940, Beneš suspected that they would not be eager to extend recognition to a Czechoslovak government in exile, especially one led by himself and committed so resolutely to the full restoration of pre-Munich Czechoslovakia. As late as August, 1939, when Beneš was to deliver his first public address in Britain at the Liberal summer school in Cambridge, it had to be a rather general discussion of democracy, since the British Foreign Office requested that Czechoslovakia not be mentioned in the speech.[5] Nor did French Premier Edouard Daladier bother to reply to the telegram pledging the Czechoslovak people's support, that Beneš sent him on France's declaration of war against Germany on September 3, 1939.

Beneš's foreboding proved amply justified. Negotiations for the recognition of a Czechoslovak government in exile, begun shortly after the outbreak of the war, ran into trouble. Although a French-Czechoslovak agreement providing for the creation of a Czechoslovak army in France was signed on October 2, 1939, by Czechoslovakia's envoy to Paris, Štefan Osuský, "in the name of the provisional government of the Czechoslovak Republic," the French government subsequently refused to follow through with the recognition of such a government.[6] Instead, on November 14, 1939, they consented to grant recognition only to a Czechoslovak national committee. In view of the reluctant stand taken by their French allies, the British could do no better, and on December 20, 1939, they in turn recognized the Czechoslovak National Committee in terms identical to those used by the French.[7] Thus, in lieu of

[4] See below.

[5] Eduard Táborský, *Pravda zvítězila* [*Truth Prevailed*] (Prague, 1947), pp. 265-66.

[6] According to Osuský and Hodža, the French premier and his cabinet changed their mind mainly because they did not want Dr. Beneš to be included. See also *Pravda zvítězila*, p. 395; and Libuše Otáhalová and Milada Červinková, eds., *Dokumenty z historie československé politiky, 1939-1943* [*Documents on the History of Czechoslovak Politics, 1939-1934*], 2 vols. (Prague, 1966), I, Nos. 7, 10, 13, 21; cited hereafter as Otáhalová and Červinková, *Dokumenty.* For the text of the Czechoslovak-French agreement see *Czechoslovak Yearbook of International Law* (London, 1942), pp. 232-35; cited hereafter as *Czechoslovak Yearbook.*

[7] *Czechoslovak Yearbook*, pp. 229-31.

a government authorized to speak for Czechoslovakia as an independent sovereign country, Beneš and his associates had to be content with a central organ of an uncertain and definitely inferior international status and clothed with a vaguely defined authority to "represent the Czechoslovak peoples."

Disappointed but by no means discouraged, Beneš decided to wait for the first suitable opportunity to raise again the issue of recognition. That opportunity came in the spring of 1940. In March, 1940, Daladier, one of the leading men of Munich and archfoe of Beneš, felt compelled to resign from the premiership and was replaced by Paul Reynaud. In April, 1940, the Germans invaded Denmark and Norway and thereby shattered the last hopes for a compromise peace cherished by pro-appeasement elements that were still strongly entrenched in both France and Britain. The influence of the opponents of Munich, especially Winston Churchill, was on the rise, whereas that of Neville Chamberlain, the main architect of Munich, seemed to be receding even prior to his resignation in early May, 1940.

Sensing that these developments tended to enhance his chances, Beneš began in April, 1940, to press the British once again for recognition of a Czechoslovak government in exile. Again he encountered difficulties and delays, stemming mainly from the subtle British insistence on a clear and public manifestation of Czech-Slovak unity, by which was really meant the participation of Hodža and Osuský in the government to be recognized.[8] However, after a series of prolonged discussions with the British Foreign Office from April to July, 1940, the British government finally recognized the enlarged national committee as the "provisional Czechoslovak government" on July 21, 1940.[9]

British recognition represented a major step forward for the Czechoslovak political exiles and a notable improvement for Czechoslovakia's cause. Beneš was well pleased with the result. "Our new government is

[8] Sir Alexander Cadogan's letter to Dr. Beneš dated May 25, 1940, in Dr. Beneš's archives; see also Otáhalová and Červinková, *Dokumenty*, I, Nos. 70, 91. Except for the delay in the recognition of the Czechoslovak government in exile that Hodža and Osuský may have caused by their exploitation of the Slovak issue, the Czech-Slovak relations created no problem during the war. While Beneš himself continued to adhere to the view that the Czechs and Slovaks were just two branches of one and the same nation, he fully respected the opposite view holding the Czechs and the Slovaks to be two different Slav nations. (See Otáhalová a Červinková, *Dokumenty*, I, No. 302). Moreover, he was quite willing to concede a substantial degree of autonomy to the Slovaks (ibid.). Thus, with the Slovak separatists being thoroughly discredited by their collaboration with the Nazis, the only danger implicit in the Slovak question appeared to be its possible misuse by the communists. As shown below, Beneš sought to avert this potential threat by a timely accommodation with the Czechoslovak communists and the Soviet Union.

[9] Text in the *Czechoslovak Yearbook*, p. 231, and Beneš, *Memoirs*, p. 110.

recognized again internationally, the international status of the Czechoslovak Republic is recognized again, our national flag again flies legitimately in the whole world," he broadcast jubilantly to the Czechoslovak people over the British Broadcasting Company on July 24, 1940. He called the recognition "the first great step toward victory."[10] Nonetheless, Beneš and his associates were well aware of certain flaws resulting from the British designation of the Czechoslovak government as provisional. While the full meaning of this "provisionality" was not quite clear, it definitely placed the Czechoslovak government in an inferior position to the other allied governments in exile, such as those of Poland, Belgium, Norway, the Netherlands, Yugoslavia, and Greece.[11] This was reflected, among other things, in the fact that, rather than a full-fledged envoy extraordinary and minister plenipotentiary, only a "delegate" of undefined status was accredited to the newly recognized Czechoslovak government.

Therefore, as soon as the threat of German invasion of Britain and the worst of the Luftwaffe's blitz had subsided, Beneš took the first steps toward inducing the British to drop the provisionality attribute and grant the Czechoslovak government in exile full *de jure* recognition. Since Anthony Eden, probably the most staunch English critic of Neville Chamberlain's appeasement policy and a good friend of Beneš from the Geneva days, had meanwhile become Britain's foreign secretary, it seemed that the prospects for an early positive response were favorable.

Beneš set the process in motion in early March, 1941, when he informally presented the British delegate, R. Bruce Lockhart, with a long memorandum spelling out his request and the reasons therefor. Once again, however, difficulties began to develop. The British objections were mainly of a legal nature. In the view of the Foreign Office lawyers, the government of Emil Hácha, Beneš's successor in the presidency—recognized by the British after Munich—had not ceased to exist even though it was currently in Nazi captivity. Also, there was a Slovak government in Bratislava to which the British had accorded *de facto* recognition in the months preceding the war.[12] How then could the provisional Czechoslovak government in exile be given full *de jure* recognition? Furthermore, the question arose as to whether the Czechoslovak government in Britain could be given jurisdiction over the Sudeten Germans, whose leaders, especially Wenzel Jaksch, objected. Finally, as Lockhart himself conceded, there were still certain doubts in the Conservative party, where some of the Munich men continued to be influential, as well as in the

---

[10] Edvard Beneš, *Tři roky druhé světové války* [*Three Years of World War II*] (London, 1942), pp. 44-47; cited hereafter as *Tři roky*.

[11] For a discussion of the issue of provisionality, see Eduard Taborsky, *The Czechoslovak Cause* (London, 1944), pp. 89-90.

[12] On the British attitude see ibid., p. 62.

British dominions, where South Africa's Gen. Jan Smuts was said to be against granting full recognition.

Thus it began to look very much like yet another protracted war of attrition. At this very moment, however, good fortune intervened in the person of Winston Churchill. On April 19, 1941, the British prime minister paid his first visit to the Czechoslovak armed forces stationed in Britain, and Beneš took advantage of the occasion to hand him a short *pour-mémoire* summarizing the Czechoslovak arguments for full recognition. Churchill was very pleased with the Czechoslovak army's spirit and performance, but he was really moved to tears when, at the conclusion of the visit, the Czechoslovak soldiers, all of whom had become exiles as a result of the shoddy treatment meted out to their country at Munich and after, bade him farewell by singing "Rule Britannia" in unison. It may well be that it was this moving encounter that prompted Churchill to act. In any case, as Lockhart told us a few days later, immediately upon his return to London Churchill gave Beneš's *pour-mémoire* to Eden with the following remark scribbled in his own handwriting: "I do not understand why the Czechs could not have the same status as the other allies. They deserve it." Eden in his turn added: "I agree," and handed it over to his Foreign Office aides for further action.

That was indeed the one touch needed to release the floodgates of recognition. Although there was to be yet another eight-week delay before the process was consummated, the *de jure* recognition—dropping the provisionality designation and placing the Czechoslovak government in exile on an equal footing with other allied governments in exile—was finally granted on July 18, 1941.[13] On the same day, the Czechoslovak government in exile was recognized officially by the Soviet Union and, on July 31, 1941, by the United States.[14] As negotiations with the United States were initiated at a time when the Czechoslovak government in Britain still carried the label of provisionality, the pertinent United States documents spoke of provisional recognition, even though the Czechoslovak government meanwhile had ceased to be provisional. However, this imperfection was set right on October 26, 1942, by an official American notification to the effect that United States recognition was meant to be full and definitive.[15]

Thus by the end of July, 1941, Beneš's endeavors to secure full recognition for his government in exile were brought to a successful conclusion.

[13] See Eden's letter to Masaryk in Beneš, *Paměti*, p. 186; *Memoirs*, pp. 125-26.

[14] For the documents on Soviet recognition see Beneš, *Paměti*, pp. 242-44; *Memoirs*, p. 157. For those on the United States recognition see *Paměti*, pp. 263-67; *Memoirs*, pp. 177-78.

[15] See Taborsky, *The Czechoslovak Cause*, p. 101.

The Struggle for the Repudiation of Munich
and Its Consequences

The main reason why Beneš was in such a hurry to obtain recognition for a Czechoslovak government in exile was to gain an official, internationally recognized position from which he could launch his offensive against the Munich *Diktat* and its consequences; for he wanted to wipe the disgraceful Munich state clean as soon as he could.

To set his struggle on a firmer theoretical basis, Beneš developed the concept of Czechoslovakia's political and legal continuity. Outlining the political program of the Czechoslovak liberation movement after Hitler's occupation of Prague in March, 1939, Beneš spelled out its very first and most fundamental principle: "Our state has legally never ceased to exist. No Czechoslovak must give up this principle of continuity either in the internal or international sphere. All that had happened since September 19, 1938, had happened illegally, unconstitutionally, and had been imposed upon us by threats, terror and violence. We shall never recognize it."[16]

Thus formulated, Beneš's theory of continuity implied several major affirmations, that:

1. the Republic of Czechoslovakia, as established in 1918, continued to exist as an International Legal Person;
2. the Slovak secession of March 1939 was null and void, and the so-called Slovak state did not legally exist;
3. the Munich agreement was invalid *ab initio*, i.e., from its very inception, and not merely because it was subsequently violated by the Nazi invasion of Czechoslovakia in March, 1939;
4. all of Czechoslovakia's territories transferred to Germany, Hungary, and Poland on the basis, and in the wake of, the Munich agreement continued, even after Munich, to be legally a constituent part of Czechoslovakia; and
5. Beneš's abdication from the presidency in October, 1938, was invalid and, therefore, he never ceased to be the legal president of Czechoslovakia.

Actually, Beneš took the very first step toward the realization of his ambitious program one day after the Nazi troops goosestepped into Prague. On March 16, 1939, he sent identical telegrams to the American president, the premiers of Britain and France, the Soviet foreign minister, and the chairman of the Council of the League of Nations protesting the German action and requesting that it not be recognized.[17]

[16] Beneš, *Paměti*, p. 156. See also a further elaboration of this concept, ibid., pp. 167-69.
[17] Text in Beneš, *Paměti*, p. 98; *Memoirs*, p. 65.

Whether or not this protest had any impact, the governments of Britain, France, the United States, and the Soviet Union did send the German government on March 17 and 18, 1939, formal notes refusing to recognize the situation brought about by the German action.[18] Thus the first and most fundamental requisite of Beneš's concept of Czechoslovakia's legal continuity was virtually conceded by the four Great Powers of the future anti-Nazi Grand Alliance a mere few days after Hitler's invasion of Czechoslovakia. Moreover, the British and the French protests made it amply clear that both countries considered Hitler's action as a "complete repudiation" and "flagrant violation" of the Munich agreement. Since, under the well-established rules of international law, violation of an agreement entitles the other parties to declare such an agreement null and void, the British and French notes provided Beneš with a valuable departure for his subsequent anti-Munich gambit.[19]

So long as the men of Munich ruled supreme in France and Britain, and were unwilling even to consider recognizing a Czechoslovak government in exile, it was evident, of course, that any attempts to push the legal-continuity issue any farther would do more harm than good. However, as soon as the political atmosphere in Britain began to clear up after the French collapse in June, 1940, and the British had agreed to recognize the Czechoslovak provisional government, Beneš felt that he ought to move one step farther. In informing the British government on July 9, 1940, of the establishment of the "provisional system of the State organization," Beneš inserted in his notification the following suavely formulated clause:

Special thanks are due to His Majesty's Government for their attitude after the events of March 15th, 1939, when they categorically refused to recognise the occupation of our country and continued to recognise our Czechoslovak Legation in its political and legal privileges as well as the other legal Czechoslovak authorities in territories subordinated to the jurisdiction of His Majesty's Government in the United Kingdom. By so doing they have solemnly emphasised the political and legal continuity of the Czechoslovak Republic.

In establishing the Czechoslovak Provisional Government we therefore are continuing and building our State machinery on the basis which has been saved by the far-sighted and generous attitude of His Majesty's Government, inspired by a sublime sense of justice and respect for international law and the sacred rights of the Nations to freedom and independence.[20]

[18] Texts of notes in *The Czechoslovak Yearbook*, pp. 226-29; F. D. Roosevelt's letter to Beneš in Beneš, *Paměti*, p. 102; *Memoirs*, p. 68.

[19] For a legal analysis of this question see Taborsky, *The Czechoslovak Cause*, pp. 17-21.

[20] Beneš, *Paměti*, pp. 159-60; *Memoirs*, pp. 108-109.

Yet, its overly flattering tone notwithstanding, Beneš's attempt to get the British officially committed to the concept of Czechoslovakia's uninterrupted legal continuity met with a polite rebuff: ". . . it cannot be presumed," read Lord Halifax's reply, dated July 18, 1940,

that His Majesty's Government necessarily share your conclusion, drawn in your letter: namely, that by their attitude after the events of March 15th, 1939, His Majesty's Government have taken any definitive attitude concerning the legal continuity of the Czechoslovak Republic. The acts of His Majesty's Government were meant to protest against the changes brought about in Czechoslovakia by German military action and to stress that in their opinion these changes had no legal basis.[21]

Moreover, the British foreign secretary made yet another reservation when he wrote:

In communicating this to you [i.e. the British willingness to recognize the provisional Czechoslovak government], I would like to make it clear that His Majesty's Government, in undertaking this act of recognition, do not intend to commit themselves in advance to recognise or support the establishment of any future boundaries in Central Europe.[22]

Lord Halifax's letter showed Beneš that persuading the British to undo the consequences of Munich and accept his theory of Czechoslovakia's legal continuity would be a long and difficult task. But whenever the undoing of Munich was at stake, Beneš never took "no," or even "maybe," for an answer. Therefore, as soon as the organization of his newly recognized government had been completed, he set to work, with the dogged determination and unrelenting persistence so typical of him, to make the British change their mind.

What followed was a series of innumerable discussions and exchanges of views on Munich and the Czechoslovak legal continuity between Beneš and the various British representatives, chief of whom were Bruce Lockhart, Philip Nichols, the newly appointed British envoy to the Czechoslovak government, and Foreign Secretary Anthony Eden.[23] Time and again during the ensuing two years, Beneš renewed his pressure, bombarding the British with every conceivable argument in support of his demands and supplying them with various memoranda and formulae suggesting possible solutions.

As negotiations kept dragging on and on without any tangible progress, even Beneš's characteristic patience began to wear thin. At one time, in a prolonged and heated session with Nichols on April 9, 1942,

[21] Beneš, *Paměti*, p. 161; *Memoirs*, p. 110.
[22] Ibid.   [23] Beneš, *Paměti*, pp. 293ff.

Beneš came close to serving the British with a virtual ultimatum. If the British were unwilling to set things right, Beneš told Nichols, then he would have to state openly that negotiations had failed and so inform Czechoslovakia's friends in the Liberal and Labour parties to show them that the responsibility for the failure lay with the British government and not with the Czechs. "Every Englishman must realize that Munich continues to stand between our nation and England, and that it will not be forgotten unless it is undone," he added. "I am afraid that you Englishmen with your lack of political imagination and foresight do not realize what could be the consequences of your attitude in postwar Central-European and overall European continental politics."[24]

Beneš's veiled threat may not have been the decisive factor, but the fact is that shortly thereafter the protracted British-Czechoslovak negotiations on Munich took a definite turn for the better. On June 4, 1942, Beneš had a long talk with Eden, who promised to do his utmost to meet Beneš's desiderata. Indeed, after two more sessions with Eden, on June 25 and July 7, 1942, an agreement was reached and subsequently embodied in the exchange of official notes between Anthony Eden and Czechoslovak Foreign Minister Jan Masaryk on August 5, 1942.[25]

The crux of Eden's letter was its statement that, as Germany had deliberately destroyed arrangements reached in 1938 concerning Czechoslovakia, His Majesty's government regarded themselves as being free from any engagements in this respect and that, at the final settlement of Czechoslovak frontiers to be reached at the end of the war, His Majesty's government would not be influenced by any changes effected in and since 1938. While the formula did not explicitly commit the British to the acceptance of the pre-Munich line as the boundary of postwar Czechoslovakia, it did amount to an official British recognition of the invalidity of all the territorial gains made in both 1938 and 1939 at the expense of Czechoslovakia, not only by Nazi Germany but also by Hungary and Poland. Moreover, it could be said to imply a virtual British promise to support Czechoslovakia in her claim to pre-Munich boundaries after the war. Finally, were it still needed after the British *de jure* recognition of Beneš's government in exile as the sole representative of the Republic of Czechoslovakia, it could be read as an implicit nonrecognition of the 1939 Slovak secession.

As Beneš then put it, in the matter of the repudiation of Munich and its consequences, he got from the British ninety percent of what he wanted. The only outstanding difference that remained was that the British considered the Munich agreement to have been invalidated only through its subsequent violation by the German action of March, 1939, and not from its very inception, as claimed by Beneš. That was also why

---

[24] Entry in this writer's diary.   [25] Texts in Beneš, *Tři roky*, pp. 161-62.

the British did not wish to express themselves one way or another on Beneš's version of the legal continuity of pre-Munich Czechoslovakia, with its implication that everything that had happened to Czechoslovakia from September 19, 1938, was illegal since it had been imposed by force and in violation of the Czechoslovak constitution. Nonetheless, they consented in advance that the concept of Czechoslovakia's legal continuity be mentioned in Masaryk's reply to Eden's letter of August 5, 1942.

Having secured a mutually acceptable settlement with Britain, Beneš turned to France, Britain's Munich partner. As he correctly anticipated, he met with no problem. General Charles de Gaulle and his French National Committee, the spokesmen for Free France, were as eager as Beneš to erase the Munich shame. On September 29, 1942, exactly four years after the Munich conference, General de Gaulle, president of the French National Committee, and Maurice Dejean, its commissioner for foreign affairs, solemnly appended their signatures to a note containing as integral a revocation of Munich as Beneš ever wanted:

> . . . rejecting the agreements signed at Munich on September 29th, 1938, the French National Committee solemnly declares that it considers these agreements as null and void from their inception as well as all other acts committed during the execution, or as a consequence, of these agreements. Recognising no territorial changes concerning Czechoslovakia which took place in 1938 and afterwards, it undertakes to do all in its power to ensure that the Czechoslovak Republic, in its frontiers of the period before September 1938, shall obtain all effective guarantees for its military and economic security, its territorial integrity and its political unity.[26]

Thus, on its fourth anniversay, the Munich Agreement stood condemned and repudiated, fully and unconditionally, by both of its signatories now fighting against the Nazi-Fascist Axis. Having never been party to the Munich settlement, the United States and the Soviet Union, the other two Great Powers of the anti-Nazi Grand Alliance, remained at all times free of any commitment in this respect and had nothing to revoke. Moreover, U. S. President Franklin Delano Roosevelt assured Beneš as early as May 28, 1939, when he received the exiled president of Czechoslovakia at his residence in Hyde Park, N. Y., that "for him there was no Munich."[27] Similarly, the Soviet government gave Beneš, on June 9, 1942, an official declaration that the Soviet Union recognized Czechoslovakia in her pre-Munich frontiers and that it never had recognized nor would recognize what had happened at Munich and after Munich.[28]

[26] The text in Beneš, *Memoirs*, p. 232.
[27] Beneš, *Paměti*, p. 116; *Memoirs*, p. 76.   [28] *Memoirs*, p. 204.

Solving the Sudeten German Problem

In Beneš's wartime thinking and strategy, Munich was tied inextricably to the problem of Czechoslovakia's German minority. Since the disloyal pro-Nazi behavior of the great majority of Czechoslovakia's Germans and its exploitation by Hitler played a major role in the destruction of Czechoslovakia during 1938 and 1939, Beneš viewed the solution of the Sudeten German problem as an integral part of his struggle for the undoing of Munich and the prevention of its recurrence. "It was clear to me immediately after Munich that when the annulment of Munich and of its consequences came in question in the future," he confides in his *Memoirs, "the problem of minorities* and especially the problem of our Germans would also have to be solved, radically and definitively."[29] As he wrote to Wenzel Jaksch, the exiled leader of the Sudeten German Social Democrats, on December 1, 1942: "The small Czechoslovak Nation cannot live with a German revolver permanently against its breast."[30]

The "radical and definitive" solution that Beneš had in mind was, of course, a drastic reduction in the size of the German minority, which he hoped to attain through a suitable combination of territorial cession and population transfer.[31] While being quite intransigent in his insistence on the recognition of Czechoslovakia's pre-Munich boundaries, Beneš was inclined, in the early years of the war, to give up some of the German-inhabited frontier areas in order to cut down the German minority. As late as January, 1943, he expressed a willingness to cede to Germany Chebsko (Egerland), Liberec (Reichenberg), and Krnov (Jägerndorf), which, taken together, represented a fairly substantial slice of the border territory.[32]

This unusual generosity stemmed from Beneš's endeavor to gain Western support for the idea of a massive population transfer, which was the cornerstone of his solution of the Sudeten German problem. Fearing that the people of the Anglo-Saxon democracies might find a compulsory translocation—involving hundreds of thousands of men, women, and children—too harsh, he hoped that a simultaneous cession of a few border areas, not crucially important from a defense viewpoint, would make his scheme less objectionable. Even so, he knew that he had to proceed with great caution. Having made his first public allusion to the possibility of postwar population transfers in a major speech at the Royal Empire

[29] Beneš, *Paměti*, p. 312; *Memoirs*, p. 210.

[30] Beneš, *Paměti*, p. 468; *Memoirs*, p. 318.

[31] At one time Beneš also played with the idea of creating a closed German territorial unit within Czechoslovakia. See also Radomír Luža, *The Transfer of the Sudeten Germans: A Study of Czech-German Relations, 1933-1962* (New York, 1964).

[32] See Feierabend, *Beneš mezi Washingtonem a Moskvou*, p. 121, and *Ve vládě v exilu*, I, 46; also Luža, *Transfer*, pp. 237-38.

Society in London on January 23, 1940, Beneš became gradually more and more outspoken as the war grew in intensity and atrocities committed by the Germans in Czechoslovakia and elsewhere were making the Germans ever more unpopular.[33]

In January, 1942, Beneš considered the situation ripe enough to begin discussing the transfer with the British government. He prepared a memorandum explaining in some detail his views on the matter. He estimated that, to begin with, some 300,000 to 400,000 Sudeten Germans would flee Czechoslovakia at the end of the war for fear of punishment. Some 1,200,000 to 1,400,000 would be transferred to Germany. An exchange of certain heavily German-populated Czechoslovak frontier districts for less populated German areas would bring about yet another decrease by some 600,000 to 700,000, so that, when the process had been completed, only about 600,000 to 1,000,000 Germans would remain. As Beneš told me, he "lent" the memorandum "privately" to Lockhart with the understanding that it was to be considered as "unwritten" unless the British were prepared to accept it. He also explained his plan to Anthony Eden at a luncheon on January 21, 1942. At that time the British were not yet ready to accept Beneš's memorandum, mainly because it also raised the thorny issue of the British recognition of Czechoslovakia's pre-Munich boundaries, and the memorandum thus remained "unwritten."

However, after the successful conclusion of negotiations for their repudiation of Munich mentioned earlier, the British also conceded Beneš's idea of a population transfer. "At the same time Minister Nichols informed us," reports Beneš in his *Memoirs*,

> that the British government had given careful consideration to our attitude *in the matter of the transfer from our Republic of minority populations which had conspired against us* and had reached the conclusion, in view of what had happened in 1938 and during the war, that at the time of the final solution of our minority problems after the victorious end of the war the British Government *did not intend to oppose the principle of transfer of the minority population from Czechoslovakia in an endeavour to make Czechoslovakia ethnically as homogeneous a country as possible.*[34]

[33] In an address at Oxford University on May 23, 1941, and a subsequent discussion with professors, Beneš recommended the adoption of a massive population transfer as the best solution of the Central-European minorities' problem, and he endorsed the idea also in his article on "The New Order in Europe" in the September, 1941, issue of *The Nineteenth Century and After*, xxx, 150 ff.

[34] Beneš, *Paměti*, p. 306; *Memoirs*, p. 206; the italics are Beneš's. The *Memoirs* do not mention the exact date of Nichols' notification. An entry in this writer's diary indicates that the first official assurance that Britain would not oppose the transfer was given Beneš orally by Anthony Eden during their meeting on July 7, 1942. See also Jaromír Smutný, *Němci v Československu a jejich odsun z*

Having gained British assent, however reluctant, Beneš turned with similar requests to the Americans and the Russians.

He raised the issue of the transfer in both discussions he had with President Roosevelt during his visit to the United States in May and June, 1943; and in both instances the American president gave Beneš his approval. "He agrees that after the war the number of Germans in Czechoslovakia must be reduced by a transfer of as many as possible," reported Beneš from Washington to his government in London after his first talk with Roosevelt on May 13, 1943.[35] And he sent another message to London after his final session with the American president on June 7, 1943: "I asked again expressly whether the United States would agree to the transfer of our Germans. He [Roosevelt] declared clearly that they would."[36]

Somewhat to his surprise, Beneš met with more hesitation when he began to discuss the matter with the Soviets. Anxious to know the Soviet attitude and to secure Soviet backing, the Czechoslovak president mentioned his idea of the transfer in several talks with Soviet Ambassadors Maisky and Bogomolov between 1941 and 1943.[37] He also talked about the transfer of the Germans with Soviet Foreign Minister Vyacheslav Molotov on June 9, 1942, during the latter's visit to London. In all of these instances the Soviet diplomats listened politely, seemed to be favorably inclined, but never really committed the Soviet Union to support Beneš's transfer plans, claiming that the Sudeten German issue was Czechoslovakia's internal affair. Eager therefore to make sure of the Soviet stand before his departure for the United States, Beneš pressed Bogomolov on March 19, 1943, to find out from Moscow whether or not Czechoslovakia could count on Soviet support in this matter.[38] However, once again the Soviet answer, brought by Bogomolov on April 23, 1943, was noncommittal.[39] It was only on June 5, 1943, a few days before Beneš's return from the United States to England, that Bogomolov finally was able to inform the Czechoslovak government that the Soviet government agreed with the idea of the transfer.[40]

Although much additional work had to be done before the promise

---

republiky [Germans in Czechoslovakia and Their Removal from the Republic], a mimeographed monograph published by Ústav Dr. Edvarda Beneše (London, 1956), p. 71.

[35] Beneš, Paměti, p. 285; Memoirs, p. 193.

[36] Beneš, Paměti, p. 289; Memoirs, p. 195.

[37] An entry in this writer's diary shows that Beneš raised the matter of the transfer in a talk he had with Maisky as early as August 28, 1941.

[38] Beneš, Paměti, p. 360; Memoirs, p. 242.

[39] Ibid.

[40] In Beneš's absence, Bogomolov contacted Hubert Ripka, State Secretary in the Czechoslovak Ministry for Foreign Affairs, and urged him to wire the message to Beneš. Beneš, Paměti, p. 362; Memoirs, p. 286.

could become a reality, the Soviet official acceptance, coming as it did on top of the positive assurances given by the other two Great Powers of the wartime Grand Alliance, clinched the matter.[41] Beneš and his government in exile had scored yet another major victory in their struggle for the undoing of Munich and the prevention of its recurrence in the future. In the end it had not been necessary to sacrifice any portion of Czechoslovakia's territory as Beneš had originally thought.

Only one thing marred Beneš's victory and caused him concern: his inability to secure the cooperation of the democratic Sudeten Germans in exile, save for a small minority, in the solution of the problem. He had meant every word when he repeated all through the war that he did not wish to harm the democratic elements among Czechoslovakia's Germans but sincerely wanted to help them remain in Czechoslovakia.[42] That was why he had reckoned in his memoranda on the transfer that some 600,000 to 1,000,000 Germans would be exempted. This was more than enough to accommodate all the Sudeten Germans who had remained loyal to the republic.[43] Unfortunately, as Beneš explains at length in his *Memoirs*, his endeavors to obtain such cooperation proved fruitless.[44]

The Search for Security Through Ties
to Poland and the Soviet Union

Designed to remove a potential fifth column from the strategically crucial border areas, the transfer of the Sudeten Germans was of the utmost importance for Czechoslovakia's security. The transfer alone was not enough, however. In her exposed geographical position and with a long and vulnerable border with Germany, Czechoslovakia could not very well be defended without outside help. Consequently, securing such help for the postwar period became one of Beneš's major wartime preoccupations. Having been betrayed by France and abandoned by Britain in 1938 and 1939, Beneš understandably felt that he had better look to the East in searching for allies, especially to those countries that would be in the direct path of any future German *Drang nach Osten*.

While by no means forgoing aid from the West, he came to the conclusion that the optimum solution for giving his country the maximum possible protection against a new Munich would be a close association with Poland backed by an alliance with Soviet Russia. Such a tripartite arrangement, he thought, would create a mighty bloc that would guarantee the safety of all its partners. At the same time a tighter confedera-

---

[41] For the whole story see Luža, *Transfer, passim*.

[42] Beneš, *Paměti*, pp. 312ff, 455ff.

[43] See also the Czechoslovak memorandum sent to the European Advisory Committee on August 24, 1944, which put the figure of the Germans eligible to retain Czechoslovak citizenship at 800,000 in Luža, *Transfer*, p. 246.

[44] Beneš, *Paměti*, pp. 312ff, 455ff.

tive link between Poland and Czechoslovakia might lessen somewhat the Soviet predominance within the bloc.

Naturally, so long as the Soviet Union played its waiting game prior to its invasion by the Wehrmacht in June, 1941, all that Beneš could do about the part of his project involving Soviet Russia was to keep the avenues of approach open—which he did by maintaining personal contacts with Ivan Maisky, Soviet ambassador in Britain throughout the entire trying period of the Nazi-Soviet rapprochement from 1939 to 1941. Hence he concentrated in the first years of the war on working out the Czechoslovak-Polish phase of his plan.

After some preliminary talks on the desirability of closer Czechoslovak-Polish ties after the war, Beneš got the negotiations started formally in November 1940 when he sent Gen. Władysław Sikorski, the Polish premier in exile, a memorandum explaining his thoughts on the establishment of a postwar Polish-Czechoslovak "confederation sui generis."[45] General Sikorski's prompt and affirmative reply of December 3, 1940, accompanied by a memorandum representing, as Sikorski pointed out, "a unanimous opinion of the Polish government," expressed complete agreement with the theses expounded in Beneš's memorandum. Shortly thereafter, mixed Czechoslovak-Polish committees were set up to work out the details of the envisaged union. In January, 1942, their efforts resulted in a Polish-Czechoslovak protocol embodying the fundamental principles upon which the Czechoslovak-Polish confederation was to be erected. The protocol provided for a common policy in foreign affairs, defense, economic and financial matters, social questions, transport, and post and telegraph; for coordination of foreign trade and customs tariffs with a view to the eventual creation of a customs union; and for the establishment of a common general staff as well as other common organs. The desire was also expressed that the confederation should embrace other states "of the European area with which the vital interests of Poland and Czechoslovakia were linked."[46]

Having laid what then seemed to be a solid foundation for a close Polish-Czechoslovak association, Beneš was ready to proceed with the second part of his plan: gaining the cooperation and alliance of Soviet Russia. He expected, of course, that there would be difficulties in the

---

[45] *Échanges de Vues sur la Collaboration Polono-Tchécoslovaque après la Présente Guerre.* See Eduard Taborsky, "A Polish-Czechoslovak Confederation," *Journal of Central European Affairs,* IX, No. 4 (January 1950), 379ff, and the same author's "Beneš, Sikorski and the Czechoslovak-Polish Relations, 1939-1942," *Central European Federalist,* XI, No. 1 (July 1963), 17ff. See also Piotr S. Wandycz, *Czechoslovak-Polish Confederation and the Great Powers, 1940-1943* (Bloomington, 1956), pp. 39-40.

[46] For a detailed study of the provisions of the protocol see Taborsky, "The Czechoslovak-Polish Confederation," *The New Commonwealth Quarterly* (July 1942), pp. 13ff; Wandycz, *Czechoslovak-Polish Confederation,* pp. 67-70.

path of Soviet-Polish cooperation, because of the tenseness of Polish-Soviet relations. But he hoped that the common struggle against the Germans and the necessity of preventing a recurrence of the pan-German menace in the future would create a sufficient community of Polish-Russian interests to allow the proposed tripartite arrangement to materialize. That seemed indeed to be the case in 1941 when, shortly after the German invasion of Russia, diplomatic relations were restored between the Soviet government and the Polish government in exile. The two countries became allies and the government of the USSR conceded on July 30, 1941, that "the Soviet-German treaties of 1939 as to territorial changes in Poland" had "lost their validity." Taking advantage of the improved situation, Beneš approached the Soviet government to inform it of his plan for a Polish-Czechoslovak confederation and to gain its support for the project. From what he learned from Maisky in London and from Zdeněk Fierlinger, Czechoslovakia's ambassador to Moscow, who had been instructed to raise the matter with the Soviet Foreign Ministry, the Soviet attitude was favorable.[47]

Less than two weeks after the signing of the Polish-Czechoslovak protocol of January 19, 1942, however, a report came from Fierlinger informing Beneš that "Soviet circles" thought that the Czechoslovak policy of cooperation with the Poles had "run ahead of the events" and was "not taking a realistic view of the future."[48] Simultaneously, Bogomolov, the Soviet ambassador to the Czechoslovak government in exile, and his aides began to buttonhole various Czechoslovak politicians in London to tell them of the doubts that those same "Soviet circles" had about the wisdom of Czechoslovakia's entering into a confederation with Poland. Though greatly dismayed by this sudden and unexpected Soviet *volte face*, Beneš persisted in his endeavors. He took advantage of Molotov's visit to London in June, 1942, to persuade the Soviet foreign minister of the desirability of the Czechoslovak-Polish confederation.[49] As Beneš told me after returning from his talk with Molotov on June 9, 1942, Molotov assured him that, provided the Poles established friendly relations with Soviet Russia, the Soviet government had no objections. But a mere five weeks later the Soviet Union reneged even on this conditional approval when Bogomolov officially informed first Jan Masaryk and then Beneš that the Soviet government was opposed to the whole idea.

In view of the Soviet refusal to go along, Beneš's cherished idea of a tripartite Czechoslovak-Polish-Soviet arrangement fell apart and the Czechoslovak president was faced with two unenviable alternatives: either to persist in his efforts to create a Czechoslovak-Polish union and

[47] See details in Taborsky, *op. cit.*, in *Journal of Central European Affairs*.
[48] From Dr. Beneš's archives.
[49] See Taborsky, *op. cit.*, in *Journal of Central European Affairs*.

incur the enmity of the Russians, or to renounce, at least for the time being, the confederative project with Poland and to seek an alliance with the Soviet Union—and thus, of course, thereby anger the Poles. Though disagreeable, the choice was clear, for Beneš wanted a Czechoslovak-Polish confederation only on the condition that it would not be opposed by the Russians, and he had made this amply clear to the Poles from the very beginning.

Thus, Beneš opted for an alliance with Soviet Russia, which was subsequently signed during his visit to Moscow in December 1943 after having overcome the initial British objections that such a treaty should not be concluded before the end of the war. Nonetheless, in spite of all the setbacks, he kept looking for some alternate form of Polish-Czechoslovak cooperation. Since the Russians evidently did not like the idea of a confederation, he came up with the idea of an alliance, hoping that this might be acceptable insofar as it did not imply such a degree of closeness as did the confederation. Though the Soviet reaction to the idea of a Czechoslovak-Polish alliance was negative at first, Beneš insisted during his ensuing negotiations for the Czechoslovak-Soviet treaty of friendship and alliance, on the necessity of bringing Poland into the Eastern system of defense. As a result, the Russians finally agreed to add a protocol to the treaty permitting a subsequent adhesion of "any third state which has common frontiers with the USSR or the Czechoslovak Republic, and which in the present war has been the object of German aggression."[50] Like so many other Soviet assurances, the protocol proved ultimately to be only a useless scrap of paper. At the time of its signature in December, 1943, however, Beneš honestly believed that, once the Polish-Soviet frontier controversy had been solved, Poland would become a fullfledged partner in the Czechoslovak-Polish-Soviet alliance system.[51]

Attempts to Find an Acceptable Modus Vivendi with Czechoslovakia's Communists

Apart from the desire to secure a strong ally against Germany, there was yet another impelling reason why Beneš gave priority to an alliance with the Soviets over a confederation with Poland. That reason lay in the troublemaking potential of Czechoslovakia's own communists. Beneš

[50] Text in Taborsky, The Czechoslovak Cause, pp. 153-54.

[51] A good deal more could be written about Beneš's wartime dealings with the Russians, but limited space does not allow further elaboration. The Czechoslovak-Soviet relations up to the end of 1943 are discussed in Beneš's Memoirs. See also this writer's "The Triumph and Disaster of Eduard Beneš," Foreign Affairs, XXXVI, No. 4 (July 1958), 669ff, and the same author's "Beneš and Stalin, Moscow 1943 and 1945," Journal of Central European Affairs, XIII, No. 2 (July 1953), 154ff, which cover also the happenings of 1944 and 1945. For the Czechoslovak communist point of view see Bohuslav Laštovička, V Londýně za války [In London during the War] (Prague, 1960), pp. 310-30 and 496-553.

was well aware of their designs to communize the country in the wake of the Nazi collapse. He knew that their chances to do so would be enhanced by such factors as the chaotic conditions bound to exist at the war's end before order could be restored, Czech-Slovak dissension that could easily lend itself to communist manipulation, the probable presence of the Red Army in Czechoslovakia, the tremendous increase in Soviet Russia's prestige resulting from the Russians' heroic fighting, and the traditional pro-Russian sympathies among the Czechoslovak masses, which rose to an unprecedented height after the Russian entry into the war. Most of all he dreaded, as if haunted by a foreboding of the February, 1948, coup, what would happen should Soviet Russia encourage, and give unreserved support to, the Czechoslovak communists in their bid to seize power. To prevent this deadly menace, Beneš conceived a strategy based on a dual approach.

First, he was resolved to do everything possible to maintain good and friendly relations with the Soviet Union. He thought that this would make it more difficult for both the Soviets and the Czechoslovak communists to turn openly against him. That was why he was so anxious to conclude a treaty of alliance and friendship with Soviet Russia as soon as possible. That was why he bowed to the virtual Soviet veto of the Czechoslovak-Polish confederation, although he knew very well how bad an impression this was bound to create in the West. That was also why, with bitterness in his heart, he agreed in 1945 to surrender Ruthenia, the easternmost province of Czechoslovakia, to the Russians and left unchallenged this and several other Soviet perfidies vis-à-vis Czechoslovakia in late 1944 and early 1945.[52]

Second, Beneš decided to seek a timely accommodation with Czechoslovakia's own communists. He considered it imperative to bring them into active cooperation in the government, make them share the responsibilities, and weaken their chances for reckless demagoguery. As soon as the communists realigned themselves behind the Czechoslovak government in exile, following the Nazi invasion of Russia, Beneš appointed several representatives of the exiled Czechoslovak communists in London to the state council as well as to various agencies of the Czechoslovak government in exile. During his visit to Moscow in 1943 he offered, unsuccessfully, two seats in the cabinet to Czechoslovak communist leaders in Moscow. To gain the communists' cooperation, he was willing to grant some of their demands beyond what he considered to be right and reasonable. Such was the case in local government reform, where Beneš yielded to communist insistence that the existing system be replaced with a network of people's committees strongly reminiscent of the USSR's soviets. It was so also in matters of economic collectivization, where he

[52] See Taborsky, "Beneš and Stalin, Moscow 1943 and 1945."

went beyond the extent of socialization that he himself viewed as a desirable maximum. Worst of all, that was so when he felt compelled during his stay in Moscow in March, 1945, to concede to the communists and their fellow travelers certain key positions in the newly formed cabinet that was to return with him to the liberated portion of Czechoslovakia.[53]

As our account of Czechoslovak politics in exile reveals, Beneš managed to attain most of the objectives that he pursued. After initial difficulties he gained full recognition for his government. He got Munich and its consequences invalidated and the pre-Munich boundaries of Czechoslovakia reaffirmed, explicitly or implicitly, by the Big Three of the victorious Grand Alliance. He obtained in advance their consent to the massive transfer of Czechoslovakia's Germans to Germany. He secured an alliance with the Soviet Union that was likely to offer the best attainable guarantee against any future danger of another Munich. Although he failed to realize his projected Czechoslovak-Polish confederation, he did keep a seat reserved for Poland in the Czechoslovak-Soviet alliance. He seemed for a while even to have succeeded in reaching a reasonable *modus vivendi* with Czechoslovakia's communists.

Subsequent developments in Czechoslovakia and their tragic culmination in the communist seizure of power in February, 1948, have, of course, cast doubts on the wisdom of Beneš's wartime policy of cooperation with the Czechoslovak communists and their Soviet mentors. Indeed, some of his political opponents began to criticize him for what they considered to be pro-Soviet, or pro-communist, leanings and wishful thinking or political opportunism even prior to his first trip to Moscow in 1943. As invariably happens, many more joined in the criticism with the easy wisdom of hindsight after things had turned for the worse in 1945 and thereafter.

However, the case of Beneš's critics stands or falls on the question of whether there was a truly viable alternative, another course of action vis-à-vis Soviet Russia and the native communists that would have yielded better results. Considering all the realities of the situation in East Central Europe between 1939 and 1945, a negative answer is clearly indicated. Indeed, an alternative approach based on firmness toward Russia and an exclusive reliance on the West was attempted by the Polish and the Yugoslav governments in exile. It resulted in failure.

Politics, it is said, is the art of the possible. In their endeavors in exile between 1939 and 1945, Beneš and his collaborators did attain the maximum of what was then possible.

[53] Ibid.

· 12 ·

THE CZECH RESISTANCE MOVEMENT

Radomír Luža
Tulane University

STRUGGLE FOR ASCENDANCY

In the wake of Munich an atmosphere of insecurity enveloped the rump-Czechoslovakia, and her independence and democratic system therefore became of immediate concern for many hitherto divergent forces. High army officers, collaborators of Edvard Beneš, former members of socialist parties, a few politicians belonging to the right-wing parties, and a host of independents united as a nucleus of opposition to the Munich capitulation. They believed in an early outbreak of armed conflict between Nazi Germany and the West that would lead to Germany's defeat and the eventual reestablishment of democratic Czechoslovakia within her pre-Munich frontiers.

After his resignation as president of the republic, Beneš took a hard look at the international situation. Before leaving the country for England in October, 1938, he discussed with his close political friends the organization of a future resistance network at home and abroad.[1] To maintain contact between Beneš and the opposition groups within the country, couriers moved frequently between Prague and London, the provisional domicile of Beneš.[2] Despite planning for underground resistance, Hitler's early decision to crush the remainder of Czechoslovakia came as an unexpected shock to almost everyone.[3]

Many Czechs and Slovaks took the destruction of the republic on March 14 and 15, 1939, as an indication that the uncontrollable German Führer was determined to pursue a violent course of action that would

---

[1] *Memoirs of Dr. Eduard Beneš. From Munich to New War and New Victory* (Boston, 1954), p. 52. Beneš resigned on October 5. This writer will not discuss the problems relating to Slovakia and the Protectorate regime as these are taken up in other chapters of this book.

[2] Ibid. Also see Václav Kural, "Hlavní organizace nekomunistického odboje v letech 1939-1941" ["Principal Organizations of the Non-Communist Resistance in 1939-1941"] in the mimeographed Prague bulletin published by the Czechoslovak Commission for the History of the Anti-Fascist Resistance *Odboj a revoluce, Zprávy*, v, 2 (1967), 5-160; hereafter cited as *Odboj*, 2, 1967.

[3] The Czechs had previously believed that the outbreak of general war would precede any possible German attempt to occupy the republic. For a comprehensive account, see Tomáš Pasák, "Vstup německých vojsk na české území v roce 1939" ["Entry of the German Troops on the Czech Territory in 1939"], *Československý časopis historický*, xvii (1969), 161-83.

result in a worldwide conflict. The Czechs met the blow of the Nazi occupation by closing ranks. On March 16, Beneš addressed protests to the United States, British, French, and Soviet governments from Chicago, proclaiming that "the Czechs and Slovaks will never accept this unbearable imposition on their sacred rights."[4] By declaring that the republic continued legally to exist, Beneš thus launched the liberation movement abroad and at home.

In the spring and summer of 1939 politically diverse clandestine groups sprang up in the Czech lands, united around the vision of a free, socially just, and democratic Czechoslovakia. These spontaneous resistance movements developed new political centers that were different from the structure of the pre-1938 party system. This gradual shift away from the traditional power structure of Czech political life was facilitated by the imprisonment and the natural self-elimination of the former leading politicians from the illegal activities. By its nature, undergound work placed the burden of activity on the shoulders of hitherto minor personalities, mostly of the younger generation. In political terms, the ignominious crumbling of the Second Republic in March, 1939, and the daily life-and-death struggle for the preservation of the Czech national existence gradually moved the political center to the left.

A major catalyst for the Czech national posture was the close association of the Sudeten German group with the Nazi system. The Henlein party endorsed the Nazi attempt to dismember the republic. Moreover, the Sudeten Germans contributed significantly to the severity of the occupation regime, aided by their long familiarity in dealing with the Czechs. Thus, in the eyes of the average Czech, the Sudeten Germans and nazism were viewed as the epitome of evil, and the fight against the German occupation became as elementary as a bedtime story of conflict between villains and heroes.

Out of the heterogeneous welter of clandestine groupings, four main units emerged to exercise a predominant influence in the first stage of the resistance that lasted until the middle of 1942.

One of these groups was the army, in which the humiliation of Munich had left a deep resentment. In September, 1938, the army leaders had even considered the installation of a military dictatorship that would refuse to capitulate. In the winter of 1938-39 profoundly disturbed army officers had held informal meetings and prepared a secret outline of a coordinated strategy against Nazi Germany. The inspirational source for these vague plans remained T. G. Masaryk's concept of an independent

---

[4] Beneš, *Memoirs*, p. 65. On March 14 the head of the Czechoslovak intelligence service, Col. František Moravec, accompanied by a group of ten intelligence officers, landed in London.

democratic state. The occupation of the country brought this ambitious scheme into an acute phase. As a result, in the summer of 1939 the military undergound spread through all of the Czech territory. The overall command joined its own central network to a multitude of spontaneous groupings and organized a vast resistance movement, the Obrana národa (Defense of the Nation—ON).[5] In June it dispatched its leader, General Sergěj Ingr, to France as its representative in the liberation movement abroad.[6]

Besides the army there was another resistance group composed of Beneš's former collaborators who grouped themselves around Prokop Drtina and created an embryonic political leadership in the spring of 1939.[7] In response to Beneš's urgings from London to coordinate all underground activities at home in the face of the rapidly approaching conflict, this organization was enlarged and reorganized into a political center, the Politické ústředí (Political Center—PÚ), in the summer of 1939. It became the supreme organ of the political leadership at home. Soon, however, it became painfully apparent that this incipient high political command, consisting mostly of personalities drawn from the pre-Munich government coalition, was amateurish.[8] By November, 1939, it was nearly destroyed by arrests. Only a few succeeded in escaping abroad. Gradually, under the influence of younger politicians and genuine resisters, the PÚ changed its character and became a full-fledged resistance movement of every political hue. Cooperating closely with the ON, it controlled the communication channels with Beneš and the military leadership in France and later in Britain, thus enjoying a position of prominence in the resistance.[9]

As early as May, 1938, a group of social democratic and leftist intellectuals had brought out a manifesto "Věrni zůstaneme" ("We Remain Faithful") in firm support of the territorial integrity of the republic.

[5] For an account of the first period of the resistance movement, see Oldřich Janeček *et al.*, eds., *Z počátků odboje 1938-1941* [*From the Beginning of the Resistance 1938-1941*] (Prague, 1969), *passim*. The organizational structure of the ON included three army headquarters in Prague, Bohemia, and Moravia; divisional headquarters in regions; and regimental headquarters in districts (*Odboj*, 2, 1967; "Obrana národa mezi 15. březnem a 1. zářím 1939" ["Obrana národa between March 15 and September 1, 1939"], *Historie a vojenství*, No. 3 [1970], 353ff).

[6] *Odboj*, 2, 1967. General Ingr became Minister of National Defense in the exile government in London.

[7] Ibid.; Jaroslav Jelínek, *P.C. Politické ústředí domácího odboje* [*P.C. Political Center of the Home Resistance*] (Prague, 1947), p. 79.

[8] Its members represented the Social Democratic party, the Czech National Socialist party, the Agrarian party, the People's party, and the National Democratic party.

[9] Vladimír Krajina, "La Résistance tchécoslovaque," *Cahiers d'histoire de la guerre*, I (February, 1950), pp. 58ff; Václav Král, *Pravda o okupaci* [*The Truth about the Occupation*] (Prague, 1962), pp. 189-95.

345

Later, after the Nazi takeover, independently of the PÚ, this group widened its basis by associating itself with left-oriented groupings from trade unions, the army, the Y.M.C.A., educational institutions, and free-masons to form what gradually emerged as the largest resistance movement, the Petiční výbor Věrni zůstaneme (Committee of the Petition "We Remain Faithful"—PVVZ). Unconnected with the petty party politics of the past, and convinced that Czechoslovakia's prewar party structure had failed badly, the movement developed a new conception of the postwar state. Its program, Za svobodu (For Freedom), sought to build a new power structure by infusing economic democracy into a new model of the democratic socialist state and boldly pushing aside the old party system. Adopted by the ON and PÚ in 1941, this program of national democratic revolution was to be carried out by the liberation government set up by the home resistance. Demands for the restoration of the "historic" frontiers and for the removal of the Sudeten Germans from Czechoslovakia formed its other common objectives.[10]

The ideological unity and action program of the democratic resistance found expression in the first months of 1940 in the constitution of the ÚVOD (Ústřední výbor odboje domácího—Central Committee of the Home Resistance) as the joint organ of the ON, PÚ, and PVVZ. For security reasons, however, the three organizations continued to act separately.[11] The ÚVOD was eventually recognized by President Beneš as the central organ of the home resistance.

The fourth unit of the resistance, the Communist Party of Czechoslovakia (KSČ), was the only political party that survived throughout the war years.[12] It followed its own program, evolving tortuously through three different stages that reflected successive Comintern lines. The KSČ embraced the idea of the national front in the spring of 1939, but changed its course abruptly in the wake of the Nazi-Soviet agreement of

[10] Karel Veselý-Štainer, *Cestou národního odboje* [*With the National Resistance*] (Prague, 1947), *passim*. The original text was modified at many meetings of the ÚVOD in 1940 and 1941. For the text see *Za svobodu do nové Československé republiky. Ideový program domácího odbojového hnutí vypracovaný v letech 1939-41* [*For Freedom toward the New Czechoslovak Republic. Ideological Program of the Home Resistance Movement in the Years 1939-1941*] (Prague, 1945).

[11] Vladimír Krajina in Ladislav K. Feierabend, *Beneš mezi Washingtonem a Moskvou* [*Beneš between Washington and Moscow*] (Washington, D.C., 1966), pp. 136-40; *Odboj*, 2, 1967.

[12] The leadership of the KSČ went into exile in 1938-39. Its center was in Moscow. Activities of the party in the Czech lands were guided by the illegal central committee. From June, 1939, until February, 1941, its contact with Moscow was maintained by a clandestine transmitter and by couriers. In the latter part of the war all contacts were broken between Moscow and the communist underground. (For a text of cables, see Gustav Bareš, ed., "Depeše mezi Prahou a Moskvou 1939-1941" ["Messages between Prague and Moscow"], *Příspěvky k dějinám KSČ*, No. 3 [1967], pp. 375-433; hereafter cited as "Depeše.")

August 23, 1939. From then until May, 1941, it described the war as a conflict between two imperialist camps and attacked Beneš and the emigrés as agents of Anglo-French capitalism. The party insisted that its duty was to oppose the war and the victory of the Anglo-French bloc and to take up the offensive against the social democratic movement. At the time, the leadership of the KSČ in Moscow went so far as to abandon its original objective to restore the Czechoslovak state.[13] In 1941 the German invasion of the Soviet Union returned the KSČ to the concept of the popular front. By early 1943 it was well on its way back to the 1938 line of promoting an independent republic. Naturally, the party resisted the German occupation from the very beginning and the undoubted bravery of the communist resisters was everywhere evident.

The self-imposed isolation of the communist underground from other resistance groups placed it in opposition to the main stream of Czech national aspirations. This did not deter the ÚVOD from seeking to cooperate with Soviet intelligence organs in Prague. After the fall of Paris these informal contacts were woven into a strong thread when the ÚVOD arranged in Prague for the systematic delivery of important reports to the Soviet Union.[14]

The remarkable unity between the liberation movements at home and abroad included the Soviet Union as a potential ally and an important factor in the postwar power structure. It also reflected the traditional pro-Russian sympathies of the Czech people, which had been strengthened by Soviet support during the crisis of Munich. After the invasion of Russia pressures toward some kind of accommodation between democratic and communist resistance forces developed a momentum of their own. Negotiations toward the constitution of a united front were well under way in the summer of 1941. They met a violent end in the wave of arrests during the fall of 1941.[15]

The one incontrovertible point about the resistance within the Protectorate was its continuing close cooperation with the liberation movement

[13] Ibid., *passim*. For the account of the role of the KSČ in the Czech resistance, see Radomír Luža, "The Communist Party of Czechoslovakia and the Czech Resistance, 1939-1945," *Slavic Review*, XXVIII (December, 1969), 561-76.

[14] *Odboj*, 2, 1967. There was a parallel development in London, where initial contacts between Czechoslovak and Soviet intelligence officers in Istanbul in January, 1941, led to the dispatch of a Czechoslovak military mission to Moscow in April, at a time when there were still normal diplomatic relations between Moscow and Berlin. Among the information passed to Moscow was the date of the Nazi invasion of the Soviet Union. See also Čestmír Amort and I. M. Jedlička, *Tajemství vyzvědače A-54* [*Secrets of Agent A-54*] (Prague, 1965), pp. 105, 122; Jan Křen and Václav Kural, "Ke stykům mezi československým odbojem a SSSR v letech 1939-1941" ["On the Contacts between the Czechoslovak Resistance and the U.S.S.R. in 1939-1941"], *Historie a vojenství* (1967), pp. 437-71, 731-71.

[15] Oldřich Janeček et al., eds., *Odboj a revoluce 1938-1945* [*Resistance and Revolution 1938-1945*] (Prague, 1965), pp. 141-44.

abroad. Beneš's leadership was endorsed unreservedly by the Czechs in the early stages of the occupation. This enthusiastic backing greatly assisted the president in his endeavor to impose himself in the West as the leader of the free Czechoslovakia in 1939-40. His popularity in the country as a trustee of the independent state soon reached an all-time high. By 1943 even the communists bowed before the high tide of the president's immense prestige. In turn, Beneš realized the vital importance of the home resistance.[16] His diplomatic actions were predicated on his claim of being the true representative of a united country. In effect, the home resistance never faltered in its unshakable conviction that the unity of the liberation movement had to be preserved under all circumstances. Until 1942, Beneš took no political decision without prior consultation with the resistance leaders. He sent them drafts of his addresses for information, and his detailed reports on the international situation served as guidelines for the underground.

The most important field of resistance activity was the gathering of intelligence. On August 12, 1939, the secret radio transmitter of the ON and PÚ started to transmit information to the Czechoslovak authorities in London. Contacts continued, with intermittent interruptions until May, 1942, when the last remaining radio groups were tracked down by the Gestapo. Not long afterward, contact was renewed by Czechoslovak parachutists who were flown from Britain, and was maintained until May, 1945.[17]

Beneš received from Germany—"often directly from the German General Staff"—extremely valuable reports which were "a source of great astonishment to the British."[18] One of the most important sources was Paul Thümmel, senior official of the *Abwehr* (German Military Foreign Intelligence Service), who was stationed in Prague until his arrest in 1942.[19] The Allied powers were provided with inside information on German war plans, the disposition of German troops, and networks of

[16] In the course of the war the Czechoslovak broadcasts from London (via the British Broadcasting Corporation's transmissions) became the most important channel linking the liberation movement abroad with the Czech people. The Nazis forbade the listening to any foreign broadcast in an enemy country and punished the violators with a sentence of death.

[17] *Odboj*, 2, 1967. The main radio network Sparta I, with eleven transmitters and eight receivers, sent some 20,000 reports to London and elsewhere, and received 6,000 cables in 1940-41 (Krajina, "La Résistance tchécoslovaque," p. 65). Detlef Brandes uses lower figures in his lucid study *Die Tschechen unter deutschem Protektorat, Part I: Besatzungspolitik, Kollaboration und Widerstand im Protektorat Böhmen und Mähren bis Heydrichs Tod (1939-1942)* (Munich and Vienna, 1969), p. 190. Contact was also maintained by couriers.

[18] Beneš, *Memoirs*, p. 158.

[19] Krajina, "La Résistance," p. 68; Amort and Jedlička, *Tajemství, passim.* Thümmel headed the section dealing with the Balkans and Near East.

German agents in Britain, the Balkans, Turkey, and the Soviet Union. The ON and, particularly, the PVVZ—through its network of postal and railroad workers and employees of the armament industries—were able to supply information on the transport of German troops through the Protectorate and the Protectorate's war production. The PÚ also gathered important political intelligence through its contacts, some of them leading up to the very office of the German Protector himself, Konstantin von Neurath. The illegal press also played a significant role until 1942 in bolstering Czech morale and in helping the resistance to achieve prominence.

During 1939-40 the flame of the liberation movement abroad was kept burning by a steady flow of thousands of Czechs, who were provided channels of escape from the Protectorate. Relief for the families of the imprisoned and deported and shelter for active resisters who had to live illegally were among the permanent features of the implacable opposition mounted against the Nazis.[20]

Spontaneous individual acts against the Nazis in the first half of 1939 had subsided in the fall.[21] There were relatively few acts of sabotage, such as the cutting of telegraph poles and electric wires, and obstruction and damage to rolling stock and rail communications. Strikes, boycott campaigns, economic sabotage, violation of delivery quotas in the countryside, slowdowns in the factories became major instruments of the opposition to the German war efforts. These pinprick tactics—and passive resistance for which no individual culprit could be held responsible— were unambiguous obstacles in the way of Nazi system.[22]

The methods and tactics of the Czech struggle corresponded to those factors reflecting the specific situation posed by the country and the historical traditions of the people. Political considerations played the main role in the resistance throughout the war, since the resistance was primarily a political warfare. As such it could only assist military operations, not supplant them.[23] Consequently, it had to find adequate forms for its activities. Unlike the ease of movements possible in most European countries, the geographical and strategic position of Czechoslovakia imposed many limitations. Landlocked as it was in the middle of Germany, the Protectorate territory formed a heartland of the Reich. The concentration of the population in industrial cities, the dense communi-

[20] Giving shelter for resisters had been punishable by death since May, 1942.

[21] Jiří Doležal, *Jediná cesta* [*The Only Way*] (Prague, 1966), pp. 60ff.

[22] From the summer of 1939 until the very last days of the war the preparation of a national uprising became a permanent factor in the planning of the military branch of the resistance. In fact, since mass insurrection was viewed as the function of the front's advance and not as an isolated operation, it was regarded as the culmination of all resistance activities.

[23] Also see Henri Michel in *European Resistance Movements 1939-45* (Oxford, 1964), II, 572ff.

cation system, and the existence of a strong German minority made the work of the Nazi security troops much easier than it was in Poland or Norway.

Except for those of Germany and Austria, the Czech resistance was the longest in Europe. Unfortunately, it was handicapped by an almost total absence of weapons and ammunition, because there had been no previous war activities in the country. With no large forest and mountain areas, there was little possibility of finding shelter in the hills. Since it was almost out of the operational range of the early type of the British aircraft, the region was unfit for the conduct of irregular warfare until the final stage of the war brought the fronts closer.

The Nazi system of occupation presented a middle way between the regime in the occupied section of western Europe and that in the east. Its form determined the nature of the resistance. A final solution of the Czech question by assimilation and extermination, decided by Adolf Hitler in the fall of 1940 as the long-range program, was subordinated to the immediate economic exploitation of the Protectorate.[24] Thus, terror had no such indiscriminate character as in Poland, and its main function was to liquidate the active and potential forces of the underground.

The Czech public soon overcame their first shock at the occupation and resorted to the traditional forms of opposition they had used with such success against the Habsburg Empire during World War I. They turned to public demonstrations under the guise of patriotic rallies and religious commemorations.

The German attack on Poland was accompanied by the arrest of Czech hostages, selected from among public figures. They were sent to the concentration camp in Buchenwald. Hitler instructed Reich Protector von Neurath to refrain from any measure that would hamper the work in the industrial complex of the Protectorate. Naturally, any possible obstruction was to be smashed ruthlessly.[25]

With the outbreak of the war Czech protest assumed politically a more effective mass character. Under the sponsorship of both the democratic

[24] The new Acting Protector Reinhard Heydrich stated the basic line of the Nazi policy in his address in Prague on October 2, 1941: "At the moment, for military and tactical reasons, we must not cause the Czechs to reach the point of explosion. . . . We must be hard . . . but we have to act in such a way as not to make them believe . . . that they would have to rise in final revolt. But the fundamental line underlying these actions must remain unmentioned—that this region must once become German." (Václav Král, ed., Lesson from History [Prague, 1962], pp. 119-20.)

[25] Radomír Luža, The Transfer of the Sudeten Germans: A Study of Czech-German Relations, 1933-1962 (New York, London, 1964), pp. 187-88; Tomáš Pasák, "Činnost protektorátní reprezentace na podzim roku 1939" ["Activities of the Protectorate Representation at the Fall of 1939"], Československý časopis historický, XVII (1969), 553ff.

and communist resistance, the anniversary of Czechoslovak independence (October 28) was celebrated by large manifestations in Prague. Scuffles between Czechs and Germans led to gunfire. Hundreds of Czechs were injured, and one was killed. The funeral of Jan Opletal, a wounded student who later died, evolved into student demonstrations in Prague on November 15, 1939.

Nazi retribution followed swiftly. On the morning of November 17 nine student functionaries of the Czech National Student Association were shot, a large number of students were sent to concentration camps, and the Czech universities were closed.[26] The outcome of the demonstrations showed that this form of struggle—precipitating ghastly reprisals—would only lead up a dead-end street. Resistance leaders became aware that continued mass actions had little relation to the reality of power at home and abroad. Reprisals against formidable Nazi repressive machinery could not be a matter of amateur conspiracy or naive optimism. It had to be an arduous effort requiring professional skill.

Crushing of the resistance structure became the focal point of the German security apparatus. Throughout the fall and winter of 1939-40 the wave of arrests seriously disrupted both the ON and PÚ. Arrests continued to play havoc almost daily in 1940 and 1941. In February, 1940, hundreds of functionaries of the Czech national gymnastic organization Sokol were arrested. In February and May, 1940, the large National Movement of Working Youth fell into the German net. The first central committee (CC) of the KSČ, with its vast regional and district network, was smashed. The Boy Scouts were dissolved in the fall of 1940. Despite these grave setbacks the reorganized ÚVOD emerged as an effective fighting force. Thus, the period from the spring of 1940 to the summer of 1941 constituted the high point of the resistance.

In the wake of the German attack on the Soviet Union in June, 1941, unrest spread among the Czech population, which expected an intensification of the war. The illegal (underground) second CC of the KSČ redoubled its effort and drew closer to the democratic forces.[27] The Nazis responded by increased arrests of members of the Sokol and other national organizations. In May, sixty officials of the former Social Democratic party were apprehended. During the summer a series of strikes occurred in Prague and other industrial cities, and individual acts of violence increased. There were slowdowns in the factories, reducing the

---

[26] [Czechoslovak] Ministry of the Interior, *Persekuce českého studentstva za okupace* [*Persecution of Czech Students during the Occupation*] (Prague, 1946), *passim*.

[27] For the communist activities, see Čestmír Amort, ed., *Heydrichiáda* (Prague, 1965), pp. 99ff. From June 22, 1941, until November 12 a total of 1,374 persons were arrested in the province of Bohemia alone because of illegal communist activities (ibid., p. 105).

productivity of the workers by 15 to 20 percent.[28] In the middle of September the boycott of the Protectorate press, instigated by the ÚVOD and assisted by the Czechoslovak section of the BBC, reduced the sale of newspapers by 70 percent. The state of affairs in the countryside was no better.[29] The situation was further complicated by the participation of several leading members of the Czech Protectorate government in the resistance movement.

As early as December, 1939, the head of the Protectorate government, General Alois Eliáš, had informed Beneš of his recognition of the president's authority, and as a key member of the resistance, Eliáš maintained contact with London until his arrest. His policy was to avoid provoking the Germans prematurely and to wait for a favorable opportunity to call a national uprising. Secretly he provided relief to the families of imprisoned resisters and collected intelligence for the exile liberation movement. He used his official authority to obstruct German demands while maintaining surface compliance with German policies. Evidence of Eliáš's illegal activities was uncovered by the Nazis, and he was put under surveillance from the spring of 1940.

In the winter of 1940-41 the Czechoslovak provisional government in London asked Britain for full *de jure* recognition of its status, and it was important for Beneš to make known to the British cabinet that he was a recognized leader at home. In April, 1941, both Protectorate President Emil Hácha and Premier Eliáš reassured Beneš of their submission to his direction. Beneš immediately sent the report to the attention of Winston Churchill and Anthony Eden.

In 1940-41 the Germans learned of Eliáš's communications with London. In a cable on June 24 Beneš had asked both Hácha and Eliáš to submit their resignations at the first favorable moment, and Eliáš had informed Beneš on August 7 that he had taken all precautionary steps for the cabinet to resign in the event of any future German provocative action.[30] This exchange was reported to Berlin by the Prague Gestapo.

In September German authorities found that the situation in the Protectorate had reached such dangerous dimensions that "the unity of the Reich was definitely in danger."[31] Hitler called Reinhard Heydrich, head of the security forces and police, and State Secretary Karl Hermann

[28] In September, 1941 (Janeček, ed., *Odboj*, p. 138).

[29] Ibid., pp. 137ff; R. Heydrich, October 2, 1941, and K. H. Frank in April, 1944, in Král, ed., *Lesson*, pp. 118-19, 156-57.

[30] Jaroslava Eliášová and Tomáš Pasák, "Poznámky k Benešovým kontaktům s Eliášem ve druhé světové válce" ["Observations on the Contacts of Beneš with Eliáš in World War II"], *Historie a vojenství*, 1 (1967), pp. 108-40; Libuše Otáhalová and Milada Červinková, eds., *Dokumenty z historie československé politiky 1939-1943* [*Documents on the History of Czechoslovak Politics*] (Prague, 1966), II, 614-15, 751-53; Brandes, *Die Tschechen*, pp. 213-14.

[31] Heydrich on October 2, 1941 (Král, ed., *Lesson*, p. 119).

Frank to a conference on September 21-22. On September 27 Heydrich was appointed Acting Reich Protector, and von Neurath was sent home on "sick leave." A civil state of emergency was decreed, and martial law was declared in the territory of the Protectorate. General Eliáš was arrested and sentenced to death.[32]

Two leaders of the ON headed the list of the first victims executed on September 28, and from then daily announcements of Czechs sentenced to death were published, reaching more than 400 by December. A large number were put to death without any trial. Thousands more were deported to concentration camps.[33] Jews were ordered to wear the star of David. Their deportation to the gas chambers got off to an early start on October 1. The main networks of the ÚVOD were destroyed, and gradually the entire team of leaders was liquidated. These measures provoked fear, alarm, and indignation among the Czechs, and made many Czechs swear that no mercy would be shown when the final victory came.[34]

Intensification of the war in 1941 confronted Beneš with the problem of providing more direct assistance to the forces at home. In the late summer of 1941 two small parties of officers and soldiers of the Czechoslovak army were dropped into the country from the Soviet Union.[35] On October 4 the first group of parachutists was dropped in Bohemia from Britain. These parties were followed by others, all seeking to establish contact with the resistance. Early in October Czechoslovak authorities in London decided to send a special group with the mission of assassinating Heydrich.[36]

On May 27, 1942, two parachutists, Jan Kubiš and Jozef Gabčík, ambushed and mortally wounded Heydrich in his car in the suburbs of Prague. Immediately, the Germans clamped martial law on the country. Mass executions, arrests, and house-to-house searches crippled the resistance. An atmosphere of terror was intentionally produced and rumors were spread that every tenth Czech would be executed. The village of

[32] General Eliáš was executed on June 19, 1942. Beneš broke all contact with Hácha and the Protectorate government. In fact, the continuing existence of the cabinet and its servile subjection to almost all Nazi demands was a help to Berlin. In 1942-43 Hácha became so seriously ill that he was unable to sign his name.

[33] From June to December, 1941, 5,162 persons were arrested in Bohemia and 5,164 in Moravia (Král, *Pravda*, p. 145).

[34] Luža, *Transfer*, p. 232. The resistance never failed in its demands for the removal of the Sudeten Germans from the territory of the future state.

[35] Antonín Benčík in *Československý voják*, xvi, Nos. 9-11, 1967. Compare Brandes, *Die Tschechen*, p. 241.

[36] For the activities of the Czech parachutists flown from England to the Protectorate, see Antonín Tichý, *Nás živé nedostanou. Historie parašutistické skupiny Antimony* [*They Will Not Get us Alive. The History of the Parachutist Group "Antimony"*] (Liberec, 1969), *passim*. Also see Amort, ed., *Heydrichiáda*, pp. 27, 283ff.

Lidice was burned down on June 10 and its 199 male inhabitants were shot on the spot, its women deported, and most of the children gassed in Chelmno in July, 1942. Actually, there was no relation between the inhabitants of Lidice and the assassination of Heydrich. The village was selected arbitrarily and obliterated as a deterrent. On June 24 the village of Ležáky was razed and all 33 inhabitants shot because some parachutists had found shelter there. On June 18, acting upon information given by a parachutist who had surrendered voluntarily two days earlier, the police and SS troops surrounded the Orthodox church of St. Charles Borromeo in Prague where seven parachutists were in hiding. They were shot to death in the ensuing fierce battle. Among them were the two who had killed Heydrich.

The Orthodox Church was dissolved, and the bishop and three clergymen and the members of the Sokol group Jindra, together with their families, who had given support to the parachutists, were executed. At the end of September, 1942, the relatives of exiled and underground leaders were sent to an internment camp in Moravia. The home resistance network was almost completely rooted out.[37]

Initiative no longer lay with the resistance. Illusions of an early end to the war and of the major role of the resistance in the new democratic republic were shattered in a savage holocaust. The decimation of the Czech resistance forces in 1941-42 moved the center of political activity to the liberation movement abroad. The decision about the future government—so far as the Czechs were concerned—no longer lay within the country. Under such conditions, the exile movement ultimately provided the nucleus of the postwar regime. Thus, skillful politicians, who had lived abroad and faced no real danger, became the leaders of the republic in 1945. The extermination of the best elements of the army, workers' movement, and intelligentsia paved the way for postwar developments.[38]

Toward National Uprising, 1942-1945

Nazi pressure slowly relaxed after revocation of the civil state of emergency on July 3. The Nazis evidently thought that the breaking-point had been almost reached and were confident that they could finish off the resistance structure by police action. Nazi measures of repression now became more sophisticated. The security apparatus began to use its net-

[37] Report by the Reich Security Main Office, August 5, 1942, at the YIVO Institute for Jewish Research, New York City; Amort, ed., *Heydrichiáda*, pp. 147ff. From May 28 to July 3 a total of 1,357 Czechs were executed and 3,188 arrested. Some 4,715,501 persons went through the process of screening.

The home resistance did not favor the plan to assassinate Heydrich because it anticipated great losses.

[38] Luža, *Transfer*, p. 222.

works of informers more systematically. K. H. Frank concentrated all the executive power in his hands in August, 1943, when he was nominated state minister. His policy consisted in applying steady and strong pressure on the resistance movement. He "discarded the practice of giving" the repressive measures great publicity although "some hundred death sentences" were passed every month.[39] Frank realized that although he was unable to crush the resistance, he could scatter its forces and curb its activity. Thus, until the late fall of 1944 sabotage was limited to a relatively few acts that did not seriously hamper the Nazi war economy or war effort.[40]

During 1942-43 the remnants of the old networks became the nucleus about which the crippled resistance forces regrouped themselves.[41] Allied victories at El Alamein and Stalingrad played an important role in the resurgence, as did the broadcasts of the BBC and of Radio Moscow. In 1943 and 1944 the movements were already planning to step up their action in unison with the advance of the Allied armies. Ties were renewed with the Slovak resistance. Valuable intelligence was supplied to London, such as the report (July, 1943) of the center of research and production of a secret German weapon—the V-1 in Peenemünde—and of the first experiments undertaken with the V-1 in East Prussia.[42]

In 1944 a plan was developed among the heterogeneous resistance forces to give them both organizational cohesion and a single center. This reorganization resulted in the formation of several large groups. The most important center was the Council of the Three (R 3),[43] which was associated with the Přípravný národně revoluční výbor (Preparatory National Revolutionary Committee—PNRV), the communist under-

[39] K. H. Frank in April, 1944, in Král, ed., *Lesson*, pp. 151ff.

[40] I follow partly the stimulating study by Jan Tesař, "Poznámky k problémům okupačního režimu v tzv. protektorátě" ["Observations on the Problems of the Regime of Occupation in the So-Called Protectorate"], *Historie a vojenství*, 2, 3 (1964), pp. 153ff., 333ff. Tesař rightly pointed out that until the outbreak of the guerrilla warfare in the wake of the Slovak uprising in the summer of 1944 and again in March, 1945, the number of German police, SS, and army units tied up by the Czech resistance amounted approximately to fifty thousand. In contrast, on April 9, 1945, the number of SS and police troops alone amounted to 89,690, not counting army and auxiliary units (ibid., pp. 349-50, 378).

[41] Reportedly 250,000 persons died during the occupation. Some 200,000 passed through concentration camps. About 68,000 Jews were exterminated (Luža, *Transfer*, pp. 262, 298; Janeček, ed., *Odboj*, pp. 212ff.).

[42] For this and other exploits of the resistance, see Veselý-Štainer, *Cestou*, pp. 101-104; Josef Grňa, *Sedm roků na domácí frontě [Seven Years on the Home Front]* (Brno, 1968), *passim*.

[43] The R 3 was built around the remnants of the ON and PVVZ and consisted of a large number of mutually unconnected groups. Communication lines of the R 3 to London were built with the help of the Slovak resistance. From April, 1944, the R 3 sheltered "Milada," a special parachutist group dropped from London. Toward the end of the war the R 3 was connected with London by six parachutist radio groups (Grňa, *passim*; and Veselý-Štainer, *passim*).

ground, and the illegal trade union movement (ROH).[44] The political attitude of the R 3 was expressed in a ten-point declaration based on the PVVZ program. As the *status quo* of 1938 appeared to be out of date, the R 3 sought wide social and economic reforms and close alliance with the Soviet Union. It called for removal of the old political parties and a more just political democracy. Unlike most other exile leaders, Beneš enjoyed its full confidence.[45] The R 3 prepared for an all-out armed struggle as the ultimate objective. The evolution of the war had drawn the democratic forces closer to the communist underground.[46] Both agreed in principle that an armed uprising should be considered as an inevitable prospect in the further development of the struggle.

In 1944 the London government was busily engaged in organizing an armed uprising in Slovakia. It favored a more cautious approach in the Czech part of the republic, since it was afraid that any large-scale guerrilla activity there would invite drastic Nazi retaliation. Conclusion of the Soviet-Czechoslovak treaty of alliance in December, 1943, was generally welcomed by the Czechs, and the advance of the Soviet front made it possible for Beneš to call for an activization of the struggle in February, 1944. Soon thereafter Czech parachute parties were dropped from the West to establish better communications with the home resistance. In a series of countermeasures the Germans succeeded in wrecking a large number of resistance networks. The PNRV, the R 3 leadership, and its Prague and Bohemian groups were badly hurt, the large communist youth movement Předvoj (Vanguard) was wrecked, and a welter of other organizations suffered serious reverses.[47] But the underground showed encouraging signs of developing a more vibrant and resistant structure than before. Assisting the underground were small groupings of Soviet soldiers who had been war prisoners and who had been aided in their flight from Nazi prisoner camps by the Czech population since 1943 and were now living clandestinely in the countryside. These dispersed bands became part of the Czech guerrilla structure. They offered expert assistance in the training of the Czech cadres and often formed a hard core of Czech partisan groups.

In the late summer of 1944 the outbreak of the Slovak national up-

[44] Janeček, ed., *Odboj*, pp. 180-234. Also see Stanislav Zámečník, "ÚRO a české Květnové povstání v roce 1945" ["ÚRO and the Czech Uprising in 1945"] in Kabinet dějin odborů, *Odbory a naše revoluce* [*Trade Unions and Our Revolution*] (Prague, 1968), pp. 9-47.

[45] Veselý-Štainer, *Cestou*, pp. 131, 155, 159-60, 211.

[46] Janeček, ed., *Odboj*, pp. 235ff; Rudolf Vetiška, *Skok do tmy* [*Leap into Darkness*] (Prague, 1966), *passim*.

[47] Veselý-Štainer, *Cestou*, *passim*; Vojtěch Mencl and Oldřich Sládek, *Dny odvahy* [*Days of Courage*] (Prague, 1966), *passim*; Doležal, *Jediná cesta*, pp. 128 ff. Some two thousand Czechs crossed the Slovak border illegally to join the Slovak insurrection.

rising spread confusion through the Nazi security system in the Protectorate. Alarmed, Frank hastened to organize a special security cover at the Moravian-Slovak border. When the partisan brigade "Jan Žižka" attempted to cross the border to Moravia, its three hundred members were engaged by a special anti-guerrilla German group numbering ten thousand. They were dispersed only after much effort in November.

Concentration of the German effort in eastern Moravia left the hilly Bohemian-Moravian borderland relatively unguarded. The first Red Army party landed there during the night of September 30-October 1, 1944, and was immediately followed by other groups. Liquidation of the gendarmerie station at Přibyslav on October 26 by a R 3 Czech-Soviet partisan unit initiated the final period of insurgency on Czech territory. The Nazi apparatus was taken off guard, and Frank tried almost desperately to reorganize the repressive system hitherto directed against illegal resistance and unfit to be used against partisan warfare. However, a streamlining and strengthening of the German security apparatus made it possible for the Germans to disorganize the partisan front during the ensuing winter. The Nazi counteroffensive hit hard at the guerrilla terrain. In effect, in the late winter and spring of 1945 the Red Army partisan detachments were waging guerrilla warfare on both sides of the Bohemian-Moravian highlands. Despite the presence of the Czech communist political commissars, recruitment from the ranks of the local population, and close cooperation with other democratic groupings, the units remained a part of the Red Army and were run from partisan headquarters at the Ukrainian front.[48]

With insurgency on the rise, centralization of the underground forces exerted a great impact on the Germans. In addition, the example of cooperation between London and the Slovak resistance in the Slovak uprising did not fail to make a deep impression on Frank,[49] who watched for any sign of concerted mass action as a series of new parachute parties were landed, this time transported by the U.S. air force from its Brindisi base.

The advance of the Soviet and Allied armies and reports of impending political negotiations between the London and Moscow exile centers speeded up the conclusion of an agreement among the main resistance forces on the establishment of a central organ. Negotiations toward such an arrangement had started in the spring and summer of 1944, but were broken off because some of the major resistance figures were either killed

[48] Doležal, *Jediná cesta*, pp. 144ff.
[49] I follow Tesař, "Poznámky," *Historie a vojenství* (1964), pp. 354ff. According to a recent still inadequate estimate some 120 partisan groups numbering 7,500 men operated in the Protectorate in the spring of 1945 (Doležal, *Jediná cesta*, p. 179). Only in Moravia between August 19, 1944, and April 13, 1945, were the partisans engaged in some 300 actions (Doležal, p. 190).

or arrested. In 1945 a rather colorless and heterogeneous central body called the Czech National Council (Česká národní rada—ČNR) arose out of consultations among the R 3, the ROH, the communist underground around the fourth CC of the KSČ, and other associated movements. Other organizations such as the military group Alex and the conservative-oriented Central National Committee were left out.[50] Professor Albert Pražák, the chairman of its central organ, was a mere figurehead who had never been an active member of the resistance. Some other members of the ČNR were certainly not resistance leaders and owed their appointment mainly to obscure party considerations. With some exceptions, the council was a group without real distinction. In its structure it reflected the incoming party system more than the democratic revolutionary spirit of the resistance. The resistance's message of readiness for action and personal sacrifice—making conduct in the liberation struggle the ultimate political criterion—was thus disregarded by the resistance itself.

Apart from the individual, localized, and sporadic outbursts that had erupted in various areas from 1939 and had been swiftly and easily suppressed, real guerrilla campaigns developed only in the fall of 1944. Then, with the reverses of the late fall, armed struggle was reduced to marginal proportions until the middle of April, 1945, except in western Moravia and eastern Bohemia[51] where partisan warfare presented a real threat to the German communications system. Soviet parachute groups enjoyed a significant advantage, since their core was composed of specially trained and well-equipped regular soldiers. Yet neither the Red Army nor the London government provided any significant military supplies to the resistance, but continued instead to stress intelligence activities. The R 3, which had been in constant contact with the Czechoslovak government from 1943, vainly urged it to send arms to the resistance. Finally, London dispatched several groupings with communications material. It was only at the beginning of April, 1945, that some weapons were dropped.

Negligible aid from abroad—unlike the generous assistance given to the French or Dutch resistance—seriously hampered the armed struggle of Czech resisters. Isolated in the heart of the Reich, without caches of weapons, the home guerrilla groups were dependent on foreign aid.

[50] See Veselý-Štainer, *Cestou, passim*; Otokar Machotka, ed., *Pražské povstání 1945* [*Prague Uprising 1945*] (Washington, D. C., 1965). Veselý-Štainer, who became a member of the ČNR and was one of the few strong personalities of the R 3, was organizing the partisan warfare outside of Prague and could not influence the working of the ČNR.

[51] Tesař, "Poznámky," p. 376. The Nazis set up specially trained anti-guerrilla units and established a center of anti-partisan activities, the so-called *Bandenbekämpfungsstab*.

Moreover, neither the KSČ in Moscow, the Red Army, nor the Soviet partisan groups operating in the Czech lands developed any contact with the illegal communist party. For a long time, the Moscow communist center even withdrew its recognition from the illegal fourth CC.[52] This still-unexplained halt in material support from abroad helped to build up tensions between the London government and the home resistance, particularly in the R 3. The resistance was unable to create larger areas of insurrection until the end of April. Yet, on receiving the first military supplies it engaged in widely dispersed, small-scale raids that harassed German army detachments and their communications. It thus developed a special type of armed struggle that closely reflected the conditions peculiar to the Czech territories.

In April, 1945, guerrilla warfare was clearly the main form of the resistance struggle. In time, some rural areas came under the control of the partisans. An inherent part of this national revolutionary situation was its implicit challenge to the established economic and political order. Since the main political currents in the resistance espoused similar aims, and all backed the authority of President Beneš, their mutual competition and political disputes presented no serious immediate problem. The everpresent Nazi terror and wide national consensus tended to play down any differences. However, the question of the postwar political system was very much on the minds of the resistance leaders.

The prospect of victory developed a momentum of its own, reflecting the popular aspirations for profound social, economic, and political changes. Furthermore, the immense pressure for a permanent solution of the Sudeten German question made a radical transformation of the republic's national structure almost inevitable. Exulting in their new role as the exponents of the national aspirations of the masses, the communists made use of this potentially revolutionary situation. In general, their espousal of guerrilla warfare and the public awareness of the wider political implications in the Soviet presence in the republic helped to bolster the communist claim to leadership in the future state. The skillful operations of the then popular Red Army partisan detachments certainly did not harm the prestige of the communist underground. The dominating communist influence in the coalition government, promulgated in Košice on April 4, 1945, was not lost upon the politically conscious Czech population and gave a tremendous boost to the communist resistance.

Guerrilla battles raging in many wooded areas from April on, and the approaching Allied armies, acted as explosive agents, thrusting aside the

---

[52] Veselý-Štainer, *Cestou, passim*; Janeček, ed., *Odboj, passim*. In 1945 the R 3 served as channel of communications of the illegal communist underground to Moscow.

Nazi regime in a series of eruptions. Starting on May 1 in the city of Přerov, separate, spontaneous local uprisings spread across the country. National committees took over the administration of their towns and removed German inscriptions from public buildings. Germans were disarmed. Czechoslovak flags were hoisted. Liberated towns and communities emerged as isolated islands in German-occupied territory. The overall picture was one of constant flux as the population in town after town rose while German troops were reintroducing their control of the recently liberated sections. Uprisings threatened the lines of communication of the retreating army group under the command of Marshal Ferdinand Schörner. Every violent measure brought on German acts of reprisal. Burned villages and the killings of civilians and resisters exacerbated the mood of the country.

In the midst of this growing tide of regional uprisings, the resistance movements centered in Prague discussed the final measures for the take-over of the capital. The ČNR opposed any premature action. Yet on May 4 there were clashes in the city, and the mood of the population threatened to get out of control. Shortly after noon on May 5 the Prague radio was seized by the Czechs, who broadcast urgent appeals for help. Fighting broke out in the city as groups of Czech protectorate police and armed patriots occupied public buildings. The seizure of the Prague radio station and the first acts of the uprising were prepared by military group Alex. One of its leaders, General Karel Kutlvašr, became the commander of Prague and with his staff was responsible for the military conduct of the operations.[53] That afternoon the ČNR assumed political control of the revolt and subordinated General Kutlvašr to its military commission. During the night of May 5-6 over sixteen hundred barricades were erected throughout the streets of Prague. The city was in Czech hands except for a few sections held by the SS and the German army.

For three days an unequal battle raged between some thirty thousand Czech men and women and about thirty-seven thousand to forty thousand German troops backed by tanks and artillery. An appeal from the city for Allied assistance went unheeded. In fact, the Czechoslovak government in Košice and the Soviet Union followed the revolt in dead silence. American troops waiting less than fifty miles from Prague made no move.[54] The ČNR ably directed the uprising to a relatively successful

[53] This appears also to have been recognized by Karel Bartošek in his study, written from the communist point of view, *Pražské povstání 1945* [*Prague Uprising 1945*] (Prague, 1965), pp. 22ff. See also the comprehensive account by Stanislav Zámečník, "České květnové povstání" ["Czech May Uprising"], *Historie a vojenství*, No. 2 (1970), pp. 267-301.

[54] The United States Army was prevented from advancing toward Prague on the direct order of General Dwight D. Eisenhower, who was anxious to maintain

end aided as it was by the favorable international situation. On May 8 the capitulation of the German garrison in Prague was signed after more than two thousand Czechs had lost their lives. Early in the morning of May 9 the first detachments of the Red Army reached the city and were enthusiastically greeted by the population.[55]

When the exile government returned to Prague on May 10 the cabinet coolly accepted the resignation of the ČNR and relegated its members to secondary positions as officials of the provincial national committee for Bohemia.[56] Unlike their counterparts in Slovakia, no Czech resistance representative was appointed as a member of the government. In effect, the remaining resistance leaders were reduced to a subordinate role in the public life of the republic after 1945, an exceptional feature in the history of European resistance.

The dreams of the slain and lonely resisters remained largely vain illusions. Yet the personal fate of the resisters formed only one strand in the complex pattern. Behind their political and personal frustrations lay the substance of their achievements: the moral significance of the liberation would have been nothing without the existence of the resistance. Nazi gallows and prison walls gave supreme testimony of its message of courage and sacrifice, presenting a new moral dimension to the strivings of the Czech people. No resistance movement could have significantly influenced the ultimate course of the war: the Allied armies were the military agents of the victory. But the political challenge of the Czech resistance forced Adolf Hitler himself to take note of its continuous threat to the security of the Reich. Moreover, behind the morale of resistance stood its realistic representation of the vital interests of the Czech people during the course of the war. In fact, on both the political and moral levels, it represented the dynamics of the historic challenge of the Czech nation to Nazism.

---

cooperation with the Red Army. Eisenhower complied with the request of General Alexey I. Antonov to refrain from advancing beyond the Carlsbad-Pilsen-Budějovice line. See *The Department of State Bulletin*, May 22, 1949, pp. 665-67. For the documentation regarding the advance of the U.S. forces to Prague, see U.S. Department of State, *Foreign Relations of the United States. Diplomatic Papers 1945*. Vol. IV, *Europe* (Washington, D.C., 1968), 441-42, 445-51.

[55] Bartošek, *Pražské povstání, passim*.

[56] Machotka, *Pražské povstání*, pp. 117ff. The KSČ and Moscow reportedly criticized the ČNR's acceptance of the help of the troops of the German-sponsored "Russian Army of Liberation" under General Andrei Vlasov, which happened to be near Prague at the time of the uprising, against the Germans, and its negotiations with the German army for an armistice.

· 13 ·

THE SLOVAK RESISTANCE MOVEMENT

Anna Josko
Library of Congress

THE DEMOCRATIC UNDERGROUND

The Slovak resistance movement originated in the days immediately following the Munich Agreement.[1] In October, 1938, at a secret meeting of Agrarian party leaders in Bratislava, the possibility that Hitler might go beyond the Munich agreement and break up Czechoslovakia was discussed.[2] In such an event, the Agrarian party leaders were determined to launch an underground resistance movement. For the moment, however, they decided to refrain from any overt activity lest it furnish Hitler with a pretext for new attacks on post-Munich Czechoslovakia. Subse-

---

[1] The Slovak resistance movement in World War II has been virtually ignored in Western historical literature. There is only one Western account of the Slovak National Uprising in 1944: Wolfgang Venohr, *Aufstand für die Tschechoslowakei: Der Slowakische Freiheitskampf von 1944* (Hamburg, 1969), which though journalistic in approach, is documented on the basis of both Slovak and German sources. In Czechoslovak historiography, the Slovak resistance has received wide though often conflicting treatment. The communist takeover in Czechoslovakia in 1948 took place before its history was written. Consequently, its history is a product principally of communist historians. Their attitude toward it has undergone several metamorphoses. Originally laudatory, it became very critical during the witchhunt against the Slovak nationalist (Titoist) communists in the 1950's. However, after their rehabilitation in the 1960's, it became more objective. Though biased toward the noncommunist resistance, Ferdinand Beer *et al.*, *Dejinná križovatka: Slovenské národné povstanie—predpoklady a výsledky* [*The Historic Crossroads: The Slovak National Uprising—Assumptions and Outcome*] (Bratislava, 1964), is quite informative. Similarly, Gustáv Husák, *Svedectvo o Slovenskom národnom povstaní* [*Testimony about the Slovak National Uprising*] (Bratislava, 1964), is highly polemical, but nevertheless an important source. A relatively objective account is Jozef Jablonický, *Z ilegality do povstania: Kapitoly z občianskeho odboja* [*Out of the Underground into the Uprising: Chapters of the Bourgeois Resistance*] (Bratislava, 1969). Basic to the study of the Slovak resistance is the massive, well-annotated collection of documents, Vilém Prečan, ed., *Slovenské národné povstanie: Dokumenty* [*The Slovak National Uprising: Documents*] (Bratislava, 1965). A very handy encyclopedia of facts and personalities is Miroslav Kropilák and Jozef Jablonický, *Malý slovník Slovenského národného povstania* [*Pocket Dictionary of the Slovak National Uprising*] (Bratislava, 1964).

[2] The conference was called and chaired by Ján Ursíny, agrarian deputy in the Czechoslovak parliament in Prague and brother of the present author, who also participated in the meeting.

quently, they informed trusted party members and leaders of other parties who were known to hold similar views. The leaders of the Social Democratic party proceeded in a similar fashion.

The breakup of Czechoslovakia and the establishment of the Slovak state under Hitler's aegis on March 14, 1939, removed any need for restraint by the Slovak democratic leaders. The time had come to act. They were encouraged by news of a telegram sent by Edvard Beneš to U. S. President Franklin Delano Roosevelt on March 15, in which the former president declared that the Czechs and Slovaks would never accept the suppression of their national freedom and that he proposed to fight for their liberation. In World War I, Beneš, together with Tomáš G. Masaryk and Milan Štefánik, had led an eminently successful movement abroad for the liberation of the Czechs and Slovaks from Austro-Hungarian rule. The knowledge that Beneš had placed himself at the head of a second movement for Czechoslovak liberation helped to rally the Slovak opponents of Hitler and of Jozef Tiso's government at Bratislava to the Slovak resistance movement. Beneš became a spokesman even for those Slovaks who had been his opponents in the past.

At first, Slovak resistance was on a smaller scale than Czech resistance. Although both movements had the same ultimate goal—the restoration of a democratic Czechoslovak republic—their organization and tactics differed because conditions prevailing in the Slovak state and the Protectorate of Bohemia and Moravia were different. From the first, the Czech resistance movement had a wide popular basis. Even the Protectorate government secretly cooperated with it. The Slovak government, on the other hand, was beholden to the Germans, and at first it had enjoyed a certain amount of support even among those Slovaks who had favored the former Czechoslovak government and were anti-German in sentiment. It was therefore necessary for the members of the Slovak resistance to unmask the true face of the Slovak fascist regime and erode the confidence of the Slovak people in it. A campaign of "whispering" propaganda and the dissemination of literature aimed at subverting the Tiso regime were the initial weapons of the Slovak resistance. As a result of this effort, there was a "winnowing" of minds. The initial confusion over the nature of the Tiso government disappeared, and the lines between its supporters and opponents were clearly drawn.

During the first years of the Slovak resistance, its members avoided forming organized groups. They preferred a system of individual cells, which reduced the risk of detection to a minimum.[3] Such cells were formed in all towns of note and even in many villages. Their members were self-sacrificing, bold, and confident of success. They were held to-

[3] Beer, *Dejinná križovatka*, pp. 103-107.

gether and bound to the liberation movement abroad by their common goal: the restoration of a united, indivisible Czechoslovakia with an internal structure that would accommodate the Slovaks and Czechs on a footing of complete equality. The older centralist concept of a unitary Czechoslovak nation had given way in the Slovak resistance to a desire for the recognition of the Slovaks as a distinct people in the future Czechoslovak state, enjoying the same standing in politics, culture, and social and economic affairs as the Czech people. Within the resistance this aim encountered disapproval only from a small minority of adherents of the former Czechoslovak centralist parties. Even they, however, while having reservations about the form of the future Czechoslovak state and the Slovak-Czech relationship, fully cooperated in the resistance to the Tiso government and the Germans.

Close cooperation was the supreme task of the day. The Gestapo's excesses against the Czechs in the Protectorate were emulated by the Tiso regime and its executive organs, the Central State Security (ÚŠB) and the Hlinka Guard (HG), against the Slovak resistance.[4] In turn, the Slovak resistance sought to infiltrate the Tiso government. In time it succeeded in planting its agents at every level of the regime.

Collaboration between the resistance movements in Bohemia and Moravia and in Slovakia encountered some difficulties. In the days immediately following the breakup of Czechoslovakia it was difficult to gain access to the representatives of the Czech underground. The Czechs had been deeply offended by the part played by Slovak extremists in the destruction of Czechoslovakia, and they tended at first to be distrustful of all Slovaks. Nevertheless, it was from the Czech side that the first contact was made between the two resistance movements.

On April 4, 1939, an emissary of the Czech underground arrived in Slovakia from Katowice, Poland, to establish a line of communications between the Czech and Slovak resistance and the liberation movement

---

[4] The Central State Security (Ústredňa štátnej bezpečnosti—ÚŠB), which had headquarters in Bratislava and branch offices in smaller towns, was subordinated to the Ministry of Interior. From its inception on January 1, 1940, until the outbreak of the Slovak National Uprising on August 29, 1944, it apprehended and confined about 3,000 persons at the Il'ava Penitentiary for political prisoners and sent 3,595 persons to district prisons. The number of persons held by the ÚŠB illegally in confinement, that is, without trial, either in the ÚŠB prison or district prisons, could never be determined accurately. See Igor Daxner, *L'udáctvo pred národným súdom* [*The People's Party before the Court of the Nation*] (Bratislava, 1961), pp. 89-90. The Jewish victims of the Tiso regime included 57,837 persons who were deported to Nazi death camps at Auschwitz (Oswieczim) and Lublin in Poland before October 20, 1942. Only a fraction of them survived. From the outbreak of the Slovak National Uprising until the spring of 1945, German "special detachments" (*Sonderabteilungen*), aided by the Hlinka Guard, again hunted down Jews. The number of victims of this second hunt remains uncertain.

abroad.[5] (It may be mentioned in passing that in March, 1939, when the Polish government realized that Poland might become Hitler's next victim, it reversed its former hostile policy toward Czechoslovakia and adopted a tolerant, even cooperative, attitude toward the Czechoslovak liberation movement.)

Until Poland's downfall in September, 1939, it was a center of Czechoslovak anti-German activity as well as a link in the communications between the Czech and Slovak resistance and the liberation movement abroad. During this period many Czech military and political leaders who fled Bohemia and Moravia passed through Slovakia to Poland, either to join the Czechoslovak volunteer army being organized there under Gen. Lev Prchala or to go on to France to join the more important volunteer army and political movement there. After the collapse of Poland, Hungary, albeit less friendly, served as the crossing-point to the West. The Slovak underground undertook to provide the Czech exiles, who were mostly penniless, with money, forged documents, and expert escorts across the Slovak frontier. Among the most active men in this effort, which did much to restore confidence between the Czech and Slovak resistance, were Ján Ursíny and Ján Lichner, former agrarian deputies in the Prague parliament, the former Social-Democratic senator František Zimák, and the former Social Democratic deputy Ján Pocisk.

At the end of 1939, thanks to the collaboration of Jaroslav Lípa, the Czechoslovak ambassador in Belgrade, the information headquarters of the resistance group "Zeta" was established in Bratislava.[6] It was able to coordinate the work of numerous Czech and Slovak intelligence networks and transmit intelligence to the liberation movement abroad under Beneš.[7] In this traffic important help was provided by sympathetic out-

[5] The emissary was J. Kadlec, a former lieutenant in the gendarmerie. The Czechoslovak resistance group at Katowice (former Czechoslovak Consul Vladimír Znojemský and Vice-Consul Vladimír Henzl) directed, among other things, broadcasts to Czechoslovakia.

[6] The information center *Zeta* was established by Karel Hostaša, editor of the newspaper *České slovo*, who returned to Slovakia at the behest of Lípa. In addition to Hostaša, the Zeta group comprised the newspapermen Josef Dočkal and Matej Josko, Prof. Karel Koch, and Miroslav Švanda, manager of a bookstore. In 1941 Švanda was arrested by the Gestapo and taken to Prague, where he was interrogated and tortured in the Pankrác Prison. He was executed during the persecutions following the assassination of Reinhard Heydrich. Throughout his ordeal he never betrayed his collaborators. Evidently, there were still other groups specializing in intelligence gathering (e.g., Flóra, Justícia, Obrana národa, Demec, and others). See Jablonický, *Z ilegality*, pp. 50-64 and 124-47.

[7] The management of the shoe-manufacturing concern Bat'a, which had outlets all over the world, arranged to have several radio transmitters smuggled from Turkey to Slovakia. On March 19, 1944, after the decision was made to launch the Slovak National Uprising, the Czechoslovak government in London sent an intelligence officer, Maj. Jaroslav Krátký, to Slovakia to operate the trans-

Bratislava

siders.[8] Some members of the diplomatic missions of neutral countries in Bratislava and Berlin helped to provide links. Aid was also given by some members of the Slovak diplomatic service, who were either sympathetic to the resistance or were trying to keep two irons in the fire, in the event that the fortunes of war should turn against Germany and Czechoslovakia be restored under Beneš.

THE COMMUNIST UNDERGROUND

In addition to the Slovak democratic resistance, there was also a Slovak communist resistance. Its role, especially in the years between 1939 and 1943, remains ambiguous, despite the major attention given it by present-day Slovak communist historians. After the Munich agreement, the government of the Second Czechoslovak Republic suppressed the Czechoslovak communist party (KSČ). Its leaders fled abroad, chiefly to Moscow,[9] or went underground. Left leaderless, many of the rank-and-file Slovak communists joined the totalitarian organizations of the Tiso regime—the Hlinka Slovak People's party (HSĽS), the Hlinka Guards (HG), and the official "Christian" labor unions—and thus worked actively for the regime. They paid little attention to the fact that Berlin, not Moscow, had been the midwife of the Slovak state.

In May, 1939, the Comintern instructed the Slovak communists to form an independent underground Slovak Communist party (KSS).[10] Its leadership was entrusted to three minor and obscure functionaries: Julius D'uriš, Ľudovít Benada, and Ján Osoha. They were confused by the conclusion of the Nazi-Soviet Pact on August 23, 1939, that, in the witty phrase of Louis Fischer, caught foreign communists "with their dialectics down." The confusion of the Slovak communists was further compounded by Soviet recognition of the Slovak state on September 23, 1939. Their first slogan, "For a Free Slovakia in liberated Czecho-Slovakia," soon gave way to new slogans, such as "Fight for a Free Slovakia against the German Occupants," "For an Independent Slovakia," and "A new, free Slovakia, whose state structure will be deter-

---

mitters and provide efficient liaison between London and the conspirators in Slovakia. See ibid., pp. 259-98; Kropilák and Jablonický, *Malý Slovník*, pp. 117-18; and Jozef Lettrich, *History of Modern Slovakia* (New York, 1955), pp. 203, 216-17.

[8] *Sborník Ústavu Slovenského národného povstania* [*Review of the Institute for the Study of the Slovak National Uprising*] (Banská Bystrica, 1950), II, 47.

[9] Of the Slovak communist leaders, deputies of the Prague parliament Karel Šmidke (Schmidke), Štefan Major, Karel Bacílek, and Viliam Široký went to Moscow, while the deputies Jozef Valo and Vlado Clementis went to France.

[10] *Dějiny Komunistické strany Československa* [*History of the Communist Party of Czechoslovakia*] (Prague, 1961), p. 399.

mined by the people of Slovakia in the spirit of the right of self-determination and proletarian internationalism."

In January, 1941, the watchword "For an Independent Slovakia" was significantly modified to read: "For an Independent *Soviet* Slovakia." Party directives explained that an independent Soviet Slovakia "would be able, following the example of the Baltic states, to opt for the Soviet Union, whereby the Communist revolution could penetrate farther to the West."[11] This slogan was not rescinded even after the German invasion of Russia in June, 1941, when the Soviet government hastened to repudiate its recognition of the Slovak state and other German satellites and to recognize the Czechoslovak government under President Edvard Beneš in London. The slogan continued to express the official line of the Slovak Communist party until the end of 1943.[12] In these circumstances it is not surprising that the leaders of the democratic resistance avoided close cooperation with the communist leaders until 1943, although in the lower echelons some cooperation did take place.

The Slovak underground sought to frustrate Nazi policies in Slovakia. When Hitler ordered Slovakia to join the German invasion of Poland in September, 1939, the underground agitated for resistance to the mobilization of the Slovak army. Despite past disagreements between Czechoslovakia and Poland, any union with the Germans in attacking the closely related Polish people was distasteful to Slovaks of all persuasions. Slovak soldiers mutinied or proved insubordinate at Trenčín, Ružomberok, Zvolen, Trnava, Nitra, Banská Bystrica, Brezno, Banská Štiavnica, Spišská Nová Ves, Prešov, Kežmarok, and Kremnica. They denounced Slovak participation in the invasion of Poland, as well as the Bratislava government and the Germans. On September 15, 1939, a major mutiny of about 3,500 soldiers broke out at Kremnica. They refused to obey their officers, abandoned their transport trains, and marched into the city.[13]

[11] The support given Slovak independence by the Slovak communists provoked a conflict between them and the Czech communists in the Protectorate, who claimed to represent the Communist Party of Czechoslovakia (KSČ) and to have jurisdiction over the Slovak communists. However, the leadership of the KSČ in Moscow decided the conflict in favor of the Slovaks. In a resolution on May 17, 1941, it declared that "at the present time it is incorrect to use slogans about Czech and Slovak Soviet republics," but decided that the "policy of the party must be based on the assumption of political, national, and state independence of the Slovak people" and freed the KSS from the jurisdiction of the KSČ in the Protectorate. See A. Hucková-Štvrtecká, *Činnost prvého ilegalného Ústredného výboru KSS* [*Activity of the First Underground Central Committee of the KSS*] (Bratislava, 1959), p. 72; Beer, *Dejinná križovatka*, pp. 86-88.

[12] See Beer, *Dejinná križovatka*, p. 84, footnote 160: interview with Gustáv Husák on August 29, 1963.

[13] *Slovenské národné povstanie r. 1944: Sborník príspevkov z národnooslobodzovacieho boja 1938-1945* [*The Slovak National Uprising in 1944: A Collection of Studies on the Struggle for National Liberation*] (Bratislava, 1965), p. 73.

Because of censorship, these events remained unknown abroad, and thus failed to dispel the image of Slovakia created by German propaganda as an island of prosperity and contentment in the heart of Europe. Even a part of the Slovak population was misled by the increase in Slovak industrial and agricultural production and the high level of employment, both caused by a war boom in the Slovak economy, and accepted, even if it did not wholeheartedly support, the Tiso government.

THE RESISTANCE

To combat this outlook, the Slovak underground tried to alter the image of Slovak prosperity by engaging in economic sabotage. This proved to be comparatively simple. Because of a dearth of qualified personnel, the Tiso government had been forced to employ men of doubtful loyalty in the state administration. Although the government succeeded in filling the policymaking positions with its own men, the execution of such policy was often in the hands of its opponents. It was common practice for resistance members in the state administration to compile two sets of statistics: a correct set for their own guidance and an unfavorable one for publication. They also impeded exports, withheld certain allocations from the population, and used every available means to conceal the true state of the economy from the Slovak government and population and from the Germans. The Tiso government realized the extent to which the resistance had infiltrated even the most sensitive posts in the state administration only when it was too late to correct the situation or to conceal it.[14] This is not to say, of course, that the government was either blind or indifferent to the sabotage of its war effort. Farmers were relentlessly persecuted for evading government regulations concerning farm production and compulsory deliveries of farm produce. Workers were likewise harassed for provoking crises in supply or wage conditions. The government took especially stern measures against industrial sabotage, which began as early as 1939.

In 1940 members of the underground Slovak Revolutionary Youth in Ružomberok and Liptovský Svätý Mikuláš set fire to and damaged machinery in factories. Other groups specialized in emptying the fuel tanks of train locomotives. In Bratislava systematic breakdowns of oil pumps occurred in the Apollo refinery and in the dynamite and cable factories; repairs of the Danube craft that carried German war supplies were slowed down; and the grain destined for the German army was deliberately spoiled. Later, major damage was done to the railway bridge near Kráľová Lehota, the burning of an ammunition train in Ružom-

---

[14] See the report of Aladár Kočiš, secretary-general of the Hlinka's Slovak People's Party, in *Slovák*, January 1, 1943.

berok, the explosion of munitions in warehouses near Nováky, the ever-recurring breakdowns in electric power supply and high tension lines throughout Slovakia—all these events caused the Slovak government grievous headaches.[15] In 1942, when the security organs seized a plan for other and more momentous sabotage, the government became fully aroused and promulgated a law making sabotage and terrorist activities subject to capital punishment.

There was also opposition to the government in Church circles. The bulk of the Catholic clergy supported the government but hoped that Tiso, as a Catholic priest, would guard against Nazi ideology and hold in check its principal Slovak exponents, Vojtech Tuka and Šaňo Mach. Slovak Protestant (Lutheran) ministers, with rare exceptions, were opponents of the government. They made no secret of their convictions, even outside their congregations. Arrests of Protestant ministers and lay church officers, censorship of the Protestant press, and suspension of Protestant publications were a daily occurrence. Young people, organized in the Association of Lutheran Youth, openly opposed the government at their conventions.

Slovak youth in general were at first inclined to accept the new regime, some enthusiastically and most at least without questioning its origins and purposes. In time, however, there was a sobering reaction among young people, with some becoming increasingly critical of the government. Although the Slovak youth, unlike the Czech youth, did not spearhead the resistance, it eventually joined it and often seized its leadership from the older generation.

In his Christmas broadcast of 1942, President Beneš gave the signal for intensified action by resistance groups in Slovakia.[16] In later secret directives he emphasized the "paramount importance" for members of the resistance to expand preparations for the seizure of power in Slovakia, especially by working among members of "the army, gendarmerie, police, and organs of state security generally. . . . The more people that may be won over in these organs, the more favorable the [Slovak] military units are to our purposes and the early reunification of the [Czechoslovak] lands, the better it will be for Slovakia and the Slovak people when the time for the overthrow [of the Tiso government] comes."[17] Beneš's public appeals, which gave wide publicity and encouragement to the aims sought by the Slovak resistance, did not remain without effect. In the towns and country secret national committees were formed,

[15] *Slovenské národné povstanie r. 1944*, pp. 73-74.

[16] Edvard Beneš, *Šest let exilu a druhé světové války: Řeči, projevy a dokumenty z r. 1938-1945* [*Six Years of Exile and the Second World War: Speeches, Declarations, and Documents in the Years 1938-1945*] (Prague, 1947), pp. 184-90.

[17] Prečan, *Dokumenty*, pp. 55-57, Beneš's reply of February 20, 1943, to resistance group "Klas."

and collaboration between members of the resistance and disaffected officers of the army, the gendarmerie, and the frontier guards broadened. Almost at the same time (March, 1943), news of the exploits of the Czechoslovak unit in the Soviet army at Sokolovo on the Eastern front and of defections of Slovak soldiers to the Soviets caused panic among government supporters. These desertions culminated on October 30, 1943, when 2,140 Slovak soldiers and 41 officers and noncommissioned officers went over to the Soviet side in the Melitopol-Kakhovka sector of the front on the Dnieper River. Later, most of these deserters joined the Czechoslovak army in Russia.[18]

The Tiso government responded to these events by increasing its repression of the opposition. Such measures and the change in the fortunes of war in favor of the Allies in 1943 led the leaders of the Slovak democratic resistance to try to unify and coordinate all the forces of the Slovak resistance. Their discussions with disaffected army officers about the possibility of bringing the army to the Allied side likewise revealed that the existing cell structure of the resistance was no longer adequate, and that a central political leadership on the home soil—one that the army would trust and whose orders it would accept and execute—was necessary. Several leaders, among them Dr. Vavro Šrobár, who had figured prominently in the establishment of Czechoslovakia in 1918, tried to create such a central leadership, but failed.[19] In the end, Ursíny, Lettrich, and Josko, because of their political standing and support and greater experience in underground work, had the greatest success.

THE CHRISTMAS AGREEMENT

In trying to organize a central leadership for the Slovak resistance, the leaders were faced, first of all, with the problem of communist participation. Various communist spokesmen, whether authorized or self-appointed, were ready to negotiate, but were unable to reveal an official communist program or to give guarantees that an agreement, once concluded, would be respected and carried out. Since the outbreak of war with the Soviet Union the Slovak Communist party had been disorganized by the arrests of D'uriš, Benada, Osoha, and other leaders, and apparently was out of contact with Moscow. In August, 1943, however,

---

[18] Edo Friš, *Povstanie zďaleka a blízka* [*The Uprising from Afar and Near*] (Bratislava, 1964), pp. 4-5. After the German invasion of Russia in June, 1941, the Slovak army was mobilized and sent to the Eastern front. It comprised 50,689 officers and men. However, as early as August, because of the army's unreliability and insubordination, 35,623 soldiers were withdrawn from the front. By the fall of 1941 the army at the front was reduced to, and thereafter remained at, about 16,000 men. See Kropilák and Jablonický, *Malý Slovník*, p. 233.

[19] Jablonický, *Z ilegality*, pp. 176-94; for Šrobár's memorandum to President Beneš see Prečan, *Dokumenty*, pp. 88-93.

Karel Šmidke, a former communist deputy in the Prague parliament, returned from Moscow with fresh instructions for the Slovak communists. He set up a new central committee of the Slovak Communist party and revived the network of its organizations. Among the members of the new central committee were two prominent Slovak intellectuals: Laco Novomeský, a well-known Slovak writer, and Gustáv Husák, a lawyer by training and a dedicated communist.

Negotiations between the spokesmen of the democratic and the communist resistance opened at the beginning of September. The planners reached agreement readily on the formula for the Slovak-Czech relationship ("The Czechs and Slovaks constitute two nations that are most closely related"). However, on other questions, notably the restoration of pre-Munich Czechoslovakia and the use of the Slovak army, as such, in the struggle against the Germans, no agreement was reached. Šmidke's instructions did not cover even such fundamental questions as collaboration between the Slovak resistance and the liberation movement abroad. At one point in the negotiations, the communist spokesmen actually declared that "in the absence of directives from Moscow relative to the official standpoint" they were unable to collaborate with the Czechoslovak government in London, which they did not recognize.[20]

The discussions nevertheless continued and culminated on November 20, 1943, in the adoption of a series of resolutions that became known as the Christmas Agreement of 1943. No doubt this agreement had been facilitated by the news from the fronts and by the information that President Beneš had been invited to visit Moscow to conclude a Soviet-Czechoslovak alliance treaty. The Preamble of the Christmas Agreement stated:

> Those who represent the ideological trends in Slovakia which have remained faithful to the principles of anti-Fascist democracy even after [the Žilina agreement of] October 6, 1938, and who have been conducting active resistance against the political, economic, and cultural coercion of the Slovak people, and who represent today the true opinions of all strata of the Slovak Nation, have agreed to create a common political leadership, the Slovak National Council [Slovenská národná rada—SNR], as the only representative of the political will of the Slovak Nation at home.

The principal tasks and aims of the SNR, according to the agreement, were to provide the Slovaks with uniform and central leadership in their struggle against the Nazi German and domestic dictatorships (point one) and to seize and hold all power in Slovakia until free elections could be

---

[20] Prečan, *Dokumenty*, pp. 144-45; Beer, *Dejinná križovatka*, p. 213.

371

held (point two). The agreement specifically provided that the SNR should act "in agreement with the Czechoslovak government and the liberation movement abroad" (point four). Insofar as the future political organization of Czechoslovakia was concerned, the agreement stated that "the Slovak and Czech nations, as the most closely related Slav nations, [should] shape their destinies in the Czechoslovak Republic, a common state of the Czechs and Slovaks built upon the principle of national equality." Future Czechoslovakia should lean in foreign policy and military affairs on the Soviet Union, "as the protector of the freedom and universal progress of small nations in general and Slav nations in particular." The internal organization of Czechoslovakia should be democratic and should guard against the errors of the past.[21]

President Beneš, who was informed of the negotiations leading to the agreement, and of the agreement itself, endorsed it publicly on March 29, 1944: "In general, it accords with what I said, in some respects more concretely and fully, in my speech of February 3, 1944. There are no substantial differences between us."[22]

The SNR, which originally consisted of the six signatories of the Christmas Agreement—two agrarians (Lettrich and Ursíny), one Independent (Josko), and three communists (Husák, Novomeský, and Šmidke)—was enlarged in January, 1944, to include a Social Democrat (Ivan Horvath) and a member of the Slovak National party (Peter Zaťko), and, on July 20, 1944, to include another Social Democrat (Jozef Šoltész) and another agrarian (Jozef Styk).[23] From the beginning there was a tendency within the SNR toward polarization between its Marxist and non-Marxist members. While the communists absorbed the Social Democrats, members of the non-Marxist parties coalesced into a single party, the Slovak Democrat party. (Although these mergers did not formally take place until after the outbreak of the Slovak National Uprising, the two factions will henceforth be referred to as the communists and the democrats.)

PLANNING AN UPRISING

The principal immediate task of the SNR was to organize the Slovak National Uprising (Slovenské národné povstanie) against the Germans and their Slovak henchmen. Although the communists and the democrats agreed that the Slovak army was to provide its nucleus, the uprising was to be—as its name indicated—a national one, comprising all elements of Slovak society. The Slovak army was still outwardly loyal to the Tiso government, but it was honeycombed with disaffected officers and men.

[21] Prečan, *Dokumenty*, pp. 125-26; Lettrich, *History*, pp. 303-305.
[22] Prečan, *Dokumenty*, pp. 177-81.   [23] Ibid., p. 171.

From the beginning the SNR was in touch with officers who held key positions in the army and who were ready to lead a revolt of the army against the government.

In March, 1944, with President Beneš's approval, the SNR selected Lt.-Col. Ján Golian, chief of staff of the military command at Banská Bystrica in central Slovakia, to prepare the army's coup against the government. Golian accepted the task and formed a secret Military Center (Vojenské ústredie) at Banská Bystrica to aid him in preparing the revolt.[24] It was evident at the time that Czechoslovakia would be liberated by the Soviet army, which had approached its eastern borders, rather than by the British and United States armies, which had bogged down in Italy and had not yet landed in France. It was therefore necessary to plan the uprising in conjunction with the Soviet army. The SNR envisaged two alternatives for launching the uprising: either when the Soviet advance warranted it or if the Germans threatened to occupy Slovakia.

The Anglo-American landing in France on June 6 and the launching of the great Soviet summer offensive on the White Russian front on June 22 convinced the SNR and the Military Center that the hour of the decisive struggle was close at hand. Late in June the Military Center produced a detailed plan for the military uprising, according to which the two best-equipped Slovak divisions, stationed in eastern Slovakia, were to open up the Carpathian passes for the Soviet army to penetrate into Slovakia, while the rear of the army was to safeguard the strategic center of the uprising against an anticipated German counterstroke. As the center of the uprising, the Military Center proposed a triangle formed by the towns of Banská Bystrica, Zvolen, and Brezno in rugged, mountainous central Slovakia.[25]

The timing of the uprising was of paramount importance, lest Slovakia suffer the unhappy fate of Italy, and later of Hungary, which surrendered prematurely to the Allies and then were caught and trampled between the great combatants, both equally indifferent to their fate. By the end of July the Soviet army had advanced in a narrow wedge to the Vistula River near Warsaw, thus precipitating the famous Warsaw Uprising (August 1-October 2, 1944). However, the Soviet army then halted its advance in Poland, allowed the Germans to wipe out the Warsaw Uprising, and proceeded to broaden its long and exposed flanks by launching offensives into the Baltic area and into the Balkans. Instead of advancing to the mid-Danube basin from the north, across the Carpathian Mountains, the Soviet army proposed to reach it from the south, through Rumania and the Danube Valley. The SNR and the Military Center were unaware of this change in Soviet strategy, which relegated the liberation

[24] Jablonický, *Z ilegality*, pp. 224-32; Beer, *Dejinná križovatka*, pp. 268-69.
[25] Prečan, *Dokumenty*, pp. 217-18.

of Slovakia to the final months of the war. They assumed that the Soviet invasion would take place in the summer or early fall of 1944.

To coordinate the uprising with the Soviet advance, the SNR decided to send a mission to the Soviet Union. After two unsuccessful attempts in July, the mission consisting of Šmidke and Lt.-Col. Mikuláš Ferjenčík managed to take off by plane on August 4 and landed near Vinitsa in the Ukraine. They were escorted to the headquarters of Gen. Ivan Y. Petrov, commander of the Fourth Ukrainian Front (Army), where they were interrogated by its political commissar and partisan warfare expert, Lev Z. Mekhlis, and then sent to Moscow for further interrogation. On September 5 they were permitted to return to Slovakia without having received any indication of Soviet plans of operations or a commitment to support the uprising.[26]

While awaiting their return and the arrival of the Soviet Army, the Military Center continued its preparations for the uprising. Under the pretext of "increased participation of the Slovak army in fighting the Soviets," it managed to obtain a decree from the Tiso government mobilizing additional age groups. Under the same pretext army units were quietly shifted to the strategic triangle of the uprising. Finally, under the pretext of removing military supplies, food, and medicines from areas exposed to Allied bombing (principally Bratislava), the Military Center moved them to the defensive triangle. Slovak Minister of Defense Gen. Ferdinand Čatloš, although not initiated into the conspiracy, was aware to some extent of the preparations for the uprising.[27] Neither the Tiso government nor its German "advisers" in Bratislava, however, had any inkling of what was in the offing.

PARTISAN WARFARE

In August these auspicious beginnings were threatened by the outbreak of partisan warfare, which risked the start of a German occupation

[26] Mikuláš Ferjenčík, "Slovenské národné povstanie a SSSR," ["The Slovak National Uprising and the U.S.S.R."], *Svědectví*, vi, 22 (1963), 145-54; Jablonický, *Z ilegality*, pp. 338-57; for Šmidke's report of the Moscow mission see Prečan, *Dokumenty*, pp. 1076-81.

[27] General Čatloš had been a member of the Czechoslovak Legion in Russia in World War I and a loyal officer of the Czechoslovak army under the First Republic. In 1939 he opportunistically rallied to the Tiso government, and by 1944 was ready to betray it. According to a memorandum he sent to the Soviet government through Šmidke on August 5, 1944, he proposed himself to lead the uprising. At an appropriate time, he proposed to overthrow the Tiso government, establish a military dictatorship, and lead Slovakia to the Soviet side. Unlike the SNR, however, he proposed to leave the question of Slovakia's future status until after the war for decision. For his memorandum to the Soviet government see Prečan, *Dokumenty*, pp. 262-64. See also Jablonický, *Z ilegality*, pp. 326-29, and Gustáv Husák, *Svedectvo*, pp. 164-65.

of Slovakia before preparations for the uprising were completed. As early as 1942 small groups of men—Slovak political offenders and army deserters, escaped Soviet and other prisoners of war, and Jews who feared deportation to the Nazi death camps—had taken refuge in the Slovak mountains. In 1943, they formed the first partisan groups. By 1944 they were very numerous in central and northern Slovakia, where the mountainous terrain lends itself to partisan warfare.

Both the leadership of the Czechoslovak Communist party in Moscow, in its directives of January 5, 1943,[28] and President Beneš, in his address of February 3, 1944,[29] encouraged the partisan movement in Czechoslovakia. However, a sharp difference in attitude toward the movement developed between the Slovak democratic and communist resistance. From the beginning, the democratic resistance welcomed and counted on the partisan movement for help in the struggle for national liberation, since by their nature the partisans were particularly well suited to operate behind enemy lines. Therefore, after the formation of the SNR and its decision to launch a military uprising, the democrats insisted that partisan formations be subordinated to the Military Center and act as auxiliaries of the army behind the German lines. The communists, on the other hand, saw in the partisans an instrument of social revolution and, ultimately, of the communist seizure of power in Slovakia. With this objective in mind, they concentrated on corroding the ranks of the Slovak army and on recruiting its soldiers for partisan warfare before the formation of the SNR. When the SNR decided to launch a military uprising, the communists sought to keep the partisan formations independent of Slovak military command and to place them under experienced Soviet leadership.[30]

In May, 1944, Klement Gottwald, chairman of the Czechoslovak Communist party in Moscow, made an agreement to this effect with Nikita S. Khrushchev, then secretary-general of the Ukrainian Communist party, as a result of which the partisan movement in Czechoslovakia was placed under the Ukranian Partisan Movement, directed by Mekhlis from headquarters in Kiev. On the night of July 25-26, 1944, the Ukrainian Partisan command sent the first Soviet paratroop unit under Lt. Peter A. Velichko to Slovakia to take charge of the Slovak partisan movement and stiffen its cadres with experienced Soviet partisans. Velichko was soon in touch with the Military Center, of which he asked arms. The center promised him weapons, but insisted that he await its signal for the uprising before he used them. Velichko promised to withhold action until August 20, but reserved a free hand after that date.[31]

[28] Beer, *Dejinná križovatka*, p. 217. [29] Prečan, *Dokumenty*, pp. 156-60.
[30] Husák, *Svedectvo*, pp. 182-90.
[31] Povereníctvo SNR pre informácie, *Vojenské akcie v národnom povstaní*

Meanwhile, premature sabotage by other partisan groups had aroused the suspicions of the Tiso government and its German advisers. On August 12 the government proclaimed martial law and ordered the army and gendarmerie to search the areas of the High and Lower Tatra Mountains for partisans. Thanks to timely warnings by confederates in the Slovak security organs, they escaped detection.[32] Thus, the Tiso government was lulled into a sense of security, which however proved to be very brief.

The successful defection of Rumania from the German side to the Soviet side, deftly carried out by King Michael on August 23, caused consternation in Berlin and fear lest the Rumanian example prove contagious in the other German satellites of East Central Europe. On August 24, Hans Ludin, the German minister in Bratislava, cabled the Foreign Ministry in Berlin: "After thorough reflection and discussions with pertinent quarters, in particular with President Tiso, I have asked the German general to arrange for the dispatch of several German military units to the Slovak territory."[33] On the same day, in a report to London, Golian expressed fear that the Germans would occupy Slovakia on August 27. In such an eventuality, he asked London for two parachute brigades and fighter plane assistance for the Slovak army.[34] His forebodings proved only too accurate.

THE NATIONAL UPRISING

On August 27, the partisans under Velichko in the region of Turiec intercepted a train at Turčiansky Svätý Martin in which the German military mission to Rumania under General Paul von Otto was returning from Bucharest to Berlin after the Rumanian defection. On the following day all twenty-eight members of the mission were shot by the partisans. The news of their killing outraged the Germans. On August 28 Ludin informed Tiso that Slovakia would be occupied on the following day. On August 29, at 7:15 P.M., General Čatloš announced the news of the German occupation over Radio Bratislava and ordered the Slovak army not to resist them.[35] Three-quarters of an hour later the Military Center at

[*Military Activity in the National Uprising*] (Bratislava, 1945), p. 34; Jablonický, *Z ilegality*, p. 368.

[32] Ibid., pp. 366-68; Imrich Stanek, *Zrada a pád: Hlinkovští separatisté a tak zvaný Slovenský stát* [*The Betrayal and the Fall: Hlinka's Separatists and the so-called Slovak State*] (Prague, 1958), p. 257.

[33] Prečan, *Dokumenty*, pp. 317-18.   [34] Ibid., pp. 319-20.

[35] After his broadcast (see ibid., pp. 354-55), Čatloš escaped from Bratislava and tried to join the insurgents. However, they arrested him and had him flown to Russia as a prisoner. See Jablonický, *Z ilegality*, p. 436. After the war the Soviet authorities returned him to Slovakia, where he was tried and sentenced to five years' imprisonment. However, he was released after the communist coup of 1948, having apparently satisfied the communists that he had been on their side.

had to act

Banská Bystrica telephoned a signal to garrisons all over Slovakia to resist the Germans.[36] The first armed encounter with the Germans took place on the same day in the area of Žilina. The Slovak National Uprising had begun, unfortunately, under the second, less favorable, alternative envisaged by the SNR.

The SNR came out into the open and in a proclamation issued at *SNR* Banská Bystrica on September 1 assumed the role of the supreme organ *politics* of the Slovak home resistance.[37] It restored Czechoslovak state sovereignty in Slovakia, and in the name of the Czechoslovak government in London assumed legislative and executive powers for the duration of the uprising. The primary tasks of the SNR were to direct the fighting and to replace the fascist administration and institutions of the Tiso regime with democratic ones. The expansion of its functions necessitated its reorganization. The Presidium of the SNR, which consisted of four— later eight—members and had two chairmen (Dr. Vavro Šrobár for the democrats and Karel Šmidke for the communists), was the supreme organ. A Board of Commissioners (*povereníci*) and the Plenum (assembly) of the SNR were subordinated to the Presidium. The former consisted of nine, later eleven, departments, while the membership of the latter rose from thirteen to fifty.[38] *Significance of uprising*

The uprising transformed Slovakia, which until its outbreak had been a peaceful hinterland, into a battlefront. In response to a call to arms issued by the SNR, men from all over Slovakia streamed to Banská Bystrica, the insurgent capital, to take up the struggle for Slovak freedom and honor. The uprising released tensions that had been building up in Slovakia since 1939 and was marked by great enthusiasm for the struggle. Many foreign nationals in Slovakia were caught up in the enthusiasm and joined in the struggle to strike a blow at Nazi tyranny.[39]

The Free Slovak Radio Banská Bystrica, which had announced to the world the Slovak determination to cast off the Nazi yoke on August 30, was destroyed by German bombers a few days later. It was replaced by a portable transmitter.[40] Whatever it was unable to handle was picked up by Allied broadcasts and announced to the world. In the insurgent territory, the daily press fulfilled the task. The restoration of democracy

---

[36] Prečan, *Dokumenty*, p. 357; Lettrich, *History*, p. 305.

[37] Lettrich, *History*, pp. 305-307; Prečan, *Dokumenty*, pp. 390-91.

[38] Prečan, *Dokumenty*, pp. 433-34.

[39] Jablonický, *Z ilegality*, pp. 369-75; Jiří Doležal and Jozef Hrozienčík, *Medzinárodná solidarita v Slovenskom národnom povstaní* [*International Solidarity in the Slovak National Uprising*] (Bratislava, 1959), *passim*. Altogether, about 2,000 Czechs, 3,000 Soviet citizens, 100 Yugoslavs, 400 Frenchmen, 800 Hungarians, 50 Americans and Britons, 200 members of the German minority in Slovakia, 90 Poles, and a small number of other nationals fought in the uprising.

[40] Ondrej Laciak, *Slobodný slovenský vysielač Banská Bystrica* [*Free Slovak Radio Banská Bystrica*] (Bratislava, 1961), *passim*.

in the insurgent area resulted in the revival of political activities, which placed a strain on the coalition of democrats and communists in the SNR. While the democrats sought to concentrate on the immediate task of fighting the Germans, the communists never lost sight of their ultimate goal, which was to seize a monopoly of power. Their primary efforts aimed at gaining a majority in the organs of public administration and among the people. But they failed. The best part of the population supported the democrats, without whom neither the national uprising nor its spiritual content would have come to fruition. The Slovak National Uprising emanated from and lived by the ideas of Tomáš G. Masaryk and his concept of democracy. Not Marx, but Masaryk, was the lodestar of the Slovak people in their spontaneous desire for, and manifestation of, freedom.[41]

The nucleus of the uprising was provided by the Slovak army, which the Czechoslovak government in London recognized as a part of Czechoslovak armed forces and designated the "First Czechoslovak Army." Golian, who was later promoted to the rank of brigadier-general, remained its commander until the arrival of Gen. Rudolf Viest from London on October 7. Golian then became Viest's deputy.

The military outlook for the uprising was somber from the beginning. Golian's Military Center at Banská Bystrica had estimated that the best time to launch the uprising would be when the Soviet army reached Cracow in Poland and Miskolc in Hungary.[42] As events turned out, the Soviet army did not capture Miskolc until December, and Cracow until January, 1945. It became evident then that the inopportune action of Velichko's partisans had precipitated the uprising four or five months too soon. According to Golian's statement to the Germans after his capture, the preparations for the uprising had been only about 70 percent complete at the time of its outbreak.[43] As a result, the uprising suffered irreparable losses in its initial days.

The German counterstroke against the uprising was well planned and swiftly executed. The German army converged on Slovakia from Austria, Moravia, Silesia (through the Jablunkov Pass), and Poland. Slovak garrisons in western Slovakia were surprised and disarmed almost without a struggle. An even more grievous loss was that of two well-equipped di-

[41] See Peter A. Toma, "Soviet Strategy in the Slovak Uprising of 1944," *Journal of Central European Affairs*, XIX (October, 1959), 297-98; Beer, *Dejinná križovatka*, p. 405; Prečan, *Dokumenty*, pp. 528, 890; *Čas* (Banská Bystrica), September 21, 1944; *Pravda* (Banská Bystrica), September 14, 1944; *Národnie Noviny* (Banská Bystrica), September 15, 1944; *Nad Tatrou sa blýska—Slovenské národní povstání* [*Lightning over the Tatra Mountains—The Slovak National Uprising*] (Prague-Bratislava, 1946), pp. 161-66.

[42] Miroslav Kropilák, *Účasť vojakov v Slovenskom národnom povstaní* [*Participation of Soldiers in the Slovak National Uprising*] (Bratislava, 1960), p. 25.

[43] Ibid., p. 35.

visions in eastern Slovakia, comprising about 24,000 men, through the unfortunate action of their commander, Gen. August Malár, who disregarded the signal from the Military Center to rise on August 29. Instead, he flew to Bratislava on August 30 and appealed over the radio to the army not to be drawn into "premature" action.[44] The word "premature" proved fatal to him. The Germans arrested him and later executed him. Although in close contact with the Military Center, his deputy, Lt.-Col. Viliam Talský, likewise failed to give the order in time to resist the Germans. Instead, he defected to the Soviet side, taking with him the better part of the Slovak air force (38 planes). Left leaderless, the two divisions were surrounded by the Germans on August 31 and disarmed. However, a part of the divisions, comprising about 2,000 men and subaltern officers, angered by the timidity of their superior officers, refused to lay down their arms, fought their way through the German encirclement, and joined the insurgents in central Slovakia.[45]

By the middle of September the Germans had secured both western and eastern Slovakia. In the north they had secured the valleys of the Váh and Hornad rivers, with the strategic east-west Bohumín (Oderberg)-Košice railway. The insurgent area was isolated from the Soviet army by a wide band of territory firmly held by the Germans. However, when the Germans assaulted the insurgents in their stronghold in central Slovakia, they encountered stiff resistance and their progress was slowed. They had to halt, regroup their forces, and bring reinforcements to Slovakia from other fronts until, with 40,000 men assisted by tanks, heavy artillery, and planes, they outstripped the insurgent army.[46]

With the shrinking of the circumference of the insurgent area, partisan warfare assumed increasing importance. According to the military plan, partisan units were to have been an effective support of the uprising and the army, especially by operating in the rear of the enemy. Some Slovak partisan groups had subordinated themselves to the army command even before the uprising. However, most of the partisan units limited themselves to an indispensable minimum of cooperation with the army and pursued their own activities under orders from the Ukrainian partisan headquarters in Kiev.

The Slovak communists first proposed to reorganize the Slovak army on the pattern of the Soviet army, with political commissars and party organizations. However, both the democrats and the army command resisted any politicization of the army. In October the army command agreed to the appointment of "education officers" in army units, but the communists never succeeded in dominating the military, which was headed by non-Marxist officers. To create a counter-balance, the com-

[44] Prečan, *Dokumenty*, p. 373.   [45] Kropilák, *Účast vojakov*, pp. 42-47.
[46] Ibid., pp. 51-56; Kropilák and Jablonický, *Malý Slovník*, pp. 822-31.

munists tried to build the partisan detachments into an army of their own.[47] The army-partisan conflict created a crisis in the uprising, which the SNR tried to solve by appointing a "War Council" on September 12 to coordinate all actions of the army and the partisans. Unfortunately, because of continued communist chicanery, the council, which consisted of Ursíny, Šmidke, Golian, Ferjenčík, and later Gen. Viest and Col. Alexei N. Asmolov (the Soviet liaison officer with the uprising), never completely resolved the conflict.[48]

ALLIED FAILURE TO AID THE UPRISING

The success of the uprising was predicated on the assumption that it would be given prompt and effective assistance by the Allies. Unfortunately, the Allied attitude toward the Slovak National Uprising was, to say the least, equivocal. The Western Allies had sympathy for the uprising politically, but they had little interest in it militarily, because their armies did not expect to operate in East Central Europe. On the other hand, the Soviet government was interested in the uprising militarily, because it might facilitate the western advance of the Soviet army, but it found the uprising suspect politically, because its leadership was divided between communists and democrats—the latter being, from a Marxist point of view, hostile "bourgeous nationalists."

On August 31, on receiving the news of the uprising, Jan Masaryk, the Czechoslovak foreign minister, personally called on the Allied representatives in London to ask their assistance for the Slovak insurgents. He asked the British and American representatives for (a) Allied bombings of German army objectives in Slovakia and (b) the issuance of an Allied statement according the Czechoslovak home forces combatant rights, which would put the Slovak insurgents under the protection of the Geneva Convention.[49] The U.S. State Department passed Masaryk's first request on to the American Joint Chiefs of Staff, and acted on the second itself. On September 7 it issued a statement recognizing that the Slovak insurgents "constitute a combat force operating against the Germans" and solemnly warned the Germans against violating "the rules of war"

---

[47] Husák, *Svedectvo*, p. 90: ". . . no communist can ever view a national uprising in terms of military action alone, no matter how readily he accepts the concept of soldiers being 'people in arms.' The communist cannot help investigating the proportion of class components in any struggle for national liberation. He must strive for the hegemony of the working class and the commanding role of the Party."

[48] Ferjenčík, "Slovenské národné povstanie a SSSR," p. 153.

[49] U.S. Department of State, *Foreign Relations of the United States: Diplomatic Papers 1944* (6 vols.; Washington, 1966), III, 521-22.

by taking reprisals against them.[50] The British Foreign Office issued a similar warning.

The British and American commands were reluctant to grant Masaryk's request for military assistance to the Slovaks. British and American aircraft had already bombed targets in Slovakia and had flown aid to the Warsaw Uprising, which was farther removed from their bases in Italy than Slovakia. They also landed twice at Banská Bystrica to evacuate Allied pilots shot down over German-held territory who had found refuge with the Slovak insurgents.[51] Nevertheless, on September 22, the U. S. Joint Chiefs of Staff decided to withhold aid from the Slovaks on the ground that "it would not be a reasonably feasible operation for American and British aircraft" and that "geography left only Soviet forces to do it."[52] The Chiefs of Staff declined to join the British in asking the Soviet government to help the Slovaks. Undoubtedly, American reserve toward the Slovak Uprising was influenced by the oft-expressed fear of Gen. George C. Marshall, chairman of the U.S. Joint Chiefs of Staff, that Western interference in Eastern Europe might prejudice promised Soviet assistance in the Pacific.[53]

The Soviet government never answered the British request, although it did extend limited assistance to the Slovak insurgents. On September 22, somewhat belatedly, the Soviet government followed the Ameri-

[50] U.S. Department of State, *Bulletin*, IX (September 10, 1944), p. 263; Lettrich, *History*, p. 307.

[51] Lettrich, *History*, pp. 212-13. According to Lettrich, American and British airplanes, on their second flight to Slovakia on October 6, brought the insurgents "clandestinely" a small quantity of arms and medicines. Colonel Threlfall of the British army, who accompanied the flight, is supposed to have explained to Viest and Golian that the Western Allies could not help the Slovaks because "Slovakia was in the Soviet sphere of operations," and that "there could be no Western interference in this sphere without Soviet permission." If this is actually what Threlfall said, he was mistaken. No spheres of operations had been formally agreed upon between the Western Allies and the U.S.S.R.; they were simply set by geography. The Western Allies did not need Soviet permission to give the Slovaks aid; they withheld it of their own volition. The "clandestine" nature of the token gift of Western arms to the insurgents was perhaps necessary to conceal it from the American command, not the Soviet command, for it constituted an infraction of the decision of the U.S. Joint Chiefs of Staff of September 22.

[52] *Foreign Relations*, 1944, p. 523. On October 6, on their return to Italy, American planes flew out a delegation of the SNR, consisting of Ursíny, Novomeský, and Lt.-Col. Miroslav Vesel, which proceeded to London to report to President Beneš on the state of the insurrection. As a result, Masaryk made a second appeal to the Western Allies, this time for a shipment of weapons to the insurgents. The request was turned down by the U.S. Joint Chiefs of Staff on November 17. See ibid., pp. 522-23.

[53] Cf., e.g., General Marshall's arguments during the U.S. White House conference on April 23, 1945, on United States policy toward the U.S.S.R. and Poland in Harry S. Truman, *Memoirs* (2 vols.; New York, 1955), Vol. I: *The Year of Decisions*, p. 79.

Soviet → pol suspect.

can and British statements with one of its own, which granted the "united forces resisting on Czechoslovak territory the right of a state at war with every consequence that that entailed."[54] Earlier, the Soviet command ordered the First Czechoslovak Army Corps, operating with the Fourth Ukrainian Front and Soviet forces, to try to break through the Dukla Pass in the Carpathian Mountains and establish contact with the Slovak insurgents. Unfortunately, by September 14 when the Czechoslovak army reached the pass, it was no longer guarded by the Slovak army but by the Germans. It was not until October 6, after suffering frightful casualties, that Czechoslovak and Soviet forces took it.[55]

By way of direct assistance to the Slovak Uprising, the Soviet command sent the First Czechoslovak Air Squadron (with twenty-one fighter planes), which proved of great assistance, but it refused to return the thirty-eight Slovak planes that Talský had taken to Russia. It also sent the Second Czechoslovak Parachute Brigade under Col. Vladimír Přikryl, which comprised about 2,000 well-trained and well-equipped men. Unfortunately, they arrived piecemeal over several weeks, so that they were unable to take part in combat as a unit. The Soviets also sent a quantity of small arms and 150 antitank guns, which unfortunately proved ineffective against the German heavy and medium tanks.[56]

END OF THE UPRISING

After the fall of Adm. Miklós Horthy's regime and the installation of the Nazi Arrow Cross regime of Ferenc Szálasi in Budapest on October 16, the Germans were able to hurl considerable forces against southern Slovakia from Hungary. The insurgent position then deteriorated rapidly. Banská Bystrica fell on October 27. On the following day, which by a cruel irony was the Czechoslovak national holiday, General Viest issued by radio his last situation report: "The Czechoslovak Army command announces herewith that the fight for freedom of Slovakia and all Czechoslovakia goes on and will be waged until victory is won." After paying tribute to the army's heroic feats, General Viest declared: "An organized resistance of the army as a whole is no longer possible. . . . Accordingly, starting October 29, 1944, the Czechoslovak army units

[54] Čestmír Amort, *Na pomoc československému lidu* [*To the Aid of the Czechoslovak People*] (Prague, 1960), p. 360.

[55] Earl F. Ziemke, *Stalingrad to Berlin: The German Defeat in the East* (Washington, 1968), p. 362.

[56] Kropilák and Jablonický (*Malý slovník*, p. 55) put the number of Přikryl's brigade at 2,933 on September 4, 1944. See also Ferjenčík, "Slovenské národné povstanie a SSSR," p. 153.

will adapt themselves to the given situation and undertake partisan-type warfare against the Germans."[57]

Although the uprising was quelled, the army did not capitulate. The war against the Germans continued. Only the methods changed. Some units fought independently, others merged with partisan formations and carried on both the fight and sabotage until they met the advancing Red Army and the Czechoslovak corps.

From the outbreak of the uprising until the end of the war, Slovakia ceased to be a safe hinterland for the Germany army on the Eastern front. The German communications system behind the front lines was disrupted; Slovakia was no longer a convenient supply route or an avenue of retreat for the German forces; German troops, sorely needed elsewhere to fight the Allies, were tied down in fighting the insurgents and partisans; German plans for utilizing the Slovak army in war were thwarted; lastly, the Germans suffered grievous losses in human lives and materiel in fighting the insurgents and partisans.

After the end of the uprising, in defiance of the solemn Allied warnings and in violation of the rules of war, the Germans carried out brutal reprisals against the captured insurgents and punitive expeditions against the civilian population in the former insurgent areas. This period swelled the uprising's casualties. From its beginning until liberation, 7,500 soldiers and 2,500 partisans were killed and 3,723 civilians—men, women, and children—were murdered and buried in mass graves; 900 were burned in lime kilns; 30,000 people were deported to German concentration camps; 60 communities were completely destroyed by fires and 142 were partially wiped out.[58]

František Palacký stated in his *History of the Czech People* that nations inscribe their name in history with blood. By resisting German Nazism and the fascism of Slovak vintage, by fighting for democracy and freedom, the Slovak nation has written new pages in its history with fire and blood. The Slovak National Uprising, in which the Slovak resistance in World War II culminated, became the apex of modern Slovak history, and indeed of Czechoslovak history. Together with the Warsaw Uprising, it was the most outstanding act of resistance in Europe.

[57] Prečan, *Dokumenty*, pp. 772-74 and 778; Kropilák, *Účast vojakov*, p. 113. Generals Viest and Golian, as well as the members of the American OSS mission under Lt. James Holt Green of the U.S. Navy, were captured by the Germans on November 3, 1944, in the village of Bukovec. They were interrogated in Bratislava then taken to Berlin, and executed at Mauthausen under circumstances that have never been clarified. See Lettrich, *History*, p. 217.

[58] Lettrich, *History*, pp. 217-18; Kropilák and Jablonický, *Malý slovník; Život* [*Life*] (Bratislava), August 25, 1964.

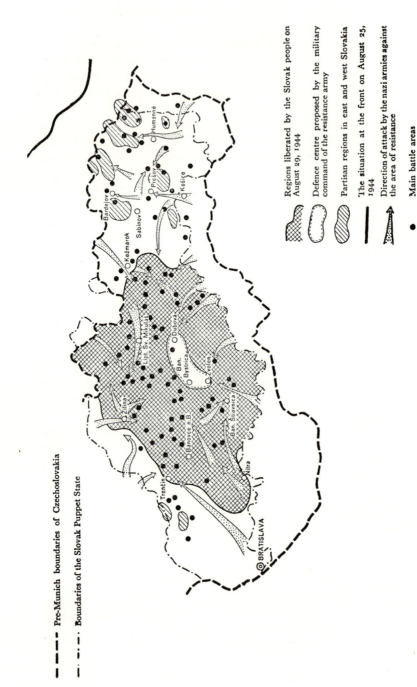

Pre-Munich boundaries of Czechoslovakia

Boundaries of the Slovak Puppet State

Regions liberated by the Slovak people on August 29, 1944

Defence centre proposed by the military command of the resistance army

Partisan regions in east and west Slovakia

The situation at the front on August 25, 1944

Direction of attack by the nazi armies against the area of resistance

Main battle areas

4. Areas of combat during the Slovak National Uprising, 1944

BRATISLAVA

Trenčín

Žilina

Bánovce n B

Ban. Štiavnica

Nitra

Ban. Bystrica

Zvolen

Dubová

Lipt. Sv. Mikuláš

Kežmarok

Sabinov

Bardejov

Prešov

Košice

Humenné

· PART THREE ·

Czechoslovakia between East and West
1945 to 1948

5. Czechoslovakia, 1945

CZECHOSLOVAKIA BETWEEN DEMOCRACY
AND COMMUNISM, 1945-1948

Radomír Luža
Tulane University

THE GOVERNMENT OF THE NATIONAL FRONT

The fate of postwar Czechoslovakia, like that of other small nations of East Central Europe, did not depend on the will and actions of her people alone. It was also affected by the actions of the great powers and their postwar relations.

In the winter of 1944-45, while the Red Army was fighting its way to Prague, Vienna, and Berlin, the Soviet Union, the United States, and Britain were making final preparations for the meeting of their leaders at Yalta. They were aware that the presence of the Soviet military might in Poland, Rumania, Bulgaria, Hungary, and Czechoslovakia meant a basic shift of power in Europe. Nonetheless, both East and West still clung to the concept of postwar coalition and were exploring the basis for a series of agreements on European and Far Eastern problems.

The policy of President Edvard Beneš, developed while he was in exile in London, had been to restore Czechoslovakia to her pre-Munich territorial integrity and reinstitute her democratic institutions. The success of this policy depended on the continued cooperation of the Allied Powers, not only until the end of the war but afterward. Only in these circumstances could Czechoslovakia hope to recover her independence and territorial integrity and restore her traditional parliamentary-democratic system. Throughout the war, therefore, Beneš had tried to promote a cooperative effort of the anti-Nazi alliance to find a permanent settlement in Europe. Alone among the exiled leaders of East Central European countries he sought both the support of the Western powers and an accommodation with the Soviet Union. The signing of the Soviet-Czechoslovak alliance treaty in Moscow in December, 1943, was conclusive proof of his determination to come to terms with Moscow, and appeared to be a guarantee of the success of his policy.

Beneš was, therefore, deeply disappointed and even shocked when reports reached him late in 1944 that Soviet authorities were promoting a movement in Ruthenia (Carpathian Ukraine)—which had been the first Czechoslovak province liberated by the Red Army—for its secession from Czechoslovakia and its attachment to the Soviet Ukraine. As early as 1939, in conversations with Ivan Maisky, the Soviet ambassador in London, Beneš had voiced his willingness to solve the question of Ruthenia in full agreement with the Soviet Union,[1] and had reiterated this view in his last talk with Stalin in Moscow in December, 1943. At the time the Soviet leaders did not regard the question as pressing, but they now apparently were determined to force a solution favorable to the Soviet Union. Czechoslovak complaints lodged with the Soviet government against Soviet activity in Ruthenia during December, 1944, proved to be of no avail.

At the same time Beneš became alarmed about the ultimate fate of Slovakia, which had been partially liberated by the Soviet army. Although the Communist Party of Slovakia (KSS) had abandoned its earlier agitation for a "Soviet Slovakia," it continued to press—with the approval of the leadership of the Communist Party of Czechoslovakia (KSČ) in Moscow—for a loose federation between Slovakia on one hand and Bohemia and Moravia on the other.

Beneš's tense concern was ended by a personal letter from Joseph Stalin on January 23, 1945, assuring the Czechoslovak government of his full support. The Soviet leader suggested, however, that the problem of Ruthenia should be solved by negotiations between the two countries that would take into account the desire of the province's Ukrainian population to join the Soviet Union. The underlying concern of Beneš, that the Soviet Union would use its control of Czechoslovak territory in disregard of its commitments, was thus relieved.[2] Soviet-Czechoslovak relations had for some time been regarded as an index of Soviet-Western relations. Undoubtedly, Stalin's decision to ease Beneš's fears on the eve of the Yalta conference was motivated, in part, by a desire to dissipate the suspicions of President Franklin D. Roosevelt and Prime Minister Winston S. Churchill, already aroused over Soviet designs in Poland and the other countries of East Central Europe occupied by the Soviet army.

Just before writing his letter to Beneš, Stalin discussed with Klement Gottwald, the exiled Czech communist leader in Moscow, the policy the KSČ should follow during and after the liberation of Czechoslovakia. Stalin advised Gottwald to accept Beneš as president, and to come to an

---

[1] Edvard Beneš, *Memoirs: From Munich to New War and New Victory* (Boston, 1954), p. 139.

[2] See the account of Eduard Taborsky, Beneš's former secretary, "Benešovy moskevské cesty" ["Beneš's Trips to Moscow"], *Svědectví*, I, Nos. 3-4 (1957), 203ff. Taborsky stated that in his wartime conversations with Soviet leaders Beneš held that Ruthenia should belong either to Czechoslovakia or to the Soviet Union. "As much as he wished" this area "to be Czechoslovak again, he was by no means ready to insist on it as the price of Soviet friendship" (p. 207). On March 24, 1945, Soviet Foreign Minister Vyacheslav M. Molotov asked Beneš to repeat in writing his acceptance of the loss of Ruthenia (p. 212).

understanding with him and his government.[3] This flexible Soviet policy essentially reflected the line set forth in the Comintern declaration of 1943, which asserted that "the great differences in the historical development of individual countries determine the differences of the various problems that the workers' class of every country has to cope with." Until the next re-examination of communist strategy in the summer of 1947, Stalin set the stamp of his approval on this thesis of national roads to socialism: "In private he even expressed the . . . view that in certain instances it was possible to achieve socialism without the dictatorship of the proletariat."[4]

During its Moscow exile the top echelon of the KSČ (Gottwald, Rudolf Slánský, Jan Šverma, and Václav Kopecký) worked out a policy line in terms of a special Czechoslovak road to socialism.[5] After broadening their reexamination to include a review of past mistakes, they determined that the party should lead and organize the national liberation struggle of the Czech and Slovak people against Nazism. In thus assuming the role of a responsible mass movement, the party acted upon the belief that after the end of the occupation it could win popular confidence under the banner of national independence.[6] In short, the communist leadership in Moscow envisioned liberation as a means of winning a predominant share of power. The irony of such an approach was that it visualized economic and social reform as being subordinate to the achievement of the primary political task: becoming the leading political force in the country. In conformity with this aim, the party tended to move cautiously. It set up broad national and democratic—instead of narrow socialist—demands. In fact, the program of the Czech home resistance—nationalization of industry, banks, and insurance companies— was much more farreaching than the initial communist platform, which merely involved confiscation of the property of Czech and Slovak traitors and hostile Germans and Magyars.[7]

During the war the principal Czech and Slovak political forces at

---

[3] Gustáv Husák, *Svedectvo o Slovenskom národnom povstaní* [*Testimony about the Slovak National Uprising*] (Bratislava, 1964), pp. 554-55; Zdeněk Fierlinger, *Ve službách ČSR* [*In the Service of the Czechoslovak Republic*] (2 vols.; Prague, 1947-48), II, 599ff.

[4] See Miroslav Soukup, "Některé problémy vzájemných vztahů mezi komunistickými stranami" ["Some Problems of the Mutual Relations between the Communist Parties"], *Příspěvky k dějinám KSČ*, IV (Feb. 1964), 13ff.

[5] Gottwald's report to the central committee of the KSČ, September 25-26, 1946.

[6] Milan Hübl, "Lidová demokracie v 1946" ["Popular Democracy in 1946"], *Slovanský přehled*, No. 2 (1966), 65-70.

[7] See Karel Kaplan, *Znárodnění a socialismus* [*Nationalization and Socialism*] (Prague, 1968), *passim*. This tendency was discernible in other European communist parties, notably in France and Italy.

home and abroad held lively discussions on the future form of the country. In the winter of 1944-45, as the Soviet army overran a large part of Czechoslovakia, the balance of the pendulum between the democratic parties represented by Beneš in London and the communists led by Gottwald in Moscow swung in favor of the communists. It was a foregone conclusion that, at the end of the war, the London cabinet would be replaced by a new government with strong communist participation.[8] In 1945, with the Soviet armies advancing across Czechoslovakia, it became urgent for Beneš to implement this agreement and to return to the liberated part of the country with a newly constituted cabinet. To determine the composition of the new government and adopt a program, it was decided to hold a conference of Czech and Slovak political parties in Moscow. The choice of Moscow rather than London for the conference was undoubtedly motivated by the fact that the Czechoslovak government needed the consent and assistance of the Soviet government to return to its homeland. It also gave the communists a considerable advantage in the ensuing negotiations.

After taking leave of Churchill and Anthony Eden on February 24,[9] Beneš, accompanied by some members of his cabinet, left London for Moscow, where he arrived on March 17. A delegation of the Slovak National Council (SNR), composed equally of Slovak Democrats and Communists, also arrived in Moscow from the liberated parts of Slovakia. However, since Bohemia and Moravia were still firmly in the grip of the Germans, the Czech home resistance was unable to send representatives. Altogether, the Czech Communist (KSČ), National Socialist, Social Democratic, and People's parties and the Slovak Democratic and Communist (KSS) parties were represented. All other prewar political movements were excluded from the conference, primarily because of their past anticommunist attitude.

Gottwald assumed the initiative at the conference, which opened on March 22 and lasted eight days, with the presentation of a draft program as the basis of the negotiations.[10] Beneš did not take part in the meetings, on the ground that as a constitutional president he stood above parties.[11]

---

[8] See the discussion Beneš had with Gottwald and other communist exiles in Moscow in December 1943, in Beneš, *Memoirs*, pp. 268-75, and, from the communist point of view, Bohuslav Laštovička, *V Londýně za války* [*In London during the War*] (Prague, 1960), pp. 310-30.

[9] See Libuše Otáhalová and Milada Červinková, eds., *Dokumenty z historie československé politiky 1939-1943* [*Documents on the History of Czechoslovak Politics 1939-1943*] (2 vols.; Prague, 1966), II, 750-51.

[10] For the minutes of the negotiations see Miloš Klimeš *et al.*, eds., *Cesta ke květnu* [*Road to May*] (2 vols.; Prague, 1965), I, 380-453. For accounts see Laštovička, *V Londýně*, pp. 496-553, and Husák, *Svedectvo*, pp. 578-89.

[11] Josef Korbel, *The Communist Subversion of Czechoslovakia, 1938-1948* (Princeton, 1959), p. 114. Korbel rightly blames Beneš for his withdrawal from

This left the London democratic exiles leaderless, since they were used to defer to him in London, even in minor matters. It also weakened their position, because Beneš enjoyed tremendous prestige, particularly in the Czech provinces. Out of fear of arousing "suspicion on the part of the communists,"[12] they discarded any joint political platform to counter the communist program. To the bewilderment of the disunited democratic camp, it soon became apparent that the negotiations were not a controversy between two political groups, one based in London and the other in Moscow: "Here for the first time there was joined the battle of two political worlds."[13] What started out as negotiations for a governmental blueprint broadened into a survey of a program of action that would change almost every aspect of Czechoslovak life.

The democratic leaders received some satisfaction from the fact that the communist draft, to some extent, incorporated points agreed upon during previous exchanges of opinion between the parties. In the main, it reflected Gottwald's conception of the necessity for agreement with the democratic parties and articulated some of the aspirations of the Czech and Slovak people. Although the democratic and communist leaders clashed on many points, in the end their common interests proved strong enough to produce a final text that was not very different from the original draft.

The sharpest controversy during the negotiations occurred between the London group and the Slovak delegation, in which Gottwald assumed the role of benevolent arbiter.[14] The Slovaks brought to Moscow a resolution passed by the SNR on March 2, which demanded what amounted to attributes of sovereignty for Slovakia: a Slovak government, parliament, and distinct army units. The London group rejected this demand. It based itself on Beneš's speech of February 23, 1945, in which the president had recognized the special needs of the Slovaks but had insisted that the definition of Slovakia's place in the Czechoslovak state—like, indeed, all constitutional questions—should be left to the elected repre-

what the President wrongly considered to be a matter of party politics. For revealing conversations between President Beneš and U.S. ambassador in Moscow, W. Averell Harriman, on March 22 and 31, 1945, see U.S. Department of State, *Foreign Relations of the United States. Diplomatic Papers 1945.* Vol. IV: *Europe* (Washington, 1968), pp. 427-29 and 430-33.

[12] Korbel, *The Communist Subversion*, p. 114.

[13] Minister Jaroslav Stránský's recollections, ibid., p. 114.

[14] Jaroslav Opat, *O novou demokracii, 1945-1948* [*For a New Democracy, 1945-1948*] (Prague, 1966), pp. 44-48; Jozef Jablonický, *Slovensko na prelome* [*Slovakia in Transition*] (Bratislava, 1965), pp. 277-85; Jaroslav Barto, *Riešenie vzťahu Čechov a Slovákov, 1944-1948* [*Solving the Relations Between the Czechs and the Slovaks, 1944-1948*] (Bratislava, 1968), pp. 30-34; and Samo Falťan, *Slovenská otázka v Československu* [*The Slovak Question in Czechoslovakia*] (Bratislava, 1968), pp. 186-200.

sentatives of the people at home to decide after the war.[15] In the end the Slovaks yielded and accepted as a compromise a somewhat ambiguously worded statement proposed by Gottwald, which he later called grandly the *"Magna Carta* of the Slovak Nation."

In the negotiations to form a new government, the communists likewise imposed their will, but managed skillfully to camouflage their victory in a seeming compromise. They did not claim the premiership or a majority of posts in the cabinet. Instead, Gottwald proposed, and the other party leaders agreed, that the government should represent a "broad National Front of the Czechs and Slovaks." In strict conformance with the rules of parliamentary arithmetic, this decision was implemented by awarding three posts in the cabinet to each of the six parties participating in the conference. The prime minister and five vice-premiers, who were the heads of the six parties, were to form an inner cabinet to direct and coordinate the government's activities. It was further decided to give posts to three non-partisan experts and to create four state-secretaryships, thus bringing the total membership of the cabinet to twenty-five.

Upon the conclusion of the Moscow conference, President Beneš and the party leaders departed for Košice, a modest eastern Slovak town recently liberated by the Red Army. They arrived there on April 3 and stayed until after the liberation of Prague on May 9. On April 4 the new government was formally installed and the next day it announced its program, which, despite its origin in Moscow, came to be known as the "program of Košice."[16]

The Košice program proposed no radical transformation of Czechoslovak society along socialist lines. It was quite free of characteristic Marxist language. On the other hand, unlike the Czechoslovak declarations of independence issued in Washington and Prague in 1918, which had been idealistic professions of faith in democracy, it said little about freedom. Its tone was sober. It threatened more than it promised.

The program opened with a government tribute to the Soviet Union and a pledge to support the Red Army until final victory. For this purpose the government announced the formation of a new Czechoslovak army, trained, organized, and equipped on the model of the Red Army,

---

[15] Edvard Beneš, *Šest let exilu a druhé světové války. Řeči, projevy a dokumenty z r. 1938-45 [Six Years of Exile and the Second World War: Speeches, Declarations, and Documents in 1938-45]* (Prague, 1946), pp. 423-24.

[16] The full text of the Košice program may be found in *Za svobodu českého a slovenského národa: Sborník dokumentů [For the Freedom of the Czech and Slovak People: a Collection of Documents]* (Prague, 1956), pp. 368-90, published by the Institute for the History of KSČ in Prague. For an English translation of point six of the program dealing with the Slovaks, see Jozef Lettrich, *History of Modern Slovakia* (New York, 1955), pp. 317-18.

with Czech and Slovak units under a unified command, and educational officers introduced into all units to extirpate fascist influences. Czechoslovak foreign policy, it said, would be based on the closest alliance with the Soviet Union on the basis of the 1943 treaty and on practical cooperation in the military, political, economic, and cultural fields, as well as in questions concerning the punishment of Germany, reparations, frontier settlements, and the organization of peace. It promised to maintain friendly relations with Poland, Yugoslavia, and Bulgaria on the "basis of Slavic brotherhood," to seek reconciliation with a democratic Hungary (after correction of injustices), and to promote a rapprochement between Hungary and Austria and their Slavic neighbors. Finally, almost as an afterthought, it thanked Britain for the aid extended during the war and promised to consolidate relations with her and the United States and promote close relations with France.

In the field of domestic policy the government pledged to hold elections at the earliest possible time for a national constituent assembly that would determine the precise form of the Czechoslovak government. In the meantime, the government guaranteed the people their political rights and set up new administrative machinery, in the form of popularly elected national committees, to administer public affairs at the local, district, and provincial levels.

The Slovaks were recognized as a distinct (*samobytný*) nation and the SNR as their legal representative and "carrier of state power in Slovak territory." The question of Ruthenia was to be settled as soon as possible according to the democratically expressed will of its people. The German and Magyar minorities were given the right of option for Czechoslovakia, with the understanding that disloyal German and Magyar citizens would be removed. The property of those who had "actively helped in the disruption and occupation of Czechoslovakia" was to be placed under national control pending a final disposal by the legislative authorities. Their land would be placed in a National Land Fund and distributed to deserving Czechs and Slovaks.

Czech and Slovak collaborators were to be deprived of voting rights and barred from all political organizations. The former agrarian party and all prewar parties not represented in the new National Front were accused of collaboration and proscribed. War criminals, traitors, and "other active, conscious helpers of the German oppressors" were to be punished without exception. President Emil Hácha and all members of the Protectorate government, as well as Jozef Tiso and all members of the Slovak government and parliament, were to be charged with high treason and brought before a "National Court." Finally, the Košice program provided for a broad system of social welfare.

In the new cabinet, according to a communist participant at the Moscow conference, the communists captured "positions which were a starting point for the assault on the actual fortress of capitalism. . . . The balance of power was such . . . from the beginning of the liberation, that the influence and weight of . . . KSČ was predominant and decisive."[17] At the Moscow conference, the communists had successfully promoted Zdeněk Fierlinger, a left-wing Social Democrat, as prime minister. From their point of view, the choice proved an excellent one. As wartime ambassador to Moscow, Fierlinger had won the confidence of the Soviet government by his display of an uncritically pro-Soviet and anti-Western attitude. As premier, he collaborated with the communists so closely that he won the popular epithet of "Quislinger."

Thanks to separate representation, the combined KSČ and KSS held eight seats in the cabinet and controlled the ministries of interior, information, education, agriculture, and social welfare.[18] The police, security, and intelligence services were in their hands. The Ministry of Defense was entrusted to Gen. Ludvík Svoboda, commander of the Czechoslovak army in Russia, as a nonparty expert. (Although a non-communist at that time, Svoboda was a loyal friend of the Soviets.) As a concession to the democratic parties, the communists agreed to the reappointment of Jan Masaryk as minister of foreign affairs. A genuinely nonpartisan personality, dedicated only to the defense of his country's interests, the son of the first president of Czechoslovakia was by family tradition, education, and experience a thoroughly Western man. Therefore, as Masaryk's assistant and watchdog the communists insisted on appointing Vlado Clementis, a Slovak communist, to the newly-created post of state-secretary for foreign affairs.

Thus far the "circumspect and purposeful course of the KSČ"[19] proved to be of particular advantage to the Communist party, whose chairman, Klement Gottwald, had given proof of his political maturity and craftsmanship. The less colorful democratic leaders let themselves be outmaneuvered. Since the central issue was one of power, it is surprising that neither Beneš nor his colleagues found it advisable to prevent the communists from assuming control of the police and security organs. A reasonable compromise on this question would have helped those forces in both camps who were willing to face up to problems affecting their common commitment to a democratic Czechoslovakia. Despite some ap-

---

[17] Bohuslav Laštovička, "Vznik a význam košického vládního programu" ["The Origin and Importance of the Košice Government Program"], *Československý časopis historický*, VIII (August 1960), 465.

[18] For the negotiations leading to the formation of the government and its composition, see Opat, *O novou demokracii*, pp. 48-50. In the SNR and its executive organ, the board of commissioners, the Communist party of Slovakia (KSS), and the Democratic party (DS) continued to share power equally.

[19] Laštovička, "Vznik," p. 463.

prehensions, however, the democratic leaders had no reason to contradict Fierlinger's observations before their departure from Moscow that "It is an immense achievement that we can return home united. . . . The ideological borderline between Moscow and London has been removed. I am aware of the fact that not a few would criticize the composition of the new cabinet . . . but I consider it an immense success that unlike other emigrations . . . we are the first to be able to put order into our affairs abroad."[20] Neither side regarded the Moscow agreement as a final settlement; both were aware that the final battle was yet to come—at home after the war.

In the Czech provinces the approaching end of the war coincided with a rising tide of guerrilla activities. Early in 1945 the largest resistance group—the Council of the Three—the illegal trade unions, and the underground KSČ established the Czech National Council as the center of Czech resistance. The council was strengthened during the first days of May by a spontaneous popular uprising that spread through those parts of the country still occupied by the Germans. The movement reached Prague on May 5, where a fierce battle broke out with German army and SS units that raged even after the official dates of German surrender at Rheims and Berlin (May 7 and 8, respectively). In the early morning hours of May 9 the first Soviet tanks arrived in Prague. On May 10 the government returned to Prague. It was followed by President Beneš amid frenetic acclamation on May 16.

The Nazi occupation was terminated. The war was over.

BETWEEN DEMOCRACY AND COMINFORM, 1945-1947

On its return to Prague, the Czechoslovak government took quick and firm hold of the levers of command. Under the Moscow agreement President Beneš had been given emergency powers to issue decrees with the validity of laws, at the request of the government, until the convocation of the National Assembly. These powers were first used to assert government authority throughout the country. The Czech National Council was dissolved.[21] The Slovak National Council, on the other hand, continued to function at Bratislava.[22] It soon became apparent,

[20] Klimeš, *Cesta*, I, 447.

[21] During the war both the Moscow and London exiles emphasized the primary importance of the home front. Upon returning to Prague, however, both united in refusing to offer the Czech resistance leaders any representation in the cabinet. See Josef Belda et al., *Na rozhraní dvou epoch* [*On the Frontier of Two Epochs*] (Prague, 1968), pp. 40-41.

[22] Apart from the fact that the SNR was recognized in the Košice program, it had functioned continuously since February, 1945. By the time the government was established in Prague in May, the SNR was well entrenched and carried on as a quasi-government.

however, that it was necessary to define its jurisdiction and the basis of its relationship to the central government at Prague, a matter that the Košice program had noted only in very general terms. The SNR took the initiative in the matter. On May 26 it adopted a proposal for the fundamental organization of the republic, in the drafting of which both Slovak communist and democratic leaders shared. The proposal envisaged a dualistic, symmetrical organization of Czechoslovakia into two federated states—Slovakia and Bohemia-Moravia—each with a government and diet of its own. A federal government and parliament were to be centered in Prague.

The previous Czechoslovak experiment in federalism—the ill-fated Second Republic in 1938-39—had not been a happy one. The proposal of the SNR therefore encountered opposition from the Czech parties, both communist and democratic. On May 31, just before the government at Prague began a discussion of the SNR proposal, the leaders of the KSČ invited the KSS leaders to a meeting at which the KSS submitted to the "unified leadership" of the KSČ and agreed to abandon the SNR plan.[23] At the cabinet meetings on May 31 and June 1, only the Slovak Democrats defended the proposal for federalization, while the Czech National Socialists and Populists pressed for the restoration of the republic's pre-Munich centralist organization; the KSČ and KSS adopted a half-way course. The discussions ended in a compromise. Federalism was discarded, but Slovakia's autonomy was assured. The resulting "First Prague Agreement" both defined and circumscribed the jurisdiction of the SNR.[24]

The government delayed a full year before implementing its pledge, given in the Košice program, to hold general elections for a constituent assembly at the earliest possible time. Meanwhile it covered the naked strength of its power in a temporary constitutional garb. On August 25, 1945, a presidential decree provided for the formation of a single-chamber, 300-member provisional national assembly. It was to be chosen not by general elections but by a complicated system of three-stage elections through the local, district, and provincial national committees—thus allowing the parties of the National Front to determine its composition.[25] The Provisional National Assembly met for the first time on October 28, 1945, the national holiday, and confirmed President Beneš in his office. In the next few days the cabinet was formally reorganized, but no significant changes were effected in its composition.

[23] Falt'an, *Slovenská otázka*, pp. 206-207; Barto, *Riešenie*, pp. 54-58.

[24] Barto, *Riešenie*, pp. 67-79; Falt'an, *Slovenská otázka*, pp. 207-12; Belda, *Na rozhraní*, p. 43.

[25] The four Czech parties received forty seats and the two Slovak parties, fifty seats each. The remaining forty seats were distributed among representatives of mass organizations.

The Provisional National Assembly's initiative remained limited. Usually, it approved unanimously and without discussion the decisions made by the party leaders at meetings of the National Front. Thus on February 28, 1946, it approved, also unanimously and without discussion, the ninety-eight presidential decrees issued from May to October, 1945, many of which affected the fundamental structure of the Czechoslovak state and society.

The delay in holding elections, however, did not indicate indifference on the part of the party leaders to public opinion. Quite the contrary. After the overthrow of Nazism all of Europe was swept by an intense popular demand for immediate reform and a certain disillusionment, or impatience, with constitutional procedures when they threatened to delay reform. Under these circumstances, to defer the pressing tasks of reconstruction and reform in order to engage in an electoral contest appeared almost frivolous to the Czech and Slovak party leaders. Their decision to preserve the interparty truce offered by the National Front and "get to work" had full public approval.

Air attacks, military operations, and the German occupation had made World War II more destructive for the Czechs and Slovaks than any previous conflict. According to an official government estimate 250,000 persons had died. In Bohemia, 3,014 houses were destroyed and over 10,000 were badly damaged; in Moravia the respective figures were 11,862 and over 19,000. In Silesia 34,986 buildings were ruined. Slovakia, because of the prolonged fighting in 1944-45, was the most seriously hit.[26] In the Czech provinces the total war damage per person was estimated at 17,000 Czechoslovak crowns (about $2,400), but in Slovakia it amounted to 35,000 crowns (about $4,900).[27] In eastern Slovakia alone 169 villages were razed and 300 damaged; 24,000 buildings were ruined or heavily damaged. The transportation system was seriously dislocated. Almost all the large factories had been badly bombed.[28] Livestock suffered heavily. Nevertheless, a large amount of food and raw materials stockpiled by the Germans during the occupation remained in the country.

The end of the war closed a struggle for the Czech nation's very existence. Since 1938 the Czechs had been humiliated and persecuted. They had also suffered from Nazi cruelties and the bloody fighting of the last days of the war. The radical mood of the country transformed resentment against the Nazis into demands for the permanent removal of all

[26] Radomír Luža, *The Transfer of the Sudeten Germans* (New York, 1964), p. 262.

[27] V. Jarošová and O. Jaroš, *Slovenské robotníctvo v boji o moc, 1944-1948* [*The Slovak Workers in the Struggle for Power, 1944-1948*] (Bratislava, 1965), p. 69.

[28] Luža, *The Transfer*, p. 262.

Germans. Popular support for the idea of expelling the Sudeten Germans caught even the Communist party by surprise. However, it swiftly went beyond the Košice program and espoused popular demands. A presidential decree on June 21, 1945, provided for the expropriation without compensation of the property of the Germans and Magyars as well as that of Czech and Slovak collaborators and traitors. The land that came within the scope of the decree involved about 270,000 farms covering 6,240,000 acres, which provided the communist minister of agriculture with a rich pork barrel from which to reward those who were willing to serve the party. By the spring of 1948 some 1,500,000 people had moved to the Czech borderlands left vacant by the Sudeten Germans, who had been removed to the American and Soviet zones of occupation in Germany in accordance with the mandate given Czechoslovakia by the Allied powers at Potsdam. After June 15, 1949, only 177,000 Germans were left in the Czech provinces.[29] This national adjustment wrought a profound change in the economic and social structure of the country. There was much disorder and violence—yet this is present in every revolutionary process. In the final analysis, the expulsion of the Sudeten Germans was a Czech national response—neither communist nor Soviet inspired—to a situation created by Nazi war policy and the Sudeten Germans themselves.

The Slovaks, led by the KSS, pressed for a similar removal of the Magyar minority from Slovakia. But it was one thing to press a claim against the Germans, who at that time were regarded as outlaws in all of Europe, and quite another to press one against the Hungarians, who were regarded as minor culprits. The Soviet Union tended to regard Hungary as a future satellite, like Czechoslovakia, and was not anxious to complicate its tasks by contributing to dissension between two of its prospective clients. At the Potsdam conference it failed to back the Czechoslovak demand for the removal of the Magyar minority. The matter was left to bilateral Czechoslovak-Hungarian negotiations. Under a mutual exchange agreement concluded between the two countries on February 27, 1946, 68,407 Magyars out of some 500,000 did leave for Hungary and a somewhat smaller number of Slovaks returned to Slovakia.[30] No large fund of land comparable to that in the Czech borderlands became available in Slovakia, a factor that had important repercussions in Czechoslovak politics.

Partly for this reason, the Czechoslovak delegation at the Paris Peace Conference in 1946 raised the demand for authorization to remove

[29] Ibid., pp. 271, 291; Karel Kaplan, "Rok československé revoluce 1945" ["Year of the Czechoslovak Revolution"], *Sborník historický*, 15 (1967), p. 115.
[30] Juraj Zvara in *Historický časopis*, No. 1 (1964), 28-49, and in *Příspěvky k dějinám KSČ* (June 1965), 409-27.

200,000 Magyars from Slovakia. But by then, the Western powers were adamantly opposed to any further population transfer, and the matter was dropped.[31] They did, however, accede to the Czechoslovak demand for a small enlargement of the Bratislava bridgehead on the south bank of the Danube River at the expense of Hungary.[32]

Meanwhile, in June, 1945, the Poles suddenly reopened the Těšín (Teschen) question. On June 19 Polish troops under General Rola-Zymierski moved up to the city of Těšín. Possibly the Poles were encouraged to revive this old thorn in Polish-Czechoslovak relations by the Soviet government, which was anxious to prod Czechoslovakia into settling the Ruthenian question. In any event, on the same day the Soviet government invited Czechoslovakia and Poland to send delegations to Moscow to discuss outstanding questions affecting their relations. On June 29, after a week of discussions, the Czechoslovak and Soviet governments signed an agreement formally transferring Ruthenia to the Soviet Union.[33] When the Czechoslovak delegation returned to Prague, Prime Minister Fierlinger announced that the Polish-Czechoslovak discussions had been indefinitely adjourned. Apart from the loss of Ruthenia and the enlargement of the Bratislava bridgehead, the pre-Munich boundaries of Czechoslovakia remained intact.

The internal position of Czechoslovakia appeared to be fully consolidated. The withdrawal of Soviet and United States troops from Czechoslovakia as early as November and December of 1945 heralded a return to normalcy. By the fall of 1945 the country had also made considerable progress in economic reconstruction. Almost everyone agreed that it had bright prospects, provided that the wartime grand alliance and the internal balance between the communist and democratic forces could be maintained.

Since it had to compete with the democratic parties, the Communist party sought to be a mass party—unlike the Communist party of the Soviet Union, which is a small elite group. The KSČ readily admitted members of former parties, drawing a line only at admitting former fascists and collaborators who, in Czech opinion, stood beyond the pale. The KSS, on the other hand, readily admitted even members of the former Hlinka People's party—indeed, it strenuously courted them. It

[31] U.S. Department of State, *Foreign Relations of the United States 1946*. Vol. IV: *Paris Peace Conference: Documents* (Washington, 1970), 727-28; A. C. Leiss and R. Dennett, eds., *European Peace Treaties after World War II* (Boston, 1954), pp. 93-96.

[32] For Article I of the Hungarian peace treaty, defining the bridgehead, see ibid., p. 274.

[33] F. Němec and V. Moudrý, *The Soviet Seizure of Subcarpathian Ruthenia* (Toronto, 1955), pp. 251-53. For the text of the Soviet-Czechoslovak treaty of June 29, 1945, on the cession of Ruthenia, see *British State and Foreign Papers*, Vol. 145 (1943-45) (London, 1953), pp. 1096-98.

posed as a Slovak nationalist party and did not hesitate to exploit religious prejudice by pointing out to the Slovak Catholic majority that the leadership of its competitor, the Slovak Democratic party, was largely Protestant. At the end of 1945 the KSS claimed a membership of 197,000, while in March, 1946, the KSČ claimed to have over 1,000,000 members.[34]

The growing strength of the Communist party was reflected in its high moral and internal consolidation. Between 1945 and 1948 the leadership of the KSČ (with Klement Gottwald as chairman and Rudolf Slánský as secretary-general) remained remarkably stable, and the party was unusually free of factional strife. The KSS experienced some internal stress, however, as its nationalist posture came into conflict with the strategy of the parent party, the KSČ. At a joint meeting of the central committees of the KSČ and KSS in Prague on July 17-18, 1945, the Czech communists sharply criticized their Slovak comrades for viewing the development from a "nationalist," instead of a "class," point of view and for allying themselves with the "reaction" in the SNR, that is, the Slovak Democrats. A resolution, passed at the meeting, demanded that the "policy of the KSS must not be to separate but to orient the party towards the progressive forces in the Czech provinces and in the central government" and delegated Viliam Široký, a dour internationalist communist, to take charge of the KSS.[35] The separation of the two parties, which was maintained for tactical reasons, thereafter became nominal.

While the Communist party was united, the Czechoslovak Social Democratic party (chairman: Zdeněk Fierlinger; secretary-general: Blažej Vilím), which had a long and distinguished history of defending the cause of the Czech working class, was increasingly rent by a tug-of-war between its right and left wings, representing its liberal-democratic and Marxian-socialist traditions, respectively. The Czech National Socialist party (chairman: Petr Zenkl; secretary-general: Vladimír Krajina), which claimed to be a socialist but non-Marxist party, suffered from no such dilemma. It came increasingly to the fore as the most resolute ad-

---

[34] Opat, *O novou demokracii*, p. 69. For a good survey of the strength, aims, and leadership of the KSČ and all parties after liberation, see Belda, *Na rozhraní*, pp. 22-39. For the KSČ, see Zdeněk Eliáš and Jaromír Netík, "Czechoslovakia," in William E. Griffith, ed., *Communism in Europe. Continuity, Change, and the Sino-Soviet Dispute* (Cambridge, Mass., and London, 1966), II, *passim*.

[35] Barto, *Riešenie*, pp. 98-100; Jarošová and Jaroš, *Slovenské robotníctvo*, p. 97. The resolution was implemented at a conference of the KSS at Žilina on August 11-12, 1945, when Široký replaced Karol Šmidke as chairman and Štefan Bašťovanský replaced Edo Friš as secretary of the party. Neither Šmidke nor Friš was a Slovak nationalist but both had been swept along by the nationalists since the Slovak uprising. Široký had not participated in the uprising, being in prison at the time. Of Slovak origin but a Magyar by education, he was a bitter enemy of Slovak nationalists whether in or out of the party. The true spokesman of the nationalists in the KSS, Gustáv Husák, saved himself, for the moment, by abjuring nationalism—also for the moment—and turning on his wartime nationalist allies, the Slovak Democrats.

versary of the communists among the Czech parties. The Czech Populist party, under the leadership of Msgr. Jan Šrámek, the wartime premier in London, was a progressive Catholic party that before the war had received its greatest support among Czech peasants, especially in Moravia. After the war it had difficulty in finding its bearings in the radical atmosphere, which affected even the countryside. The Slovak Democratic party (chairman: Jozef Lettrich; secretary: Fedor Hodža), which was largely a continuation of the Slovak branch of the proscribed agrarian party, suffered from the polarization of Slovak opinion after the war between the radical revolutionary movement and the conservative Catholic anti-communist movement. It could not compete with the communists in appealing to the former and found it distasteful and dangerous to appeal to the latter, for fear of exposing itself to the charge of catering to crypto-fascists.

In retrospect it is clear that the prolongation of the provisional regime benefited the Communist party more than the democratic parties, by allowing an unusual measure of influence in public affairs to various extra-constitutional mass organizations, such as worker, peasant, youth, resistance, and other nationwide associations, that sprang up after the liberation of the country. The general European "swing to the left" immediately after the war undoubtedly helped the Communist party gain a preponderant influence in these organizations. No instrument was more important to it than the united Revolutionary Trade Union Movement (ROH) and workers' factory councils (závodní rady). This was true at least in the Czech provinces. In Slovakia, where the working class did not have the same importance,[36] the Communist party relied more on its influence in the resistance organizations, especially the association of former partisans.

The communist plans had emphasized the necessity of gaining leadership of the working class, a traditional domain of the Social Democratic movement. In the first postwar days the communists occupied positions of power in the ROH and the workers' councils in all large factories. In this situation, the predominant influence of the Communist party with the working class,[37] combined with its control of important levers of the state apparatus, became the central fact of politics.

[36] In Slovakia 25.58 percent of the population derived an income from industry, mining, and the trades, compared to 39.5 percent in Bohemia and Moravia. On the other hand, 52.59 percent of the Slovak population worked in agriculture, forestry, and fisheries, while only 20.37 percent of the population of the Czech provinces did. See Jarošová and Jaroš, *Slovenské robotníctvo*, p. 65.

[37] In June, 1945, the prominent communist trade unionist Antonín Zápotocký became chairman of the ROH. The membership amounted to 2,249,976 on December 31, 1947. See V. Pachman, "Boj o odborovou jednotu v letech 1945-1948" ["Struggle for the Unity of the Trade Union Movement in 1945-1948"], *Československý časopis historický*, VIII, No. 6 (1960), 810.

After the party consolidated its grip on the political structure in the early summer of 1945, its initial moderation in economic affairs began to fade. President Beneš and the two socialist parties viewed the nationalization of the principal industries, banks, and insurance companies as inevitable. Moreover, the corresponding pressure exerted by the workers found widespread popular support. Under these circumstances the expropriation of German capital evolved into a wider trend that reflected a consensus of all responsible political forces. Thus, the first postwar measure of large nationalization in Europe[38] became a demonstration of a common resolve to establish collective ownership and direct state control over the chief means of production. The presidential decrees of October 24, which were mainly prepared by the Social Democratic controlled Ministry of Industry, resulted in the creation of a nationalized sector containing 61.2 percent of the industrial labor force.[39]

The nationalization decrees were the last great measures adopted without parliament's authorization. After the convocation of the Provisional National Assembly four days later, the democratic parties sought to limit the influence of the ROH and other extraconstitutional mass organizations and to confine policy-making to parliament. This encountered the opposition of the communists, who had found it advantageous to promote their aims through these organizations. They lent themselves more easily to manipulation than did the parliament, which had an orderly procedure and in which, moreover, they were a minority. The National Front began to experience increasing strains, and early in 1946 it was decided to hold general elections for the constituent assembly. May 26 was set as the date for the elections.

All parties committed themselves to maintain the National Front and the Košice program. This seemingly left no divisive issues. The electoral contest was nevertheless lively, though orderly. The difference between the parties lay in the accent they placed on specific aspects of the common program. The communists and Social Democrats stressed its social aspects and hinted that there were more to come. The democratic parties, on the other hand, maintained that the social goals of the program had largely been attained and placed a greater accent on freedom and democracy.

In Slovakia two new parties came into existence. Some of the old Slovak Social Democrats regarded the fusion of their party with the Communist party during the Slovak uprising in 1944 as a shotgun marriage, and now wished to go it alone. In January, 1946, with the assistance of

---

[38] Czechoslovakia was the second state after the U.S.S.R. to nationalize its industry and banks.

[39] Opat, *O novou demokracii*, p. 115; Kaplan, *Znárodnění*, pp. 7-58.

the Czech Social Democrats, they formed the Labor party.[40] The other new party, the Freedom party, came into existence as a byproduct of electoral strategy by the Slovak Democratic party (DS). On March 30 Lettrich, the chairman of the DS, concluded an agreement (incorrectly known as the "April Agreement") with the Catholic leaders under which the Catholics were promised representation in all organs of the DS in a ratio of 7:3 in their favor.[41] The April Agreement promised to bolster the electoral strength of the DS, because the Catholic clergy had a powerful influence in Slovakia, especially in the rural areas, but it was fraught with dangers for the party. Many Catholic politicians were unreconstructed l'udáks. Their entry pulled the party sharply to the right and proved more than some of its leaders could stomach. The dissidents, among whom was notably Vavro Šrobár, formed the Freedom party on April 1.[42] Even more important was the communists' reaction to the April Agreement. In direct retaliation for its conclusion, the KSČ, with the concurrence of the Czech parties and the KSS, pressed through a further limitation of SNR prerogatives. Under the "Second Prague Agreement" on April 11, 1946, the SNR was deprived of the important power of making personal appointments without the approval of the Prague government.[43]

While the United States remained studiedly aloof during the electoral campaign, the Soviet Union gave a pointed reminder of its interest. On May 22, almost the eve of the elections, it was announced the Soviet troops would be moved across Czechoslovak territory from Austria and Hungary to the Soviet zone of occupation in Germany. At the outcry of the democratic leaders over this crude attempt at intimidation, the troop movement was postponed, but its psychological purpose had already been attained—it reminded the Czechs and Slovaks that the Soviet army was close by and could return on short notice.[44]

The communists approached the elections with confidence. They hoped to win an absolute majority, but were not worried if they did not. On February 4, at the outset of the campaign, Gottwald assured the

[40] Marta Vartíková, *Od Košíc po február* [*From Košice to February*] (Bratislava, 1968), p. 71. Jaroslav Nedvěd, "Cesta ke sloučení sociální demokracie s komunistickou stranou" ["The Road to the Merger of the Social Democratic and Communist Parties"], *Rozpravy Československé Akademie věd*, No. 8 (1968), 46-48.

[41] Opat, *O novou demokracii*, pp. 162-66; Belda, *Na rozhraní*, p. 70; Vartíková, *Od Košíc*, p. 78.

[42] Vartíková, *Od Košíc*, pp. 74-77.

[43] Barto, *Riešenie*, pp. 138-47; Falt'an, *Slovenská otázka*, pp. 216-17.

[44] Hubert Ripka, *Le Coup de Prague: Une révolution préfabriquée* (Paris, 1949), p. 39.

party workers: "Even if it should happen, which is improbable, that we should not gain a favorable result . . . the working class, the party, and the working people will still have sufficient means, arms, and a method to correct simple mechanical voting, which might be affected by reactionary and saboteur elements."[45] In other words, if the results of the election were favorable to the communists, they would be accepted; if not, they would be "corrected."

The elections on May 26, which proved to be the last free Czechoslovak elections, passed without incident and, according to foreign observers, without any attempt at intimidation or manipulation. The ballot was secret. All citizens over eighteen years of age, except political offenders, were not only allowed, but were obliged to vote, thus assuring a heavy turnout. The results did not basically alter the existing party balance. In the Czech provinces the KSČ obtained 40.1, the National Socialists 23.5, the Populists 20.2, and the Social Democrats 15.6 percent of the vote. In Slovakia the DS obtained 62, the KSS 30.3, the Freedom party 3.7, and the Labor party 3.1 percent.[46] In the whole country the communists (the combined KSČ and KSS) secured 37.9 percent of the vote. This fell short of their hopes but was still impressive. The most surprising development was the failure of the Social Democratic party, which had at one time been the largest party in Czechoslovakia but was now the smallest. Its Slovak branch, the Labor party, likewise made a poor showing. During the electoral postmortem the democratic wing blamed the defeat on the campaign strategy of the party leadership, which had adopted an almost identical position on many issues as the communists, and demanded that in the future the party follow an independent course of action.

The most impressive gains were made by the Slovak Democrats. There is no doubt, however, that the large vote cast for the DS represented less a show of confidence by the Slovak electorate in the DS than a rebuke to the KSS. Several factors accounted for the communists' modest showing in Slovakia compared with their good record in the Czech provinces: the relative unimportance of the Slovak working class; the absence of a large reserve of confiscated land with which to entice the land-hungry peasantry, such as existed in the Czech borderlands; the greater war damages in Slovakia and consequently greater problems of reconstruction (in the winter of 1945-46 there were acute food shortages in the province); the influence of the conservative Catholic clergy, who did not hesitate to warn in their sermons against the perils of "godless" communism; and the bitter memory of the many excesses committed against the civilian population by the Red Army during its operations in Slo-

[45] Belda, *Na rozhraní,* p. 60.
[46] Ibid., pp. 72-73; Opat, *O novou demokracii,* pp. 178-89.

vakia in 1944-45, for which the injured took revenge by voting against the "Russian party," that is, the communists.[47]

The communists did not mistake the fact that the large vote for the DS was really a vote against them, and at once took steps to correct the situation. "We have not won yet, the struggle continues," said Gottwald in reporting the results of the election to the central committee of the KSČ on May 30,[48] and he made it clear that the first target in the continuing struggle must be the DS. In order to limit its influence, Gottwald proposed to abolish what was left of Slovak autonomy—"even if we thereby violate formal national rights or promises or guarantees. . . . The Slovak comrades will no doubt understand."[49]

For the assault against the DS, Gottwald proposed four concrete steps: to limit further the prerogatives of the SNR, to launch a drive against the ľudáks camouflaged in the DS, to punish Jozef Tiso, and to take steps against the Slovak Catholic clergy, for the adoption of which the KSČ secured the concurrence of the National Front of the Czech parties on June 12 and the National Front of the Czech and Slovak parties two days later.[50] The first step was implemented in the "Third Prague Agreement" on June 27, 1946, which placed the legislative powers of the SNR under government control and the Slovak commissioners under the appropriate ministers in Prague.[51] In practice, Slovakia reverted to the position that it had held before the Munich agreement in 1938: that of a simple administrative unit, like Bohemia and Moravia. This latest advance of centralism placed added strains not only on the relations between the KSS and DS but also—since it was supported by all Czech parties—between the Czechs and Slovaks as a whole.

The National Front had been somewhat shaken by the electoral contest. However, all parties still professed loyalty to it and it was continued. The Eighth Congress of the KSČ in March, 1946, had endorsed the strengthening of the National Front and had directed the party to implement further the national and democratic revolution.[52] (The KSČ never failed to stress that whatever the future model of the republic, it would correspond closely to special Czech and Slovak conditions.[53]) On July 2

[47] The same factors operated against the communists, to a smaller extent, in Moravia. The communist share of the vote in Moravia was 34.5 percent as against 43.3 percent in Bohemia.

[48] Belda, *Na rozhraní*, p. 74.

[49] Vartíková, *Od Košíc*, p. 80; Jarošová and Jaroš, *Slovenské robotníctvo*, p. 157; Barto, *Riešenie*, p. 159.

[50] Barto, *Riešenie*, p. 160; Belda, *Na rozhraní*, p. 80.

[51] Belda, *Na rozhraní*, p. 83; Opat, *O novou demokracii*, pp. 193-95; Barto, *Riešenie*, pp. 170-71; Falťan, *Slovenská otázka*, p. 222.

[52] Opat, *O novou demokracii*, pp. 135-36.

[53] Gottwald on July 8, 1946, in presenting the "construction program" of his

the cabinet was reshuffled to conform with the results of the elections. Fierlinger yielded the premiership to Gottwald, as the representative of the largest party. Of the twenty-five cabinet posts, the KSČ received seven, the KSS one and one state secretaryship, the National Socialists four, the DS three and one state secretaryship, and the Czech Populists and Social Democrats three posts each.[54]

The parties were impelled to maintain a solid front by, among other things, the opening of the Paris Peace Conference on July 29. Three days earlier Gottwald and a delegation had returned from Moscow with the good news that the Soviet government had not only promised to support Czechoslovak claims at the conference but had also waived the provision of the Potsdam agreement that entitled it to claim German "external assets" in Czechoslovakia. Moreover, Gottwald revealed that the Soviet government had promised to support Czechoslovak economic plans by concluding a long-term trade treaty. On the other hand, the United States government had granted Czechoslovakia a credit of $50 million in June to buy American surplus war supplies in Europe. However, in September, before the credit was exhausted, the United States abruptly suspended it because the Czechoslovak delegates at the peace conference had applauded the Soviet delegate when he inveighed against American "economic imperialism."[55]

Czechoslovakia had been caught in the first cross fire of the cold war. On July 10, Soviet Foreign Minister Vyacheslav Molotov fired the first

new government to the National Assembly. See Opat, *O novou demokracii*, pp. 197-200. Also in September, 1946, and on October 4, 1946.

[54] Ibid., pp. 191-96; Belda, *Na rozhraní*, pp. 84-86. While claiming the premiership and a proportionate share of posts in the central government, the communists were extremely reluctant to accept the results of the elections in the Slovak National Council and the board of commissioners. It was not until August 7, after bitter wrangling between the KSS and the DS, that the DS was allowed to take 60 percent of the seats in the SNR and 9 out of 15 posts on the board of commissioners. The communists fought tooth and nail against relinquishing the commissariat of interior, which controlled the police. In the end they agreed to relinquish it, not to a DS member but to a nonparty expert, Gen. Mikuláš Ferjenčík. Moreover, contrary to the principle that the strongest party should get the chairmanship of the board, which Gottwald had invoked to claim the premiership, this important post was retained by the communist Husák. See Vartíková, *Od Košíc*, pp. 109-11; Jarošová and Jaroš, *Slovenské robotníctvo*, p. 163.

[55] James F. Byrnes, *Speaking Frankly* (New York, 1947), pp. 143-44; Ripka, *Le Coup*, p. 41. In addition to the insult at the peace conference, the Americans were angered by a Czechoslovak deal with Rumania, under which Prague resold American goods to the Rumanians at a profit, and by the Czechoslovak failure to compensate American citizens for the loss of property in Czechoslovakia through nationalization. The American rebuff was a great blow to Masaryk, who had to explain it in a secret cabinet meeting on October 7. See Belda, *Na rozhraní*, pp. 120-21; U.S. Department of State, *Foreign Relations of the United States 1946*, Vol. VI: *Eastern Europe: The Soviet Union* (Washington, 1969), pp. 216, 220ff.

shot in the East-West struggle for Germany, by calling for the formation of a German national government and questioning the French right to the Saar. United States Secretary of State James F. Byrnes replied in his famous Stuttgart speech on September 6, by also calling for a German national government and by repudiating—in effect—the Potsdam agreement on the Oder-Neisse boundary and thus, by implication, reopening the whole question of the eastern settlement. Czechoslovak isolation from the West and dependence on the East had increased.

This development boded ill for the first important measure of the Gottwald government—the Two-Year Economic Plan for 1947-48, which the National Assembly approved on October 24.[56] The plan, which proposed to raise the standard of living ten percent above the pre-war level, was oriented toward the long-range coexistence of the private and nationalized sectors of the economy and was predicated on the assumption that Czechoslovakia's traditional trade ties with the West would continue. At that time the Soviet Union faced gigantic problems of reconstruction and was in no position to provide economic aid to Czechoslovakia or to furnish, in exchange for Czechoslovak exports, the kind of goods and services she needed to realize her economic plans. The promised Soviet-Czechoslovak trade pact did not materialize until December, 1947.

The next important measure of the Gottwald government was political: it staged the trial of Monsignor Tiso as a deterrent to Slovak separatists. The trial, which opened in Bratislava on December 3, 1946, ended in March of the following year with Tiso's conviction of treason and a sentence of death. As calculated by the communists, the sentence placed the DS in a difficult position. The leaders of the party, chairman of the SNR Lettrich and Vice-Premier Ján Ursíny, were Protestants and former agrarians. They had led the Slovak resistance against Tiso's government during the war and had little sympathy for him, but they were put under pressure by the party's Catholic wing to save him. When the government considered Tiso's appeal for mercy on April 16, the DS ministers moved to commute the sentence to life imprisonment. They were seconded by the Czech Populist ministers, who demurred at hanging a fellow priest. However, the other ministers held firm for execution.[57] On the recommendation of the cabinet, President Beneš declined the appeal for mercy, and on April 18 Tiso was hanged.

Since the removal of the Sudeten German minority the "Slovak question," that is, the problem of satisfactorily adjusting relations between the Czechs and Slovaks, had become the foremost internal question in the country. The trial of Tiso, by deeply offending conservative Catholic

---

[56] Belda, *Na rozhraní*, p. 95; Opat, *O novou demokracii*, p. 204.
[57] Belda, *Na rozhraní*, pp. 172-73.

opinion in Slovakia, aggravated this concern. It was to trouble the Third Czechoslovak Republic until its end—and, indeed, continued in a different form afterward.

In the spring of 1947 the Communist party adopted the goal of winning at least fifty-one percent of the votes in the next elections and thus gaining a majority in the National Assembly. This angered the other parties, but it did indicate that the communist leadership did not yet wish to take over all power, but was committed to the maintenance of the National Front. There were radical elements in the party that criticized the leadership for not following the Bolshevik way. Simultaneously, there were anticommunist groups in the country, biding their time. Both segments, however, represented politically insignificant forces. The predominant majority of the people wholeheartedly endorsed the objectives of the National Front to liberate men from economic and social domination within a democratic society.

These hopeful expectations, predicated on the belief that Czechoslovakia could eventually become the show window of a new, more humane system and the bridge between East and West were shattered in the summer of 1947 by Stalin's new policy line,[58] which called for consolidating the Soviet hold on Eastern Europe and drawing clear lines of combat with the West. On June 5, at Harvard University, U.S. Secretary of State George C. Marshall made his historic offer of American aid to Europe. Czechoslovakia was eager to share in the American aid, which it needed to complete the Two-Year Economic Plan successfully. On July 4 and 7 the cabinet and inner cabinet, respectively, voted unanimously to accept an invitation to send a delegation to a preliminary conference of European states in Paris to discuss the Marshall Plan.[59] Immediately after the cabinet made its intention known, a government delegation led by Premier Gottwald left for Moscow where it was scheduled to negotiate mutual trade problems and to discuss the possibility of concluding a Franco-Czechoslovak treaty. When the delegation arrived in Moscow on July 9, it was given an ultimatum by Stalin to choose between East and West. On the following day the Prague government reversed its decision to send a delegation to Paris.[60] It had chosen the Soviet alliance.

[58] Jaroslav Opat, "K metodě studia a výkladu některých problémů v období 1945-1948" ["On the Method of Study and Explanation of Some Problems in the Period of 1945-1948"], *Příspěvky k dějinám KSČ* (February, 1965), 65-83.

[59] Belda, *Na rozhraní*, pp. 121-22; Opat, *O novou demokracii*, pp. 236-38.

[60] Ripka, *Le Coup*, pp. 51-55. Apparently, the Czechoslovak acceptance of the invitation to go to Paris was in part a result of a misunderstanding brought about by Soviet inefficiency. Masaryk sought advance Soviet approval for accepting the invitation, but Bodrov, the Soviet chargé d'affaires in Prague, lacked instructions. Failing to get a reply from Moscow in time, the Czechoslovak government announced its acceptance—only to be told by Moscow that it must not go to Paris. See Belda, *Na rozhraní*, pp 122-25. Masaryk, who clung to relations with the

At the end of September, the Information Bureau of the Communist parties (Cominform), including the KSČ, was founded at Szklarska Poreba in Poland as the institutional device of the communist international control system.[61] The delegates aimed "to apply the final touches to a general plan for easing the 'National Front' allies out of power and establishing a Communist dictatorship" in Eastern Europe.[62] The Cominform, then, was founded at the moment when "the Soviet Union had finally decided to take under her direct control a number of East European states," particularly Czechoslovakia.[63] The secretary general of the KSČ, Rudolf Slánský, informed the conference that the first task of the party was "to deal a death blow to reaction in Slovakia,"[64] and added ominously: "It will be necessary to throw reactionary forces out of the National Front."[65] The road was opened for the Stalinist takeover in Czechoslovakia.

From the Cominform to the Prague Coup

By the fall of 1947 the struggle for power in East Central Europe was almost decided. Czechoslovakia remained the sole exception. It still had a coalition government. During the summer her hitherto favorable economic development suddenly ceased. A severe drought caused the harvest to fall to one-half of its normal level. As the leading party in the government, the communists received the major blame for the deteriorating economic situation. Feeling that the tide of public opinion was turning against them, they sought to postpone the elections that they had proposed in the spring. The democratic parties, on the other hand, aware that their chances in an electoral contest had improved, pressed for holding them at an early date. After much bickering it was decided to hold them in May, 1948.

As the parties girded for another electoral struggle, the communists displayed a wide arsenal of political and psychological weapons. In August they proposed that the owners of property in excess of one million

West, was crushed by the humiliation. For more information see Josef Belda et al., "K otázce účasti Československa na Marshallově plánu" ["On the Question of the Czechoslovak Participation at the Marshall Plan"], *Revue dějin socialismu*, VIII (1968), 81-100.

[61] *For a Lasting Peace, for a People's Democracy*, November 10, 1947.

[62] Eugenio Reale, who participated at the conference as the delegate of the Communist party of Italy, in Milorad Drachkovitch and Branko Lazitch, eds., *The Comintern: Historical Highlights* (New York, 1966), p. 260.

[63] Vladimir Dedijer, *Tito* (New York, 1953), p. 292.

[64] The minutes of E. Reale in Drachkovitch and Lazitch, *The Comintern*, p. 254; Jarošová and Jaroš, *Slovenské robotníctvo*, p. 232.

[65] Conference of the Nine Communist Parties, p. 118, quoted in Korbel, *Communist Subversion*, p. 186.

Czechoslovak crowns pay a "millionaires' tax" to provide aid to the ailing rural districts. Millionaires had never been numerous in Czechoslovakia and their ranks had been further reduced by the war and the subsequent expulsion of the German minority. Even the Social Democrats demurred at supporting so demagogic a measure. However, when communist propaganda succeeded in arousing popular support for it, the Social Democrats hastened on September 11 to conclude an agreement with the KSČ providing for their cooperation. The social democratic leadership thus sought to bind the KSČ to their own democratic practices. However, a large number of party members sharply criticized the agreement and Minister Václav Majer even tended his resignation.[66]

A strident note crept into communist propaganda. The communist press began systematically to impugn the loyalty of the other parties to the republic and to vilify their leaders. The public was shocked by the revelation on September 10 of an abortive attempt on the lives of noncommunist ministers Jan Masaryk, Petr Zenkl, and Prokop Drtina, who had received parcels containing bombs. The communist Minister of Interior Václav Nosek and the communist-dominated police showed a curious lack of interest in the case. Instead, with much fanfare, the Slovak Commissioner of Interior, Mikuláš Ferjenčík, announced on November 14 the discovery of a plot by the l'udák underground to assassinate President Beneš and overthrow the republic. Subsequently, the police linked the alleged plot to the l'udák exiles Karol Sidor and Ferdinand D'určanský. Widespread arrests, ultimately of more than 500 persons, followed. Among the arrested were three DS members of the National Assembly and a secretary of Vice-Premier Ján Ursíny. Although Ursíny himself was not implicated in the plot, he was forced to resign from the cabinet.

The affair served as a smoke screen behind which the communists prepared to purge the Slovak board of commissioners of its DS majority and to restructure the National Front of Slovak parties to make it more responsive to their wishes.[67] To set the stage for this coup, they arranged for the Slovak Trade Union Council (SOR—the Slovak counterpart of ROH) to meet in Bratislava on October 30 and for the Slovak Peasant Union to meet there two weeks later. At its October 30 meeting the SOR passed a resolution blaming the board of commissioners for the breakdown in food distribution and a failure to safeguard the security of the state and calling for its dismissal. Another resolution called for the re-

[66] Nedvěd, "Cesta ke sloučení," p. 56; Belda, Na rozhraní, pp. 154-67; Opat, O novou demokracii, pp. 242-45.

[67] For the Slovak November crisis see Jarošová and Jaroš, Slovenské robotníctvo, pp. 221-52; Vartíková, Od Košíc, pp. 147-62; Lettrich, History, pp. 249-51. For Gottwald's formula to solve the crisis, see Václav Král, ed., Cestou k únoru [The Road to February] (Prague, 1963), p. 270.

organization of the Slovak National Front to include trade union, resistance, and peasant organizations. On the following day, in response to this "voice of the people," the communist chairman of the board of commissioners, Husák, four other communist commissioners, and the nonparty Commissioner of Interior Ferjenčík resigned from the board. Husák declared that the board was thereby dissolved and opened negotiations with the minute Freedom and Labor parties, until then unrepresented on the board, to form a new one. The DS leaders naturally protested against this novel constitutional concept whereby a minority could dismiss the majority from the cabinet. They refused to resign from the board or to admit the mass organizations into the National Front.

The government in Prague then stepped into the situation, but to the dismay of the communists the National Socialists and Populists refused to associate themselves in a communist measure of coercion against the DS. On November 18, after prolonged negotiations, a new board of commissioners was formed in which the DS was deprived of its majority and the Freedom and Labor parties received representation.

The Slovak "November crisis" proved to be a dress rehearsal for the Prague "February crisis." The communists had effectively used their control of the police and mass organizations and had ruthlessly exploited every weakness in the ranks of the DS to achieve their objective. The democratic parties were alerted to what was in store for them. An early symptom of their reaction was the reassertion by the Social Democratic party of its independence of the KSČ. At its congress at Brno on November 16 the procommunist Fierlinger was removed as chairman of the party and replaced with centrist Bohumil Laušman.[68] The democratic parties were encouraged by this development to believe that the Social Democratic party would cooperate with them. Laušman, however, personified the inability of the party to decide whether to fight on the side of the Communist party for social demands or on the side of the democratic parties for democracy. Under his leadership the party wavered in Hamlet-like indecision between the communist and democratic parties.

The communists increased their pressure on the other parties through the winter of 1947-48, with each issue exacerbating the political atmosphere and widening the divergences between the two camps.[69] The noncommunist parties made common complaint about police use of false confessions and *agents provocateurs*. Accusations levelled at the KSČ for attempting to monopolize control of the police engendered popular

[68] Nedvěd, "Cesta ke sloučení," pp. 58-59.
[69] The KSČ raised demands for the nationalization of private trade and for new land reform. In February, 1948, it was defeated in an attempt to prevent an increase in the salaries of public servants. It continued to use the security apparati to increase pressure, and managed to hush up an investigation of the attempt against the lives of three democratic ministers.

411

demands for the preservation of basic democratic freedoms. The time remaining for any possible settlement was running out. In November, 1947, the upper echelons of the KSČ began concerted action according to a plan based on their experience in the Slovak crisis. This involved a call by the ROH for a meeting of the workers' factory councils and peasant committees to formulate new popular demands. The party would then endorse their program, which would be adopted subsequently by all the mass organizations and those personalities within the existing parties who had secretly been won over by the communists. The ensuing "renovated" National Front would draw up a unified list of candidates for the elections.[70] The new alliance would then mount an electoral campaign aided by the mass media of communication, national committees, and police machinery—all controlled by the party.[71]

On February 12, 1948, the ROH issued a call to the workers' factory councils to meet in Prague on February 22, an action that convinced the democratic leaders that the communists were about to move. In a cabinet meeting the following day, the National Socialist ministers precipitated a crisis by protesting against the demotion and transfer of eight high noncommunist police officers by Minister of Interior Nosek. All ministers except the communists approved a motion introduced by the National Socialists to instruct Nosek to reinstate the police officers and desist from further personnel changes in the police forces. The communists were placed in a minority position in the cabinet and appeared isolated. Encouraged by their success, the National Socialists decided to take the offensive against them and try to upset their timetable. On February 20 the National Socialist ministers, followed by the Populist and Slovak Democratic ministers, resigned from the cabinet in protest against the failure of Nosek to carry out the cabinet decision of February 13 in the police matter. The "latent crisis" was thus transformed into "open crisis."[72]

[70] According to a confidential survey of public opinion taken by the communist-controlled Ministry of Information, the KSČ faced a loss of eight to ten percent in the next election. See Ripka, *Le Coup*, p. 190.

[71] Miroslav Bouček, *Praha v únoru* [*Prague in February*] (Prague, 1963), pp. 25, 149; Karel Kaplan in *Historica* (Prague, 1963), v, 241.

[72] The literature on the February crisis is quite extensive. Among the communist accounts and documentary collections are: Belda, *Na rozhraní*, pp. 223-62; Bouček, *Praha*, pp. 143-254, and *Únor 1948: Sborník dokumentů* [*February 1948: A Collection of Documents*] (Prague, 1958); Král, *Cestou*, pp. 329-410; Jiří Veselý, *Prague 1948* (Paris, 1958), pp. 71-190, which is a French adaptation of his *Kronika únorových dnů* [*Chronicle of the February Days*] (Prague, 1958); and Alois Svoboda *et al.*, *Jak to bylo v únoru* [*What Happened in February*] (Prague, 1949), *passim*. A Czech National Socialist account may be found in Ripka, *Le Coup*, pp. 201-316, of which there is an English translation, *Czechoslovakia Enslaved* (London, 1950), and a Social Democratic one in Bohumil Laušman, *Kdo byl vinen?* [*Who is to Blame?*] (Vienna, n.d.), pp. 108-54. President Beneš's side of the story is told in detail by the head of his chancellery,

The dramatic return of two old adversaries, U.S. Ambassador Laurence A. Steinhardt and Soviet Deputy Minister of Foreign Affairs and former ambassador to Czechoslovakia Valerian A. Zorin, to Prague on February 19 appeared to give the crisis an international dimension. Steinhardt declared to the press that the door to the Marshall Plan was still open to Czechoslovakia.[73] Zorin arrived ostensibly to expedite deliveries of grain, which the Soviet government had promised in December to alleviate the food shortage. The Western press speculated widely that he had really come to Prague to direct the communist takeover. Actually, no evidence ever turned up indicating that he had directly intervened in the crisis.[74] He did not have to. Gottwald and his associates had matters well in hand.

The ministers who had resigned constituted a minority, since neither the Social Democrats nor nonparty ministers Jan Masaryk and Ludvík Svoboda had been consulted and thus had not resigned. Consequently, Gottwald remained legally in power. The ministers who had resigned counted on President Beneš to refuse to accept their resignations. In that case, they would compel Gottwald either to call new elections or to carry out the decision of the cabinet in the police matter. They thought in strictly parliamentary terms, regarding their resignation as a mere cabinet affair, and called on their supporters "to remain calm under all circumstances." But the communists refused to abide by the rules of parliamentary democracy. While the democratic ministers and parties passively awaited Beneš's decision, the communists used their control of mass organizations and the police to take over power.

On the morning of February 21 Gottwald addressed an organized mass meeting in the Old Town Square in Prague. He accused the resigned ministers of having formed a "reactionary bloc" in the cabinet to obstruct

---

Jaromír Smutný, in "Únorový převrat 1948" ["February Revolution, 1948"], *Doklady a Rozpravy*, Nos. 12 (1953); 19 (1955); 21 (1955); 25 (1956); and 28 (1957); published by the Institute of Dr. Edvard Beneš in London. Accounts by Western scholars may be found in Korbel, *Communist Subversion*, pp. 206-35, and Paul E. Zinner, *Communist Strategy and Tactics in Czechoslovakia, 1918-1948* (New York, 1963), pp. 204-16. Among the numerous accounts by Western journalists, perhaps the best may be found in Dana Adams Schmidt, *Anatomy of a Satellite* (Boston, 1952), pp. 108-21.

[73] Report of ČTK, the Czechoslovak News Agency, in Král, *Cestou*, p. 347. Steinhardt informed Czechoslovak officials that the United States would consider favorably an application for a credit of $25 million to purchase American cotton. See Schmidt, *Anatomy*, p. 110. Although Czechoslovakia experienced great economic difficulties at the time, the economic weapon was quite inadequate to affect the crisis.

[74] According to Belda, *Na rozhraní*, p. 265, Zorin assured Gottwald that "the Soviet Union would not allow Western powers to interfere in the internal affairs of Czechoslovakia." Since, however, none of the Western powers intervened in the crisis, the Soviet Union did not have to do so either. Although the crisis had international repercussions, it was a purely internal one.

the popular policies of the communists. They had precipitated the crisis, he alleged, to prevent the holding of elections, the outcome of which they feared. By their action they had "excluded themselves from the National Front," and the communists could have no further dealings with them. They would be replaced "with new people, who had remained faithful to the original spirit of the National Front." Gottwald put his proposal for the "renovation" of the cabinet into a resolution that was approved by acclamation, and on the spot a workers' delegation was "elected" to carry this expression of the "will of the people" to the president.

At the same time the communists deployed the instruments of their takeover—party activists, workers' militia, the police, and "action committees"—in Prague and outside it, according to a carefully prepared plan. On February 24 armed workers lent Prague a certain spurious aura of Petrograd in 1917, but their military value was slight, if any. In the event of an armed conflict with the other parties, the communists relied on the police, particularly on specially trained police regiments composed exclusively of communists. On the morning of February 21 the police assumed guard over the Prague radio station, post and telegraph offices, and railway stations. The most original instrument of the communist takeover was the action committees, which had been secretly organized earlier among men within and outside the KSČ whom the party could trust. Action committees sprang up in every government bureau, factory, and town—in fact in every organized body in the country—and proceeded to purge them of democrats.[75]

By mass demonstrations centered on Prague and the mere threat of violence, the communists isolated and silenced the democratic parties, split the Social Democratic party, and awed the president. In such an unprecedented situation, naturally, the majority of the population expected word from Beneš—word that never came. After resisting the communist demands for five days, Beneš yielded. On February 25 he accepted the resignation of the democratic ministers and simultaneously appointed a new cabinet handpicked by Gottwald, which—in addition to communists and Social Democrats—included some members of the National Socialist, Populist, and Slovak Democratic parties, who had secretly agreed to cooperate with the communists. The façade of the National Front was thus maintained.

The only force that could have prevented the communist takeover was the army. But the army under General Svoboda, a friend of the communists, remained neutral throughout the crisis. In any event, Beneš never considered opposing force by force. The behavior of the noncommunist

---

[75] The purge involved some 28,000 persons. See Karel Kaplan, *Utváření generální linie výstavby socialismu v Československu* [*The Formation of the General Line of the Construction of Socialism in Czechoslovakia*] (Prague, 1966), p. 27.

party leaders was, if possible, even worse. While the communists were brilliantly using the instruments of power, "the non-Communist parties . . . had no organization, no plan"[76] and finished in complete disarray, despite the support they enjoyed from the helpless and baffled majority of the Czech and Slovak people. By their precipitate and ill-considered resignation, the democratic ministers had made it possible for the communists to take over power by constitutional means. They were not forced out of the government by the communists; they had walked out of it.

Meanwhile, the zealous Husák had anticipated Gottwald's coup at Prague with one of his own at Bratislava.[77] But the events in Bratislava lacked the drama of those in Prague, because they constituted, more or less, only a mopping-up operation, designed to complete what had been left undone in November. Unlike Gottwald, Husák did not have to contend with Beneš. Moreover, while Prague was swarming with foreign correspondents who had come to observe and report on the death of Czechoslovak democracy, none troubled to go to the provincial backwater of Bratislava. Husák, therefore, dispensed with the elaborate *mise en scène* that Gottwald felt compelled to arrange at Prague. Unlike the DS ministers in Prague, the DS commissioners in Bratislava did not resign; they had to be expelled from the board. On February 21, without awaiting the outcome of the cabinet crisis in Prague, Husák wrote them that the resignation of the DS ministers from the central government bound them to resign too, and against the eventuality that they might dispute this ruling he posted policemen at the doors of their offices to turn them away. They did not choose to resist, for the DS had been emasculated and cowed in November and had nothing left with which to fight. The communists took a majority of seats on the board (eight out of fifteen), and distributed the rest among the other parties (including two pliant DS members) and representatives of the communist-controlled mass organizations. Action committees completed the mop-up.

After appointing the new government on February 25 Beneš retired to his country residence at Sezimovo Ústí and withdrew from further participation in the conduct of state affairs. The communists were left the sole masters of the republic—free to reorganize it according to their beliefs and concepts.

[76] Kaplan, *Historica*, v, 250ff.
[77] For the Slovak side of the crisis see Vartíková, *Od Košíc*, pp. 181-84; Jarošová and Jaroš, *Slovenské robotníctvo*, pp. 265-67; Lettrich, *History*, pp. 259-60.

· 15 ·

SOLUTION OF THE MINORITIES PROBLEM

Ludvík Němec
Rosemont College

In East Central Europe numerous historical migrations had resulted in a confluence of various ethnic groups that had little in common except the land they inhabited. Thus, in 1918 and again in 1945, Czechoslovakia inherited ethnic groups that had lived for centuries on its territory.[1] The future of these minorities became an integral part of wartime plans for the reconstruction of the Czechoslovak Republic.

Although in the course of the war the idea of transferring these minorities from Czechoslovakia was accepted in principle by all the Great Powers, it remained to be seen what their reaction would be when they were confronted with a workable plan for its implementation.

At the end of July, 1944, the European Advisory Committee of Britain, Soviet Russia, and the United States, meeting in London, requested the Allied governments to submit their proposals for the capitulation of Germany. In its reply on August 24, 1944, the Czechoslovak government in exile submitted a memorandum proposing a concrete plan for the transfer of its German minority: some 1,600,000 Germans were to be removed to Germany and about 800,000 reliable Germans were to retain their citizenship.[2] These totals assumed that about 250,000 would be war

---

[1] There are no official census figures on nationality in Czechoslovakia after 1930. The following table presents the statistics from the 1930 official census. The second column of figures shows the estimates made in May 1947 by the U.S. Bureau of the Census. The last column gives 1950 estimates. All figures have been rounded to the nearest thousand.

Population Distribution Among the Various Nationalities

Nationality	1930	1947	1950
Czechs ⎱ Slovaks ⎰	9,722,000	11,090,000	⎰ 8,428,000 ⎱ 2,838,000
Germans	3,305,000	250,000	Numbered among others
Magyars	604,000	600,000	580,000
Ruthenians	118,000	100,000	161,000
Poles	100,000	110,000	Numbered among others
Jews	110,000	⎱ 50,000	Numbered among others
Others	46,000	⎰	333,000
Total	14,004,000	12,200,000	12,340,000

See Vratislav Bušek and Nicolas Spulber, eds., *Czechoslovakia* (New York, 1957), pp. 32-33; Miroslav Blažek, *Hospodářská geografie Československa* [*Economic Geography of Czechoslovakia*] (Prague, 1954).

[2] Radomír Luža, *The Transfer of the Sudeten Germans. A Study of Czech-German Relations, 1933-1962* (New York, 1964), p. 246.

casualties and that another 500,000 would escape before the end of the war. The transfer would take about two years, with some compensation assured for the immovable properties of the transferees. This principle was to be inserted as an armistice condition of the Reich's capitulation to make certain that the idea of a transfer was recognized and accepted by the Germans. The same text of a workable plan was delivered to the governments of all the Great Powers on November 23, 1944.

The reaction of the Western powers was marked by an attitude of caution. While the British government pondered the plan "with care and sympathy," the United States advised that it be carried out "under international auspices, gradually and in an orderly manner."[3] The Soviet government reaffirmed its support of the plan, to which it had already assented in 1943. Further negotiations with Britain followed.

The Czechoslovak government regarded agreement by the Great Powers as a basic precondition for the plan, because of their responsibility to the great number of people to be affected by the transfer. The Great Powers viewed the transfer as a necessary evil, closely related to the solution of the problems of postwar Europe. They hoped that by carrying out the plan, some measure of balance would be achieved in East Central Europe.

The concept of the transfer became part of the official program of the new Czechoslovak government set up at Košice. It was incorporated into Košice program of April 5, 1945. The program assured those members of the German and Magyar minorities in Czechoslovakia who had *actively* fought against nazism and fascism of full rights as Czechoslovak citizens. As for other members of the German and Magyar minorities, it provided as follows:

> Czechoslovak citizenship of other Czechoslovak citizens of German or Magyar nationality will be cancelled. Although they may again opt for Czechoslovakia, public authorities will retain the right of individual decision in the case of each application. Those Germans and Magyars who will have been prosecuted and condemned for a crime against the Republic and the Czech and Slovak people, will be declared to have forfeited their Czechoslovak citizenship and, unless they are under sentence of death, will be expelled from the Republic forever.[4]

[3] Ibid., pp. 247-48.

[4] Ústav dějin KSČ, *Za svobodu českého a slovenského národa: Sborník dokumentů k dějinám KSČ v letech 1938-1945* [*For the Freedom of the Czech and Slovak People: A Collection of Documents for the History of the Communist Party of Czechoslovakia in 1938-1945*] (Prague, 1956), pp. 378-79; Theodor Schieder, ed., *Dokumentation der Vertreibung der Deutschen aus Ost-Mitteleuropa* (Bonn, 1957), IV/1, pp. 184-203.

The program was regarded as being relatively moderate, since it offered the right of option and thus handled the minority question cautiously.[5] However, the communists did not yet fully appreciate the radical mood of the country. During the Nazi occupation national feelings had been so aroused that the expulsion of the Germans and Magyars assumed the status of a crusade. It was regarded as a protest against the sufferings of the past rather than as a mere political arrangement.[6]

In May, 1945, Czechoslovakia drew up the balance sheet of her losses: 250,000 persons dead and more than 100,000 with some permanent injury. Material damage, including the destruction of many public and private properties, was estimated at 1,284.5 billion Czechoslovak crowns.[7] Indignation against the Germans was so intense that the idea of transfer became the only alternative acceptable to the Czech people.

It is important to note the different moods prevailing in Slovakia and in the Czech lands fully to understand their different reactions to, and acceptance of, the Košice program. The Slovaks were indignant against the Magyars with whom they had had painful experiences during the existence of the Slovak state. They had not forgotten that their compatriots in the southern regions, incorporated within Hungary in 1938, had suffered at the hands of the Magyar authorities. Toward the Germans, the Slovak attitude was pragmatic.[8] On the whole, it must be remembered that the Slovaks were patriots in their own right,[9] no matter how one may evaluate their often puzzling relationship with the Czechs. The Czechs had more justification for being adamant enemies of the Germans, which explains why the solution to the problem of the German minority took precedence among the Czechs over other minority problems in the period immediately following the war.

The Sudeten Germans seemed to be more surprised than the Magyars at the amount of Czech and Slovak animosity[10] they had generated. They were therefore unprepared for the events that followed. The collapse of Nazi Germany, the presence of the Soviet and American armies, and the complete overhaul of the Czechoslovak administrative apparatus had created an executive vacuum in the period immediately following the

[5] Klement Gottwald, *Spisy* [*Works*] (Prague, 1950-61), XI, 245ff.

[6] Ygael Gluckstein, *Stalin's Satellites in Europe* (London, 1952), pp. 194ff.

[7] Leopold Chmela, *The Economic Aspects of the German Occupation of Czechoslovakia* (Prague, 1948), pp. 4-7, 135ff.

[8] M. S. D'urica, *La Slovacchia è le sue relazioni politiche con la Germania* (Padova, 1964), *passim*.

[9] B. S. Buc, *Slovak Nationalism* (Middletown, Pa., 1960), *passim*; Július Mésároš, "Die Idee der slawischen Schicksalsgemeinschaft in der slowakischen nationalen Bewegung in der zweiten Hälfte des 19. Jahrhunderts," *Historica*, X (Prague, 1965), pp. 159-211.

[10] Alfred Bohman, *Die Ausweisung der Sudetendeutschen dargestellt am Beispiel des Stadt- und Landkreises Aussig* (Marburg, 1955), pp. 45-46ff.

government's return to Prague on May 10, 1945. During this time some towns meted out "short justice" to collaborators. Germans were abused and summary executions took place, actions that the foreign news media quickly discovered and reported. That there was harsh treatment in the handling of the German people can be seen from such measures as the limiting of food rations, the closing of all German schools,[11] and the introduction of compulsory labor[12] to clean up war damages and restore the national economy. These measures were intended to be an interim, rather than a final, solution to the German question.

President Edvard Beneš exhorted the Czechs and Slovaks to act with reason and patience. He insisted that no final settlement, especially one that involved a transfer, could be reached without the sanction of the Great Powers, and such agreement might be withheld if the people were not more circumspect in their actions.

On July 3, the Prague government requested the three Allied powers to place the question of the transfer[13] on the agenda of the approaching Potsdam conference (July 17-August 2, 1945).[14] On July 22, Prague[15] submitted its completed plan to the Great Powers for the orderly removal of the Germans. On July 25, the question was put on the agenda and a subcommittee was appointed to draw up a draft of the question. After a discussion on July 31, the transfer was approved and it became Article XII of the Potsdam Declaration.[16] It emphasized that "any transfers that take place should be effected in an orderly and humane manner," and stated:

> Since the influx of a large number of Germans into Germany would increase the burden already resting on the occupying authorities, they consider that the Allied Council in Germany should in the first instance examine the problem with special regard to the question of the equitable distribution of these Germans among the several zones of occupation. They are accordingly instructing their representatives on the Control Council to report to their Governments as soon as possible the extent to which such persons have already entered Germany

---

[11] Schieder, ed., *Dokumentation*, IV/1, pp. 79-80, 95.

[12] Presidential decree of Sept. 19, 1945.

[13] Department of State, *Foreign Relations of the United States. Diplomatic Papers: The Conference of Berlin (The Potsdam Conference), 1945* (2 vols.; Washington, 1960), I, 646-47. Hereafter *Foreign Relations: The Potsdam Conference.*

[14] William D. Leahy, *I Was There* (New York, 1950), pp. 414ff; Herbert Feis, *Between War and Peace. The Potsdam Conference* (Princeton, N.J., 1960), pp. 269-70; Johann W. Brügel, "Die sudetendeutsche Frage auf der Potsdam Konferenz," *Vierteljahrshefte für Zeitgeschichte*, X (Jan. 1962), 56-61.

[15] Luža, *Transfer*, p. 278.

[16] Department of State, *Foreign Relations: The Potsdam Conference*, II, 383, 387, 398, 523, 536, 1543-51.

from Poland, Czechoslovakia and Hungary, and to submit an estimate of the time and rate at which further transfers could be carried out, having regard to the present situation in Germany. The Czechoslovak Government . . . are at the same time being informed of the above, and are being requested meanwhile to suspend further expulsions pending the examination by the Governments concerned of the report from their representatives on the Control Council.[17]

This appeared to be a rebuke to those governments, such as the Czechoslovak, that had tolerated harsh actions against their minorities. On the other hand, the Czechs viewed the nationality section of the Košice program as being too lenient and discarded part of it. Under the Czechoslovak presidential decree of August 2, 1945, all Sudeten Germans were considered to be Reich German citizens and had to prove their loyalty to Czechoslovakia before being allowed to apply for Czechoslovak citizenship. All supporters of the Nazi regime were to be prosecuted at special courts. Under decrees of May 19, June 21, and October 25, all German property was confiscated.[18]

Such property was recognized by the Paris Conference on Reparation in 1945 as Czechoslovak assets and was not charged to the Czechoslovak reparation account.[19] On August 16, 1945, the Czechoslovak government sent a note to the three powers assuring them that it would faithfully comply with the Potsdam instructions, but suggesting that the transfer be completed within a year. Shortly afterward it sent the Allied Control Council in Berlin a report that estimated the number of the German minority considered as subjects for transfer to be 2,500,000. This excluded those Germans who had already fled and excepted German women in mixed marriages as well as antifascists.[20] It was estimated that about 223,000 Germans had fled to the American Zone and about 150,000 to the Soviet Zone.[21] The Allied Control Council agreed to implement the recommendations of this report in full as requested by Prague.

On January 8-9, 1946, a series of meetings were held in Prague be-

[17] The matter is treated in Article 12 of the "Protocol of Proceedings" and Section 13 of the "Report on the Tripartite Conference of Berlin," ibid., 1511.

[18] Luža, *Transfer*, p. 271.

[19] Article 6 (on German External Assets), paragraphs A and D of the final act of the Paris Conference on Reparation, signed Dec. 21, 1945, *The Department of State Bulletin*, XIV (Jan. 27, 1946), 117.

[20] See Schieder, ed., *Dokumentation*, IV/1, pp. 97-99, 245-48. Professor Luža (*Transfer*, p. 284) arrived at a total estimate of 3,320,000 Germans before Munich. His estimate is based on the confidential memorandum of the Prague Foreign Ministry made available to him.

[21] These are Professor Luža's statistics, ibid., again based on the Memorandum. Statistical data vary greatly according to the source of information. German statistics are always higher.

tween American and Czechoslovak officials to complete plans for the organized transfer. It was agreed that each trainload would include 1,200 persons in 40 heated cars. The Czechoslovak government was to provide sufficient food for the trip and for three additional days. Families were to be kept together, clothing was to be adequate, and every person was to be permitted to take with him personal belongings totaling 30 to 50 kilograms and an allowance of 1,000 Reichsmarks.

The actual transfer was executed according to the following schedule: beginning on January 25, 1946, one train moved daily; after February 25, two trains; after April 1, four trains. Later, the daily rate peaked at six trains. On July 15 the rate was reduced to four trains per day and in November to only three trains per week. This reduction was necessitated by the inability of the distribution centers in Germany to handle the influx with sufficient speed. Thus from January 25 to November 30, 1946, the total of Germans removed to the American Zone was 1,334,856.[22] In Berlin, Soviet Marshal Sokolovsky at first refused to implement the decision of the Allied Control Council, but after direct negotiations, held in May and June of 1946 at Prague's insistence, the transfer was carried out in the Soviet Zone as well in accordance with the provisions of the Potsdam agreement. This phase of the transfer involved a total of 786,482 persons. The anti-Nazis, numbering about 100,000, were the last to be transferred. The whole transfer procedure cost over 500 million Czechoslovak crowns.[23]

The Czechoslovak authorities, mindful of world opinion, made every effort to carry out the transfer according to the principles laid down at Potsdam. Their actions were noted by foreign correspondents, official observers, and diplomatic representatives. On the completion of the transfer, Gen. Lucius Clay, the U.S. representative on the Allied Control Council in Berlin, praised the manner in which the transfer had been handled by the Czechoslovak government, as did Soviet General Leljushenko.[24] The ambassadors of all the Great Powers likewise expressed their appreciation of the effective organization of the transfer. One may conclude therefore that it was indeed effected "in a humane manner."[25] One aspect, which perhaps casts a shadow over the transfer procedure, was the expropriation without compensation of all the properties of the transferees except their personal belongings. It must be said in justice, however, that President Beneš had proposed compensation, but his plan was rejected by the Czechoslovak communists and some ex-

[22] Ibid., pp. 284ff.   [23] Ibid., pp. 286-87.

[24] Joseph B. Schechtman, "Resettlement of Transferred Volksdeutsche in Germany," *Journal of Central European Affairs*, VII (Oct. 1947), 262-84.

[25] Joseph B. Schechtman, "Postwar Population Transfers in Europe: A Study," *The Review of Politics*, XV (April 1953), 156ff.

tremists. It is also cause for wonder that the powers occupying Germany tolerated this injustice. This was perhaps due to the postwar atmosphere in which the victor sought to exact justice in proportion to the guilt of his victim.

Besides the organized transfer, there were voluntary emigrations of Germans from Czechoslovakia, amounting to about 30,000 persons by June, 1949. With the creation of the two German states in 1949, the time came to stabilize the situation. The first movement toward this end came in a memorandum of U.S. Maj. Gen. G. P. Hays on November 3, 1948, which informed the Czechoslovak government that in the future any transferred Germans would have to be provided with a military entry permit. This action was designed to stop the endless and illegal influx of German latecomers from Czechoslovakia. This group involved former German war prisoners who had been released in small units and by January 1, 1949, numbered 7,568 persons.[26]

Finally, what may be called a philanthropic emigration should be mentioned. On October 26, 1949, the Bonn government applied to the Allied High Commission for the transfer of some 20,000 Germans in order "to reunite these persons with their relatives."[27] By agreement with Prague, a total of 16,832 Germans were removed by April 28, 1951. After all the transfers there still remained in Czechoslovakia about 165,000 registered Germans. This indicates how difficult it is in practice to achieve a truly national state.

One interesting feature of the Potsdam conference was its concentration on the Germans. The handling of their satellites was left to the various states. As a result, the question of the Magyar minority reverted to the Czechoslovak government, which applied the principle of collective responsibility to the Magyars since they had, at the time of the Munich crisis, manifested a desire to be united with the country of their origin and had exploited the weaknesses of the republic toward this end, with the full support of Nazi Germany. The removal of the Hungarian minority was envisaged in the Košice program and reaffirmed by the decision of the political parties of the National Front on April 11, 1946, which established the principle that Czechoslovakia was to be a national state of Czechs and Slovaks only.

The extent of the Magyar minority problem can be seen from the following statistics: according to the 1921 census it involved 635,000; the 1930 census, 572,000; the 1938 census, 650,000; and the 1946 census 700,000 persons.[28] The increase between the 1938 and the 1946 cen-

---

[26] Luža, *Transfer*, p. 306.

[27] Schieder, ed., *Dokumentation*, IV/2, pp. 540-44; Jozef Jablonický, *Slovensko na prelome* [*Slovakia in Transition*] (Bratislava, 1965), pp. 396-409.

[28] Kalman Janics, "How Many Hungarians Are There in Czechoslovakia?" *Uj*

suses can be attributed to the Slovak reoccupation of territories that had been ceded to Hungary in 1938-39. The Czechoslovak government was handicapped in its attempt to resolve this problem because Budapest was initially unwilling to accept any removal of Hungarians from Slovakia.

The arbitrary expulsion of the Magyars, their deprivation of civil rights, and the confiscation of their property, seemingly justified by the Košice program, so alarmed Budapest that a Hungarian delegation arrived in Prague in the autumn of 1945 to discuss this issue. At the official conference in December, 1945, Dr. Vlado Clementis, State Secretary in the Czechoslovak Foreign Ministry, made a proposal to "exchange the Slovaks of Hungary desirous of leaving the country, for an analogous number of Hungarians designated by Prague, all other Hungarians from Slovakia to be expelled later."[29] The Hungarian delegation accepted the idea of an exchange, but categorically refused to approve any expulsion. In their second conference, held on February 27, 1946, at Tatranská Lomnica in Slovakia, the Hungarian delegate agreed that Czechoslovakia could "expatriate as many Hungarians as there were Slovaks in Hungary naturally desirous of returning to establish themselves in Czechoslovakia."[30] In return, Prague pledged to suspend expulsion, halt the confiscation, and make compensation for what had already been taken.

The exchange was to begin in August, 1946. However, the Hungarian government adopted delaying tactics in the hope that the Paris Peace Conference would oblige the Czechoslovak government to grant civil status to the Magyar minority in Czechoslovakia, and that the exchange would then become unnecessary. The Czechoslovak delegation to the Paris Peace Conference held to the plan for the unilateral expulsion of 200,000 Magyars in addition to the exchange previously agreed upon, but did not insist upon the confiscation of their properties. The conference recognized Czechoslovakia's right to insist on the principle of a national state and acknowledged the principle of an exchange of population, but rejected any further unilateral transfer.[31] Article 5 of the Peace Treaty of 1947 with Hungary stipulated that

1. Hungary shall enter into negotiations with Czechoslovakia in order to solve the question of those inhabitants of Magyar ethnic

---

Szó (Bratislava, Dec. 4, 1968), reported in English in Czechoslovak Press Survey, May 24, 1968, New York, Radio Free Europe.

[29] Etienne Kertesz, "Tout est calme sur les bords du Danube," *Courier de l'Occident* (Paris, Oct. 15, 1949); Martin Vietor, "K problematike okupácie južného Slovenska" ["Concerning the Problems of the Occupation of Southern Slovakia"], *Odboj a revoluce*, No. 2 (Prague, 1966), pp. 46-84.

[30] Association Hongroise des Affaires étrangères, *La déportation des Hongrois de Slovaquie* (Budapest, 1947), pp. 5ff.

[31] Jan Masaryk, *Ani opona ani most* [*Neither a Curtain Nor a Bridge*] (Prague, 1947), pp. 13ff.

origin, residing in Czechoslovakia, who will not be settled in Hungary in accordance with the provisions of the Agreement of February 27, 1946, on exchange of populations.

2. Should no agreement be reached within a period of six months after the coming into force of the present Treaty, Czechoslovakia shall have the right to bring this question before the Council of Foreign Ministers and to request the assistance of the Council in effecting a final solution.[32]

This provision of the peace treaty, although it restricted the original proposals of the Czechoslovak government to a minimum, at least put the question before an international forum. However, the only concession that Czechoslovakia obtained from Hungary in the peace treaty was the cession of the Danubian bridgehead area on October 15, 1947. Thus the opposition of the peace conference postponed the ultimate solution of the Magyar minority problem to an uncertain future date.

To whittle down the Magyar ethnic minority, the Czechoslovak government scattered a part of it over the country, especially in the Sudeten borderland regions. The dispersal was carried out under the provisions of presidential decree No. 88/1945 concerning "The Mobilization of Manpower," which authorized the recruiting of laborers for a limited time to perform urgently needed public works. This action began on November 17, 1947, and was effected with the help and support of the army. It was brought to an end on February 25, 1948.

On the whole, the program was unsuccessful because many Magyars preferred to escape or pass secretly into Hungary. This operation was, of course, designed to camouflage the compulsory internal resettlement, for in some cases family members as well as workers were evacuated from their homes by force and the promise of receiving property as compensation in their new homes. Hungary protested vehemently against these tactics and intensified its propaganda campaign in a series of insulting attacks against Czechoslovakia. The attempt to liquidate the Magyar minority was unsuccessful. During the period from 1945 to 1947, only about 92,000 persons are known to have left Czechoslovakia.[33] Between 1947 and the spring of 1948, about 68,000 Magyars were resettled in Hungary.[34] War losses and unrecorded emigrations were probably con-

[32] Amelia C. Leiss and Raymond Dennett, eds., *European Peace Treaties After World War II* (Boston, 1954), p. 276; Joseph A. Mikuš, *Slovakia: A Political History 1918-1950* (Milwaukee, 1963), pp. 210ff; Dalibor M. Krno, *Our Peace Talks with Hungary* (Chicago, 1950), pp. 282ff.

[33] Bušek and Spulber, *Czechoslovakia*, p. 33.

[34] These data are taken from Juraj Zvara, *Riešenie maďarskej národnostnej otázky na Slovensku* [*The Solution of the Hungarian Nationality Question in Slovakia*] (Bratislava, 1967), *passim*.

siderable, yet according to recent calculations,[35] the Hungarian minority in Czechoslovakia still numbers between 720,000 and 740,000.

Attention should also be given to the Polish minority. At the Paris Peace Conference of 1919, the Polish delegation claimed from Czechoslovakia the Silesian district of Těšín and the Slovak districts of Orava and Spiš. A plebiscite was to decide this problem. It was never held. Instead, on July 28, 1920, the Ambassadors' Conference allotted the Slovak districts to Poland in compensation for Těšín's coal basin. On February 11, 1924, the Commission on Delimitation cut from Slovak territory 25 villages (12 in Orava and 13 in Spiš) together with their 24,700 inhabitants. In 1938, Poland occupied the remainder of Orava and Spiš that it claimed in 1919, that is, a strip of land to the north of Čadca, Námestovo, and the western part of Javorina. After the Nazi invasion of Poland, all of this land, including about 35,000 inhabitants, reverted to the Slovak state by the terms of the German-Slovak treaty of November 21, 1939. In 1945, the Czechoslovak state returned to its pre-Munich frontiers. Thus, the Polish minority in the republic[36] remained the same as it had been in pre-Munich days, amounting to about 100,000 persons. It enjoyed the full civil rights promised by the Košice program.

Finally, the Jewish religious minority should be mentioned. According to the 1930 census, there were 356,830 Jews classed as Czechoslovak citizens. This included 76,301 Jews in Bohemia, 41,250 in Moravia and Silesia, 136,737 in Slovakia, and 102,542 in Ruthenia.[37] Some Jews declared themselves to be of German nationality: 35,657 in the Czech provinces and 10,075 in Slovakia and Ruthenia; 87,489 were listed as Czechoslovaks, and of this number 30,000 Jews were in the territory incorporated by Hitler in 1938, from which all except 2,649 fled to post-Munich Czechoslovakia. Upon the disintegration of Czechoslovakia on March 15, 1939, it was estimated that there were 118,310 Jews in the Protectorate and 89,000 in the Slovak Republic. Since 30.3 percent of the Jews in the Czech provinces proclaimed themselves to be Germans, it may be estimated that in that area, 20,500 German Jews were murdered by the Nazis. As 7.3 percent of the Slovak Jews were of German

[35] Czechoslovak Press Survey, May 24, 1968, New York, Radio Free Europe.

[36] Václav Beneš, "Psychology of Polish-Czechoslovak Relations," *The Central European Federalist*, xv (June 1967), 21-28; Adam Bromke, "Poland and Czechoslovakia: The Hesitant Alliance," ibid., 9-20; Piotr S. Wandycz, *France and Her Eastern Allies, 1919-1925. French-Czechoslovak-Polish Relations from the Paris Conference to Locarno* (Minneapolis, 1962), *passim*; Ladislav Feierabend, *Ve vládě v exilu* [*In the Government-in-Exile*] (2 vols.; Washington, 1965-1966), I, 72-84.

[37] Erwin Winkler, *Die Tschechoslowakei im Spiegel der Statistik* (Carlsbad-Leipzig, 1937), pp. 12, 58.

nationality, more than 6,000 German Jews there became Nazi victims. Since only about 22,000 Czech Jews survived in the Czech countries, one can construct the following comparison with the 1930 census:

JEWISH INHABITANTS OF THE CZECH PROVINCES BY YEAR

Year	Country	Jewish inhabitants	Difference
1930	Czech provinces	117,551	———
1939	Protectorate	118,310	+759
1943	Protectorate	15,550	−102,760
1945-1946	Czech provinces	22,000	−96,310

The decrease between 1930 and 1945 gives some indication of the cruel fate of the Jews in the Czech provinces. Summarized from the detailed statistics of Prof. Radomír Luža,[38] the final outcome was that 33,499 Jews emigrated to different countries and 68,000 were exterminated. In Slovakia, somewhere between 28,000 and 35,000 (approximately 31,500) Jews survived to 1945. For this area, the comparison with the 1930 census is shown below.

JEWISH INHABITANTS OF SLOVAKIA BY YEAR

Year	Country	Jewish inhabitants	Difference
1930	Slovakia	136,737	———
1939	Slovak Republic	89,000	−47,737
1945	Slovakia	31,500	−105,237

The difference between the figures from 1930 and those from 1945 includes 68,000 Jews estimated to have suffered extermination and about 30,000 thought to have been deported.[39] There is some difficulty in establishing these figures for 1945 because statistics are not available for the Jews who were in Ruthenia, which had been annexed by Hungary in 1939 and joined to the Soviet Union in 1945. The 1930 census figures indicate that there were at that time 102,542 Jews in Ruthenia, a great number of whom escaped to Slovakia where they shared the common Jewish tragedy. Only those few who emigrated to Israel or elsewhere escaped.

The after-effects of these solutions to the problem of ethnic minorities in Czechoslovakia are evident even today. The suffering inflicted upon these peoples and the feelings of resentment that it engendered brought

[38] For the conclusive statistics challenging those of German authors, see Luža, *Transfer*, pp. 293-300.

[39] Ibid., pp. 298-300.

a tragic end to the centuries-old ethnic symbiosis that had been a feature of Central European history. The political decision to safeguard a new national state in 1945 by separating it from the turmoil and hostility of minority groups precluded any beneficial cultural integration and prevented the area from absorbing any significantly large minority in the manner of that preeminent "melting pot"—the United States.

All nations of the world can learn a lesson from the experience of the Czechoslovak Republic. Although the country was in theory committed to the principle "live and let live," it was unsuccessful in its efforts to make it practical in its national life because of the interference of outside influences that, in advocating the politics of race and nationality, disturbed the balance of equality that is essential to harmonious life in society. Although exercises of patriotism and nationalism by any individual are as valid as his natural right to belong to his nation, they become invalid in those areas where their exercise violates the rights of others. This is a lesson that could well be learned by the cultural[40] revanchists, who have poisoned the postwar atmosphere with their unfortunate propagandistic writings, and by the political[41] revanchists, who employ the old antagonistic tactics to discredit the Czechoslovak Republic before the international forum. They forget that the treatment of the minorities in Czechoslovakia between 1945 and 1948 was caused in large measure by their counterparts and carried out to wash away the guilt shared collectively by all of them. If this lesson has become a part of the heritage of Europe, then *felix culpa*.[42] Germany and her supporters have produced at least this one beneficial effect, and this tragedy has had a purpose and a meaning.

[40] Literature of this stripe is widespread indeed. Luža deals with it on pp. 301-16.

[41] Antonín Šnejdárek, "The Beginning of Sudeten German Organizations in Western Germany after 1945," *Historica*, vii (Prague, 1964), 235-52; Boris Čelovský, "The Transferred Sudeten Germans and Their Political Activity," *Journal of Central European Affairs*, xvii (July 1957), 127-49.

[42] See the *Exultet*, traditionally sung by the deacon in the liturgy of the Easter Vigil on Holy Saturday, which expounds the thought that without Christ's sacrifice on Good Friday there would have been no resurrection on Easter Sunday (*Liber Usualis Missae et Officii* [Roma-Tornaci, 1921], pp. 654-55). This thought would coincide with a retrospective on the whole problem of minorities and especially on the transfer of some of them, calling for greater sanity on the part of future potential aggressors and for more patience for all for the sake of peace and justice.

· 16 ·

POSTWAR ECONOMIC DEVELOPMENT

Jan M. Michal
State University of New York at Binghamton

In the first three postwar years Czechoslovakia's economy underwent farreaching structural and institutional changes. Great shifts in economic structure were necessary to overcome the consequences of war and the German occupation. Therefore, the following discussion will cover, first, the main economic aspects of the German occupation of the Czech lands and the resulting special problem of postwar economic reconstruction and reconversion. Since changes in economic institutions in the first postwar years were connected with the introduction of a new economic system, based partly on nationalized, partly on private enterprise, the new system will be the subject of the second part of the paper. In the last part, Czechoslovakia's economic performance from the end of World War II through 1947 will be considered, with some comments being made on subsequent trends.

OCCUPATION AND WAR
1939 TO 1945, AND THEIR ECONOMIC AFTERMATH

The dismemberment of prewar Czechoslovakia began after the Munich Agreement in September, 1938. By the turn of that year, Czechoslovakia had lost 29 percent of her territory, 33 percent of her population, and approximately 40 to 45 percent of her industrial capacity.[1] The new borders cut through the main railroads and other transport and communications facilities. This was an additional blow to the economy of the remaining Czechoslovak territory. Despite these difficulties, and despite uncertainty as to the economic and political future, the economy still continued to operate with fewer disruptions than many economists had expected.

In March, 1939, Hitler's armies marched into the Czech lands, imposing a German protectorate in Bohemia-Moravia, while a separate, German-dominated state was set up in Slovakia. The proved viability of the

---

[1] Data from Graham Hutton, *Survey after Munich* (Boston, 1939). In some industries the loss of output through the annexation of the border regions by Hitler was much heavier than is suggested by the above-mentioned average for the whole industry. Thus, Czechoslovakia lost 100 percent of the sheet glass output, 98 percent of china output, 63 percent of paper output. Ibid., p. 126.

Czechoslovak economy under difficult circumstances may have been one of the reasons why Hitler decided to assign the so-called Protectorate a special role: to supply his war machinery with heavy industrial products. Whereas most cabinet members of the new Protectorate were Czechs—to maintain some appearance of autonomy—the minister of economic affairs was a German, Walter Bertsch. The Germans also took over the nongovernmental economic organizations, such as the Federation of Industries. In addition, special offices headed by high SS officers were set up to supervise the management of war-important industries, such as the Office for Coal (Kohlenwirtschaftsstelle). A system of labor exchange offices drafted labor. Those who were not sent to work in Germany itself—practically all young people born in 1924—were drafted for work in mines and steel and armament works in the Protectorate: employment in mining increased from 93,000 workers in 1937 to 156,000 in 1944; employment in iron and steel industries (metallurgy and steel- and iron-using industries, mainly armaments) increased from 362,000 to 769,000.[2] By combining this forcible draft of labor with the death penalty for economic sabotage, and special rations of food, textiles, cigarettes, and other products, plus higher wages for workers in heavy industries, the Germans succeeded in stepping up the output of key products in the Protectorate.

In 1943 production of crude steel reached 2.7 million metric tons compared with 2.3 million in Czechoslovakia in 1937, the year of highest prewar military preparedness, and 2.3 million in 1929, the prewar peak prosperity. Output of hard bituminous coal reached 24.6 million metric tons in 1943, compared with 16.7 million in 1937 and 16.5 million in 1929.[3] On the other hand, consumer goods industries were starved of labor, capital, and raw materials, and their output dropped. Yet a major part of consumer goods was directed by the occupation authorities to the German armed forces. The resulting great shortage of goods on the domestic market, combined with a relatively moderate increase in real wages, created serious inflationary pressures. By applying strict price controls and rationing, the German authorities suppressed open price inflation but allowed a tremendous excess liquidity and demand to accumulate.

The "normal" pattern of foreign trade was disrupted as much as the "normal" pattern of output, especially after the creation of a customs union between the Protectorate and the German Reich on October 1,

[2] Vilem Brzorad, "Fuel, Power, and Producers Goods Industries," in Vratislav Bušek and Nicolas Spulber, ed., *Czechoslovakia* (New York, 1957), p. 300.

[3] Figures for 1937 and 1943 from *United Nations Statistical Yearbook 1952*, pp. 103-224. For 1929, from *Statistical Handbook of the Czechoslovak Republic* (London, n.d., probably 1940), pp. 50-51.

1940. In Slovakia, the distortion of the patterns of output and trade, and thus the problem of postwar reconversion, were somewhat less serious than in the Czech lands. On the other hand, physical war damage, and the problem of postwar reconstruction, were heavier in Slovakia.[4]

It has frequently been assumed in Western literature that in Czechoslovakia as a whole, economic losses from World War II were less severe than those in other belligerent or occupied countries. However, if one takes into account the reckless wartime depletion of natural resources, the great distortion of the pattern of output, employment, and trade, and the disruption of the monetary system, in addition to physical destruction and losses in territory and population,[5] the economic consequences of war appear to have fallen as heavily on Czechoslovakia as on Europe as a whole.[6]

This is reflected in the great gap between prewar and postwar output in Czechoslovakia. A meaningful comparison with other European countries cannot be found in the otherwise most useful *Economic Surveys of Europe*. These publications of the Economic Commission for Europe in Geneva, use 1938, for the most part, in reference to prewar output. Yet, as I have pointed out, for Czechoslovakia 1938 was anything but a "normal" year. To fathom the gap between prewar and postwar output one has to go back to 1937 as the point of departure.[7]

It would be very time-consuming to try to recompute the various index numbers for Europe on the basis of 1937 = 100 in order to compare the

[4] Whereas physical destruction in the Czech lands was limited mostly to bombing damage, for instance of the Vitkovice Steel Works, the Škoda Works in Plzeň, and the German-built synthetic gasoline works in the former Sudetenland, great parts of eastern Slovakia were devastated by land war.

[5] Because of the loss of Ruthenia to the U.S.S.R. (taking into account some very minor adjustment of other boundaries in Czechoslovakia's favor), the territory was reduced from 54,250 square miles in 1937 to 49,354 square miles in 1945, that is, by 9 percent. Ruthenia's economy was based mostly on forestry, agriculture, and salt mining, so that this loss of territory did not have much impact on industrial output. The losses in population were much more serious, as is discussed in the text.

[6] Readers interested in a more detailed assessment of the wartime economic developments are referred to an official publication of the Czechoslovak government *Státní hospodářství za války a po válce* [*The National Economy during the War and after the War*] (Prague, 1946). Socio-economic trends in the Czech lands in 1938-45 have been described by Václav Král, *Otázky hospodářského a sociálního vývoje v českých zemích v letech 1938 až 1945* [*Questions of Economic and Social Development in the Czech Provinces in 1938-1945*] (Prague, 1957). Nonclassified statistics for the Czech lands up to April, 1944, can be found in *Statistisches Jahrbuch für das Protektorat Böhmen-Mähren*, published by the Statistical Office in Prague.

[7] One single year, 1937, is, of course, far from being an entirely satisfactory base, since this was a period when several industries and exports had not yet fully recovered from the Great Depression. Industrial output was approximately 3 percent and the volume of export 26 percent below the peak prosperity levels of 1929; yet heavy industries experienced a boom because of the intensified defense effort.

Czechoslovak and European economic trends in real terms. Further-more, for many countries, and especially for Czechoslovakia, many sta-tistics for 1945 are subject to a wide margin of error; only some basic output figures can be considered to be reasonably accurate.[8]

Under the circumstances, Czechoslovakia's changing share in the Eu-ropean production of some basic commodities seems to be the least dis-torting illustration of the relative economic impact of World War II.

In Table 1 the U.S.S.R. and Germany have been excluded from the un-

TABLE 1.

CZECHOSLOVAK INDUSTRIAL OUTPUT IN PERCENT OF EUROPEAN OUTPUT

(excluding Germany and U.S.S.R.)
Selected Products

Product (units based on absolute figures)		1937	1945	1946	1947	1948
Hard coal	(tons)	4.26	3.99[a]	3.96	4.23	4.33
Electric power	(KWH)	3.69	3.37[a]	3.55	4.00	4.21
Pig iron and ferroalloys	(tons)	5.99	4.78[a]	5.11	6.02	5.50
Crude steel	(tons)	6.25	5.04[a]	5.99	6.81	6.54
Cement	(tons)	4.74	—	3.89	5.00	4.94
Cotton yarn	(tons)	6.01	—	—	5.09	5.15
Wool yarn	(tons)	4.90	—	—	5.33	5.19
Footwear[a]	(pairs)	12.69	—	9.38	12.65	14.60
Passenger automobiles[b]	(units)	2.10	—	1.44	2.40	3.58
Rayon filament yarn	(tons)	1.79	2.33[a]	1.93	2.06	2.08
Sugar[a, c]	(tons)	15.44	—	16.49	14.27	9.43

[a] Based on figures from *United Nations Statistical Yearbook, 1949-50* (New York, 1950).
[b] As percent of output of France, Italy and the United Kingdom only.
[c] Based on crop years.

Sources: Unless stated otherwise, based on production figures in *Economic Survey of Europe, 1948*, Economic Commission for Europe, Geneva, 1949.

derlying output figures for Europe, mainly because no reliable data are available for those two countries for the period immediately following the war. Furthermore, the inclusion of Germany, with her near collapse of industrial output in 1945, would distort the European trend. Czecho-slovakia's share in "European" output in Table 1 appears to be lower in 1945 than it was in 1937, even in those heavy industry products (steel, coal) that had been given top priority under the German occupation. It

[8] Until May, 1945, data for the new Czechoslovak territory had to be brought together from four sources (disregarding very minor territorial changes besides the loss of Ruthenia to the Soviet Union): the Statistical Office in Prague, covering the so-called Protectorate of Bohemia and Moravia; the Statistical Office in Bra-tislava, covering the wartime Slovak state; the German Statistical Office, covering the Czech border regions (Sudetenland); and the Hungarian Office, covering the southern Slovak regions previously lost to Hungary. Four different currency units were used on the Czechoslovak territory until May 1945. This makes it extremely difficult to compute meaningful aggregates in money terms.

is very likely that Czechoslovakia's share in the "European" output of light industry products decreased even more sharply, although no definite conclusion is possible because of a lack of figures for 1945. The fall in Czechoslovakia's share in 1945 relative to 1937 tends, of course, to contradict the widespread belief that Czechoslovak industry had the advantage of starting its postwar recovery from a level of output that was closer to the prewar output than that of most other belligerent or occupied countries. Another conclusion to be derived from Table 1 is Czechoslovakia's stagnant or falling share of output in 1946. The lag in Czechoslovak coal output (and of some other products) behind the European trend in that year was caused by several factors, among them the dismantling of some industrial complexes by the Red Army and the disinvestment (negative net investment) discussed below. Yet the main cause was the great loss of population in 1946.

Population (without Ruthenia) developed as follows:[9]

1937a	1945a	1946a	1947a	1948a
14,447,000	13,534,000	12,075,000	12,265,000	12,339,000

a End of year.

The 6.4 percent decrease in population between December, 1937, and December, 1945, was caused mainly by war casualties, deportations, and executions, which were not compensated for by the natural increase in population.

The 10.8 percent decrease from December, 1945, to December, 1946, was a result mainly of the transfer of the greatest part of Czechoslovakia's German population to Germany. The majority of the transferred population had been active in industry. After having adjusted to this loss of (mostly skilled) industrial labor, Czechoslovakia's share in the European output of industrial products (listed in Table 1) went up again in 1947, but leveled off or went down for some of these products in the upheaval of 1948.

Czechoslovakia's share in the chief European crops is given in Table 2. Again, Germany and the U.S.S.R. have been excluded from the underlying figures for Europe. This table should be interpreted with even more caution than Table 1 since it reflects, among other things, the instability of crops in various parts of Europe. In contrast to its share in the output of main industrial products, Czechoslovakia's share in main European crops in 1945, relative to its prewar output, was higher for wheat and rye but lower for barley and potatoes. In 1946 Czechoslovakia's share went down for all the crops listed, except potatoes. Again, the loss in population may have been one of the causes. Yet, a dramatic, general fall in

---

[9] *Statistická ročenka Republiky Československé 1958* [*Statistical Yearbook of the Czechoslovak Republic 1958*]. 47.

TABLE 2.

CZECHOSLOVAK MAIN CROPS IN PERCENT OF EUROPEAN OUTPUT

(excluding Germany and U.S.S.R.)

Crop	1934-38 Average	1945	1946	1947	1948
Wheat	3.96	5.52ᵃ	4.25	3.88	4.07
Rye	11.26	13.28ᵃ	12.13	10.66	10.39
Barley	9.51	7.36ᵃ	7.32	6.71	7.90
Potatoes	9.53	7.74ᵃ	11.60	5.42	6.64
Sugar beets	12.30	—	14.05	8.66	11.27

[a] Based on figures in *United Nations Statistical Yearbook 1948*.

Sources: Unless otherwise stated, based on data in *Yearbook of Food and Agricultural Statistics 1949*, Washington, D.C., 1950.

Czechoslovakia's share in European crops occurred only in 1947 when a disastrous drought reduced the yields much below the level of 1937 and even of 1945.[10] In 1948 the crops had still not recovered to the 1946 level. Here an additional factor entered the picture: the impact of the collectivization of agriculture after February, 1948.

But let us turn back to the direct consequences of war. Despite the great margin of error for 1945-46, it may be useful to provide some aggregate figures. The pertinent data are not readily available in the postwar official statistical yearbooks[11] which cover the period since 1948 only.

In the absence of reliable estimates of gross national product for the period under study, the available series of national income figures provide the most aggregative measure of national output. Table 3 provides two national income series: under the usual Western definition and under the Marxian definition. The latter excludes some final services.[12] The two

[10] According to *Hospodářské noviny* No. 18/1965, the yields (in 100 kg per hectare) developed as follows:

	1937	1945	1946	1947	1948
Wheat	17.1	12.7	15.0	10.4	16.4
Rye	16.0	11.6	14.4	13.9	15.5
Barley	17.0	11.9	13.6	11.4	15.4
Sugar beets	285.8	204.9	239.7	130.0	235.0
Potatoes	134.8	94.7	131.8	71.9	110.1

[11] From 1957 until 1962, *Statistická ročenka Republiky Československé*; after 1962, *Statistická ročenka ČSSR*. No postwar statistical yearbooks were published by the Statistical Office in Prague until 1957, except the short 1948 *Statistical Digest*.

[12] The difference between these two concepts of national income has been explained in the available literature in English, for instance by Nicolas Spulber, "National Income and Product," in V. Bušek and N. Spulber, eds., *Czechoslovakia* (New York, 1957), pp. 227ff; by Alton, Holešovský, Lazarčík, Sivák, and

433

indexes of industrial output,[13] one of gross value of agricultural output and one of the quantum and dollar value of exports and imports, are also included in Table 3. This table indicates the low starting base of reconstruction: in 1945, the quantum of exports and imports was more than nine tenths; industrial output approximately one half; animal production almost one half; and vegetable output a good third below the 1937 levels. No national income figures are available for 1945, but in 1946 real national income—under the usual Western definition—was still 17 percent below the 1937 level.

There were two main obstacles to extricating the output from the postwar lows: a disrupted transportation system and a very severe suppressed inflation. Under the strict wartime price control, *official* prices were not allowed to rise fast. At the end of the war (April, 1945) the wholesale price index stood officially at 152 on the basis of 1937 = 100, and the cost of living index, based on the income of a worker's family in Prague, at 181 (see Table 4). However, the volume of liquid assets in the economy was far in excess of the amount commensurable with the output of goods and services at official prices. Table 4 provides some figures on currency circulation, current accounts (demand deposits, which, together with currency circulation, constitute money supply under the conventional definition), and savings deposits, indicating the trends in highly liquid assets. From the end of 1937 until the end of 1944, currency circulation—in Czech koruny (K) and Slovak koruny (Ks) taken

---

Wynnyczuk in *Czechoslovak National Income and Product 1947-48 and 1955-56* (New York, 1962), pp. 72-78; and by this author in *Central Planning in Czechoslovakia* (Stanford, Calif., 1960), pp. 211-37.

Neither of the two national income series in Table 3 is a good measure of changes in real net national output. Stádník's computation of national income under the usual Western definition may tend to overrate the speed of postwar recovery by including the unduly swollen public sector. In some communications of the State Planning Office (some of which have been quoted by Spulber, *op. cit.*) attempts seem to have been made to reduce this possible upward bias by revising upward the estimates for 1937 and 1947 relative to 1948. The three variants of national income figures under Western definition compare as follows:

BILLIONS OF KORUNY (PREWAR Kč, POSTWAR Kčs) AT CURRENT FACTOR COST

According to:	1937	1946	1947	1948
UN *Statistical Yearbook 1948*, p. 371	60.0	155.4	194.4	213.1
Spulber, *op. cit.*, p. 243	58.6	155.4	194.4	213.1
"Revised series," unofficially reported	62.0	163.0	194.4	213.1

The higher estimate for 1946 in the "Revised series" has been explained by the inclusion of the income of the German population before their transfer to Germany (which allegedly is not included in Stádník's estimate that provided the basis for the other two series). No explanation has been offered for the higher 1937 figure in the "Revised series."

[13] Construction of these indices has been described in Western literature, for instance, by this author in "Problems of Measuring Industrial Output in Czechoslovakia," Miloslav Rechcigl, ed., *The Czechoslovak Contribution to World Culture* (The Hague, 1964), pp. 373 ff.

TABLE 3.

TRENDS IN CZECHOSLOVAKIA'S AGGREGATE OUTPUT AND FOREIGN TRADE, 1937-48

	1937	1945	1946	1947	1948
1. National income, Western definition, in billions of koruny, at constant 1937 prices index, 1937 = 100	62.0	—	51.6	59.1	61.1
	100	—	83	95	99
2. National income, Marxian definition, in billions of koruny, at constant 1937 prices index, 1937 = 100	56.5	—	—	51.4	59.8
	100	—	—	91	106
3. Index of industrial production, 1937 = 100					
general	100	—	—	87	102
mining	100	—	—	104	113
metals and engineering	100	—	—	97	116
chemical industry	100	—	—	102	125
textile industry	100	—	—	60	77
food industry	100	—	—	65	77
4. Index of gross value of industrial production, 1937 = 100	100	50	69	88	108
5. Index of agricultural production, average, 1934-38 = 100	—	—	84	67	78
6. Index of gross value of agricultural production, 1936 = 100	—	62	78	76	76
vegetable output	—	63	83	59	84
animal products	—	58	71	84	67
7. Index of quantum of imports, 1937 = 100	100	—	35	77	99
8. Index of quantum of exports, 1937 = 100	100	—	26	56	75
9. Index of current dollar value of imports (excluding UNRRA) 1937 = 100	100	4	54	151	198
10. Index of current dollar value of exports 1937 = 100	100	4	69	137	180

Sources:

1. "Revised series," communication of the State Planning Office (cf. fn. 12 in text), deflated by the State Planning Office as follows:

	1937	1946	1947	1948
National income deflator	100.0	315.5	329.1	348.7

This deflator is said to have been obtained from an index of wholesale prices, using the arithmetic average of 1937 and of the current weights. The deflator reflects the increase of prices in foreign trade, but obviously disregards the black market prices.

2. Same communication of the State Planning Office. It is noteworthy that in *Hospodářské noviny* No. 18/1965 the corresponding index figure for 1948 was given at only 97.

3, 5, 7, 8, 9, and 10. United Nations, *Statistical Yearbook 1949-50*, pp. 134, 99, 374, 368, respectively.

4 and 6. *Hospodářské noviny* No. 18/1965.

together—increased seven times. No figures are available to this author on the increase of demand deposits, but there are indications that it may have been as fast as the increase in currency circulation, so that the total money supply also increased roughly seven times.

On the other hand, net national product of final goods and services at current official prices at the end of the war was approximately the same

TABLE 4.

CURRENCY CIRCULATION, DEPOSITS, PRICES, AND WAGE RATES

	Dec. 1937	Dec. 1944	April 1945	Oct. 1945	Nov. 1945	Dec. 1945	Jan. 1946	Dec. 1946	Dec. 1947	Dec. 1948
1. Currency circulation (in billions of koruny, excluding holdings of the issuing authority; end of period)	8.0	55.5	——	(56)a	——	28.2	——	46.6	61.7	75.6
2. Demand deposits (current accounts) (in billions of koruny, end of period)										
National Bank	7.5b	—	——	——	——	2.2	——	10.1⎫	(54)	——
All other banks	8.3b	—	——	——	——	8.8	——	33.0⎭		——
3. Time deposits (in billions of koruny, end of period)	57.1b	—	——	——	——	——	——	14.1b	(25)	——
4. Blocked accounts (in billions of koruny, end of period)										
Current	——	—	——	——	70.1	65.8	——	71.3	(70)	——
Savings	——	—	——	——	193.2	192.0	——	163.8	(151)	——
5. Official wholesale price index, 1937 = 100, monthly average	100	—	152	159	161	207	275	310	316	335
6. Official index of cost of living in Prague, 1937 = 100, monthly average	100	—	181	192	194	230	339	341	319	325
7. Hourly wage rates in manufacturing (in koruny, monthly average)	3.45c	5.69d	5.69	6.42	6.42	10.43	10.43	10.65	10.92	10.96
8. Approximate index of "real" wage rates in manufacturing; 1937 = 100, monthly average (based on Row 7 deflated by the official cost of living index, Row 6) [Caution! This index is not a satisfactory indication of the trend in the actual purchasing power of earnings. See last part of chapter]	(100)	—	(91)	(97)	(96)	(131)	(89)	(91)	(99)	(98)

a Rough approximation by the author for September, 1945, based on the trend in increase in the circulation of notes (from 41.6 billion koruny [Czech and Slovak, assuming parity ratio] in December, 1944, to 47.5 billion in September, 1945; *United Nations Monthly Bulletin of Statistics* [July 1947], p. 96).

b Figures for 1937 from *Statistical Digest of the Czechoslovak Republic 1948* (Prague, 1948), p. 80; not fully comparable with the rest of the series.

c Yearly average, 1939. For 1937, statistics are available only for wage rates in Prague. If the movement of the rates in Prague can be considered to be characteristic for the whole country, the 1939 rate for the whole country would not be very different from the corresponding figures for 1937.

d Yearly average, 1944.

Sources:
1. *Monthly Bulletin of Statistics*, United Nations, December, 1949, p. 137.
2. *International Financial Statistics*, International Monetary Fund, January, 1948, pp. 48-49.
3. Ibid., except for 1937; see footnote b.
4. *Statistical Digest of the Czechoslovak Republic 1948*, Prague, 1948, p. 81.
5, 6. *Monthly Bulletin of Statistics, United Nations*, June, 1947, p. 126. Ibid., December, 1949, p. 170.
7. Ibid., January, 1947, p. 74; June, 1947, p. 116; August, 1949, p. 154.
8. Figures in parentheses are rough estimates by the author.

as in 1937. (In *constant* 1937 prices it was probably only 55 to 65 per-cent of the prewar output.) The great gap between the sevenfold in-crease in money supply and the practically unchanged current value (at official prices) of final output is in itself an indication of excess liquidity that, of course, tends to lead to black markets. Yet the actual scope of suppressed inflation was even greater, for savings deposits also increased very sharply. A great part of this increase was the frozen, unsatisfied, accumulated demand for goods and services that would have been quick-ly translated into effective demand if rationing and the drastic penalties for black marketing had been relaxed. Thus, a great part of the inflated volume of time deposits was also to be considered as excess liquidity (excess purchasing power) in addition to the unduly inflated money supply.

Roughly speaking, the total of liquid assets in Czech and Slovak koruny (disregarding liquid assets in Reichsmark, Hungarian pengö, and other monies) between the end of the war and the currency reform of November, 1945, may have amounted to some 300 billion koruny (in-cluding currency circulation, demand and time deposits, and some short-term bills). This was several times more than the then annual output of final goods and services at current controlled prices.

It was imperative to deal with this huge excess liquidity in order to re-place the harsh wartime coercion to work by financial incentives and to do away with almost comprehensive rationing. The government attacked the problem from three sides.

First, part of the excess liquidity was wiped out by a levy on net wealth (capital levy) and a much heavier, steeply progressive levy on the in-crease in wealth of "natural and juridical persons" between January 1, 1939, and November 15, 1945. The yield of this one-time levy on house-hold wealth alone was over 18 billion koruny. Unfortunately, no data are available to this author as to the yield of the levy on companies ("juridi-cal persons").

Second, another major part of the remaining excess liquidity was frozen by the currency reform of November, 1945. A new currency unit (Kčs) was introduced at the ratio of 1 K = 1 Ks = 1 Kčs. All holdings in K and Ks paper money had to be deposited (with the exception of 500 K or 500 Ks converted into Kčs for each member of household and and a monthly payroll converted into the new currency for firms and in-stitutions). All demand and time deposits in old currencies were then blocked. The total of blocked accounts amounted to 263 billion K and Ks (see Table 4). Transfers among the blocked accounts were allowed for a limited time to meet obligations (such as life insurance benefits and tax payments) that had originated prior to the currency reform. On the other hand, certain amounts of old currencies could be unblocked and converted into the new currency in special cases. In July, 1947, liabilities of all financial institutions from blocked accounts were transferred to a Currency Redemption Fund. The fund also received the proceeds from the sale of confiscated German property and other reparation claims. From these proceeds the fund was supposed to finance the progressive unblocking (and conversion) of accounts in old currencies.[14] However, at the time of the second currency reform in May, 1953, all blocked claims, together with the entire internal debt, were repudiated by the new communist government without publication of the final balance sheet of the Currency Redemption Fund.

Third, it was assumed that money supply (in the new currency), after payment of the capital levies and the blocking operations, would amount to approximately three times the prewar money supply. Believing tacitly in a crude kind of quantity equation of exchange, with price levels supposedly moving parallel with money supply, the authorities argued that official prices should be established at a level approximately three times higher than prewar prices. This, it was claimed, would bring the official and the black market prices closer, thus facilitating a progressive relaxation of price controls and rationing. In fact, the Price Control Office allowed wholesale and retail prices to rise rapidly in the two months following the currency reform, as is reflected in Table 4. To avoid an unfavorable impact of these price increases on Czechoslovak exports and the balance of payments, the Czechoslovak koruna was devalued on November 1, 1945, from 3.414 U.S. cents to 2.000 U.S. cents (official dollar price, mid-point, thus increasing from 29.52 to 50.00 koruny).

These operations were not fully successful in dealing with the excess liquidity. Rationing, price controls, and black markets continued to exist throughout the period under study. A failure to stabilize the monetary situation in 1946 and 1947 will be discussed in more detail in the final part of this chapter.

ECONOMIC SYSTEM

The basic features of the postwar economic system were laid down in the Košice Program of April 5, 1945—a proclamation of the political parties of the National Front, including the communists. It stated that the property of "traitors and collaborators with the Nazi occupation" would be confiscated; the entire financial and credit system, insurance companies, natural and energy resources, and key industries would be placed under the control of the state; and the economy would be planned.

[14] The currency reform of November, 1945, was based on presidential decrees No. 91/1945 and No. 95/1945 of *Sbírka zákonů*. The Currency Redemption Fund was created on the basis of law No. 141/1947 of *Sbírka zákonů*.

When the war and the German occupation were over, these principles started to be translated into law. The proposed control by the state was secured by four nationalization decrees in October, 1945, as described below. In manufacturing, nationalization went far beyond the "key" industries, but agriculture, handicrafts, domestic and foreign trade, and practically the whole service sector remained under private ownership, except for the confiscation of some firms and farms owned by Germans and "collaborators."[15] After the nationalization had been completed, one half of national income still originated in privately-owned enterprises.[16] Although the share of the combined government and nationalized sectors in national output was almost twice as large as, for instance, that in France or Austria or Britain at that time, Czechoslovakia's economy still was not a typically socialist economy in comparison with the post-February 1948 situation under the communist government, when the socialist sector embraced more than nine tenths of national output.[17]

The scope of nationalization in mining, production of energy, and manufacturing (except food industry) was determined by the Decree of the President of the Republic No. 100/1945 of the Collection of Laws and Ordinances (*Sbírka zákonů a nařízení*). Mining, energy, metallurgy, metal rolling, armament, cement, cellulose, and gramophone record industries were completely nationalized. In these sectors no private enterprise was to be allowed in the future. Firms in other industrial sectors were nationalized only if their employment exceeded a certain limit, varying from 500 employees in metal working, electrical appliances, optics, cotton spinning, and some other industries, down to 150 employees in china, ceramics, and timber industries.[18] The critical employment level was determined largely on the 1938-40 average, but in industries that were expanding during the war (steel, for instance), on the 1942-44 average. In some sectors private enterprise was to be allowed even if the firms concerned were to exceed the above-mentioned employment limits in the future.

The owners of nationalized firms, except Germans, Hungarians, and

[15] According to Bušek and Spulber, *Czechoslovakia*, p. 435, 513 trading companies and 2,475 industrial firms were already nationalized in September, 1945. Expropriation in agriculture and forestry will be described later.

[16] According to Spulber, the share of the "socialist sector" (i.e. government-run enterprises plus nationalized enterprises) in national income before February 1948 was 50.3 percent. *Op. cit.*, p. 234.

[17] In 1965, national income (Marxist definition) originating in the socialist sector amounted to 171 billion Kčs; income originating in nonsocialist sectors (including the private plots of members of unified agricultural cooperatives) to 7 billion Kčs, at constant prices of April 1960 (*Statistická ročenka ČSSR 1966*, p. 126).

[18] Productive capacity rather than employment was used as criterion for nationalization in some industries, e.g. glass.

collaborators with the occupants, were to receive compensation through a special "Fund of Nationalized Property."[19] The fund had the right to disburse its obligations in special securities, with interest and amortization service financed from the profits of nationalized enterprises. A clear distinction was made between government-owned and government-run enterprise (for instance, railroads, post offices, and the tobacco monopoly) and the new "national corporations." The latter were supposed to stand on their own feet financially, applying commercial principles and paying taxes. Although the Czechoslovak state became the legal owner of nationalized enterprises, it did not assume their liabilities. On the other hand, the nationalization decrees stated, in rather vague terms, that "surpluses of national corporations would be transferred to the State."

The scope of nationalization in food industries was determined by presidential decree No. 101/1945. The output of sugar (except cooperative sugar factories) and of alcohol was completely nationalized. Breweries were subject to nationalization if their output in 1937 exceeded 150,000 hectolitres; flour mills if their daily capacity exceeded 60 tons of grain; margarine factories if they employed more than 150 workers; and chocolate and candy factories if they employed more than 500 employees between 1938 and 1940. The basic organization of national corporations was similar to that in other industries, but they came within the jurisdiction of the minister of food supplies rather than of the minister of industry.

The national corporations were managed by 17 general directorates (trust-like organizations) and 12 regional directorates. It would go beyond the scope of this study to discuss the organization of management at the directorate level and of individual national corporations. It should be mentioned, however, that several aspects of the 1945 nationalization violated generally accepted principles of efficiency in economic theory. For instance, national corporations had to buy their inputs and sell their outputs through operating markets in which they were supposed to compete with the private sector, with imported goods, and with one another. Thus, a "workable" amount of competition was supposed to continue to exist in the national economy; but competition from imports was extremely limited in view of severe quantitative restrictions on imports and exchange controls, and competition from the remaining private firms was often illusory.

[19] Compensation claims against the fund were later repudiated by the communist government, except for the claims of some foreign nationals. By 1956 compensation agreements for nationalized property had been negotiated with the United Kingdom, France, Belgium, Luxembourg, Switzerland, the Netherlands, and Sweden, totaling 85 million U.S. dollars. Bušek and Spulber, *op. cit.*, pp. 363-64.

In terms of employment weights, the percentage of nationalization varied between 50 and 100 percent in producer goods industries and between 3 and 50 percent in consumer goods industries.[20] Thus, supplies of many products from private enterprises were relatively unimportant, and competition among sellers was practically limited to competition among national corporations. Yet, the directorates of national corporations could easily become vehicles for monopolistic collusion. As long as centralized price control was in force, this monopolistic power could not readily result in price increases, but it had some other unfavorable consequences. For instance, some nationalized industries tended to be negligent in quality control, in meeting the dates of delivery, and in other essential business practices. Another feature conflicting with efficiency principles was the choice of criteria for nationalizing certain industries and enterprises: employment limits were often unrelated to the degree of competition, to the economies to scale to be realized, and to the ability of the industries concerned to raise the capital necessary for reconstruction and modernization. Furthermore, nationalization decrees often were stretched in a legally dubious manner to cover as many enterprises as possible. This, combined with political pressures, created fears of further nationalization among the remaining private entrepreneurs, thus limiting the growth of the most efficient firms with the greatest potential of expansion.

Incorporated banks (joint-stock banks) were nationalized by presidential decree No. 102/1945, and privately-owned insurance companies by decree No. 103/1945. In view of the previous control by the central bank, and of the previous cartelization of the financial institutions, nationalization did not change the existing market structure in these sectors as dramatically as it did in industry.

A significant expropriation, but no large-scale nationalization or collectivization, took place in agriculture. In 1945, 1.8 million hectares of agricultural land, mostly of German ownership, was confiscated. About two-thirds of this land was subdivided into small lots and allocated to small landowners or to settlers in the border regions. The settlers usually received ownership rights to parcels of up to 13 hectares (24.7 acres) from Julius Ďuriš, the communist minister of agriculture. This, however, did not prevent the communist government from forcibly collectivizing this land in the post-1948 period. Further expropriation took place under the provisions of a 1947 law revising the land reform that had been undertaken shortly after World War I. Private holdings of agricultural land were limited to 50 hectares. Part of the 1947 expropriations (of almost 1 million hectares, including, however, forests) was allocated to

[20] Spulber, *op. cit.*, p. 220.

441

small farmers and farm workers; another part was managed by "national administrators," with the ownership remaining undecided. After all of these measures had been carried out between 1945 and 1947, holdings of less than 5 hectares (14.7 acres) comprised more than half of agricultural land. The size of an average farm was no doubt much below the economic optimum. In contrast to agricultural land, most of the forests confiscated in 1945 (approximately 1.2 million hectares) were allocated to the State Forest Administration—an institution that was already in existence in Czechoslovakia between the two World Wars.[21]

Since all national corporations were supposed to operate through the market, their existence did not in itself make it necessary to introduce widespread direct central planning. The principle of planning was advocated on other grounds:

1. It was argued that (relatively free) markets alone could not take care of the great structural changes that were necessary during the reconstruction period. A similar argument led to the establishment of central planning institutions in several other European countries, for instance France and the Netherlands.

2. In view of her heavy dependence on foreign trade, Czechoslovakia was hit extremely hard by the Great Depression of the 1930's. The number of officially registered unemployed jumped from 41,000 in 1929 to 920,000 in February, 1933,[22] and the rate of unemployment among wage and salary earners topped 25 percent. The painful memory of this near collapse of moderately regulated private enterprise economy, combined with, in 1945, a still understandable lack of confidence in the stabilizing effect of fiscal and monetary policies on Keynesian lines, led many Czechoslovaks to believe that a planned economy is a good alternative to a heavy reliance on the allocational role of domestic and foreign markets.

3. Most socialists thought it a good idea to supplement, but not to eliminate, the allocational role of the profit motive with output plans for the sake of a more equable distribution of income.

4. In all probability the Communist party considered the mostly noncoercive and indirect planning of the first postwar years to be a springboard for further socialization and more comprehensive, direct planning.

[21] Figures in this paragraph are from Ernest Koenig, "Agriculture," in Bušek and Spulber, ed., *op. cit.*, pp. 247-51.

[22] *Statistická příručka Československé Republiky—Statistical Handbook of the Czechoslovak Republic* (London, n.d., published by the Czechoslovak Ministry of Foreign Affairs in exile, probably in 1940), pp. 134-35.

Systematic planning became operative on January 1, 1947, under the Two-Year Economic Plan Act of October 25, 1946, No. 192/1946 of the Collection of Laws and Ordinances, but central planning agencies had already been set up in 1945: the Economic Council in August, the State Planning Office in November. The former was supposed to draft broad economic programs; the latter, with its Slovak branch, the State Planning and Statistical Office in Bratislava, to work out more detailed economic plans. Furthermore, various ministries, the National Bank, the State Price Control Office, offices for the protection of labor, economic groups of the Federation of Industries, and other corporate organizations inherited from the Germans and from the prewar republic performed various planning tasks. The State Statistical Office was entrusted, together with the State Planning Office, with the statistical control of the plan's implementation.

To understand the nature of economic planning in Czechoslovakia from 1945 through 1947, it is necessary to distinguish clearly between the initial setting up of the plans and their implementation.

The former had one aspect in common with Soviet planning: a number of output targets were set up in physical units and their mutual consistency was supposed to be secured through material balances. However, the problem of consistency between the planned supplies and the planned uses was much easier than in the U.S.S.R. The Two-Year Plan in Czechoslovakia for 1947 and 1948 contained only 142 basic targets, compared with several thousand compulsory targets in the U.S.S.R. Prior to the introduction of direct central planning in Czechoslovakia in 1948, a more detailed specification of outputs was left to the interplay of market forces and to contracts between enterprises.

The main objectives of the Two-Year Plan were to surpass, by the end of 1948, the 1937 level of industrial output (net) by one tenth; to reach the 1937 level of agricultural output and transportation; to speed up the construction of housing and industrial plants; and to reduce the gap between the lesser developed regions in Slovakia and southern Bohemia on the one hand and the economically more developed remainder of the country on the other. The plan contained investment ceilings in rather aggregative terms. Total fixed investment for the two-year period was not to exceed 69.9 billion koruny, of which 10.2 billion were earmarked for public (government-run) construction (railroads, waterworks, and the like) and 57.7 billion for national corporations and private enterprises taken together. The latter figure was subdivided by main economic sectors (industry and handicrafts, 25.4 billion koruny; agriculture, 5.2 billion; transportation, 15 billion; housing, 14 billion). Total investment maximum was also subdivided by major regions (Slovakia was supposed to use not more than 22.1 billion koruny for the new fixed investment). Investments not provided for under the plan were not supposed to be carried out unless they used only locally available materials and man-power, without detracting from the inputs reserved for the planned investment projects. It is noteworthy that the law concerning the Two-Year Plan referred to investment targets in terms of maximum cost, probably to safeguard a certain level of consumption. However, the plan did not state explicitly the price base underlying the investment maxima, nor did it contain any suggestions as to the sources for financing the investment (such as private, corporate, and public domestic saving, possibly also capital imports).

Finally, the plan foresaw an increase in employment by 270,000 workers in industry, 90,000 in construction, and 230,000 in agriculture and forestry.[23]

The above-mentioned features of the Two-Year Plan show some similarity to the macroeconomic planning of the French or the Yugoslavs. However, such planning was rather crude in Czechoslovakia. No attempt was made to apply a closed system of national accounts when computing the aggregate targets.

The implementation of the plan was also somewhat similar to the French "indicative" system of planning. The managers of both national corporations and private enterprises had a great deal of freedom in choosing their pattern of output. There were no bonuses for fulfilling the "basic targets." The managers were to a large extent responsive to the profit motive (within the constraint of controlled prices). They were, however, restricted in their choice of material inputs by the continued rationing of some basic materials. On the other hand, they had much leeway in combining the primary factors: labor and capital. Labor was hired in the open market, but again at controlled wage rates. The wartime draft of labor was essentially abolished. The greatest part of capital funds—in contrast to the central planning under the communist government after February, 1948—was not provided through the government budget but came from the internal sources of the enterprises and from bank loans. Needless to say, rates of interest were controlled by the central bank.

The law concerning the Two-Year Plan stated explicitly that government enterprises, national corporations, and private enterprises would be given equal opportunities in their operation. This was not quite so in practice. Some public enterprises and some national corporations were

---

[23] Figures on the Two-Year Plan are from law No. 192/1946 of the *Sbírka zákonů* and from a chapter, "The Two-Year-Plan," by Jaroslav Krejčí in *Statistical Digest of the Czechoslovak Republic 1948*, pp. 81-92.

directly or indirectly subsidized by the government. Yet, by and large, until February, 1948, the Czechoslovak postwar economic system can be legitimately described as a combination of public, nationalized, and private enterprise, operating in the framework of mostly noncoercive planning through regulated markets.

Economic Performance

How did this hybrid economic system perform? There are, of course, many criteria of economic performance. We shall discuss very briefly only the following:

Growth in national output and in civilian consumption
Stability of employment and prices
Productivity, allocational efficiency, and plan fulfillment
Efficiency in foreign trade and external balance
Distribution of income and wealth

Growth in Output and Consumption

The period under study is too short and too exposed to extraordinary influences to allow a meaningful evaluation of the growth performance of the first postwar "mixed" system. Furthermore, the available sources of data on the actual growth in national income that will be used to measure national output in the absence of available estimates of the gross national product provide conflicting figures. National income, computed by the Economic Commission of Europe (ECE) in terms of constant 1938 dollar prices, showed up to 1947 a relatively slower increase, but in 1947-48 a much faster increase than indicated by the official estimates in constant 1937 koruny (quoted in Table 3, line 1). The differences between these two series seem to be too large to be explained by the different price base. A relatively minor part of the difference in trend over 1937-47 is probably due to the ECE's failure to deduct from the 1937 national income the share of Ruthenia (approximately 2.5 percent) to make it comparable with the postwar figures. This omission, however, does not help to explain the great divergence in the 1947-48 growth in the "real" national income according to official and ECE estimates.

For the sake of record it may be useful to reproduce here the conflicting series, as well as another Western recomputation by Alton *et al.*, which, however, has not been deflated to a constant price base.

The ECE series, in terms of *constant* prices, shows a greater percentage increase from 1947 to 1948 than the other two series show in terms of current prices, although a substantial part of the rise in money terms

445

	Czechoslovakia's National Income, at factor cost, Western definition		
	1937	*1947*	*1948*
1. Official computation, *current* prices (billions of koruny)	62.0	194.4	213.1
index 1947 = 100	31.9	100	109.6
2. Alton *et al.*, *current* prices (billions of koruny)[24]	——	196.8	231.6
index 1947 = 100	——	100	117.6
3. Official computation, *constant* 1937 prices (billions of koruny)	62.0	59.1	61.9
index 1947 = 100	104.9	100	104.7
4. ECE computation, *constant* 1938 prices (billions of U.S. dollars)[25]	2.69	2.01	2.40
index 1947 = 100	133.8	100	119.4

was due merely to inflation.[26] Thus, one is inclined to believe that the ECE series overrates the 1947-48 growth.

All these computations of *total* national income disregard, of course, the great loss of population, especially in 1945 and 1946. Therefore, the growth in per capita income at constant prices is a somewhat better— though by far not a perfect—indication of the growth performance. The pertinent figures can be found in Table 5. While *total* real national income reached, roughly, the prewar level in 1948, on a per capita basis the prewar level was clearly surpassed in 1947. Table 5 also shows the faster increase of Czechoslovak per capita income relative to the European average. It may be of interest to give here ECE figures on per capita incomes in selected European countries in 1947 (in 1938 dollars): Switzerland, 451 (highest in Europe); United Kingdom, 363; France, 207; Czechoslovakia, 165; Poland, 114; Austria, 96; Italy, 70; Bulgaria, 51.

What is important is not only the rate of growth in national income

[24] Thad Paul Alton, Václav Holešovský, Gregor Lazarčík, Paul D. Sivák, and Alexej Wynnyczuk, *Czechoslovak National Income and Product 1947-1948 and 1955-1956*, p. 73.

[25] *Economic Survey of Europe in 1948* (Economic Commission for Europe, Geneva, 1949), p. 235. Although the ECE published the underlying figures at current prices in national currencies for a number of countries, it published only the already converted and deflated dollar figures for Czechoslovakia.

[26] As the official figures imply, out of the 9.6 percent increase in national income over 1947-48, 4.9 percent was due to price increases. If a similar deflater were applied to Alton's figures: out of the 17.6 percent increase, 7 percent was price increase and approximately 10 percent an increase in real terms, compared with the 18 percent "real" increase claimed by ECE figures.

TABLE 5.

Some Indicators of Economic Performance (in European Comparison), 1937-48

	1937	1946	1947	1948	Increase in percent		
					1947 over 1946	1948 over 1947	1948 over 1937
1. Per capita national income (at factor cost)							
A. Czechoslovakia, in constant 1937 koruny	4,297	3,995	4,869	4,953	12.1	1.0	15.3
B. Czechoslovakia, in constant 1938 dollars	176	(144)	165	195	(11.5)	18.1	11.1
C. Europe, excluding USSR and Germany, in constant 1938 dollars	181[a]	(159)	169	186	(6.3)	10.0	10.2[a]
2. Per capita personal consumption (at factor cost)							
A. Czechoslovakia, in constant 1937 koruny	3,853	3,770[b]	4,410[b]	4,270[b]	17.0	−3.2	10.8
B. Czechoslovakia, in constant 1938 dollars	141	——	132	(146)	——	10.6	10.4
C. France, in constant 1938 dollars	198[a]	——	166	182	——	9.6	−8.1
D. Italy, in constant 1938 dollars	84[a]	——	86	84	——	−3.3	0.0
3. Output per man-year in industry, index							
A. Czechoslovakia, 1937 = 100	100	(78)	89	99	(14.1)	11.2	−1
B. Europe, excluding USSR, Germany, and some countries with low industrial production, 1938 = 100	—	86[a]	90[a]	97[a]	4.7	10.8	−3[a]
4. Terms of Trade, index							
A. Czechoslovakia	100	172	124	120	−28	−3	20
B. Norway	100	101	99	98	−2	−1	−2
C. Switzerland	100	108	107	101	−1	−6	1
D. United Kingdom	100	101	95	94	−6	−1	−6

[a] 1938, or increase over 1938, or based on 1938 = 100, whichever is applicable.

[b] In addition to personal (individual) consumption, one should allow for the rapidly increasing "collective" consumption (free social services). Figures in parentheses are approximations by the author.

Sources:

1A; 2A: Previously mentioned unpublished study by the State Planning Office in Prague.

1B; 1C: Economic Survey of Europe in 1948, p. 235.

2B; 2C; 2D: Computed on the basis of the Economic Survey of Europe in 1948, pp. 45, 235.

3A; 3B: Economic Survey of Europe in 1948, p. 7.

4A; 4B; 4C; 4D: Obtained by dividing unit value of export index by unit value of import index, United Nations Statistical Yearbook 1949-50, pp. 378-79.

but also its sources. It is well known that in the 1950's a relatively fast rate of growth was engineered mainly by unusually high inputs of labor and capital; that is, by mobilizing labor and by enforcing a very high rate of saving and investment at the expense of current consumption. This was not so in 1946-47. On the contrary, personal consumption, as shown in Table 5, increased in 1946-47 substantially faster than national income (for 1947-48 there is again a conflict between ECE and official figures on the intertemporal change in personal consumption). At the same time, government consumption also increased faster than national income.

The faster increase in total current consumption relative to national income and product came mainly from three sources:

1. Czechoslovakia received large United Nations Relief and Rehabilitation Administration (UNRRA) supplies (8.0 billion koruny from July, 1945, to June, 1946, 6.4 billion from July, 1946, to June, 1947, and 1.5 billion from July, 1947, to June, 1948, in terms of current prices). These deliveries are not included in regular Czechoslovak import statistics.[27]

2. Imports exceeded exports in 1947 and 1948. The current account in the balance of payments showed a net deficit of 3.3 billion koruny in 1947 and of 2.2 billion in 1948.

3. Gross investment was probably so low that it did not cover the depreciation of capital stock with the resulting use of some assets in 1946. The figures on net investment in the unpublished material of the State Planning Office are conflicting; but at least one of the studies claims that in 1946 there was a net disinvestment of 5.6 billion koruny (at current factor cost). *Economic Survey of Europe in 1948*, p. 45, also indicates that in 1946 net investment was negative (disinvestment amounted to 10 percent of the Czechoslovak national income). According to the same source, the net investment rate in 1947 was zero, and in 1948, only 3 percent of national income.

The negative net investment rate in 1946, and the low rate in 1947-48 obviously tended to undermine the future growth potential. However, one has to bear in mind that the capital-labor ratio did not decrease, since population decreased faster than capital stock. Nevertheless, a shrinking or a stagnating stock of fixed capital made it difficult to apply modern technology and to change the economic structure. One of the planned structural changes was, as previously mentioned, industrialization of Slovakia. Slovakia's national income developed as follows:[28]

	Billions of Koruny at current factor cost	Share in Czechoslovakia's national income (percent)
1946	32.3	19.8
1947	37.7	19.4
1948	43.5	20.4

[27] Cited from the previously mentioned, unpublished national income study by the State Planning Office.

[28] Ibid.

Slovakia's share was thus higher than in prewar times (when it was, according to Mrs. Pryor's contribution to this volume, approximately 18 percent). Although I have no figures concerning net investment in Slovakia, I would venture to conjecture that it was positive, and that the 1946 disinvestment was concentrated in the border regions of the Czech lands (Sudetenland).

Finally, a few words about the composition of national income by sectors of origin. Unfortunately, I do not know of any study based on constant prices or constant factor cost. The State Planning Office computed (in 1949) the sectoral shares based on *current* factor cost as follows:[29]

	Percent of National Income			
	1937	*1946*	*1947*	*1948*
Agriculture and forestry	20.5	21.3	18.3	17.6
Industry and handicrafts	36.7	38.8	40.8	42.3
Construction	4.8	3.2	4.8	5.2
Transport	7.3	8.4	8.1	7.8
Trade, banking, and other services, except government and housing	15.4	13.3	12.1	11.8
Central, regional, and local government	11.6	11.9	12.9	12.5
Housing	3.7	3.1	3.0	2.8

These shares reflect not only changes in the real composition of national net output but also changes in relative prices. Their significance is therefore limited. Nevertheless, I am reproducing these figures here for the benefit of future researchers who would care to compute sectoral deflators.

Stability of Employment and Prices

Again, the period under study is too short, and the available statistical information too scanty, to make a definite conclusion as to the stability of the postwar mixed system.

Total employment of wage and salary earners developed as follows:[30]

	Wage- and Salary-Earners			
	1945	*1946*		*1947*
	December	*June*	*December*	*June*
Nongovernment employment (including nationalized industries)	2,759,000	2,837,000	2,578,000	2,731,000
Government (including post office, railroads, and local authorities)	505,000	652,000	612,000	616,000
Total	3,264,000	3,399,000	3,191,000	3,348,000

[29] Ibid. Percentages are based on the following totals of national income in billions of koruny at current factor cost: 1937, 62.0; 1946, 163.0; 1947, 194.4; 1948, 213.1.

[30] *Statistical Digest of the Czechoslovak Republic 1948*, p. 37. Unfortunately, the pertinent figures are available only until June 1947.

449

According to most indications, voluntary unemployment was very low, and most of it was seasonal, in winter.

The employment figures cited above are based on the number of persons enrolled under the compulsory health insurance and other public insurance, and do not include independent farmers, other entrepreneurs, and their helping family members. The total of all economically active persons was much higher. The exact figure is difficult to come by, because statistical treatment of the 1947 census was not completed for Moravia when the 1948 Statistical Digest was published.[31]

Despite the lacunae in available statistics it is fairly safe to state that, on the whole, full employment prevailed during the period under study. However, there was a noticeable shift from nongovernment to government employment, and there was a shortage of labor in some branches of production.

Movement in officially controlled prices is reflected by the indexes in Table 4, lines 5 and 6. Compared with prices in most other countries on the continent of Europe, officially controlled prices in Czechoslovakia in 1946-47 were fairly stable.[32] Black market prices were still approximately two times higher than official prices, but they tended to fall, until the political turmoil set in in the winter of 1947-48.

On the whole, the stability record of the mixed system in Czechoslovakia was no worse, if not better, than the record of most other European countries at that time.

Productivity, Allocational Efficiency, and Plan Fulfillment

Index of productivity of labor in industry (measured somewhat inaccurately by output per man-year) is given in Table 5. As the table indicates, this index increased in a fairly parallel way with the European average. No reliable estimates are available concerning the overall productivity of labor and of fixed capital. Since total net output increased, while the stock of capital remained practically the same, in 1947-48, one could conjecture that productivity of capital tended to increase. However, one would have to allow for changes in unused productive capacity and in other variables to come to a valid conclusion. This would go beyond the scope of this study.

Allocational efficiency eludes statistical measurement. Under pure and perfect competition, when no firm has the monopolistic power to increase the price of products or the monopolistic power to depress the price of inputs, and under a given socially acceptable distribution of income, higher rate of profits would tend to indicate allocational efficiency. Pure and perfect competition has, of course, never existed in any country, and certainly not in Czechoslovakia during the period under study.

---

[31] Cf. ibid., pp. 20-21.
[32] Cf. *Economic Survey of Europe in 1948*, Chapter 2.

Nevertheless, since all sectors faced mostly the same state-controlled prices, typical monopolistic profits were limited and profitability tended to indicate, by and large, relative efficiency. The following computation by the State Planning Office[33] of the national income by ownership classes may be of interest in this connection.

Billions of Koruny, at Current Factor Cost

	1947			1948		
	Wages and salaries	"Profits"	Total income (excluding rent)	Wages and salaries	"Profits"	Total income (excluding rent)
"Socialist sector" (including government and nationalized enterprises)	92.8	8.7	101.5	113.5	11.6	125.1
Small independent farmers, craftsmen, and professionals not employing salaried labor	1.0	28.9	29.9	1.0	30.6	31.6
"Capitalist sector" (private enterprise employing salaried labor)	38.2	18.9	57.1	31.7	18.7	50.4
Total	132.0	56.5	188.5	146.2	60.9	207.1
Rent (for all sectors)			5.9			6.0
Total national income			194.4			213.1

Unfortunately, this computation suffers from many analytical weaknesses. First of all, the "socialist sector" includes also administration proper, where profits were zero, and public utilities such as railroads, where profits were intentionally low, or negative. This lowers unduly the relative "profitability" ("profits" as percent of income originating) in the socialist sector. Another serious weakness of this computation is that "profits" include explicit and implicit interest on capital, implicit rent (explicit rent has been given on the last line for all sectors together), and implicit return on the labor of self-employed persons. The implicit returns on factors were, of course, much more important in the nonsocialist sectors, so that the relative profitability of these sectors, as reflected by the above table, is inflated. Despite all of these and other problems of comparison on the basis of available statistics, profitability of socialist enterprises in 1947-48 seems to have been relatively lower, and stagnating, whereas profitability of the "capitalist" sectors seems to have been relatively higher, and increasing.[34] This can be taken as an indication that the private business sector operated more efficiently than

[33] Previously cited unpublished computations of the State Planning Office.

[34] After deducting income originating in central and local governments (23.2 billion Kčs in 1947, 24.7 billion in 1948) from total income originating in the "socialist sector," "profits" (including interest on capital) amounted in 1947 to 11.1 percent, and in 1948 to 11.5 percent of the remaining nongovernmental income originating in the socialist sector. On the other hand, "profits" in the capitalist sector (including interest on capital, implicit rents, and implicit rewards for the owners' labor) amounted in 1947 to approximately 33 percent and in 1948 to approximately 37 percent of the income originating in that sector.

the nationalized industries. Minister of Industry Bohumil Laušman, a Social Democrat who was one of the engineers of the first postwar nationalization in Czechoslovakia, himself admitted it in a published study.[35]

To assess the efficiency of the whole system, one would have to inquire into the reasons for the lagging profitability and efficiency of the nationalized industries. One reason may have been a difficulty of transition. Another, probably more important, reason was the method of appointing directors of nationalized industries and managers of nationalized enterprises. Some were selected by political bargaining among the four political parties of the "National Front" rather than on the basis of qualification and performance. In carrying out their duties, they often had to observe political expediency rather than the requirements of economic efficiency.

Nevertheless, the economy as a whole avoided such massive misallocations and inefficiencies as occurred later under comprehensive direct central planning. Competition between the sectors and from imports, though rather limited, still put some pressure on both nationalized and private enterprises to minimize cost, or at least to avoid a sharp increase in cost. The profit motive, which was definitely present in the nonsocialist sector and was not quite absent in the socialist sector, induced the enterprises to adjust the pattern of output to the pattern of demand. Unlike effects that arose in the 1950's and 1960's, there was no tendency toward large unsalable inventories of some products and chronic shortages of many others. The mixed system operated, over the period under study, without shocking disproportions in the pattern of output.

The limited space of this article does not allow an adequate inquiry into another important question: the effectiveness of the Two-Year Plan and its contribution to the avoiding of imbalances in output. Table 6 provides figures on the fulfillment of selected targets in 1947. Items that fell short of the target were housing, some sectors of transport, and the output of farm products, hit hard by drought. The percentage of plan fulfillment for most other targets varied from 90 to 110. If one allows for the hasty computation of the plan without adequate statistical information and experience, indirect planning appears to have been moderately successful in reconciling the preferences of the planners with those of the producers in the nationalized and private sectors, as well as with the preferences of private consumers, although consumer sovereignty was already curtailed by price controls and rationing.

Efficiency in Foreign Trade and External Balance

In contrast to domestic output, foreign trade over the period under study was almost entirely based on private enterprise. There were, of course, extensive foreign exchange controls, and imports and exports were sub-

[35] Bohumil Laušman, *Řeknu pravdu* [*I Shall Tell the Truth*] (Prague, 1947).

TABLE 6.

FULFILLMENT OF THE PLAN, 1947 (SELECTED TARGETS ONLY)

		Output		Rounded Percent of Plan Fulfillment
		Planned	*Actual*	
Mining and Energy				
Hard coal	(million tons)	16.4	16.2	99
Brown coal	(million tons)	21.8	22.4	103
Coke	(million tons)	3.9	4.1	106
Iron ore	(million tons)	1.5	1.4	91
Electricity	(million kwh)	6.8	6.7	99
Gas	(million cubic meters)	359.5	370.5	103
Manufacturing				
Pig iron	(million tons)	1.3	1.4	106
Crude steel	(million tons)	2.2	2.3	104
Rolled steel products	(million tons)	1.5	1.6	108
Railroad freight cars		12,524	13,777	110
Locomotive engines		230	234	102
Passenger cars		11,500	9,372	82
Motorcycles	(1,000 units)	50	40	79
Wireless sets	(1,000 units)	136	163	120
Copper and its alloys	(tons)	5,494	5,954	108
Lead and its alloys	(tons)	8,220	8,227	100
Aluminum alloys	(tons)	2,850	1,979	69
Ball and roller bearings	(1,000 units)	829	1,034	125
Phosphate fertilizers	(1,000 tons)	380	344	90
Nitrate fertilizers	(1,000 tons)	129	132	103
Sulphuric acid	(1,000 tons)	93	90	96
Soda	(1,000 tons)	15	14	94
Ammonia	(1,000 tons)	24	26	109
Plate glass	(1,000 tons)	133	126	95
Bricks	(million units)	637	698	110
Cement	(1,000 tons)	145	84	58
Cellulose	(million q)	2.0	2.4	115
Sawn timber	(million m³)	2.8	3.0	107
Cotton yarn	(1,000 tons)	53.0	59.0	112
Worsted yarn	(1,000 tons)	4.8	6.7	140
Dairy butter	(1,000 q)	305	191	63
Malt	(million q)	1.8	.8	44
Beer (sales)	(million hl.)	8.0	8.9	111
Building and Construction				
Housing (total dwelling units)		61,056	28,744	47.1
New housing (dwelling units)		30,132	13,481	44.7
Reconstruction (dwelling units)		30,924	15,263	49.4

TABLE 6. (*cont.*)

FULFILLMENT OF THE PLAN, 1947 (SELECTED TARGETS ONLY)

		Output		Rounded Percent of Plan Fulfillment
		Planned	Actual	
Agriculture (Area in 1,000 hectares)				
Wheat		830	813	98
Rye		799	718	90
Barley		634	563	89
Potatoes		651	601	92
Sugar beet		186	182	98
Fodder plant		2,377	1,910	80
Crops				
Wheat	(million tons)	1.5	.8	56
Rye	(million tons)	1.3	.9	72
Barley	(million tons)	1.0	.6	63
Potatoes	(million tons)	9.1	4.4	48
Sugar beet	(million tons)	4.8	2.5	53
Fodder plants	(million tons)	10.4	3.3	32
Livestock				
Beef cattle	(million units)	4.1	3.7	92
Swine	(million units)	3.4	2.8	84
Milk	(million hl.)	25.6	18.1	71
Transportation				
Railroad				
in gross ton-kilometres (billion)		2.3	2.5	111
in net ton-kilometres (billion)		9.0	12.5	139
number of persons carried (million)		—	316	132
Road motor traffic				
quantity of goods transported (million tons)		22	17	78
persons carried (million)		102	173	169
River traffic				
quantity of goods transported (million tons)		—	.9	32
Air traffic				
persons carried	(1,000)	233	136	61
kilometres flown	(million)	6.0	4.9	83

ject to licensing by the Ministry of Foreign Trade within existing trade agreements. These controls were mostly negative in nature, preventing certain deals. Positive decisions to export or to import were left largely to private initiative. Foreign trade was characterized by a rapid increase, as has been indicated in Table 3, and by a great flexibility in adjusting exports and imports to the new situation in Europe and in the world. This is reflected by rapid changes in the geographic pattern of exports and imports, as given in Table 7. Trade shifted from Germany, the most

TABLE 7.
CZECHOSLOVAK FOREIGN TRADE

A. Special Imports (excluding UNNRA), in millions of koruny (Figures in parentheses denote percentage shares of the 10 most important supplying countries)

	1937	1945 (May–December)	1946	1947	1948
Total	10,980 (100.0)	604 (100.0)	10,239 (100.0)	28,633 (100.0)	37,716 (100.0)
	Germany 1,903 (17.3)	U.S.S.R. 198 (32.8)	Switzerland 1,087 (10.6)	United Kingdom 3,358 (11.7)	U.S.S.R. 5,888 (15.6)
	United States 962 (8.8)	Switzerland 135 (22.4)	U.S.S.R. 979 (9.6)	United States 2,916 (10.2)	United Kingdom 3,816 (10.1)
	United Kingdom 695 (6.3)	Hungary 106 (17.5)	Sweden 914 (8.9)	Switzerland 2,217 (7.7)	Yugoslavia 2,394 (6.3)
	France 685 (6.2)	Austria 45 (7.5)	United Kingdom 909 (8.9)	Sweden 2,001 (7.0)	Netherlands 2,035 (5.4)
	Netherlands 628 (5.7)	Germany 44 (7.4)	United States 852 (8.3)	U.S.S.R. 1,777 (6.2)	Poland 2,024 (5.4)
	Rumania 532 (4.8)	Sweden 30 (5.0)	Yugoslavia 652 (6.4)	Netherlands 1,664 (5.8)	Sweden 1,996 (5.3)
	Austria 457 (4.2)	Yugoslavia 11 (1.8)	Hungary 587 (5.7)	Yugoslavia 1,355 (4.7)	United States 1,820 (4.8)
	Sweden 418 (3.8)	Rumania 4 (0.7)	Netherlands 493 (4.8)	Belgium 1,328 (4.6)	Switzerland 1,784 (4.7)
	Yugoslavia 411 (3.7)	United States 0.1 (0.0)	Germany 415 (4.1)	Italy 1,152 (4.0)	Rumania 1,471 (3.9)
	Switzerland 360 (3.3)	United Kingdom 0.1 (0.0)	Austria 407 (4.0)	France 1,000 (3.5)	Belgium 1,157 (3.1)

B. Special Exports (including re-exports) in millions of koruny (Figures in parentheses denote percentage shares of the 10 most important buying countries)

	1937	1945 (May–December)	1946	1947	1948
Total	11,923 (100.0)	471 (100.0)	14,345 (100.0)	28,596 (100.0)	37,648 (100.0)
	Germany 1,801 (15.0)	Switzerland 153 (32.5)	Switzerland 2,112 (14.7)	Switzerland 2,926 (10.2)	U.S.S.R. 6,006 (16.0)
	United States 1,112 (9.3)	United States 118 (25.0)	U.S.S.R. 1,721 (12.0)	Netherlands 2,458 (8.6)	Poland 2,643 (7.0)
	United Kingdom 1,039 (8.7)	U.S.S.R. 64 (13.6)	Sweden 1,149 (8.0)	Sweden 2,086 (7.3)	Yugoslavia 2,609 (6.9)
	Austria 877 (7.3)	Austria 35 (7.4)	United States 1,083 (7.6)	United Kingdom 1,841 (6.4)	Netherlands 2,415 (6.4)
	Sweden 654 (5.5)	Sweden 29 (6.2)	Germany 1,004 (7.0)	Belgium 1,817 (6.4)	Switzerland 1,789 (4.8)
	Germany 596 (5.0)	Germany 11 (2.3)	Netherlands 782 (5.5)	Yugoslavia 1,772 (6.2)	Austria 1,538 (4.1)
	Hungary 577 (4.8)	Hungary 8 (1.7)	Belgium 716 (5.0)	U.S.S.R. 1,445 (5.1)	Sweden 1,486 (3.9)
	Yugoslavia 546 (4.6)	Yugoslavia 6 (1.3)	Norway 652 (4.6)	United States 1,251 (4.4)	United Kingdom 1,358 (3.6)
	Netherlands 457 (3.8)	Turkey 5 (1.1)	Austria 650 (4.5)	Italy 1,246 (4.4)	Rumania 1,189 (3.2)
	Switzerland 409 (3.4)	Rumania 0.2 (0.0)	Denmark 571 (4.0)	Austria 1,008 (3.5)	United States 1,168 (3.1)

C. Special Exports and Imports by Commodity Groups (Brussels Nomenclature) in per cent of total imports and exports as given (i.e. excluding bullion and specie)

IMPORTS

	1937	1945	1946	1947	1948
I. Live animals	2.0	13.4	0.9	0.3	1.3
II. Foodstuffs, beverages	11.1	4.7	21.3	19.0	28.9
III. Raw materials	57.5	59.2	51.3	57.3	48.8
IV. Finished products	29.4	22.7	26.5	23.4	21.0

EXPORTS

	1937	1945	1946	1947	1948
I. Live animals	0.1	......	0.0	0.1	0.0
II. Foodstuffs, beverages	8.1	2.1	21.4	11.0	4.5
III. Raw materials	20.3	39.6	16.4	15.0	13.8
IV. Finished products	71.5	58.3	62.2	73.9	81.7

Sources: 1937–47: Prokop Macháň, *Československý zahraniční obchod* [Czechoslovak Foreign Trade] (mimeographed) RFE (Munich, 1961). *Měsíční přehled zahraničního obchodu Republiky Československé* [Monthly Survey of the Foreign Trade of the Czechoslovak Republic], December, 1948.

important prewar partner, toward neutral and Allied countries until the relatively liberal trade policy was radically changed in 1948, with the U.S.S.R. emerging as by far the greatest trading partner. The pattern of trade by large commodity groups changed less dramatically, as is also indicated in Table 7. However, within these large commodity groups, a more detailed composition of exports and imports was also changing rapidly.[36]

Privately-owned export and import firms tried to sell in the highest-priced export markets and to buy in the lowest-priced import markets (within the constraints of nonconvertibility of certain currencies and of the previously mentioned licensing). Led by the profit motive, they also tried hard to adjust the commodity pattern of exports to the desires of foreign buyers. This was probably one of the factors in the noticeably improved terms of trade, relative to 1937, as indicated by the pertinent index in Table 5, section 4. This index reflects not only changes in the relative prices of exports and imports but also changes in their composition. The unusually favorable terms of trade in 1946 were due, *inter alia*, to the fact that Czechoslovakia could obtain a great part of the imported, relatively high-priced food and raw materials free of charge through UNRRA. In 1947-48, the terms of trade deteriorated in comparison with 1946 terms in Czechoslovakia as well as in most other industrial European countries, mainly because of the increase in the world price of food and materials relative to the price of exports of finished manufactures. Nevertheless, Czechoslovakia's terms of trade remained more than one-fifth better than in prewar terms. This was a more favorable situation than in most other European countries, and it can be taken as some indication of efficiency in Czechoslovakia's trade.

A more meaningful indicator of changing (static) efficiency in foreign trade—changes in gains from trade—again eludes statistical measurement. However, it is noteworthy in this connection that, in contrast to the situation in the 1950's, the export-import firms were not heavily subsidized from the state budget. Yet, they realized money profits, and merchandise trade was nearly balanced. The reader can derive the bal-

---

[36] Cf. Prokop Macháň, *Československý zahraniční obchod* [*Czechoslovak Foreign Trade*] (RFE Evaluation and Analysis Department, Munich, 1961). This is a most comprehensive compendium of Czechoslovak foreign trade statistics between 1945 and 1960, with substantial statistical information also on prewar trade from 1918 to 1937 and on wartime trade from 1938 to 1944. The weak spot is the year 1948. Macháň's figures for that year cover only nine months (January-September). Therefore, *Měsíční přehled zahraničního obchodu Republiky Československé* [*Monthly Survey of the Foreign Trade of the Czechoslovak Republic*] of December, 1948, is a better source of statistical information for that year.

ance of visible trade by comparing export and import figures in Table 7. There was a surplus in merchandise trade in 1946, and a slight deficit in 1947-48. Data on the whole current accounts in the balance of payments, from national income computations,[37] are as follows (in billions of koruny):

	1947			1948		
	Gross credit	Gross debit	Net	Gross credit	Gross debit	Net
Merchandise payments[a]	28.0	29.5	—1.5	36.6	36.1	0.5
"Invisible" trade and all other current transfers	1.6	3.4	—1.8	3.3	6.0	—2.7
Current account total	29.6	32.9	—3.3	39.9	42.1	—2.2

[a] Excluding UNRRA and (relatively small) reparation deliveries, but including part of transport cost.

Relatively small differences between merchandise payments as given above and the figures on imports and exports in Table 7 can probably be explained by differences in valuation and by the time-lag between reporting output of exportables for national income accounts and reporting the exports at the time they crossed the border for trade statistics. On the other hand, the above net totals on current account are almost identical with the current account totals in the balance of payments according to United Nations statistics. (A discrepancy between the 2.2 billion koruny total net debit in 1948, as given above, and the 2,118 million total net debit according to UN statistics, can possibly be explained by rounding; the subdivision of "current account" is, however, quite different in the UN statistics, which include UNRRA deliveries as debits on goods accounts and as credits on donations account).

Current account was balanced by movements of private capital, official capital, and gold as follows (net sectoral credits [+] or debits [—] in millions of koruny):[38]

	Current Account								
	Goods and transport	Other services	Investment income	Donations	Total	Private capital	Official capital	Monetary gold	Errors and omissions
1937	+1,272	—330	—514	—9	+409	—274	—321	—63	+249
1947	—6,791	—886	—14	+4,439	—3,252	—16	+3,245	—187	+210
1948	—319	—1,432	—107	—260	—2,118	—106	+1,656	+217	+351

[37] Previously quoted computation by the State Planning Office.
[38] *United Nations Statistical Yearbook 1949-1950*, p. 382.

The reserves of gold and foreign exchange held by the Czechoslovak National Bank moved (in billions of koruny at official exchange rates and official gold parity) at the end of the years given, as follows:[39]

1945	1946	1947	1948	1949
2.6	5.3	4.8	4.1	3.0

The sudden increase in official international reserves in 1946 was due, *inter alia*, to a partial restitution of Czechoslovak gold confiscated under the German occupation. While the ratio of international reserves to imports was substantially lower in comparison with the prewar ratio, by this as well as by most other criteria, official holdings of foreign exchange and gold in 1946-47 were at least as adequate in Czechoslovakia as in most other European countries that had suffered under the war or under the German occupation. Czechoslovakia started to lose international reserves after the government first accepted, and then refused to participate in the Marshall Plan in the spring of 1947 (a more substantial loss of reserves occurred in 1948-49). Nevertheless, Czechoslovak external economic relations over the period under study were in reasonably good shape, and they did not put an undue constraint on domestic economic development.

Distribution of Income and Wealth

Compared with prewar conditions, a substantial shift occurred in the *functional* distribution of national income from entrepreneurial income and from explicit property income to wages, salaries, and pensions. The shares of these three broad categories changed, in terms of current factor cost, as follows:[40]

	Percent of national income			
	1937	1946	1947	1948
Wages, salaries, social security payments, all other pensions	59.0	67.9	68.2	68.5
Entrepreneurial incomes (including farmers' incomes and profits of nationalized enterprises)	32.2	28.6	28.5	28.4
Property incomes (explicit rent and explicit interest)	8.8	3.5	3.3	3.1
	100.0	100.0	100.0	100.0

[39] According to the *Monthly Bulletin of the Czechoslovak National Bank*, as cited by Edward Ames in Bušek and Spulber, *op. cit.*, pp. 375, 383.

[40] From a previously quoted computation by the State Planning Office.

Substantial research has been done on the distribution of *personal* income by members of the Czechoslovak Institute of Labor (*Československý ústav práce*), an institution affiliated with the Central Council of Trade Unions (ÚRO). Unfortunately, only fragments of this research are available.[41] They tend to indicate a strong tendency toward a more equal distribution of money income before taxes.[42] This tendency toward equalization was probably even more pronounced in terms of real income, in view of the progressive taxation and of substantial free social services. While real income was probably somewhat more unequally distributed in 1946-47 than in the late 1950's and early 1960's, it was probably more equally distributed in Czechoslovakia than in most other European countries at that time.

The imposition of the previously mentioned tax on wealth in connection with the currency reform of 1945 provided some interesting data on the distribution of wealth. Out of the total property holdings reported by natural persons (excluding property of corporations) in the amount of 315.2 billion koruny, 27.4 percent was property of independent farmers, 23.7 percent property of entrepreneurs in nonfarm sectors, 2.1 percent property of members of liberal professions, 6.7 percent property of rentiers, 8.1 percent property of recipients of old-age pensions, and 40.1 percent property of wage and salary earners. Allowing for the nonreportable minima of property (40,000 koruny for a married couple), one can estimate that even before the imposition of capital levies more than a half of the total wealth of natural persons (households) was held by wage and salary earners (working and retired). After the payment of capital levies (in the total amount of 18.2 billion koruny), the distribution of household wealth definitely shifted in favor of wage and salary earners. It is also noteworthy that Slovakia's share in the reported wealth of households was only 15.1 percent. However, all of these figures[43] should be interpreted with caution. In view of the steeply progressive rates of the capital levies there was a strong inducement to underreport property, and the degree of underreporting probably varied from occupation to occupation and from region to region.

---

[41] For instance, Vítězslav Velímský, *Mzdový vývoj podle dat národního pojištění* [*Wage Development in the Light of Data of National Insurance*] (Prague: October, 1949, mimeographed).

[42] One factor of this tendency toward equalization was, of course, the reduced income of entrepreneurs relative to the income of employees. Another factor was the narrowing difference between the average income of salary earners (including executives) on one hand and the average income of wage earners, on the other. According to Velímský, *op. cit.*, the average income of salary earners in November, 1946, was 146.9 percent of wage earners' average income. In November, 1947, it was only 136.5 percent.

[43] From the *Statistical Digest of the Czechoslovak Republic 1948*, pp. 111-12.

I have tried to outline, without claim to analytical and statistical accuracy, the economic performance of the postwar system in Czechoslovakia from May, 1945 until February, 1948. My outline indicates, I hope, that this mixed system, combining public with private enterprise and limited market forces with substantial, but mostly noncoercive, planning, functioned reasonably well under the difficult conditions of postwar economic reconversion and recovery: the growth, stability, and productivity record of Czechoslovakia was by no means worse, if not better, than in most other European countries at that time. Czechoslovakia succeeded in avoiding a serious balance of payments problem and secured a distribution of income that was more equal than in prewar times and probably more equal than in most other European countries. The crisis of February, 1948, which put an end to this system, was more of a political than an economic nature.

· 17 ·

SUMMARY

The Czechoslovak Republic was born in 1918 on the ruins of the Austro-Hungarian monarchy, but the seeds of Czechoslovak independence had been planted in the nineteenth century, when the Czechs and Slovaks, like all peoples of East Central Europe, experienced a national revival. The Slovak revival was soon stunted by the Austro-Hungarian Compromise (*Ausgleich*) of 1867, under which Emperor Francis Joseph I gave the Magyars a free hand against the non-Magyars of Hungary, in return for Magyar loyalty to the Habsburg dynasty. Thereafter, as a result of the Hungarian policy of magyarization and their singularly unenlightened social policies, the Slovaks regressed rather than progressed. The Czechs, on the other hand, made rapid progress in the much freer atmosphere of the Austrian half of the empire, until by 1914 they had attained levels of social, economic, and cultural development second only to those of the Germans among the peoples of the empire. However, they had failed to achieve their political ambition, which was to secure for the kingdom of Bohemia a place in the empire analogous to that of the kingdom of Hungary after the *Ausgleich*. Therefore, the Czechs grew increasingly disaffected. However, they did not contemplate withdrawal from empire, because before 1914 the only alternative to their association in the weak Habsburg empire appeared to be their incorporation in the powerful German empire.

It was not until after the outbreak of World War I, which opened the prospect of Germany's defeat and Austria's disintegration, that some Czech leaders began to contemplate the possibility of Czech and Slovak independence. At first, they tended to remain passive and to look to Russia for liberation. Only one among them, Prof. Tomáš G. Masaryk, was not content to wait passively for Russian liberation, but developed from the first an active program for Czech and Slovak liberation, which was oriented as much to the Western Allies as to Russia. Late in 1914, at the advanced age of sixty-four, Masaryk left Austria-Hungary to launch the supreme adventure of his eventful life—the organization of the movement for Czechoslovak independence abroad. Masaryk's efforts, in which he was assisted by Edvard Beneš and Milan R. Štefánik, were eventually eminently successful. In 1918, after considerable hesitations, the Allied powers recognized the Czechoslovak National Council of Paris under Masaryk as a trustee of the future Czechoslovak government, and thereby committed themselves to support Czechoslovak independence.

461

Meanwhile, Czech politicians at home maintained a cautious wait-and-see attitude until the outbreak of the Russian Revolution and the American entry into the war in 1917 put the demand for national self-determination into wide currency. At first cautiously but later boldly, they began then to demand not only the restoration of the historic state rights of Bohemia but, speaking for the "politically gagged" Slovaks, the creation of a Czechoslovak state. In July, 1918, the leaders of the Czech parties formed the Czech National Committee in Prague under Karel Kramář to speak with one voice for the Czechs and Slovaks. On October 18, 1918, Masaryk declared Czechoslovak independence in Washington, and on October 28, as the Habsburg empire began to break up from within, the Czech National Committee followed suit by declaring it in Prague. A few days earlier, its delegates had left Prague for Geneva to meet there with Beneš and coordinate the moves of the Prague committee and the Paris council. The outcome of the Geneva conference was the formation of the first Czechoslovak government, with Masaryk as president and Kramář as prime minister. On November 14, a "revolutionary national assembly," consisting of the Czech deputies to the former Austrian Reichsrat and the diets of Bohemia, Moravia, and Silesia and forty (later fifty-five) Slovak representatives who had been coopted, confirmed the government in office and adopted a provisional constitution.

By January, 1919, when the Paris peace conference opened, the Czechoslovak government was already well established. Ably represented at the conference by Beneš, Czechoslovakia secured Allied confirmation of all her essential claims in the treaties of St. Germain and Trianon, except her territorial dispute with Poland over Těšín and the Slovak border districts of Orava and Spiš. This claim was adjusted by the Allies only later, not quite to the satisfaction of either Poland or Czechoslovakia, and remained a thorn in their relations. Despite this disappointment, Czechoslovakia was among the new nations of East Central Europe undoubtedly the most satisfied with the Paris peace settlement and, consequently, the most attached to the *status quo*.

Meanwhile, the Revolutionary National Assembly, anxious to consolidate the new state and impress the Allied peacemakers with its viability, proceeded to draft a permanent constitution. In retrospect, it may appear to have been an error for the assembly to undertake this task, for it represented only a limited range of opinion in the country. The mandate of the Czech deputies dated from the last Austrian election in 1911. Since then Czech opinion had shifted considerably to the left. The Slovak deputies likewise were not fully representative of Slovak opinion, for they had not been elected but picked by Šrobár, principally from the Slovak Protestant minority, which had been historically sympathetic to the Czechs.

462

Even more unfortunate was the absence of any representatives of the national minorities in the assembly. The assembly was not unaware of this weakness. In November, 1918, the Czech political leaders invited the (Sudeten) German parties to join the Prague National Committee. Unfortunately, at that time the Germans expected to be incorporated into Austria or Greater Germany and did not want to prejudice this prospect by dealing with Czechoslovakia, which they regarded as an "ephemeral state" (*Saisonstaat*). Therefore, they declined to send their representatives to Prague. Representatives of the other national minorities (Hungarians, Poles, Ruthenians) were not invited to Prague, because at that time they were not fully incorporated into Czechoslovakia and their future status was uncertain. Since the national minorities did not take part in the drafting of the constitution, they never felt committed to support it. The Slovak Catholic majority likewise felt reservations about it. Even the Czech communists were hostile to the "bourgeois" republic until the adoption of the "popular front" tactic by the Comintern and the signing of the Soviet-Czechoslovak alliance in 1935, when they rallied to it. All of these factors constituted weaknesses in the structure of the Czechoslovak state, which were revealed at the time of its great trial, during the Munich crisis of 1938. However, it should be stressed that Czechoslovakia did not break up from *within* under the pressure of her discontented national minorities, as Neville Chamberlain alleged in March, 1939, but was dismembered from *without* by hostile foreign nations.

As drafted, the Czechoslovak constitution of 1920 reflected principally the views of the Czech middle class, which was the backbone of the First Czechoslovak Republic. Strongly democratic and egalitarian in outlook, the Czech middle class looked to France for inspiration. Like most continental peoples at that time, the Czechoslovak constitution-makers had little familiarity with British and American constitutional practices, and took the constitution of the French Third Republic as their model. Like its French model, the Czechoslovak constitution was highly centralist. It was based on the principle of Czechoslovak unity, that is, it assumed that the Czechs and Slovaks were a single "Czechoslovak" people, speaking—theoretically—a single "Czechoslovak" language. Although the Czechs and Slovaks were obviously the creators and carriers of the Czechoslovak state, they were designated as the country's "state people" (*Staatsvolk*) only indirectly, in the constitution's preamble. The constitution itself guaranteed the civil, linguistic, and religious rights of all the citizens of the republic, including the minorities, but did not recognize the minorities as legal entities. Unlike the French constitution which accorded suffrage to men only, the Czechoslovak constitution provided for universal suffrage and direct and secret ballot.

Like its French model, the Czechoslovak constitution concentrated most powers in the national assembly. The powers of the judiciary and of the president were limited. Nevertheless, thanks to his prestige as a philosopher-statesman and the country's liberator, Masaryk exercised a strong influence. Beneš, who succeeded him in 1935, likewise enjoyed great prestige and influence. If the First Republic had endured, however, with the passing of the liberators, Czechoslovak presidents were likely to become figureheads, like the presidents of the French Third Republic.

Like France, Czechoslovakia also adopted proportional representation in her electoral system. This had as a result the rise of numerous political parties, none of which was strong enough to hold power alone. It was therefore necessary to form coalition governments. Czechoslovakia, however, was no replica of France. Unlike French politics, Czechoslovak politics was marked by unusual moderation, stability, and continuity. This was due in part to the rise of an extra-constitutional organ, which prevented the unbridled strife among parties such as marred French parliamentary life. Shortly after the adoption of the constitution in 1920, the heads of the five parties then forming the government coalition began the practice of meeting in private and deciding issues before they reached the floor of the parliament. Known according to the number of parties in the government coalition as the "Five" or "Six" or "Seven," this shadow cabinet lasted, with short interruptions, as long as the First Republic—indeed, it outlived it, reemerging after World War II in the guise of the National Front.

Members of the parliament were subject to rigid party discipline and obliged to vote as instructed by their party leaders. Infractions of party discipline could be, and sometimes were, punished by expulsion from the party and loss of parliamentary mandates. The institution of the "Five" (*Pětka*), which became a peculiar feature of Czechoslovak politics, has often been criticized as unconstitutional and undemocratic, but it did have the virtue of assuring stability of Czechoslovak parliamentary life. In no small measure, it was due to this institution that parliamentary democracy survived in Czechoslovakia after it had collapsed in every European country east of the Rhine.

Czechoslovakia's foreign policy in the interwar period likewise showed remarkable continuity and stability. More than the foreign policy of any other European country, it bore the personal stamp of a single man—Edvard Beneš, who served as foreign minister from 1918 until he succeeded Masaryk as president in 1935. Even then, however, he kept a close hand on its formulation.

Czechoslovakia was a status quo nation *par excellence*. The basic motivation of Beneš's policy was defensive. He sought to preserve what he had gained for Czechoslovakia at the Paris peace conference. Not unnaturally, therefore, he oriented Czechoslovak foreign policy toward the League of Nations and the Western powers, which had been victorious in World War I and had, consequently, the greatest interest in preserving the status quo. So long as the Western powers dominated European politics, Czechoslovakia appeared to be safe from all danger, despite her strategically exposed position. Of her five neighbors—Germany, Austria, Hungary, Rumania, and Poland—all but Rumania were unfriendly. Intelligent, hard-working, and knowledgeable, Beneš toiled ceaselessly to appease their hostility and to foil their revisionist designs on Czechoslovakia's territory.

The most persistent threat to Czechoslovakia's integrity was the militant revisionism of Hungary. To contain it, Beneš took a prominent part in promoting the Little Entente with Yugoslavia and Rumania in 1921. To appease Austria's bitterness, he shared in various international schemes to prop up her tottering economy, and eventually succeeded in developing good working relations with her. With Germany, which was Czechoslovakia's principal trading partner, Beneš sought to maintain "correct" diplomatic relations. His effort was facilitated by the fact that the revisionist agitation of Weimar Germany was directed in the east principally against Poland rather than Czechoslovakia, and that the Weimar Republic took no interest in the Sudeten Germans. Therefore, Beneš declined to follow the example of Poland and conclude an alliance with France directed against Germany. It was not until 1924, during a relaxation of Franco-German tensions following the Ruhr crisis, that Beneš concluded an alliance with France. Although Germany refused to exchange with Poland and Czechoslovakia guarantees analogous to those she exchanged with France and Belgium at Locarno in 1925, German-Czechoslovak relations continued to be polite.

Czechoslovakia's relations with Poland were permanently affected by their conflict over Těšín. Periodic attempts at reconciliation, made from both sides, as well as attempts of French diplomacy to mediate between the two countries, all failed. The Polish-Czechoslovak agreement of 1925 was voided by Piłsudski's rise to dictatorial power in the following year. Piłsudski would not forgive Těšín. Thereafter, neither side made any earnest attempt at reconciliation, which proved ultimately detrimental to both countries.

Hitler's rise to power in Germany in 1933 presented a grave threat to Czechoslovakia. He had made his hostility to the Versailles system, of which Czechoslovakia was a part, well known. However, Germany's threat to Czechoslovakia was implicit rather than explicit. Germany had lost no territory to Czechoslovakia under the Versailles treaty, and Hitler at first showed no interest in the Sudeten German minority. Nevertheless, Beneš's reaction to his rise to power was very wary. Unlike Piłsudski, he

465

was not prepared to seek or trust an agreement with Hitler, but tirelessly worked to strengthen and expand Czechoslovakia's alliances. He followed the conclusion of the Franco-Soviet alliance in 1935 by immediately concluding a Czechoslovak alliance with the Soviet Union, which was to become operative when France honored her commitment to defend Czechoslovakia. Czechoslovakia had no alliance with Britain, but Britain was committed to defend France in the event of a war with Germany. On paper, Beneš's alliance system thus appeared to be perfect: a German attack on Czechoslovakia would automatically bring to her rescue France, the Soviet Union, and Britain.

However, when the Czechoslovak alliance system was put to a test during the great Munich crisis in 1938, it failed completely to function. France refused to act without Britain, and the Soviet Union without France. Britain was determined not to be drawn into war over Czechoslovakia, and proceeded to extricate France from her commitment to help her. When Hitler threatened to invade Czechoslovakia, her Western friends and allies not only failed to come to her rescue but assisted in her dismemberment, while the Soviet Union and her Little Entente allies passively looked on.

Like all successor nations of the Habsburg empire, Czechoslovakia faced serious economic problems after her establishment. She had inherited about 80 percent of the industries of the Habsburg empire, but the partition of the empire deprived them of their natural markets. The war had not directly affected Czechoslovak territory, but had strained the Habsburg finances and inflated its currency. Like all successor states, Czechoslovakia had to assume part of the financial obligations of the defunct empire. As an allied nation, she did not have to pay the Allied powers reparations but, what amounted to the same thing, "liberation" costs. In apportioning the reparations and liberation fees, the Allied powers were guided principally by the successor nations' ability to pay. As potentially the most prosperous among them, Czechoslovakia had to shoulder the largest part of the burden. She was, therefore, saddled from the beginning with a considerable foreign debt.

Under the energetic guidance of Alois Rašín, she set about putting her finances in order. By drastic measures, Rašín managed to stabilize the Czechoslovak currency and restore solvency to the new state in a remarkably short time. A political and economic conservative of the pre-Keynesian school, Rašín placed perhaps an undue importance on a sound currency and recognized no relationship between financial and social policy. Being eminently a trading nation, Czechoslovakia needed a stable and strong currency, but Rašín's deflationary policy was so harsh that it had painful side effects: unemployment and suffering among the working classes. This explained in part the strong swing to the left in the first

Czechoslovak parliamentary elections in 1920. In 1923 Rašín was assassinated by an unbalanced communist youth, who had been inflamed by communist agitation against his policy. His murder, incidentally, constituted a rare case of violence in Czechoslovak politics, which was sometimes marred by violent words but rarely by violent deeds. The policies of Rašín's successors remained in the main the same; they placed an accent on fiscal responsibility, discipline, and hard work. Thanks to these qualities, Czechoslovakia recovered a relatively high degree of prosperity in the 1920's. Unfortunately, it was not evenly spread throughout the country.

Czechoslovakia was to some extent overindustrialized, but industry was unevenly distributed in the country. Historically, industry was concentrated in the western (Czech) provinces; Slovakia and Ruthenia were predominantly agrarian provinces. Industry sprang up in Slovakia and, to a much smaller extent, in Ruthenia, under the paternal guidance of the Hungarian government, only in the last decade of the nineteenth century and the early years of the present century. It was made possible by generous tax exemptions, preferential railroad rates, and outright subsidies. After 1918, when these artificial stimuli were removed and the young Slovak industry was exposed to the competition of the highly developed Czech industry, it inevitably succumbed. Slovakia and Ruthenia were reduced primarily to the role of food and raw materials producing appendages of the industrial Czech provinces, a role for which they were by their mountainous character not best suited. This had the undesirable effect of aggravating an old Slovak and Ruthenian social problem—rural overpopulation and unemployment or underemployment. The problem was further compounded by the fact that at the same time the traditional safety valve of Slovak and Ruthenian social discontent—emigration—was stopped by adoption of restrictions on immigration in the United States and other overseas countries. In consequence, social restlessness increased in Slovakia and Ruthenia, which was reflected in the growth of the Communist party in their rural areas.

The Sudeten area had traditionally been the center of Bohemia's highly developed consumer industries, especially textiles and glass. After 1918 these lost many of their markets in other parts of the former Habsburg empire. The growth of protectionism among the successor states forced a partial shift in emphasis in Czechoslovak industrial production, from consumer goods to heavy industrial goods, especially machinery and armaments, and a reorientation of Czechoslovak exports from East Central Europe to Western Europe and the overseas. The shift had the undesirable effect of increasing the social and political discontent of the Sudeten Germans. Czechoslovakia followed the general trend toward protectionism by adopting high tariffs on farm products, which protected her farmers but because it forced food prices up was resented by the workers. It also prevented closer economic ties with Czechoslovakia's Little Entente allies, Yugoslavia and Rumania, which depended on the export of farm products for their prosperity.

As an industrial nation depending heavily on foreign trade for her prosperity, Czechoslovakia was very hard hit by the advent of the World Depression in the 1930's. It was only toward the end of the decade that, thanks to the growing demand for armaments, both for Czechoslovak defense and export abroad, her economic situation somewhat improved. The depression deepened social and political tensions in Czechoslovakia, but it must be repeated that it was not these but foreign intervention that led to her downfall.

The Munich Agreement, by depriving Czechoslovakia of one-third of her territory containing some of her most important industrial centers and most fertile farm land, left her economically crippled. However, even worse was its strategic and political impact. By depriving Czechoslovakia of her natural defenses, it left her at Germany's mercy. The betrayal of the country by the Western powers and the capitulation of their government threw the Czech people into complete confusion and despondency. Deeply hurt, they turned almost revengefully on their old leaders, cherished notions, and democratic traditions. The prestige of President Beneš, who resigned and went into exile, suffered an eclipse. The old Slovak and Ruthenian demands for autonomy, which had been stubbornly resisted until Munich, were granted thereafter almost gladly. The hitherto unitary state was transformed into an ill-defined Czech-Slovak-Ruthenian federation. The ill-fated Second Republic had come into existence.

Emil Hácha, a non-party bureaucrat, was chosen to replace Beneš as president, and Rudolf Beran, an Agrarian party leader who had criticized Beneš for refusing to seek an agreement with Hitler, became prime minister. After Munich Czechoslovakia's western friends washed their hands of her. The Beran government tried as best it could to adjust to the new situation. It made pathetic attempts to appease Germany by reorienting Czechoslovakia's foreign policy to comport with Hitler's notions of a "New Order" in Europe and her domestic policies to harmonize with his *Weltanschauung*. The democratic system was for all practical purposes scrapped, and an absurd semi-authoritarian system introduced.

All attempts to appease Hitler failed, however, for he did not regard the Munich Agreement as a definite settlement but only as a step toward the complete destruction of Czechoslovakia. He hesitated only about the best way of doing it, alternately considering political and military means. In the end, about mid-February, 1939, he decided upon the Slovak radicals as a convenient tool of his policy. For some time, they had clamored for going beyond the autonomy accorded Slovakia after Munich and for establishing an independent Slovak state. The inevitable end came in mid-March.

On March 10, after getting wind of the intentions of the Slovak populist radicals, the Prague government sent troops into Slovakia, deposed the Slovak provincial government under Msgr. Jozef Tiso, and appointed a new one under Karol Sidor. Much to the astonishment and annoyance of the Germans, Sidor refused to heed their suggestion that he declare Slovakia's independence and secession from Czechoslovakia. Therefore, they turned to Tiso, who was Sidor's rival for the leadership of HSĽS. On March 13 Hitler summoned Tiso to Berlin, and gave him the choice of declaring Slovakia's independence or seeing it annexed by Hungary, the Slovaks' historical enemy. Tiso chose the former course. On March 14 the Slovak Diet heeded his advice, and declared Slovakia independent. While Slovakia was launched on a new career as an independent state under German protection, Ruthenia was occupied and annexed by Hungary.

Meanwhile, the bewildered President Hácha solicited an interview with Hitler to discuss the Slovak situation. However, when he arrived in Berlin in the night of March 14, he was told that the Slovak situation was no longer subject to discussion, because the Slovaks had declared their independence and Germany had recognized it. Instead, he was presented with an ultimatum for the Czechoslovak army to capitulate and was bullied into signing a document placing Bohemia and Moravia under German protection. On March 15 the German army occupied the two provinces.

The March events of 1939 had a less depressing effect on the Czechs than Munich had. In a sense they clarified the situation. Hitler's perfidy had demolished the thesis of the appeasers and vindicated Beneš: no agreement with Hitler was possible. When Beneš announced from his American exile that he was placing himself at the head of a new movement abroad to liberate and restore Czechoslovakia, as he had done in World War I, his prestige with the Czechs was restored. The Czech national solidarity reasserted itself. They closed their ranks to face their historical enemy, Germany, as they had often done in the past.

Almost immediately after the German occupation of Bohemia and Moravia the Czechs began to form resistance organizations. The Czech resistance was at first confined to democratic organizations, the Czech communists beginning to resist the Germans only after the Soviet entry into the war. Unlike the Polish, Yugoslav, and Greek resistance movements, the Czech resistance never suffered an east-west, communist-nationalist schism. Although the communists maintained their own network, they cooperated with the democratic resistance to the end of the war. This was due in no small measure to the diplomatic skill of Beneš, who managed to secure not only Allied recognition of his exile government in London, but also by concluding an alliance treaty with the Soviet Union in December, 1943, securing Soviet blessing during the war, and winning a promise of support after the war.

In imitation of the Czechoslovak legions in World War I, Czech and Slovak exiles formed volunteer units to fight alongside the Allies against Germany in World War II. In 1939 a volunteer unit was formed in Poland to fight with the Polish army. After the Polish collapse, it retreated to the Soviet Union where it was interned until the German invasion in 1941. It was then reactivated and became the nucleus of the Czechoslovak "Eastern Army," which returned home in 1944 fighting alongside the Red Army. In 1939 a volunteer army was also formed in France. After the French debacle, it was evacuated to Britain where it remained until the Allied landing in France in 1944. The Czechoslovak "Western Army" then saw service on the Western front before returning home in 1945. A Czechoslovak volunteer unit also fought with the British Eighth Army in the Middle East and Africa.

Because of the occupation and direct control of Bohemia and Moravia by the Germans and the vigilance of the Gestapo, the Czech resistance was long confined to the gathering of intelligence, keeping communications with the exile government in London open, sabotage of industrial production, and occasional attacks on German officials. The gentle rolling countryside of Bohemia and Moravia, the absence of rugged mountains and dense forests, a good network of roads, railroads, and communications, and their great distances from Allied-controlled territory made them unsuitable for guerrilla warfare. Only in the final days of the war when the Soviet and American armies invaded Moravia and Bohemia did a wave of Czech insurrections break out, culminating in the Prague uprising in May, 1945.

The situation was quite different in Slovakia. The confusion of spirit that prevailed in all of Czechoslovakia after Munich lasted in Slovakia longer than in Bohemia and Moravia. Unlike the Protectorate of Bohemia and Moravia, the Slovak State was not occupied by the Germans until August, 1944. Until then, although a helpless German satellite, Slovakia controlled her internal affairs. It was one thing to resist foreign occupants and quite another a native government, even one that was compromised by collaboration with Germany.

The Slovak people had accepted with incredulity the independence suddenly thrust upon them by the Germans. They had never sought independence, because they had no confidence in their ability to maintain it. Father Tiso's and Karol Sidor's hesitations about accepting independence in March, 1939, had not been motivated by any reluctance to part company with the Czechs but by lack of confidence in their ability to administer a modern state. However, the Czechs had been excellent schoolmasters in Slovakia. In the short space of twenty years, they had trained sufficient basic cadres of Slovak administrators, judges, lawyers, doctors, and technicians, so that when they left in 1939 there was no breakdown of the administration or services. This came to the Slovaks as a great revelation, and greatly boosted their self-confidence.

Part of the Slovak population sincerely rallied to the Tiso regime. Another part, consisting of democrats who disliked its fascist features and the Protestants who disliked its identification with Catholicism, opposed it and looked to the restoration of the Czechoslovak Republic. The communists accepted the idea of Slovak independence but opposed the regime. The bulk of the population adopted a cautious wait-and-see attitude until 1943, when the Battle of Stalingrad and the Allied landing in Italy opened the prospect of Germany's defeat. Two resistance movements, one democratic and one communist, then sprang up. In the Christmas Agreement of 1943 the democrats and communists agreed upon a common program of struggle for the restoration of a democratic Czechoslovakia, with two distinct nations, the Czechs and the Slovaks, and formed the Slovak National Council to direct the struggle.

Slovakia, with her rugged mountainous terrain and deep forests, was eminently suited for guerrilla warfare, which began as early as 1942. In 1944, at the approach of the Soviet front, the Slovak National Council prepared plans for a large-scale insurrection, involving the Slovak army, which was designed to take Slovakia over to the Allied side. Unfortunately, in August, 1944, the Germans, disquieted by the upsurge of partisan warfare and the Rumanian defection, occupied Slovakia and thereby precipitated the Slovak National Uprising before the preparations for it were completed. The uprising failed after two months of heavy fighting, which nevertheless caused the Germans considerable inconvenience and loss. The Slovak National Council, which had directed the uprising, survived the defeat. It reemerged later in the Soviet-occupied part of Slovakia.

Meanwhile, in March, 1945, Beneš and the exiled government moved from London to Moscow. There the exiled leaders of the democratic and communist parties and representatives of the Slovak National Council agreed upon the Košice program for postwar Czechoslovakia. Although it reflected communist views, it was not explicitly a Marxist program. At the time the communists claimed to be pursuing a specific "Czechoslovak way to socialism," and disclaimed any desire for a monopoly of power. In the first National Front government, which was agreed upon at the same time, they did not claim the premiership or a majority of posts. They did, however, make sure of getting the ministry of interior, which would give them the control of the police.

Upon returning to Prague in May, 1945, the National Front government took charge of the situation, without encountering any opposition. The Czech National Council, which had emerged in the final days of the war to direct the struggle against the Germans, was dissolved, but the Slovak National Council continued to exercise a large measure of authority in Slovakia. The authority of the government was at first based on decrees issued over the signature of President Beneš. In October, 1945, a national assembly was selected by the parties, but its authority remained slight. In the tradition of the prewar "Five," it confirmed automatically decrees which the party leaders in the National Front had decided upon.

Freed from normal political concerns, the government was able to tackle the tasks of consolidating the restored state with energy. Because of the total defeat of Germany and her allies, it encountered no difficulty in recovering control of the territory of pre-Munich Czechoslovakia. There was only one exception—Ruthenia, which was abandoned to the Soviet Union, tacitly from the outset and formally, by treaty, in June, 1945. The Sudeten German minority was expelled, which the Allied powers authorized at the Potsdam conference. The government wanted also to expel the Hungarian minority, but failed to get Allied authorization for it. The plan was first postponed and later abandoned altogether. War damages, which were considerable in Slovakia and parts of Moravia but slight in Bohemia, were energetically repaired. The inflated currency was reformed and stabilized. Large-scale industry and banking were nationalized, as envisaged in the Košice program. Some industries were transferred from the Sudeten area to Slovakia. Despite the loss of Sudeten German labor, production spurted up. By 1946 the country showed heartening signs of economic recovery.

With conditions in the country reasonably stabilized, the government felt obliged to legalize the basis of its power by holding elections into a constituent assembly. The National Front was maintained. Only parties represented in it were permitted to participate in the elections, which were to be held in May, 1946.

Since the end of the war, the communists had strengthened their positions in the country through dexterous use of mass organizations. They were strengthened also by the knowledge that they had the backing of the Soviet Union. The democratic parties, on the other hand, were weakened by the decimation and demoralization of the Czech middle class under the German occupation, and lack of assurance of Western backing. France and Britain were discredited by the part they had played at

Munich. In any event, they had little power. The United States, on the other hand, had power but little interest in Czechoslovakia. Despite official denials, the Americans showed disquieting signs of a readiness to accept the lines of demarcation between the Western and Soviet armies at the end of World War II as permanent lines of division between Western and Soviet spheres of influence in Europe, and to write off East Central Europe. President Beneš summed up Czechoslovakia's position accurately when he remarked that she did not lie between East and West but between Russia and Germany. Much as the Americans might sympathize with Czechoslovakia, it was more important for them to back Germany.

The communists entered the elections confident of their ability to win a majority, which would entitle them to form a cabinet alone. However, the results of the elections fell short of their expectations. With 38 percent of the vote, they emerged as the strongest party, which entitled them to take the premiership but not to hold power alone.

The electoral contest had strained the relationship of the parties in the National Front. Still, all parties, including the communists, professed loyalty to the principle of national-front (i.e., coalition) government. A change came about in 1947 when a disastrous drought at home and the beginning of the cold war abroad combined to increase tensions between the communist and democratic parties. The formation of the Cominform signaled the communist decision to end their cooperation with democratic parties in national fronts, and to liquidate the latter as a dangerous fifth column of the Western "imperialists" in the Soviet sphere.

In Czechoslovakia, the decision was implemented in two stages. First, in November, 1947, the Slovak Democratic party was emasculated. Next, in February, 1948, the Czech democratic parties were eliminated. In both instances, the communists used the same tools—mass organizations to pass "spontaneous" resolutions and the police forces to enforce them. Only the frail and ailing figure of President Beneš then stood in the way of a communist monopoly of power. After a brief resistance, he bowed to a communist show of force in Prague, as he had bowed to Hitler's show of force at Munich ten years earlier. The communists had arrived to power by a bloodless coup.

Victor S. Mamatey

· SELECTED BIBLIOGRAPHY[1] ·

Compiled by
Radomír Luža

PRIMARY SOURCES

Published Official Documents

Akten zur deutschen auswärtigen Politik 1918-1945. Aus dem Archiv des Auswärtigen Amtes. Series B: *1925-1933.* 3 vols. Göttingen, 1966-68.

Bohemia and Moravia. Protectorate. *Sammlung der Gesetze und Verordnungen, 1939-1945.* Prague, 1939-45.

─────. Statistisches Zentralamt. *Statistisches Jahrbuch für das Protektorat Böhmen und Mähren.* Prague, 1941-44.

Czechoslovak Delegation to the Peace Conference 1919. *Mémoires.* Paris, 1919.

    Eleven memoranda containing the Czechoslovak claims to the Peace Conference; printed only for the use of the Conference; published later by Hermann Raschhofer, ed. *Die Tschechoslowakischen Denkschriften für die Friedenskonferenz von Paris, 1919-1920.* Berlin, 1937.

Czechoslovak Ministry of Foreign Affairs. *Archiv diplomatických dokumentů československých* [*Archives of Czechoslovak Diplomatic Documents*], Prague, 1928.

[Czechoslovak] Ministry of Information. *Československo a norimberský proces. Hlavní dokumenty norimberského procesu o zločinech nacistů proti Československu* [*Czechoslovakia and the Nuremberg Trial. Principal Documents of the Nuremberg Trial for Nazi Crimes against Czechoslovakia*]. Prague, 1946.

─────. *Český národ soudí K. H. Franka* [*K. H. Frank on Trial before the Czech People*]. Prague, 1946.

    Valuable material on the period of 1938-45 used at K. H. Frank's trial in 1946.

─────. *Zpověd K. H. Franka. Podle vlastních výpovědí v době vazby u krajského soudu trestního na Pankráci* [*Confession of K. H. Frank. According to his Own Depositions at the Regional Criminal Court at Pankrác*]. Prague, 1946.

    Valuable for the Sudeten German and Nazi policies in 1933-45.

[Czechoslovak] Ministry of the Interior. *Lidice. Čin krvavého teroru i porušení zákonů a základních lidských práv* [*Lidice: Act of Terror and Violation of Laws and Basic Human Rights*]. Prague, 1946.

[1] No objective and impartial study could have been published in Communist-dominated Czechoslovakia in the period 1948-68. Since about 1963 Czechoslovak historiography has sought a more judicial approach to historical evidence.

I have attempted to select only those sources which seem to be particularly relevant to the subject or are written in a Western language. The listing is intended to be more suggestive than comprehensive, thus not all source material cited in the text is surveyed in the bibliography.

Documents pertaining to the burning of the small town Lidice in June, 1942.

―――. *Persekuce českého studentstva za okupace* [*Persecution of Czech Students during the Occupation*]. Prague, 1946.

A documentary collection on the October and November, 1939, demonstrations in Prague and on the closing of Czech universities on November 17, 1939.

Czechoslovak Republic. *Sammlung der Gesetze und Verordnungen des tschechoslowakischen Staates, 1918-1938*. Prague, 1918-38.

―――. State Statistical Office. *Manuel statistique, 1928-1948*. Prague, 1928-48.

In 1934-38 as *Annuaire statistique de la république tchécoslovaque*. In German *Statistisches Handbuch*, 1921-32, and *Statistisches Jahrbuch*, 1934-38. In 1939-47 suspended.

―――. *Statistisches Jahrbuch der Tschechoslowakei, 1958*. Prague, 1959.

Les Événements survenus en France de 1933 à 1945. Témoignages et documents recueillis par la Commission d'enquête parlementaire. 9 vols. *Rapport de M. Claude Serre, député, au nom de la Commission d'enquête parlementaire*. 2 vols. Paris, 1947ff.

Basic for the French policies.

Documents on British Foreign Policy 1919-1939. Edited by E. L. Woodward and Rohan Butler. First Series. Vols. I-XVII: 1919-25. Second Series. Vols. I-XI: 1930-38. Third Series. Vols. I-X: 1938-39. Series Ia. Vols. I-II: 1925-29. London, 1946-70.

Hungarian Ministry for Foreign Affairs. *Hungary and the Conference of Paris*. 5 vols. Vol. II: *Hungary's International Relations before the Conference of Paris*. Vol. IV: *Hungary at the Conference of Paris*. Budapest, 1947.

A good presentation of the Hungarian views.

International Military Tribunal. *Trial of the Major War Criminals before the International Military Tribunal, Nuremberg, 1945-46*. 42 vols. Nuremberg, 1947-49.

Czechoslovak materials are not always very accurate. See vols. X, XXV-XXXV, XXXVII-XL.

Ministère des Affaires Etrangères, *Documents diplomatiques français (1932-1939)*. Première série: 1932-35. Seconde série: 1936-39. Paris, 1963-68.

Ministero degli Affari Esteri. *I Documenti Diplomatici Italiani*. Seste Serie: 1918-22. Settima Serie: 1922-35. Ottava Serie: 1935-39. Nona Serie: 1939-43. Rome, 1952-.

Ministry for Foreign Affairs of the Czechoslovak Republic and the Ministry for Foreign Affairs of the Union of Soviet Socialist Republics. *New Documents on the History of Munich*. Edited by V. F. Kločko *et al.* Prague, 1958.

A biased selection of diplomatic reports.

Ministerstvo inostrannych děl SSSR. *Dokumenty vneshnei politiky SSSR* [*Documents on Soviet Foreign Policy*]. Vols. I-XV: 1917-32. Moscow, 1958-69.

Ministerstvo zahraničních věcí ČSR a Ministerstvo zahraničních věcí SSSR. *Československo-sovětské vztahy v době Velké Vlastenecké Války 1941-1945. Dokumenty a materiály* [*Czechoslovak-Soviet Relations in the Time of the Great Patriotic War, 1941-1945. Documents and Materials*]. Prague, 1960.

A short biased selection of diplomatic documents; of no great importance.

Těsnopisecké zprávy o schůzích Národního shromáždění republiky Československé [*Stenographic Reports on Sessions of the Czechoslovak National Assembly*]. 1918-38. Prague, 1919-39.

After the first election in 1920 the reports on sessions of the Chamber of Deputies and of the Senate were published separately.

Těsnopisecké zprávy o schůzích Prozatimního Národního shromáždění republiky Československé [*Stenographic Reports on Sessions of the Provisional National Assembly of the Czechoslovak Republic*]. Prague, 1946.

The reports continue in 1946-48 as [*Stenographic Reports on Sessions of the Constitutional National Assembly*].

Tesnopisecké zprávy Snemu Slovenskej krajiny [*Stenographic Reports of the Diet of the Slovak State*]. Bratislava, 1939-45.

Tisky k těsnopiseckým zprávám o schůzích Národního shromáždění republiky Československé [*Printed Matters Appended to the Stenographic Reports on Sessions of the Czechoslovak National Assembly*]. 1918-38. 1945-48.

The volumes are attached to the stenographical reports of the various national assemblies in the period of 1918-48.

Trials of War Criminals before the Nuremberg Military Tribunals under Control Council Law No. 10. 15 vols. Nuremberg, 1946-49.

For Czechoslovakia, see volumes IV, XII-XIII.

U.S. Department of State. *Documents on German Foreign Policy, 1918-1945, from the Archives of the German Foreign Ministry*. Series C. Vols. I-V: 1933-37. Series D. Vols. I-XIII: 1937-41. Washington, D.C., 1949-66.

——————. *Papers Relating to the Foreign Relations of the United States 1914-1946*. Washington, D.C., 1922-70. Since 1932 the collection has been entitled *Foreign Relations of the United States. Diplomatic Papers*.

Ústav pro mezinárodní politiku a ekonomii. *Dokumenty československé zahraniční politiky 1945-1960*. [*Documents on Czechoslovak Foreign Policy, 1945-1960*]. Prague, 1960.

A selection of public papers.

The Year-book of the Czechoslovak Republic. 1929-38. Prague, 1929-38.

Published Unofficial Documents

Amort, Čestmír, ed. *Heydrichiáda* [*Period of Terror Following the Assassination of Heydrich*]. Prague, 1964.

A collection of documents on the German persecution in 1942.

——————. *Na pomoc československému lidu: Dokumenty o čs.-sovětském přátelství z let 1938-1945* [*To the Rescue of the Czechoslovak People:*

Documents of Czechoslovak-Soviet Friendship in 1938-1945]. Prague, 1960.

Bareš, Gustav, ed. "Depeše mezi Prahou a Moskvou, 1939-1941" ["Messages between Prague and Moscow, 1939-1941"], *Příspěvky k dějinám KSČ*, No. 3 (1967), 375-433.

Contains cables exchanged between the Moscow Communist center and the illegal Communist party in the Protectorate.

Beneš, Edvard. *Boj o mír a bezpečnost státu [Struggle for Peace and the Security of the State].* Prague, 1934.

A compilation of Beneš's speeches, 1924 to 1934.

————. *Problémy nové Evropy a zahraniční politika československá [Problems of New Europe and Czechoslovak Foreign Policy].* Prague, 1924.

A compilation of Beneš's speeches to 1924.

————. *Šest let exilu a druhé světové války. Řeči, projevy a dokumenty z r. 1938-1945 [Six Years of Exile and the Second World War: Speeches, Declarations, and Documents in the Years 1938-1945].* Prague, 1946.

————. *Světová války a naše revoluce [The World War and Our Revolution].* Vol. III. Prague, 1929.

Bílek, Bohumil. *Fifth Column at Work.* London, 1945.

A valuable collection of documents on the subversive activities of the Henlein party in 1938, based on Czech archives.

César, Jaroslav, and Otáhal, Milan, eds. *Hnutí venkovského lidu v českých zemích v letech 1918-1922 [Movement of the People in the Countryside in the Czech Lands in 1918-1922].* Prague, 1959.

A part of the collection of documents selected from the communist standpoint.

Doležal, Jiří, and Křen, Jan, eds. *Czechoslovakia's Fight 1938-1945. Documents on the Resistance Movement of the Czechoslovak People, 1938-1945.* Prague, 1964.

A one-sided collection aiming to prove the communist thesis of the leading role of the Communist Party.

Gajan, Koloman, ed. *Německý imperialismus proti ČSR 1918-1939 [German Imperialism against the Czechoslovak Republic, 1918-1939].* Prague, 1962.

A collection of selected documents; reflects the Czech viewpoint.

Klimeš, Miloš, *et al.*, eds. *Cesta ke květnu. Vznik lidové demokracie v Československu [On the Way to May: The Origin of People's Democracy in Czechoslovakia].* 2 vols. Prague, 1965.

An important collection on the pre-1945 development; selection reflects the communist viewpoint.

Kocman, Alois, ed. *Souhrnná týdenní hlášení presidia zemské správy politické v Praze o situaci v Čechách 1919-1920 [Weekly Surveys of the Reports of the Presidium of the Provincial Administration in Prague on the Situation in Bohemia in 1919-1920].* Prague, 1959.

A part of the major collection of documents covering the early postwar period.

————, *et al.*, eds. *Boj o směr vývoje československého státu [The Struggle for the Direction of the Development of the Czechoslovak State*]. 2 vols. Prague, 1965-69.

A useful collection of documents on Czechoslovak foreign and domestic policies in the formative period, from October, 1918, to May, 1921.

Král, Václav, ed. *Das Abkommen von München 1938. Tschechoslowakische diplomatische Dokumente, 1937-1939.* Prague, 1968.

A collection of hitherto unpublished Czechoslovak documents on the Munich crisis, including some private papers of Foreign Minister Kamil Krofta.

————. *Cestou k únoru. Dokumenty [On the Way to February. Documents].* Prague, 1963.

A biased selection of documents on the activities of the Czech Socialist party in 1945-48. The editor is well known for his unscrupulous distortion of evidence to justify past and present party policies.

————. *Die Deutschen in der Tschechoslowakei 1933-1947. Dokumentensammlung (Acta Occupationis Bohemiae et Moraviae).* Prague, 1964.

A collection of documents on Czech-German internal relations, from Hitler's rise to power to the expulsion of the German minority from Czechoslovakia.

————. *Lesson from History. Documents Concerning Nazi Policies for Germanisation and Extermination in Czechoslovakia.* Prague, 1962.

A few well selected documents on the policies of Henlein, Frank, and Heydrich from 1938 to 1944.

————. *Politické strany a Mnichov [Political Parties and Munich].* Prague, 1961.

Documents on the policies of various Czech parties in the 1938 crisis; selection reflects pro-communist slant.

Malá, Irena, and Štěpán, František, eds. *Prosincová generální stávka 1920 [The December General Strike, 1920].* Prague, 1961.

Documents on the communist attempt to overthrow the Czechoslovak democratic regime.

Masaryk, Tomáš G. *Cesta demokracie: Soubor projevů za republiky [The Path of Democracy: A Collection of Speeches in the Era of the Republic].* 2 vols. Prague, 1933-34.

A compilation of Masaryk's speeches, 1918-23.

Mnichov v dokumentech [Munich in Documents]. 2 vols. Prague, 1958.

A biased selection of useful material on domestic policies.

Novák, Oldřich, *et al.*, eds. *KSČ proti nacismu. KSČ v dokumentech nacistických bezpečnostních a zpravodajských orgánů [The Communist Party of Czechoslovakia against Nazism. The Communist Party of Czechoslovakia in the Documents of the Nazi Security and Intelligence Organs].* Prague, 1971.

Orlík, Josef, ed. *Opavsko a severní Morava za okupace. Z tajných zpráv okupačních úřadů z let 1940-1943 [The Region of Opava and Northern Moravia during the Occupation. From the Secret Reports of the Occupation Authorities in 1940-1943].* Ostrava, 1961.

Otáhalová, Libuše, and Červinková, Milada, eds. *Dokumenty z historie československé politiky 1939-1943* [*Documents on the History of Czecho-slovak Politics 1939-1943*]. 2 vols. Prague, 1966.

Still a not entirely reliable selection referring mainly to the relations of international diplomacy to the Czechoslovak liberation movement in the West and to contacts between the exile movement in London and the home front.

Prečan, Vilém, ed. *Slovenské národne povstanie; dokumenty* [*The Slovak National Uprising; Documents*]. Bratislava, 1965.

A good comprehensive collection.

Royal Institute of International Affairs. *Documents on International Affairs. 1934-1950.* Edited by Stephen Heald and John W. Wheeler-Bennett. London, 1935-54.

Each volume contains a section on Czechoslovakia.

[Slovak Government]. *Pred súdom národa; proces s Dr. J. Tisom, Dr. F. Ďurčanským a A. Machom v Bratislave v dňoch 2. dec. 1946-15. apr. 1947* [*Facing the Trial of the People: The Trial of Dr. J. Tiso, Dr. F. Ďurčanský, and A. Mach in Bratislava from December 2, 1946-April 15, 1947*]. 5 vols. Bratislava, 1947.

Contains the partial transcripts of the trials of the wartime leaders of the Slovak state.

Štefánik, Milan R. *Zápisníky M. R. Štefánika* [*The Notebook of M. R. Štefánik*]. Prague, 1935.

An important source for the study of the Czechoslovak actions abroad during World War I.

Wynne, Waller, Jr. *The Population of Czechoslovakia.* Washington, 1953.

A brief compilation of population statistics reports.

Za svobodu do nové Československé republiky. Ideový program domácího odbojového hnutí vypracovaný v letech 1939-41 [*For Freedom toward the New Czechoslovak Republic. Ideological Program of the Home Resistance Movement Elaborated in 1939-1941*]. Prague, 1945.

The text of the program of the Czech democratic resistance.

BOOKS

Adler, H. G. *Theresienstadt 1941-1945; das Antlitz einer Zwangsgemein-schaft.* Tübingen, 1960. 2nd rev. ed.

A detailed, exhaustive study of the Jewish concentration camp at Terezín.

Alton, Thad P., *et al. Czechoslovak National Income and Product, 1947-48 and 1955-1956.* New York, 1962.

A concise study.

Alexander, Manfred. *Der deutsch-tschechoslowakische Schiedsvertrag von 1925 im Rahmen der Locarno-Verträge.* Munich-Vienna, 1970.

Amort, Čestmír, and Jedlička, I. M. *Tajemství vyzvědače A-54* [*Secret of Agent A-54*]. Prague, 1965.

A not always reliable but interesting story of Paul Thümmel, the Nazi *Abwehr* official who worked for the Czechoslovak intelligence service.

Barto, Jaroslav. *Riešenie vzťahu Čechov a Slovákov, 1944-1948* [*Solving the Relations between the Czechs and the Slovaks*]. Bratislava, 1968.

On the changing legal status of Slovakia from 1944 to 1948.

Bartošek, Karel. *Pražské povstání 1945* [*Prague Uprising 1945*]. 2nd rev. edition. Prague, 1965.

A valuable study; not unfrequently tainted with communist bias.

Basch, Antonín. *Germany's Economic Conquest of Czechoslovakia*. Chicago, 1941.

An illuminating study of German methods of penetration into and seizure of Czechoslovak economy.

de Battaglia, Otto Forst. *Zwischeneuropa. Von der Ostsee bis zur Adria*. Frankfurt a.Main, 1953.

Gives a general survey of Czechoslovakia in 1939-52 on pp. 187-322.

Bauer, Otto. *The Austrian Revolution*. London, 1925.

A brilliant analysis by the Austrian socialist leader who was a promoter of the right of self-determination for small nations in the Habsburg Empire.

Beer, Ferdinand, *et al. Dejinná križovatka. Slovenské národné povstanie—predpoklady a výsledky* [*Historic Crossroads: The Slovak National Uprising—Assumptions and Outcome*]. Bratislava, 1964.

A comprehensive account written by communist historians.

Belda, Josef, *et al. Na rozhraní dvou epoch* [*On the Frontier of Two Epochs*]. Prague, 1968.

A communist account of the main trends of the developments in Czechoslovakia during 1945-48.

Benčík, Antonín, *et al. Partyzánské hnutí v Československu za druhé světové války* [*The Partisan Movement in Czechoslovakia during World War II*]. Prague, 1961.

This strongly tendentious volume provides some useful data on partisan warfare.

[Beneš, Edvard]. An Active and Responsible Czechoslovak Statesman. *Germany and Czechoslovakia*. 2 vols. Prague, 1937.

A concise analysis of Czechoslovak foreign policy and its relations to Germany; also examines the Czechoslovak policy at the Versailles Peace Conference.

Beneš, Edvard. *Memoirs of Dr. Eduard Beneš. From Munich to New War and New Victory*. Boston, 1954.

The most useful reminiscences giving an account of Beneš's activities in 1938-45.

———. *Mnichovské dny. Paměti* [*Days of Munich. Memoirs*]. Prague, 1968.

This is the enlarged complete version of Beneš's *Memoirs* including a discussion of the crisis of Munich; of basic importance for the understanding of Beneš's policies during 1938-45.

———. *Souvenirs de guerre et de révolution, 1914-1918; la lutte pour l'indépendance des peuples*. 2 vols. Paris, 1928.

This French translation is the only complete text of the original version of this valuable war memoirs.

Blažek, Miroslav. *Hospodářská geografie Československa* [*Economic Geography of Czechoslovakia*]. Prague, 1954.

A useful guide to the post-1945 republic.

Bokes, František. *Dejiny Slovenska a Slovákov od nejstarších čias po oslobodenie* [*History of Slovakia and the Slovaks from the Oldest Times to their Liberation*]. Bratislava, 1964.

The only substantial synthesis of Slovak history to 1920; factual and objective.

Borovička, Josef. *Ten Years of Czechoslovak Politics*. Prague, 1929.

An informative survey of the formative period of the Czechoslovak state.

Borský, Lev. *Znovudobytí samostatnosti české* [*Reconquest of Czech Independence*]. Prague, 1928.

Memoirs of a right-wing patriot.

Bosl, Karl, ed. *Handbuch der Geschichte der böhmischen Länder.* Vol. III: *Die böhmischen Länder im Habsburgerreich 1848-1919.* Vol. IV: *Der tschechoslowakische Staat im Zeitalter der modernen Massendemokratie und Diktatur.* 4 vols. Stuttgart, 1968-70.

This vast scholarly enterprise by German historians presents the most up-to-date study available in any language; includes exhaustive bibliography.

Bouček, Miroslav. *Praha v únoru 1948. O práci pražské stranické organizace v únorových dnech 1948* [*Prague in February 1948. On the Activities of the Prague Party Organization during February, 1948*]. Prague, 1963.

A biased account of the February communist takeover as seen through the eyes of the Prague communist regional organization under the leadership of Antonín Novotný.

Braddick, Henderson B. *Germany, Czechoslovakia, and the "Grand Alliance" in the May Crisis, 1938*. Denver, 1969.

This is a short survey of the May crisis not without merit.

Bradley, John F. N. *La Légion tchécoslovaque en Russie, 1914-1920*. Paris, 1965.

An informative study; a full scholarly treatment has still to be written.

Brandes, Detlef. *Die Tschechen unter deutschem Protektorat.* Part I: *Besatzungspolitik, Kollaboration und Widerstand im Protektorat Böhmen und Mähren bis Heydrichs Tod (1939-1942).* Munich-Vienna, 1969.

The most up-to-date thorough discussion based on primary evidence and sound scholarship.

Brod, Tomáš, and Čejka, Eduard. *Na západní frontě. Historie československých vojenských jednotek na Západě v letech druhé světové války* [*On the Western Front. History of the Czechoslovak Military Units in the West during World War II*]. 2nd rev. edition. Prague, 1965.

Well-documented but still one-sided.

Brügel, Johann W. *Ludwig Czech. Arbeitsführer und Staatsmann.* Vienna, 1960.

A perceptive short biography of the leader of the German Social Democratic party in Czechoslovakia until 1938.

————. *Tschechen und Deutsche 1918-1938.* Munich, 1967.

An exhaustive review of Czech-German relations.

Buchválek, Miroslav, *et al. Dějiny Československa v datech [History of Czechoslovakia in Dates].* Prague, 1968.

A very handy encyclopedia of Czechoslovak history.

Buk, Pierre [Weisskopf, F. C.]. *La Tragédie tchécoslovaque. De septembre 1938 à mars 1939. Avec des documents inédits du livre blanc tchécoslovaque.* Paris, 1939.

A well-informed discussion of the Munich crisis written from the Czech point of view.

Burgess, Alan. *Seven Men at Daybreak.* London, 1960.

A popular account of the assassination of Reinhard Heydrich in Prague in May, 1942.

Bušek, Vratislav, and Spulber, Nicolas, eds. *Czechoslovakia.* New York, 1957.

A useful guide providing valuable data; focuses on the post-1948 era.

Butvin, Jozef, and Havránek, Jan. *Dějiny Československa [History of Czechoslovakia].* Vol. III. Prague, 1968.

A substantial survey of Czech and Slovak history from 1781 to 1918.

Byrnes, Robert F. *Bibliography of American Publications on East Central Europe, 1945-1957.* Bloomington, Ind., 1957.

Čapek, Karel. *President Masaryk Tells His Story.* New York, 1935.

An immensely interesting autobiography as told to the foremost Czech writer.

Celovsky, Boris. *Das Münchener Abkommen von 1938.* Stuttgart, 1958.

A systematic, exhaustive, and somewhat pedestrian treatment of the diplomatic background of Munich; a strict traditional diplomatic history.

Černý, Bohumil. *Most k novému životu. Německá emigrace v ČSR v letech 1933-1939 [The Bridge to a New Life: The German Emigration in the Czechoslovak Republic in 1933-1939].* Prague, 1967.

César, Jaroslav, and Černý, Bohumil. *Politika německých buržoazních stran v Československu v letech 1918-38 [Policy of German Bourgeois Parties in Czechoslovakia in 1918-1938].* 2 vols. Prague, 1962.

Contains much information.

Československá akademie věd. Historický ústav. *Bibliografie československé historie za léta 1955-1961 [Bibliography of Czechoslovak History for the Years 1955-1961].* 5 vols. Prague, 1957-64.

The annual collection began in 1904 under the title of *Bibliografie české historie [Bibliography of Czech History].* So far the period of 1942-54 has not been covered for Czech history, nor 1945-54 for Slovak history.

Československá akademie věd. Sekce historická. *25 ans d'historiographie tchécoslovaque, 1936-1960.* Prague, 1960.

A bibliographic guide through all aspects of Czech and Slovak history; a presentation at the occasion of the Eleventh International Historical Congress in Stockholm.

————. Ústav dějin evropských socialistických zemí. *Češi a Poláci v minu-*

losti [*Czechs and Poles in the Past*]. 2 vols. Prague, 1964-67.

A scholarly survey of Czech-Polish relations from the beginning to 1945.

Československá revoluce v letech 1944-1948. Sborník příspěvků z konference historiků k 20. výročí osvobození ČSSR [*Czechoslovak Revolution in 1944-1948. Memorial Volume of Contributions at the Conference of Historians on the Occasion of the Twentieth Anniversary of the Liberation of the Czechoslovak Socialist Republic*]. Prague, 1966.

In a series of articles Czech and Slovak historians deal with the main problems of the postwar period.

Československá vlastivěda [*A Study of Czechoslovakia*]. 10 vols. in 12. Prague, 1929-36.

A mine of information although the contributions are of uneven quality. Volume IV deals with history.

Chaloupecký, Václav. *Zápas o Slovensko 1918* [*Struggle for Slovakia 1918*]. Prague, 1930.

An informative account of the diplomatic and military struggle for the control of Slovakia between the Czechoslovak and Hungarian governments.

Chmela, Leopold. *The Economic Aspects of the German Occupation of Czechoslovakia*. Prague, 1948.

An elaboration of the assessment of Czechoslovak losses and damages compiled by Czechoslovak authorities; the author was the director of the Czechoslovak National Bank.

Chmelař, Josef. *The German Problem in Czechoslovakia*. Prague, 1936.

————. *Political Parties in Czechoslovakia*. Prague, 1926.

Lucid surveys.

Císař, Jaroslav, and Pokorný, František. *The Czechoslovak Republic. A Survey of Its History and Geography, Its Political and Cultural Organisation, and Its Economic Resources*. Prague, 1921.

A useful introduction.

Codresco, Florin. *La Petite Entente*. 2 vols. Paris, n.d. [1931?].

A comprehensive treatment.

Craig, Gordon A., and Gilbert, Felix, eds. *The Diplomats 1919-1939*. Princeton, N.J., 1953.

Contains the noteworthy contribution by Paul E. Zinner on the diplomacy of Beneš.

Čulen, Konštantín. *Pittsburghská dohoda* [*The Pittsburgh Agreement*]. Bratislava, 1937.

A well documented but biased account of the Czechoslovak Pittsburgh Agreement of 1918 and its repercussions in Czechoslovak politics; by a Slovak autonomist.

————. *Po Svätoplukovi druhá naše hlava: Život Dr. Jozefa Tisu* [*After Svatopluk our Second Head of State: The Life of Dr. Jozef Tiso*]. Cleveland, 1947.

An admiring biography of Dr. Tiso, the head of the German-sponsored Slovak state; contains much inside information.

Dami, Aldo. *La Ruthénie subcarpathique*. Genève-Annemasse, 1944.

A general account up to 1944.

Danáš, Jozef. *Ľudácky separatizmus a hitlerovské Nemecko*. Bratislava, 1963.

One-sided account covering the period of 1938-1940.

Daxner, Igor. *Ľudáctvo pred národným súdom 1945-1947* [*The People's Party before the Court of the Nation 1945-1947*]. Bratislava, 1961.

A propagandistic account of the postwar trials by the presiding communist judge.

Deák, Francis. *Hungary at the Paris Peace Conference; the Diplomatic History of the Treaty of Trianon*. New York, 1942.

An analysis from the Hungarian viewpoint.

Dérer, Ivan. *Slovensko v prevrate a po ňom* [*Slovakia during the Revolution and After*]. Bratislava, 1924.

Important for the establishment of the Czechoslovak rule in Slovakia.

———. *Slovenský vývoj a ľudácka zrada* [*Slovak Development and the People's Party Betrayal*]. Prague, 1946.

An examination of the policies of the Hlinka party in prewar Slovakia.

Diamond, William. *Czechoslovakia between East and West*. London, 1947.

A contemporary observer describes the situation in 1945-46. This should be supplemented by more recent studies.

Dobrý, Anatol. *Hospodářska krize československého průmyslu ve vztahu k Mnichovu* [*Economic Crisis of Czechoslovak Industry with Regard to Munich*]. Prague, 1959.

Deals with the main trends of Czechoslovak industrial development during 1918-38.

Dolejší, Vojtěch. *Noviny a novináři. Z poznámek a vzpomínek* [*Newspapers and Journalists. From Notes and Recollections*]. Prague, 1963.

A slanted account on the Czechoslovak press from 1918 to 1948 by an orthodox former editor of the *Rudé právo*.

Doležal, Jiří. *Jediná cesta. Cesta ozbrojeného boje v českých zemích* [*The Only Way. The Way of the Armed Struggle in the Czech Lands*]. Prague, 1966.

A good account of the activities of the Czech underground in 1939-45; based on broad documentation.

Drug, Štefan. *Vladimír Clementis; kultúrny publicista* [*Vladimír Clementis; a Cultural Journalist*]. Bratislava, 1967.

A well-written biography of the prominent Slovak victim of the Stalinist purges.

Ducháček, Ivan. *The Strategy of Communist Infiltration: The Case of Czechoslovakia*. New Haven, 1949.

A lucid short presentation of communist methods used in the February takeover.

D'urica, Milan S. *La Slovacchia e le sue relazione politiche con la Germania 1938-1945*. Vol. I. Padua, 1964.

The volume covers Slovak-German relations in the post-Munich period till the outbreak of World War II; contains a valuable collection of eighty-five documents; written from the separatist Slovak viewpoint.

D'určanský, Ferdinand, ed. *Právo Slovákov na samostatnosť vo svetle dokumentov* [*The Slovaks' Right to Independence in the Light of Documents*]. Buenos Aires, 1954.

A slanted account reflecting the Slovak separatist viewpoint.

Dzvoník, Michal. *Ohlas Veľkej októbrovej socialistickej revolúcie na Slovensku, 1918-1919* [*Echo of the Great October Socialist Revolution in Slovakia, 1918-1919*]. Bratislava, 1957.

On social disturbances in Slovakia after the armistice, which the author sees as an "echo" of the Bolshevik revolution.

Encyclopédie tchécoslovaque. Edited by Oscar Butter and Bohuslav Ruml. 4 vols. Prague, 1923-29.

A detailed, unfinished, multi-volume work; describes the economy of the country.

Erdely, Eugene V. *Germany's First European Protectorate. The Fate of the Czechs and the Slovaks.* London, 1941.

Should be supplemented by more recent studies.

Eubank, Keith. *Munich.* Norman, 1963.

A well-balanced account of the Munich crisis.

Falťan, Samo. *Partizanská vojna na Slovensku* [*Partisan Warfare in Slovakia*]. Bratislava, 1959.

On partisan warfare in World War II from the communist point of view.

————. *Slovenská otázka v Československu* [*The Slovak Question in Czechoslovakia*]. Bratislava, 1968.

On Czech-Slovak relations from 1918 to 1948 by a prominent Slovak communist.

Feierabend, Ladislav K. *Ve vládách Druhé republiky* [*In the Cabinets of the Second Republic*]. New York, 1961.

Memoirs of a Czech agrarian politician who was a member of the Czechoslovak, Protectorate, and London exile governments.

————. *Ve vládě Protektorátu* [*In the Protectorate Government*]. New York, 1962.

————. *Z vlády doma do vlády v exilu* [*From the Government at Home to the Government in Exile*]. New York, 1964.

————. *Ve vládě v exilu* [*In the Government in Exile*]. 2 vols. Washington, 1965-66.

————. *Beneš mezi Washingtonem a Moskvou. Vzpomínsky z londýnské vlády od jara 1943 do jara 1944* [*Beneš between Washington and Moscow. Recollections of the London Government from Spring, 1943, to Spring, 1944*]. Washington, 1966.

————. *Soumrak československé demokracie* [*The Twilight of Czechoslovak Democracy*]. Washington, 1967.

Fierlinger, Zdeněk. *Ve službách ČSR* [*In the Service of the Czechoslovak Republic*]. 2 vols. Prague, 1947-1948.

Illuminating memoirs of the well-known pro-communist politician describing his diplomatic activities in 1937-45. The book was withdrawn from the market in 1948 because it did not correspond to the new Stalinist line.

Fischer, Josef, and Patzak, Václav, and Perth, Vincenz. *Ihr Kampf. Die wahren Ziele der Sudetendeutschen Partei*. Carlsbad, 1937.
A perceptive account of the clandestine activities of the Henleinist leaders in 1933-37.

Friedman, Otto. *The Break-up of Czech Democracy*. London, 1950.
A still valuable examination of the destruction of the democratic regime in 1948.

Friš, Edo. *Myšlienka a čin. Úvahy o Československu 1938-1948* [*Thought and Action. Observations on Czechoslovakia, 1938-1948*]. Bratislava, 1968.
An analysis by a sharp-minded Slovak communist leader.

———. *Povstanie zd'aleka a blízka* [*The Uprising from Afar and Near*]. Bratislava, 1964.
An account by a wartime resident of Moscow.

Fuchs, Gerhard. *Gegen Hitler und Henlein. Der solidarische Kampf tschechischer und deutscher Antifaschisten von 1933 bis 1938*. Berlin, 1961.
Reflects the communist viewpoint.

Gajan, Koloman. *Německý imperialismus a československo-německé vztahy v letech 1918-1921* [*German Imperialism and Czechoslovak-German Relations in 1918-1921*]. Prague, 1962.
One-sided but based on little-known sources.

Gajanová, Alena. *ČSR a středoevropská politika velmocí 1918-1938* [*The Czechoslovak Republic and the Central European Policy of the Great Powers 1918-1938*]. Prague, 1967.
This comprehensive, thoughtful, but overly descriptive treatment centers on the 1920's.

———. *Dvojí tvář: z historie předmnichovského fašismu* [*Two-Face: History of pre-Munich Fascism*]. Prague, 1962.
A biased but valuable contribution to Czechoslovak internal politics under the First Republic.

Gedye, G.E.R. *Betrayal in Central Europe*. New York, 1939.
First-hand reporting at its best on the Munich crisis from Prague by a sympathetic English correspondent.

George, Pierre. *Le Problème allemand en Tchécoslovaquie (1919-1946)*. Paris, 1947.
A short account, sympathetic to Czechoslovakia; by a communist professor at the Sorbonne.

von Glaise-Horstenau, Edmund. *The Collapse of the Austro-Hungarian Empire*. London-Toronto-New York, 1930.
The standard work on the last two years of the Habsburg Empire by the former nationalist head of the Austrian War Archives.

Germany (Federal Republic). Bundesministerium für Vertriebene, Flüchtlinge und Kriegsgeschädigte. *Dokumentation der Vertreibung der Deutschen aus Ost- Mitteleuropa*. Edited by Theodor Schieder. Vol. IV, 1-2:

Die Vertreibung der deutschen Bevölkerung aus der Tschechoslowakei.
2. Beiheft: *Ein Tagebuch aus Prag 1945-46* by Margarete Schell. Bonn,
1957.
> A well-documented presentation of the German viewpoint.

Gottwald, Klement. *Spisy [Writings].* 15 vols. Prague, 1950-61.
> The collective writings and speeches have not much value because some
> articles and speeches were left out or were abbreviated and cut by the
> editors.

Graca, Bohuslav. *14. marec 1939 [March 14, 1939].* Bratislava, 1959.
> A presentation of the post-Munich development in Slovakia.

Grant Duff, Shiela. *A German Protectorate; the Czechs under Nazi Rule.*
London, 1942.
> A still useful volume.

Grečo, Martin. *Martinská deklarácia [Declaration of Martin].* 2nd ed.
Turčiansky Svätý Martin, 1947.
> Slovak political activity during World War I and immediately after-
> ward.

Griffith, Joan and Jonathan. *Lost Liberty? The Ordeal of the Czechs and
the Future of Freedom.* New York, 1939.
> A good on-the-spot report from Prague in 1938.

Griffith, William E., ed. *Communism in Europe. Continuity, Change, and
the Sino-Soviet Dispute.* 2 vols. Cambridge, Mass., and London, 1966.
> The second volume includes a perceptive article on Czechoslovakia.

Grňa, Josef. *Sedm roků na domácí frontě [Seven Years on the Home Front].*
Brno, 1968.
> An honest and absorbing account by one of the leaders of the Resist-
> ance movement in 1939-45.

Groscurth, Helmuth. *Tagebücher eines Abwehroffiziers, 1938-1940.* Stuttgart, 1970.
> Gives information on the situation in the Sudeten area in the fall of
> 1938.

Gruber, Josef, ed. *Czechoslovakia; a Survey of Economic and Social Conditions.* New York, 1924.

Hajda, Jan, ed. *A Study of Contemporary Czechoslovakia.* Chicago, 1955.
> An account of Czechoslovak society during the period of 1930-55.

Hájek, Jiří S. *Mnichov [Munich].* Prague, 1958.
> An orthodox communist account.

Hájek, Miloš. *Od Mnichova k 15. březnu [From Munich to March 15].*
Prague, 1959.
> A biased but still informative survey of the history of the post-Munich
> rump republic; partly superseded by the study by Lukeš.

Hajšman, Jan. *Maffie v rozmachu [Mafia at Its Height].* Prague, 1933.
> Reminiscences on the struggle of the Czech secret anti-Austrian or-
> ganization in the last two years of the war.

Hamšík, Dušan, and Pražák, Jiří. *Bomba pro Heydricha [The Bomb for
Heydrich].* Prague, 1963.

The assassination of Heydrich has evoked several books. This one is a well-written and popular account.

Hassinger, Hugo. *Die Tschechoslowakei. Ein geographisches, politisches und wirtschaftliches Handbuch.* Vienna, Leipzig, Munich, 1925.

A pro-German, informative, and thoughtful survey.

Henderson, Alexander. *Eyewitness in Czecho-Slovakia.* London, 1939.

A still useful account including material on the events of 1938-39 by the London *Daily Herald* correspondent.

Herben, Jan. *T. G. Masaryk: Život a dílo presidenta Osvoboditele* [*T. G. Masaryk: Life and Work of the President-Liberator*]. 5th ed., Prague, 1946.

The most comprehensive biography of T. G. Masaryk.

Hitchcock, Edward B. *"I Built a Temple for Peace": The Life of Eduard Beneš.* London, 1940.

This laudatory biography belongs to the better works on Beneš.

Hoch, Charles. *The Political Parties in Czechoslovakia.* Prague, 1936.

A concise survey.

Hoensch, Jörg K. *Geschichte der Tschechoslowakischen Republik 1918 bis 1965.* Stuttgart, 1966.

———. *Die Slowakei und Hitlers Ostpolitik. Hlinkas Slowakische Volkspartei zwischen Autonomie und Separation, 1938/39.* Cologne-Graz, 1965.

An objective and well-documented study of Nazi policy in Slovakia during 1938-39.

———. *Der ungarische Revisionismus und die Zerschlagung der Tschechoslowakei.* Tübingen, 1967.

A solid work with considerable material.

Hodža, Milan. *Federation in Central Europe.* London, 1942.

Memoirs of the Czechoslovak premier; frank and revealing only for the period before World War I.

———. *Slovenský rozchod s Maďarmi r. 1918* [*The Slovak Break with the Hungarians in 1918*]. Bratislava, 1929.

A collection of Hodža's papers and articles on his mission to Budapest in 1918.

Holotíková, Zdeňka, and Plevza, Viliam. *Vladimír Clementis.* Bratislava, 1968.

A biography of the former Czechoslovak Foreign Minister, executed in December, 1952.

Horecky, Paul L., ed. *East Central Europe: A Guide to Basic Publications.* Chicago, London, 1969.

Contains historical bibliography on Czechoslovakia.

Hoření, Zdeněk. *Antonín Janoušek: Predseda revolučnej vlády Slovenskej republiky rád* [*Antonín Janoušek: Chairman of the Revolutionary Government of the Slovak Soviet Republic*]. Bratislava, 1964.

A panegyric.

Houdek, Fedor. *Oslobodenie Slovenska* [*Liberation of Slovakia*]. Bratislava, 1929.

Reflects pro-Czechoslovak viewpoint.

Houdek, Fedor. *Vznik hraníc Slovenska* [*The Genesis of the Boundaries of Slovakia*]. Bratislava, 1931.

Drawing of the Slovak boundary at the Paris Peace Conference.

Hruban, Mořic. *Z časů nedlouho zašlých* [*From the Recent Past*]. Ed. by Jan Drábek. Rome-Los Angeles, 1967.

Interesting reminiscences of one of the leaders of the Czech Populist party.

Husa, Václav. *Geschichte der Tschechoslowakei*. Prague, 1963.

A communist propagandistic presentation.

Husák, Gustáv. *Svedectvo o Slovenskom národnom povstaní* [*Testimony about the Slovak National Uprising*]. Bratislava, 1964.

A slanted account by the present communist leader.

Hutak, B. *With Blood and with Iron. The Lidice Story*. London, 1957.

Ivanov, Miroslav. *Nejen černé uniformy. Monology o atentátu na Reinharda Heydricha* [*Not Only Black Uniforms: Monologues on the Attempt on Reinhard Heydrich*]. Prague, 1965.

A popular account based on original research.

Jablonický, Jozef. *Slovensko na prelome. Zápas o víťazstvo národnej a demokratickej revolúcie na Slovensku* [*Slovakia at the Breaking-Point. The Struggle for Victory of the National and Democratic Revolution in Slovakia*]. Bratislava, 1965.

A serious study tainted with Communist bias on the activities of the Communist party of Slovakia in 1944-45.

————, and Kropilák, Miroslav. *Slovník Slovenského národného povstania* [*Dictionary of the Slovak National Uprising*]. 2nd rev. edition. Bratislava, 1970.

A useful encyclopedia of facts and personalities in the Slovak Resistance in World War II.

————. *Z ilegality do povstania. Kapitoly z občianskeho odboja* [*From the Underground into the Uprising. Chapters from the Bourgeois Resistance*]. Bratislava, 1969.

So far the best study on the activities of the democratic Slovak Resistance until the outbreak of the Uprising.

Jackson, G. D. *Comintern and Peasant in East Europe, 1919-1930*. New York, 1966.

Contains a chapter on Czechoslovak peasants.

Jacoby, Gerhard. *Racial State; The German Nationalities Policy in the Protectorate of Bohemia and Moravia*. New York, 1944.

A good survey.

Jahn, Egbert. *Die Deutschen in der Slowakei, 1918-1929: Ein Beitrag zur Nationalitätenproblematik*. Munich-Vienna, 1971.

Jaksch, Wenzel. *Europas Weg nach Potsdam. Schuld und Schicksal im Donauraum*. Stuttgart, 1958.

A slanted personal account of Czech-German relations in the last fifty years by a Sudeten German social democratic leader. English translation, *Road to Potsdam*, published in 1963.

Janeček, Oldřich *et al.*, eds. *Odboj a revoluce 1938-1945. Nástin dějin česko-*

slovenského odboje. [Resistance and Revolution 1938-1945. An Outline of the History of the Czechoslovak Resistance]. Prague, 1965.

A synthesis by the authors of the projected three-volume history of the Resistance; without a bibliography or notes.

———. *Z počátků odboje 1938-1941 [Beginnings of the Resistance, 1938-1941]*. Prague, 1969.

A reliable examination.

Jaroš, Václav, ed. *Šest let okupace [Six Years of Occupation]*. Prague, 1946.

A collective account of the German occupation from 1939 to 1945.

Jarošová, V., and Jaroš, O. *Slovenské robotníctvo v boji o moc, 1944-1948 [The Slovak Workers in the Struggle for Power, 1944-1948]*. Bratislava, 1965.

A slanted discussion of the efforts of the Slovak Communist party to win power in Slovakia.

Jelínek, Jaroslav. *PÚ. Politické ústředí domácího odboje. Vzpomínky a poznámky novináře [PC. Political Center of the Home Resistance. Reminiscences and Notes by a Journalist]*. Prague, 1947.

Written by a participant; a general account.

The Jews of Czechoslovakia. New York, 1968.

A symposium of articles discussing Jewish contributions to the Czechoslovak state.

Jung, Rudolf. *Die Tschechen. Tausend Jahre deutsch-tschechischer Kampf.* Berlin, 1937.

An anti-Czech and anti-Semite volume surveying some aspects of German-Czech relations; the author was an exiled leader of the Nazi party in Czechoslovakia.

Kabinet dějin odborů. *Odbory a naše revoluce. Sborník studií [Trade Unions and Our Revolution]*. Prague, 1968.

A valuable series of articles referring to the Czech revolutionary trade unions in 1944-48.

Kalina, Antonín S. *Krví a železem dobyto čs. samostatnosti [Czechoslovak Independence Was Conquered by Blood and Sword]*. Prague, 1938.

The first volume of a projected two-volume study on American policy toward the Czech liberation movement in World War I; by a conservative author who argues a well-documented thesis that the existence of the Czechoslovak legion in Siberia was the most important factor making for the U.S. recognition of the Czechoslovak political demands.

Kalista, Zdeněk. *Stručné dějiny československé [Concise History of Czechoslovakia]*. Prague, 1947.

With Krofta's work, this is the best survey by a known Czech historian.

Kaplan, Karel. *Znárodnění a socialismus [Nationalization and Socialism]*. Prague, 1968.

A thoughtful Marxist analysis of Czech society in 1945-46.

Karlgren, Anton. *Henlein-Hitler a československá tragedie [Henlein-Hitler and the Czechoslovak Tragedy]*. Prague, 1945.

A Czech edition of a Swedish book generally sympathetic to Czechoslovakia; published originally in Sweden in June, 1939.

Kárník, Zdeněk. *Socialisté na rozcestí. Habsburk, Masaryk či Šmeral? [The Socialists at the Crossroads. Habsburg, Masaryk or Šmeral?]*. Prague, 1968.
A factual monograph on the Czech Social Democratic party in 1917-18.

―――. *Za československou republiku rad: Národní výbory a dělnické rady v českých zemích, 1917-1920 [For a Czechoslovak Soviet Republic: National Committees and Workers' Councils in the Czech Lands, 1917-1920]*. Prague, 1963.
Propounds the dubious thesis that in 1917-20 there was a conscious movement in the Czech lands to establish a Soviet Republic.

Kennan, George F. *From Prague after Munich. Diplomatic Papers 1938-1940*. Princeton, N.J., 1968.
A collection of Kennan's reports from Prague.

Kerner, Robert J., ed. *Czechoslovakia. Twenty Years of Independence*. Berkeley and Los Angeles, 1940. 2nd edition in 1949.
A standard survey.

Kertesz, Stephen D., ed. *The Fate of East Central Europe. Hopes and Failures of American Foreign Policy*. Notre Dame, Ind., 1956.
This comprehensive symposium deals with American foreign policy in East Central Europe; emphasis is on the post-1945 development.

Kiesewetter, Bruno. *Die Wirtschaft der Tschechoslowakei seit 1945*. Berlin, 1954.
A useful account.

Kirschbaum, Joseph M. *Slovakia: Nation at the Crossroads of Central Europe*. New York, 1960.
With anti-Czech slant; the author is a former official of the Slovak state.

Kladiva, Jaroslav. *Kultura a politika [Culture and Politics]*. Prague, 1968.
A monograph on the cultural and ideological scene in 1945-48.

Klepetář, Harry. *Seit 1918 . . . Eine Geschichte der tschechoslowakischen Republik*. Moravská Ostrava, 1937.
A generally reliable study by an informed Sudeten German democrat.

Kolařík, J. *Peníze a politika: Karel Engliš, bojovník o stabilizaci [Money and Politics: Karel Engliš, a Fighter for Stability]*. Prague, 1937.
A biography of the famed Czechoslovak finance minister; important for the economic development of the First Republic.

Kopecký, Rudolf. *Československý odboj v Polsku v r. 1939 [Czechoslovak Resistance in Poland in 1939]*. Rotterdam, 1958.

Kopecký, Václav. *ČSR a KSČ. Pamětní výpisy k historii Československé republiky a k boji KSČ za socialistické Československo [The Czechoslovak Republic and the Communist Party of Czechoslovakia. Memoirs on the History of the Czechoslovak Republic and the Struggle of the Communist Party of Czechoslovakia for a Socialist Czechoslovakia]*. Prague, 1960.
A biased account by a communist leader.

―――. *Gottwald v Moskvě [Gottwald in Moscow]*. Prague, 1948.
A personal laudatory account by a communist leader.

Korbel, Josef. *The Communist Subversion of Czechoslovakia, 1938-1948. The Failure of Coexistence*. Princeton, N.J., 1959.
A case study of a democratic country subverted by communist forces.

Kozeński, Jerzy. *Czechosłowacja w polskiej polityce zagranicznej w latach 1932-1938* [*Czechoslovakia in Polish Foreign Policy in the Years 1932-1938*]. Poznań, 1964.

A noteworthy study based on broad documentation.

Král, Václav. *Intervenční válka československé buržoazie proti maďarské sovětské republice r. 1919* [*Interventionist War of the Czechoslovak Bourgeoisie against the Hungarian Soviet Republic in 1919*]. Prague, 1954.

Stalinist historiography at its worst.

———. *Otázky hospodářského a sociálního vývoje v českých zemích v letech 1938-1945* [*Questions of Economic and Social Development in the Czech Lands in 1938-1945*]. 3 vols. Prague, 1957-59.

A strongly biased study providing a wealth of source material.

———. *Pravda o okupaci* [*The Truth about the Occupation*]. Prague, 1962.

A general account written from the communist viewpoint; the author uses little-known sources but tends to neglect the basic principles of historical scholarship.

———. *Spojenectví československo-sovětské v evropské politice, 1935-1939* [*Czechoslovak-Soviet Alliance in European Politics, 1935-1939*]. Prague, 1970.

A study of diplomatic relations based on unpublished documents.

Kramer, Juraj. *Iredenta a separatizmus v slovenskej politike, 1919-1938* [*Irredentism and Separatism in Slovak Politics, 1919-1938*]. Bratislava, 1957.

On the role of Hungarian revisionist propaganda and its Slovak henchmen in Slovak politics.

———. *K dejinám priemyslu na Slovensku za prvej ČSR* [*History of Industry in Slovakia during the First Czechoslovak Republic*]. Bratislava, 1955.

A short survey.

———. *Slovenské autonomistické hnutie v rokoch 1918-1929* [*Slovak Autonomist Movement in 1918-1929*]. Bratislava, 1962.

A communist analysis of the Slovak autonomist movement. See also the abbreviated German version in *Historica*, VII, 115-44.

Krebs, Hans. *Kampf in Böhmen*. Berlin, 1936.

An interesting anti-Czech historical account by a Nazi leader.

Křen, Jan. *Do emigrace* [*Into Exile*]. Prague, 1963.

A biased but comprehensive study of the political activities of the Czechoslovak exile movement up to September 1939.

———. *V emigraci. Západní zahraniční odboj 1939-1940* [*In Exile. The Liberation Movement in the West, 1939-1940*]. Prague, 1969.

This second volume of the planned history of the Czechoslovak exile movement treats the political activities of the emigration in France and Great Britain during the period from the outbreak of World War II until the defeat of France.

Krofta, Kamil. *Dějiny československé* [*Czechoslovak History*]. Prague, 1947.

An excellent survey by a prominent historian who happened to become foreign minister.

Krofta, Kamil. *A Short History of Czechoslovakia*. New York, 1934.

A shorter version of the original Czech text.

―――. *Z dob naší první republiky* [*During the Times of our First Republic*]. Prague, 1939.

A study of the internal and diplomatic developments; focuses on the post-1935 period.

Kropilák, Miroslav. *Účast vojakov v Slovenskom národnom povstaní* [*Participation of Soldiers in the Slovak National Uprising*]. Bratislava, 1960.

An attempt to correct the earlier communist denigration of the part of Slovak soldiers, as distinguished from partisans, in the uprising of 1944.

Kvaček, Robert. *Nad Evropou zataženo* [*Clouds over Europe*]. Prague, 1966.

In this accurate, meticulously documented, and comprehensive first volume of a planned history of Munich, the author examines Czechoslovak foreign policy in the period between 1933 and the fall of 1937.

―――. *Osudná mise.* [*The Fateful Mission*]. Prague, 1958.

Discusses the events in connection with Lord Runciman's mission to Prague in the summer of 1938.

Kuhn, Heinrich, *Biographisches Handbuch der Tschechoslowakei*. 2 vols. 2nd rev. edition. Munich, 1969.

Contains a wealth of biographical data on the post-1948 period.

―――. *Handbuch der Tschechoslowakei*. Munich, 1967.

An extremely informative factual survey of the post-1945 political system.

―――. *Der Kommunismus in der Tschechoslowakei*. Cologne, 1965.

A scholarly presentation of the history of the Communist Party of Czechoslovakia; contains many documents.

Lacko, Michael, ed. *Slovak Bibliography 1945-1965. Slovak Studies*, vol. VII. *Bibliographica*, Cleveland-Rome, 1967.

Laffan, Robert G. D. *The Crisis over Czechoslovakia. January to September 1938. Survey of International Affairs*, vol. 2, 1938. London, 1951.

The standard work on the subject; a pedestrian and painstaking treatment.

Laštovička, Bohuslav. *V Londýně za války. Zápasy o novou ČSR 1939-1945* [*During the War in London: Struggles for a New Czechoslovak Republic 1939-1945*]. Prague, 1960.

A biased account by a leading communist official.

Laušman, Bohumil. *Kdo byl vinen?* [*Who Was Guilty?*]. Vienna, 1953.

Observations on the period of 1945-48 by a former chairman of the Social Democratic party; written in exile.

Lemberg, Eugen, and Rhode, Gotthold, eds. *Das deutsch-tschechische Verhältnis seit 1918*. Stuttgart, Berlin, Cologne, Mainz, 1969.

A symposium of uneven articles.

Lettrich, Jozef. *History of Modern Slovakia*. New York, 1955.

A concise study of post-1918 Slovakia. The best work in a Western language.

Lipscher, Ladislav. *Ľudácka autonomia: ilúzie a skutočnost* [*The Ľudák*

Autonomy: Illusions and Reality]. Bratislava, 1957.

A one-sided account.

———. *K vývinu politickej správy na Slovensku, 1918-1938* [*On the Development of Political Administration in Slovakia, 1918-1938*]. Bratislava, 1966.

A well-documented study of provincial, county, and district administration in Slovakia under the First Czechoslovak Republic.

Lipták, Ľubomír. *Ovládnutie slovenského priemyslu nemeckým kapitálom, 1939-1945* [*Seizure of Control of Slovak Industry by German Capital, 1939-1945*]. Bratislava, 1960.

———. *Slovensko v 20. storoči* [*Slovakia in the Twentieth Century*]. Bratislava, 1968.

Reflections on the problems of Slovakia by a prominent Slovak communist historian.

Lockhart, Bruce R. H. *Comes the Reckoning*. London, 1947.

A lucid description of the British attitude toward Beneš and the Czechoslovak state during World War II by the British representative to the Czechoslovak government in London.

Lukeš, František. *Podivný mír* [*A Strange Peace*]. Prague, 1968.

A very good examination of the post-Munich rump republic.

Luža, Radomír. *The Transfer of the Sudeten Germans. A Study of Czech-German Relations, 1933-1962*. New York and London, 1964.

Lvová, Míla. *Mnichov a Edvard Beneš* [*Munich and Edvard Beneš*].

A carefully documented examination of the political and diplomatic activity of President Beneš during the days between September 19 and October 5, 1938.

Macartney, Carlile A. *Hungary and Her Successors. The Treaty of Trianon and its Consequences 1919-1937*. London, New York, 1937.

A study of the Trianon settlement by the foremost authority on Hungary.

Machotka, Otokar, ed. *Pražské povstání 1945* [*The Prague Uprising, 1945*]. Washington, 1965.

A collection of articles by the non-communist participants.

Machovec, Milan. *Tomáš G. Masaryk*. Prague, 1968.

This is the first serious study of the personality and thoughts of the first president of the republic published after 1948.

Machray, Robert. *The Little Entente*. London, 1929.

A detailed study.

———. *The Struggle for the Danube and the Little Entente, 1929-1938*. London, 1938.

This thorough volume sheds light on Czechoslovak diplomacy.

Mainuš, František. *Totální nasazení: Češi na pracích v Německu, 1939-1945* [*Total Mobilization: Czech Labor in Germany, 1939-1945*]. Brno, 1970.

A valuable survey.

Mackenzie, Compton. *Dr. Beneš*. London, 1946.

A laudatory biography of Beneš as a politician and diplomat.

Malypetr, Jan, *et al.*, eds. *Die Tschechoslowakische Republik, ihre Staatsidee in der Vergangenheit und Gegenwart*. 2 vols. Prague, 1937.

A valuable symposium of articles to bolster the Czechoslovak case.

Mamatey, Victor S. *The United States and East Central Europe, 1914-1918. A Study in Wilsonian Diplomacy and Propaganda*. Princeton, N.J., 1957.

A standard work on the subject.

Masaryk, Thomas G. *The Making of a State: Memories and Observations, 1914-1918*. New York, 1927.

An important source; vivid war memoirs of the President.

Masarykův slovník naučný; lidová encyklopedie všeobecných vědomostí [*Masaryk's Encyclopedia: A Popular Encyclopedia of Universal Knowledge*]. 7 vols. Prague, 1925-33.

An important source with a wealth of facts and data.

Mastny, Vojtech. *The Czechs under Nazi Rule: The Failure of National Resistance, 1939-1942*. New York, 1971.

Biased toward the Resistance.

May, Arthur J. *The Passing of the Hapsburg Monarchy 1914-1918*. 2 vols. Philadelphia, 1966.

A voluminous study by one of the best experts on Austria.

Medvecky, Karol A. *Slovenský prevrat* [*Slovak Revolution*]. 4 vols. Trnava, 1930-31.

A full-length study of the Slovak problem during World War I and the transition period, based on extensive documentation.

Mercier, Marcel. *La Formation de l'état tchécoslovaque*. Paris, 1923.

One of the few French accounts; brief, and sympathetic to Czechoslovakia.

Michal, Jan M. *Central Planning in Czechoslovakia*. Stanford, 1960.

A critical analysis focusing mainly on the post-1948 era.

Mikuš, Joseph A. *Slovakia in the Drama of Europe: A Political History, 1918-1950*. Milwaukee, 1963.

A slanted account by a former diplomat of the Slovak state.

Mosley, Leonard. *On Borrowed Time: How World War II Began*. New York, 1969.

Contains a highly colored, journalist account of Czechoslovak developments from Munich to March, 1939.

Mráz, Andrej. *Dejiny slovenskej literatury* [*History of Slovak Literature*]. Bratislava, 1948.

A standard work.

Molisch, Paul. *Die sudetendeutsche Freiheitsbewegung in den Jahren 1918-1919*. Vienna, 1932.

A standard account from the German nationalist viewpoint.

Němec, František, and Moudrý, Vladimír. *The Soviet Seizure of Subcarpathian Ruthenia*. Toronto, 1955.

An important eyewitness account; Němec was the Czechoslovak delegate in Ruthenia in 1944.

Němec, Ludvík. *Church and State in Czechoslovakia*. New York, 1955.

Nicolson, Harold G. *Peacemaking 1919. Being Reminiscences of the Paris Peace Conference.* Boston, 1933.

By now a classic in its field.

Nittner, Ernst, ed. *Dokumente zur Sudetendeutschen Frage 1916-1967.* 2nd rev. edition. Munich, 1967.

A slanted selection of various documents and texts to bolster the Sudeten German cause.

Noguères, Henri. *Munich: "Peace for Our Time."* New York, 1965.

By a French journalist.

Nosko, Július. *Vojaci v Slovenskom národnom povstaní [Soldiers in the Slovak National Uprising].* Bratislava, 1945.

On the participation of the Slovak army in the Slovak National Uprising, by one of the participants.

Novák, Arne. *Stručné dějiny české literatury [A Short History of Czech Literature].* Olomouc, 1946.

An authoritative and monumental work.

Olivová, Věra. *The Doomed Democracy: Czechoslovakia in a Disrupted Europe, 1914-1938.* London, 1972.

A competent survey of the history of the first Czechoslovak Republic in its European context.

——— and Kvaček, Robert. *Dějiny Československa od roku 1918 do roku 1945 [History of Czechoslovakia from 1918 to 1945].* Prague, 1967.

A survey of political history.

Olšovský, Rudolf, *et al. Přehled hospodářského vývoje Československa v letech 1918-1945 [A Survey of the Economic Development of Czechoslovakia, 1918-1945].* Prague, 1961.

The first comprehensive post-1948 treatment.

Opat, Jaroslav. *O novou demokracii, 1945-1948. Příspěvek k dějinám národně demokratické revoluce v Československu v letech 1945-1948 [For a New Democracy, 1945-1948: A Contribution to the History of the National Democratic Revolution in Czechoslovakia in 1945-1948].* Prague, 1966.

A provocative analytical study.

Opočenský, Jan. *The Collapse of the Austro-Hungarian Monarchy and the Rise of the Czechoslovak State.* Prague, 1928.

A concise and valuable study of the birth of the republic in 1918.

d'Orieval, François. *Le Danube était nôtre. La cause de la Slovaquie indépendente.* Paris, 1968.

A summary account of the wartime Slovak state, sympathetic to it.

Osvobození Československa Rudou Armádou 1944-1945 [Liberation of Czechoslovakia by the Red Army, 1944-1945]. 3 vols. Prague, 1965.

A detailed work.

Otáhal, Milan. *Zápas o pozemkovou reformu v ČSR [The Struggle for Land Reform in Czechoslovakia].* Prague, 1963.

A serious Marxist study valuable for its bibliography and data.

Ottův slovník naučný [Otto's Encyclopedic Dictionary]. 28 vols. Prague, 1888-1909.

For the post-1918 period to be supplemented by the *Ottův slovník naučný nové doby; dodatky* . . . [*Otto's Modern Encyclopedic Dictionary; Supplements* . . .]. 6 vols. Prague, 1930-40.

Still the best reference work on Czech and Slovak affairs.

Papoušek, Jaroslav. *Rusko a československé legie v letech 1914-1918* [*Russia and the Czechoslovak Legion in 1914-1918*]. Prague, 1932.

An outstanding survey by one of the best European experts on Russia; analyzes the relationship of Russian foreign policy to the Czechoslovak liberation movement under three Russian regimes.

Paulová, Milada. *Tajný výbor (Maffie) a spolupráce s Jihoslovany v letech 1916-1918* [*A Secret Committee (Mafia) and Cooperation with the Yugoslavs in 1916-1918*]. Prague, 1968.

A meticulous and exhaustive study of the Czech underground in World War I; by a prominent Czech historian; forms the third volume of a vast study started in 1937.

Perman, Dagmar. *The Shaping of the Czechoslovak State: Diplomatic History of the Boundaries of Czechoslovakia, 1914-1920*. Leiden, 1962.

A basic, detailed, scholarly study of the formation of the Czechoslovak Republic.

Peroutka, Ferdinand. *Budování státu; československá politika v letech popřevratových* [*Building of the State: Czechoslovak Politics in the First Postwar Years*]. 5 vols. in 6, 2nd edition. Prague, 1934-36.

A monumental and invaluable work by a noted liberal journalist; an indispensable, if not always accurate, source.

Pešek, Boris P. *The Gross National Product of Czechoslovakia in Monetary and Real Terms, 1946-59*. Chicago, 1965.

Peters, Gustav. *Der neue Herr von Böhmen. Eine Untersuchung der politischen Zukunft der Tschechoslowakei*. Berlin, 1927.

One of the few good critical studies presenting the German point of view.

Pichlík, Karel, *et al. Červenobílá a rudá: Vojáci ve válce a revoluci, 1914-1918* [*Red-white and Red: Soldiers in War and Revolution, 1914-1918*]. Prague, 1967.

A substantial work on Czech and Slovak soldiers in the Austrian army as well as the legions with the Allied armies.

———. *Zahraniční odboj 1914-1918 bez legend* [*Resistance Movement Abroad, 1914-1918, without Legends*]. Prague, 1968.

A close examination of the political struggle of Czechs and Slovaks abroad during World War I.

Plaschka, Richard G. *Cattaro-Prag. Revolte und Revolution. Kriegsmarine und Heer Österreich-Ungarns im Feuer der Aufstandbewegung vom 1. Februar und 28. Oktober 1918*. Graz-Cologne, 1963.

A clear and balanced work; particularly important for its account of the October 28 bloodless takeover in Prague.

Plevza, Viliam. *KSČ a revolučné hnutie na Slovensku 1929-1938* [*The Com-*

498

munist Party of Czechoslovakia and Revolutionary Movement in Slovakia, 1929-1938]. Bratislava, 1965.

A detailed treatment reflecting the communist viewpoint.

[Prague]. Borkovský, Ivan, et al. Dějiny Prahy [History of Prague].

A popular work; deals with the postwar period on pp. 539-668.

Prečan, Vilém. Slovenský katolicismus pred Februárom [Slovak Catholics before February]. Bratislava, 1961.

On the political activity of the Slovak Catholic clergy from 1945 to February, 1948.

Preidel, Helmut, ed. Die Deutschen in Böhmen und Mähren. Ein historischer Rückblick. Gräfelfing near Munich, 1952.

A collection of articles of uneven value reflecting the Sudeten German point of view.

Pułaski, Michał. Stosunki dyplomatyczne polsko-czechosłowacko-niemieckie od roku 1933 do wiosny 1938 [Polish-Czechoslovak-German Diplomatic Relations from 1933 to Fall, 1938]. Poznań, 1967.

A penetrating examination of the pre-1939 diplomatic scene.

Purgat, Juraj. Od Trianonu po Košice: K maďarskej otázke v Československu [From Trianon to Košice: On the Hungarian Question in Czechoslovakia]. Bratislava, 1970.

Covers the period from 1918 to 1945.

Rabl, Kurt. Das Ringen um das sudetendeutsche Selbstbestimmung 1918-1919. Munich, 1958.

A one-sided nationalist account.

Rajchl, Rostislav. Štefánik, voják a diplomat [Štefánik, Soldier and Diplomat]. Prague, 1948.

A balanced biography of one of the founders of modern Czechoslovakia.

Raschhofer, Hermann. Die Sudetenfrage. Ihre völkerrechtliche Entwicklung vom ersten Weltkrieg bis zur Gegenwart. Munich, 1953.

A legalistic analysis of the events in 1918, 1938, and 1945 from the nationalistic German viewpoint; by a former promoter of Nazism in the Czech lands.

Rapoš, Pavol. Priemysel na Slovensku za kapitalizmu [Industry in Slovakia under Capitalism]. Bratislava, 1957.

On the decline of industry in Slovakia under the First Republic; a biased account.

Rašín, Alois. Financial Policy of Czechoslovakia during the First Year of its History. Oxford, 1933.

A presentation by the first Czechoslovak Minister of Finance.

Rechcigl, Miloslav Jr., ed. The Czechoslovak Contribution to World Culture. The Hague, 1964.

Studies and essays on Czechoslovak culture, the arts, and sciences.

―――. Czechoslovakia: Past and Present. 2 vols. The Hague and Paris, 1968.

A valuable symposium of articles on political, social, economic, and international aspects, and essays on the arts and sciences; mostly by Czech and Slovak scholars living abroad.

Reimann, Paul. *Geschichte der Kommunistischen Partei der Tschechoslowakei.* Hamburg, 1931.

A classic study by a communist official; prohibited in Stalinist Czechoslovakia.

Říha, Oldřich, and Mésároš, Július, eds. *Přehled československých dějin* [*Survey of Czechoslovak History*]. 3 vols. in 4. Prague, 1958-60.

A synthesis of Czech and Slovak history from their national awakening to 1945; volume III covers period of 1918-45; biased in approach but full of factual information.

Ripka, Hubert. *Czechoslovakia Enslaved: The Story of the Communist Coup d'Etat.* London, 1950.

A vivid eyewitness study by one of the most talented democratic politicians who was a noted historian himself.

————. *Munich: Before and After.* London, 1939. Reprinted in 1969.
Still useful.

Robbins, Keith. *Munich 1938.* London, 1968.

A disappointing volume by a student of A.J.P. Taylor.

Rönnefarth, Helmuth K. G. *Die Sudetenkrise in der internationalen Politik. Entstehung-Verlauf-Auswirkung.* 2 vols. Wiesbaden, 1961.

A slanted comprehensive study based on broad documentation.

Rotkirchen, Livia. *The Destruction of Slovak Jewry. A Documentary History.* Jerusalem, 1961.

Deals with the Jewish problem in Slovakia; there are no Czechoslovak studies on this question. In Hebrew, with an English introduction.

Royal Institute of International Affairs. *Survey of International Affairs, 1933-1946.* Edited by Arnold J. Toynbee, et al. London, 1934-1954.

An invaluable aid; the volumes contain sections dealing with Czechoslovakia.

Rudnický, Jozef F. *Československý štát a Slovenská Republika* [*The Czechoslovak State and the Slovak Republic*]. Munich, 1969.

Recollections of a Slovak journalist, who was one of Hodža's confidants; contains inside information.

Schmidt, Dana Adams. *Anatomy of a Satellite.* Boston, 1952.

The story of how the communists took over Czechoslovakia and how they ruled it; by a veteran foreign correspondent.

Seibt, Ferdinand. *Bohemica. Probleme und Literatur seit 1945. Historische Zeitschrift.* Sonderheft 4, 1969-70. Ed. by Walther Kienast. Munich, 1970.

Selver, Paul. *Masaryk, a Biography.* London, 1940.

So far the best study on T. G. Masaryk in English.

Seton-Watson, Robert W. *A History of the Czechs and Slovaks.* London, 1943. Reprinted 1965.

A standard study.

————. *The New Slovakia.* Prague, 1924.

The result of the investigation of the post-1918 situation in Slovakia. Critical of the centralist system.

————, ed. *Slovakia, Then and Now. A Political Survey*. London, Prague, 1932.

A comprehensive survey of Slovak affairs in the 1920's by twenty-five prominent Slovaks.

Sidor, Karol. *Andrej Hlinka, 1864-1926*. Bratislava, 1934.

The only substantial biography of the Slovak autonomist leader; a mine of information on Slovak politics before World War I and immediately afterward.

————. *Moje poznámky k historickým dňom* [*My Notes on the Historic Days*]. Middletown, Pa., 1971.

Personal reminiscences of the events of March 14, 1939.

————. *O vzniku slovenského štátu* [*On the Origins of the Slovak State*]. Bratislava, 1945.

Recollections of a Slovak nationalist leader.

————. *Šesť rokov pri Vatikáne* [*Six Years at the Vatican*]. Scranton, Pa., 1947.

Memoirs of the former minister of the Slovak state to the Vatican in 1939-45.

————. *Slovenská politika na pôde pražského snemu, 1918-1938* [*Slovak Politics in the Prague Parliament, 1918-1938*]. 2 vols. Bratislava, 1943.

A survey of Slovak politics.

Slovenská akadémia vied. Historický ústav. *O vzájemných vzťahoch Čechov a Slovákov. Konferencie Historického ústavu Slovenskej akadémie vied* [*About Mutual Relations between Czechs and Slovaks. A Conference of the Historical Institute of the Slovak Academy of Sciences*]. Bratislava, 1956.

A collection of interesting contributions.

————. *Slovenské národné povstanie roku 1944. Sborník príspevkov z národnooslobodzovacieho boja 1938-1945* [*Slovak National Uprising of 1944. A Review of Contributions on the Struggle of the Liberation Movement in 1918-1938*]. Bratislava, 1965.

A symposium of articles by communist historians trying to correct the Stalinist deformation of the interpretation of the Slovakian uprising.

Slovenská akadémia vied a umení. *Slovenská vlastiveda* [*A Study of Slovakia*]. 5 vols. Bratislava, 1943-48.

A basic reference aid.

Slovenský náučný slovník; príručná encyklopedia vedomostí [*Slovak Encyclopedic Dictionary*]. 3 vols. Bratislava, 1932.

Provides a wealth of data.

Šolle, Zdeněk, and Gajanová, Alena. *Po stopě dějin: Češi a Slováci v letech 1848-1938* [*On the Trail of History: Czechs and Slovaks from 1848 to 1938*]. Prague, 1969.

An interpretation of Czech and Slovak history.

Smutný, Jaromír. *Únorový převrat 1948* [*The February Upheaval of 1948*]. 5 vols. Doklady a rozpravy: Nos. 12, 19, 21, 25, 28. London, 1953-1957. (Mimeographed.)

A balanced account of the role of Beneš in the February coup by his close collaborator.

Sobota, Emil. *Co to byl Protektorát* [*What the Protectorate Was*]. Prague, 1946.

A penetrating analysis by an author who was executed by the Nazis in 1945.

——. *Das tschechoslowakische Nationalitätenrecht.* Prague, 1931.

A detailed study by a noted expert.

Soják, Vladimír, ed. *O československé zahraniční politice 1918-1939: Sborník statí* [*About Czechoslovak Foreign Policy 1918-1939: A Collection of Studies*]. Prague, 1956.

A strongly biased and partly outdated account; still useful for its data.

Soukup, František. *28. říjen 1918. Předpoklady a vývoj našeho odboje domácího v čs. revoluci za státní samostatnost* [*October 28, 1918: The Conditions and Development of Home Resistance in the Czechoslovak Revolution for State Independence*]. 2 vols. Prague, 1928.

An overlong personal account of a Social Democratic leader.

Šprinc, Mikuláš, ed. *Slovenská Republika, 1939-1949* [*The Slovak Republic, 1939-1949*]. Scranton, 1949.

A collection of articles on the German-sponsored Slovak state by Slovak separatist exiles; informative.

Šrobár, Vavro. *Osvobodené Slovensko: Pamäti z rokov 1918-1920* [*Liberated Slovakia: Memories of the Years 1918-1920*]. Bratislava, 1928.

First volume of the projected but uncompleted memoirs of the years 1918-20, by the eminent Slovak leader who played a crucial role in establishing Czechoslovak rule in Slovakia.

——. *Pamäti z vojny a väzenia, 1914-1918* [*Memories of War and Imprisonment, 1914-1918*]. 2nd ed., Turčiansky Svätý Martin, 1946.

——. *Z môjho života* [*Out of My Life*]. Prague, 1946.

Reminiscences of pre-World War I Slovak politics.

Stanek, Imrich. *Zrada a pád: Hlinkovští separatisté a tak zvaný Slovenský stát* [*The Betrayal and the Fall: Hlinka's Separatists and the So-called Slovak State*]. Prague, 1958.

One-sided; discusses the activities of the Slovak separatists.

Státní hospodářství za války a po válce [*The National Economy during and after the War*]. Prague, 1946.

A governmental publication mainly useful for the wartime data.

Štefánek, Anton. *Základy sociografie Slovenska* [*Basic Sociography of Slovakia*]. Bratislava, 1944.

In *Slovenská vlastiveda*, vol. III. A mine of sociological and statistical information.

Strauss, Emil. *Die Entstehung der Tschechoslowakischen Republik.* Prague, 1934.

An account by a German Democrat.

——. *Tschechoslowakische Aussenpolitik.* Prague, 1936.

Strháň, Milan. *Kríza priemyslu na Slovensku v rokoch 1921-1923* [*The*

Crisis of Industry in Slovakia in 1921-1923]. Bratislava, 1960.

A study of the crisis and liquidation of industry in Slovakia.

Ströbinger, Rudolf. *A/54-Spion mit drei Gesichtern*. Munich, 1966.

A popular account of the activities of the Nazi *Abwehr* official Paul Thümmel who worked for the Czechoslovak Intelligence Service.

Sturm, Rudolf. *Czechoslovakia. A Bibliographic Guide*. Washington, 1967.

Of not much value to the historians.

Svoboda, Ludvík. *Cestami života* [*Roads of My Life*]. Vol. I. Prague, 1971.

The first volume of the reminiscences of the Czechoslovak president is surprisingly candid and interesting.

Szklarska-Lohmannowa, A. *Polsko-czechosłowackie stosunki dyplomatyczne w łatach 1918-1925* [*Polish-Czechoslovak Diplomatic Relations in 1918-1925*]. Wroclaw, 1967.

An informative account.

Szulc, Ted. *Czechoslovakia since World War II*. New York, 1970.

A survey by the *New York Times* reporter.

Taborsky, Edward. *Czechoslovak Democracy at Work*. London, 1945.

An analysis of the democratic system in Czechoslovakia.

————. *Pravda zvítězila* [*The Truth Prevailed*]. Prague, 1947.

This is the diary of the second liberation movement abroad by a close collaborator of Beneš; it treats the beginning of the post-1938 period.

Textor, Lucy Elisabeth, *Land Reform in Czechoslovakia*. London, 1923.

Thompson, Laurence. *The Greatest Treason: The Untold Story of Munich*. New York, 1968.

A journalistic account; tries to rehabilitate the British appeasers by finding fault with Czechoslovak policy.

Thomson, Harrison S. *Czechoslovakia in European History*. Princeton, N.J., 1944; rev. ed., 1953.

A standard work.

Thunig-Nittner, Gerburg. *Die Tschechoslowakische Legion in Russland. Ihre Geschichte und Bedeutung bei der Entstehung der 1. Tschechoslowakischen Republik*. Wiesbaden, 1970.

A significant study.

Tichý, Antonín. *Nás živé nedostanou. Historie parašutistické skupiny Antimony* [*They Don't Get Us Alive: History of the Parachutist Group "Antimony"*]. Liberec, 1969.

A good account of the activities of the Czech parachutists flown from England to the Protectorate in 1941-43.

Tobolka, Zdeněk. *Politické dějiny československého národa od r. 1848 až do dnešní doby* [*Political History of the Czechoslovak People from 1848 to the Present Time*]. 4 vols. in 5. Prague, 1932-1937.

An exhaustive and pedestrian study.

Trapl, Miloš. *Politika českého katolicismu na Moravě 1918-1938* [*The Policy of Czech Catholicism in Moravia, 1918-1938*]. Prague, 1968.

A concise short study of the policies of the Moravian wing of the Populist party.

Turčan, Pavel, and Pavlenda, Viktor. *Le Dévelopement économique de la Slovaquie au sein de la Tchécoslovaquie socialiste.* Bratislava, 1963.
> On the post-1945 industrialization of Slovakia.

United Nations Relief and Rehabilitation Administration, European Regional Office. *Agriculture and Food in Czechoslovakia.* London, 1946.
———. *Industrial Rehabilitation in Czechoslovakia.* London, 1947.
———. *Foreign Trade in Czechoslovakia.* London, 1947.
———. *Transport Rehabilitation in Czechoslovakia.* London, 1947.
> These are informative accounts with helpful data and facts.

Urban, Rudolf. *Die sudetendeutschen Gebiete nach 1945.* Frankfurt a.M., Berlin, 1964.
> A detailed survey.

Ústav dějin Komunistické strany Československa. *Dějiny Komunistické strany Československa* [*History of the Communist Party of Czechoslovakia*]. Prague, 1961.
> A typical product of Stalinist hagiography.

———. *Na obranu republiky proti fašismu a válce. Sborník dokumentů k dějinám KSČ v letech 1934-1938 a k VI., VII. a VIII. svazku spisů Klementa Gottwalda* [*For Defense of the Republic against Fascism and War: A Collection of Documents on the History of the Czechoslovak Communist Party in 1934-1938 and on Volumes VI-VIII of the Writings of Klement Gottwald*]. Prague, 1955.

———. *Příruční slovník k dějinám KSČ* [*A Pocket Dictionary for the History of the Communist Party of Czechoslovakia*]. 2 vols. Prague, 1964.
> Biased; contains useful information.

———. *Za svobodu českého a slovenského národa. Sborník dokumentů k dějinám KSČ v letech 1938-1945 a k IX., X., a XI. svazku spisů Klementa Gottwalda* [*For the Freedom of the Czech and Slovak Nations: A Collection of Documents on the History of the Czechoslovak Communist Party in 1938-1945 and on Volumes IX-XI of the Writings of Klement Gottwald*]. Prague, 1956.
> A one-sided selection to prove the predominant role of the KSČ in the Resistance.

———. Knihovna. *Československá revoluce 1945-1948 a Únor 1948* [*The Czechoslovak Revolution: 1945-1948 and February, 1948*]. Prague, 1968.
> A valuable bibliography for the period 1945-48.

Ústav dějin socialismu. Knihovna. *Bibliografie k dějinám ČSR a KSČ 1917-1938. Historiografická produkce za léta 1945-1967* [*Bibliography of the History of the Czechoslovak Republic and the Communist Party of Czechoslovakia, 1917-1938: The Historiographic Production for 1945-1967*]. Edited by Helena Engová et al. 4 vols. Prague, 1968.

Vallette, Geneviève. *Munich, 1938.* Paris, 1964.
> A journalistic account.

Vartíková, Marta. *Od Košíc po Február. Politika slovenského Národného frontu od košického obdobia do februárových udalostí (1945-1948)* [*From Košice to February: Policy of the Slovak National Front from the*

Period of Košice up to the February Events, 1945-1948]. Bratislava, 1968.

A biased examination of the role of the National Front in Slovakia as the spearhead of the communist takeover.

Vávra, Ferdinand, and Eibel, Ján. *Viedeňská arbitráž: dôsledok Mnichova [The Vienna Arbitration: A Consequence of Munich]*. Bratislava, 1963.

German-Italian arbitration of the Czechoslovak-Hungarian frontier in Vienna on November 2, 1938.

Venohr, Wolfgang. *Aufstand für die Tschechoslowakei: Der slowakische Freiheitskampf von 1944*. Hamburg, 1969.

So far the only Western account of the Uprising by a German journalist; based on Slovak and German documents.

Veselý, Jindřich. *Prag Februar 1948*. Berlin, 1959.

This German edition of *Kronika únorových dnů* reflects the Stalinist point of view.

Veselý-Štainer, Karel. *Cestou národního odboje. Bojový vývoj domácího odbojového hnutí v letech 1938-45 [With the National Resistance: A Development of the Struggle of the Home Resistance Movement, 1938-1945]*. Prague, 1947.

Memoirs of a resistance leader; basic to understanding of the Czech Resistance.

Vietor, Martin. *Dejiny okupácie južného Slovenska, 1938-1945 [History of the Occupation of Southern Slovakia, 1938-1945]*. Bratislava, 1968.

Hungarian policy in the occupied portion of Slovakia.

————. *Slovenská sovietská republika [Slovak Soviet Republic]*. Bratislava, 1959.

Overblown account of the shortlived Slovak Soviet Republic of 1919.

Vnuk, František. *Dr. Jozef Tiso, President of the Slovak Republic*. Sidney, 1967.

A brief scholarly presentation of Tiso as a Slovak patriot; written from the separatist viewpoint by one of the best experts on Slovakia.

————. *Kapitoly z dejin Komunistickej strany Slovenska [Chapters in the History of the Communist Party of Slovakia]*. Middletown, Pa., 1968.

Hostile but well-informed; has an English summary.

————. *Neuveriteľné sprísahanie: Vojenské a politické akcie proti Slovenskej Republike v roku 1944 [The Incredible Conspiracy: Military and Political Activity against the Slovak Republic in 1944]*. Middletown, Pa., 1964.

A hostile view of the Slovak National Uprising of 1944; English summary.

Vojenský historický ústav. *Za svobodu Československa. Kapitoly z dějin československé vojenské jednotky v SSSR za druhé světové války [For the Freedom of Czechoslovakia: Chapters from the History of the Czechoslovak Military Unit in the U.S.S.R. in the Course of World War II]*. 3 vols. Prague, 1959-61.

A detailed account of the Czechoslovak Army's activities in the U.S.S.R.

Vondráček, Felix J. *The Foreign Policy of Czechoslovakia, 1918-1935.* New York, 1937.

A reliable examination of Czechoslovak diplomacy.

Vozka, Jaroslav. *Hrdinové domácího odboje [Heroes of the Home Resistance].* Prague, 1946.

A popular account; not without merit.

Wandycz, Piotr S. *Czechoslovak-Polish Confederation and the Great Powers 1940-1943.* Bloomington, Ind., 1958.

A useful survey of the Polish-Czechoslovak negotiations in London.

———. *France and Her Eastern Allies, 1919-1925. French-Czechoslovak-Polish Relations from the Paris Peace Conference to Locarno.* Minneapolis, 1962.

A basic study; based on broad documentation; throws new light on Beneš's policy toward Germany and France.

Wanklyn, Harriet G. *Czechoslovakia.* New York, 1954.

A balanced survey of the population, economy, and geography.

Weirich, M. *Staré a nové Československo [Old and New Czechoslovakia].* Prague, 1938.

An account of the economic development in the interwar period.

Wheeler-Bennett, John W. *Munich: Prologue to Tragedy.* New York, 1948.

A solid study; to be supplemented by more recent works.

Willars, Christian. *Die böhmische Zitadelle. ČSR-Schicksal einer Staatsidee: Abrechnung und Ausblick.* Vienna-Munich, 1965.

An attempt to reinterpret the idea of the Czechoslovak state.

Wiskemann, Elizabeth. *Czechs and Germans. A Study of the Struggle in the Historic Provinces of Bohemia and Moravia.* London, New York, Toronto, 1938. 2nd ed. in 1967.

A classic in its field.

———. *Germany's Eastern Neighbours. Problems Relating to the Oder-Neisse Line and the Czech Frontier Regions.* London, New York, Toronto, 1956.

Generally favorable to the Polish and Czechoslovak points of view.

Young, Edgar P. *Czechoslovakia: Keystone of Peace and Democracy.* London, 1938.

An informative survey.

Za svobodu. Obrázková kronika československého revolučního hnutí na Rusi 1914-1920 [Toward Freedom: Illustrated Chronicle of the Czechoslovak Revolutionary Movement in Russia, 1914-1920]. 4 vols. Prague, 1925-29.

A detailed popular account of the activities of the Czechoslovak legion until its return from Russia home; contains many documents.

Zauberman, Alfred. *Industrial Progress in Poland, Czechoslovakia, and East Germany, 1937-1962.* London, New York, 1964.

A solid study.

Zeman, Zbynek A. B. *The Break-Up of the Habsburg Empire 1914-1918. A Study in National and Social Revolution.* London, 1961.

A comprehensive examination.

Zinner, Paul E. *Communist Strategy and Tactics in Czechoslovakia, 1918-1948*. New York, 1963.
A thoughtful analysis.

Zvara, Juraj. *Riešenie maďarskej národnostnej otázky na Slovensku* [*Solving the Hungarian Nationality Question in Slovakia*]. Bratislava, 1967.
Czechoslovak policy toward the Hungarian minority in Slovakia in 1945-48.

ARTICLES

Armstrong, Hamilton Fish. "Armistice at Munich," *Foreign Affairs*, XVII (January, 1939), 197-290.

Belda, J., Bouček, M., Deyl, Zd., and Klimeš, M. "K otázce účasti Československa na Marshallově plánu" ["On the Question of Czechoslovak Participation in the Marshall Plan"], *Revue dějin socialismu*, VIII (1968), 81-100.

Bodensieck, Heinrich. "Das Dritte Reich und die Lage der Juden in der Tschecho-Slowakei nach München," *Vierteljahrshefte für Zeitgeschichte*, IX (July, 1961), 249-61.

———. "Der Plan eines 'Freundschaftsvertrages' zwischen dem Reich und der Tschecho-Slowakei im Jahre 1938," *Zeitschrift für Ostforschung*, X (September, 1961), 462-76.

———. "Die Politik der Zweiten Tschechoslowakischen Republik," *Zeitschrift für Ostforschung*, VI (April, 1957), 54-71.

———. "Zur Vorgeschichte des 'Protektorats Böhmen und Mähren.' Der Einfluss volksdeutscher Nationalsozialisten und reichsdeutscher Berufsdiplomaten auf Hitlers Entscheidung," *Geschichte in Wissenschaft und Unterricht*, No. 12 (1968), 713-32.

Břach, Radko. "Československá zahraniční politika v politických proměnách Evropy 1924" ["Czechoslovak Foreign Policy in the Political Transformations of Europe, 1924"], *Československý časopis historický*, XVIII, No. 1 (1970), 49-83.

———. "Francouzský alianční systém a Československo na počátku roku 1924" ["The French Alliance System and Czechoslovakia at the Beginning of 1924"], *Historie a vojenství*, No. 1 (1968), 1-21.

Bradley, John F. N. "The Allies and the Czech Revolt against the Bolsheviks in 1918," *Slavonic and East European Review*, XLIII (June, 1965), 275-92.

Broszat, Martin. "Das Sudetendeutsche Freikorps," *Vierteljahrshefte für Zeitgeschichte*, IX (January, 1961), 30-49.

Brown, MacAlister. "The Third Reich's Mobilization of the German Fifth Column in Eastern Europe," *Journal of Central European Affairs*, XIX (July, 1959), 128-48.

Brügel, Johann W. "Die Aussiedlung der Deutschen aus der Tschechoslowakei," *Vierteljahrshefte für Zeitgeschichte*, VIII (April, 1960), 134-64.

———. "German Diplomacy and the Sudeten Question before 1938," *International Affairs*, XXXVII (July, 1961), 323-31.

Brügel, Johann W. "Die sudetendeutsche Frage auf der Potsdam Konferenz," *Vierteljahrshefte für Zeitgeschichte*, x (January, 1962), 56-61.

Burian, P. "Demokratie und Parlamentarismus in der ersten Tschechoslowakischen Republik," in Hans-Erich Volkmann, ed. *Die Krise des Parlamentarismus in Ostmitteleuropa zwischen den beiden Weltkriegen* (Marburg, 1967).

Černý, Bohumil, "Schwarze Front v Československu," *Československý časopis historický*, xiv, No. 3 (1966), 328-57.

Clemens, Walter C., Jr. "Great and Small Powers Collaboration to Enforce the Status Quo: France and Czechoslovakia against the Vienna Protocol," *East European Quarterly*, ii (January, 1969), 385-412.

Deák, Ladislav. "Siedmy marec 1936 a Malá Dohoda" ["March 7, 1936 and the Little Entente"], *Československý časopis historický*, xvii, No. 3 (1969), 323-50.

Eliášová, Jaroslava, and Pasák, Tomáš. "Poznámky k Benešovým kontaktům s Eliášem ve druhé světové válce" ["Observations on the Contacts of Beneš with Eliáš in World War II"], *Historie a vojenství*, No. 1 (1967), 108-40.

Ferjenčík, Mikuláš. "Slovenské národné povstanie a SSSR" ["The Slovak National Uprising and the U.S.S.R."], *Svědectví*, vi, No. 22 (1963), 145-54.

Gasiorowski, Zygmunt J. "Beneš and Locarno: Some Unpublished Documents," *Review of Politics*, xx (April, 1958), 209-24.

———. "Polish-Czech Relations 1918-1922," *The Slavonic and East European Review*, xxxv (1956), 172-93.

Gorovský, Karel. "Bohumír Šmeral," *Revue dějin socialismu*, ix, x, Nos. 6, 1 (1969, 1970), 893-922, 112-39.

Heiber, Helmut. "Zur Justiz im Dritten Reich. Der Fall Eliáš," *Vierteljahrshefte für Zeitgeschichte*, iii (July, 1955), 275-96.

Hemmerle, Josef. "Schrifttumsverzeichnis zur Geschichte der Sudetenländer und der heutigen Tschechoslowakei in Auswahl 1945-1953," *Zeitschrift für Ostforschung*, iv, No. 1 (1955), 145-60.

Hoensch, Jörg K. "Účast Telekiho vlády na rozbití Československa (březen 1939)" ["Participation of the Teleki Cabinet in the Destruction of Czechoslovakia, March, 1939"], *Československý časopis historický*, xvii, No. 3 (1969), 351-74.

Holdoš, Ladislav. "Niektoré problémy československého zahraničného odboja vo Francúzsku v rokoch 1939-1940" ["Some Problems of the Czechoslovak Resistance Abroad in France in 1939-1940"], *Historický časopis*, xvii, No. 3 (1969), 379-419.

Hornová, A. "Charakteristika ekonomiky tzv. Slovenského štátu" ["Characteristics of the Economy of the So-Called Slovak State"], *Ekonomický časopis*, ii (1954), 337-48.

Hyndrák, Václav. "Polsko a československá krize na podzim 1938. Materiály" ["Poland and the Czechoslovak Crisis in the Fall of 1938"], *Historie a vojenství*, No. 1 (1968), 84-98.

Janáček, František, *et al.* "Nová orientace" ["New Orientation"], *Historie a vojenství*, No. 4 (1969), 629-73.

————. "Pakt, válka a KSČ. První týdny po 23. srpnu a 1. září 1939" ["The Pact, War, and the Communist Party of Czechoslovakia. The First Weeks after August 23 and September 1, 1939"], *Historie a vojenství*, No. 3 (1969), 425-57.

Janeček, Oldřich. "Zrod politiky národní fronty a moskevské vedení KSČ" ["Origin of the Policy of the National Front and the Moscow Leadership of the KSČ"], *Revue dějin socialismu*, IX, No. 6 (1969), 803-47.

Jelínek, Yeshayahu. "Slovakia's Internal Policy and the Third Reich, August 1940-February 1941," *Central European History*, IV (September, 1971), 242-70.

Kamenec, Ivan. "Snem Slovenskej republiky a jeho postoj k problému židovského obyvateľstva na Slovensku v rokoch 1939-1945" ["The Diet of the Slovak Republic and its Attitude toward the Problem of the Jewish Population in Slovakia in 1939-1945"], *Historický časopis*, No. 3, XVII (1969), 329-60.

Kaplan, Karel. "Hospodářská demokracie v letech 1945-1948" ["Economic Democracy in 1945-1948"], *Československý časopis historický*, XIV (1966), 844-61.

————. "Poznámky k znárodnění průmyslu v Československu 1945" ["Notes on the Nationalization of Industry in Czechoslovakia 1945"], *Příspěvky k dějinám KSČ*, No. 6 (1966), 3-23.

Kárník, Zdeněk. "Založení KSČ a Kominterna" ["Foundation of the Communist Party of Czechoslovakia and the Comintern"], *Revue dějin socialismu*, IX, No. 2 (1969), 163-200.

Kisch, Guido. "Documents: Woodrow Wilson and the Independence of Small Nations in Central Europe," *Journal of Modern History*, XIX (1947), 235-38.

Kořalka, Jiří. "Jak se stal německý lid v Československu kořistí fašismu" ["How the German People in Czechoslovakia Became Prey to Fascism"], *Československý časopis historický*, III, No. 1 (1955), 52-81.

Kozeňski, Jerzy. "The Nazi Subjugation of Slovakia (March-September 1939)," *Polish Western Affairs*, VII, No. 2 (1971), 326-50.

Krajčovičová, Natália. "Slovenská národna rada roku 1918" ["The Slovak National Council in 1918"], *Historický časopis*, XVII (1969), 177-97.

Krajina, Vladimír. "La résistance tchécoslovaque," *Cahiers d'histoire de la guerre*, I (February, 1950), 55-76.

Křen, Jan, and Kural, Václav. "Ke stykům mezi československým odbojem a SSSR v letech 1939-1941" ["On the Contacts between the Czechoslovak Resistance and the U.S.S.R. in 1939-1941"], *Historie a vojenství* (1967), pp. 437-71, 731-71.

Křížek, Jurij. "Příspěvek k dějinám rozpadu Rakouska-Uherska a vzniku Československa" ["A Contribution to the History of the Collapse of Austria-Hungary and the Birth of Czechoslovakia"], *Příspěvky k dějinám KSČ*, No. 5 (September, 1958), 13-120.

Kvaček, Robert. "Československo-německá jednání v roce 1936" ["Czechoslovak-German Negotiations in 1936"], *Historie a vojenství*, No. 5 (1965), 721-54.

Kybal, Vlastimil. "Czechoslovakia and Italy: My Negotiations with Mussolini. Part I: 1922-1923, Part II: 1923-1924," *Journal of Central European Affairs*, xiv (January, 1954), 352-68; (April, 1954), 65-76.

Laroche, Jules. "La question de Teschen devant la conférence de la Paix 1919-1920," *Revue d'histoire diplomatique*, lxii (1948), 8-27.

Laštovička, Bohuslav. "Vznik a význam Košického vládního programu" ["The Origin and Importance of the Košice Government Program"], *Československý časopis historický*, viii (August, 1960), 449-71.

Lemberg, Hans. "Karel Kramářs Russische Aktion in Paris 1919," *Jahrbücher für Geschichte Osteuropas*, xiv (September, 1966), 400-28.

Lipscher, Ladislav. "Klub slovenských poslancov v rokoch 1918-1920" ["The Club of the Slovak Deputies in 1918-1920"], *Historický časopis*, xvi (1968), 133-68.

Lipták, Ľubomír. "Maďarsko v politike slovenského štátu v rokoch 1939-1943" ["Hungary in the Policy of the Slovak State, 1939-1943"], *Historický časopis*, xv (1967), No. 1.

————. "Príprava a priebeh salzburských rokovaní roku 1940 medzi predstaviteľmi Nemecka a Slovenského štátu" ["Preparations and Course of the Salzburg Negotiations between the Representatives of Germany and the Slovak State"], *Historický časopis*, xiii (1965), 329-65.

Lockhart, Robert R. H. "The Second Exile of Eduard Beneš," *Slavonic and East European Review*, xxvii (November, 1949), 39-59.

Lukeš, František. "Poznámky k čs.-sovětským stykům v září 1938" ["Notes on Czechoslovak-Soviet Relations in September, 1938"], *Československý časopis historický*, No. 5 (1968).

Luža, Radomír. "The Communist Party of Czechoslovakia and the Czech Resistance, 1939-1945," *Slavic Review*, xxviii (December, 1969), 561-76.

Lvová, Míla. "Československá otázka v diplomatických spisov horthyovského Maďarska" ["The Czechoslovak Question in the Diplomatic Documents of Horthy's Hungary"], *Historický časopis*, xv (1967), Nos. 1-2.

————. "K otázce tzv. objednaného ultimáta" ["On the Problem of the So-Called Ordered Ultimatum"], *Československý časopis historický*, xiii (1965), 333-49.

Mamatey, Victor S. "Documents: The United States Recognition of the Czechoslovak National Council in Paris, September 3, 1918," *Journal of Central European Affairs*, xiii (April, 1953), 47-60.

"T. G. Masaryk 1850-1950," *Journal of Central European Affairs*, x (April, 1950), 1-52.

Mastný, Vojtěch. "Design or Improvisation? The Origins of the Protectorate of Bohemia and Moravia in 1939," *Columbia Essays in International Affairs* (1966), pp. 127-53.

Nedvěd, Jaroslav. "Cesta ke sloučeni sociální demokracie s komunistickou stranou v roce 1948" ["The Road to the Merger of the Social Democratic and Communist Parties"], *Rozpravy Československé Akademie věd*, No. 8 (1968), 3-93.

Odložilík, Otakar. "Modern Czechoslovak Historiography," *Slavonic and East European Review*, xxx (1952), 376-92.

Olivová, Věra. "Československá diplomacie v době rurské krise roku 1923" ["Czechoslovak Diplomacy during the Ruhr Crisis of 1923"], *Československý časopis historický*, VI (1958), 59-70.

———. "Československá zahraniční politika a pokus o restauraci Habsburků v roce 1921" ["Czechoslovak Foreign Policy and the Attempt at Habsburg Restoration in 1921"], *Československý časopis historický*, VII (1959), 675-92.

———. "Československo-sovětská smlouva z roku 1935" ["Czechoslovak-Soviet Treaty of 1935"], *Československý časopis historický*, XIII, No. 3 (1965), 477-99.

Opat, Jaroslav. "K metodě studia a výkladu některých problémů období 1945-1948" ["On Methods and Explanation of Some Problems of the Period 1945-1948"], *Příspěvky k dějinám KSČ*, V (1965), 65-84.

Pachman, Vl. "Boj o odborovou jednotu v letech 1945-1948" ["The Struggle for the Unity of the Trade Union Movement in 1945-1948"], *Československý časopis historický*, VIII, No. 6 (1960), 793-813.

Palecek, Anthony. "Anthony Švehla; Czech Peasant Statesman," *Slavic Review*, XXI (December, 1962), 699-708.

Pasák, Tomáš. "Aktivističtí novináři a postoj generála Eliáše v roce 1941" ["The Activist Journalists and the Attitude of General Eliáš in 1941"], *Československý časopis historický*, XV (1967), 173-92.

———. "Činnost protektorátní reprezentace na podzim roku 1939" ["The Activity of the Protectorate Leadership in the Fall of 1939"], *Československý časopis historický*, XVII (1969), 553-73.

———. "Vstup německých vojsk na české území v roce 1939" ["Entry of German Troops into Czech Territory in 1939"], *Československý časopis historický*, XVII (1969), 161-83.

———. "Vývoj Vlajky v období okupace" ["Development of the Vlajka during the Occupation"], *Historie a vojenství*, No. 5 (1966), 846-95.

Pichlík, Karel. "Die Entstehung der Tschechoslowakei," *Vierteljahrshefte für Zeitgeschichte*, No. 2 (1969), 160-80.

Prečan, Vilém. "Nacistická politika a Tisův režim v předvečer Povstání" ["Nazi Policy and the Tiso Regime on the Eve of the Uprising"], *Historie a vojenství*, No. 6 (1969), 1082-1146.

Rimscha, Hans von. "Zur Gleichschaltung der deutschen Volksgruppen durch das Dritte Reich," *Historische Zeitschrift*, CLXXXII (1956), 29-63.

Schiefer, Hans. "Deutschland und die Tschechoslowakei von September 1938 bis März 1939," *Zeitschrift für Ostforschung*, IV, No. 1 (1955), 48-66.

Seymour, Charles. "Czechoslovak Frontiers," *Yale Review*, XXVIII (1938), 273-91.

Skilling, Gordon H. "The Comintern and Czechoslovak Communism: 1921-1929," *American Slavic and East European Review*, XIX (April, 1960), 234-47.

———. "The Czechoslovak Struggle for National Liberation in World War II," *Slavonic and East European Review*, XXXIX (December, 1960), 174-97.

Skilling, Gordon H. "The Formation of a Communist Party in Czechoslovakia," *American Slavic and East European Review*, XIV (October, 1955), 346-58.

———. "Gottwald and the Bolshevization of the Communist Party of Czechoslovakia 1929-1939," *Slavic Review*, XX (December, 1961), 641-55.

———. "Revolution and Continuity in Czechoslovakia 1945-1946," *Journal of Central European Affairs*, XX (January, 1961), 357-77.

Sládek, Oldřich. "Gestapo v boji proti první vlně výsadků vyslaných z Anglie v operačním období 1941-1942" ["The Gestapo in the Struggle against the First Wave of Parachutists Flown from England in the Operational Period of 1941-1942"], *Historie a vojenství*, No. 2 (1969), 247-301.

———. "Gestapo v boji proti druhé vlně výsadků vyslaných z Anglie v operačním období 1942-1943" ["The Gestapo in the Struggle against the Second Wave of Parachutists Flown from England in the Operational Period of 1942-1943"], *Historie a vojenství*, No. 3 (1969), 458-90.

Strháň, Milan. "Živnostenská banka na Slovensku 1918-1938" ["The Trade Bank in Slovakia, 1918-1938"], *Historický časopis*, XV (1967), 177-218.

Szporluk, Roman. "Masaryk's Idea of Democracy," *Slavonic and East European Review*, XLI (December, 1962), 31-49.

Taborsky, Edvard. "Beneš, Sikorski and the Czechoslovak-Polish Relations, 1939-1942," *Central European Federalist*, XI (July, 1963), 17ff.

———. "Beneš and the Soviets," *Foreign Affairs*, XXVII (January, 1949), 302-14.

———. "Beneš and Stalin; Moscow, 1943 and 1945," *Journal of Central European Affairs*, XIII (July, 1953), 154-81.

———. "Benešovy moskevské cesty" ["Trips of Beneš to Moscow"], *Svědectví*, I (1957), 193-214.

———. "A Polish-Czechoslovak Confederation; A Story of the First Soviet Veto," *Journal of Central European Affairs*, IX (January, 1950), 379-95.

———. "The Triumph and Disaster of Eduard Beneš," *Foreign Affairs*, XXXVI (July, 1958), 669-84.

Tesař, Jan. "K problému nacistické okupační politiky v Protektoratu v r. 1939" ["On the Problem of the Nazi Policy of Occupation in the Protectorate in 1939"], *Historie a vojenství*, 1 (1969), 40-85.

———. "Poznámky k problémům okupačního režimu v tzv. protektorátě" ["Notes on the Problems of the Regime of Occupation in the So-Called Protectorate"], *Historie a vojenství*, Nos. 2, 3 (1964), 153-91, 333-85.

Toma, Peter A. "The Slovak Soviet Republic of 1919," *American Slavic and East European Review*, XVII (April, 1958), 203-15.

———. "Soviet Strategy in the Slovak Uprising of 1944," *Journal of Central European Affairs*, XIX (October, 1959), 290-98.

"La Tchécoslovaquie pendant la guerre," *Revue d'histoire de la deuxième guerre mondiale*, XIII (October, 1963), 1-92.

Uhlíř, Dušan. "Republikánská strana lidu zemědělského a malorolnického ve vládě panské koalice" ["The Republican Party of the Agrarian and Small Peasant People in the Cabinet of the Gentlemen's Coalition"], *Československý časopis historický*, XVIII (1970), 195-236.

————. "Konec vlády panské koalice a republikánská strana v roce 1929" ["The End of the Cabinet of the Gentlemen's Coalition and the Republican Party in 1929"], *Československý časopis historický*, XVIII (1970), 551-92.

Ullman, Walter. "Czechoslovakia's Crucial Years, 1945-1948: An American View," *East European Quarterly*, I (September, 1967), 217-30.

Ústav dějin KSČ and Ústav dějin KSS. "Přehled o složení nejvyšších orgánů KSČ v letech 1920-1945" ["A Survey of the Composition of the Highest Organs of the KSČ in 1920-1945"], *Příspěvky k dějinám KSČ*, V (October, 1965), 757-84.

Vietor, Martin. "Príspevok k objasneniu fašistického charakteru tzv. slovenského štátu" ["A Contribution to the Understanding of the Fascist Nature of the So-Called Slovak State"], *Historický časopis*, VIII, No. 4 (1960), 482-508.

Vital, David. "Czechoslovakia and the Powers, September 1938," *Journal of Contemporary History*, I (October, 1966), 37-67.

Vnuk, František. "Munich and the Soviet Union," *Journal of Central European Affairs*, XXI (October, 1961), 285-304.

Voláková, Radmila, and Fučíková, Lenka. "Československý ozbrojený zahraniční odboj—počátek československé armády. Výběrová bibliografie . . ." ["The Czechoslovak Armed Resistance Abroad—the Beginning of the Czechoslovak Army. Selected Bibliography . . ."], *Historie a vojenství*, No. 1 (1969), 130-216.

————. "Soupis publikací Památníku Osvobození a výběr z vědecké produkce Vojenského historického ústavu v Praze (1919-1969)" ["A List of the Publications of the Memorial of Liberation and a Selection of Scholarly Production of the Military Historical Institute in Prague, 1919-1969"], *Historie a vojenství*, No. 1 (1970), 99-137.

Wallace, William V. "The Foreign Policy of President Beneš in the Approach to Munich," *Slavonic and East European Review*, XXXIX (December, 1960), 108-36.

————. "The Making of the May Crisis of 1938," *Slavonic and East European Review*, XLI (June, 1963), 368-90.

Watt, D. C. "The May Crisis of 1938: A Rejoinder to Mr. Wallace," *Slavonic and East European Review*, XLIV (July, 1966), 475-80. W. V. Wallace's reply, *ibid.*, pp. 481-86.

Weinberg, Gerhard L. "The May Crisis, 1938," *Journal of Modern History*, XXIX (September, 1957), 213-25.

————. "Secret Hitler-Beneš Negotiations in 1936-1937," *Journal of Central European Affairs*, XIX (January, 1960), 366-74.

Werstadt, Jaroslav. "Literatura a dokumenty k dějinám našeho osvobození" ["Literature and Documents on the History of Our Liberation"], *Český časopis historický*, XXXII (1926), 211-20, 656-63; XXXIII (1927), 213-20.

Zámečník, Stanislav. "České květnové povstání" ["The Czech May Uprising"], *Historie a vojenství*, No. 2 (1970), 267-301.

————. "Komunistická koncepce povstání a otázky národní fronty v českých zemích" ["The Communist Concept of Uprising and Questions of the National Front in the Czech Lands"], *Historie a vojenství*, No. 2 (1968), 161-94.

Zinner, Paul E. "Marxism in Action: The Seizure of Power in Czechoslovakia," *Foreign Affairs*, XXVIII (July, 1950), 644-58.

Zuberec, Vladimír. "Príspevok k dejinám vzniku agrárnej strany na Slovensku (1918-1921)" ["A Contribution to the History of the Origin of the Agrarian Party in Slovakia, 1918-1921"], *Historický časopis*, XV (1967), 573-99.

Zvara, Juraj. "K problematike postavenia maďarskej národnostnej skupiny v ČSR v období boja za upevnenie l'udovej demokracie a rozšírenie moci robotnickej triedy 1945-1948" ["On the Problems of the Situation of the Hungarian National Group in Czechoslovakia during the Period of the Struggle for the Strengthening of the People's Democracy and the Expanding of the Power of the Working Class, 1945-1948"], *Historický časopis*, XII (1964), 28-49.

———. "Maďarská otázka v ČSR v letech 1948-1954" ["The Hungarian Question in the Czechoslovak Republic, 1948-1954"], *Příspěvky k dějinám KSČ*, V (June, 1965), 409-27.

SELECTED LIST OF PERIODICALS AND NEWSPAPERS

Periodicals

There are articles scattered in such various journals and publications as:

Acta Universitatis Carolinae. Philosophica et Historica. 1958-.

Bohemia- Jahrbuch des Collegium Carolinum. 1960-. Annual volumes.

Böhmen und Mähren. 1939-44.

Bratislava. 1927-37.

Canadian Slavic Studies; Revue canadienne d'études slaves. 1967-.

Československý časopis historický. 1952-.

Český časopis historický. 1895-1940; 1947-49.

Dějiny a současnost. 1959-69.

Der Donauraum. 1956-.

East European Quarterly. 1967-.

Historica-Historical Science in Czechoslovakia. 1959-. Annual volumes.

Historické štúdie. 1957-. Annual.

Historický časopis SAV. 1952-. Under other titles: 1940-41; 1945-46; 1948-52.

Historie a vojenství. 1952-. Former title *Válka a revoluce*, 1947-51.

Jahrbücher für Geschichte Osteuropas. Neue Folge. 1953-.

Journal of Central European Affairs. 1940-61.

Journal of Modern History. 1929-.

Le Monde slave. 1917-38.

Naše doba. 1893-1947.

Naše revoluce. 1924-38.

Österreichische Osthefte. 1958-.

Osteuropa, 1951-.

Příspěvky k dějinám KSČ. 1957-. Since 1968 entitled *Revue dějin socialismu.* Suspended in 1970.

Revue d'histoire de la deuxième guerre mondiale. 1950-.

Revue des études slaves. 1921-. Annual.

Sborník historický. 1953-. Annual.

Slavic Review. 1961-. Previously *American Slavic and East European Review.* 1941-61.

Slavonic and East European Review. 1922-.

Studia historica slovaca. 1963-. Annual.

Svědectví. 1957-.

Mitteilungen. 1862-1941. Published by the Verein für Geschichte der Deutschen in den Sudetenländern.

Vierteljahrshefte für Zeitgeschichte. 1953-.

Vojensko-historický sborník. 1932-39.

Zahraniční politika. 1922-38.

Zeitschrift für Ostforschung. 1951-.

Newspapers

Bohemia. 1928-38. Prague. National German.

Čas. 1944-48. Bratislava. Slovak Democratic.

Čechoslovák. 1939-45. London. Weekly.

Central European Observer. 1923-48. Prague. Since 1933 bi-weekly.

České slovo. 1907-45. Prague. Since 1945 under the title *Svobodné slovo.* Czech Socialist.

Československý boj. 1939-40. Paris. Weekly.

Gardista. 1939-45. Bratislava. Separatist.

Grenzbote. 1871-1945. Bratislava.

Lidové listy. 1922-39. Prague. Since 1945 under the title *Lidová demokracie.* Populist.

Lidové noviny. 1893-1945. Brno. Since 1945 under the title *Svobodné noviny.* Liberal and independent.

Ľudová politika. Bratislava. Ceased to appear in 1938. Populist.

Národní deník. Bratislava. National Democratic.

Národní listy. 1861-1941. Prague. Conservative after 1918.

Národnie noviny. Martin. The oldest Slovak paper.

Národní osvobození. 1923-39; 1945-48. Prague. Progressive, independent.

Národní politika. 1883-1945. Prague. Conservative, independent.

Der neue Tag. 1939-1945. Prague. Nazi.

Práce. 1945-. Prague. Labor.

Prager Presse. 1921-38. Prague. Official.

Prager Tagblatt. 1875-1938. Prague. Liberal.

Pravda. 1944-. Bratislava. Slovak Communist.

Právo lidu. 1897-1938; 1945-48. Prague. Social Democratic.

Přítomnost. Prague. Liberal weekly. Suspended in 1938. Under the title *Dnešek* in 1946-48.

Robotnícke noviny. Bratislava. Suspended 1938. Social Democratic.
Rudé právo. 1920-38; 1945-. Prague. Communist.
Slovák. 1919-45. Bratislava. Ľudák.
Slovenská politika. Bratislava. Agrarian. In 1939-1945. Ľudák.
Slovenský denník. 1919-38. Bratislava. Agrarian.
Venkov. 1906-39. Prague. Agrarian.
Die Zeit. 1935-38. Henleinist.